Forbes MediaGuide 500

1994

Forbes MediaGuide 500

Forbes MediaGuide 500 is published annually by Forbes Inc. as a supplement to *Forbes MediaCritic,* a quarterly
Editorial correspondence should be sent to
MediaGuide 500, P.O. Box 762, Bedminster, NJ 07921 Phone: 908-781-2078
Subscription correspondence should be sent to
MediaGuide Subscriptions Dept. c/o Forbes Inc., 60 Fifth Ave., New York, NY 10011
or call 1-800-825-0061
ISSN: 1067-4918 ISBN: 08281-9952-3

TABLE OF CONTENTS

PREFACE

WHEN RUMORS SPREAD IN 1980 THAT NEWS-caster Walter Cronkite might run for president, one colleague remarked, "Why in the world would Cronkite want to be President...and give up all that power?"

The power of the press—to expose, to inform, and to influence—is indeed enormous and has been for more than 200 years. From reprinting the first copies of the Constitution in 1787 to spreading anti-slavery tracts in the mid-1800s to investigating the Nixon White House in the 1970s, the press has proven, along with the presidency, one of our nation's most powerful institutions.

Although the press, which, due to an explosion in formats we now call the media, cannot send troops to foreign lands or sign or veto legislation, it differs most markedly from the presidency in one key respect: It does not have to answer to the people. Perhaps this is the quality Cronkite's colleague envied, for if people don't like the president or other elected officials, they can vote them out of office. But the media? Who votes on them? Still, news organizations cannot afford to be indifferent to what consumers think of their products, which, after all, they are in the business of selling.

To help news consumers discern which journalists do a good job (and which don't), *MediaGuide* commenced publication in 1986. Bought by Forbes Inc., in 1992, the annual underwent a slight name change—to *Forbes MediaGuide 500.* The 500 in the title refers to the nation's 500 most influential journalists. We read thousands of articles and essays in every major newspaper, magazine, and specialized journal. *MediaGuide* is a veritable consumers' guide to the nation's leading journalists—the only one of its kind.

This 1994 volume, the second issued under the Forbes imprint, supplements our new quarterly, *Forbes MediaCritic.* Edited by the same team, *MediaCritic* contains full-length articles examining the news media's performance. Readers familiar with previous editions of *MediaGuide* will discover some major changes. To begin with, we now divide the journalists we rate into five categories: Politics & Culture; Business & Economics; Science & Technology; Foreign; and Commentary.

We have also changed the criteria we use to determine which journalists to include in the *Guide.* Past editions reviewed journalists the editors considered the *best,* which meant that even the lowest-rated journalists were well regarded. The present edition features journalists we consider the most *influential.* This makes for a greater range in quality, as an influential journalist may not deserve to be well regarded. An explanation of how we assess the influence of journalists, and of our rating criteria, can be found in the "Rating Guide" on pages 40-41.

In the chapter titled "Best of 1993," an altogether new section appears: the top 10 quotes of the year. Here we highlight the most intriguing, provocative, and entertaining passages written by journalists in 1993.

Throughout this volume you will see something never before included in any previous edition—pictures in the form of the top political cartoons of the year. We include this journalistic art because it deserves recognition in its own right and also because it illustrates the myriad issues journalists covered in 1993.

One last new item appears in the book: biographical sketches. These sketches highlight the milestones of each journalist's career.

MediaGuide begins with a review of the major stories of 1993 and then our selection of the Top 10 articles of the year in each of the five categories. The bulk of the volume consists of what previous editions have always offered: critical, hard-hitting reviews of individual journalists. We invite you to flip through the book and let your eye fall on the foreign correspondent or the political columnist or the business writer that you most like—or dislike.

So welcome to the 1994 *Forbes MediaGuide 500.* We might not have the power of a Cronkite (or a President), but we aim to help news consumers keep tabs on some of the media powers that be.

19 THE YEAR IN REVIEW

William Jefferson Clinton had barely been inaugurated as the 42nd president of the United States on January 20, 1993, when his nominee for attorney general, Zöe Baird, was forced to withdraw. The rejection followed the disclosure that she and her husband had hired illegal aliens as domestic help. The controversy that kept Baird employed in the private sector sprung from a story leaked to *The New York Times,* where it appeared on the front page. However, it was not Beltway journalists who were outraged by the Baird story—indeed, for many denizens of Washington this was a "non-story." Rather, the incident provoked the ire of a talk-show culture (starring Rush Limbaugh) whose increasing power would affect other events throughout the year.

The new President hoped to refocus public attention on his plans for the economy and health care, but another imbroglio eclipsed the Baird fiasco: the contentious debate over homosexuals in the military. As the Baltimore *Sun*'s Carl Cannon reported in our first issue of *MediaCritic* (Fall 1993), Clinton's campaign promise to end the ban on gays in the military drew scant attention from the campaign press corps. The downplaying resulted in large part from the press corps' agreement with Clinton on the issue and its belief that his proposed policy would spark little controversy—a judgment later events proved wrong. By the summer, Clinton and Sen. Sam Nunn [D-GA], the chief congressional opponent of the President's new policy, would forge a compromise that took the matter out of the news. During his initial days in office, however, Clinton took a lot of heat generated from this story. Together with the Baird disaster and several broken campaign promises—including harbor for Haitian refugees and a tax cut for middle-income earners—the President endured negative commentary from pundits right and left, as well as on the coast-to-coast talk show circuit. As *The Washington Post*'s media writer Howard Kurtz put it on the last day of January, "In the blink of a news cycle, the new president [went] from *Time*'s 'Man

of the Year' to punching bag of the week."

Smoldering tension between the White House and the press corps helped inspire Clinton to get his message out "unfiltered" by such means as holding town-hall meetings outside Washington. Clinton had yet to call a single press conference with the White House press corps when he flew to Detroit on February 10 to conduct his first town-hall session. Three weeks later the President announced his national service plan—on MTV. The traditional press continued to be tough on Clinton, as the following account of the Detroit event in *The Wall Street Journal* reveals. The account also demonstrates the growing tendency for news stories to contain as much interpretation and even opinion as they do news. "Mr. Clinton opened himself up to charges of disingenuousness with his answers to some questions. He made it appear that it was his preference to delay the decision about gays to serve in the military; in fact he was forced into the delay by opposition from Capitol Hill and the joint chiefs of staff."

In February Congress passed and President Clinton signed into law the family-leave act, which President Bush had opposed. But the major Washington story in the first weeks of Clinton's tenure was his proposed budget. The package sought tax increases and spending cuts in order to reduce the deficit and, in theory, boost the economy. News organizations followed the ins and outs of the budget process for the next six months, turning in often competent performances. However, these reports generally failed to discuss the budgetary gimmicks employed in 1993—as in years past—by politicians of both parties. (For more on this subject, see Tony Snow's article in the Winter 1994 issue of *MediaCritic.*)

On February 26, a homemade bomb exploded two floors beneath the World Trade Center in New York City, killing seven and injuring more than 1,000. As is now routine when natural disasters and terrorist acts occur, CNN appeared immediately on the scene and enabled the world to look on. When a suspect tried to collect a $400 deposit on a rented van used to transport the bomb, federal authorities were able to crack the case. Authorities charged Sheik Omar Abdel-Rahman and several Muslim followers.

On February 28, news organizations turned their attention to Waco, Texas, where agents from the U.S. Bureau of Alcohol, Tobacco, and Firearms attempted to raid the compound of David Koresh and his Branch Davidian cult. Four agents and two cult members died in the raid, and CNN and other news teams kept watch as the feds contemplated their next move. That came by order of Attorney General Janet Reno (the President's third choice for the job) on the morning of April 19, when the FBI assaulted the compound with tanks and tear gas. The fiery disaster leveled the place, killing 85 cult members, many of them children. That night Reno—the daughter of two journalists and the sister of a *Newsday* columnist—took every available television opportunity to explain that she had made the decision to enter the compound and that responsibility rested entirely with her. With her "buck-stops-here" performance, Reno became a media darling: *Newsweek* remarked that she had "turned a real disaster into a Beltway triumph," and *Time* chirped that "the capital is all agog at the new attorney general's outspoken honesty."

Only in the fall, as the facts of her decision-making became available, did the press commence some Reno revisionism. The Attorney General had said in April that she based her decision to storm the compound on charges of child abuse by Koresh. Yet, an internal Justice Department review released in October found no such evidence. Furthermore, the review said nothing regarding Reno's April assertion that the exhaustion of specially trained FBI agents had made the assault necessary. Under the headline, "Reno Contradicted in New Report on Decision to Attack Waco Cult," *The New York Times* reported the results of the internal review. Thereafter Reno's star fell inside Washington, thanks in part to White House officials who considered her too soft on crime—and who willingly leaked such nuggets to the media. In December the "CBS Evening News" stated that White House officials viewed the Attorney General as "a loose cannon" and that she may have become "a liability" to the administration.

Late April marked the end of Clinton's first hundred days in office, and the press obliged with mixed reviews. It is hard to fault the press for evaluating Clinton's first three months, since Clinton himself effectively invited such reviews by promising "an explosive hundred-day action period" that would be "the most productive...in recent history." Still, more press skepticism about the relevance of this first-hundred-days measure would have been welcome. After all, the measure comes from Franklin D. Roosevelt's first hundred days in 1933, which, unlike the same period 60 years later, was a time of depression that indeed facilitated an "explosive action" presidency—unlike any other in this century.

Even as Bill Clinton experienced an often critical press, his wife Hillary Rodham Clinton enjoyed the opposite. As the *Post*'s Kurtz noted, this was due in part to a public affairs office that skillfully gave and denied interviews, depending on the friendliness of the reporters. As the First Lady spearheaded the health-care reform effort throughout the spring, summer, and fall, the glowing clips on her mounted, enough to fill an oversized scrapbook. In *MediaCritic*'s debut issue (Fall 1993), Stephen Rodrick, now at *Boston Magazine*, examined the "Hillary journalism," identifying her principal cheerleaders (*Time*'s Margaret Carlson and *Newsweek*'s Eleanor Clift) and discussing areas of inquiry—such as HRC's record as a lawyer—that the press had largely ignored. By year's end, as the story concerning her and her husband's 1980s involvement with the Madison Guaranty Savings & Loan and the Whitewater Development Corporation gained steam, Ms. Clinton's legal work of the past decade began to interest the press, which now seemed ready to reassess its earlier, rosy portrait of the First Lady.

On April 25, hundreds of thousands of homosexuals gathered in Washington to march for gay rights. Although the march made the front pages and led the network news, the media overlooked a central part of the event. Most news outlets—with the notable exceptions of C-SPAN and *The Washington Times*—provided a sanitized version of the march, leaving out such demonstrators as topless lesbians, leather-clad exhibitionists, and cross-dressers. In the May 17 issue of *The Nation*, Andrew Kopkind wrote that the "approving media" must have missed "the thousands of 'Lesbian avengers' roaring past the White House...and on to the Washington Monument grounds in the early hours of the night before." The *Post's* Kurtz observed that the coverage of the march reflected a more general tendency: When reporting stories involving sex, race, and ethnicity, the press tends to "delete key details for fear of offending some portion of their audience." This approach, he added, "often leaves the public in the dark" even as it erodes press credibility "with those who discover they're not getting the full story." What Kurtz grasped was the influence of "politically correct" views upon newsrooms and news coverage, an influence that would be evident in other ways during the year. In a number of newspapers, including *USA Today* and the *Los Angeles Times*, diversity committees reviewed stories to ensure that they contained the right mix of sources, defined in terms of race, ethnicity, sex, and in some cases, sexual orientation. (For more on "mainstreaming," as diversity-in-sourcing is also called, see the article by *The American Spectator's* Christopher Caldwell in the Fall 1993 issue of *MediaCritic*.)

In Southeast Asia, the Cambodian elections held in May came off without a hitch—a somewhat surprising turn of events. The expensive UN effort to disarm the nation had proved ineffectual, and as elections approached, near anarchy prevailed in rural areas. Uli Schmetzer of the *Los Angeles Times* reported bandits dressing up as Khmer Rouge fighters before undertaking their raids. In retrospect, the elections appeared to reflect the resolve and bravery of the war-weary Cambodians, as they put in power a coalition government that included everyone but the Khmer Rouge, who had threatened to disrupt the vote.

Back in Washington, the President's budget plan advanced in Congress. But May also witnessed "Hairgate" in which the President, while on board Air Force One, allegedly tied up the Los Angeles International Airport for 45 minutes to get a $200 haircut from a fancy Hollywood barber. (Amid charges of Clinton's arrogance and elitism, *Newsday's* Jonathan Schell later obtained relevant records showing that the President's haircut had caused no airport traffic delays. Alas, his finding received little notice in the media.) A week later came "Travelgate," with the White House firing its entire travel staff amid accusations of mismanagement. The White House Counsel's office used the FBI to provide cover for the firings, as the bureau's press office—departing from its usual practice of refusing even to confirm the existence of an investigation—issued a release indicating that a "criminal investigation" of the travel office was underway. Attorney General Reno then admonished both the White House and the FBI for improper conduct.

To rescue a White House seemingly in disarray, President Clinton hired former Nixon, Ford, and Reagan adviser and spin-master deluxe David Gergen, who worked as an editor at *U.S.News & World Report* and as a commentator on PBS's "MacNeil/Lehrer News Hour." Gergen's appointment shocked Democrats who wondered why a Republican needed to be recruited to counsel the first Democratic President since Carter. It also shocked Republicans, especially when Gergen admitted he had voted for Clinton, a long-time friend. By mid-summer the White House staff was operating more smoothly. Gergen himself received good reviews from his former press colleagues—Tom Rosenstiel of the *Los Angeles Times* tentatively elevated him to "the pantheon of presidential 'wise men' who left a mark on their times." However, Michael Kelly emerged as arguably the journalist savviest about Gergen. His October 31 *New York Times Magazine* cover piece (see "Best Stories of 1993," page 17) effectively analyzed "Gergenism"—the qualities of non-partisan insidership that enabled Gergen's star to rise in both political and journalistic Washington. By year's end, as the White House encountered the stormy weather brought on by allegations of Clinton's extramarital affairs while governor of Arkansas, the burgeoning Madison/Whitewater scandal, and a health-care plan seemingly in political trouble, rumors circulated that Gergen might take another turn through the revolving door between politics and journalism.

Despite his public affairs skills, Gergen could not rescue the nomination of Lani Guinier to head the Justice Department's Civil Rights Division. An April 30 *Wall Street Journal* op-ed by the attorney Clint Bolick, headlined "Clinton's Quota Queens," instantly transformed the debate. Although the term "quota queen" appeared nowhere in the article, it proved more important than the text in that it negatively defined the nominee in a crisp soundbite. A University of Pennsylvania law professor who specialized in voting rights, Guinier had written complicated law-review articles that defied easy summary. Most journalists reported them only to the extent they bore on the controversy over her nomination, and the often cryptic treatment of her academic writings prevented her views from receiving a full public airing. At the same time, it appeared that the President himself had not paid adequate attention to her writings before he nominated her. When, shortly, Clinton said that he had finally read, and in part disagreed with, her law-review articles, he withdrew her nomination. While the Guinier story felled a few forests in the telling, the press—revealing an institutional bias by which it scants the work of the federal agencies—proved uninterested in reporting the civil rights policies made on a day-to-day basis by the new administration.

On June 6, a Chinese freighter carrying 300 illegal aliens ran aground off New York. Seven died after jumping overboard but the rest made it to America, where immigration authorities debated their future. Back in Washington, the Senate approved Clinton's budget plan. Meanwhile, the President, after weeks of seeming indecision, named Judge Ruth Bader Ginsburg to the Supreme Court to replace Associate Justice Byron White, who had announced his retirement three months earlier. When ABC News White House correspondent Brit Hume opened the press queries about the nomination by asking the President about "a certain zig-zag quality" to his decision-making, an angry Clinton cut off the news conference by chastising reporters. In a complaint echoed throughout the year, the President accused the media of focusing too heavily on Beltway gossip and "who's-in-who's -out" journalism, and of engaging more in negativity than explanation. A case could be made that Clinton received more negative press coverage than had his predecessor. The non-partisan Center for Media and Public Affairs found that from January through May, 64 percent of all references to Clinton by network news reporters or by those they interviewed were negative. Conversely, during the comparable period in 1989, only 41 percent of such references to President Bush were negative. Clinton and his staff, moreover, were surprised by the negative coverage the President received, based on the assumption that journalists are predominantly Democrats and, thus, more liberal than conservative. There can be little doubt the President was experiencing the tendency of the press to play an adversarial role—regardless of the party controlling the White House.

In July Bosnia's Muslim-led government rejected a plan that would have divided the nation into three ethnically separate republics. In the United States, floods ravaged the Midwest. The Mississippi River overflowed its banks, leaving 48 dead, some 70,000 others displaced, and causing $10 billion in property damage. As *The Christian Science Monitor* noted, in one of the year's best headlines, "Miss Ain't Behavin'."

Traveling to Japan for the Group of Seven Summit, Clinton received favorable press but achieved little in terms of an improved trade policy with the host nation. Clinton's visit occurred on the eve of major political change in the host country—as later in July Japanese voters ousted Prime Minister Kiichi Miyazawa. The downfall of his Liberal Democratic Party, which had dominated the government for 38 years, reawakened interest in the political process. But while the LDP lost control of the Diet, the traditional opposition Socialist Party lost more than half of its seats to fledgling neo-conservative parties. By year's end, few expected the coalition government headed by Miyazawa's successor, Morihiro Hosokawa, to survive in its current form. While most of the media concentrated on the superficial political results, only a few judicious souls noted that access to Japan's markets remained under the watch of the country's all-powerful yet anonymous bureaucrats.

Washington's most dramatic event of the year occurred on July 20 when the body of Associate White House Counsel Vince Foster was found, gun in hand, in a park on the Virginia side of the Potomac River. The presidential adviser had committed suicide, or so it seemed to almost everyone at the time. A former law partner of Hillary Rodham Clinton at the Rose Law Firm in Little Rock, Arkansas, Foster had close ties to both Clintons, and especially to the First Lady. After he died, reports of his depression surfaced, and a note torn into 27 pieces that was found in his briefcase charged that the editors of *The Wall Street Journal* "lie with impunity." The press seemed to accept the President's take on Foster's suicide as a mysterious event beyond explanation. And with grave introspection, journalists wondered whether they helped to make Washington hell for those who serve in high-ranking posts. By any reasonable standard, the *Journal*'s editorial remarks about Foster were fairly tame. The paper said that Foster's legal efforts on behalf of the First Lady's health-care task force "cut some legal corners" and that Ms. Clinton had asked Foster about "Travelgate." Moreover, the *Journal*'s editorials focused less on Foster than on what it called "the Rose [Law Firm] clique" that advised the President. (Other Rose alumni and close friends of Hillary's—Webster Hubbell and William Alexander—worked in the Justice Department and the White House Counsel's office, respectively.) By year's end, the press had to rethink its position on Foster's suicide, not to mention the "Rose clique." Thanks in large part to the relentless curiosity of *The Washington Times*'s Jerry Seper, more information was uncovered. Among other things, certain files in Foster's office—including one containing Whitewater items—had been removed by White House Counsel Bernard Nussbaum before federal authorities conducted their investigation in July. The suggestion of a White House diversion of key evidence renewed press interest in the Madison/Whitewater story, in which the Rose Law Firm was involved, leading to a rush of stories in late 1993 and early 1994. While the police in August had ruled Foster's death a suicide, evidence surfaced that led some journalists to doubt whether he had in fact taken his own life.

On August 5, the House passed the President's budget plan by two votes. A day later the Senate followed suit, with Vice President Al Gore casting the tie-breaking ballot. No Republican in either chamber voted for the plan, and only White House deals appeasing House Democrats who wanted more spending cuts drew enough of them into the President's camp. Clinton received more good news when the Senate easily confirmed Ruth Bader Ginsburg as the 107th Supreme Court Justice, and the first appointed by a Democratic president in more than a quarter century. Vacancies on the High Court occur on average once every two years, and Clinton will likely have one or two more opportunities to shape the Court. The President, meanwhile, moved slowly in filling the more than 100 vacancies he inherited on the lower federal courts, and it was not until fall that the Senate confirmed the first of his lower court nominees.

When Pope John Paul II visited the U.S. in late summer, two "conflict" themes pervaded press coverage: disagreement within the Catholic Church over matters of sexuality and gender; and disagreement between the Pope and the President over abortion. While "certainly part of the essential background" of the Pope's visit, observed *The New York Times*'s Peter Steinfels, these topics unjustifiably "came to dominate the foreground," as they obscured much about his visit and his message. "The Pope," Steinfels noted, "repeatedly lamented the loss of belief in objective truth and in universally valid principles of morality." As it happened, the Pope also gave advance notice of the encyclical on morals that the Vatican published later in the year. Although a major moral and religious event, the press largely neglected it, thus demonstrating its frequent blind spot to things not of this world.

On September 13, President Clinton stood beside Israeli Prime Minister Yitzhak Rabin and PLO leader Yasir Arafat as they joined together in an improbable handshake of potentially historic importance. Under the pact reached by the two men through secret negotiations in Norway, both Israel and the PLO would recognize each other's existence and agree to partial autonomy for Palestine in lands occupied by Israel. Peace did not come as quickly as the agreement promised, however, as deadlines for taking certain actions passed unmet.

September saw formal announcement of two major initiatives of the Clinton administration: a plan to "reinvent government," fashioned under the direction of Vice President Gore; and the long-awaited health-care package, the handiwork of a task force led by Hillary Rodham Clinton. Gore's reinvention effort received wide coverage but quickly faded from public view as debates over health care and the pending North American Free Trade Agreement heated up. The President's health-care-reform plan, on the other hand, promised to be much on the public's mind in 1994 and perhaps beyond.

"Nothing the president has done—or is likely to do—better defines aspirations of the Clinton presidency," wrote *The Washington Post*'s Steven Pearlstein and Dana Priest on October 28, "than [its] massive health care plan....Woven through the 1,300-page health plan is a liberal's passion to help the needy, a conservative's faith in free markets and a politician's focus on the middle class." Middle-income earners were certainly among those the President hoped to reach with his plan. Indeed, as *The Wall Street Journal*'s Paul Gigot pointed out, Clinton's pollster Stanley Greenberg had advised as early as 1991 that the Democratic Party needed a major new program that would show middle-class Americans that government can work for them, too. At the heart of the President's plan lay a commitment to universal health coverage, and the Clintons considered themselves direct heirs to FDR. "We have to build on what President Roosevelt tried to do," said Hillary Rodham Clinton, "when he introduced the Social Security Act and thought the second part of it would be health security." In reporting the developments in health-care reform, the press sometimes indulged in certain "myths," as Fred Barnes argued in the first issue of *MediaCritic* (Fall 1993). In this and a similar piece he wrote earlier in the year for *The American Spectator* (see "Best Stories of 1993," page 32), Barnes questioned whether in fact "a health-care crisis" even exists.

When Katherine Ann Power surrendered to federal authorities on September 15, those under 30 probably had no idea who she was. While a student at college in the late 1960s, Power joined student radicals opposed to the Vietnam War. Taking a step beyond non-violent marches and sit-ins, she and her friends tried to fund their protests by robbing a Boston bank. During the holdup, they shot and killed police officer Walter Schroeder. Power went underground, and eventually embarked upon a new life in Oregon. When she turned herself in, she asked that her actions 24 years earlier be viewed in the context of the "illegal" war the government was conducting at the time. Power said that she was tired of living with "shame and hiddenness," that she wanted to live with "full authenticity" in the present, and that she had been trying to "grow as a person of peace." This rhetoric of self-absorbed victimhood did not impress the Massachusetts judge, who sentenced her to eight to 12 years in prison. But Power's rhetoric impressed numerous news outlets, which told her life story in such a sympathetic fashion as to suggest she already had suffered enough. So entranced by her biography, *The Wall Street Journal* failed to mention Schroeder until the 30th paragraph of its front-page story. With the *Journal*'s performance in mind, one of the slain police officer's nine children told the packed Boston courtroom the day Power was sentenced, "For reasons I will never comprehend, the press and the public seem far more interested in the difficulties that Katherine Power has inflicted upon herself than in the very real and horrible suffering she inflicted upon my family." In recounting Power's life, the press also fixated on the violence of the 1960s radical extremists, slighting, as Margaret Spillane of *The Nation* argued, "the ordinary heroes" of the era who peacefully pursued "the unglamorous day-to-day work of radical social change."

In September civil disorder broke out in Russia. Parliament, claiming to be the legitimate government, impeached President Boris Yeltsin, and for a moment it appeared the historic move from communism to capitalism might come to an end. Because Yeltsin controlled the army, he prevailed in the violent battle with Parliament in early October. Dozens of Russians died when army tanks blasted the parliament building, setting it ablaze. Yeltsin suffered a setback in the December elections in which voters, while approving the President's proposed constitution, expressed their support for the highly nationalistic Vladimir Zhirinovsky. By year's end, the idea held by so many in the West, including journalists, that only "shock therapy" could move Russia toward a market economy was finally discredited.

October saw the awarding of a joint Nobel Peace Prize to African National Congress President Nelson Mandela and South African President F.W. de Klerk. The Nobel marked the culmination of a long, painful process to end nearly a half-century of apartheid. The year began with an agreement to form a multi-racial constitutional congress, and it ended with the realization of that goal. But violence persisted, mostly between supporters of the Inkatha Freedom Party, which favors autonomous regions, and the ANC, which favors a strong central government. By year's end, the Inkatha Freedom Party had formed a coalition, which included conservative Afrikaner groups, that vowed not to take part in any constitutional talks that did not promise autonomous zones.

On October 3, 18 U.S. soldiers were killed in a disastrous effort to abduct aides of Somali clan-leader Mohamed Farah Aidid. The idea of saving starving Somalis no longer seemed so compelling to many Americans. Images of the hungry and dying had led the U.S. to intervene in 1992. Images of a dead American soldier being dragged through the streets of Mogadishu and of a helicopter pilot held captive now led the U.S. to seek withdrawal. At the end of the month, President Clinton set a March 31, 1994, deadline for removing U.S. troops from Somalia. As with the Persian Gulf War in 1991, Americans debated the influence of television—and the images portrayed—upon foreign policy. In the Western Hemisphere, meanwhile, an army-backed group blocked U.S. troops from docking in Haiti. Constitutional questions regarding war powers arising in connection with Somalia, Haiti, and Bosnia occupied both the President and Congress.

The year's top business story arrived in the autumn announcement that cable giant Viacom had made an offer to purchase Hollywood's last independent movie studio, Paramount Communications. Excited media cartographers began fervently mapping the information superhighway, and when home-shopping guru Barry Diller, chairman of QVC, soon launched his hostile counter-offer, the story became the Superbowl of business. Journalists proclaimed the return of merger-mania and hostile takeovers and a return to the "go-go 1980s." All eyes watched Diller and Viacom's Sumner Redstone as they scrambled to line up investors and beef up their bids. Daily reports flowed from the courtroom battleground where media giants waged an apparent war for the future of entertainment and communications. Diller celebrated Christmas with some victories in the legal sparring, but Redstone and Viacom emerged triumphant in February 1994. Elsewhere on Wall Street, the Dow set record highs seemingly every other day, climbing almost to 4000 by year's end.

In the year's four major elections, Republicans claimed victory. In June Richard Riordan won the mayoral race in Los Angeles. And in November George Allen and Christine Todd Whitman won the gubernatorial races in Virginia and New Jersey, respectively, and Rudolph Giuliani, in a rematch of 1989, defeated New York City Mayor David Dinkins. Ed Rollins, Whitman's chief campaign adviser, spoiled her victory by boasting to reporters that he had spent $500,000 to suppress the African-American vote. He claimed that Republicans had paid Democratic precinct workers in black areas to sit on their hands on election day. The story turned out to be a lie. While the Rollins story drew press interest from coast to coast, a story of real chicanery—in Philadelphia—drew hardly any. A solid investigative series in *The Philadelphia Inquirer* revealed that voter fraud permeated a pivotal state senate election in November. As *Philadelphia Magazine*'s Larry Platt discusses in the third issue of *MediaCritic* (Spring 1994), this "Philadelphia Story" was no lie.

Arguably the most important legislative event of the year took place in November, when Congress approved NAFTA. While the national debate was waged more in terms of politics than economics, economists themselves tended overwhelmingly to favor the pact, although most of them thought its effects—for good and for bad—would be limited. Why did they support NAFTA? As Sylvia Nasar reported in *The New*

York Times, they thought it would be good for Mexico. Given that poor nations need to export in order to industrialize, open access to the rest of North America would strengthen the hand of a pro-American, pro-free-market government in Mexico. Another professional group also tended overwhelmingly to favor NAFTA—the pundit class. It was hard to find an anti-NAFTA editorial page, columnist, or talk-show pundit. Among the few were Mark Shields and Alexander Cockburn. Shields succinctly explained his brethren's support of NAFTA. "There are no $35-a-week Tijuana bureau chiefs to steal their jobs," he remarked, and they "are more worried about whether they are going to the Vineyard." In a stroke of political genius—although it was not seen that way in advance—the Clinton White House suckered Ross Perot into a debate with Vice President Gore on CNN's "Larry King Live." Perot failed to make the best performance, setting back both the anti-NAFTA cause and perhaps his own political aspirations.

Speaking in the city where Martin Luther King had been assassinated 25 years earlier, President Clinton warned black ministers in Memphis on November 13 that King would be horrified to see an America that had won the Cold War and secured civil rights for all citizens now torn apart by crime and violence. This emerged as the President's most emotional, and probably most effective, speech of the year. In turn, Congress soon passed the Brady bill, which requires a waiting period for handgun purchases. Public concern over crime increased as the year ended, with the news media—and television especially—often failing to put facts in perspective. As Princeton University's John J. DiIulio, Jr., pointed out in a *New York Times* op-ed, crime rates in most places have remained stable or dropped for at least a decade. The main problem lies in the inner cities, where violence has never been worse—and where its victims have never been younger. Crime and welfare, in addition to health care, promised to be the most hotly debated domestic issues in 1994.

As Christmas approached, the media came bearing not exactly frankincense and myrrh to the Clintons. Some news outlets, most notably *The Washington Post* and *The Washington Times,* began publishing frequent stories on Vince Foster, Madison, and Whitewater. To compound the Clintons' yuletide woes, some Arkansas state troopers then decided to go public with their stories alleging extramarital affairs—and misuse of office—on the part of then-Governor Bill Clinton. The troopers' story first appeared on December 19 in David Brock's 11,000-word essay in the January 1994 *American Spectator. The Wall Street Journal* boycotted the story, while a reluctant *New York Times* was forced to refer to it when the First Lady stepped forward to denounce the allegations as "outrageous." Some liberal opinion journalists dismissed the charges by questioning the medium in which it first appeared. *The American Spectator,* they protested, is a conservative, anti-Clinton monthly, not a "mainstream" news organization. On December 21, however, the mainstream *Los Angeles Times* published the troopers' story in a lengthy, well-reported piece by William Rempel and Douglas Frantz.

The troopers' story revived the question of whether, or to what extent, journalists should report on the private lives of government officials. This was not the only press issue debated in 1993, a year that saw *Time* and *USA Today* publish dubious photos (see former *New York Times* staff writer John Corry's piece in the Winter 1994 issue of *MediaCritic*), and NBC President Michael Gartner lose his job when it was discovered that "Dateline NBC" had rigged the explosion of a GM pick-up truck. Some of these press issues doubtless will be debated again in 1994—more grist for our mill here at *MediaCritic* and *MediaGuide 500.*

It is relatively easy to predict which of the major stories of 1993 will continue to make headlines in 1994. It is, of course, a different matter to judge which issues and events from 1993 might interest historians 50, 100, and 200 years hence. President Clinton's health-care reform effort, the top priority of his presidency, ranks as one possibility. Another is the carnage in Bosnia and the West's so-far restrained response to it. Still another is Russia as it emerges with evident difficulty from more than seven decades of communist rule.

Perhaps the only thing we can predict with certainty is that throughout 1994 we'll keep track of the major stories and how the media's most influential journalists cover them.

THE BEST STORIES & COLUMNS OF 1993

Throughout the year, we at *Forbes MediaGuide 500* read thousands of articles in newspapers, magazines, and journals. From this mountainous pile of news and commentary we set aside the most outstanding pieces. We reread these works to determine the best, and then select the Top 10 articles by print journalists in each of five categories: Politics & Culture; Business & Economics; Science & Technology; Foreign; and Commentary. The articles in each category are listed in *alphabetical* order by journalist, *not* by the order in which we might rank them. To do justice to the works cited, we briefly summarize each article. Following these 50 selections is a list of the year's Top 10 quotes by journalists as found in their written compositions.

The following articles and quotes stand out for many reasons, including their descriptive power, depth of analysis, and quality of writing. They represent the very best of America's journalism.

POLITICS & CULTURE

Paul M. Barrett
The Wall Street Journal
February 2, 1993
"David Souter Emerges as Reflective Moderate on the Supreme Court"

In this remarkable profile of Justice David Souter, Barrett reveals as much about the inner workings of the Supreme Court as he does about its most solitary member and the importance of his role. "As [Souter's] third term unfolds, the man who was called a 'stealth nominee' has surprised legal scholars who had questioned his credentials and seemingly narrow life experience as a reclusive bachelor. He is becoming a major force on the conservative court by means of independent thinking and strong personal alliances with other justices. Should President Clinton appoint one or more liberal justices, some scholars predict that Justice Souter would emerge as the anchor of a moderate center on a divided court." Barrett enhances this sharp assessment with insightful and sometimes witty anecdotes about Souter himself. "Though sometimes stuffy in his legal prose, Justice Souter isn't pompous in person. Asked why he sings along with the chief justice at Mr. Rehnquist's annual Christmas carol party, he replies, 'I have to. Otherwise I get all the tax cases.'" Barrett rounds out this colorful piece with a smart discussion of Souter's work in the 1992 abortion case, *Planned Parenthood v. Casey*. "The Souter-O'Connor effort provided Justice Kennedy with the alternative to overruling Roe for which he had been groping. He joined their opinion and added a section of his own. The core of the cooperative product was Justice Souter's assertion that 'to overrule under fire in the absence of the most compelling reason to reexamine a watershed decision would subvert the Court's legitimacy beyond any serious question.' He called on combatants in the abortion clash 'to end their national division by accepting a common mandate rooted in the Constitution.'"

Richard E. Cohen
National Journal
July 24, 1993
"Ted's Turn"

In this savvy, three-dimensional profile of Senator Edward M. "Ted" Kennedy [D-MA] and the unique opportunity afforded him by Clinton's planned emphasis on social issues, Cohen portrays an effective lawmaker and the optimistic prospects for his legislative agenda. "For Kennedy, the next few months offer a chance to make a fresh start. If he succeeds, he could reestablish himself as the congressional Democrats' leading voice on domestic policy, burnish his credentials as a legislative activist and lift a lingering cloud of personal problems. And he could strengthen his position in a tough reelection race next year. The next phase of Clinton's program includes much of the unfinished agenda of the 1960s, for which Kennedy has carried the torch during years when his efforts were often scorned or ignored." With health-care reform—Kennedy's pet issue for many years—finally on the national policy agenda, Cohen provides a timely evaluation of the Senator's influence and his relationships with other members of Congress and his congressional staff. Kennedy, he observes, "knows where the congressional power levers are located and is not shy about pulling them....His hope for action this year rests on the assumption that the President and congressional leaders will agree on an accelerated schedule—starting, he said, with Clinton's possible announcement of a 'statement of principles'.... Kennedy aides, who emphasize that he is more committed to broad goals than to a specific mechanism for reform, have worked with White House officials on the details of such a declaration." Cohen's marvelous, behind-the-scenes profile depicts both the Massachusetts Senator and his impact on policy.

Thomas B. Edsall
The Washington Post
January 3, 1993
"The Special Interest Gambit"

Crafting a savvy analysis of how President Clinton will have to change his party's discourse—and the party itself—if he wants to succeed, Edsall carefully starts the reader on the rocky path toward 1996. "Bill Clinton, elected to the presidency with a fragile 43 percent plurality, faces the enormous task of using the power of the White House to rebuild the battered image of the Democratic party. His chance of winning a second term, in the assessment of his key political strategists, is very likely to be closely linked to the public's perception of his party....Clinton is engaged in a subtle strategy: It requires challenging such liberal interests as feminist and black organizations while maintaining a commitment to racial and sexual diversity. The inherent danger of the strategy is the risk of appearing duplicitous, of seeking to have it both ways." The President must, according to Edsall, "prevent his image from melding into the longtime liabilities of the Democratic Party. He is determined to distance himself from policies seen as redistributing income and tax dollars from the working class to the poor." In this exceptional evaluation of the campaign strategy that won the Arkansas Governor the White House, Edsall examines how Clinton the campaigner brought together different factions within the party, and must now recast the defining orthodoxy to cement his tenuous coalition of support. "The election results show that the coalition Clinton put together could potentially form the base of a revived Democratic party. But it must be significantly enlarged, primarily among white voters, if it is going to reach 50-percent-plus-one in 1996. More than any Democratic presidential candidate in the past 20 years, Clinton restored the biracial alliance that is crucial to victory." Edsall's stellar essay shows the reader how.

Michael Kelly
The New York Times Magazine
OCTOBER 31, 1993
"THE GAME"

For this first cover story of the revamped Sunday *Times Magazine,* Kelly expands an earlier profile of David Gergen to provide a knockout punch that says as much about Washington and the way the capital works as it does about President Clinton's top media adviser. "If perception is reality, what is the point of any differences at all—between Republicans and Democrats, between journalists and Government officials, between ideologues and copywriters, between the chatterers of television and the thinkers of the academy, between Washington and Hollywood?" In this stunning indictment of Washington "insiders" and their penchant for redefining themselves, Kelly describes Gergen's various political and ideological affiliations, noting that "in most places, this sort of performance could win one a reputation for opportunism. It does that in Washington too, but here the tag is meant as a compliment. Possessing a large degree of what the Washington columnist and talk-television star Michael Kinsley has called 'intellectual, uh, flexibility' is no sin here. Wrong lies in the opposite direction, in the gaucherie of displaying passionately held convictions....A man like Gergen, unafraid to admit that his loyalties and convictions are no more than outerwear, is always welcome at the table." Kelly then reviews the political history of the past 30 years to help explain the evolution of Washington and the presidency until it reached its present form. "The President in 1993 seems to have lost the option of exercising dignity or restraint in support of his policies. The conversation of politics now is carried on the vernacular of advertising. The big sell, the television sell, appears to be the only way to sell. Increasingly, and especially in Washington, how well one does on television has come to determine how well one does in life.... Washington has become a strange and debased place, the true heart of a national culture in which the distinction between reality and fantasy has been lost....The standards and boundaries that have been eroding for years have at last faded almost completely away." In this unflattering portrait of both Gergen and Washington, Kelly presents a dazzling political primer for the 1990s.

John Merline
Investor's Business Daily
SEPTEMBER 7, 1993
"WHO PAYS FOR OUR HEALTH CARE?"

Relying on several different studies, Merline provides a devastating report revealing health-care costs hidden in taxation. "American families pay an average $4,500 annually for health care—other people's health care, that is. In contrast, the average family spends about $2,400 a year to pay the direct cost of its own care....Families that carry private insurance pay almost 90 percent of the nation's $900 billion health-care tab, although they spend only one-third of that on themselves. This method of funding health care not only has important implications for a family's budget, but the health-care market as well, contributing to the rapid rise in costs, economists say." Moreover, Merline discovers, "some analysts fear these problems might get worse under President Clinton's reforms, which would ask working Americans to subsidize insurance coverage for those currently uninsured. Currently, the typical family's health-care budget includes not only the direct cost of paying insurance premiums and out-of-pocket medical costs, but also the payroll and income taxes levied to fund public health-care programs. The cost of these government programs—both in real terms and as a share of total health-care spending—has been growing rapidly over the years. In 1960, the federal government paid only 9 percent of the nation's health-care costs. Today, it picks up more than 30 percent of the tab. The rise was largely attributable to the explosive growth in the federal Medicare and Medicaid programs, both of which were created in 1965. Spending on Medicare has increased nearly 400 percent in real, inflation-adjusted, terms since 1970. Medicaid's costs have climbed by even more over those years." Merline's powerful assessment pinpoints who now pays for government-run health care and who will do so in the future: working families.

Charles Murray

The Wall Street Journal

OCTOBER, 29, 1993

"THE COMING WHITE UNDERCLASS"

With a backbone of chilling statistics, Murray's compelling article defines the threat of rising illegitimacy in the white community, and he also offers solutions. Arguing that while society as a whole has survived a level of 68 percent illegitimacy within the African-American community—which still represents a small proportion of the overall population—it will not survive remotely similar levels in the white community, where the rate has now reached 22 percent. "In raw numbers, European-American whites are the ethnic group with the most people in poverty, most illegitimate children, most women on welfare, most unemployed men, and most arrests for serious crime." Despite the media's obsession with the disproportionate increase of illegitimate children born to professional mothers, the problem is not with the real-world Murphy Brown's. "Women with family incomes of $75,000 or more contribute 1 percent of white illegitimate babies," Murray notes, "while women with family incomes under $20,000, contribute 69 percent." Murray sees a microcosm in the black community of the past generation, where "the values of unsocialized male adolescents [become] norms—physical violence, immediate gratification and predatory sex." Positing that the white community will hit the "critical mass" point when the illegitimacy rate reaches 25 percent, Murray urges a new approach to combat the problem. "The child deserves society's support," he reasons. "The parent does not." While he endorses universal medical coverage for children, he suggests that the government end economic benefits for single mothers, thus forcing them to seek aid from their families, communities, or churches. He urges, among other solutions, a reintroduction of "social stigma" for unwed parents, and laws to ease adoption. "The long steep climb in black illegitimacy has been calamitous for black communities and painful for the nation," he concludes. "It cannot survive the same epidemic among whites." In this provocative article, Murray pulls no punches.

Art Pine

Los Angeles Times

APRIL 5, 1993

"LINGERING DEATH OF AN AIR BASE STALLS RECOVERY"

While other journalists were content to report the closing of military bases using only Pentagon press releases, Pine traveled to Beeville, Texas, to craft an eye-opening dispatch of how the town tried to redevelop a Navy air base. His stunning exposé reveals how the government's inefficiency in closing superfluous installations costs both jobs and revenue. "Like many communities are finding across the country, the biggest challenge in the base-closing nightmare is not necessarily seeing the local base shut down. It's getting the government to turn over the property so the community can put its recovery plan into action quickly enough to reduce the economic impact of the closure. In Beeville, the Pentagon's obligation to first offer the parcel to other federal agencies was expected to take only a few months to fulfill. It wound up occupying most of a year." And that, Pine explains, was only the beginning. "Efforts to obtain an 'interim' lease to enable commercial tenants to use portions of the base pending final disposition ran into difficulties that added months to the transfer process. And new legislation concerning the Pentagon's liability for environmental damage has slowed the process even more. As a result, the Chase Field project already has lost three prospective tenants, with an estimated 100 to 300 new jobs, and Brad Arvin, executive editor of the Beeville/Bee County Redevelopment Council, said other potential employers are getting edgy as well." Pine culls great detail, but wastes no words in this evocative story of how the government gets in the way in spite of itself.

David Shaw

Los Angeles Times

SEPTEMBER 15-17, 1993
"COVERING CLINTON: DID MEDIA RUSH TO JUDGMENT OR MERELY REFLECT REALITY?"

Filled with candid comments from Washington press mavens, this high-spirited three-part series explores the personal feelings that fueled the generally negative media coverage of President Clinton during his first eight months in office. Shaw offers a rare glimpse of White House reporters as they impatiently fidget and whine that the President's haircut will make them late for dinner. "'This guy is the worst...absolutely the worst,' says [Ann] Devroy of the [*Washington*] *Post.* 'Clinton has no concept of the traditional middle-class virtue of not keeping other people waiting. He is extraordinarily self-absorbed.'" Such attitudes, Shaw finds, show themselves in the coverage of seemingly innocuous matters. "The press corps erupted in outrage [over the firing of the White House travel-office staff]. They shouted questions and charges, demanded explanations, described the firings as a massacre and accused the White House of cronyism, nepotism, McCarthyism and every other pejorative -ism that came to their perfervid minds." Although Shaw allows journalists to justify their coverage, he invites White House officials to present their side as well. Highlighting the negative characterization of George Stephanopoulos's shift from communications director to full-time presidential adviser, Shaw paraphrases Paul Begala, another presidential adviser. "Only the Washington press corps are so solipsistic that they would regard a shift from spending most of one's time with the press to spending all one's time with the President as a demotion." Masterfully debunking the glamour and mystique of the White House beat, Shaw shows the human, often petty motivations, of the journalists who cover the President.

Pat Towell

Congressional Quarterly

JULY 24, 1993
"MONTHS OF HOPE, ANGER, ANGUISH PRODUCE POLICY FEW ADMIRE"

Constructing a stellar evaluation of the politics and the policy of President Clinton's shift on gays in the military, Towell provides an even-handed review of the affair and its impact on the armed forces. "For all the fanfare and denunciations, President Clinton's effort to liberalize the military's ban on gay soldier's will do no more or less than this: It will make life a little easier, and less risky, for homosexuals intent on belonging quietly to an organization that remains determined to bar homosexual conduct." As others in the press corps echo either the administration or gay-rights' groups, Towell focuses on the nitty-gritty of Clinton's retreat and how the compromise came to pass. "Even though Clinton's plan drew few enthusiastic backers and a bevy of critics, it gained considerable political momentum during the week of July 19, largely because it carried the endorsement of the Joint Chiefs of Staff." In four days of testimony before Congress, "Pentagon officials made it clear that Clinton's policy essentially continued the prohibitions on homosexual conduct in the policy that had been in effect since 1981. And in a memo to Clinton, Attorney General Janet Reno maintained that Clinton's revision would make it easier to defend the Pentagon's gay ban in court." Towell takes the reader through the entire history of the issue that led to the fashioning of the policy. And the *CQ* reporter leaves no question as to who ultimately prevailed. "Clinton announced his decision before an audience of senior officers in an auditorium on a military base in Washington. While he lauded the efforts of gay rights advocates, none of them were present."

Ralph Vartabedian
Los Angeles Times
JULY 11-13, 1993
"THE ENEMY WITHIN"

In three exhaustive, front-page articles, Vartabedian pens an eye-opening examination of outmoded regulations within the defense industry, as its security needs change with the end of the Cold War. From an assessment of internal security clearances and costs to an exploration of how to preserve the necessary secrecy for certain technologies, he covers all the bases in this exceptional series detailing how outdated rules sometimes strangle both the system and its workers. "Intent on rooting out every possible mole or worker vulnerable to blackmail, the government delves deeply into employees' private lives. Disqualifications can be based on family ties, sex practices, alcohol or drug use and spending habits, among other factors. At its worst, critics claim, the system discriminates against people with foreign kin—with especially painful results for Asian-Americans. They say those deemed untrustworthy often are given no explanation and offered no appeal, raising constitutional questions. A denied or revoked clearance becomes a permanent blot on a personnel record: it must be disclosed on every future clearance application." Vartabedian adds that "the creation [and maintenance] of a massive industrial security bureaucracy" costs $13.8 billion annually, "enough to rebuild every skyscraper in downtown Los Angeles every year." Vartabedian's vigorous critique casts national security in a new light.

BUSINESS & ECONOMICS

Laurie P. Cohen and Michael Siconolfi
The Wall Street Journal
MAY 21, 1993
"ART OF INFLUENCE: HOW ONE MAN MADE LAZARD FRERES A FORCE IN MUNICIPAL BONDS"

In a front-page exposé, Cohen and Siconolfi provide both a detailed account of how a modern-day Manhattan Midas makes his money and a broader look into influence-peddling by state and local politicians. "In 1990, Lazard Frères & Co. didn't manage the underwriting of a single municipal-bond issue in New Jersey," the article begins. But in 1992, "the investment-banking boutique ranked No. 1 in the state—by a long ways." How? In exploring this mystery, Cohen and Siconolfi reveal how Lazard partner Richard P. Poirier Jr. schmoozed and networked his way into the innermost sanctums of government in the Garden State. Like many states, New Jersey does not award underwriting jobs based on competitive bidding, leaving politicians to hire whom they please. Poirier, the pair reports, helped raise large sums for the Democratic State Committee and became very friendly with Democratic Governor Jim Florio's chief of staff. Profitable state-bond work soon followed. As Cohen and Siconolfi explain, such practices are standard fare in localities where politicians choose underwriters, because "winning lead-managing mandates is particularly lucrative for Wall Street investment banks; lead underwriters typically keep about 50 percent of the fees for underwriting bonds, with the co-managers sharing the rest." By exposing Poirier's unseemly relationship with the governor's aides, coupled with Lazard's explosive jump to the fore in state-bond work, Cohen and Siconolfi spark a controversy that becomes a major issue in Florio's failed reelection bid.

George Gilder
Forbes/ASAP
OCTOBER 25, 1993
"DIGITAL DARKHORSE NEWSPAPERS"

Taking a very contrarian viewpoint, the visionary Gilder boldly predicts that newspapers will emerge the big winners of the ongoing Information Revolution. At a time when many think they hear the death knell sounding for the daily bugle, Gilder hears the future whispering a different verdict. "The ultimate reason why newspapers will prevail in the Information Age is that they are better than anyone else at collecting, editing, filtering and presenting real information, and they are allying with the computer juggernaut to do it." Despite maneuverings by the likes of Barry Diller and John Malone, Gilder doesn't consider TV a medium that will translate well in the coming communications nirvana. The battle for Paramount appears to him a gigantic exercise in futility, and he witheringly chastises its glory-seeking participants. "Most of these leaders in the goldrush toward multimedia are getting it wrong. Fixated by market surveys that map demand for existing video, they are plunging down dead-ends and cul-de-sacs with their eyes firmly focused on the luminous visions in their rearview mirrors." The streamlined computerized newspapers of the future, Gilder contends, will lay strong claim to scarce advertising dollars—welcome news to an industry still wracked by an advertising depression. "Viewers who are seriously interested in [an] advertised item can click on it and open up a more detailed presentation, or they can advertise their own desire to buy a product of particular specifications." With such striking meditations, Gilder brushes close against the fences of fancy, occasionally running across the fields of the absurd. But this provocative article's claims about the future of information challenge the most basic assessments of culture and society, and point imaginatively in a new direction.

George Hager

Congressional Quarterly

MAY 8, 1993
"SPRINGTIME RITUAL: CUTTING MONEY PIE INTO 13 PIECES"

DECEMBER 11, 1993
"A NEW DYNAMIC"

Steering readers through the corridors of the Capitol, Hager's two related accounts reveal the Byzantine manner in which congressional barons divvy up the funds flowing into the treasury. In the first piece, Hager describes the toils and troubles of "the so-called college of cardinals"—the 13 subcommittee chairmen of the House Appropriations Committee, a baker's dozen of the most powerful people in Washington. Springtime, Hager reports, finds them tired and irritable as they struggle to guard their fiefdoms while trying to meet Presidential spending requests that surpass the budget limits proscribed by law. The process can become quite taxing, a clash "between the green-eyeshade, detail-conscious world of the appropriators and the big-think, broad-picture realm of the budget drafters." In the second article, Hager shows how the dominion of these potent cardinals is challenged by "a force whose powers in some ways seem to rival their own"—namely, a veteran staff accountable not to these subcommittee chairmen but only to the chairman of the full committee, in this case Rep. William H. Natcher [D-KY]. Committee staff members, Hager explains, "wield enormous influence of their own over money matters and, by extension, over policy matters." Because the average tenure for these staff members exceeds two decades, "the result is a staff that rarely changes, no matter who moves into a subcommittee chairmanship—or even into the committee's top spot." As a consequence, voters have far less control over the legislative process than they imagine. With his remarkable snapshot of these obscure power brokers, Hager exposes a puissant cabal of unelected Washington insiders directing the flow of billions of tax dollars.

Diana B. Henriques and Dean Baquet

The New York Times

OCTOBER 10-12, 1993
"TAINTED TRADE" SERIES

Brandishing the Freedom of Information Act, the investigative duo of Henriques and Baquet marches through reams of confidential Agriculture Department records and court documents to provide a damning account of bureaucracy run amok. The pair chronicles incompetence, waste, logrolling, and fraudulent practices since the late 1980s by large agricultural concerns and their government patrons in Washington. On Day One of this hard-hitting three-part series, Henriques and Baquet probe abuses in programs aimed at bolstering crop exports. "From 1986 through 1989," they write, "one large Agriculture Department program to help the United States compete against the Europeans awarded $1.38 billion—more than half its payouts—to four multinational corporations, two of them based in Europe." In a subsequent article, the pair blasts the "cozy relationship between Corporate Agriculture and the Federal Government" by revealing how one company used a low-cost loan from the U.S. Agency for International Development to build a plant and corner the Iraqi rice market. Saving their most explosive information for the series finale, Henriques and Baquet expose a practice by which the Agriculture Department—in direct violation of a 1986 executive order—permits companies known to have defrauded the government to participate in lucrative federal programs. "Records show [that] top department officials—including the Secretary of Agriculture in the Bush Administration [Clayton K. Yeutter] and his most senior aides—have refused to comply or have prolonged the process for years." Countless hours spent poring through reams of classified papers and public records pay huge dividends for Henriques and Baquet as the two tear the cover off egregious mismanagement in the nation's capital.

Carol J. Loomis
Fortune
MAY 3, 1993
"DINOSAURS?"

"Jurassic Park" may have inspired many journalistic flights of fancy in 1993, but a different motivation moves Loomis to investigate "Dinosaurs." Demonstrating in this cover story her unique ability to recognize shifts in the business landscape, she examines the fundamental question of why some successful companies eventually fail. This article should keep Bill Gates awake at night, fraught with worry, as Loomis describes how three of the century's mammoth corporations—IBM, General Motors, and Sears—are today "painfully and wheezingly gasping for breath." As recently as the 1960s, she notes, "IBM was...a monarch, about to launch its famed 360 family of computers....GM was then widely suspected of trying to hold its market share down, so as not to rouse the dogs of antitrust. Sears absolutely ruled retailing; the company was bigger in merchandise sales than its next four rivals combined." But along the way, she shows, the three companies faltered. The dynamism that propelled each to the pinnacle of the business world, Loomis argues, yielded to excessive caution. All "thought themselves protected from competitive harm by economies of scale," which led in turn to paralyzing layers of bureaucracy. An arrogant sense of security impeded each company's ability to size up competitors' threats or to make critical decisions. Before anyone could realize what was happening, Microsoft, Japanese carmakers, and Wal-Mart knocked them off their perches. Firing a warning shot at corporate titans who would grow comfortable and lethargic in their success, Loomis displays a masterful vision of American business writ large.

Gretchen Morgenson
Forbes
AUGUST 16, 1993
"FUN AND GAMES ON NASDAQ"

Ending her stint at *Forbes* with a decided bang, Morgenson gives readers the lowdown on "the hanky-panky" behind NASDAQ, the equities market in which shares are traded via computer and telephone, rather than at some central exchange. The over-the-counter market has pulled even with the New York Stock Exchange in terms of shares handled, and "NASDAQ claims to be the home for companies of the future," trading stocks like MCI Communications and Intel Corp. But Morgenson looks beyond the rise of this up-and-coming exchange to see something insidious. "NASDAQ volume is more profitable for the brokers than is stock-exchange volume. Because it is more profitable for brokers, they have more incentive to push NASDAQ stocks." Morgenson chronicles numerous instances of NASDAQ trickery as brokers enrich themselves at the expense of unwitting investors. Ripping the "clubby world of NASDAQ trading" where traders routinely bilk their clients, she describes the scheme of trading ahead of customers' orders, which "can have the effect of driving the price of a stock up when you want to buy and down when you want to sell. On the New York and the American exchanges, this is illegal." One source estimates that only 38 percent of NASDAQ's volume is customer trading—the rest is by brokers for themselves. After crunching the numbers, Morgenson concludes that the auction system at the major exchanges gets investors better prices than the faceless, computer-linked world of NASDAQ trading. Any investor dealing in O-T-C stocks would be wise to check out Morgenson's farewell story from *Forbes*.

Scot J. Paltrow
Los Angeles Times
JUNE 22, 1993
"PARTNERS IN A TROUBLED VENTURE"

JUNE 23, 1993
"AS ENERGY FUNDS STUMBLED, COMPANIES REAPED BENEFITS"

A flurry of internal records released in a class-action suit brought against Prudential Securities provided Paltrow the ammunition to write this definitive, two-part assessment of the 1980s Prudential-Bache (as it was then known) limited-partnership scandal. Spending the first half of 1993 wading through a sea of documents, Paltrow pieces together an imbroglio that rivals any before seen on Wall Street. More than 130,000 investors, he reports, poured money into extremely risky oil and gas ventures touted by Pru-Bache brokers as extraordinarily safe investments. "The firm fired up its salespeople with promises of lavish European vacations, bonuses and commissions far higher than they got for selling municipal bonds or stocks. It assured brokers that the investments had been thoroughly researched both by Pru-Bache and its mighty parent company, Prudential Insurance." Adroitly assembling confidential Prudential memos, sales pamphlets, and instruction manuals for brokers, Paltrow shows how the firm attempted to hide the risk involved. He also chronicles the questionable relationship between Prudential executives and the tiny Louisiana wildcatting company "inexplicably assigned" to handle their oil and gas business. The Louisiana company, a firm with an established track record of failure, staged "lavish hunting trips and European and Mexican vacations—including one 10-day trip to London on which a senior Pru-Bache executive ran up a tab of $34,000. All the perks were charged to the partnerships and ultimately paid by investors." Paltrow's Prudential profile hits home because he *doesn't* rely on mawkish anecdotal accounts of investors losing their shirts to prove his point. After bunkering down on the court's paper mountain, Paltrow emerges with a powerhouse series leaving few questions unanswered about the company's shady financial practices.

Mark Robichaux
The Wall Street Journal

AUGUST 27, 1993
"CABLE FIRMS PUSH TO SHORT-CIRCUIT '92 LAW"

SEPTEMBER 28, 1993
"SCRAMBLED PICTURE: HOW CABLE-TV FIRMS RAISED RATES IN WAKE OF LAW TO CURB THEM"

When the cable reregulation law took effect in September, consumers cried murder as rates that were supposed to fall rose instead. Critics savaged Congress and the Federal Communications Commission for crafting rules that blew up in everyone's face. Before implementation of these rules, Robichaux finds himself in the distinct minority of journalists who refuse to swallow whole the notion of reregulation as viewers' salvation. In an article just before the law takes effect, he cautions that many cable companies are working to undercut it. The latter article, penned just weeks after the law's implementation, confirms Robichaux's earlier speculation. "Cable companies are finding loopholes in the new law to raise rates rather than reduce them," he states. "Some used lapses in the law to raise a variety of charges to offset any rate reductions." Robichaux explains an aspect of the issue that many journalists failed to consider. "While opposing the bills in Congress, cable operators had predicted that rates would go up, not down if the bills were passed. Since then, they have labored to make that prediction come true, raising rates and telling consumers the cable law is to blame." Rather than just fault the industry, Robichaux fingers lawmakers and the FCC for devising vague regulations rife with loopholes. "Congress wrote the legislation...in terms so narrow and strictly defined that the FCC had little discretion to make desirable changes. In addition, the FCC had too little time and staff to draft rules for enforcing the new act." Where other journalists voice surprise at the reregulation imbroglio, Robichaux provides a thorough assessment of why the law went awry, targeting suspects in both industry and government.

John W. Verity
Business Week

FEBRUARY 8, 1993
"GUESS WHAT: IBM IS LOSING OUT IN MAINFRAMES, TOO"

JUNE 7, 1993
"THE MIDGETS, THE MAMMOTH, AND THE MAINFRAMES"

For all the problems IBM has suffered and that journalists have chronicled, one stands out—unswerving devotion to the mainframe computer, which the press loves to describe as woefully obsolete. Hold on a minute, says Verity, "Clearly, the mainframe is not dead." Indeed, in two related articles, he shows that the still-lucrative and intensely competitive mainframe industry poses new problems for its Goliath. Having suffered many blows at the hands of personal computers, IBM must now weather an attack on a different front. A frantic IBM, Verity reveals, is "losing [market] share in a shrinking market." However, although annual purchases have dropped nearly 30 percent since 1990, mainframes continue to be IBM's cash cow: $5.1 billion in sales, he notes, "is still a healthy piece of change for any company. And gross margins of as much as 60 percent are nothing to sneer at." Competitors, who not so long ago waited to see IBM's new line in order to ape it, now blaze trails in mainframe technology, with IBM playing ignominious catch-up. The ponderous Big Blue, Verity explains, finds itself too slow to adapt to a fast-moving marketplace. Having seen its market share slip from 85 to 68 percent in just four years, IBM may be shooting itself in the foot. Smaller and more flexible companies, Verity's articles brilliantly show, are discovering there's gold in them thar mainframe hills.

Kirk Victor
National Journal
JULY 3, 1993
"BUYER BEWARE"

Kudos to Victor for delving into a weighty transportation issue largely ignored by every major press organ outside of *The Journal of Commerce*. Tackling the freight-undercharge crisis in the trucking and shipping industry, Victor examines the complicated and controversial topic with fairness and clarity. After deregulation in 1980, shippers negotiated lower rates with truckers hauling their goods, though often without filing the agreed-upon new rates with the Interstate Commerce Commission, as required by law. Trustees for trucking companies that have gone bankrupt have targeted "deep-pocketed shipping customers," attempting to recover the difference between the new rates and those still on file. "The pot of loot that's at stake here is certainly nothing to sneeze at," writes Victor. "The total could reach $32 billion, according to the ICC. A half-million 'undercharge' claims have already been filed." Despite the mighty fortunes hanging in the balance, the issue's complexity likely scared off other journalists. No wonder, then, that most media outlets take a pass later in the year when the Supreme Court invalidates most undercharge claims. Victor deserves commendation for alerting readers to a dispute with serious ramifications for other industries, as well as for the principles of negotiated settlements.

SCIENCE & TECHNOLOGY

Lawrence K. Altman
The New York Times
JANUARY 12, 1993
"WHEN AN IMPORTANT DRUG IS SCARCE"

With an astute examination of the pharmaceutical industry, Altman explores what happens when the producer of a critical drug fails to meet demand. Stressing the dilemma plaguing the U.S. drug industry, this veteran doctor-journalist argues persuasively that "because many drugs are made by only one company, a serious manufacturing or financial problem could leave the United States vulnerable to a sudden disruption in the supply of standard drugs." Digging deeper, Altman covers the recent shortage of nitroglycerin pills as well as two other shortages: one that involved a drug used "to treat a parasitic infection of the brain that is common among AIDS patients"; and another that involved "two anti-tuberculosis drugs." Tuberculosis, he adds, "is now surging in incidence, and for a time the shortage hampered efforts to control the disease." Altman also probes the issue of monopolies among the pharmaceutical companies. "It is widely believed that when a drug goes off patent, the monopoly ends, resulting in increased competition and lower prices. But that is often not the case. Some drugs are still made exclusively by one manufacturer, although they are no longer protected by that patent." In a year of scare-stories about runaway pharmaceutical prices, Altman questions a major industry on behalf of the people who depend on their products to survive.

Natalie Angier
The New York Times
AUGUST 31, 1993
"THEY'RE SMART, FOR FISH, AND A MODEL OF DIVERSITY"

For the third year in a row, Angier's work on animal behavior wins her top honors. Her superior piece on cichlids, a most diverse and speciated fish, gets this year's prize. "The date is a dud and both parties know it," Angier writes of the cichlids' amusing mating rituals. "Yet as long as they are stuck with each other...they make a wan effort to flirt. He lunges lazily toward her. She quivers gently in response....He circles around, charges her again and tries to nip her, but now she's getting bored with the charade and moves away from him. Reacting likewise, he drifts off to the opposite end of the tank. For a few moments they are each lost in the inscrutable vastness of fish thought. And then it happens. The female opens her plump, sensual carved lips into the widest, roundest, most perfect, least courteous gape of a mouth that can be imagined: a fish yawn." Using these mating rituals as an intro into the cichlids' survival habits, Angier piles up detail after fascinating detail. "People are especially taken with the [cichlids'] courtship and fry-rearing practices. Most [other] fish lay eggs and abandon them, or the father may remain and watch the eggs until they hatch. But among cichlids, both parents often engage in protracted parental care. They brood their eggs in their mouths, and even after the fry are born, they protect the little fish by taking them back into the safety of their mouths when predators approach. 'They'll suck the fry back in as though they're sucking in strands of spaghetti,' [one researcher says]....In some species, both parents also feed their fry with their own flesh, allowing the young fish to nibble at the scales and nutritious mucus cells in the surface of their bodies." Through such remarkable descriptions, Angier makes readers care about these extraordinary little creatures and what their actions say about the natural world.

Malcolm W. Browne
The New York Times
May 4, 1993
"City Lights and Space Ads May Blind Stargazers"

In this depressing but entertaining article, Browne focuses on the manmade debris cluttering the skies that impedes astronomers' efforts to peer into the universe. The latest threat to stargazers is a plan to sell advertising on satellites in space. "America's great observatories now face the possibility that huge commercial billboards may soon be rocketed into orbit, while cities fearful of crime are flooding the night sky with even brighter lights. Added to this plague of light pollution, astronomical observatories also face increasing interference from such mundane sources as radio-operated garage-door openers." The recession, Browne reveals, has made some astronomers more receptive to commercializing the heavens. "The economy has...reduced Federal financing of several branches of science, leading some Government scientists to work with promoters on such projects as commercial advertising in space." Browne discusses how the brightly illuminated satellite billboards would disable observatories and how stargazers, in search of darker skies, may need to retreat to Hawaii or "the mountains of northern Chile." But "stray visible light is merely one of the plagues of astronomy," Browne explains. "Another is a thickening global smog of radio interference," which has increased greatly in recent decades because of powerful broadcasting stations, automobile computers, fluorescent lights, and the use of many small appliances. In his woeful conclusion, Browne quotes a researcher who throws up his hands and says, "'I guess it's possible that eventually we'll be chased away to the moon if we want to continue doing astronomy.'"

David L. Chandler
The Boston Globe
June 7, 1993
"Can We Remodel Mars? Should We?"

Straddling the border between science and science fiction, Chandler pens an eye-opening piece on the possibility of altering the climate of Mars to make it more similar to that of the Earth—and thus habitable by humans. At present, the Martian climate is too cold by about 100 degrees Fahrenheit to sustain human life. But if the temperature were raised—something scientists believe to be within the grasp of today's technology—then a runaway greenhouse effect could create rivers, oceans, and an environment suitable for living creatures. "The key to making Mars into a pleasant place for humans to live is to harness the very phenomenon with which we may be threatening the survival of our own planet: Global warming induced by the addition of 'greenhouse gases' to the atmosphere." Chandler addresses the copious scientific and ethical issues, such as "whether Mars now harbors any kind of life. If there is an indigenous life, however primitive—some scientists believe isolated pockets of simple microbes might still live there—does that mean we should not tamper with the planet?" The ultimate decision of whether "to terraform Mars will be made by colonists many decades from now, [one scientist] said, not by those who remain on Earth. 'Nothing anybody decides today will have any influence whatever.'" Perhaps so, but the idea itself, as Chandler ably conveys it, is enough to fire the imagination of even the most hidebound Earthling.

Alan M. MacRobert
The Boston Globe
MARCH 29, 1993
"THE SKY IS FULL OF SIGNS OF SPRING"

"When you wish upon a star..."—look out, it might be a planet! In his wonderful *Globe* "Star Watch" column tracing the configuration of stars and planets in the springtime sky, MacRobert, an editor at *Sky & Telescope*, focuses his lens on Jupiter and how different the solar system would be if the giant planet were a star. "It missed out only because it's not massive enough," he explains. "If it had another 80 times more [mass], the heat and pressure at its core would be enough to ignite the nuclear reaction that makes the sun shine, and Jupiter would light up as a red dwarf star." And how might Jupiter's elevation to stardom affect life on Earth? "In addition to our familiar bright sun, we'd have a lesser one that would nevertheless dazzle the eye and maintain perpetual twilight whenever it had the sky to itself. Spring would be a season of constant light for the next few years. In the fall, on the other hand, we'd have two suns of different colors in the daytime sky, and after they both set in the west, autumn nights would be as dark as usual. The season of perpetual light and the season of double-sun days would shift around the calendar in a 12-year cycle, so that spring, summer, fall and winter would experience each condition twice per generation. It would be a much more interesting world." MacRobert shows his disappointment in a single-sun solar system with this final sentence: "We are celestially deprived by having only one sun, and Jupiter makes a pretty poor substitute." This heavenly article conveys all the wonders of the night sky.

Jeffrey Salmon
Commentary
JULY 1993
"GREENHOUSE ANXIETY"

In this spectacular piece, Salmon cautions against rushing to judgment on global warming. "On the face of it, the greenhouse effect would seem to be an unlikely candidate for the apocalypse," he writes, adding that President Clinton has committed the U.S. to a goal of a 20 percent reduction in carbon dioxide (CO_2) emissions by the year 2000. This would cause prices of energy-producing fuels to skyrocket, and, since the U.S. emits only 30 percent of the Earth's greenhouse gases, stabilizing CO_2 emissions worldwide "would require a fundamental restructuring of the global economy." Salmon goes on to reveal that "whatever role might be played by global warming in domestic and international politics, there is *no* solid scientific evidence to support the theory that the Earth is warming because of manmade greenhouse gasses." Brilliantly explicating the scientific aspects of the issue, Salmon discloses that "the actual greenhouse effect is a natural phenomenon, existing for eons before humans ever appeared on the scene." He explains that the estimates which approximate a one-half degree rise in the temperature per year "are based on computer simulations of future climate change....In fact, every greenhouse forecast...is the result of computers attempting to model the myriad factors that influence climate change....To gain an idea of how reliable [computer] models are, consider how poorly they predict climate changes we have *already* experienced. And if they are incapable of accounting for the past, how will they be able to predict the future?" Concluding this provocative essay, Salmon ponders the fallout caused by the global-warming controversy. "Undoing the harm this has done to the credibility of the scientific community may be the work of generations."

Barry Siegel
Los Angeles Times
NOVEMBER 7, 1993
"2 BABIES, 1 HEART AND A DILEMMA"
NOVEMBER 8, 1993
"A FATHER'S UGLY FALL FROM GRACE"

In this fascinating pair of stories, Siegel portrays the heart-wrenching circumstances of

Siamese twins who shared a malformed heart and the media circus that erupted over the decision to separate them. He narrates the story of the Indiana couple's odyssey through the medical establishment and how the father—"a good ol' boy" and "violent substance abuser" with a criminal record—manipulated the press to gain fame and money. The doctors would have to kill one of the babies to allow the other to live, Siegel explains, and even then the odds for survival were extremely low. Although doctors urged the couple to let nature take its course, the parents opted for the operation. More than 100 journalists who soon descended on the family and hospital portrayed the parents as heroes defying the experts, and the father basked in the attention. Along with trying to sell the movie rights to the story, he spent money raised for the $300,000 operation on "a used Chevrolet" and "a three-day cocaine binge." Siegel focuses not just on the parents and the babies but on the doctors and the major social issues the case raised. "Was it fair to pour unlimited resources into an almost certainly futile effort, while failing to provide basic care to many thousands of children? Do we have a responsibility to serve as moral agents for the good of society, not just the interest of one family? Or should we instead ignore the needs of the community and pursue the health care of the individuals at hand?" Stepping back, Siegel examines the case from myriad angles and wonders who is to blame. "Was it the news media's fault, for egging everyone on with a fairy tale about courageous folks battling impossible odds? Was it the health-care system's fault, for allowing doctors no recourse when families—even dysfunctional, manipulative families—demand expensive and nearly futile treatment? Or was it [the doctor's] own fault for failing to slam the gate quickly and firmly?" While no easy answers emerge, Siegel dramatically relates the entire story, skillfully highlighting the emotions of all the individuals involved and the complex ethical issues of the tragic case.

David Stipp
The Wall Street Journal
MARCH 22, 1993
"CANCER SCARE"

"After Jim Swide [of Ukiah, California] recently emptied a bag of sand into his two-year-old daughter's sandbox, some words caught his eye: 'may contain...crystalline silica...known to the state of California to cause cancer.'" Thus Stipp begins his fascinating account of California regulations that claim common beach sand causes cancer. "Crystalline silica, the primary ingredient of sand and rocks, looms as perhaps the scariest cancer demon ever," Stipp writes. "It is in countless products: pharmaceuticals, bricks, paper, jewelry, putty, paint, plastics, household cleansers—not to mention bags of sand for toddlers' backyard boxes. Soil is laced with the stuff, so is dust in the air....The idea that much of the planet's surface is a deadly chemical may sound like the stuff of science fiction. But it is true: For several years, crystalline silica has been classified as carcinogenic." Stipp notes, however, that the evidence comes largely from injections of silica in animals. "The listing of silica as a probable human carcinogen was based chiefly on five rat experiments. But at least five similar studies in hamsters and mice, all reported by 1986, found no evidence of cancer.) Stipp concludes that "the official lumping of beach sand in the same category as carcinogens such as dioxin...suggests as nothing before that the regulatory system tends to cry wolf when it comes to cancer." In fairly presenting this controversial matter, Stipp's eye-opening article highlights a major regulatory issue.

William Tucker
Reader's Digest
JUNE 1993
"THIS IS NO WAY TO SAVE THE EARTH"

In this revealing piece, Tucker describes what "has gone badly awry" with the Superfund program, which Congress established in 1980 to pay for the clean-up of toxic-waste contamination. At the program's outset, Superfund investigators made dramatic and vital discoveries, such as locating "valleys filled with chemical drums, unfenced dump sites littered with explosives, [and] fissures where toxins oozed out of the earth." But in the past decade, Tucker contends, "the program has spun out of control," as the government has sued everyone "capable of shelling out large sums of money." As one example of the unfair lawsuits, personal hardships, and legal gridlock the Superfund program has caused, Tucker cites the case of Helen Kramer, a 93-

year-old widow from Mantua, New Jersey, "who allowed an old gravel pit on her farmland to be used as a landfill. She accepted chemical waste only when it was legal to do so. Then the EPA named the landfill as a hazard and sued her. Kramer had to declare bankruptcy to keep her house." Tucker also describes the case of Ron Stevens of Memphis, Tennessee, who in 1977 sold nine used transformers for a profit of $250. After some of them ended up at a waste site more than 10 years later, Superfund officials "threatened [Stevens] with a lawsuit...[because] the transformers contained a few ounces of oil with PCBs which can harm wildlife. The EPA told him he could settle for $250,000." In 1993, Tucker explains, lawmakers began holding hearings to consider reforms of the Superfund program. "As President Clinton told a joint session of Congress, it's time we use 'Superfund to clean up pollution for a change and not just pay lawyers.'" In this eye-opening article, Tucker succinctly lays out the entire story.

Michael Waldholz

The Wall Street Journal

March 30, 1993

"Pricing Health Care: Drug Makers' Images Are Self-Induced"

Surveying the scarred image of American drug companies, Waldholz's trenchant piece answers clearly his own question, "How can anyone justify carping at companies that spend as much as $1 billion a year to cure disease?" Mostly, he reasons, the drug companies brought on their own problems through their secretive cultures and poor choices of public battles. "The companies...simply have been unable to explain that discovering new medicines is extraordinarily expensive and fraught with a high rate of failure—only one in eight experimental medicines makes it out of human testing and onto pharmacy shelves." But Waldholz judges the companies guilty as charged regarding price hikes. "A recent congressional study found that some companies boosted prices of old medicines 100 to 150 percent between 1982 and 1990." When the drug industry fought a proposal to provide a drug-insurance benefit for elderly people on Medicare, it ran head-on into the massive senior-citizen lobby, again inflicting on itself massive harm. "The great irony is that if the elderly had been covered by a Medicare drug benefit, the drug makers could have gotten away a lot longer with increasing prices to the privately insured. Now, agreeing to a Medicare drug benefit merely looks self-serving, as a way to generate more revenue." Pulling no punches, Waldholz smartly appraises the damage the drug industry has inflicted on itself.

FOREIGN

Mark Danner

The New Yorker

December 6, 1993

"The Truth of El Mozote"

Extraordinary and immense, Danner's article on the 1982 massacre of hundreds of Salvadoran peasants in El Mozote by U.S.-trained Salvadoran army units contains a distinct point of view—that the U.S. government unjustly whitewashed the entire affair. From start to finish, this exhaustive piece supports Danner's contention that the handling of the incident reflects the indelicate balance between hard-nosed foreign policy and unpleasant reality during the Reagan administration. "That in the United States [the massacre] came to be known, that it was exposed to the light and then allowed to fall back into the dark, makes the story of El Mozote—how it came to happen and how it came to be denied—a central parable of the Cold War." Danner provides a detailed history of the event from myriad angles, including military accounts, rebel broadcasts, reports that appeared in the U.S. press, and the horrifying experiences of Rufina Amaya Márquez, the sole survivor of the massacre. "Rufina could not see the children; she could only hear their cries as the soldiers waded into them, slashing some with their machetes, crushing the skulls of others with the butts of their rifles." Danner reveals how reporters from *The New York Times* and *The Washington Post* visited El Mozote, saw evidence of the massacre, and reported it, and how junior State Department officers tried to reach the village, but turned back when their Salvadoran army escorts refused to continue, about an hour shy of their destination. Danner quotes extensively from the State Department report—which claimed no evidence of the massacre was found, but failed to mention that investigators never made it to the village—which was used to discredit the accounts in the *Times* and the *Post*. Danner also finds through his own reporting that the State Department officials who investigated the massacre strongly felt that something nefarious involving the army had occurred, but because of the political nature of the event, they failed to convey their impressions in their findings. Danner's balanced and fresh reporting qualifies this story as the definitive history of an ugly and important event, which, had it been publicized, might have altered the course of U.S. policy in Latin America.

Tony Horwitz
The Wall Street Journal
JULY 6, 1993
"RISE IN KNEECAPPINGS SHOWS A DIRTY SECRET OF LONG CIVIL STRIFE"

Through numerous compelling anecdotes from Northern Ireland, Horwitz portrays the anarchy that results when government institutions collapse. By focusing on the increasingly common and excruciatingly painful practice of "kneecapping"—shooting through the knees or elbows to maim rather than kill—Horwitz describes how vigilante justice quickly turns "habitual and thuggish." Belfast presents a prime example of this breakdown of public order, and "the maiming... reflects one of the dirty secrets of this long, dirty conflict: Protestants and Catholics now target their own almost as often as they target each other, or the police." In fact, says Horwitz, the thuggishness has largely superseded the ideological causes that spawned the violence. "In the mean streets of Belfast, giving young men guns and the license to use them—as in Bosnia and Somalia—has mutated political passions, often reducing this struggle to a cynical war between well-armed urban gangs." Debunking the oft-made argument that the police are ineffective battling common crime, Horwitz observes, "Most of those kneecapped aren't undetected criminals; they are lawbreakers awaiting trial." He further adds that, "crimes now deemed to merit kneecapping include failure to pay dues to paramilitary groups." While Horwitz focuses on Belfast, where such groups are gradually falling out of favor, his masterful and expansive analysis highlights the danger of allowing powerful but unaccountable groups to selectively enforce the law when government institutions cannot.

Christina Lamb
Financial Times
APRIL 30, 1993
"A BLIND EYE TO THE ENEMY WITHIN"

In this highly insightful assessment of the Brazilian economy and the first fiscal plan of Brazilian President Itamar Franco—which calls for massive spending from empty government coffers to stimulate an inflationary economy—Lamb persuasively argues that the new program falls far short of what's needed to overhaul the nation's economic system. She shows how Brazilian politics survives the ongoing economic free-fall and explains why the international community wants nothing more to do with the world's ninth largest economy and fifth largest country. "For years, Brazil has been living with levels of inflation considered by most economists to be unsustainable....[It] has become institutionalized. Daily or monthly indexes are issued for everything from construction materials to rents....95 percent of the money supply is in bank accounts which are indexed at the daily inflation rate." Lamb posits that because of this indexing, which adjusts the values of goods, services, and money to match the inflation rate, Brazilian voters never feel the effects of inflation. She reasons that real solutions will come only after a total national breakdown—which may not be far off. "Anyone who has driven on a Brazilian road or tried to make a phone call from Rio can see that the infrastructure is collapsing. The country...holds the world record for the number of deaths in traffic accidents last year." Lamb's incisive portrait of the devastated Brazilian economy will shock even the soberest of readers.

Gary Marx
Chicago Tribune
JANUARY 14, 1993
"SOMALIAN MISSION FRUSTRATES MARINES"

In this riveting piece on the intense violence confronting Marines just five weeks into their Somalia mission, Marx articulates the anxiety of young soldiers in a style that brilliantly recalls the "New Journalism" that produced some of the finest writing from Vietnam. "'Drop your weapon,' [Marine Sgt. Ralph] Guerrero shouted. The gunman turned toward Guerrero, raised his rifle—and paused. 'I could have killed him...' said Guerrero after the Somali surrendered and was taken into custody. 'We came here to feed people, and I keep telling my people that this is not a war...but they are trying to kill us.'" Appearing immediately after the first Marine death, this piece eloquently portrays the troops' battered morale. "American soldiers often get stoned by Somali kids; others are cursed by Somalis in crude English....Other Somalis point their index finger and thumb at the American GIs, mimicking a gun and pulling the trigger." Marx's effort comes fully alive when he switches to a real-time, moment-by-moment narration from a Marine patrol. "Bullets ricochet off a concrete wall within feet of a dozen Marines. They return fire. One Marine lays down a burst of covering fire while six men move across a field toward a group of Somalis. Guerrero confiscates two AK-47 rifles and takes six prisoners. Suddenly, the Marines are under fire from three different directions. Guerrero calls in reinforcements, a pair of M-1 tanks and two armored personnel carriers. The gunmen flee, but Marine command tells Guerrero to release the six prisoners." Masterfully combining style and observation, Marx conveys a chilling reality from the streets of Mogadishu.

John Simpson
The Spectator
JULY 17, 1993
"LEAVE US TO DIE IN PEACE"

This concise article conveys both the despair and optimism of Sarajevo residents trapped in a brutal war. Beginning with his own dash across a sniper alley simply to escape the "claustrophobia of the Holiday Inn," Simpson vividly reports the almost-surreal incidents of compassion among the victims in the besieged city, and the twisted, self-conscious justifications offered by soldiers in the hills. One Muslim woman he meets allows her Serbian next-door neighbor to receive telephone calls from her son on the siege lines. "'I always used to put him through,' the woman told me. 'They were decent enough people, even though they were Serbs. And we all have to live together, don't we?'" Simpson finds Serbian soldiers "unwilling to recognize themselves as the killers and maimers of children and women and old men. ...'We aren't besieging Sarajevo,' one of them insisted; 'we're just here to protect our Serbian villages from those bloody Muslims.'" Back in the streets he finds a badly disheveled 72-year-old woman alone in her bombed-out basement apartment. "'I'm all alone, you see. I'm an orphan....I only have two friends in the whole world: a man who brought me this wood—he's a Serb, but Serbs can be good men too—and a woman who shares her sugar with me.' She flicked her hands distractedly at the ants, and tears filled her eyes again. 'I can't even wash myself, so even though I'm ill, I'm ashamed to go to the doctor. And when the shells go off, I think I'm going to die.'" By focusing on individuals and allowing them to speak for themselves, Simpson captures the tragedy, the absurdity, and the ongoing horrors of the war in Bosnia.

Jonathan Stevenson
Foreign Policy
SUMMER 1993
"HOPE RESTORED IN SOMALIA"

Reflecting on the UN's diplomatic approach in Somalia, Stevenson offers an outstanding analysis of why the mission deteriorated almost from day-one into a morass of deadly confusion. With a fresh look at the decentralized, "clan-based" political structure of the war-torn African nation, Stevenson explains how the clan system exacerbated the plight of refugees trying to escape fighting and drought during the past three years. "As the victims lost their children to malnutrition and atrocities, they staggered to Mogadishu in the hope that food would arrive by sea. But with local clans exclusionary by nature and already frazzled from all the violence, the newcomers could not secure food from their fellow Somalis." Stevenson argues that the UN's failure to respect local customs contributed to early tensions with residents. "The U.S. soldiers were not well briefed about Somali peculiarities. They skinnydipped in full view of the Muslim natives, never realizing that Somalis would take offense. The soldiers were also instructed not to talk to the Somalis, fueling misunderstandings." Stevenson shows further UN missteps that subverted the exhaustive efforts of envoy Mohammed Sahnoun, who served in 1992 and was the only UN representative to fully grasp the nation's clan structure and the need to work with it—rather than against it. "Because [former dictator Mohammed] Siad Barre had favored his own clan, the Marehan, so heavily and abused others so brutally, each rebel group vengefully sought to take Siad Barre's power for itself." Formulating an in-depth explanation of events, Stevenson provides the definitive portrait of the chaos, warfare, and failed diplomacy in Somalia.

Anne Swardson

The Washington Post

NOVEMBER 23, 1993

"UNSPEAKABLE CRIMES: THIS STORY CAN'T BE TOLD IN CANADA. AND SO ALL CANADA IS TALKING ABOUT IT"

In this sensational, yet thoughtful piece, Swardson describes both the abduction and murder of two Canadian teenage girls and the legal issues raised by the Canadian court's injunction against publicity about the case. Karla Homolka and Paul Teale were charged separately for the kidnapping, rape, torture, and murder. Afraid that public dissemination of the grisly details would prevent a fair trial, Teale's prosecutors asked Ontario Court Justice Francis Kovacs to censor press coverage of Homolka's trial. The judge agreed and allowed members of the Canadian press into the courtroom only under the condition that they print just the plea and the sentence. "Foreign media were barred from the courtroom entirely because, the judge said, the ban could not be enforced against them. The general public was kept out as well—Kovacs said he feared people would tell U.S. media what had happened." The judge's ban inspired rampant speculation and rumors throughout Canada, Swardson notes, and brazenly challenging the ruling, she provides a full account of the facts read at Homolka's trial. A Canadian distributor shredded copies of a British paper that carried similar details, and Canadian cable systems blacked-out an episode of "A Current Affair" that dealt with the case. Prudently arguing that such bans prevent reasonable public debate and encourage sensationalism, Swardson makes the strongest possible case against court-ordered injunctions simply by highlighting their ineffectiveness and printing the truth.

Andrew Tanzer

Forbes

AUGUST 2, 1993

"THIS TIME IT'S FOR REAL"

In this broad survey of Chinese consumer markets, Tanzer expertly utilizes statistics and the insight of foreign merchants to illustrate both the nation's tremendous hunger for Western goods and the corresponding range of business opportunity. Despite the paradox of a burgeoning consumer market in a country where the government reports the per-capita income at less than $400 a year, Tanzer notes that "nearly every independent study by academics and multilateral agencies puts incomes, adjusted for black market activity and purchasing power parity, at three or four times that level." On top of that, Tanzer adds, Chinese citizens still enjoy huge state subsides and "spend less than 5 percent of household income on housing, health care, education and transportation combined, compared with 30 percent to 40 percent in other Asian countries." Moving beyond figures, Tanzer draws extensively from the experience of advertisers in China who recognize encouraging trends all around them, such as the dramatic growth in the number of households with refrigerators—"great for chilling that Coke and Pabst"—and the fact that China has become the world's largest market for TV sets. "'[Chinese] consumers want to show off that they can afford to spend money,' says James Wong, general manager of DDB Needham Advertising's Beijing office. 'They leave the tags on sunglasses and labels on the sleeves of suits.'" With this business-oriented glimpse of China, Tanzer effectively demonstrates that despite the huge divergence in lifestyle and income among China's 1 billion people, the consumer boom has just begun.

Stefan Wagstyl

Financial Times

MAY 14, 1993

"PEACE IS IMPOSED ON A STILL TROUBLED PUNJAB"

In this compelling piece on the return of relative calm to the Punjab region of India, Wagstyl finds that "terrorism has been suppressed only by one of the toughest police campaigns seen in India....In the first four months of this year 38 died in terrorist attacks, compared with 1,518 last year and 2,591 in 1991." Wagstyl smartly reports that Punjabis, though concerned that strong-arm tactics fail to address terrorist demands for an independent Sikh state, welcome the return of both order and economic opportunity. Leading with the story of Madan Singh Bharara, a bicycle manufacturer, Wagstyl focuses on one salient detail: Bharara could recently add two new shifts at his factories because workers no longer fear traveling at night. "A key issue is jobs in the Punjab, especially for educated youths who no longer want to stay on their parents' farms and who might be tempted to become militants." Wagstyl credits K.P.S. Gill, the Sikh police chief who upon taking office in 1991 began to confront the militant bands of terrorists. "Mr. Gill turned conventional wisdom on its head by withdrawing the army from front-line positions and replacing it with the police. He also armed his men with semi-automatic weapons and taught them to shoot terrorists." Despite widespread concerns of human-rights groups about police abuse, Wagstyl states, "most Punjabis are less interested in Mr. Gill's methods than in his results. In Chandigarh, in nearby villages and in Ludhiana, the state's industrial center, the overwhelming feeling is of relief that terrorism seems beaten." Wagstyl's sharp analysis and keen reporting vividly describe the changing climate of the Punjab region.

Teresa Watanabe
Los Angeles Times
OCTOBER 30, 1993
"STACKING THE BIDS IN JAPAN"

In this insightful and exhaustively reported piece, Watanabe provides a detailed glimpse of the backroom dealings of the Japanese construction industry and bureaucracy as the two entities engage in a practice called *dango*—or bid-rigging—which involves payoffs to politicians and cooperation among firms. Emphasizing that the entrenched system will be tough to change, Watanabe employs stunning statistics and connects her story to a larger issue—the penetrability of the Japanese market. "For much of the last century [dango] carried a benevolent meaning—to take turns at the trough so no one would starve, to subordinate personal interests for the good of the group....Today, the dango system protects one of Japan's largest and most influential constituencies: 515,000 contractors and 6 million construction workers, including the relatives of an estimated 30 percent of the Japanese Parliament." The threat to thousands of small firms that couldn't exist without dango, Watanabe smartly points out, overrides concern about the considerably higher prices that result from the inefficiencies and payoffs. "Dango is said to boost prices by 16 to 33 percent, raking in excess profits of anywhere from $48 billion to $99 billion—more than the entire revenue raised by the Japanese consumption tax." Despite talk among politicians about opening Japanese markets, Watanabe finds unshaken confidence among business people. "Over fried rice in a Tokyo snack bar recently, three construction executives echoed breezy confidence: Japanese technology is tops, reams of required paperwork are all but unintelligible to outsiders, and the labor market is controlled by local 'bosses' who will not supply workers to just anyone." Combining fresh anecdotal evidence with her focused survey of the forces supporting the system, Watanabe reveals the daunting task facing foreign firms seeking to penetrate the Japanese market.

COMMENTATORS

Fred Barnes
The American Spectator
MAY 1993
"WHAT HEALTH CARE CRISIS?"

With the Republican establishment cowering under the seeming moral weight of President Clinton's crusade for health-care reform and the media feeding the public medical horror stories, Barnes takes the controversial stand of claiming that no crisis in health care exists. He energizes the debate on nationalizing the health-care industry by making a subtle, though monumentally important, distinction. "Will someone please tell Bill Clinton that having no health insurance is not the same as having no health care?" Barnes argues that health care is available to all Americans—hospitals have no choice. "Turning away patients isn't an option. Federal law requires medical screening of everyone requesting care at a hospital emergency room." Though admitting the American health-care system has problems—notably that many people lack insurance and access to primary-care—Barnes on the

whole offers a stirring defense. "Health care may (or may not) be too costly. But it's the best health care system in the world—not arguably the best, but the best." He warns against looking to other nations for model systems by pointing out their chief flaws, like chronically long waiting lists and poor service in Canada and England. Price controls and fee caps in Japan, he writes, breed impersonal service and "assembly-line treatment." He quotes a health professor who says that Tokyo outpatient physicians see an average of 49 patients per day, and 13 percent see over 100. In volunteering for the role of tempest in the health-care teapot, Barnes lays the groundwork for principled opposition to sweeping health-care changes.

Sidney Blumenthal
The New Yorker
October 25, 1993
"Why Are We in Somalia?"

In this brilliant assessment, Blumenthal details the succession of political errors and misjudgments that led to U.S. involvement in Somalia. "In trying to relieve the famine, we plunged directly into the murderous cockpit of Somali politics....The humanitarian role could not have been more political. Preventing the recurrence of the crisis that had brought us into Somalia required nothing less than establishing a quasi-neo-colonial United Nations trusteeship." The "Letter from Washington" columnist minutely examines the policy pressures and varying circumstances that led to President Bush's decision to intervene in the first place, and crisply recounts the chain of events that led to the U.N. hunt for General Mohamed Farah Aidid. Blumenthal also examines the political stakes and ramifications for the White House. "Bill Clinton's ultimate promise is the revival of domestic social policy [in the U.S.]. For better or worse, foreign policy encroaches....More at risk than anything else in the Somali crisis is Clinton's authority. His political interest has become the identifiable national interest. It has been placed in jeopardy by a history of miscalculation, cloaked in good intentions that Clinton wrapped around himself." In this provocative, nuanced essay, Blumenthal provides a comprehensive history of the U.S.-UN-Somalia story.

David S. Broder
The Washington Post
February 24, 1993
"Beware the 'Trust' Deficit"

Backing up his argument with solid analysis, the grand old man of Washington political journalism crafts an airtight indictment of President Clinton's economic program, stating quite plainly that "his plan just doesn't achieve its advertised goals." Broder decimates the President's "reliability" on this issue. "People are discovering that Clinton really played fast and loose with the facts in last year's campaign. When reporters challenged the assumptions and the internal mathematics of Clinton's campaign-season economic plan, 'Putting People First,' the Democratic nominee brushed off the questions. When Republicans said he was being deceptive, he issued indignant denials that ring hollow today." Broder explains specifically that "when the Bush campaign ran ads based on the calculation that Clinton could finance his campaign promises only by raising taxes on every family earning more than $36,600 a year, this is what the Democratic nominee said: 'It is blatantly false....It is a disgrace to the American people that the president of the United States would make a claim that is so baseless, that is so without foundation, so shameless in its attempt to get votes under false pretenses.'" Broder then announces, "last week Clinton, unembarrassed, put forward a revised program requiring tax increases the administration says will affect most families making over $30,000, one-sixth below the threshold George Bush had forecast. Clinton claims he has been forced to these steps by the unexpected $346 billion size of the deficit he inherited. But last July, he told *Business-Week* the deficits would approach $400 billion." White House officials "have conceded," Broder states, that "the higher tax bites actually begin at a figure closer to $20,000 than to $30,000." In this devastating assessment, Broder gets the goods on Clinton, hanging the new President with his own rhetoric.

Alexander Cockburn
Los Angeles Times
October 5, 1993
"A Democratic Russia Goes Up in Smoke"

Providing a succinct and clear-headed view of the burning of the Russian Parliament and the suspension of the constitution, this biweekly *Nation* columnist was the only journalist to recognize both the implications and the root cause of the uproar in Moscow. Upending the popular Western image of President Boris Yeltsin as the besieged selfless reformer, Cockburn works vigorously to establish the credibility of the legislature, an element in the story most others dismissed summarily. "The Russian Congress...had authentic democratic credentials," he states. "The deputies elected to it in March 1990, had faced the voters under conditions far from the one-party rituals of the past. It was this same Congress of People's Deputies that awarded Yeltsin his own political ascendancy and his executive post. [Ruslan] Khasbulatov and [Alexander] Rutskoi stood shoulder to shoulder with Yeltsin on the balcony of the Russian White House to denounce the attempted putsch of 1991. It was this Congress that brought not only this executive presidency into being, but also the Constitutional Court, modeled on the U.S. Supreme Court." But, argues Cockburn, "amid rising public resentment at his leadership, Yeltsin undertook the equivalent of suspending the Congress, the court and the constitution....Yeltsin dissolved Parliament on Sept. 21 because he was at the end of his tether. The breathing space and popular license of the approval he had won with his victory in April's referendum had been squandered." Cockburn then explains why in this sterling assessment: "economically, Russia remains stricken, plunged ever deeper into ruin by Yeltsin's team, coached by the same gang of international advisers whose failures in Poland recently prompted that nation's voters to give their biggest cheer to the former Communist Party." In simple but hard-hitting prose, Cockburn gives a perspective seldom seen in the mainstream media.

Rowland Evans &
Robert Novak

The Washington Post

MARCH 1, 1993
"CLINTON'S CORPORATE DEPENDENTS"

Following the Chamber of Commerce's about-face on Clintonomics and its endorsement of the President's "soak-the-rich taxes," Evans & Novak keenly assess the political implications of these actions. "The President has launched more than just another battle of the budget but seeks to shape the political landscape for a dozen years into the future, as Franklin D. Roosevelt and Ronald Reagan did. Integral to his plan is not to defeat business interests but to make them heavily dependent on government for survival. While Republicans are trapped in their sterile, green-eyeshade discussions of budget cuts, Clinton is playing for the big prize. Business leaders are asked to join the President's campaign for a program that increases the burden of taxes and regulation. In return, they are offered government dependency: subsidies, protection and co-operation. The takers are not reticent. Detroit's Big Three, much of the Silicon Valley and beleaguered corporations like the Boeing Co. are rushing into dependency." As usual, the pair's provocative analysis goes beyond mere events, noting that, "as Roosevelt proved, creators of new coalitions need not actually solve economic problems. What they need is a wide and deep base of supporters who cannot do without the government. When the U.S. Chamber of Commerce decided to play that game, Bill Clinton scored a big one." In one succinct column, Evans & Novak capture the essence of this pivotal decision.

Molly Ivins

Fort Worth Star-Telegram

APRIL 21, 1993
"AN ENDING MADE FOR TV MOVIES"

Making strong points from start to finish, this forthright Texan pens the definitive word on the siege and destruction of the Branch Davidian compound in Waco. "When the final confrontation with authority was forced—by the authorities, not by [David] Koresh—the mass suicide was predictable. It is part of a cult pattern." In this powerful essay, Ivins crafts a sharp argument on how the conflagration could have been avoided. "There was no reason for it to happen in Waco. Koresh was still talking to outsiders, to his lawyers. He wasn't hurting anyone. Maybe he wouldn't have come out after he finished his manuscript. So what? They'd already thrown a fence around the place. All they had to do was put one guard by a gate and wait. Who needed the million-dollar-a-day operation with the choppers and the M-60s? 'They could be in there for months!' said the alarmists. And who would that have hurt?" Ivins rails strongly against the government and indicts it in no uncertain terms. "The FBI and Alcohol, Tobacco and Firearms agents responsible for this fiasco have no right to claim Koresh was unreasonable, that he wouldn't negotiate or cooperate, because they never tried it. They went in there in the first place with guns blazing and apparently killed some of their own agents. When someone comes at you firing weapons, it is not an invitation to reasonable negotiation." Despite a late-year request by *The Nation* to run for the Senate in 1994, this feisty Texan might be more influential hurtling missiles at Washington than being part of it.

Mickey Kaus
The New Republic
FEBRUARY 15, 1993
"THE GODMOTHER"

In this superlative critique of the Children's Defense Fund and founder Marian Wright Edelman's skillful labors as a lobbyist, Kaus attacks the propositions at the heart of the CDF philosophy. "The trouble begins with Edelman's founding insight: that people who don't want to talk about blacks or the poor can be mobilized by talk of helping children....The federal government's most important welfare program is Aid to Families with Dependent Children. It sends cash to poor single parents, mainly women. CDF's literature says the program was 'designed to be a safety net for children deprived of parental support due to the death, illness, incapacity or absence of a parent.' But AFDC's checks go to the mothers, not the children, and the mothers as well as the children live off them. Thus the great half-century-long debate over AFDC has centered on whether, by supporting single mothers who don't work, the program encourages single parenthood and dependency." Kaus effectively redefines the issue. "That's not a debate about children," he states. "It's a debate about adults. Cast welfare as a children's issue, CDF-style, and poof! the crucial questions of work and dependency disappear....Indeed, you can read through CDF's thirty-three-page report on 'Child Poverty in America,' and its 114-page report on 'The State of America's Children' without coming across any acknowledgment that welfare dependency might even be a legitimate concern." After examining how the organization stifles important and open social debate, Kaus concludes by posing this query: "Are American taxpayers more likely to open their wallets for someone with an unvarnished analysis of the underclass problem, or someone who tries to overwhelm analysis with emotionalism about children?" With welfare a top legislative concern in 1994, Kaus helps to reshape the debate.

Joe Klein
Newsweek
NOVEMBER 15, 1993
"NEW YORK'S ROUGH RIDE"

Critiquing the New York City mayoral campaign as seen through the prism of *The New York Times*, Klein provides trenchant observations on each. He torpedoes the conventional wisdom about this contest. "Don't be fooled: nothing much happened in New York this year. David Dinkins and Rudy Giuliani ran, essentially, the same campaigns they ran four years ago. Dinkins ran as a healer. Giuliani ran as a not-black person. A tiny sliver of the electorate changed its mind, rejected Dinkins and elected Giuliani. This had something to do with the fact that they had just lived through four years of David Dinkins as mayor. Being New Yorkers, if they had just lived through four years of Giuliani as mayor, they probably would have elected Dinkins in what, no doubt, would no be hailed as a triumph of liberalism and an affirmation of faith in Bill Clinton, NAFTA and Barbra Streisand. All of which will come as something of a disappointment to the folks at *The New York Times* and the other enlightened, progressive sorts (including Bill Clinton) who worked overtime attempting to portray the campaign as a crossroads in American ethnic history." Klein further clarifies the contribution by the "paper of record" to the polarization of the city. "It was about *race*, they said...but that's only part of the story....The paper now seems intent on tossing away a century's worth of sobriety in pursuit of a trendy, disingenuous *correctness* on matters racial....*The Times* celebrated Giuliani's victory with, among other things, a front-page account of Dinkins voters' reactions: 'Many predicted...[the] loss will translate into a tougher, smarter battle for the empowerment of people of color.'...The paper seemed to be accepting the nonsensical line put forward by some black militants: that all non-Caucasians have common interests and constitute an emerging electoral majority. This sort of group obsession is worse than wishful thinking: it is dangerous racial stereotyping. It's also a fundamental misreading of the realities of urban life." In this thoughtful column, Klein offers a tough, honest appraisal of both city and media politics.

Paul Craig Roberts
The Washington Times
June 22, 1993
"Whacking Capital and Jobs"

In addition to taking the Clinton administration to task for raising the marginal capital-gains tax rate, Roberts deconstructs the National Competitiveness Act, which is supposed to help businesses get capital. "This act gives the federal government the job of providing startup capital to entrepreneurs. It establishes the U.S. Department of Commerce as investment banker for startup companies. All-knowing bureaucrats will allocate capital by making loans, purchasing preferred stock, and guaranteeing the dividends of venture capital companies." Roberts excoriates the government for removing the capital from capitalism, noting Washington "will do this with taxpayer money, of course, thus completing the separation of risk and reward from accountability. The taxpayers will be able to lose a lot of their hard-earned tax dollars so that people who have never been in business can identify 'critical technologies,' 'outreach to economically depressed areas,' and allocate risk capital to 'socially and economically disadvantaged individuals.' In other words, the government will have a new political slush fund to distribute in political ways for political purposes. In place of a capitalistic process of wealth creation, there will be another mechanism for redistributing taxpayers' incomes to the politically favored." Direct, concise and provocative no one in journalism does this kind of economic commentary better than Roberts.

George F. Will
Newsweek
May 3, 1993
"Jon Will's Aptitudes"

On the occasion of his oldest child's 21st birthday, Will reflects on a life that medical science doubted would advance so far. His touching essay on son Jon, born with Down syndrome, may have been the year's most moving article. "Jon lost, the moment he was conceived, one of life's lotteries," writes his father, noting that his son lives each day saddled with extraordinary and wrenching burdens unknown to most people. One of Down syndrome's great tragedies is how it limits the ability to articulate. We alleviate the loneliness and desolation of our individual existence, Will explains, through communication in friendship and intimacy. But his son, while possessing the same feelings, must struggle to cast off "the many burdens attendant on personhood. The shadow of loneliness must often be somewhat darker, the sense of apartness more acute, the sense of incompleteness more aching for people like Jon." Will marvels at his child's eternally agreeable disposition. "He does not 'suffer from' Down syndrome. It is an affliction, but he is happy....Happiness is a species of talent, for which some people have superior aptitudes." All of which, Will suggests, provide clues that pierce the veil of human nature. "It is an interesting commentary on the human condition that one aspect of Jon's abnormality—a facet of his disability—is the fact that he is gentleness straight through. But must we ascribe a sweet soul to a defective chromosome? Let us just say that Jon is an adornment to a world increasingly stained by anger acted out." And such painfully poignant columns are adornments to a world often lacking proper perspective.

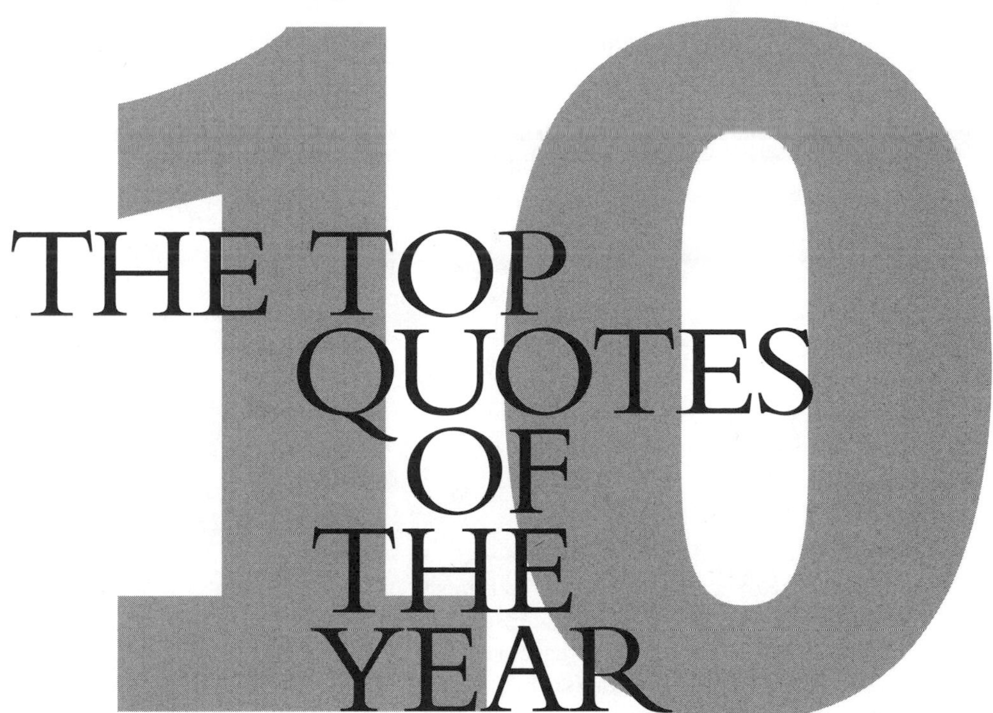

THE TOP QUOTES OF THE YEAR

"Bill Clinton is a man of many tomorrows....'Don't stop thinking about tomorrow' has become his mantra. He's even said he'd hang it as a sign in the Oval Office. The great thing about tomorrow is that it never comes, and by the time it does you can reschedule the rhetoric, claiming that it is necessary to adapt to new circumstances. Thus has Clinton rationalized his somersaults of the past month. Tomorrow is an endless alibi."

— **Alexander Cockburn**
Los Angeles Times
January 24, 1993

"Washington and Hollywood have always been drawn to each other because of their common interest in performance and image, and their complementary insecurities: the Hollywood elite wants to be seen as serious, and the Washington elite wants to be seen as glamorous."

— **Maureen Dowd**
The New York Times
May 9, 1993

"The coming age of bandwidth abundance in glass and in air [which will allow more space for more channels] converges with an era of supercomputer powers in the sand of microchips. We should build our systems of the future—the cathedrals of the information age—on this foundation of sand. It will not disappoint us."

— **George Gilder**
Forbes ASAP
September 13, 1993

"The morning after the 1990 earthquake [in the Philippines], then-President Corazon Aquino flew into Cabatuan, where a high-rise school had collapsed and crushed scores of students. Although cries could still be heard from children trapped in the rubble, soldiers stood mutely, disaster workers sipped soft-drinks and crowds milled about. 'Who's in charge here? Isn't anybody in charge?' the President angrily demanded. In four years I never found out the answer."

— **Bob Drogin**
Los Angeles Times
August 3, 1993
in his farewell column
as Manila bureau chief

"That's like setting a limit on gluttony, but excluding dessert."

— **John Judis**
In These Times
May 17, 1993
on Clinton's decision to allow corporations, when computing tax deductions, to exempt stock options from CEO salaries exceeding $1 million

"North Koreans may be freezing, hungry, and impoverished, but they are intensely nationalistic....Radios in the North have no tuning dials but are all set on the same government propaganda frequency. Lacking any other information, the populace swallows the hard-line preachings of the Kim dynasty hook, line, and sinker."

— **Colin Nickerson**
The Boston Globe
March 21, 1993

"Wilt Chamberlain took his ball and went home yesterday."

—**William Power**
The Wall Street Journal
February 17, 1993
on the ex-basketball star's withdrawal of the initial public offering of stock in his company, Wilt Chamberlain's Restaurants Inc., right after the stock plummeted

"Silicon Valley's digerati and Hollywood's more analog moguls now woo each other with the sort of passion you see only when the pheromones of Really Big Money are wafting in the breeze."

— **Michael Schrage**
Los Angeles Times
March 18, 1993
on the computer and entertainment industries' attempts to define the next stage in the communications revolution

"The Administration stumbled and fumbled so often in the early going that if the White House had been a restaurant its *plat du jour* would have been flounder."

— **David Shaw**
Los Angeles Times
September 15, 1993

"This is a talkative presidency. The President seems himself characterized by a horror of silence....Often he seems to think that he has acted when he has merely spoken."

— **Leon Wieseltier**
The New Republic
July 19 & 26, 1993

Introductory Offer

Newspapers! Magazines! TV! News is everywhere, with thousands of journalists racing to give it to you every second. But amid this information overload, which journalists can you trust to give you the whole story? Which ones should you beware of? The new FORBES *MediaCritic* will help you find answers to these questions. FORBES *MediaCritic* will steer you through today's fast-paced, news-filled world.

Coming to you four times a year, the new FORBES *MediaCritic* will explore how the media covers the most important topics of the day. It will examine major stories covered by the media and help you judge how well journalists do their job. It will also help you get a handle on all the information you receive every day. To become media-savvy and media-smart, get FORBES *MediaCritic*. It's for readers who want the best that journalism has to offer.

INVESTOR'S BUSINESS DAILY TAKES ON THE WALL STREET JOURNAL
Forbes MediaCritic
THE BEST AND WORST OF AMERICA'S JOURNALISM
FATAL ATTRACTION: JOURNALISTS & TRIAL LAWYERS
RACE, DOUBLE STANDARDS & THE NEW YORK TIMES
by William McGowan
RIP-OFF IN CABLE RATES & CABLE BILL COVERAGE
$7.95
ALSO:
RICHARD VIGILANTE on the asbestos panic in New York City's schools & FRED BARNES on bigoted reporters
NEW THIS ISSUE:
CRITIC'S CORNER
Tony Snow: Budget Gimmicks
Paul Sheehan: The Tarnishing of Notre Dame Football

Also...

With your paid subscription of $29.95 you will in addition receive the FORBES *MediaGuide 500* (a $19.95 value). *MediaGuide 500* gives you critical, nonpartisan reviews of the nation's top 500 journalists and how they covered the year's major stories.

For more info or to order your subscription, call 1-800-825-0061.
Also available at Barnes & Noble, Crown and other leading bookstores.

7CG41T

THE RATING GUIDE

"Look here! These pencils will do more to create opinion than a hundred thousand mobs. While I speak to these pencils, I speak to millions of men."
Liberator, *February 1, 1861*

SO SAID ABOLITIONIST WENDELL PHILLIPS TO A group of reporters as hecklers tried to disrupt a Boston anti-slavery meeting in 1861. Phillips well understood that "these pencils" symbolized the power of the press—the power to record and influence the flow of events. A fair question for these "pencils"—in Phillips's age as well as our own—is how well do they perform their jobs?

At *Forbes MediaGuide 500*, we ask this question of 500 print journalists whom we deem the nation's most influential. In determining influence, we employ two criteria. One is the *size* of the audience that reads the publication in which the journalist appears; the larger the audience, the more likely the journalist will make our list. The second criterion is the *nature* of that audience; a journalist read by political Washington ranks as a top candidate for inclusion. Note that influence is not synonymous with quality; it is judged less by what one writes than by whom and by how many one is read.

To indicate the quality of the 500 journalists reviewed in this volume, *MediaGuide* uses a star rating system that appears on the facing page. In determining how well or poorly a given journalist has done his or her job in 1993—and thus deciding which rating to give—we use the basic standards accepted by most news organizations. *For reporters, these include accuracy, fairness, balance, and thoroughness. We also use four additional standards: depth of reporting, quality of analysis, grasp of subject matter, and quality of writing.*

What these standards mean in practical terms can be expressed in the following questions: Can readers trust the information the reporter provides? Does the reporter ask the right (or most important) questions of the sources cited? Does the reporter give enough information to enable readers to form their own judgments? Does the reporter understand the complexity of an issue and explain nuances and subtleties? Does the reporter know the historical background and major issues of his or her beat? Can the reporter distinguish between relevant and irrelevant details? Does the reporter allow personal views to slant or distort the story? Finally, and perhaps most crucial, does the reporter meet these standards *consistently*?

For commentators, the standards include accuracy, grasp of subject matter, depth of analysis, soundness, fairness, and persuasiveness of argument, quality of writing and consistency with which quality work is produced. The best commentators offer original insights and well-argued opinions. Some distinguish their columns by their facility with language—their use of satire, for example, or their ability to turn a phrase. And, perhaps most important, the best commentators inform. As *New York Times* columnist William Safire advised Mikhail Gorbachev when the former Soviet leader embarked on a new (and, as it turned out, short-lived) career as a columnist in 1992, "Slip in a little news....You get around and hear things; train yourself to spill them in your column." Too many commentators fail to report; too many look into themselves for their columns when they should be hitting the phones—or the streets—in search of fresh information. The more a columnist engages in reporting and presenting "newsy nuggets," as Safire put it, the more likely his or her pieces will be worth reading.

All ratings are based on work published between January 1, 1993, and December 31, 1993. The reviews found below the ratings convey a sense of the journalist's strengths and weaknesses. As Wendell Phillips stated more than a century ago, journalists speak to millions and help to "create opinion" around the world. With these evaluations, we aim to provide an accurate picture of how well "these pencils" do their job.

REPORTERS	RATING	COMMENTATORS
A byline not to be trusted.	F Fails most criteria.	A byline not to be trusted.
Fails some criteria. Slanted, superficial.	½★ Poor.	Fails some criteria. Slanted, superficial.
Barely meets criteria. Seldom offers anything new.	★ Mediocre.	Barely meets criteria. Seldom offers anything new.
Meets basic criteria. Shines intermittently.	★½ Adequate.	Meets basic criteria. Shines intermittently.
Reports and writes capably; offers useful analysis.	★★ Good.	Provides insight and sometimes strong argument.
Offers above-average reporting and often sharp analysis.	★★½ Very good.	Takes on big topics and delivers skillful arguments.
Demonstrates superior reporting, writing, and analytic skills.	★★★ Excellent.	Provides superior arguments strengthened by sound reporting.
Displays superlative reporting, writing, analytic skills, is unquestionably fair, and provides sharp insight.	★★★½ Exceptional Approaching the Very Best.	Writes provocative, well-informed, and powerfully argued pieces on a wide variety of subjects.
Consistently offers magnificent reporting and writing, as well as provocative and penetrating analysis.	★★★★ Outstanding Pacesetters for the Entire News Media. A byline not to be missed.	Consistently provides fascinating insight and magnificent and provocative writing.

THE HIGHEST RATED JOURNALISTS OF 1993

★★★★

Angier, Natalie	*The New York Times*	Sci. & Tech.
Gilder, George	*Forbes ASAP*	Bus. & Econ.
Keller, Bill	*The New York Times*	Foreign
Loomis, Carol J.	*Fortune*	Bus. & Econ.
Mahar, Maggie	*Barron's*	Bus. & Econ.
Pollack, Andrew	*The New York Times*	Foreign
Waldmeir, Patti	*Financial Times*	Foreign

★★★ ½

Bacon, Kenneth	*The Wall Street Journal*	Bus. & Econ.
Broder, David S.	*The Washington Post*	Commentary
Dobrzynski, Judith H.	*BusinessWeek*	Bus. & Econ.
Drogin, Bob	*Los Angeles Times*	Foreign
Easterbrook, Gregg	*Newsweek*	Sci. & Tech.
Evans & Novak	*Creators Syndicate*	Commentary
Fabrikant, Geraldine	*The New York Times*	Bus. & Econ.
Gallagher, James P.	*Chicago Tribune*	Foreign
Henriques, Diana B.	*The New York Times*	Bus. & Econ.
Kaye, Lincoln	*Far Eastern Economic Review*	Foreign
Kelly, Michael	*The New York Times*	Pol. & Culture
Merline, John	*Investor's Business Daily*	Pol. & Culture
Morgenson, Gretchen	*Worth*	Bus. & Econ.
Opall, Barbara	*Defense News*	Pol. & Culture
Paltrow, Scot J.	*Los Angeles Times*	Bus. & Econ.
Raspberry, William	*The Washington Post*	Commentary
Steinfels, Peter	*The New York Times*	Pol. & Culture
Taylor, Alex, III	*Fortune*	Bus. & Econ.
Taylor, Stuart, Jr.	*The American Lawyer*	Pol. & Culture

★★★

Altman, Lawrence K.	*The New York Times*	Sci. & Tech.
Anders, George	*The Wall Street Journal*	Bus. & Econ.
Andrews, Edmund L.	*The New York Times*	Bus. & Econ.
Baker, Russell	*The New York Times*	Commentary
Barnes, Fred	*The New Republic*	Commentary
Barrett, Paul M.	*The Wall Street Journal*	Pol. & Culture

Bartley, Robert L.	*The Wall Street Journal*	Commentary
Bovard, James	*Freelance*	Commentary
Browne, Malcolm W.	*The New York Times*	Sci. & Tech.
Byron, Christopher	*New York*	Bus. & Econ.
Cockburn, Alexander	*The Nation*	Commentary
Coll, Steve	*The Washington Post*	Foreign
Covault, Craig	*Aviation Week & Space Technology*	Foreign
Cowan, Alison Leigh	*The New York Times*	Bus. & Econ.
Darlin, Damon	*Forbes*	Bus. & Econ.
Dempsey, Judy	*Financial Times*	Foreign
Edsall, Thomas B.	*The Washington Post*	Pol. & Culture
Engelberg, Stephen	*The New York Times*	Pol. & Culture
Farhi, Paul	*The Washington Post*	Bus. & Econ.
Farrell, Christopher	*BusinessWeek*	Bus. & Econ.
Fialka, John J.	*The Wall Street Journal*	Pol. & Culture
Ford, Peter	*The Christian Science Monitor*	Foreign
Foreman, Judy	*The Boston Globe*	Sci. & Tech.
Forsyth, Randall W.	*Barron's*	Bus. & Econ.
Fraser, Damien	*Financial Times*	Foreign
Freudenheim, Milt	*The New York Times*	Bus. & Econ.
Fulghum, David A.	*Aviation Week & Space Technology*	Pol. & Culture
Gigot, Paul	*The Wall Street Journal*	Commentary
Greenhouse, Linda	*The New York Times*	Pol. & Culture
Haberman, Clyde	*The New York Times*	Foreign
Hentoff, Nat	*The Village Voice*	Commentary
Hoagland, Jim	*The Washington Post*	Commentary
Holley, David	*Los Angeles Times*	Foreign
Horgan, John	*Scientific American*	Sci. & Tech.
Ibrahim, Youssef M.	*The New York Times*	Foreign
Ivins, Molly	*Fort Worth Star-Telegram*	Commentary
Jones, Clayton	*The Christian Science Monitor*	Foreign
Kamm, Henry	*The New York Times*	Foreign
Kaus, Mickey	*The New Republic*	Commentary
Klein, Joe	*Newsweek*	Commentary
Kolata, Gina	*The New York Times*	Sci. & Tech.
Kristol, Irving	*The Wall Street Journal*	Commentary
Kurtz, Howard	*The Washington Post*	Pol. & Culture
Lancaster, John	*The Washington Post*	Pol. & Culture
Leo, John	*U.S.News & World Report*	Commentary
Leopold, George	*Defense News*	Pol. & Culture
Levin, Doron P.	*The New York Times*	Bus. & Econ.
Lewis, Anthony	*The New York Times*	Commentary
Maggs, John	*The Journal of Commerce*	Bus. & Econ.
Marsh, David	*Financial Times*	Foreign
Mathews, Jay	*The Washington Post*	Pol. & Culture
McArdle, Thomas	*Investor's Business Daily*	Bus. & Econ.
McGough, Robert	*The Wall Street Journal*	Bus. & Econ.

Moberg, David	*In These Times*	Bus. & Econ.
Moffett, Matt	*The Wall Street Journal*	Foreign
Morrocco, John D.	*Aviation Week & Space Technology*	Sci. & Tech.
Mortimer, Edward	*Financial Times*	Commentary
Nash, Nathaniel C.	*The New York Times*	Foreign
Nicholson, Mark	*Financial Times*	Foreign
O'Rourke, P. J.	*Rolling Stone*	Commentary
Parks, Michael	*Los Angeles Times*	Foreign
Perry, James M.	*The Wall Street Journal*	Pol. & Culture
Proctor, Paul	*Aviation Week & Space Technology*	Pol. & Culture
Quinn-Judge, Paul	*The Boston Globe*	Pol. & Culture
Roberts, Paul Craig	*The Washington Times*	Commentary
Robichaux, Max	*The Wall Street Journal*	Bus. & Econ.
Rodriguez, Paul M.	*The Washington Times*	Pol. & Culture
Rosenberg, Howard	*Los Angeles Times*	Pol. & Culture
Royko, Mike	*Chicago Tribune*	Commentary
Safire, William	*The New York Times*	Commentary
Schlessinger, Jacob M.	*The Wall Street Journal*	Foreign
Schmemann, Serge	*The New York Times*	Foreign
Schrage, Michael	*Los Angeles Times*	Bus. & Econ.
Sciolino, Elaine	*The New York Times*	Pol. & Culture
Seligman, Daniel	*Fortune*	Commentary
Silverberg, David	*Defense News*	Pol. & Culture
Simpson, John	*The Spectator*	Foreign
Smith, Randall	*The Wall Street Journal*	Bus. & Econ.
Sowell, Thomas	*Forbes*	Commentary
Starr, Barbara	*Jane's Defence Weekly*	Pol. & Culture
Sterngold, James	*The New York Times*	Foreign
Stewart, James B.	*The New Yorker*	Bus. & Econ.
Summers, Harry	*Los Angeles Times*	Commentary
Tanner, James	*The Wall Street Journal*	Bus. & Econ.
Tanzer, Andrew	*Forbes*	Foreign
Towell, Pat	*Congressional Quarterly*	Pol. & Culture
Tyler, Patrick E.	*The New York Times*	Foreign
Vartabedian, Ralph	*Los Angeles Times*	Pol. & Culture
Verity, John	*BusinessWeek*	Bus. & Econ.
Wagstyl, Stefan	*Financial Times*	Foreign
Waldholz, Michael	*The Wall Street Journal*	Sci. & Tech.
Waldman, Peter	*The Wall Street Journal*	Foreign
Watanabe, Teresa	*Los Angeles Times*	Foreign
White, Joseph B.	*The Wall Street Journal*	Bus. & Econ.
Wilford, John Noble	*The New York Times*	Sci. & Tech.
Will, George F.	*Newsweek*	Commentary
Williams, Carol	*Los Angeles Times*	Foreign
Wines, Michael	*The New York Times*	Pol. & Culture
Zachary, G. Pascal	*The Wall Street Journal*	Bus. & Econ.

★ POLITICS & CULTURE ★

Jill Abramson

The Wall Street Journal

★½

Deputy Washington bureau chief. Now writing considerably less in her new position, Abramson produced adequate, if not fully satisfying, stories prior to her promotion. In her limp 1-4 effort examining the management of Bill Clinton's inaugural, Abramson highlights organizer Rahm Emanuel, providing more information about the finances and contributions than either the planned events or the contributors. Although she and co-author Hilary Stout confuse the reader in a 3-18 article about medical firms lobbying the new administration on health care, they provide one intriguing tidbit: "The explosive growth in health lobbying is mirrored by a boom of health-industry campaign contributions during the past election cycle." In her evocative and carefully reported 6-4 effort, co-authored by Gerald F. Seib, Abramson profiles four former aides of Robert F. Kennedy, 25 years after his assassination. Although the four have since gone different ways politically, they all recall RFK's ability to inspire confidence in government and hope for the future. The article suggests that, despite the cataclysmic events of 1968, the Democratic party had more unity and direction around the time of Kennedy's death than during the next two decades. Abramson's 7-20 portrait of Harvard Law School's first coed graduating class of 1959 offers a conventional look back at the bad old "sexist" days. The piece includes reporting on the experiences of Ruth Bader Ginsburg's female classmates. Abramson's most spirited effort appears in *The New Yorker* 5-24. She and co-author Jane Mayer, who are writing a book about the Clarence Thomas-Anita Hill hearings of 1991, strongly challenge the case made by author David Brock. They are particularly persuasive in their presentation of information about where they feel he fell short. Unfortunately, *The New Yorker*'s refusal to print Brock's reply helped to short-circuit debate on the controversy. For Abramson, however, this article stands out in an otherwise mediocre year. A capable reporter, Abramson seems capable of far more.

Henry Allen

The Washington Post

★★

"Style." With a discerning eye and irreverent literary style, Allen tackles topics as diverse as politics, the Holocaust, and the creation of the universe. Although amusing and provocative, he sometimes tends to get caught up in his prose, running out of ideas while the words keep coming. In his 1-19 roundup of events preceding the inauguration, Allen fawningly parrots Clinton press flacks. Of a luncheon attended by regular people who met Clinton during the campaign, he writes, "They were the ultimate Bill Clinton crowd, everything his magnum-grade security required to show itself in the bitten lip, the frowning pauses, the three-quarter smile of wonderment. They couldn't stop talking about his sincerity." Please. Allen shows far more depth in his 4-20 piece considering why, of all places, Washington, D.C. should have a Holocaust Memorial Museum. While he never sufficiently answers this question, he provides a moving description of the museum's exhibits and their effects on visitors. "Holocaust photographs are nothing new, they hardly seem real anymore. But the sense of reality tingles quite vividly at the sight of the Hollerith machine. There, glowering with the bustling potential you remember of old sewing machines, is the IBM computer that sorted *lebensunwertes Leben*, life unworthy of life, into stacks of punch cards." In his sardonic 6-16 attack on those who find the term "Big Bang" a "sexist, sexual and undignified" way to describe the primal moment, Allen wonders, "Is it possible that the creation was inherently ugly and sexist and disrespectful, an eruption that turned the universe into the equivalent of a desert island populated by nothing but hockey fans, Navy fliers and flannel-shirt feminists?" For his 9-19 portrait of filmmaker Martin Scorsese, Allen quotes his subject generously, providing eyes so his readers might also see the master speak. As Scorsese describes an inspirational scene from the Stanley Kubrick movie "Barry Lyndon," "[the director] leans forward, frowning with astonishment at what's inside his head. His hands carve away at the air as if he's proposing an ice sculpture." Seldom breaking new ground, Allen often illuminates what previously existed in the shadows of his readers' vision.

Jonathan Alter

Newsweek

★★½

A competent writer, the liberal-leaning Alter follows developments in the media, particularly as they relate to politics. Despite occasional lapses, his column, "Between the Lines," often yields sharp and penetrating insights. The infamous rigged GM crash video on "Dateline NBC" inspires Alter to reflect on the dual career of NBC News president Michael Gartner, 3-8, who came up as a newspaperman and still writes columns on First Amendment and press ethics issues. Alter devastatingly finds "two public Michael Gartners." "The first [the newspaperman] crusaded against the use of anonymous sources; the second did little to stop their use at NBC News. The first Gartner might have written a column about the GM story, pointing out how the pressure to produce good pictures...could slowly infect—even corrupt—a news organization. The second Gartner is all for television news—as long as General Electric's money goals are met first." Alter proves equally astute in his 2-8 examination of the press's intense focus on President Clinton's early mistakes. "When Clinton makes a more serious blunder than on gays in the military, the media will have trouble moving to an even higher threshold of attention and outrage." Alter's 11-1 reflection on Bill Clinton and John F. Kennedy shrewdly points out that while Kennedy was president "during a time of Michael-row-your-boat-ashore earnestness," his approach to life was defined by "ironic detachment." By contrast, Clinton is president when the culture is saturated with "Lettermanesque irony," but he himself is "full of almost indiscriminate 1960s enthusiasm." In Alter's best column of the year, 11-29, he confronts liberals who accuse the National Endowment for the Arts of censorship. "Describing the battle over government funding of controversial art as a 'censorship' issue," he observes, "is loopy. Declining to use taxpayer dollars to fund art is hardly the same as suppressing it." Alter stumbles in his 11-15 column defending Hillary Rodham Clinton's rhetorical blast at the health-insurance industry. "She's right substantively," he says, but provides little evidence to show why. This lapse noted, Alter knows how to write snappy, engaging prose on political topics in the news—and on the news business itself.

R. W. Apple, Jr.

The New York Times

★★½

Washington bureau chief. Although Apple has to keep an eye on his staff as well as on Beltway politics, he still manages—thanks to his extensive experience covering American politics—to shed light on the complexities of the political scene. Instead of two or three insights per article, however, with his added duties Apple now provides only one. He comes up short in a rather standard 1-29 examination of the candidates' various uses of the media. Yet after probing the question of voter participation on individual issues, he incisively observes, that "with the whole county wired, ordinary voters in Kansas with time on their hands often have a better grip on events in Washington" than the pollsters or the politicians. On 2-19, he shrewdly appraises President Clinton's plans for economic change—"pull this string or that, and the whole thing might unravel quickly, no matter how skillful the knitting that put it together in the first place"—but he provides no assessment of the economics behind the politics. His 5-28 effort suffers from a hyperbolic lead on the political importance of the House's passage of the President's fiscal package. "Standing on the burning deck, President Clinton sailed his ship to victory in the House of Representatives tonight." Yet Apple goes on to

explain smartly how Clinton might maneuver through his programs. "Mr. Clinton will need to continue repairing his bridges to the moderate and conservative Democrats who, having backed him last year because they considered him one of them, have come to see him as an apostate. As they did under President Ronald Reagan, who wooed them so effectively, they hold the balance in both houses and the country at large." Two soul-searching exercises, 6-5 and 8-13, on Lani Guinier and Vince Foster, respectively, seem inappropriate for the front pages. Apple searches more for answers than for news in these apologias, the first for Clinton, the second for the Washington press corps. Similarly, his 10-13 effort is less news analysis than a woeful recap of the situations in Haiti, Somalia, and Bosnia, and the powerlessness of the U.S. and UN to do anything about them. Although serviceable, this kind of work does not contain the high-quality analysis Apple can produce.

Peter Applebome

The New York Times

★★★

Southeast. Tracking economic, political, and social issues in the American South, Applebome provides a readable blend of facts, quotes, and insightful analysis that reflects a rare sensitivity to the people and history of the region. In nearly all his columns, he delves into the meaning of events and what they represent in the larger picture. In his fascinating 1-27 piece, Applebome explores how southern state governments use the Confederate battle flag, and he gives clear voice to Southerners' own questions about the flag's symbolism. Should Alabama and Georgia, he asks as his central question, continue to incorporate into their state flags a symbol that, for African Americans, represents oppression and slavery? "In the region that William Faulkner described as a place where 'the past is not dead, it isn't even past,'" he notes, "the questions touch a live wire." Unfortunately, in both his 4-6 article on a tourist's murder in Florida and a 5-26 piece on the acquittal of a Louisiana man who shot an innocent Japanese student he thought was going to assault him, Applebome highlights the sensational nature of reports on these incidents in the foreign press while underplaying the problem of high crime rates in the U.S. He pens an original 6-5 column describing how cumulative voting—one of the highly criticized ideas advocated by the withdrawn Justice Department nominee Lani Guinier—is in operation and running smoothly in several voting districts around the country. Applebome's best pieces directly take on the politics of race and economics in the South, such as his 8-21 article on rural ghettos. "Almost 20 percent of black elected officials nationwide come from Mississippi and Alabama alone. But many of them have come to political power only to inherit the dust of economic abandonment. 'You're in charge, but how much can you do?' said [former Jonestown, MS mayor] Bobbie Walker, who recently lost her bid for re-election." In his 1-2 piece, Applebome turns the financial woes of a small Georgia college into front-page news. "Morris Brown College has never loomed large on the national stage," he admits, but as it fights to stay afloat, it "has come to symbolize many of the issues facing America's private black colleges"—while enrollment gains for private black colleges have far exceeded the national average, most are financially strapped due to low tuition, low endowment, and few wealthy alumni. In his comprehensive 11-27 article on economic growth in the southeast, Applebome tempers a portrait of manufacturing expansion in the region with disturbing statistics on the widen- ing income disparity between rich and poor. With his consistently informative and provocative articles, Applebome sets the pace for regional correspondents in the United States.

Terry Atlas

Chicago Tribune

★

Diplomatic correspondent. Only occasionally reaching beyond the superficial, Atlas seldom adds to the political debate. In one of his more promising efforts, a 3-31 dispatch co-authored by Mitchell Locin, the pair provides a convincing explanation of why President Clinton will likely back Yeltsin no matter what the cost. "The recriminations over 'Who lost Russia?' would echo through the rest of Clinton's term and beyond, much as the debate over 'Who lost China?' hung over Democrats in the 1950s." Although this idea gained currency in the autumn when Clinton decided to back Yeltsin after the latter dissolved Parliament, Atlas provided nothing as original or stimulating for the rest of the year. Another Russian-summit essay, co-authored by Howard Witt, 4-4, yields only a touchy-feely prognosis of what might be accomplished at the Vancouver summit. "There is a very good reason why Yeltsin and Clinton are not dwelling on the nuclear issues that transfixed the world during every previous superpower summit. If they did, they would only get depressed." Atlas tries to pull together information on the complex Bosnia story for his 5-9 dispatch but offers only a peripheral sense of geopolitics, and not much new at that. While he positions his 6-28 effort as news analysis, stating that "in sending 23 Tomahawk cruise missiles slamming into the heart of the Iraqi capital in Sunday's early hours, President Clinton was responding forcefully to those who doubted his resolve in foreign affairs and viewed him as a weak military leader." Yet Atlas provides scant information to support this assessment. Focusing as much on Clinton's apparent need to assert power as on recent developments in the Caribbean nation, his 10-19 essay presents a respectable overview of Clinton's balancing act on Haiti. In his conventional 7-4 assessment of whether the U.S. should support the UN in its peacekeeping military role, Atlas never explores whether the UN should be doing this job, nor does he examine the costs to the U.S. As with much of his work, this dispatch adds little to the reader's understanding.

B. Drummond Ayres, Jr.

The New York Times

★½

National correspondent. Ayres writes beautifully, his evocative dispatches vividly conveying a real feel for scenes and situations. Only seldom, however, do they answer questions about major issues. In his 1-14 examination of the Virginia grand jury's refusal to indict Sen. Charles S. Robb [D-VA] on charges in an electronic eavesdropping case, Ayres raises more questions than he answers, his data too preliminary to pass as "news analysis." He peers into the crystal ball in his 3-15 effort on Ross Perot's future, but he doesn't see much. Although he notes that Perot "wants to use [United We Stand] to bring pressure at all levels of American politics, even down to school board elections," Ayres fails to assess what role his organization might play in the upcoming elections. Two follow-ups on Perot, 3-22 and 5-28, contain little more than who said what on the "war of the words" between Perot and Congress and between Perot and Clinton, respectively, over the deficit. Ayres fashions a well-rounded 10-26 dispatch of Washington, D.C., Mayor Sharon Pratt Kelly's request to use the National Guard to supplement the police. However, he neglects to examine the proposal itself in great detail, nor does he look at its implications for other urban mayors. His work on the Midwest flooding during the summer, 7-16, 7-17, and 7-19, showcased his writing skills. "The Missouri and Mississippi Rivers, both surging to maximum crests in the great Midwest flood of 1993, joined muddy forces today at their nexus just north of here, then swept down on this city's sodden, weakened system of protective levees. The extra water pouring into the Mississippi from the Missouri swelled the nation's greatest river to a record crest, or maximum depth, of 47 feet as it roiled southward of the Gateway Arch. Some small berms on the suburban outskirts of the city were topped, forcing emergency evacuation of several hundred homes." Ayres again uses his powerful prose to convey the receding of the waters, 8-10, and the first stages of rebuilding. If only Ayres's political reports matched his fine feature writing.

FOREPLAY

Charles R. Babcock

The Washington Post

★★

Investigations. Babcock doesn't hit pay dirt with his continual inquiries, but it isn't for lack of trying. A versatile reporter, he ferrets out nuggets on diverse subjects and weaves them together to fashion informative articles. Zeroing in on fundraising, 1-14, Babcock and co-author Michele L. Norris get to the nitty-gritty of which corporations are contributing to the inauguration, and how much they're paying. Turning to congressional fundraising, Babcock crafts a forward-looking 3-12 article hinting that potential reform bills may change the game. "With President Clinton promising to sign a campaign finance reform bill that would limit spending to $600,000, [Rep. Robert] Matsui [D-CA] and other House incumbents know they may be raising money the old-fashioned way for the last time." Babcock tackles one of the year's hot-button issues, with a 4-21 dispatch on health care that details pertinent information in a report by the General Accounting Office (GAO), which found that doctors with financial interests in MRI centers "were twice as likely to refer patients for MRI scans as doctors who did not have investments in such facilities." Rep. Fortney "Pete" Stark [D-CA], who is pushing for a bill that would prohibit most doctors from investing in businesses to which they refer patients, cited the GAO report at a congressional hearing. An earlier law sponsored by Stark, Babcock notes, already limits some physician referrals. Unfortunately, he fails to examine how the new bill might fit in with the administration's ideas on health care, except to note briefly that "the Clinton administration has proposed extending the federal ban to other doctor-owned facilities." Following up with a more specific 7-7 examination of an MRI-referral study from the patient's point of view, Babcock fails to offer a sense of the bigger health-care picture. The information for his 9-3 dispatch about GOPAC's involvement in raising funds for Rep. Newt Gingrich [R-GA] to plan and teach a college course at Kennesaw State College was provided by a "Democratic activist" with an obvious ax to grind. As one professor tells him, "the original concern was 'whether the college was an appropriate forum for a political leader to advance his own political ideology.'" Although he sometimes fails to provide enough context, the sleuthing Babcock is a natural for his beat.

Dan Balz

The Washington Post

★½

Politics. The quality of Balz's portfolio varies markedly. When he takes time to carefully craft his dispatches, he can be informative, but his quick news flashes seem slapdash and rarely satisfy. In his 2-14 effort, Balz surveys several governors who have raised taxes early in their terms, as President Clinton plans to do. However, his analysis sheds little light on how a tax increase might play out on the national level. In his revealing, well-written 5-9 *Magazine* essay, Balz examines how Clinton chose his cabinet. "Very often a president's Cabinet represents little more than an assortment of individual expertise and political paybacks, brilliant minds and occasional hacks, a stew without a recipe. In the case of this Cabinet, however, the main ingredient is Clinton himself. Throughout the campaign, he promised to assemble a Cabinet that looked like America. When he finally completed his task it was clear that he wanted more than a group that mirrored the country. He wanted a Cabinet that reflected Bill Clinton as well.... Clinton's Cabinet was assembled as much to reflect a set of values as a set of policies." Balz goes on to explore how this approach helped in some ways to short-circuit the selection process. Although he offers a timely 10-18 dissection of how crime and the role guns play in urban violence are changing long-standing political relationships, he fails to address the question of whether gun control will solve the problems of inner-city crime. In his 8-8 analysis of Sen. Robert Kerrey's [D-NE] switch from a 'no' to a 'yes' vote on the budget, Balz expends considerable energy describing the key players in the White House who lobbied him heavily, but not much effort uncovering Kerrey's intellectual odyssey. He reveals, 9-29, the plans of the National Policy Forum, a nationwide set of GOP committees seeking consensus on major issues. This skimpy dispatch, however, fails to evaluate the Forum's chances of success, nor does Balz examine its grassroots competitor, United We Stand. Balz's skills definitely show in his longer pieces, but in his shorter ones he should be a little more meticulous, crafting his dispatches instead of just banging them out.

James A. Barnes

National Journal

★★½

Politics. Barnes tells Beltway denizens nearly everything they need to know about a given subject. While he may seem tedious to readers beyond the capital, the names he mentions all play an integral role on the Washington scene. This Beltway focus weakens his 1-23 article, an evaluation of the power of some conservative Christian organizations—such as the Christian Coalition, an offshoot of Pat Robertson's organization—that actively lobby and support candidates. Though Barnes carefully examines their activities in D.C., he virtually ignores their local operations. He gives a strong 4-10 rundown, both conceptually and organizationally, of United We Stand and Ross Perot. However, he fails to answer the big questions: will Perot run in 1996, and if not, who will United We Stand nominate (the group claims definite plans to run a presidential candidate in the next election)? Barnes presents mind-numbing detail on the logistics of campaign reform, 5-8, and although he tries to augment the numbers with political analysis and quotes, the article would leave a Beltway outsider gasping for air. Barnes provides an inside look, 6-12, at the growing idea of "parent power" within the conservative political movement. The article teems with information on the emerging foundations and organizations that emphasize "family values," but Barnes neglects to assess the political impact of these new groups. In his 7-31 effort, he explodes the media myth that President Clinton's core support lies among moderate Democrats. He finds that party liberals think the President is doing a reasonably good job and are willing to cut him some slack in the early days of his tenure. Barnes's useful 9-4 handicapping of the GOP field for 1996 draws upon a wide variety of sources and demonstrates his political acumen. The writing even shows some flair. "Contenders will rise and fall like Lazarus, but for now most of the interest in the party is focused on Dole." Despite occasional dryness, Barnes's dispatches often sparkle.

Paul M. Barrett

The Wall Street Journal

★★★

Supreme Court, law, justice. With his revealing profiles of Supreme Court justices, as well as discerning takes on the implications of their decisions, Barrett proves a tough reporter to match on this beat. In his superb 2-2 profile of Justice David Souter, Barrett yields fresh insight and information about Souter's judicial philosophy and lifestyle. "Though sometimes stuffy in his legal prose, Justice Souter isn't pompous in person. Asked why he sings along with the chief justice at Mr. Rehnquist's annual Christmas carol party, he replies: 'I have to. Otherwise I get all the tax cases.'" In an equally laudable and incisive 4-27 profile of Justice Clarence Thomas, Barrett places the Anita Hill controversy in context and perspective, treating the incident briefly but fairly. On 3-24, he examines how lower courts can misinterpret the Supreme Court's fuzzy rulings, especially those on punitive damages. In this penetrating article, Barrett demonstrates the relevance of reporting how the Court's decisions are treated by judges below—something other reporters on this beat rarely do. In his trim 7-22 account of Ruth Bader Ginsburg's confirmation hearings, Barrett focuses on her preference for the "strict scrutiny" standard in sex-discrimination cases before broadening the discussion. "Judge Ginsburg's view could come into play in potential disputes over workplace policies that favor or disfavor women, as well as controversies over restrictions on abortions." In his 10-4 piece, Barrett analyzes the different writing styles of the justices, noting that "Louis Brandeis, who served on the high court from 1916 to 1939, quipped that the justices are about the only people in Washington who 'do their own work.' In reality, most court members these days edit their law clerks' work, content to insert their own little touches while assuring that the opinions accurately reflect their views on the issues." Barrett then identifies whose touches are whose, and which justices actually write their own opinions. These kind of pieces show that Barrett goes the extra mile.

Barbara Benham

Investor's Business Daily

National issues, Washington. Benham delivers timely information and, on occasion, pen-

etrating insight. Because she focuses more on facts than analysis, however, her work can be dry. Benham's 1-12 dispatch on Leon Panetta's Senate confirmation hearings for the post of budget director displays this tendency. By focusing only on his testimony and failing to incorporate much pertinent background information, she deprives her account of depth and resonance. Her 2-8 survey explores why deficit estimates always differ so drastically from the original predictions. Despite this intriguing premise, she clutters the piece with too many variables and theories and is unable to make sense of some of her information. Benham pens a respectable 3-3 assessment of how Clinton's youthful cabinet looks to the public at large, noting that, "Richard Nixon, meanwhile, had one of the youngest White House staffs in history. Dick Cheney was only in his late 20s when he became Nixon's chief of staff." Unfortunately, Benham doesn't examine how younger staffs have performed in comparison to older ones. She crafts an information-laden 5-10 article on the new Labor Department method of calculating the unemployment rate, and its potential effects. "The new approach, which is scheduled to come on line early next year, might produce a higher unemployment rate, early findings suggest. A higher unemployment rate would have several consequences, mainly political and psychological. Voters might judge Washington more harshly, should the unemployment rate jump one month to the next for esoteric reasons....A higher unemployment number could have economic consequences, too, though subtle ones. It could dampen consumer confidence by increasing workers' concerns about losing their jobs." Benham spent much of the remainder of the year following the housing market. Three efforts, 6-3, 8-26, and 10-20, typify this work. Examining the apparent upswing of home sales and starts, she presents a variety of angles, carefully blending data, quotes, and analysis. When she can provide such dispatches consistently, Benham will become a must-read.

Richard L. Berke
The New York Times
★★

Washington. Berke's talent for gathering information enables him to turn up a new fact or two on the stories he covers. In his pithy, but superficial, 1-12 assessment of Ross Perot, he describes the Texan's appearance at a United We Stand conference. "It was part nightclub comedian, part self-promoter, part college professor, part shrewd businessman, and part bumpkin." In his weak 3-11 effort on the administration's plan to invest money in towns where military bases have closed, he offers few specifics on how much money will be invested, what the government will actually be investing in, or the kinds of jobs for which the government will help laid-off workers retrain. He demonstrates his skill at compiling information under pressure by providing a balanced 5-20 dispatch on Travelgate, carefully explaining the positions of both the White House and Barney Brasseaux, a member of the staff who lost his job. In two follow-ups, 5-21 and 5-22, Berke shows similar care in presenting and interpreting information. Despite the damning material he reports, he never inserts a point of view. He also provides detail on a Stanley Greenberg poll showing that Perot's constituents are not going to go away. In this nicely rounded 7-8 dispatch, Berke's interviews with a few participants yield a sense of why the United We Stand members are a force to be reckoned with. However, his amusing 8-2 evaluation of Perot's talk-show performances—hawking his economic plans and critiquing Clinton's budget—is less political analysis than a review of Perot, who, Berke contends, dodged the specifics of question after question. If Berke felt this way about every politician, he couldn't be a political reporter. Despite his overall fairness and eye for detail, Berke should dig a little deeper, and think a little harder.

Jeffrey H. Birnbaum
The Wall Street Journal
★

Congress. Providing only the most basic information, Birnbaum's curt and cursory dispatches seldom convey the detail necessary for one to see the big picture. In his pithy 1-20 dispatch examining Bill Clinton's performance during his first hours in office, Birnbaum offers an early criticism of the new President. "Although [Clinton] spent hour upon hour talking about problems in the nation's economy, he was able to avoid making even a single comment that could be construed as a newsworthy nugget about what he might propose in order to solve them." He follows Clinton around for a week, even reaching the Oval Office, but since Birnbaum presents little information in this 3-9 essay, aside from Chelsea's ills and a golf game that never materialized, it's hard to buy his assessment that "Unlike George Bush, he has a clear vision of what he wants to do. Unlike Ronald Reagan, he possesses a true command of the details of his many initiatives. And unlike Jimmy Carter, he is a consummate politician." In his superficial 6-2 report, Birnbaum swallows all the administration's political excuses for delaying the unveiling of its health-care program, never examining the possible proposals nor exploring the White House's possible trouble developing it. In a strange 7-23 essay on Rep. Dan Rostenkowski [D-IL], head of the Ways and Means Committee and presently under investigation, Birnbaum and co-author David Rogers seem to bemoan the death of the old patronage system and Chicago machine, rather than take a critical look at Rostenkowski. On the administration's plan for "reinventing government," 9-7, Birnbaum and co-author Timothy Noah posit that the plan will work because it's Clinton who introduces it. "Today, for the 11th time this century, a president will propose how, finally, to make government work better. This time, though, it might—just might—happen.... Clinton will be especially eager to push his plan to remake government as a way of offsetting the image that he is just an old-fashioned tax-and-spend Democrat, an image some Republicans tried to pin on him during the summer budget debate." Covering a Clinton speech in North Carolina, 10-13, Birnbaum stresses the President's need to clarify his agenda, arguing that, "there was more than semantics at work here." Yet Birnbaum provides no substantive evidence of any new policies advanced herein by the President. Like many of Birnbaum's articles, this one offers little "more than semantics."

Joan Biskupic

The Washington Post

★

Supreme Court. Often showing a knack for conventional legal analysis, Biskupic turns in a barely passable portfolio in her first full year on this beat for the *Post.* An occasional tendency to emphasize the politics of a ruling as opposed to its legal aspects detracts from her reporting on Supreme Court decisions. Although not fancy, her 3-20 dispatch, co-authored by Ruth Marcus, on Justice Byron White's decision to retire presents a solid overview of his tenure on the Court. Biskupic shows signs of developing subtlety, 10-11, reporting a job-bias case that Solicitor General Drew S. Days III will argue before the Court. Inappropriately, she seems to applaud his politics, casting Days as the rescuer of discrimination law in the wake of the Bush administration. Biskupic's politics also show through in the overblown lead to her 7-6 review of the Rehnquist court: "It has been five years since a conservative majority formed on the Supreme Court, and its message to the American people is clear: Take your big problems elsewhere." The implied message that a conservative court seems bad, a liberal court good—after all, you can take your big problems to it—seems a bit oversimplified. After examining the papers of the late Thurgood Marshall, 5-24, Biskupic discusses the Court's shift in several civil-rights cases, but she uncovers little that's new. Her quick 9-2 peek at the new justice, Ruth Bader Ginsburg, never gets beyond the superficial. Although Biskupic reports adequately, her powers of interpretation fall short.

Katherine Boo

The Washington Post

★½

"Outlook" section editor. The squalor of D.C.'s darkest side comes through clearly in Boo's *Magazine* articles, but to no great effect. Despite solid reporting, her conclusions often outrun or overlook her evidence. In her 6-20 article, Boo jumps to defend the Clinton administration even though, as she says, "[it's] trolling for an apologist." Heralding the first 100 days, she adds, "judging Clinton's appointees isn't all a calculus of outsize resumes and early promise. From a few of those infamous late-night policy convocations, some actual achievements have escaped." She lists as accomplishments a series of initiatives—such as lifting the gag order on abortion at federally funded clinics—that have been around so long that their implementation would have been all but assured un-

der any Democrat. In her riveting 4-18 essay, Boo paints a face on the residents of the Sheridan Terrace housing project in Washington, D.C. "Conditions are so grim at Sheridan today that the famously brave local Domino's Pizza won't deliver here anymore....Six years ago, refurbishing Sheridan Terrace would have cost taxpayers less than the salaries of a dozen assistant administrators [at the Department of Public Assisted Housing]. Today, the job will run the District, by its own estimate, $23 million." Boo nearly succeeds with her intimate 9-26 portrait of a 16-year-old ex-convict, Alonzo Washington, who is trying to learn a trade and become responsible for his infant son. Boo weakly blames Washington's problems on the juvenile-detention system, "a system that invests tens of millions a year to lock up kids for a while, then abandons them, at 15, 16, 17, in the center of their temptations." She disregards the point of the teenager admitting that the fear of reentering that system keeps him in line. In her compelling 4-25 portrait of grandmother Hannah Hawkins and her unique after-school program called Children of Mine, Boo finds old-time remedies working on modern problems. "With no salary, no public funds, little self-consciousness and a lot of religion, Hawkins and a cadre of volunteers have been fiercely working their emotional alchemy on a group that includes some of the most hard-to-reach kids." Despite her narrative skills, Boo's strong reporting too often falls victim to either her weak analysis or her silence on solutions.

Max Boot
The Christian Science Monitor
★★½

Congress. A solid reporter and sturdy analyst, even in his Washington roundup columns, Boot unearths facts that other reporters miss. His 1-29 summary of Washington abounds with quirky information, on Native Americans for instance, that seldom receives coverage. In his 2-4 piece, Boot offers salient detail on the Family and Medical Leave Act and the politics surrounding it that might impede its passage, as well as further information on the conflict-of-interest charges swirling around Commerce Secretary Ron Brown. His superb 3-22 effort matches anything that Supreme Court reporters yielded on Clinton's opportunity to appoint a new associate justice, the politics involved in the decision, and the record of retiring Justice Byron White. "Although White reached generally conservative conclusions during his 31 years on the high court, constitutional scholars say he did not hew to any specific ideology." Boot then goes on to explore this angle by examining White's work on landmark cases during his tenure. In an important 6-30 dispatch, Boot reveals the discontent of the Black Caucus at their treatment by the Clinton administration and their dismay at the Clinton budget. "Caucus members, normally the most loyal Democrats in Congress, have broken ranks with their party recently, even going so far as to open talks with GOP senators on an alternative budget deal." Also eye-opening is Boot's 7-29 effort on the transportation bill. By illuminating the battle over the $40 billion transportation bill between Rep. Norman Mineta [D-CA] and Rep. Bob Carr [D-MI], he provides a valuable civics lesson on how Congress really works. Boot shows how deals get made, political alliances shift, and feuds ensue, all before a vote can be taken. His surprisingly skimpy 8-3 profile of the newly nominated FBI director Louis Freeh imparts little sense of the nominee, because Boot crams in too many other items, such as references to J. Edgar Hoover, the tarnished image of the bureau, and the troubles of William Sessions. Always able to get his foot in the door, Boot knows his way around the Beltway.

John M. Broder
Los Angeles Times
★★

Washington, national security. With his inside sources and judicious use of quotes, Broder provides articles brimming with information. Seldom turning his hand at analysis, however, he deprives his work of an extra dimension. In his important 2-19 article, Broder dissects President Clinton's economic proposals to show why "some of his budget cuts are illusory at best." He logically explains that some alleged cuts—such as fees for government services—"are actually feebly disguised tax increases" and that many other cuts will never be enacted. But such keen analysis seldom appears in Broder's work. In a 4-1 essay, co-authored by Doyle McManus, the pair presents a frank, though superficial, discussion of the importance of Russia to Clinton and his new administration. Never questioning the course the President has taken, they instead evaluate the political implications of supporting Yeltsin and supplying aid. Broder's solid 5-1 review of Clinton's speech at the University of New Orleans, in which the President defended his first 100 days and outlined his national service program, provides excellent detail as well as an assessment of the program's potential problems. In his 6-8 piece, he imparts an early look at the role David Gergen might play as White House counselor. "Gergen's standing thus equals or surpasses that of White House chief of staff Thomas (Mack) McLarty....It also adds another senior aide with direct access to President Clinton and spreads Clinton's horizontal organization chart even wider. Gergen... joins Hillary Rodham Clinton and Vice President Al Gore in the innermost White House circle of advisors." Broder follows Clinton to the United Nations to craft a strong 9-28 report on Clinton's speech to the General Assembly. Along with a healthy selection of quotes from the speech itself, Broder examines some nuances of the debates raging within the administration over Clinton's foreign policy. The only thing Broder misses is a range of reaction to the speech. Similarly, his 10-8 coverage of Clinton's announcement that more troops will be sent to Somalia never strays from the straight and narrow, barely hinting at the controversy to come. Perhaps the development of stronger analysis would help to broaden Broder's scope and strengthen his talents.

Ronald Brownstein
Los Angeles Times
★★½

National political correspondent. Brownstein specializes in assessing politics. While few can match his superb writing, his evaluations sometimes lack fresh insight. In his 1-11 essay, Brownstein examines the policy fare for the new administration, listing new buzzwords—charter schools, green taxes, managed trade—to add to the common lexicon. Although carefully summarizing the Clinton agenda, he presents few new items of any significance. "Disputes over abortion could still set off sparks in 1993 if congressional Democrats decide to seriously pursue legislation codifying the legal right to abortion." He broadens the ideological fight over Lani Guinier to a struggle for the soul of the administration, 5-26. Although he gets points for actually quoting some of Guinier's writings, Brownstein gets nothing fresh from either President Clinton or the nominee. In his solid 6-14 political overview of a president not fully in control of his party, Brownstein defines how the "powerful centrifugal impulse [of Democrats fighting among themselves] may now pose as great a threat to Clinton as the unstinting criticism from Ross Perot and the GOP leadership in Congress." Despite again failing to present much new information, he superbly encapsulates the party's problems and how they might affect the elections in 1994 and 1996. Brownstein's 8-7 essay credibly tracks the political risks undertaken by Clinton in his economic program. While he neglects to address the actual economics—thereby presenting only half the story—he capably outlines the political tightrope Clinton is walking. More his old self in his 10-6 dispatch, Brownstein crafts an excellent discussion of how two issues, health care and NAFTA, have shaped Clinton's presidency. "The two episodes reflect what is emerging as the central goal of Clinton's presidency: creating a new system of government programs and guarantees that will give working Americans the sense of personal security they need to face the challenges of economic flux and change." Brownstein never addresses how Clinton will achieve this goal, but he effectively underlines new demands placed on the U.S. by the expanding global economy. Utilizing his skill at yielding political assessments, Brownstein recasts the debate—as he often does when he's at his best.

Jackie Calmes
The Wall Street Journal
★★

Congress, taxes. In a year when taxes moved to the forefront of the debate on the nation's direction, Calmes supplies no-nonsense dispatches that showcase her acute sense of politics. Rarely, however, does she address the tough economic questions. In her lucid 4-30 essay, Calmes defines the political stakes of Clinton's economic package and outlines which provisions Congress might change. She notes shrewdly that "the final bill will differ in several key respects from Mr. Clinton's plan, owing to gripes about its particulars from his own party. The president then must de-

cide whether he goes to the mat for his proposals, or whether, as someone who has studied Ronald Reagan's successful first year, he will follow Mr. Reagan's 1981 example of accepting a rewritten bill and declaring victory." As Clinton's economic package faces a tough audience in the Senate, she and co-author David Wessel craft a solid 5-28 update, but they never assess the economic implications of Clinton's ideas. In her pithy 6-28 review, Calmes provides fresh detail on so-called reduction measures, the differences between the House and Senate versions, and who voted for which and why. Her quick 7-2 profile of Sen. Russ Feingold [D-WI], who is getting rid of the freebies—such as "calendars, mugs, bookends, a rosary, and Clinton-Gore lapel pin in the shape of Minnesota"—showered on him by companies and lobbying firms, fails to adequately profile the Senator. Known "for his high ethical standards," Feingold backs legislation to ban all gifts from lobbyists. "But," Calmes wonders, "Washington being Washington, the question often asked is whether the senator—who accepted $460,000 in contributions from political action committees to help win his seat—represents a new attitude, or the kind of practiced self-righteousness that Washington excels at." By including a smattering of congressional and White House reactions, her 9-22 dispatch cleverly recaps the political maneuvering following Rep. Richard Gephardt's [D-MO] announcement of his opposition to NAFTA. A second 10-25 effort on NAFTA reveals another Clinton political tradeoff—dropping customs fees in order to garner more GOP votes. But before improving on this beat, Calmes must delve into the realm of economics. Otherwise, she gets—and gives—only half the story on taxation and Congress.

Carl M. Cannon

The Baltimore Sun

★★½

White House. A diligent reporter with a sharp eye for the odd fact, Cannon provides reliable accounts of the daily story at 1600 Pennsylvania Avenue. While he does not routinely plumb the depths of policy debates, he composes politically savvy news analyses. In his 4-2 story reporting President Clinton's speech—"short on specifics, but full of soaring imagery"—on the role of the U.S. in helping Russia build a free-market economy, Cannon notes perceptively that many of the President's proposed activities "are... already occurring daily between the two nations, and it remains to be seen whether such [a] minimalist approach will encourage the beleaguered Russian reformers, no matter how warm and evocative Mr. Clinton's words sounded." In his solid 6-15 account of Clinton's nomination of Ruth Bader Ginsburg to the Supreme Court, Cannon points out that the search, amazingly, "dragged on for a longer period than any since the Civil War." In his 3-28 assessment of the new administration after its ninth week, Cannon astutely employs the remark of a Republican—former Reagan White House Chief of Staff Kenneth Duberstein. "'[Clinton] gets an A-plus as a salesman,'" Duberstein says. "'He stumbled at the start, but he has gotten his economic message across. People think he is trying and is someone who cares about them.'" Cannon quotes another Republican (and frequent source of his), Martin C. Anderson, Reagan's first domestic policy adviser, who says that Clinton's budget numbers "don't add up." In his 6-27 piece on Clinton's practice of government by "trial balloon," Cannon shows how the new White House floats ideas and even potential nominations in the press to see how well—or poorly—they might be received. Relying on his many sources, Cannon crafts a well-balanced 8-8 account of the events immediately following passage of the budget, complete with Clinton advisor Paul Begala hugging folks in the White House. Canvassing the difficulties Clinton faces in trying to govern from "the center," Cannon discusses the President's style of leadership. "Mr. Clinton is finding out that representing the majority can be a thankless job—and that the nation's political institutions are not set up to deal very well with non-ideological decisions." With informative and often insightful articles, Cannon carefully chronicles Clinton's first year in office.

Lou Cannon

The Washington Post

Los Angeles. For this experienced reporter, the Golden State continues to yield a rich lore of stories. Time and again, Cannon displays an acute understanding of both California politics and Los Angeles affairs. His coverage of the second Rodney King trial, while not groundbreaking, remains balanced and direct. In his 4-18 report on the verdict convicting two police officers and acquitting two others, Cannon manages to capture the mood of the city without detracting from the meat of the story. And his well-crafted 1-10 story on Gov. Pete Wilson [R-CA] holds the attention of folks inside the Beltway, as Cannon manages to cover Wilson's State of the State speech and budget proposal, detail the problems behind the state's economic upheaval, and analyze the political challenges confronting the beleaguered Governor. In a series of reports on the Los Angeles mayoral race, Cannon's work proves less satisfying. While well-written, his 6-10 profile of newly elected Republican Mayor Richard Riordan lacks the depth and perception found in Cannon's best work. This recap of the campaign will disappoint most Washington political junkies. Failing to fully delineate the differences between the candidates, he does not provide an adequate discussion of the core issues. Cannon also disappoints in his colorful 5-17 front-page story on the "two troubled cities" of Los Angeles. Contrasting a "middle-aged, somewhat graying around the temples, and highly stable" white community with a second, "voiceless city" of Hispanics and Asians detracts from Cannon's otherwise thoughtful analysis. Moreover, his assertion that a large percentage of the city's population is "disenfranchised by lack of citizenship" fails to take into account the vexed issue of illegal aliens. Cannon also declines to address the concerns of the voters of his first L.A., unfairly criticizing them for refusing to foot the bill for services they don't use. In discussing a proposal to raise taxes to pay for more police, he blames its defeat on "tax-conscious white homeowners in the San Fernando Valley, some of whom are protected by private security systems." Thankfully, such bias is the exception rather than the norm in Cannon's reporting. He usually turns in the kind of concise yet substantial dispatches that engage readers on the opposite coast.

Margaret Carlson

Time

★

Deputy Washington bureau chief. Now part of CNBC's "Capitol Gang" talkfest, Carlson has more visibility than ever. Unfortunately, she rarely offers new information or anything beyond conventional analysis. Her 2-8 effort on Hillary Rodham Clinton delivers little that hadn't been seen elsewhere, and while this well-written dispatch shows how hard the folks at the administration are working, it lacks much hard news. Carlson largely succeeds, 5-10, in portraying the First Lady as everywoman—no doubt the image the White House wanted conveyed. "To millions of women, Hillary Clinton's career-and-family balancing act is symbolic struggle. Never mind that she has plenty of help, including more top officials on her staff than Al Gore has. Hillary still has something in common with women everywhere: a day that contains only 24 hours, and responsibilities that extend way beyond what happens in the office. Family duties fall primarily to her—from attending soccer games and helping Chelsea with her homework to shopping and organizing birthday parties. She's also looking after her mother, who is staying at the White House while recovering from the death of Hillary's 82-year-old father....The First Lady's plea is familiar to any working woman. 'We are trying to work it out that we have some more time just for ourselves. The job eats up every spare minute.'" Carlson reiterates this view of the First Lady in the June *Vanity Fair*—even using some of the same phrasing! Her 8-2 work on the suicide of Vince Foster offers little that couldn't be learned from TV news. Her 9-13 effort spotlights Vice President Al Gore but, again, there's not much new information to be gleaned. Although adequate as an overview, the piece represents a typical Carlson offering.

Edwin Chen

Los Angeles Times

Health care, Washington. Keeping a steady head during the raging debate over health-care reform, Chen reports developments clearly and precisely. He seems to take for granted the need for massive reform, however, and thus misses the larger debate over whether such reform represents the best approach to controlling costs and improving care. In his 2-14 dispatch, Chen deftly encapsulates the problem of what a federal package should cover. "The task

promises to set off a high-stakes struggle among medical specialties and other providers that could bog down the entire initiative....In designing a core package of benefits, the Administration must not only strike a balance among high-powered, competing interest groups, but also guard against offering too much—or too little. Too rich an array of benefits could bankrupt a system already teetering on the brink of collapse. Too skimpy a package invites a Faustian bargain: If people lack certain medical coverage, they are likely to delay seeking care until their illnesses require far more expensive treatments." Chen renders a credible 5-1 effort updating his readers on how the administration might require taxpayers to pay for health-care reform. His 6-1 profile of Ira Magaziner unfortunately reveals much less about Magaziner's record than the comparable effort in the May *Washington Monthly*. Although Chen provides an adequate sense of the health-care task-force guru, he takes too much at face value. In his 9-28 report, Chen exposes administration lowballing of estimates on the amount business (and everyone else) will have to pay to finance President Clinton's health-care plan—not 7.9 percent of payroll but 8.5 percent. Chen comes close to questioning the need for reform, 10-3, relating a recent *Times* poll that seems to indicate the public's support for health-care reform. Chen observes that some of the positive public opinion may reflect the skill with which Clinton "exploited" public anxiety on the subject, but he doesn't really go anywhere with this provocative idea. At least Chen's getting closer to the debate of true importance.

George J. Church

Time

★★

Senior writer. Packing so many details, charts, and polls into his articles that they rival multimedia presentations, Church provides in-depth analyses of national issues and White House concerns. He focuses more on domestic than foreign affairs this year and, with mixed success, takes risks making predictions. In his 11-15 assessment of the NAFTA debate, Church jocularly discusses the administration's strategy. "[President Clinton] and [Vice President] Gore had been trying to find some whiz-bang event that would impress an apathetic public. They were intrigued by White House poll findings suggesting that for all the fervor of his supporters, [Ross] Perot also arouses considerable antipathy—so much so that public support for NAFTA rises sharply when people find out the jug-eared Texan is against it." In his 2-22 piece predicting key targets for budget cuts, Church goes out on a limb—and falls off. "Clinton is likely to take a hard whack out of funding for the space station, at the risk of offending Senators from California, Texas and Florida, but will not similarly slash money for the Texas-based Superconducting Supercollider. No point in giving the Texans an additional grievance." As it turned out, the supercollider was killed in October. However, Church's 10-18 analysis concerning the U.S. presence in Somalia proved right by year's end. "Aspin had turned down a request...for reinforcements...that could have rescued the Rangers in the Oct. 3 fire fight much sooner. Aspin eventually confirmed that, and gave his reason: at a time when the U.S. was considering dispatching a peace-keeping force to Bosnia, he did not want to make it look as if the nation was increasing rather than reducing, its force in Somalia.... Aspin...may have permanently damaged his effectiveness." In his 5-24 preview of health-care reform, Church shows that his real expertise lies in presenting detailed surveys of major policy topics. "Elementary prudence—not to mention Clinton's usual habit of seeking to accommodate everybody—would seem to have dictated trying to bring the major interest groups aboard from the start, at least to the extent of listening to their views and thus giving them a stake in a plan they could feel they had helped shape. Instead, the White House turned the job over to a 511-member task force whose very names were kept secret." Although his stories are seldom riveting, Church presents balanced and *Time*ly overviews of current events.

William Claiborne

The Washington Post

Covering everything from Midwest floods to Mideast peace negotiations, Claiborne takes a practical approach to complicated issues. He remains particularly adept at illustrating how decisions made on Capitol Hill affect people on Main Street. In his 7-30 report from the National Conference of State Legislators, Claiborne examines the need to balance "conflicting federal and state interests in an era of deficit reduction." Citing an "ever-growing list of rules and regulations," he illustrates the impact of costly government mandates on state budgets. Here Claiborne paints a convincing picture of a bureaucratic and irresponsible federal government. Similarly, his 8-12 story on Iowa flood victims portrays frustrated homeowners caught in a government-imposed "Catch-22." In order to qualify for low-interest federal loans to repair their homes, Claiborne notes, they must incur the additional expense of raising their foundations above flood-plain level. Too often, however, Claiborne fails to adequately sift through information before incorporating it into his work. He blends a good amount of useless material into his otherwise newsworthy series, 3-30, 6-20, 6-26, 6-28, and 7-13, on the closing of military installations across the country. In these redundant accounts of how targeted communities will suffer, Claiborne overlooks the larger issue of making necessary cuts in defense spending. His 6-26 installment, co-authored by Kent Jenkins, portrays Charleston, South Carolina, as a city in danger of losing "not only many jobs, but its place in naval lore." Not only overly sentimental, the piece fails to convey the city's historical significance. Claiborne's Israel dispatches, 9-12 through 9-24, reveal little evidence of any singular knowledge of the region and offers one quote after another in lieu of sophisticated analysis. Although he captures the mood of the country in the wake of the Israeli-Palestinian peace accords, his accounts of a Jewish population skeptical of concessions with the PLO become repetitive. Claiborne displays more insight in his thorough 5-9 profile of David Koresh. Co-authored by Jim McGee, this highly readable portrait offers a detailed account of Koresh's transformation from troubled adolescent to self-proclaimed prophet. In addition to these stories, Claiborne still finds time to report on Bosnia, the JFK assassination, and health-care reform. While he may chalk up more frequent-flier miles than any other journalist in the business, Claiborne's juggling act allows for little more than a thumbnail sketch of any one subject.

Eleanor Clift

Newsweek

½★

Washington. Clift never adds anything substantive to the policy debates in the nation's capital—even from her chair on "The McLaughlin Group." Worse, she sometimes plays the role of cheerleader for the new administration, particularly for the First Lady. In her 2-22 effort, Clift highlights "women's issues" receiving greater attention in Washington—child care, "the glass ceiling," diversity in the Cabinet—but fails to inform the reader of anything new concerning the difficulties between the sexes on Capitol Hill. Her 5-31 essay on the budget focuses less on Congress and lawmakers' maneuverings than on how backroom dealing is affecting President Clinton politically. This exercise lacks substantive information on economic policy. Clift and two co-authors spend a week with the President and document, in a 7-12 report, their seven memorable days. Judging from the sometimes breathless prose, they seem taken with their assignment—and also themselves. Their inside view, while informative, doesn't get to the nitty-gritty of policy formation. In an odd 8-30 profile of Bernard Nussbaum, Clinton's lawyer, Clift positions him as the administration scapegoat for his bad advice to Clinton on Zöe Baird and Lani Guinier, among others. She spends so much time detailing what people blame him for that she neglects to tell the reader about anything Nussbaum's done right. "How can someone of Nussbaum's obvious intelligence and ability turn into a hapless incompetent overnight? Corporate litigators are the bulldozers of the legal world, running over whatever is in their way. Political lawyering is more subtle." In her disappointing 3-29 piece, Clift adds nothing to the debate over health-care reform. Instead, she simply cheers the First Lady's public relations initiatives. "Hillary [Rodham Clinton] is mounting a campaign of her own to counter the often phony grassroots opposition ginned up by special-interest groups." Clift re-reports this story, 4-26, and re-re-reports it, 9-20. As the First Lady's fortunes wax and wane in the media, Clift can always be counted on to herald Hillary's

DON WRIGHT · RIBUNE MEDIA SERVICES

comebacks. While her admiration for the First Lady may be laudable, this heroine worship seriously impedes her ability to report independently and fairly. Memo to Editors: Keep Clift off this story.

Adam Clymer
The New York Times
★½

Congress. With his keen eye for the absurdities of politics, Clymer has a strong talent for storytelling, but not for examining policy. In his colorful 4-19 profile of Sen. Bob Dole [R-KS], Clymer compellingly describes the Minority Leader's political skills as well as his sense of humor. "Senator John Chafee of Rhode Island recalled how Mr. Dole broke up Mr. Clinton and Republicans at a caucus; the President was given a mystery novel titled *Murder in the Senate* and observed that he was troubled that the victim had been a Democrat. Mr. Dole quipped, 'Yes, it had a happy ending.'" In his 8-9 piece, Clymer analyzes the role of Sen. George Mitchell [D-ME] in helping to pass the budget bill: "The very characteristics that deny Mr. Mitchell attention—the control of his temper, the willingness to yield center stage and the sometimes tedious command and explication of detail—were essential to success. It was the weeks of prodding that made this one of the signal victories of Mr. Mitchell's four and a half years as majority leader." In a detailed 2-10 profile of Rep. Dan Rostenkowski [D-IL], Clymer provides an intriguing portrait of a man in a defensive posture. However, because he fails to clearly define the nature of the House Post Office scandal and Rostenkowski's rumored involvement, the reader doesn't learn why the Chicago Congressman is in such a position. Clymer's 5-28 article examines the "extravaganza of inconsistency" within Congress, which—despite searching for ways to cut the budget—appropriated $1.2 billion *more* than the military had asked for. Although he muddles the explanation, Clymer notes amusingly that "the Pentagon is smiling all the way to the bank." His 10-13 report from a Pennsylvania hearing on health care with Sen. Harris Wofford [D-PA] disappoints, as Clymer takes the number of people who attended—three dozen—and translates this into broad support for health-care reform. Where Clymer's profiles satisfy, his political dispatches leave the reader wanting more.

Richard E. Cohen
National Journal
★★½

Congress. With a deeper sense of politics now strengthening his smart, direct reporting, Cohen renders solid analysis that informs and provokes. In his 1-3 *Washington Post* op-ed, he rebukes those who would throw out the parties in favor of a national referendum and electronic town halls. He notes incisively: "Demands by critics—press lords and others—for 'change' and for instant solutions to complex conflicts can only compound the difficulty of governing and eventually add to public frustration." Cohen provides a fine 3-4 portrait of how GOP senators may be able to operate effectively despite constituting the minority. He cites as a case in point the fight over the motor-voter bill, which Republicans felt was vastly improved by their labors. In his smart 5-29 article, Cohen argues that despite Clinton's overwhelming victory in the electoral college —370-168—his margin of support nationwide was far slimmer. "A new study of votes by congressional district reveals that Clinton won only 257 of the 435 districts; Bush won 178." Furthermore, "the new president's worst showings came mostly in the South and West," or in his own backyard. Cohen crafts a savvy, three-dimensional profile of Sen. Ted Kennedy [D-MA], 7-24, remarking on the unique opportunity afforded him by Clinton's planned emphasis on social issues for the balance of the year. "For Kennedy, the next few months offer a chance to make a fresh start. If he succeeds, he could reestablish himself as the congressional Democrats' leading voice on domestic policy, burnish his credentials as a legislative activist and lift a lingering cloud of personal problems. And he could strengthen his position in a tough re-election race next year. The next phase of Clinton's program includes much of the unfinished agenda of the 1960s, for which Kennedy has carried the torch during years when his efforts were often scorned or ignored." But Cohen's dense 8-7 account of the "ego-driven politics" behind the House-Senate negotiation over Clinton's deficit reduction plan confuses more than enlightens. Although it may be a chaotic process, its retelling should not be. This piece, however, marks the exception, as Cohen usually delivers the goods.

Lyle Denniston

The Baltimore Sun

★½

Supreme Court. While not the smoothest of writers, Denniston adequately covers the high court and the Justice Department. Like others on his beat, he often uses political terms that do not easily apply to judicial decisions, and his news analysis, though competent, seldom stands out. In his 1-22 story on the 20th anniversary of *Roe v. Wade*, Denniston confuses the issue with his overuse of metaphor. The piece begins by portraying Justice Harry Blackmun, who wrote the majority opinion in Roe, as "the quiet man at the storm center of the abortion controversy." Several paragraphs later, Denniston writes that "the nation's courts are moving away from the center of the storm as it blows into Congress, state legislatures, and city councils." Literally, that means Blackmun is blowing into Congress and other lawmaking chambers—an amusing image but not one that Denniston intended. His otherwise competent 2-14 analysis of what Clinton intends to achieve judicially through his Supreme Court nominations suffers from his use of terms like "liberalism," which are usually understood to convey a political meaning. Unless Denniston thinks law can be reduced to politics, he must be referring to liberalism (and conservatism) not in a political but in a judicial or jurisprudential context—something he should make plain. His 3-20 analysis of Justice Byron White's career contains inaccuracies—a Court opinion dated 1985 was actually handed down in 1986—but also some marvelous anecdotes. Told of the news media's unhappiness over Court rulings adversely affecting First Amendment rights, White said: "Well, the bastards deserve it." In his best piece of the year, Denniston delivers a 4-4 treatment of the Court's tangled church-state jurisprudence. Citing an Illinois man who describes himself as the national spokesman for American Atheists, Inc. as an example, Denniston shows that some people have become professional plaintiffs, always on the watch for lawsuits they can bring charging some public school, city council, or county government with a First Amendment violation. With so much litigation over so many fine points, he notes, it's no wonder the Court's decision-making jumps all over the map. In his 5-15 profile of Justice Antonin Scalia, Denniston again indulges his preference for simplistic political labels. Scalia, for example, leads "the conservative revolution." Worse, however, while Denniston correctly observes that Scalia tilts against the Court's "balancers," he fails to describe what it means for a judge to engage in "balancing." Denniston's stories on the Ginsburg nomination and confirmation, 6-15, 7-19, and 8-4, cover the facts but too eagerly predict what is impossible to predict—her performance as a Justice. And while his 9-18 dispatch on Clinton's slow-to-get-going judicial selection process awkwardly begins with a passive construction, it manages to convey the President's preoccupation with "diversity" in judge-picking. A long-time reporter on this beat, Denniston provides most of the basics but little more.

Ann Devroy

The Washington Post

★½

White House. Coasting for much of the year, Devroy rarely employs her considerable reporting talents on this beat—and supplies few insights. In her otherwise pedestrian 2-15 essay examining President Clinton's potential economic proposals, she concludes sharply, "Overall...the president hopes to come up with $500 billion

of spending cuts and tax increases over four years. That is approximately the same amount of deficit reduction that Bush and Congress agreed to in 1990 before the recession and soaring health costs made mincemeat of their economic projections." Characteristically, Devroy provides minimum detail in her 3-31 essay on the potential repeal of the Hyde Amendment, which prohibits Medicaid funding of abortions. Although more a moral issue than a financial one, she does note that the AMA "lists the average cost of a birth in a hospital at $3,200 and an abortion as less than half that." Unfortunately, she gives no indication of whether repealing the amendment would ultimately cost or save the government money. In her 4-17 piece, she presents the White House's effort to keep a low profile on Clinton's meeting with gay rights leaders. "Was Clinton willing to meet with gays, but only if the rest of the country couldn't see it? Willing to support much of the gay civil rights agenda, but not be seen in a gay-rights march? White House officials denied such interpretations." In her 6-25 account of the tug-of-war over gays in the military, Devroy excerpts "an emotional letter" from the gay-rights group ANGLE urging Clinton not to "'bend to the voices of bigotry.'" She also quotes an ANGLE activist, but no one opposed to lifting the ban. In her 10-12 essay, she details Mack McLarty's attempt to get White House staffers to define their work in written job descriptions, so as to facilitate a corporate-type management review. Noting that former White House Chief of Staff Sam Skinner tried this and lost his job, Devroy concludes snidely by knocking McLarty. "Officials describe [the Chief of Staff] as trying to make the White House run efficiently, as holding many phone sessions and luncheon meetings with members of Congress on health care and other issues. But if he has a central role in the White House, it has not been visible." Pithy perhaps, but Devroy can do better.

Helen Dewar

The Washington Post

★½

Senate. Although Dewar pens strong, crisply defined overviews of senatorial politics and infighting, her Democratic leanings occasionally show. In her 3-18 report, she delivers a flavorful view of the Senate debate over the Motor Voter Bill, but reveals her preferences. Citing no sources, she notes that, "while Democrats argued that the provision would encourage participation in elections by low-income or jobless people, Republicans argued publicly that it could lead to coercion by public officials and complained privately that it probably would lead to registration of more Democrats." She then quotes Senate Majority Leader George Mitchell [D-ME] calling a GOP maneuver "'cruel,'" but includes no response from Republicans beyond their congratulating themselves for their unity. In her disappointing 6-25 effort, Dewar skims the substantive issues that divide Ross Perot and Congress over deficit reduction, favoring instead rhetorical flourishes. "Perot and the Senate were more than just a hundred yards apart. They were on different planets, separated by the infinite space that divides the holiness of lofty crusades from the often compromised purity of governance." Her lackluster 9-17 article on the retirement of Sens. Dennis DeConcini [D-AZ] and David Durenberger [R-MN] at least incorporates a light summary of the new candidates fighting for their seats. Dewar delivers a solid 10-2 overview of the First Amendment debates in Congress, from flag burning to television violence. Although she offers little new, she provides a useful review of the debate. But she and co-author David Von Drehle disappoint with a 5-3 profile of Sen. Sam Nunn [D-GA]. The piece covers all the gossip surrounding Nunn's decision not to support Clintonomics—including his jealousy of Clinton over winning the White House—but adds nothing to the reader's knowledge. It seems as though she and Von Drehle think Nunn just ought to be supporting the President. If Dewar could better distance herself from her own politics, she could do a better job covering the Senate's politics.

Edwin Diamond

New York

★★½

Media. While the New York City tabloid wars provide a steady stream of juicy media news this year, Diamond's best work comes when he takes a critical pen to his own industry. Attacking what he considers the sorry journalistic standards of the 1990s, Diamond illustrates how old-fashioned reporting has given way to sloppiness and sensationalism. He examines what qualifies as "news," the process of reporting news, and the not-so-fine line between fact and fiction. In his insightful 4-5 column on ABC's coverage of the war in Bosnia, Diamond discusses the "conventional thinking about what viewers will watch, as well as what TV news should try to give them." Comparing the "ethnic cleansing" in Bosnia to the genocidal policies of Adolph Hitler, Diamond praises Peter Jennings and ABC News for "turning over some thoughts that normally ought to be on the agenda of White House policymakers and Congress." In his 1-11 column, Diamond explores local television coverage of the New York City mayoral race. Noting that a rubber chicken brought to a debate by Conservative Party candidate George Marlin dominated the news, Diamond astutely points out that "journalistic fact and journalistic fancy" often receive equal media attention. In the quest for the all-important picture, television has practically abandoned reporting the issues; the press relies so heavily on commentary, he notes, it puts a spin on nearly everything. In his biting 3-15 analysis of NBC News president Michael Gartner's resignation following the controversy over the rigged explosion of a GM truck on "Dateline," Diamond discusses what he calls the "dirty little secret about the media today." He blasts both NBC's slipshod ethical enforcement and Gartner's mismanagement of the crisis, concluding cynically that "neither Gartner's resignation nor all of NBC's reaffirmations of proper guidelines will have much deterrent effect on the shape of what passes for news these days on TV and in print." Usefully examining the increase in the publishing of false information, 5-3, Diamond warns that "the news workers of the nineties are in danger of sliding back down the evolutionary tree." He cites numerous examples—such as J. Edgar Hoover's alleged cross-dressing—of how "fantastic tales are legitimized by sheer repetition and then distributed far beyond the modest scope of the original source." With the current "ends justify the means" approach influencing today's journalism, Diamond maintains an appreciation for good, honest reporting. The multifaceted Diamond still sparkles.

Cathryn Donohoe

The Washington Times

★★

"MetroTimes" writer. "Irreverent wit" does not begin to describe Donohoe's noisy rampages. Although she tackles everything from ancient history to the latest elections, she sometimes spreads herself too thin, and her insights seem scarcer and less original than last year's. Her one-liners, however, sometimes hit the bull's-eye. Nowhere else will you find the writing on the Dead Sea Scroll fragments described, 4-29, as "a set of tiny tracks from some paleo-chicken (forgive us, O Lord)." Nor would most people know, had they not read her 4-14 piece on filling out the 1040 income tax form, that "if you read the list on Page 13, 'Examples of Income You Must Report,' you'll see you're headed for deep, deep trouble if you're not up front about 'embezzled or other illegal income.'" Some jokes fall flat, however, such as her sophomoric 2-8 reference to Clinton's "White House that seemed on the verge of defining itself as, well, a waffle house." Donohoe's more serious 3-26 piece on Russian President Boris Yeltsin's near-coup in March sensitively conveys the despair of the Russian emigrés she interviews, such as David Fox-Rabinovitz, a 44-year-old computer programmer now living in Maryland. "[He] is so estranged from his former home he celebrates his exit the way one would the moment of one's birth: 'I left,' he says, 'on 31 December 1989, on the eve of the New Year, at 4 o'clock p.m.'" Despite such poignant quotes, Donohoe's failure to report on Russian politics and her broad generalizations about the Russian people render the article disjointed. In her 2-4 piece on Hazel O'Leary, Donohoe provides an illuminating catalog of the new Energy Secretary's long-standing political connections. However, she reveals virtually nothing about O'Leary's character, offering only a curt remark by a former colleague—"'Hazel's rough, isn't she?'" In her 10-28 article on the Virginia elections and the Democrats' portrayals of the Republican candidates as devotees of the 'religious right,' Donohoe notes perceptively, "What is most intriguing about the conservative response is that Catholics, normally wary of working with Protestants whom they connect with nativist prejudice against the influence of

Rome, have been quick to defend the evangelicals." Such comments, along with her flashes of wit, make Donohoe's articles entertaining if not always fulfilling.

Maureen Dowd
The New York Times
★★½

White House. Dowd certainly has her share of fans, her flippant style of writing so popular that it has spawned countless imitators on many different beats. As clever as her writing is, though, it can't always mask the occasional frivolity of her subjects. Dowd cooks up a tasty inaugural appetizer, 1-3, examining the changes in the electorate's feelings toward presidents as they move from making campaign promises to enacting policy. In her 2-8 review of President Clinton's troubles choosing an attorney general, she incorporates many quotes from analysts but doesn't quite pull it all together. Emphasizing Hollywood in a trifling 4-5 collection of gossip, Dowd offers mere scraps from the Vancouver summit. Her 5-9 article lists who's coming to Washington from Hollywood, but fails to examine what effect, if any, this might have on policy. However, she does provide one perceptive insight on the new East-West axis. "Washington and Hollywood have always been drawn to each other because of their common interest in performance and image, and their complementary insecurities: the Hollywood elite wants to be seen as serious, and the Washington elite wants to be seen as glamorous." In her informative 10-26 dispatch, this former New York metro reporter returns to the city's political beat, where she finds Mayor David Dinkins during the last moments of a close campaign with Rudolph Giuliani. In addition to getting a sense of the race, the reader learns of the Mayor's campaign style. "With a flair for changing clothes that Cher might admire and a fastidiousness about hangers that Joan Crawford would envy, Mr. Dinkins brought along his usual array of jackets—a black silk windbreaker, a Rangers jacket and a pinstriped suit, slipping in and out of various looks during the morning." In a balanced and vivid 8-18 account of Captain Gregory Bonham's trial for assaulting Lieutenant Paula Coughlin in the infamous Tailhook gauntlet, Dowd takes care not to judge. Dowd proves more effective when covering hard news. On that beat, Dowdism is the style, not the star.

Thomas B. Edsall
The Washington Post
★★★

Politics. Edsall regains his fine form this year, astutely analyzing the shifting political fortunes of both parties, from the national to the local level. Although he sometimes glosses over economic issues, he perceptively defines the differences between Republicans and Democrats. In his outstanding 1-3 appraisal, Edsall clearly correlates Bill Clinton's chances of success with his ability to change his party's discourse. The President "faces the enormous task of using the power of the White House to rebuild the battered image of the Democratic party....It requires challenging such liberal interests as feminist and black organizations while maintaining a commitment to racial and sex diversity. The inherent danger of the strategy is the risk of appearing duplicitous, of seeking to have it both ways." In his 2-21 lead, Edsall cuts to the heart of the matter on Clintonomics. "President Clinton has wrapped in the rhetoric of moderation an economic program that is, in fact, designed to overturn the anti-government ideology that underpinned the conservative revolution of the early 1980s." But while Edsall constructs a credible political analysis of Clintonomics, he, like many of his colleagues, sidesteps the economics. In two solid articles on the senatorial campaign in Texas, 6-5 and 6-6, Edsall defines the problems a Kay Bailey Hutchison victory would mean for Clinton, such as opposition to his economic proposals from a *just-elected* senator. In his sharp 9-22 overview, Edsall emerges as one of the few to point out that "reception of [Republican candidate Christine] Whitman's economic program this week will be crucial in determining the direction of the New Jersey gubernatorial campaign." Exploring how the New York City mayoral contest typifies changing urban politics, Edsall's well-crafted 10-17 effort considers the demographic changes that have helped to shift traditional big-city liberal ideology towards the center. Edsall distinguishes himself as one of the rare political reporters who can move easily between the local, state, and national arenas. Greater concentration on economics would lift him to the highest echelons of the journalistic profession.

Timothy Egan

The New York Times

★★½

Northwest correspondent. With very balanced accounts of emotional issues—from the timber summit to the sesquicentennial of the Oregon Trail—Egan often qualifies the information provided by his sources. He shows the same care in reporting less volatile stories. In his 4-2 piece on the overblown efforts of loggers and environmentalists to sell their respective cases to the Washington luminaries visiting the timber summit, Egan humorously portrays the Oregonians' attempts to control both the medium and the message. "White House aides are despairing at reports that many of these unschooled local types spent Wednesday in an intensive course on how to speak in sound bites." In his riveting three-part series on the 150th anniversary of the Oregon Trail, 5-30, 5-31, and 6-1, Egan describes how Native Americans and pioneers peaceably shared the land prior to the Indian Wars, which took place just over 100 years ago. The 6-1 installment keenly recalls how recently these wars ended, particularly in the psyche of Native Americans. "Not a day goes by when the consequences of those wars, the reduced reservations, the lingering distrust between tribes that sided with whites and those who fought, are not felt along the old Oregon Trail." Pulling up just shy of bashing, Egan reaches a bit in his 8-17 piece on the seemingly insurmountable and ever-changing barriers facing American apple growers in their efforts to penetrate the Japanese market. "Apples are to Japanese and American trade policy what intercontinental missiles were to the cold war." This example of Japanese barriers against agricultural imports hardly merits Cold War comparison. Egan picks up a quirky 6-7 story on the power of owners' boards in suburban developments. Homeowners Lee and Barbara Jones run afoul of their board for painting their house "mauve with deep purple trim—combined with just a hint of teal around the windows....When the Joneses refused to submit a new color scheme last fall, following [a court's] judgment [against them], the court ordered that money be taken from their checking account and Mrs. Jones's wages and turned over to the homeowners association." Despite the amusing detail, Egan fails to provide sufficient legal explanation of the judge's ruling. Such lapses prove rare. With his shrewd and somewhat irreverent style, Egan provides vivid and entertaining snapshots of everyday life in the Pacific northwest.

Michael Elliott

Newsweek

★½

National affairs. With his simplistic analysis of Clinton administration foreign policy, Elliott offers insufficient background material to allow readers to draw their own conclusions. He seldom digs beneath the level of public statements and popular images to provide a more thoughtful perspective. In his vague 9-27 piece on the Israeli-PLO peace plan, Elliott starts out assuming that the U.S.—as primary broker of the plan—would have to raise the money to rebuild Palestine. He provides an unlikely assessment of what that entails, oddly comparing a refugee nation to a crumbling superpower. "How much cash is needed? Less than many think. The State Department reckons that the Palestinians need about $2 billion in aid in the first five years of peace —compare that with the $28 billion which in April the Group of Seven industrial countries thought was needed to rebuild Russia." In his 11-1 piece on the Clinton administration's internal debate on how to redefine NATO, Elliott isolates two underlying principles: "Don't Gloat"—NATO should not be used to flaunt Cold War victory; and "Big Brother"—it should be used to spread support for burgeoning democracies in Eastern Europe and Russia by including them in the alliance. Rather than concluding the piece with a detailed account of why the administration favors the latter approach, Elliott strangely inserts, "Why should military security be the most pressing concern of the new Democracies in Europe? And the answer is: it isn't." Who said it was? His 10-25 search for reasons behind the lack of direction plaguing the Clinton foreign-policy team lacks critical assessment of the major players. In his 10-18 article, however, Elliott articulately surveys events leading to a two-track policy in Somalia following a disastrous October battle in the streets of Mogadishu.

"[Clinton] called for a doubling of troops and, this time, armor and gunships to protect them. Their job is to hunt for [General Mohamed Farah] Aidid—assuming, of course, he isn't invited to a political conference first." Such irreverence suits Elliott, whose generally timid analysis often ends up unnecessarily non-confrontational.

Stephen Engelberg
The New York Times
★★★

Washington. Organized, thorough, and literate, Engelberg easily makes the transition this year from Warsaw bureau chief to the national desk. In his probing 6-1 piece on apparent turmoil within Ross Perot's United We Stand America, Engelberg ably balances statements from inside and outside the organization. He explains that the turmoil may have motivated Perot's recent attacks on the administration. "Although none of Mr. Perot's advisers will say so, the increasingly public grumbling by once-committed Perot supporters may have been a major factor in the timing of Mr. Perot's latest televised assault on President Clinton... [which] shifted attention from complaints within United We Stand America to the increasingly testy relations between Mr. Perot and Mr. Clinton." In his 10-20 piece, Engelberg looks at the charges of impropriety that crop up against Robert Oakley, a longtime diplomat who served as President Clinton's Somali envoy through March. The allegations, he notes, show that Oakley stands to profit from a contract with a Lebanese construction company if a flight ban to the Beirut airport is lifted. Engelberg then reveals that Oakley and an associate delivered a report to the State Department urging removal of the ban. In his compelling 8-23 piece on Saudi Arabia's cash crisis, Engelberg presents a literate and concise explanation of the situation. "When foreign countries buy weapons through the Pentagon, they put money in a foreign military sales trust fund....A few years ago, the Saudis maintained a multibillion-dollar surplus in their account. But Pentagon officials said the surplus disappeared after the gulf war." In his 9-12 profile of Poland's Prime Minister Hanna Suchocka, Engelberg notes the role fate has played in the political careers of eastern Europeans. "Three years after martial law was imposed [in 1981], Suchoka was among the handful of [Parliament] deputies who voted against stripping Solidarity of its legal status, a move that would have ended her political career had Communism not collapsed. She left the Democratic Party soon after, and retired from Parliament at the end of her term, in 1984." Unafraid to step on toes, Engelberg shows his mettle in his late-year investigations of the Clintons and the Whitewater affair. Offering not just clues but conclusions, Engelberg delivers consistently readable and informative work.

James Fallows
The Atlantic

Washington editor. Despite his reputation, Fallows rarely provides insight into current political events. His know-it-all tone can irritate, especially since he seldom offers anything new or of much interest. His 2-14 *Los Angeles Times* article exemplifies this, with Fallows contrasting presidents who overanalyze and fail with presidents who oversimplify and succeed. A former speechwriter to Jimmy Carter, Fallows ought to know; but his point is hardly an original one. In his February *Atlantic* effort, he tells readers everything they never wanted to know about computers, expending considerable space and energy with complaints about DOS and its shortcomings before getting to the good stuff on the new generation of computers. Fallows uses his April essay to debunk an MIT study published in *Operations Research* magazine claiming both that the American casualties in Vietnam did not have a class-based element and that American soldiers went to Vietnam in equal proportions across the class spectrum. Arguing his points strongly—even arrogantly—Fallows jumps on his own bandwagon. "Their [1992] study is presented largely as a rebuttal to an article I wrote eighteen years ago called 'What Did You Do in the Class War, Daddy?' It appeared in *The Washington Monthly*, and it argued that because the sons of the nation's economic, professional, and political elite were generally spared the costs of the Vietnam War, the war went on longer than it otherwise would have." While there can be no doubt that Fallows's work helped to blast conventional assessments of the time, his thesis has become quite widely accepted since the

1970s, and thus his "response to" remark seems both overstated and smug. "The MIT study is preposterous....I'm waiting for someone to ask me what 'sophistry' means. I'll pull out my copy of *Operations Rescue* magazine and say 'See for yourself!'" In his gossipy June dispatch on changes in Malaysia, Fallows crafts a mere diatribe against its sultans, who are now falling out of favor, yet says nothing about the country's dramatic economic resurgence that may have contributed to the sultans' disrepute. A former resident, Fallows trips over his ego in assuming the reader will find credible his retelling of five-year-old rumors—whispered to him on the putting green—about the king beating his caddy to death with a golf club. Some real reporting would be more informative.

John J. Fialka
The Wall Street Journal
★★★

National Security. Thanks to his outstanding writing and reporting skills, Fialka brings unique insight to various national security issues. Using sources judiciously, he thoroughly investigates military matters both domestic and international. In his 1-19 story on Iraq's efforts to rearm after its Persian Gulf defeat, Fialka cuts to the quick. "A look at the ease with which Iraqi operatives used borrowed money, bogus stories and a tangle of front companies to bring Baghdad chemical weapons, guided missiles and a host of nuclear-related equipment shows how porous the U.S. export-control system is." Fialka opens story after story with captivating, no-nonsense prose. "North Korea," he writes, 2-25, "is experimenting with biological weapons and is likely hiding evidence of nuclear weapons activity from international inspectors, including enough material to make at least one nuclear weapon, according to Central Intelligence Agency officials." Following up this story with an exceptional 5-24 article, Fialka demonstrates his ability to fill his work with compelling statistics. "Changes in North Korea's military are the second part of the puzzle. In the late-1980s, as other major military forces in the world began to shrink, U.S. analysts were startled to find North Korea's army had grown 23 percent. The nation of 22 million has a staggering 1.2 million under arms." Effortlessly switching from building bombs to taking them apart, Fialka writes several well-researched pieces on Russian disarmament, noting, 3-9, "An $800 million U.S. program to help Russia dismantle its nuclear weapons has moved at a glacial pace, encumbered by Pentagon red tape, Russian secrecy, mutual suspicion and the difficulty of getting experts from both sides to understand the other's system." With his solid analysis and clear prose, Fialka displays the rare talent to make the beginning, middle, and end of his stories equally intriguing.

Howard Fineman
Newsweek

Washington. Although Fineman rarely plumbs the depths of policy, he can occasionally be original. He provides basic news summaries, which contain few sharp insights. In his intriguing 6-21 piece, Fineman follows the route of the Clinton-Gore 1992 campaign bus tour, and finds disaffected voters. Unfortunately, he doesn't go anywhere with this idea in that he fails to put his evocative quotes and stories into any kind of context. In his 3-8 article, Fineman assesses key interest groups—such as the energy and defense industries, seniors, and doctors—challenging Clinton's economic plan, but delivers only bare thumbnail sketches. His coverage of the gay rights march in Washington, 5-3, suffers from the same problems afflicting other dispatches on this story. Fineman emphasizes the mainstream participants without even mentioning the more vocal and confrontational gay rights groups, ACT-UP and Queer Nation, until the close—and then only to dismiss them. His simplistic 7-5 effort on the Congressional Black Caucus seeks to define the group's complexity by recycling stereotypes, courtesy of an unnamed source. There are "a half dozen 'Malcolms' who reject all compromise in the manner of Malcolm X. [Caucus chairman Rep. Kweisi] Mfume [D-MD] plays this role when he has to. And there are an equal number of 'Angelas,' sisters to the 'Malcolms,' on the model of one-time radical Angela Davis. Rep. Maxine Waters of California, well known for her heated rhetoric, is the caucus' members' nominee in this category. But there are also a few 'Jeff Davises,' a mocking reference to the president of the Confederacy, mainly from newly created and

often rural districts in the South. They are quite sensitive to their rural constituents, many of whom are white, and looking for deals to make with conservative Democrats." And so on. Fineman renders an equally superficial 11-8 article, lumping all evangelical Christians into one group—all thirsty for power and of the same socially conservative views. This, Fineman maintains, even while quoting Sen. Mark Hatfield [R-OR], who is a social liberal *and* an evangelical. There's precious little to be learned from Fineman.

Philip Finnegan

Defense News

★★

Washington staff writer. Showing improvement, perhaps from a sharpened focus, Finnegan spends considerable time this year concentrating on military issues related to the Middle East. Analyzing new defense programs, he examines the U.S. role in fostering a new sense of security in what remains an uncertain political environment. His impressive 1-18/24 report on the state of the Desert Storm alliance after the latest air strikes against Iraq finds that "pressure on Turkey and Arab nations to stop supporting coalition actions against Iraq is growing." In his 3-1/7 dispatch, Finnegan investigates Iran's purchase of three Russian submarines, which could potentially ignite a regional arms race. Despite such a danger, he finds that most countries "in the Persian Gulf ultimately are likely to rely on U.S. military might to defeat any submarine intruder." His excellent 5-31/6-6 summary thoroughly analyzes the Egyptian government's defense-aid lobbying efforts in Washington. Finnegan reveals that the Egyptians, aware of U.S. budgetary constraints, are trying to find new ways to stretch existing aid dollars through increased spending flexibility. Such flexibility, Finnegan notes, includes purchasing U.S.-surplus military equipment and moving toward a completely integrated Western-style defense force. In his 6-28/7-4 article, Finnegan and co-author David Silverberg skillfully examine the current Chinese public relations blitz designed to convince the world that the Chinese are reforming their military. The pair uncovers some of the truth behind the hype: "China's real military budget is in fact two to three times its stated size and is somewhere between $15 billion and $30 billion." Finnegan's engaging 11-15/21 piece reports that the lifting of sanctions on South Africa has freed its defense industry to pursue export sales. The anticipated victory of the African National Congress (ANC) in the April 1994 election should not prove an impediment to sustained increases in arms exports, because the ANC realizes that South Africa needs exports to fuel growth. More the reporter than analyst, Finnegan nonetheless brings greater insight to his beat this year, especially in covering events in the Middle East.

Thomas Fleming

Chronicles

★★½

Editor. Part provocateur and part historian, Fleming persistently challenges the status quo. Aggressively conservative, he presents exceptionally well-written and forceful arguments, placing his subjects in historical and theological contexts. In his June examination of the American judicial system, Fleming defends the police officers accused of beating Rodney King. Using the case as a springboard to harshly criticize the "tyrannical government," which provides "special privileges" to some groups while denying others their basic liberties, he concludes that "the entire American regime is now built upon a foundation of inequality and redistribution, and any challenge to that regime will be met by the unrestrained power that has already been used against... God-knows-how-many religious crackpots and tax protesters." Fleming's thoughtful July discussion of lawbreaking and vigilantism focuses on the case of the murdered abortion-doctor David Gunn. Conceding that abortion will not be re-criminalized in the near future, he contends that Gunn's killer was taking the logic of disobedience to its "diabolical conclusion." Fleming rejects such extreme behavior, reasoning that "we are not called upon to lead other people's lives for them, to make their choices, to keep them from folly, and it would be a vain religion or a merely academic philosophy that preached such a doctrine." In his comprehensive August article, Fleming applies this "mind your own business" ideology to governments as well. Arguing against intervention in Yugoslavia, he concludes, "when each of the sides can have its own country, its own identity, its own religion, only then will there be peace." Intent on clearing up misconceptions, Fleming discusses the conflict from the Serbian perspective, which he claims the Western press has ignored. While this anecdotal piece clarifies the complex history of atrocity and revisionism conducted by the region's warring ethnic groups, Fleming fails to convince that the Serbians have been misunderstood. Ardently nationalist again in his November essay opposing NAFTA, Fleming derides internationalism as an "outdated foreign fad." He also predicts that the agreement "will be the symbolic act of betrayal around which a nationalist political movement will be organized." Exercising a rare command of language, Fleming passionately defends unpopular causes. In taking a creative approach to his subjects, Fleming yields work that proves scholarly, readable, and provocative.

Douglas Frantz

Los Angeles Times

★½

Investigative projects. As with any investigative reporter, the deeper Frantz digs, the more likely he is to find something. The opposite is also true, and Frantz digs deepest at the end of the year. In his simplistic 4-11 review of Rep. Tom Foley's [D-WA] remarks concerning health-care reform on CNN's "Evans & Novak," all Frantz had to do was either get a transcript or watch the program. He at least puts the Speaker's remarks in the context of the political fight to come over this issue. There's evidence of digging in a 6-30 effort, in which Frantz stunningly reveals that only after the World Trade Center bombing did federal and local authorities translate "critical documents." These documents, he points out, had been in their possession more than two years and detailed the terrorist intentions of some Islamic militants in this country. In his no-nonsense 7-20 dispatch, Frantz briskly recounts the testimony of former House Post Office head Robert Rota, which implicates Rep. Dan Rostenkowski [D-IL] as having received more than $21,000 in cash in exchange for expense vouchers and stamps. Frantz provides a thorough 8-10 summary of the plan to loosen U.S. rocket-technology sales abroad —if no security risk exists—in order to stem the loss of jobs in the aerospace industry. His 10-9 examination of the FBI report on the Waco, Texas, incident recounts not just the report but the response to it from both sides of the aisle. However, Frantz adds only marginally to the available information. He cites criticism from Rep. Don Edwards [D-CA], head of a House subcommittee overseeing the FBI, who argues that the government has learned nothing from the disaster. With co-author William Rempel, 11-7 and 11-12, Frantz helps break—and untangle—the story of the Clintons' connection to Madison Guaranty, a failed Arkansas savings and loan. In their 12-21 report, he and Rempel recount the Arkansas troopers' allegations of then-Governor Clinton's extramarital affairs. The story contains some notable facts—such as that Clinton made dozens of cellular phone calls to the same woman in 1990. Hot on the scandal trail, Frantz seems poised to do some deeper digging in 1994.

Thomas L. Friedman

The New York Times

★★½

White House. Although Friedman excels at viewing world politics through the Beltway prism, he would do better to incorporate more economic analysis into his work. In his balanced 3-24 roundup of President Clinton's remarks defending his personal support for Russian President Boris Yeltsin on the eve of the Vancouver summit, Friedman provides a broad smattering of views outlining the high risk of this strategy, adding substantially to the collective body of knowledge. In his 4-8 article, he buys into the conventional wisdom of Bosnia as an ethnic problem—ignoring the more provocative view of Bosnia as an economic-disaster-turned-civil-war espoused by various economists. As a former Middle East correspondent, Friedman displays his expertise in an informative 9-2 assessment of the Israelis and Palestinians trying to work out the last-minute obstacles to peace. "Israeli and Palestinian officials said their agreement in principle on Palestinian self-rule in the Gaza Strip and the West Bank town of Jericho was ready for signing. But they said the event was being held up by the snags on separate statements providing for mutual recognition between Israel and the PLO." And Friedman provides a valuable 10-25 critique of the shift in Clinton's Somalia policy, explaining the President's plan for U.S. troops to act less

as policemen. However, Friedman doesn't relate how the President will play the hardball needed with the UN and with General Mohammad Farah Aidid for his policy to succeed. Moreover, his editors often squander Friedman's considerable analytic skills by assigning him to spot news stories. His solid, newsy 5-20 overview of Clinton trying desperately to push his economic plan through Congress suffers from an absence of Friedman's trademark analysis. His analytic skills remain similarly unused in his 6-1 snapshot evoking Clinton's emotionally charged Memorial Day appearance at the Vietnam Veterans Memorial. Memo to Editors: Keep Friedman fully employed on foreign issues!

Sara Fritz

Los Angeles Times

★★

Congress. Fritz spends most of 1993 covering one of the year's hot-button issues: health-care reform. Although she fails to examine many intricacies of the debate, she always provides a clear view of both the raw data in use and where President Clinton is going with it. In her 2-22 effort, Fritz smartly explains the gap between what the public thinks is wrong with health care and what the government can or will fix. "While a recent study shows that most Americans would like to see the government crack down on what they view as the inequities and profiteering inherent in the current system, the President's health specialists are talking instead about imposing a new health care plan that would limit medical expenditures and ration care." On 3-7, Fritz pinpoints the logic of Clinton's admonition of the drug companies—invoking President Kennedy's discipline of the steel industry in 1962 as a basis for comparison—and gives several reasons why this industry presents such an irresistible target: "While Medicare and private health insurance policies cover most other medical costs, prescription medicine is an out-of-pocket expenditure for most Americans. Members of Congress receive more complaints from citizens about drug prices than any other element of health care spending." Fritz's informative 5-23 demographic breakdown of the uninsured showcases her grasp of statistics. "Census data shows that in 1991, 85 percent of the uninsured lived in households headed by either full-time or part-time workers, nearly three-fourths live in households earning more than $10,000 a year and more than half were under the age of 30. One in 10 lives in a family earning more than $50,000 a year." But despite the massive detail she provides, Fritz doesn't take the next step of probing why such diverse groups are uninsured. Attempting to examine the broader implications of Clinton's health-care reform on the economy by briefly consulting just three economists, her 7-6 article falls short. Although adequate, this kind of work fails to highlight Fritz's true talents.

David A. Fulghum

Aviation Week & Space Technology

★★★

Washington military editor. An experienced reporter with excellent insights, Fulghum provides valuable analysis of defense-technology conversion and arms proliferation. And he excels at untangling the intricacies involved in American strategic and peace-keeping goals in the post-Gulf War Middle East. In his 3-29 report, Fulghum perceptively describes the increasing involvement of U.S. government labs in defense conversion. "As defense reductions gather steam during the next five years, the labs will have to prove their commercial utility or risk being shut down." This leaves only a small window of time, Fulghum points out, for the successful completion of defense conversion. Congress may not provide the funds necessary to assess technologies suitable for release to the private sector, and thus, he notes, may scuttle the whole program. In his well-focused 5-10 report, Fulghum addresses efforts to defeat new radar-tracking systems that may be deployed in the Middle East through upgrades in the U.S. EF-111 electronic warfare aircraft. The source of greatest concern, he contends, is China, which plans to "improve the Soviet [radar] design by incorporating illegally-obtained U.S. Patriot missile technology." Fulghum's fascinating 6-7 article chronicles attempts by the Air Force to reduce the radar signature of the A-10 attack aircraft that was so successful during the Gulf War. Reductions in the A-10's radar signature, he adds, would enhance survivability during low-altitude attacks. In his engrossing 7-5 dispatch, Fulghum analyzes the disappointingly low success rate (67 percent) on a recent Tomahawk cruise-missile attack on Iraq. Because earlier attacks were more successful, he wonders whether this indicates a statistical aberration or a more serious problem. Fulghum provides a fascinating 10-11 appraisal of the armed services' efforts to convert a Cold War strategic spy aircraft into part of an integrated low-observable ballistic-missile and aircraft-defense system. This technology, he points out, will allow early warning of attacks by even the most advanced aircraft and missiles. Fulghum's crisp style and sharp analysis place him a notch above many of his colleagues. An essential source for information on the latest defense technologies, Fulghum always explains how they fit into U.S. defense plans.

Michael Fumento

Investor's Business Daily

★★

National issues, Los Angeles. While Fumento clearly defines the complex problems of modern life and politics, he sometimes fails to examine thoroughly the implications of some of the solutions he offers. In his 1-8 investigation of ways to save endangered species, Fumento sets up the problem superbly, but fails to fully explore whether market forces could play an effective role. Two essays on the media suffer in a similar manner. In his 3-26 article on the abuses of network newscasts, Fumento says little that hasn't been said before. And although his 5-10 effort recycles much of his previous work on the subject, he offers one insightful comment. "In its self-criticism, the media usually concentrate on sensationalism." Instead of examining the smaller inaccuracies that creep into news reports and stories, the self-critics, Fumento contends, concentrate on the more egregious examples—like the infamous GM pickup-truck manipulation by NBC's "Dateline." He comprehensively explores Clinton's national service program, 6-7, discussing its relatively small size—the plan would affect less than 1 percent of the nation's college students—as well as its costs. Fumento's 7-14 essay on Ruth Bader Ginsburg suffers from poor organization, as he holds all the "nagging questions" about her record until the close of the article. Taking his cue from the hit novel and movie "Jurassic Park," Fumento crafts an eye-opening 8-26 article that clearly distinguishes the boundaries between fact and fiction on the idea of genetic engineering. "The actual definition of biotechnology is the application of biological systems and organisms to technical and industrial processes. But the more popular definition is that it is genetic engineering, or removing genes from one organism and inserting them into another." Although he doesn't always go the distance, Fumento seldom fails to inform or provoke.

Barton Gellman

The Washington Post

★½

Defense. If there were a contest for the journalist who spread the most military gossip in 1993, Gellman would certainly emerge as a finalist. One can picture him huddling with military aides in dark Pentagon corridors, snickering and telling stories about their bosses. However, when Gellman rises above such trivial pursuits he can provide crisp, astute analysis of complex military issues. In his lightweight 4-1 article on relations between the military and the White House, he writes, "A whole series of apocryphal anecdotes also have made the rounds and fed military disaffection. There was the story of Chelsea Clinton's refusal to ride to school with a military driver. (Didn't happen.) Or the one about Hillary Rodham

OHMAN-TRIBUNE MEDIA SERVICES

Clinton's ban on uniforms in the White House. (Also didn't happen.)" His 6-20 story covers more inconsequential turf wars. "Graham Allison, [Defense Secretary Les] Aspin's choice to be assistant secretary for plans and policy, is accused in one story of saying he had a graduate student who could produce a better document than [Gen. Colin] Powell's National Military Strategy." Still, Gellman's penchant for dishing the dirt can make for lively moments, as in his 3-13 article about President Clinton's visit to an aircraft carrier. "Ambivalence is no frame of mind for a warship. But there seemed to be no better word for the mood that filled the hangar deck here today." Although notable for the number of sailors and fliers willing to go on record questioning their commander-in-chief, the article amounts to little more than talking heads sounding off. Gellman drops most of this gossip in the second half of the year, replacing it with a focus on substantive issues. In his excellent 10-6 article on Somalia, he writes, "Sunday's destruction by Somali militiamen of an American Ranger company, which suffered unit casualties unlike any seen in the U.S. Army since Vietnam, caught U.S. forces in Mogadishu without adequate contingency plans to rescue or reinforce the surrounded and outgunned force, according to new details of the firefight emerging yesterday." Likewise, Gellman's excellent 10-10 overview on affairs in Somalia, co-authored by Thomas W. Lippman, should be required reading for all UN officials. When Gellman has action to report, he often rises to the occasion. Unfortunately, he seldom seeks action, but Gellman's new posting in Jerusalem should alleviate this shortcoming.

David Gelman
Newsweek
★★

Senior writer, society and lifestyle. A fresh and gutsy reporter, Gelman tackles cultural topics with flair and command. As *Newsweek*'s pop-psychologist-in-residence, he tends to simplify the complex. In his 5-17 cover story on children who survived the Branch Davidian fiasco in Waco, Texas, Gelman emphasizes the human side of tragedy. "For them, all is confusion....These kids are not just orphaned, but emptied of moral certitude." Another group of troubled kids—California's Spur Posse—draws his attention, 4-12, when Gelman and co-author Patrick Rogers analyze aggressive sexual behavior among male teenagers. Instead of blaming the boys, he criticizes parents and schools for failing to educate youngsters. "To educators, knowing about sex is not the same as appreciating what it means. They note that besides avoiding the subject themselves, parents in many states have tried to discourage schools from talking about it." Much of Gelman's work dwells on sexuality and homosexuality, as in his alarming 1-11 AIDS message that "many young gays carry a conviction of indestructibility." Gelman's 11-8 feature suggests that teenagers find homosexuality both chic and confusing. "Psychologists say the media fascination with sexual athleticism and androgynous pop icons...help promote experimentation among teenagers. One Boston teenager thought she was a lesbian until she found herself enjoying a relationship with a man." In his 8-2 article, Gelman takes a familiar look at brutality in America. "Our national icons tend to be men who excel at violence, from John Wayne to Clint Eastwood. The danger, psychiatrists say, is that the constant repetition of violence and violent imagery desensitizes us in much the way a therapist desensitizes a phobia patient: by deliberate exposure to what's scary. When do we stop feeling helpless and start doing something?" Although sometimes superficial, Gelman's portrayal of contemporary America as a dysfunctional society seldom fails to provoke.

Jeff Gerth
The New York Times

Washington. While structural problems and choppy prose plague his work, Gerth delivers solid investigative reporting on the business affairs of government officials and institutions. And he conscientiously follows the money, even if he doesn't draw the most coherent maps. In his lengthy 5-27 piece, Gerth exposes the business empire of the Stephens family in Arkansas. He includes the Worthen National Bank, which "lent more than $2 million to the [Clinton presidential] campaign when it was on the ropes." Although offering evidence of incomplete disclosures to regulators, Gerth's points get bogged down in his explanations. "As for Worthen, in which family members own more than a fourth of the stock, the Fed is trying to determine whether the Stephens group, the family's holding company, exercises a controlling influence in the bank, according to Worthen officials." Gerth takes a stale 1-16 look at an investment by incoming Treasury Secretary Lloyd Bentsen. While he notes that the investment "violated no laws or ethical strictures," Gerth purports to reveal how a career in government can lead to favorable business opportunities. Gerth rehashes this heavily reported story from the 1988 presidential campaign because it "represents precisely an aspect of the Washington system that Mr. Clinton has vowed to change." Turning his eyes overseas, Gerth pens an informative and compelling 8-22 piece on Saudi Arabia's cash crunch. The crunch, he explains, stems from the nation's decision to spend massive sums on social security and infrastructure. "In the 1980s, the fiscal policies of the Saudis began to resemble those of the United States....No goal was too costly. Saudi officials decided to turn deserts into wheat fields using price supports and water drained from ancient aquifers. Saudi Arabia is now the sixth largest exporter of wheat in the world." A solid 11-2 piece, co-authored by Stephen Engelberg, reveals the details of the federal investigation into dealings among principals of Madison Guaranty, the failed Arkansas savings and loan, and Whitewater Development Co., a speculative land-development firm owned jointly by the Clintons and the head of Madison, James McDougal. Gerth explores factors driving the investigation, including those of the personal relationship between McDougal and the Clintons. "Mr. McDougal contended that he had helped the Clintons in numerous ways, from agreeing to hire Mrs. Clinton to do additional legal work at Madison to paying on Mr. Clinton's behalf portions of the loans on the [Whitewater-owned] Ozark property." Although he breaks important stories,Gerth might benefit by investing more effort in presenting his well-detailed reports.

Bill Gertz

The Washington Times

★★½

National Security. Gertz doesn't mince words in his coverage of national security issues. Aided by his excellent Pentagon sources, he specializes in breaking news, and generally provides solid, workmanlike stories. In his 3-13 article on military-base closings, he bluntly describes the realities of defense cutbacks. "Defense Secretary Les Aspin announced plans yesterday to close 31 major military bases in 15 states as a cost-saving measure that will result in the loss of 81,000 civilian and military jobs over six years." He uncovers the startling fact that some states, which voted for the Democratic ticket in 1992 were spared the largest cuts—and a few were spared cuts entirely. "Also, four states that backed Mr. Clinton in the presidential election—Illinois, Georgia, Missouri and Washington—will each see gains in defense jobs for between 2,000 and 7,000 workers under the proposal." In his 7-13 article on U.S. involvement in the civil war in the Soviet state of Georgia, he makes fine use of his inside sources. "U.S. Special Forces personnel were sent to the strife-torn former Soviet republic of Georgia earlier this year in a covert operation to protect Georgian President Eduard Shevardnadze....The covert training program is designed to protect Mr. Shevardnadze and other members of his government against kidnapping and assassination plots by radical nationalists associated with the former Gamsakhurdia regime." Gertz uncovers another remarkable fact in his 9-14 story on the supposedly emasculated Russian military. "Russia's military continues to modernize its huge nuclear force, and its elite Strategic Rocket Forces recently conducted a large exercise that included a mock attack against the United States." Although Gertz's accounts include all the pertinent details, his matter-of-fact style sometimes makes for dry reading. His 10-8 account of a bloody Somali firefight in which many U.S. soldiers died includes the relevant information but none of the emotion of this tragic event. This drawback aside, Gertz's "just-the-facts-ma'am" approach makes him essential reading for basic information.

Josh Getlin

Los Angeles Times

★★

Although he covers a grab-bag of issues, Getlin is at his best when describing people. Despite an occasional indulgence in truisms, he has a knack for tracking down colorful indi-

viduals, and when he zeroes in on a particular person, his subjects almost come to life. In his 2-14 piece on New York City judge Judith Sheindlin, Getlin brilliantly captures her personality. "Tart, tough-talking and hopelessly blunt, Sheindlin runs her court with an impatience that borders on rage....'I can't stand stupid, and I can't stand slow,' she snaps. 'I want first-time offenders to think of their appearance in my courtroom as the second-worst experience of their lives...circumcision being the first.'...Some family court judges approach their $90,000-a-year jobs with caution, conciliation and tact. They take great pains not to offend anyone. Sheindlin tore up that script long ago." Getlin's 2-18 profile of Hazel Johnson, an environmental activist in the impoverished Altgeld Gardens housing project in Chicago, conveys the pathos of people living in "a toxic doughnut." "Crammed into an isolated project, they're plagued by high rates of cancer, puzzling birth defects, and the strong belief that nobody else gives a damn." Recounting a meeting with Chicago housing officials that project residents had sought for 10 years, Getlin portrays Johnson's stamina. "Weaker souls would have given up and moved away, yet Johnson continues to search for answers—even as an estimated 26 million pounds of hazardous air chokes her neighborhood each year." Unfortunately, in his articles on more general issues, Getlin does not weave in information with the same sympathetic enthusiasm. His 5-24 piece on the takeover of book-selling by mega-bookstores, which he blandly calls "a Darwinian shakedown," offers no new insight. In his 10-3 piece on immigration, however, he notes shrewdly, if unoriginally, that "Americans have long supported the idea of immigration. They only have trouble with the latest newcomers, whomever they happen to be." With his knack for vivid portrayal of personalities, Getlin would do best to stick with profiles.

William Glaberson

The New York Times

Media. Perhaps Glaberson was absent the day they taught that news stories should have a beginning, middle, and end. In reporting what's new in the news, he usually gets off to a promising start, but his accounts lack development and slowly dissipate, resulting in little more than lengthy and muddled monologues. An able fact gatherer, Glaberson presents plenty of statistics in his 3-29 discussion of the interconnection between New York City's four daily papers. Although he raises some salient background issues overlooked in the coverage of the city's newspaper wars—such as eroding circulation and competition for advertising dollars—his report becomes tedious when he fails to add insight to his data. He proves more successful in his 8-16 study of the introduction of electronic newspaper editions into the changing news market. Clearly doing his homework, Glaberson discusses the impact that on-line newspapers could have on publishers, advertisers, and consumers. He goes on to note the potential of these publications to provide services such as community "bulletin boards," up-to-date news reporting, and expanded local coverage. Uncharacteristically direct, Glaberson examines "whether they will someday cannibalize print newspapers, serve as a companion to them or never become more than a niche market." When he strays from reporting the business side of the news business, Glaberson tends to reveal a liberal political leaning. In his 11-14 attempt to assess the effects of the Newspaper Guild strike on workers who lost their jobs when the union failed to settle with the *New York Post*, he becomes downright maudlin in his portraits of former workers seeking "closure." Glaberson confronts a similar problem in his 5-25 treatment of the press coverage of health-care reform. Challenging the media to "reduce the policy discussion to human terms," his story reads more like a rallying cry to his fellow journalists, whom he credits for bringing the health-care question to the top of the American agenda. Here Glaberson makes a value judgment based on his own ideology, presuming that the need for reform diminishes the media's responsibility to report the political debate surrounding it. While he addresses a variety of significant news-industry concerns, Glaberson too often fails to clarify the issues, as his ideas become lost in a profusion of data.

Malcolm Gladwell

The Washington Post

★★½

New York bureau chief. With smooth reporting skills, clear

writing, and perceptive insights, Gladwell moves this year from science to the Big Apple. He shines brightest in his opinion and analytic pieces, such as his perceptive 2-7 account of the return home from prison of rapist Donald Chapman. In telling the story of a small New Jersey town's terror at Chapman's presence, Gladwell deftly examines the universal conundrum of how to treat incorrigibly vicious criminals. His 3-21 "Outlook" piece on New Jersey's assault-weapons ban astutely questions the traditional wisdom behind this legislation, arguing that assault weapons are no more lethal than other guns. Their main characteristic "is that they are ugly," Gladwell asserts, which is probably why they "have such special appeal to drug dealers and killers....All that assault bans do is say that it's okay to have a violent killing fantasy based on culturally familiar and acceptable figures like cowboys and policemen but not okay to have violent killing fantasies based on culturally unacceptable figures like terrorists or Colombian drug lords." In his 9-18 column, Gladwell artfully depicts the economic growth of New York City neighborhoods that were in danger of becoming "urban moonscapes" before 1980, when a large influx of immigrants began to revitalize these areas. Just when he seems to be getting a handle on the city, he seems to lose it as he struggles to get a grip on the mayoral contest. His 10-27 piece calls the campaign "a race that seems sometimes to belong on a psychiatrist's couch"—as if other political races of this era do not. And Gladwell considers Republican challenger Rudolph Giuliani's campaign "a weird kind of protest politics," implying that nostalgia for a less crime-ridden era is new. Responding to a *New York* article that criticized Giuliani's brusque treatment of a homeless man—saying the candidate would appear warmer if he offered the man food or a chair—Gladwell eloquently notes, "In the...Giuliani rebellion, the homeless don't get a sandwich or a seat. They get a lecture." Only Gladwell's 7-4 "Outlook" piece on Independence Day proves a dud, irritating not for its cynicism about the American Revolution but for its flippancy and insincere self-mockery. In debunking the revolutionaries' image as idealistic freedom fighters, he makes too many glib comments, such as that Paul Revere "clearly beat his horse" and that the Boston Tea Party turned the harbor into a "Superfund site." Still, Gladwell can take a bow for a successful first year as New York bureau chief, and the polish he adds to the Big Apple.

Ari L. Goldman

The New York Times

★½

Religion. While he also covers some local and regional stories, Goldman provides readable but often incomplete stories on his main beat. His 1-3 article on the remarkable growth of Korean churches in the U.S.—from 200 churches 35 years ago to roughly 4,000 today—reports that many Korean emigrés of Buddhist and Confucian background visit U.S. churches and end up converting. Presbyterian churches attract most of the converts, Goldman writes, but he fails to relate their theological orientations or doctrinal concerns. On 2-7, Goldman travels to Scarsdale, New York, to report on the spread of Mormonism in the northeast. Their numbers, he reports, have more than doubled, from 35,000 in 1975 to 80,000 today, as Utah Mormons who moved east have proselytized, especially among single parents and members of minority groups. Although he quotes professors of religion and longtime Mormons, Goldman, unfortunately, talks to none of the recent converts. Clearly, he writes his best work on Jewish communities of faith. Goldman provides comprehensive 1-29 and 2-1 reports on the split in the Lubavitch Hasidic community in Crown Heights, Brooklyn, between those who consider the Grand Rebbe Menachem Mendel Schneerson the Messiah and those who claim the 90-year-old spiritual leader merely has the qualities to be the Messiah. On 7-7, Goldman straightforwardly reports a New York State Court of Appeals decision declaring unconstitutional a public school for handicapped children in the village of Kiryas Joel, where nearly all residents belong to the Satmar Hasidic sect. Although the school is not religious, Goldman explains, it was established by the state in response to a request by the Hasidic Jewish citizens of the town. He explains that, according to the court, the state thus endorsed a religion in violation of the First Amendment. Goldman follows this story with a well-sourced 7-8 look at the future of the now-in-

question school. The case comes before the Supreme Court in 1994, and a decision could put Kiryas Joel on the national map. Perhaps this year Goldman will file some stories on the case that live up to its big-league status.

Walter Goodman

The New York Times

★★½

Television. Intelligently covering TV, Goodman always delves beneath the surface with originality and wisdom. He analyzes what's on, who produces it, and who watches it. But he mixes heavy prose with a wit so dry it often fails to amuse, and his cerebral style weighs down his complex, cynical pronouncements about what's wrong with the world. Rating news reporters' interviews of Hillary Rodham Clinton, 9-27, Goodman inserts a superfluous disclaimer. "One hopes that no sexist imputation will be drawn from the fact that the male interviewers...were softer than the female interviewers." A stronger editorial hand would rescue Goodman's provocative ideas from his tangled prose. In his 7-7 column on parental-warning labels for violent programs, Goodman insightfully points out the hypocritically self-congratulatory tone of TV executives as they announce the policy they had fought hard against. But the reader must trudge through awkward phrases like "bespeaks the set of mind" and sudden metaphors like "the process of spiritual conversion," a reference to networks' growing commitment to reduced TV violence. Goodman's 10-17 critique of what "Parson [Dan] Rather" said at an annual convention of the Radio and Television News Directors Association is a paragon of biting social commentary. "What makes Mr. Rather's brave denunciation of the commercial television mentality ring hollow," Goodman notes, "is his refusal to utter an unkind word about the brains or taste of the great American audience, those co-conspirators of their own exploitation." Goodman's harsh skepticism is enjoyable when his humor hits the mark, as in his 4-29 piece about "experts" interviewed on TV news and talk shows. "What the experts are peddling, along with the usual mix of unexceptional observations and pop formulations, is themselves....They are cultivating their gardens. The fertilizer is a blend of real troubles and the usual ingredient." Goodman reliably reviews documentaries and other challenging TV fare, providing a valuable resource to intelligent viewers. With his critical armor, Goodman shields himself from the tube's hypnotic rays—and helps readers to do the same.

Michael R. Gordon

The New York Times

★½

Washington. Seldom digging beneath the surface, Gordon's coverage of military matters provides little more than the issues discussed in daily Pentagon briefings. And even that coverage rarely tells the whole story. In his 3-28 "news analysis," Gordon offers none, stopping short at wondering where future defense cuts will come from. "The main question is not so much how the 1994 budget will be received by Congress but where the Pentagon will go from here in refashioning the American military." His 8-9 dispatch on potential replacements for Gen. Colin Powell is basically a laundry list of names without context. To his 1-18 article on George Bush's missile raid on Iraq, Gordon does bring a measure of political acumen. "With Mr. Clinton's inauguration 72 hours away, the decision to use cruise missiles, instead of manned aircraft, reflected the political imperative that no American pilots be shot down and captured in a raid over Iraq." Gordon provides a both revealing and lurid 4-24 account of the investigation of the 1991 Tailhook convention. "Naval aviators and their guests also engaged in consensual oral sex and sexual intercourse in full view of other participants," he notes. "In addition, the aviators shaved the legs and pubic areas of some women, apparently with their consent." With a 12-1 article on Russian disarmament efforts, Gordon ends the year on a high note. "While the end of the cold war has dispelled the threat that poison gas, germ weapons and nuclear warheads from the former Soviet Union posed to the United States, Russia's difficulties in cutting its arsenal may slow global arms control efforts and add to the risk that dangerous weapons may fall into the wrong hands." The initiative Gordon shows in this particular effort is, unfortunately, all too rare.

Linda Greenhouse

The New York Times

★★★

Supreme Court. With abortion—the issue she can't seem

to cover evenhandedly—on the judicial back burner, Greenhouse can display her expertise on this beat without also indulging her bias. Carefully incorporating politics where appropriate, she provides a comprehensive 3-3 review on the legalities of President Clinton's decision to continue repatriating Haitian refugees. In her 5-27 dispatch, Greenhouse correctly identifies the reason for the Justices' chagrin over the divulgence by the Library of Congress of the late Thurgood Marshall's papers. The Court's concern, she explains, is "driven in part by the natural desire of many organizations to shield their internal workings from public view....But there is something else at work here: a belief among judges that to strip any court of its mystique is also inevitably to strip it of some of its authority and legitimacy." In her 6-2 effort, Greenhouse provides a superb account of new decisions, crisply extrapolating one important ruling on criminal law. "Overturning a murder conviction, the Supreme Court ruled unanimously today that regardless of the evidence, a criminal conviction is invalid if the judge did not instruct the jury properly on finding guilt beyond a reasonable doubt....The Court held that mistaken jury instructions on reasonable doubt could never be disregarded as 'harmless error,' even if it appeared that the guilty verdict was not the product of the mistake." A nuanced 7-22 review of Ruth Bader Ginsburg's confirmation testimony before the Senate Judiciary Committee displays the same thoroughness. Although Greenhouse falls short in predicting Ginsburg's future opinions on the basis of her first dissent, 9-2, she still supplies a solid roundup of the cases before the Court. And she crafts an insightful 11-10 dispatch defining how the Court has made sexual harassment easier to prove by throwing out the "severe psychological injury" requirement that many states require. When objective—and she usually is—Greenhouse proves an excellent reporter, one of the top analysts of the Supreme Court.

Lloyd Grove
The Washington Post
★★

Style. Grove's beat is the Beltway, but his true mission seems that of providing *People* magazine-style profiles of the Washington set. With his vast array of sources and his nervy tenacity in using them, he can cover the inside scene and its players with impressive breadth and detail. Yet many of Grove's columns are too short and flip, leaving them lite without bite. In his choppy 1-7 piece on the significance of Rhodes scholarships to the incoming administration, Grove tries to squeeze too much out of this trivial pursuit. The same holds true for his weak 1-16 column on Bill Clinton's post-election negative press coverage. Grove poses five questions and fails to answer a single one. His 5-27 piece on an anonymous news source raises no deep issues, and his 7-2 and 7-7 columns on Hillary Rodham Clinton are pure fluff. In his meatier pieces, however, Grove scratches below the surface—as in his adept 4-4 account of the political battle between the White House and Senator Richard Shelby [D-AL]. Although several senators admired Clinton's strong-arm tactics, Grove presents Clinton's team as vindictive, manipulative, and petty. "The White House revenge play...has been 'quarterbacked' by Clinton's legislative affairs director, Howard Paster, with assists from political director Rahm Emanuel...[who] is no stranger to the revenge business, having once sent an enemy a rotting fish." In his thorough 3-2 profile of Clinton chum Susan Thomases, Grove doesn't flinch from calling her "Hillary's blunt instrument of enforcement." He takes time to paint her portrait with opinions from both admirers (mostly Hillary) and detractors (everyone else), punctuating this readable and measured account with inside stories of Thomases's "fits" of temper. The celebrity-hunting Grove can always turn a phrase. During the inaugural week festivities, Grove attended a party for Al Gore hosted by *The New Republic*, the journal which featured a "Clinton Suck-Up Watch" in 1992. Grove muses, 1-20, that a "Gore Suck-Up Watch" may be next—until editor Martin Peretz confides to him his affection for the Vice-President, who had been a student of his at Harvard. "Over the cocktail party chatter," Grove quips, "one could hear that great big sucking sound that Ross Perot used to talk about, only this time it wasn't jobs going to Mexico." With his sardonic style and flashes of wit, Grove never bores and sometimes hits the mark.

Richard Harwood

The Washington Post

★★½

Media. Now semi-retired, this former *Post* ombudsman opens most columns with a perceptive idea, the quality of the column hanging on whether he develops this idea or simply abandons it. In his 1-30 effort, Harwood begins, "Americans are acutely class conscious only in the sense that virtually all of us are acutely conscious of being middle class. We envy more than we hate the rich. We pity more than we despise the poor." Rather than focus on nuances of class, however, Harwood showcases the elite new power group now populating Washington, leaving his provocative opener unexplored. His more successful 4-17 column probes the connection between violence and television. Quote-filled and data-packed, he cites one study that shows rising aggression rates in a remote Canadian village after the introduction of TV. He uses another study revealing that in the television-saturated U.S. and Canada, homicide rates almost doubled from 1945 to 1975, while during the same period in South Africa—a country, he notes, with no TV before 1975—the homicide rate *dropped* 7 percent. The issue poses a dilemma for those in the media who argue that TV news shapes how people think and act but deny that TV induces violence. Although offering no solutions, Harwood shrewdly frames the issue. His sensible, if predictable, 5-11 column surveys the historical roots of the suppression of free speech to place in context the absurdity of recent university policies restricting offensive language. "Do the 'South Pacific' lyrics—'she is broad where a broad should be broad'—represent 'sexist' speech that should be prohibited, as some have suggested?" And because one speech code bans utterances based on "Vietnam-era status," Harwood then questions whether calling the President a "draft evader" could be grounds for offense. In his 9-25 article, Harwood argues that newspapers vary considerably in the news they print, in part because of the idiosyncrasies of editors. A week later, however, he seemingly contradicts himself in his 10-2 lament decrying "a sameness and a blandness about our newspapers" resulting from the homogenization of editors. Although less consistent than in recent years, Harwood still provides provocative nuggets that keep the brain whirring.

Michael Hedges

The Washington Times

★½

Investigations. Hedges finds himself on the firing line this year, as various sources asserted—incorrectly, as it turned out—that he was preparing an exposé on Vince Foster, right before the White House counsel committed suicide. Because he covers so many stories, however, it's difficult for Hedges to provide depth, much less turn up the startling information required on this beat to be a star. For example, Hedges begins his 1-4 article by evocatively relating the anger of the mobs waiting for UN Secretary General Boutros Boutros-Ghali in Somalia. Yet he does not explain why they are so angry at the UN or whom they support. With the unenviable task of examining the mess in Waco, Texas, as the cleanup at the torched compound begins, Hedges provides a workmanlike and informative 4-22 roundup. But he offers little unique in his 7-20 effort on the firing of FBI Director William Sessions, for alleged improprieties, and on the hiring of Louis Freeh. Hedges shows some talent in rendering a trim 8-12 profile of Robert Bennett, lawyer to political VIPs such as former Defense Secretary Caspar Weinberger and Rep. Dan Rostenkowski [D-IL]. Although he doesn't quite get a sense of the man, Hedges does a solid job detailing Bennett's legal abilities. His most potent article, 2-27, describes how "alien smugglers" can easily get people—including potential terrorists—into the U.S., simply by claiming political asylum. "In March 1980, President Carter signed a law allowing persons from any nation to declare themselves political refugees and get a hearing. 'That opened the floodgates,' said one official. Last year alone, 103,000 claimed political asylum in the United States." Coming one day after terrorists bombed New York's World Trade Center, Hedges would have had a scoop if his editors had run this just two days earlier.

Keith Henderson

The Christian Science Monitor

★½

What do the *CSM*'s reporters in Massachusetts, Michigan, Missouri, and Vermont have in common? They are all the same person—Keith Henderson. Although his wide-ranging stories saluting the downtrodden or forgotten prove readable and original, they rely almost exclusively on interviews and often lack depth. In his 5-21 piece on the reluctance among Hispanics in Lawrence, Massachusetts, to get involved in schools and in politics, Henderson insightfully quotes school-board member Ralph Carrero. "'In many Latin American countries, teachers are viewed with lots of dignity and respect. Parents don't question them—the teacher knows best....Their perception of government may be as a corrupt entity—that it's better not to let government know who you are.'" Unfortunately, Henderson provides no other viewpoints. Despite recycling various clichés—such as "gun-toting youngsters" and "boarded-up store fronts"—Henderson's 3-8 article on Detroit and a new generation of urban black activists presents an optimistic portrait of the Michigan city. Writing more pessimistically from flood-ravaged St. Louis, 7-30, Henderson effectively quotes the city's beleaguered new mayor who, when asked who's in charge, replies, "'The water's in charge. All we can do is respond.'" In his meandering 9-27 piece on a painter at work in South Royalton, Vermont, on a 48-foot-long mural commemorating the Underground Railroad, Henderson digs up an intriguing historical tidbit. "One Vermont judge, Theophilus Harrington of Middlebury, refused to return a slave to his reputed owner unless the man could produce a document from the 'original proprietor.' When asked what that meant, Judge Harrington was said to have proclaimed, 'a bill of sale from God Almighty!'" For thoughtful anecdotes like these, Henderson's flaws may be forgiven.

Philip J. Hilts
The New York Times
★

Health. You would never know by reading Hilts that health care was a hot topic in 1993. His bland reports reveal neither expertise nor enthusiasm for the subject. In his 7-2 report, Hilts offers little more than a superficial overview of new FDA guidelines for blood banks. Although he touches on controversy here, he doesn't quite get to the bottom of the debate. In his 11-16 dispatch on the FDA's proposed rule changes for reporting the side-effects of drugs, Hilts merely regurgitates information from press releases and news conferences. Taking a potentially interesting example of a disastrous experiment by the National Institutes of Health for a new hepatitis B treatment, Hilts kills the reader's curiosity with dull prose and unoriginal material. Hilts's feature articles reveal an ability to hold the reader's attention, suggesting that laziness may lie at the root of his lifeless reports. He pens a particularly provocative 3-29 study of plagiarism. Discussing the American Historical Association's move to redefine the term, Hilts poses some provocative questions regarding the "threshold for plagiarism." Analyzing the gray area between the deliberate duplication of words and the more subtle adaptation of another's work, Hilts presents a thorough report on the debate surrounding an Amherst professor accused of borrowing both the ideas and the actual language from another historian. Again thought-provoking in his 7-19 story on particle pollution, Hilts provides uncharacteristic detail when he explores a form of pollution caused by microscopic airborne particles that "rivals the death toll of some cancers." His frustrating 9-14 profile of Surgeon General Joycelyn Elders supplies basic information on her appointment and confirmation but lacks any compelling analysis. Citing one supporter after another in praise of her "populist style," Hilts declines to adequately address the substantial controversy surrounding her nomination. As far as the conservative opposition goes, Hilts quotes only conservative Christian groups, failing to interview even one Senator who voted against her. This slanted story remains unredeemed by its leaden prose. Although he can overcome his pedestrian style when he does some digging, Hilts relies on the latest government press release to do his work for him.

Steven A. Holmes
The New York Times
★

State Department. A newcomer to this beat, Holmes supplies very little beyond the bare bones. In his superficial 1-16 dispatch, he stresses the politics of President Clinton's backtracking on his campaign pledge to make asylum easier for Haitians. Yet he neglects to provide sufficient background on the actual situation. In his cur-

sory 3-27 effort listing who is getting what in terms of ambassadorships, Holmes notes that Clinton is appointing more career foreign service officers to plum assignments. However, he doesn't examine whether these positions constitute mere tokens or reflect a broader trend toward a meritocracy at the State Department. In his skin-deep 4-1 essay, he never questions Clinton's desire to restore aid—despite popular demand for budget cuts—to population-control groups on the international level. Holmes yields adequate 5-2 and 5-6 updates on the series of talks between the Arabs and Israel on the issues of Middle East peace but provides scant analysis about the exceedingly complex proceedings. His 6-26 effort merely recounts a regular daily briefing with State Department spokesman Michael McCurry, who mentions U.S. dissatisfaction with the peace process. Holmes leaves even the basic questions of U.S. involvement in the negotiations unanswered. His reliance on briefings shows in his 8-25 article on the State Department's decision that China violated a missile agreement. Holmes presents virtually no evidence that led the department to that conclusion. In his 10-12 snapshot, he provides a bit more background on the incident in Port-au-Prince harbor, where U.S. troops failed to come into port due to a surly mob on the dock. However, he adds little new to the reader's understanding of the situation. To better serve his readers, Holmes must flesh out his material by developing both better contacts and stronger analytic skills.

Janet Hook

Congressional Quarterly

★★½

Senior writer. Assigned mostly to special projects in the second half of the year, Hook impresses with her crisp writing style and ability to ferret out information. She yields an astute 7-24 assessment of the potential turmoil in the House Ways and Means Committee if Rep. Dan Rostenkowski [D-IL] is indicted and forced to step aside as chairman. "A change in the chairmanship could transform the character of the committee, erode its power and possibly touch off a bitter internal struggle over its long-term leadership. And much is at stake for the rest of Congress and the country. The Ways and Means chairman has tremendous influence over some of the most far-reaching issues on the national agenda: taxes, trade, health and welfare." With detail and intelligence, Hook's 9-18 piece explains why the debate over health-care reform should prove fractious and contentious. The issue, she mentions, "will touch so many constituencies that virtually every member will try to be part of the action." In her comprehensive 10-9 essay on the influx of women in Congress, Hook opens with a revealing anecdote. "When President Clinton signed family leave legislation in February, it was a sweet victory for the small band of women in Congress who had pushed the issue for years. All the fanfare about 1992 being the 'Year of the Woman' in politics seemed to bear fruit quickly in the first major law of 1993. But the Rose Garden ceremony was also a quiet reminder that a single 'Year of the Woman' couldn't make a dent in two centuries of men dominating American politics. The only members of Congress who spoke at the ceremony were men—Democratic leaders and members who controlled committees that wrote the bill." Hook provides a succinct story on the fight over votes for NAFTA, 11-6, but, uncharacteristically, she adds little new to the subject. Still, with her sources and insight, Hook remains a reporter to watch at *CQ*.

Gwen Ifill

The New York Times

★

White House. Coasting after a promising year on the campaign trail, Ifill offers spot news dispatches that often lack depth. Although she writes well, she needs a wider variety of sources to give the reader a better sense of events and of policy debates. Her 1-28 effort on the gay ban in the military provides only a vague sense of where the battle lines are drawn, as she covers too briefly the various positions. In her 3-19 fluff bio of President Clinton's Chief of Staff Mack McLarty, Ifill never examines his qualifications or indicates his preparedness for this job. Instead she rattles off his techniques for motivating people. In another article on the President's staff, 5-5, Ifill merely reports Clinton's "mea culpa" on staff problems and policy snafus. She makes no real effort to fill in the blanks on this issue, such as who might be McLarty's second deputy; nor does she examine possible causes of the staff's problems, such as inexperience or the pursuit of too many initiatives at once. In her 8-4 dispatch, Ifill provides detailed background on the events leading up to Clinton's 19-minute economic address to the nation. While delivering an overview of the administration's internal wrangling over the speech and its content, she fails to place these matters in a larger context. And she only parrots the administration line in her 10-15 article examining U.S. policy on the restoration of President Jean-Bertrand Aristide's regime to Haiti. Because she fails to ask enough questions, this dispatch neither informs nor stimulates. Ifill has to dig more.

Marshall Ingwerson

The Christian Science Monitor

★★

Washington. Although his work sometimes lacks hard data, Ingwerson offers valuable and timely observations. In his 1-20 effort, he clearly defines the incoming President's political advantages—such as a majority in both Houses of Congress—and disadvantages. "The challenges before President Clinton are... more difficult than those that confronted Mr. Bush," he writes. "While Bush set out mainly to soften the hard edges of the Reagan Revolution, the Clinton agenda involves numerous domestic changes that cannot be broached without asking for sacrifice from large segments of the public. He was clearly elected to bring change, yet unlike Franklin Roosevelt he does not have a Depression-scale crisis forcing a public consensus around strong action." In his provocative 2-3 article, Ingwerson draws intriguing parallels between Clinton and Reagan, defining the ambitious goals of their first 100 days. He presents Reagan's domination of Congress as a standard for Clinton to match in getting his programs passed. Using lobbyists as political analysts, 3-22, Ingwerson concludes smartly that "the president's economic program will face more trouble in the Senate this week than it had in passing the House of Representatives last week. But not much more trouble, according to lobbyists who work the Senate." In his 7-6 report on health care, he notes that while single-payer reforms are unlikely to pass Congress, "the Clinton overhaul of health care may allow for single-payer, single-plan systems at the state level. In some rural states, covering up to a quarter of the United States population, single-plan systems may even be difficult to avoid, according to some health-care analysts." Ingwerson then explains why: Some states "have medical facilities spread so thinly that the [managed] competition envisioned in the Clinton plan is impractical." His superficial 10-5 review of who wins and loses under health-care reform and other proposals reads like an administration press release. This is a piece that could have benefited from the writer's impressive interpretive skills. Such skills, when fleshed out with more hard facts, would give Ingwerson's work an edge.

Michael Isikoff

The Washington Post

★★

Justice Department. Polite to a fault, Isikoff gently covers legal issues and major social and political stories. Although he presents facts clearly, he seldom digs deeply. In his 4-20 show of sympathy for government officials after they botch the siege in Waco, Texas, Isikoff assumes the role of apologist. "There was an undercurrent of exasperation among the FBI team. For weeks, agents had been seeking to reason with and cajole [David] Koresh into ending the standoff....Nothing worked. Koresh made several promises or suggestions that he was about to leave; he broke each promise." Isikoff follows up with a glowing 4-29 summation. "[Attorney General Janet] Reno emerged virtually unscathed.... Members [of the House Judiciary Committee] committee warmly praised Reno for her handling of the matter, especially her quick and forthright acceptance of responsibility for the FBI's assault shortly after the raid went awry." Isikoff's 12-13 puff piece on Louis Freeh sounds like a press release for the FBI director. "In a defiant visit to the home turf of the Sicilian Mafia, a heavily guarded Freeh conducted a whirlwind and at times emotional tour of this ancient city....Today's events were especially satisfying for Freeh, who came here in large part to commemorate his friend [Giovanni] Falcone. His motorcade's first stop on the road in from Palermo was the site where Falcone's motorcade was blown up in May 1992. Freeh laid flowers at the site." In his 9-16 article suggesting the crumbling of President Clinton's drug policy, Isikoff fails to examine the deeper implications. Citing a review by the National Security Council, he remarks, "despite record worldwide seizures of cocaine in each of the last four years, there has been no dip in the price or purity of the drug or the number of cocaine-related hospital emergencies." Still, Isikoff doesn't ask tough questions about plans for a drug program that might work. Refreshingly, Isikoff covers key aspects of Clinton's handling of the nomination of Lani Guinier, 6-4, explaining the seldom-noticed point that "the articles that led to Guinier's demise are not easily simplified....While advancing novel and intellectually challenging ideas is rewarded within the academic audience that Guinier was addressing, her articles were dynamite in the political arena." Following Guinier's forced withdrawal as a nominee, 6-5, Isikoff seems to elevate her to martyr status. "A crowd of supporters, including Jesse L. Jackson, surrounded her in the hallway and erupted into applause. Some groped to touch her hands." Many readers may well scoff at Isikoff's cozy Washington coverage.

Douglas Jehl
The New York Times
★★½

White House. For hard information, Jehl emerges as the *Times* reporter of choice on this beat. Although he lacks the delightful style of a Maureen Dowd, he packs in the data and wastes nary a word. He can, however, be dry. In his well-rounded 3-14 report on CIA Director R. James Woolsey's recommendations to the administration to cut neither staff nor funding too precipitously, he concisely encapsulates the situation. "If intelligence agencies' main cause came to be the cold war, they say, that should not obscure that the agencies were created with Pearl Harbor in mind. Even without a Soviet Union, Mr. Woolsey told lawmakers, the United States must still reckon with a bewildering array of threats, from terrorism to North Korean nuclear weapons, and at a time of great instability in the world. What might seem dispensable now could quickly become essential, he said, and it would be particularly unwise for intelligence agencies to be forced to dismiss those entrusted with their most sensitive secrets." Jehl's 4-15 follow-up, though arid, culls its information from classified sources, and gives a logical rationale for the short-term boost in funding for the intelligence agencies. "Nearly all of the new spending, Administration officials said today, is to be devoted to launching one or more spy satellites that can take the place of several older ones, saving money in the future." In his 5-23 piece, Jehl's own logical reasoning for keeping the intelligence community funded echoes that of Woolsey's—and is no less compelling. "If an open world leaves less reason to worry about the Russians, it appears more prone to unpredictability. For intelligence agencies, it probably raises more questions than it solves." For his informative 8-12 roundup of Clinton's anti-crime proposal, he gathers data from all sources, including the NRA. And testing his mettle under fire, Jehl reports from Mogadishu, providing a vivid, on-the-spot dispatch, 10-13, replete with detail on strategy. A versatile, dogged reporter, Jehl will do well for the *Times* at the White House.

David Johnston
The New York Times
★★

Justice Department. Providing trustworthy accounts of official Justice news, Johnston also relies, for better or worse, on anonymous law-enforcement sources to craft major stories. While not the keenest legal analyst, he rises at year's end to the

The Ice Sculpture

challenge of covering the Clintons' involvement with Madison Guaranty, the failed Arkansas savings and loan, and the Whitewater Development Corporation. The recipient of the leaked news that an internal Justice report critical of FBI Director William Sessions's administrative practices has been forwarded to Attorney General William Barr, 1-16, Johnston thoroughly discusses the issue of Sessions's future at the bureau, a political hot potato that will soon be tossed to the incoming Clinton administration. In his strong 3-10 account of the first day of Janet Reno's Senate confirmation hearings, Johnston not only summarizes her testimony but points out that "her emphasis on practical law-enforcement, more than her views on crime and justice, seemed to define the differences between Ms. Reno and former Attorneys General." A 5-1 profile of Reno adheres to the conventional wisdom on the new Attorney General, remarking that she "seems to have emerged [from the Waco disaster] not only unscathed but also with her recognition and popularity enhanced." Johnston, however, seems aware of the dangers of writing premature hagiography; toward the end of the piece he recognizes that Reno "has had few substantive accomplishments in her first two months." Five months later, as a new and less admiring conventional wisdom about Reno emerges, Johnston and co-author Stephen Labaton produce a lengthy 10-26 story that gives Reno critics full-throated but mostly anonymous voice—a fact that diminishes the story's impact. Based on "interviews with dozens...of former and current lawyers" at Justice—virtually none of them named—the pair contends that "Reno's stewardship has resembled a shakedown cruise under a novice captain." As the Madison/Whitewater story leaps to the top of the news in December, Johnston leaps after it, becoming the first reporter to recognize, in his 12-22 story, the potential for conflict between the White House and the Justice Department over matters relating to a criminal investigation. While sharper analysis could enhance his work, Johnston remains a solid reporter who can be counted upon to pursue the daily news story.

Sheila Kaplan

Legal Times

★★

Lobbying. With an irreverent and ironic tone, Kaplan entertainingly covers Washington's corridors of power. But she relies on largely anecdotal information, and her revealing articles and "Lobby Talk" columns are sometimes long and repetitive. Practically mocking Bill Clinton's pledge to stem the influence of Washington lobbyists, Kaplan's 1-11 piece surveys the sponsor list of inaugural-week events. This list contains major firms and companies—such as Skadden-Arps, Boeing, and Waste Management Inc.—but most notable are the justifications they offer for their involvement. No one, of course, admits to trying to curry favor with the new administration. "'It's a historic event—a major American celebration,' says Stephen Lambright [an Anheuser-Busch vice president]. 'We're happy to be helping to bring it to the American people.'... And a spokesman for the American Bankers Association says [his] group's loan 'is certainly an indication of our good faith.'" Almost a year later, 12-27, Kaplan exposes several White House officials who easily dodged new lobbying restrictions introduced by President Clinton. Ronald Plesser, for example, who oversaw the incoming administration's review of the FCC, immediately reentered private practice as a lobbyist for telecommunications interests. "Plesser's way around the restrictions? For the first six months, he lobbied only Congress, which is permitted, and masterminded the strategy for lobbying the administration." In her severe and thorough 5-31 critique of the Agency for International Development, Kaplan finds rampant waste, conflicts, and questionable ethics. Unfortunately, she offers numerous examples of every charge, where one or two would suffice. Noting that drug-giant Merck received a $3.2 million AID grant to provide measles vaccines in Russia, she remarks, "Sounds impressive. But for the same money, UNICEF, which has handled similar AID contracts in recent years, could have inoculated between four and five times as many children." In her sharp 11-1 "Lobby Talk" column, Kaplan reports on a four-day Department of Energy strategy meeting held at the plush facilities of Fluor Daniel, a DOE construction contractor. "'How can you talk frankly about contractors when they're in the room?' asks Daniel Gutt-

man, an energy lawyer and partner at D.C.'s Spiegel & McDiarmid. 'This is an appearance problem. The government has a trillion feet of wasted space. Is this the only place you can have your strategy planning meeting?'" Although she sometimes edges toward cynicism, Kaplan consistently offers fresh and shrewd insight.

Jon Katz

Rolling Stone

★★

Media. As *Rolling Stone*'s bad boy of journalism, Katz attacks the mainstream media at every turn. In his 5-27 criticism of objectivity, he goes after the very foundation of modern journalism. Noting that most Americans regard the press as biased anyway, Katz contends that journalists "ought to be diverse and they ought to be fair, not neutral." He frames his argument around Randy Shilts, a gay reporter who for many years covered AIDS for the *San Francisco Chronicle*. He praises Shilts—who would die of AIDS in February 1994—for having "fused strong belief with the gathering of factual information and marshaling the arguments, the way the founders of the modern press did." True to his words, Katz makes no pretense of neutrality, dismissing any argument for objective reporting. In his 4-15 story on the technological trends affecting the industry, Katz describes electronic bulletin-board systems as "the purest journalistic medium since smoke signals." Here he examines how interactive computer systems may revolutionize journalism by putting Americans in control of their news, making the traditional "gatekeepers" obsolete. Katz warns that "for journalists such interaction means surrendering control and sharing power, things that journalists are trained not to do." Does Katz support the interpretation of information only when journalists are the ones who are doing it? In his 8-19 criticism of the Washington press corps, he attacks the journalistic establishment. Remarking that "transparent flattery, social bribery and vengeance seem perfectly acceptable journalistic ethics among the White House press," Katz chides reporters for attempting to compensate for their limited access to the President by avoiding big stories and exaggerating unimportant ones. In his 11-25 essay on how the media outlets have ignored young people, Katz defends 1990s popular culture. He rightfully points out the hypocrisy of mainstream journalism, which "thinks that the most interesting things in [kids'] lives are dumb and dangerous, yet continually tries to exploit and market them." But in refusing to acknowledge the potentially detrimental effects of some forms of adolescent entertainment, Katz falls into the same trap as those who criticize it. Katz's engaging rhetoric packs a punch, and although some of his ideas may be off the wall, it's always entertaining to watch him bounce them around.

Michael Kelly

The New York Times

★★★½

Sunday *Magazine* staff writer. Few journalists can match Kelly's analysis of Washington politics—or his influence upon it. Two *Magazine* cover stories this year set the terms of discussion inside the Beltway—and beyond. In "Saint Hillary," 5-23, Kelly seeks to understand the First Lady in terms of both her goals and her ideas. Hillary Rodham Clinton, he writes, "is searching for not merely programmatic answers but for The Answer. Something in the Meaning of It All line...[and] looking for a way of looking at looking at the world that would marry conservatism and liberalism, and capitalism and statism, that would tie together practically everything....What Mrs. Clinton seems—in all apparent sincerity—to have in mind is leading the way to something on the order of a Reformation: the remaking of the American way of politics, government, indeed life." Kelly deftly captures the First Lady's pursuit of virtue—as defined by this child of the 1960s—but he doubts whether the culture of liberty, affirmed by '60s radicals, can allow much of what the First Lady now seeks. With the premier 10-31 cover story of the redesigned *Magazine*, Kelly revamps and expands his 5-30 profile of David Gergen. This fascinating piece packs a punch and says as much about Washington (including the press corps) and the way Washington works as it does about Gergen. "If perception is reality, what is the point of any differences at all—between Republicans and Democrats, between journalists and Government officials, between ideologues and copywriters, between the chatterers of television and the thinkers of the academy, between Washington and Hollywood?" In his 4-25 effort on Waco, Texas, Kelly makes pertinent observations by quoting psychiatrist Robert Coles about the judgmental nature of the media on such events. "'The press,' he said, suffers from 'an arrogant faith in rationalism and a determination to jump on anyone in authority,' which makes it 'appallingly gullible' to 'the plague of experts. God save us from them all, that descends on every tragedy, the psychiatric experts and the religious experts and the mediation experts, all of them shrieking, 'If you had only listened to me!' and all of them paying homage to the great delusion of our times, that social scientists will deliver us from irrational madness and the random hand of fate.'" In his 6-6 dispatch, Kelly helps to refine the debate over ideology. "The myth was that President Clinton would painlessly lead America into a post-cold-war age of New Politics, in which the old divisive 'false choices' of left versus right would merge into a new middle ground of happy consensus." With this kind of portfolio, Kelly's star is certainly on the rise in Washington.

Julie Kosterlitz

National Journal

★½

Health, welfare, pensions, environment and energy. Perhaps because of the breadth of her beat, Kosterlitz has trouble getting to the heart of the matter on any one subject. She typically reports a hefty amount of information, but sometimes has difficulty making sense of it. In a 1-16 article, one of her better efforts, Kosterlitz clearly discerns a gap on health-care reform between the assumptions of policy experts and the expectations of the public. "The main problem," she explains, "is that the public and the experts have expectations of health reform that are vastly different and potentially directly at odds.... The achievements of health care reform, no matter how real, are likely to be largely intangible to individuals, while the sacrifices will be all too concrete." Thus Bill Clinton's political risk looms quite large. Unfortunately, Kosterlitz seldom delivers such insight. Although informative, her 3-6 effort on the problems with the Pension Benefit Guaranty Corp. (the federal agency set up in 1974 to guarantee the pension benefits of private companies) never fully explains the problems and leaves the reader confused. In her 5-1 review, Kosterlitz examines the potential of health-care reform and the proper role of government, but the piece suffers from her poorly organized data. Fortunately, Kosterlitz organizes more carefully her 7-10 dispatch on the health-care system in Minneapolis, which has more HMOs than any other city in the country, and is now refining that approach still further. She also details how Clinton, in planning a new health-care system, might avoid some of Minneapolis's mistakes. In her 10-9 essay, Kosterlitz examines the complexity in the Clinton health-care plan. However, as with so much of her portfolio, she only dances around that central idea. Because this particular plan is so complicated—"an ingenious mix of public, quasi-public and private-sector involvement"—no one, least of all the government, will ultimately be held accountable.

Clifford Krauss

The New York Times

★

Congress. Moving from the State Department, Krauss is hobbled by his unfamiliarity with Congress and by his lack of sources. He rarely reports events beyond those that take place in open session of Congress, never overhearing the cloakroom conversations. The purpose of Krauss's 5-3 story on Rep. Gerald Kleczka [D-WI] and his internal debate over whether to support President Clinton's budget package remains as obscure as the Congressman. "The 49-year-old Representative explained that his work on the Ways and Means Committee was separate from the process by which Congress approves spending. He pledged to take out a sharp knife when spending bills came to the House floor later this year." Krauss takes glib shots at "Big Science," 6-28, but draws no blood. "Simply put, the very lawmakers who came of age marveling at 'Star Trek' and 'The Right Stuff' have scaled back their dreams of shaping the universe with space colonies across the galaxy. The Age of Tang has given way to the Age of [Ross] Perot, and the budget deficit is the new target of choice." On the rare occasion Krauss delves deeper into an issue, like in his 11-23 news analysis of the Brady Bill, he makes blanket statements without substantiation. "And if nothing else, the experience of states suggests that the waiting

period to buy a gun gives a chance to let passions cool: a dismissed employee angry at his boss, a wife enraged with her husband, a troubled person contemplating suicide in a moment of anguish." In one of his better efforts, 5-29, Krauss examines the flurry of deal-making surrounding the passage of President Clinton's budget package. "The intensity of the Administration lobbying was so fierce that some of the 38 Democrats who broke with their party have expressed fear that they may be punished by their leaders and the White House for years to come." A freshman on the congressional beat, the reader can only hope more experience on the Hill will improve Krauss's accounts of federal lawmaking.

Howard Kurtz

The Washington Post

★★★

Media. With the release of his new book, *Media Circus*, Kurtz stepped confidently into his role as ringmaster of the press, deftly balancing new media trends with occasional clowning around. His breezy style consistently entertains, but he sometimes overstuffs his articles with quotes, which, however meaty, take up space that could be better used for analysis. In his provocative 5-9 piece on the dangers of reporting news that reinforces negative stereotypes, Kurtz explains the press's failure to show the "fringe" element at the Washington gay rights march. "Fear of igniting a backlash has produced a new skittishness in the mainstream media, a powerful urge to skirt sensitive subjects and airbrush ugly realities. Unfortunately this approach often leaves the public in the dark, eroding our credibility with those who discover they're not getting the full story." Kurtz tackles a related theme in his 7-4 report on the rise of tabloid TV news that relies on "blood, guts and gore" to lure viewers. "The tabloid format features MTV-style quick cuts, brief stories, bold graphics, slow-motion footage, dramatic music, grieving relatives and flamboyant reporters who inject themselves into the news." He reveals the absurdities of the press, 4-24, rushing to assess President Clinton's first hundred days in office, noting *National Review*'s staging the first First-100-Days luncheon on day 84, because, according to *NR*'s publisher, "'It benefits to be the first one out there.'" His 9-17 piece bewailing the lack of left-liberal columnists defending Clinton suffers from his assumption that the President *is* a liberal and *is* to the left and therefore *deserves* their defense. Although Kurtz quotes a stack of pundits, his case falls flat. He regains his footing with a solid 6-29 portrait of John Chancellor, whose 40-year career at NBC personified the growth and stature of TV news. "And yet Chancellor is the first to recognize that the era he helped define no longer exists." As the new era evolves, Kurtz's sharp eye will no doubt keep focusing on the upcoming acts in the ever-changing media circus.

Stephen Labaton

The New York Times

Justice Department. Although he has proven adept at reporting on economic policy, Labaton adds little to the coverage of Justice, probably because he is new to the beat. In his serviceable 3-8 effort, Labaton outlines President Clinton's opportunity to name more than 100 federal judges. Notwithstanding the information he provides, Labaton offers little sense of the criteria—other than the "diversity" yardstick—Clinton might use in filling these vacancies. Furthermore, Labaton gives no clue what diversity might mean substantively for the courts, the law, or the country. He uses his 4-29 article to relate Treasury Secretary Lloyd Bentsen's comments indicating that Stephen E. Higgins, head of the ATF, is on his way out because of the botched February raid on David Koresh's compound in Waco, Texas. However, Labaton puts neither Bentsen's remarks nor the tragic events in political context. As it turned out, Higgins lasted five more months, with Labaton chronicling his departure in a workmanlike 9-28 dispatch. He sounds as confused as everybody at the Justice Department in his barely adequate 5-18 overview of the internal tumult over the Waco probe. Labaton yields a solid 8-4 roundup of the court decision allowing alleged Nazi war criminal John Demjanjuk to return to the U.S. Yet, Labaton says little about the legal complexities, which seem to elude him. In his 10-14 story, he fails to answer fully why the IRS—of all organizations—caved in to the Church of Scientology on its tax-exempt status after nearly 40 years of legal battles over the exemption. Labaton provides background on the squabbling, but little on the reconciliation, leaving the reader in the dark. Judging from his strong work in years past, Labaton—with a little time and seasoning—should soon set the pace at Justice.

John Lancaster
The Washington Post
★★★

Military. At ease writing about G.I.s in Somalia and generals in Washington, Lancaster provides absorbing accounts of the 1990s military. A stellar reporter, he is not afraid to challenge the reader with his exhaustive knowledge of defense topics. Lancaster's 1-17 story effectively conveys the confusion and ambiguity of the Marine mission in Somalia. "To hear the policy makers tell it, the U.S. military presence in Somalia is strictly humanitarian, a selfless mission of mercy to protect food supplies for starving thousands. Tell it to the Marines. Children spit at them, pelt them with stones and call them names. Few have ever seen a starving Somali. And sniper fire is a regular feature of life at the Marines' main encampment in Mogadishu, a ruined soccer stadium that the grunts have renamed Fort Apache." Carefully examining the hardship of married life in the Marines, 8-14, Lancaster relates the fact that combining young, newly married recruits with dangerous assignments in Somalia and the Persian Gulf can be a prelude to divorce. In his 7-20 piece, he cuts to the chase on the issue of gays in the military, calling President Clinton's "don't ask, don't tell" decision ultimately futile. "Advocates on both sides of the debate described the president's new policy—which rests on the seemingly contradictory principle that homosexuality is acceptable but homosexual behavior is not—as a sure-fire recipe for protracted litigation." While most military reporters wrote the cursory "new chairman of the Joint Chiefs of Staff" story when Gen. Colin Powell stepped down, Lancaster wrote an important 3,000-word 9-21 piece on the new chairman, Gen. John Shalikashvili. The story provides context on the kind of leadership expected of the new chairman. "Shalikashvili arrived in his NATO post in June 1992. From his headquarters in Mons, Belgium, he has watched the upheavals that accompanied the collapse of communism with a sense of déja vù, inveighing against the 'dark side' of nationalism and, associates say, privately agonizing over the carnage in Bosnia." When Lancaster tracks down sources on his new beat in Cairo, he will likely be an important voice in the Middle East.

George Leopold
Defense News
★★★

Washington staff writer. An excellent and wide-ranging defense reporter, Leopold brings his strong analytical skills to bear on such topics as arms control, non-proliferation, and defense conversion. Moving late in the year from *Defense News* to *Electronic Engineering Times,* his lucid style makes for clear explanations of a variety of technical matters. In his 1-11/17 *DN* dispatch, Leopold confidently examines the START II agreement, highlighting a move away from traditional nuclear-bomber payloads. The Pentagon has already issued a draft report, Leopold notes, detailing a conversion from nuclear to conventional payloads. He peers into his crystal ball, 2-15/21, to project the future of the Arms Control and Disarmament Agency (ACDA) and its role in arms control, noting shrewdly that "some experts worry that Clinton's pledge to counter weapons proliferation could fall victim to bureaucratic infighting, and that ACDA could be left twisting in the wind." Leopold provides a concise and prescient 3-29/4-4 report on the Russian military's reticence about intervening in the latest clash between President Boris Yeltsin and parliament. "Military leaders wary of political involvement after the failed 1991 coup against former Soviet President Mikhail Gorbachev have little choice but to remain neutral in a power struggle likely to continue indefinitely." Leopold succinctly reports, 4-5/11, on the progress of defense-industry conversion. Companies that can shift workers between commercial and defense production, he contends, will be better able to compete and survive in the post-Cold War era. Leopold points out that failure to completely convert to flexible production may force some contractors out of business, thereby accelerating unemployment and the loss of valuable technical expertise. Taking an intelligent 5-10/16 look at the quandary facing NATO in "out-of-area" regions, Leopold explains that,

traditionally, NATO countries cooperated in the defense of Western Europe. Now they face a crisis in Yugoslavia and remain unsure as to what their role—and especially Germany's—should be in stopping the conflict. Moving easily from subject to subject, Leopold effectively covers all the topics he takes on.

Neil A. Lewis

The New York Times

★★½

Legal issues. Although sometimes lacking the nuance so vital to excellence on this beat, Lewis's workmanlike efforts on legal issues invariably inform. His 3-11, 3-31, 4-8, and 4-11 dispatches keep the reader posted over the NAACP's search for a leader. The series culminates in a solid profile of the man who got the job—the Rev. Benjamin F. Chavis, Jr. Lewis succinctly portrays both Chavis and his goals for the organization. Probing the views of Lani Guinier, 5-5, Lewis examines the politics surrounding her nomination, accurately forecasting the stormy weather that eventually wrecked her candidacy. He notes that the "first salvo was fired by Clint Bolick, a friend of Justice [Clarence] Thomas's who wrote in a *Wall Street Journal* op-ed article that Ms. Guinier was a radical exponent of quotas." But Lewis doesn't provide enough hard information for the reader to make an intelligent decision regarding Guinier's views. In his revealing 5-14 effort, he does report in depth on Guinier's writings, observing that one of her main ideas, cumulative voting, "exists mainly today in the corporate world." Lewis provides a 6-2 bird's-eye view of President Clinton's waffling over Guinier, and delivers a 6-3 follow-up on the decision to jettison the nominee. Finally, he writes a 6-4 roundup of the political fallout, as politicians all over Washington wash their hands of the matter. In tandem, these three dispatches provide sharp insight. Lewis's 7-23 dispatch during Ruth Bader Ginsburg's confirmation hearings details a heated exchange between the nominee and Sen. Orrin Hatch [R-UT]. Asked her views on the death penalty, Ginsburg replied, "'[It] is an area I have never written about.' Senator Hatch persisted. 'It's not a tough question.' Judge Ginsburg said asking her to signal how she might vote on an issue that was certain to come before a court 'is something you must never ask a judge to do.' 'But that's not what I asked you,' Mr. Hatch replied. 'I asked you is it in the Constitution?'" At which point, Sen. Howard M. Metzenbaum [D-OH], recalling testimony of Justice Anthony M. Kennedy in 1987, noted, "'This is not the first time we have had a nominee who has declined to respond on this question.'" In his sharp 8-14 roundup, Lewis provides a complete picture of the D.C. Court of Appeals decision dictating that government computer files must be saved. "The unanimous court ruling won praise from historians and journalists who said it recognized how much of the Government's business is conducted on the computer. Paper files, while not obsolete, no longer provide a complete record of government action." A top-notch journalist, Lewis's byline usually deserves attention.

Paul Lewis

The New York Times

★★★

United Nations. Providing enriching context and precise detail, Lewis's acute reporting consistently reveals the finer points of UN diplomacy. In his well-organized 1-27 story on a highly critical report issued by Secretary General Boutros Boutros-Ghali regarding Israel's reluctance to comply with a resolution demanding the readmittance of 400 expelled Palestinians, Lewis finds the results predictable. "The Secretary General's recommendation was seen by diplomats here as an open invitation to the PLO and its Arab supporters to demand mandatory sanctions against Israel, and the PLO promptly circulated its draft." Offering fine-grained insight, 4-19, Lewis reveals the strong and deep-running sentiments for immediate action following the latest cease-fire breakdown in Bosnia. "The decision to impose new trade sanctions on Yugoslavia [which supports the war] was reached because France and a group of third world Council members successfully called an elaborate Russian bluff aimed at frightening the Security Council into delaying the vote again." In his 10-21 piece on a Russian threat to veto any effort by the Security Council to impose sanctions on Libya if it refuses to turn over the accused hijackers of Pan Am Flight 103, Lewis wonders why President Boris Yeltsin would defy Western governments that supported him during the recent coup. Arguing unpersuasively that Russian generals may be behind the threat, Lewis oddly ignores a perfectly reasonable explanation. "Russia's objection to the current draft resolution is that it would prevent Libya from using its overseas assets to pay off [its Russian] debts, which amount to more than $1 billion...." Lewis's 7-21 dispatch from Baghdad, offers vivid details on the effects of sanctions, as the Iraqi government takes steps to comply with UN demands to have them lifted. "In meetings with foreigners these days, [Iraqi] Government spokesmen no longer speak of the embargo as a hurdle they have to overcome. On the contrary, they emphasize Iraq's lack of foreign currency to buy food and medicine, and the hardship this inflicts." With a sharp ear and discerning eye, Lewis masterfully covers both front-room and backroom diplomacy at the UN.

Charles M. Madigan

Chicago Tribune

Washington. Covering public opinion polls, Madigan keeps his fingers on the pulse of the nation regarding hot-button topics but seldom offers much insight. In his 3-14 effort, he supplies a glimpse of Ross Perot and United We Stand, pointing out the flaws of Perot's polling techniques. "Because it's for TV, the questions in the video referendum are simplified to the point at which everything becomes a choice between 'yes' and 'no.' And the wording of some of the questions is so loaded that it would draw fire from any sophisticated pollster. Most of the questions seem aimed at drawing a 'well, of course, I'd do that' response." Despite the fancy statistics in Madigan's emotional 4-5 piece on the National Commission on Children, a four-year study on improving children's "health and well-being," he offers few policy recommendations. And he fails to put in context a 6-1 breakdown of *Tribune* poll results of Illinois voters still griping about gridlock in Washington. He provides results of various surveys, 9-22, that seem to indicate the public wants both health-care reform and universal coverage, but he supplies little information on the specifics. Madigan's best work, an 8-15 opinion article on gun control, doesn't address the question of illegal guns in the inner city but raises a provocative issue. "The *Tribune*'s 'Killing Our Children' series has provided such a long and depressing litany of gun violence that those stories alone should provide enough steam to move gun control legislation through the state legislature, at the very least. But that is not going to happen. The unfortunate fact is that if the society cared that much about the lives of urban poor, if it felt some collective responsibility or perhaps, even some sense of love for children who are victims of violence, they wouldn't be living those awful lives anyway. Gun violence is at the end of their problems, not the beginning." Now that sounds like the beginning of an intriguing premise. If he could flesh out the vital issues he handles, Madigan's work would carry more clout.

Jim Mann

Los Angeles Times

★★

National security, Washington. After broadening his strategic base to include most of the Pacific Rim, Mann loses just a bit of steam. Because he's still learning the ins and outs of the internal affairs of some of these Asian nations, Mann hasn't developed the expertise to fully assess all the major issues. While he doesn't come out and say so in his 1-28 effort, he suggests that Bill Clinton's decision not to meet with Japan's Prime Minister Kiichi Miyazawa early in his administration—due to a lack of a concrete Japan policy—shows not only rudeness but an ignorance of how business and politics are conducted in Asia. Mann notes that "Japanese officials are making little effort to hide their irritation with the American pressure to have Miyazawa bring something tangible to Clinton," but he doesn't examine the long-term strategic problems this may cause. Instead, Mann provides a bird's-eye view of the shift on U.S. policy towards Japan on trade, with some cursory analysis of the change. Again, however, he incorporates little about what the long-term effect on relations might be. His 2-3 and 10-3 dispatches on potential CIA director R. James Woolsey's Senate confirmation hearings and on employee buyouts at the CIA, respectively, showcase Mann's reporting skills. "Like thousands of other Americans in this time of corporate belt-tightening, Jim Waller has just taken a buyout, a one-time cash payment as an incentive to retire early. 'I'm 54.

I had put in 34 years,' Waller said....That would all seem very ordinary, except for one thing. Waller's employer is not just another company but as it is known to insiders, 'The Company': the CIA." Mann's work on China displays, as usual, great insight. In his 5-29 article, he comprehensively recounts the conditions attached by Clinton to the next (1994) reaffirmation of China's most-favored-nation status. And in a solid 9-30 report, Mann combines myriad factors to present a fairly clear picture of the complexities of restoring full relations with China after Tiananmen Square. As a former Beijing bureau chief, Mann has an exceptional handle on such issues, and it's only a matter of time before he applies himself equally well in covering news from other countries in the region.

Ruth Marcus

The Washington Post

★½

White House. Second banana on this beat after Ann Devroy, Marcus has made a fairly smooth transition from covering the Supreme Court. Because she's new, though, she hesitates to put events in context and sometimes reveals her own prejudices. In an impressive and balanced 1-21 look at the events of the day as President Clinton takes the oath of office, Marcus and co-author Devroy squarely detail the passing of the guard. A 3-7 examination co-authored by Dan Balz of the White House scramble to ready the State of the Union address simply gushes. "Less than 10 minutes into the speech, they realized Clinton was doing the unthinkable: He was ad-libbing the State of the Union, moving far afield of the text that had been distributed. On the open phone line between the Capitol and the war room, [Mandy] Grunwald marveled to [George] Stephanopoulos, 'He's riffing. He's making this up'....Clinton aides Michael Waldman and Gene Sperling, who had been part of the all-night team reworking the speech, exchanged high-fives like jubilant fans at a basketball game." In her tough 4-26 review of Clinton's "rambling" speech to the Newspaper Association of America, Marcus puts the President's claims in perspective. "Clinton said he had only broken one campaign pledge—tax cuts for the middle class—and blamed the tax increases he has proposed on unforeseeable deficit projections. He did not mention his campaign positions on such issues as forcibly returning fleeing Haitians and stronger steps to stop Serb aggression in Bosnia." On the road with Clinton and Gore, Marcus covers a whistle stop in Cleveland that provides a PR opportunity to tout "Reinventing Government," but her lackluster 9-10 dispatch mentions only what they did and who they saw, not what their actions and words might mean. In a solid 7-1 profile, Marcus captures a good sense of the White House counsel, Bernard Nussbaum, and reviews his tenure in the post. Marcus maintains careful treatment of disasters on Nussbaum's watch—such as the withdrawn nominations of Zöe Baird and Lani Guinier—while noting his former success as a mergers and acquisitions litigator. Now Marcus need only transfer that meticulous caution and balance to her other dispatches.

John Mashek

The Boston Globe

Washington. Because he frequently swallows any premise whole, Mashek's undiscerning reviews of Washington politics add little to the mix. His 1-11 summary of what Ross Perot has been doing and what he might do proves lightweight at best. Similarly, Mashek provides virtually no substantive information in his 2-21 dispatch about what was discussed at a seminar on the 1992 presidential debates, sponsored by the Washington Program of Northwestern University. What were the problems of the 1992 debates, and why did folks squabble over the rules? What effect might proposed legislation have? Mashek doesn't find out. And he makes only one imaginative point in his 3-4 examination of Republican strategy: The GOP is returning to the grassroots, via Chairman Haley Barbour's barnstorming tour of various groups. Well, at least that's somewhat newsy. The rest of the piece consists of who's hiring whom. In his 6-11 effort, Mashek completely accepts the premise that because Perot has United We Stand behind him, he'll be around for a while. Mashek skims over the rumblings of serious discontent in the organization, dismissing it as sour grapes. His superficial 7-8 report discloses that the Democratic Leadership Council finds Perot voters open to

Clinton. Yet Mashek defines no issues that might attract them, nor what Clinton might do to woo them. And a thin 10-3 profile of Haley Barbour reveals only one new fact—Barbour and Democratic consultant Bob Beckel sometimes meet for drinks. Mashek simply needs to ask more questions.

Jay Mathews

The Washington Post

★★★

New York. Always digging beneath the surface, Mathews files engaging reports that consistently turn up fresh details and make smart points. In his 6-19 profile of Martin Ginsburg, Mathews deftly portrays the husband of Ruth Bader Ginsburg, the newly nominated Supreme Court justice. "The truly unusual partner, in the view of their friends was Marty, a man so in love and so blessed with unshakable (and to some annoying) self-confidence that he could tailor his life to fit his wife's without a single regret." But Mathews offers no doe-eyed tribute. "Marty had no problem with Ruth graduating at the top of her Cornell class while he played golf and hovered near the bottom." In one masterful stroke, 2-28, Mathews describes the essence of Medco, a mail-order prescription service, and the controversy surrounding it. "Medco promises lower costs through economies of scale, sophisticated computer services and a new program called 'Prescriber's Choice,' in which Medco pharmacists call doctors and urge them to change their prescriptions to brands that have cut deals with Medco for lower prices." Mathews amusingly tells his story of disappointment and tedium, 1-26, while participating in market research for an automaker. "The questionnaire pushed me much further than I wanted to go....I began to feel some of the same emotions I had during the presidential election: Please don't ask me for the 89th time what I think, just do something!" In his 8-1 effort, Mathews uncovers a little-known meeting-of-minds between Jerry Richardson—CEO of Flagstar Inc., which owns Denny's Restaurants—and NAACP official Charles Davis over the company's hiring and promotion practices. The two joined forces a year before the Annapolis, Maryland, incident that led to discrimination charges against the company. "That small gesture, and the unusual relationship it forged between Richardson and Davis, has become the key to the $3.7 billion food service company's chances of riding out a storm of protest." A prolific writer, Mathews often breaks new ground with his business coverage and feature articles.

Tony Mauro

USA Today
Legal Times

★★½

Supreme Court. With his dignified, informative, and at times insightful, reviews, Mauro brings depth to the daily once derided as "McPaper." In his pithy 1-12 *USA Today* summary of the Supreme Court docket, Mauro concentrates on *Alexander vs. U.S.*, in which bookstore-owner Ferris Alexander's sale of four magazines and three videos deemed obscene cost him assets of $25 million. Usefully placing the case in context, Mauro draws a strong conclusion. "First Amendment advocates say the government's treatment of Alexander—and seizure of his property—is a frightening form of censorship that could cast a chill over legitimate expression as well as obscenity. By destroying Alexander's books and tapes, they say, the government keeps Alexander from expressing himself in the future based on past crimes—a classic 'prior restraint' the court has deemed unconstitutional for 60 years." Two quick 3-22 roundups on the Supreme Court report the political pressures on Clinton to appoint judicial liberals to the Court in order to shift its balance. In his 4-8 newsblurb, Mauro explains why 117 lower-court vacancies, left unfilled, make more work for other judges, thereby slowing down the justice system. As Lani Guinier comes under fire, Mauro crafts an acceptable 6-4 roundup that explores less her views than what she hopes her views might accomplish in solving "'the next generation' of problems in ending race discrimination." In a major 8-16 scoop in *Legal Times* (in which Mauro's "Courtside" column appears every other week), Mauro breaks the story of the Court's attempt to keep law professor Peter Irons from publishing *May It Please the Court*, a compilation of tapes and transcripts of the Court's most famous arguments. Although fuzzy on the legal issues, Mauro methodically explains the process by which Irons obtained the tapes, as well as the Court's

penchant for secrecy. "This is a Court," he notes, "that won't even allow a justice's doodlings to be auctioned off at a charity function." In an engaging 10 11 *LT* effort, Mauro reveals that certain groups—such as the National Legal Center in the Public Interest and the ACLU—sponsor fancy breakfasts (and sometimes "drab" lunches) to lobby Supreme Court reporters so that their pet issues get better coverage. Mauro's in-depth, behind-the-scenes reporting in *Legal Times* dovetails nicely with his more straightforward accounts in *USA Today*.

Jim McGee
The Washington Post
★★½

Investigations. Specializing in extensive probes, McGee often relates these examinations of various issues in a series of articles. One such series, entitled "The Appearance of Justice," 1-10 through 1-15, constitutes a comprehensive six-part report on questionable Justice Department practices. McGee examines, for example, "the use of simultaneous or successive indictments in conservative jurisdictions" against distributors of pornography—even though three federal courts have proclaimed the tactic unconstitutional. He also explores the failure of the Justice Department to monitor the work of some U.S. Attorneys. In one case that he treats at length, the Department failed to rebuke a Los Angeles prosecutor for lying to a federal judge. The judge, McGee notes, later dismissed a major racketeering case "with prejudice"—meaning it could not be re-filed—on that very account. Although long, the series is well-reported, and at year's end the Justice Department altered some practices in ways that pleased McGee, as well as the *Post*, which, in an editorial, lauded the work of its investigative ace. McGee's other work proves solid, if not quite as riveting. His spot coverage of the World Trade Center bombing supplements the filings of his paper's New York bureau. In his 3-3 dispatch, McGee summarizes known facts, and his 3-12 effort advances the story, as he writes that "a senior law enforcement official said investigators were looking at transfers or deposits 'just under $10,000' suggesting a pattern aimed at evading federal rules requiring that banks report to the government cash transactions of $10,000 or greater." He carefully notes that so far no involvement of foreign governments or terrorist organizations has been proved. His pithy 4-1 overview relates who's been arrested and who's still at large. McGee and co-author William Claiborne craft an exceptional 5-9 profile of Vernon Howell, examining how he became David Koresh and turned the Branch Davidian group into his own personal fiefdom. "The engine of Koresh's ascendancy was his talent for proselytizing," they write. "The entire enterprise depended on a steady flow of new members into Waco, followers who would turn over their income and often their savings to the cult." A bloodhound reporter, McGee relentlessly pursues his quarry, often turning up information that intrigues and provokes.

Doyle McManus
Los Angeles Times
★½

National security, Washington. Although he fails to provide the in-depth information necessary on this beat, McManus pens adequate reports on the complicated questions facing world policy-makers. In his 1-13 review of various global crises Bill Clinton will face as president, McManus supplies simplistic, and somewhat confusing, views of who's saying what about which areas, such as Somalia and Bosnia. In noting that some liberals are urging intervention in the Balkans, while many conservatives are not, he culls a memorable quote from Sen. Joseph I. Lieberman [D-CT]. "'It isn't hawks and doves anymore. It's internationalists and isolationists.'" McManus follows up with a 2-14 story that compiles some early evidence that Secretary of State Warren Christopher and others will be running the show because of Clinton's inexperience. "The proposal for new negotiations over Bosnia, announced last week, was the first major foreign policy initiative of Clinton's 3-week-old administration. But the President was, by design, almost 500 miles away." McManus and co-author John M. Broder craft a frank but superficial 4-1 discussion of the importance of Russia to Clinton and his new administration. The pair never questions the course the President has taken, but instead evaluates the political risk and implications both of supporting Yeltsin and of supplying aid. A similar lack of skepticism hampers McManus's 6-13 effort, as he accepts without inquiry the prescription of aid to Russia. Moreover, he concentrates on the painfully slow speed with which the country might get the aid, despite Clinton's pushing. His quick 7-22 review of the U.S. decision not to use military force in Yugoslavia, despite pleading from Bosnia, lacks a sense of the deeper strategic issues involved. With balance and care, McManus assesses in a 10-8 effort Clinton's "exit strategy" for Somalia (by March 31, 1994), and explores the military and strategic utility of such a tactic. This kind of work shows that McManus *can* plumb the depths when he sets his mind to it.

Timothy McNulty

Chicago Tribune

★★

White House. Although some of his articles on foreign affairs lack depth, McNulty remains a sharp White House watcher. In his 2-26 story, he hints at trouble for Boris Yeltsin. "There is a sense that Yeltsin, like his predecessor, Soviet leader Mikhail Gorbachev, may be ruling on borrowed time. The summit date is one week before a Russian referendum on whether to assign more power to Yeltsin or to the increasingly contentious Russian parliament." This purely political assessment, however, reveals less about Yeltsin and his circumstances than it does about the new partnership between Bill Clinton and the Russian president. McNulty points to a flaw in the Clinton health reform plan, 4-22: "Creating a larger number of generalists or family practice doctors is key to the health-care reforms expected to be unveiled in May by the Clinton administration. Generalists are the linchpin of the reform envisioned by the president's task force on health care. Such primary-care providers are essential in restraining health-care costs because they are the gatekeepers, the first to see a patient and make the decision whether further and more expensive treatments or a visits [sic] to the specialist are necessary." The problem, as McNulty points out, is that only 30 percent of practicing physicians are GPs. In his ambitious 7-27 essay, he deems the "politics of meaning" framework of Michael Lerner and Hillary Rodham Clinton too "esoteric." But this poorly written op-ed flits between a phone conversation with Lerner and McNulty's own thoughts. A former Middle East correspondent, McNulty should have plumbed the depths of the peace accords; instead his efforts were disappointingly shallow. In his workmanlike 9-5 overview of the agreement, McNulty seems as piqued as the U.S. government at being a wallflower at the dance. And his basic 10-8 summary merely recounts the meeting between Yitzhak Rabin and Yasir Arafat to work out specifics of what was "achieved" in Washington. These latter efforts suggest that McNulty best serves the reader when covering domestic politics.

John Merline

Investor's Business Daily

★★★½

National issues, Washington. An astute observer of both politics and economics, Merline emerges as the reporter to beat on the issues of taxation and health-care reform. In his sharp 1-12 study of the economic effects of a higher gas tax, Merline provides a memorable introduction, in which he identifies the section of the population that will suffer most. "The first campaign promise President-elect Clinton might break is his pledge not to raise taxes on the middle class." Again, in his 2-26 examination of the budget, Merline pulls no punches in attacking Clinton's economic proposal. He zeroes in on sev-

Thanksgiving at the Bobbitts

eral questionable budget "cuts" the President has recommended. "One of the biggest, and most obvious, tricks was to count $21 billion raised through a tax on Social Security benefits as a spending cut." In his balanced 4-15 essay, Merline examines problems with Medicare to expose the potential pitfalls of government-run health care. "For example, the original [1965] forecast for Medicare's Hospital Insurance program—often called Medicare Part A—predicted that spending in 1990 would be a little over $9 billion. The actual spending level for 1990 was $67 billion." In his 5-13 dispatch, he raises another key point on health care—one that few reporters have tackled. "Critics note that Clinton's plan focuses all that money on only one of the many contributors to health—namely, access to medical care. And most experts believe that access plays a relatively minor role in a person's overall health." Although Native Americans, Merline states, receive government-sponsored health care, many suffer abominable health. For his stellar 9-7 article, Merline gathers data from an array of studies and finds the real costs of health care hidden in taxation. "American families pay an average $4,500 annually for health care—other people's health care, that is. In contrast, the average family spends about $2,400 a year to pay the direct cost of its own care....This method of funding health care not only has important implications for a family's budget, but the health-care market as well, contributing to the rapid rise in costs." Illuminating another key aspect of Clinton's proposals, Merline's 10-20 essay draws a sharp bead on the new health-care plan. "The reform plan also calls for additional spending by the National Institutes of Health to research such things as 'unintentional injuries, learning and cognitive development, reproductive health including contraceptive development and use, and child abuse and neglect.' Clinton would also mandate that health insurance companies provide coverage for a generous array of services, including treatment for mental health problems, substance abuse, family planning, home care for the elderly and more. This expansion of what comes under the health-care umbrella has led many analysts to wonder how Clinton can make good on his pledge to cut the share of the economy devoted to health care." No one puts things as succinctly as Merline.

Eugene H. Methvin

Reader's Digest

★★

Senior editor. Methvin writes what many American readers love most: stirring accounts of good- and evil-doers. His pathos-filled stories usually escape relegation to pulp journalism through his diligence in relating them to larger issues. In his January piece on the Geneva Works steel mill in Provo, Utah, Methvin dramatically recounts how Washington lawyer and ex-EPA official Joe Cannon—with the help of Sen. Orrin Hatch [R-UT]—worked to save thousands of jobs in the floundering steel industry in the late 1980s. Knowing an intriguing detail when he finds one, Methvin notes that "Hatch is a Pittsburgh native who spent years as a union member in the city's building trades." After stating that union work rules "had killed productivity," Methvin demonstrates that it was rank-and-file workers who made the plant successful again, as they partook readily in profit-sharing and their new liberty to perform a variety of tasks. Methvin's September essays on a Seattle arsonist and executed child-molester Westley Allan Dodd offer the sensationalist type of coverage that lesser journalists might produce. While the arson tale plays like a fast-paced detective story, the article on Dodd descends to a voyeuristic foray into spine-tingling deviance. In his June effort on juvenile justice, Methvin argues for harsher punishments for serious habitual offenders. "For a certain small proportion of incorrigible young predators who pose a deadly danger to society...sure rehabilitation is beyond our capability." Methvin, however, overlooks the fact that "sure rehabilitation" for *any* criminal remains beyond the justice system's grasp. In his 4-3 *American Spectator* review of Jimmy Carter's new book, *Turning Point*, Methvin shares with the former President a high esteem for the late *Atlanta Journal* columnist, John Pennington, whose exposé of fraudulent voting practices helped Carter reclaim a stolen victory in his race for the Georgia State Senate in 1962. Amusingly, Methvin compares Americans' "grassroots political competence" in this saga with the ingrained political passivity of Russians, and he praises Carter's rise to the presidency as a sign of the health of the American political system. Methvin then gives a jarring aside, maintaining that the virtue of grassroots democracy is a "point to ponder for those liberals who would rather trust five lawyers in Washington to create rights for us instead of" the hundreds of thousands of elected state and local officials. Huh? This odd misplaced comment detracts from an otherwise thoughtful review. Methvin should avoid attempts at humor and stick to his more conservative, gentlemanly prose, which has served him so well over the years.

David C. Morrison

National Journal

★★

Defense. Scouring both the globe and the nation one step ahead of his competitors, Morrison makes obscure issues on national defense both timely and understandable. Although he suffers a tendency to highlight the obvious, he uses his military expertise to good effect in stories notable for their lucidity. Ahead of the curve in his 5-1 article on North Korea, Morrison yields a keen insight. "Now bereft of allies, Pyongyang in February again retired into sullen, hermetic isolation after a brief opening to the outside world....Of all the potential flash points in Asia, the Korean imbroglio is the one guaranteed to involve American forces." Morrison capably covers other remote but intriguing issues in the Pacific, such as his 6-12 piece on Guam's desire to snap American apron strings and his 7-3 examination of pacifism in Japan. "Save among Shinto zealots on the emperor-worshiping right-wing fringe, the old samurai spirit seems to be all but extinguished here." On issues closer to home, Morrison still manages to find new angles on familiar stories. In his 3-6 piece on the defense industry, he vividly examines the impact of military downsizing on small subcontractors. "Although their vital signs may not be monitored as closely as those of the defense giants, tens of thousands of Pentagon subcontractors are also at risk. These smaller firms catch serious colds, if not fatal pneumonia, when the climate gets chilly for the major firms." For all his insight and originality, however, Morrison too often belabors the obvious. In his 2-13 article he makes the understatement that President Clinton "seems to be widely held in contempt by the officer corps." Likewise, Morrison mentions nothing new in his 1-23 article on the break-up of Czechoslovakia, drawing a banal conclusion: "Nationalism is another earmark of nationhood." These weaker efforts aside, Morrison remains one of *National Journal*'s better reporters.

Neil Munro

Defense News

★★½

Washington staff writer. An expert on the essential, albeit mundane and often overlooked topics of both defense logistics and command, control, and communications technologies, Munro also displays a solid grasp of the operation and procurement of defense computing systems. His fascination with computers plainly shows in his 1-25/31 report, in which he skillfully surveys initiatives undertaken to protect the U.S. military's information systems from attack. These systems, Munro explains, are essential during wartime and would be likely targets for enemy electronic warfare specialists. His solid 3-15/21 dispatch offers a quick and concise view of a proposed Pentagon program to help manage the flow of information between battlefield commanders. Such improvements, he maintains, will enhance U.S. war-fighting capabilities and reduce U.S. "friendly-fire" casualties. In his 4-12/18 effort, Munro ably discusses plans to improve coordination between Defense Department mission-planning programs, which seek to reduce both interservice redundancies and costs and to increase the effectiveness of military missions. He provides a well-focused 5-17/23 overview of a difficult and tedious topic—computer management studies. Reporting the halt of a planned centralization of defense-related computer procurement and software design, Munro explains that these functions will remain with the armed services. In his 7-12/18 follow-up, Munro continues his solid coverage of the Defense Department's computer system, noting that the Clinton administration's plan to suspend the consolidation of the armed services' computing systems threatens the possible cost savings. His timely 11-15/21 piece reports a classified Defense Department program that might replace a series of satellite-based sensors with a less expensive mix of ground-, air-

and satellite-based sensors. Satellites "fly over the North Pole daily, allowing them to monitor missile tests in northern Russia from a distance of several thousand miles," providing the U.S. with valuable defense information. Munro also shows how the new sensor technology may reduce defense costs. With his eye for obscure details, Munro remains the expert on Defense Department computer systems.

Frank J. Murray

The Washington Times

★½

White House. Although he offers scant creative analysis, Murray provides adequate information in his no-frills, no-nonsense dispatches. His 1-26 retelling of President Clinton's desire to lift the gay ban in the military includes most of the familiar arguments as well as Murray's pedestrian conclusion. "It also seemed clear that [Clinton] would become the focus of persistent demonstrations by homosexual activist groups if he reneged on this promise." In his muddled 6-18 account of Clinton's economic press conference carried live only by NBC, Murray recounts the Q&As but provides little background. However, he does provide a serviceable 7-24 overview of Vince Foster's suicide, relating the dismay of Dee Dee Myers as she calls other staff members' concern about the late White House counsel. Still, Murray seems at his best when reporting with an enterprising air. His discouraging 4-29 review of Clinton's first 100 days never smacks of partisanship, although the lead comes close. "President Clinton's first 100 days in office were more fizzle than the explosion he promised. But he could have done worse —William Henry Harrison died on Day 32 of his administration." Murray lifts this effort above the ordinary by examining the details of Clinton's 100-day celebratory booklet and contending that the President's accomplishments can be misleading. Digging deep in his 10-7 dispatch, Murray reveals the concern within the Secret Service of finding a new director to replace John Magaw. Murray also points out the internal fear of declining morale and chain-of-command within the service. In an intriguing sidenote, Murray reports that "the [*Washington*] *Times* asked White House officials about reports that then-Associate Counsel Vincent Foster visited Mr. Magaw in February to ease out the highly respected director and create a vacancy." Few others reported this move of Magaw to the beleaguered ATF. But these dispatches were exceptions. To break new ground, Murray will have to prove more resourceful and imaginative.

Salim Muwakkil

In These Times

★★½

Senior editor. Intelligently delving into factions within the African-American community, Muwakkil delivers penetrating and multifaceted accounts of inter- and intra-racial issues from a left perspective. As both a reporter and analyst, he explores nuances of explosive subjects often ignored or downplayed by the mainstream media. In his intriguing 2-22 column on the Congressional Black Caucus (CBC), Muwakkil investigates factors behind "intramural dissent" in the CBC, which led to the first contested race for the position of chairman. "There is a growing clamor," he notes, "within the black political establishment for a more activist agenda" to provide an effective voice for impoverished African Americans. Discussing the popularity of African-American public figures who have made anti-Semitic remarks, 6-14, Muwakkil reports that many blacks criticized Nation of Islam leader Louis Farrakhan's recent conciliatory gestures toward the Jewish community. "Conciliation is equated with selling out in black America in the '90's," Muwakkil states, "and 'sell-out' is a major epithet." In his outstanding 8-23 article on "black homophobia," Muwakkil cites an impressive array of those both for and against African-American gay activists. Cleverly juxtaposing the anti-gay-rights sentiment of a middle-aged community activist with young rap singers' violent homophobic lyrics, he illustrates the endemic hostility toward homosexuality in the black community. But it's his analysis of "the construction of black masculinity as hard, aggressive, machismo-identified and *cold*" and his linking of black gay-bashing to other black-on-black violence that makes for arresting reading. Muwakkil, however, can be a bit uneven in his use of research findings. His 4-19 piece on "the criminal just-us system" makes dramatic use of findings from a 1989 New York study that showed whites comprised 7 percent of those arrested in drug busts but 47 percent of those in state-funded drug treatment slots. The piece ends by citing an unconvincing second study of a job training program aimed at reducing recidivism. The latter study contains a design flaw that Muwakkil overlooks: The more successful group volunteered, whereas the less successful group chose *not* to volunteer—a fact which undermines the validity of the findings. Such drawbacks aside, Muwakkil's unconventional columns provide a valuable perspective on race relations and racial issues in the United States.

Seth Mydans
The New York Times
★★

Los Angeles. Focusing on gang wars, racial unrest, and firearm proliferation, Mydans tends to strengthen negative stereotypes of Los Angeles. Even so, he consistently delivers careful and comprehensive stories. In the aftermath of the Rodney King and Reginald Denny beatings and trials, Mydans covers the legal, sociological, and psychological consequences of these racially charged events. In preparing for the outcome of the King trials, 4-10, Mydans cogently observes of neighboring Koreans, "Like many others, Miss [Elizabeth] Hwang's family is armed now—with a Glock-17 pistol, a Baretta and a shotgun—and they plan to barricade themselves in their store to fight off looters." As tension builds during the trial of the officers accused of beating King, 4-13, Mydans seems to pour more gas on the fire. "There is a feeling of menace in the air here at the edge of the Jordan Downs housing project, where few teen-agers ever expect to have a job....Moody young men said that nothing would stop people like them from venting their anger as they did last year." In his more optimistic 5-2 article, Mydans detects a possible sign of change in the inner cities. "As they age into their 20s and 30s, some gang leaders around the country have begun what they call 'trucing.' Tiring of the continuing killings, concerned for their own children and tempted by the celebrity of national attention, some of the leaders are leaving the streets for the talk shows to call for peace." In his 6-27 article, Mydans ably examines some of the tensions between natives and newcomers. "Anti-immigrant feelings are... colored by a perception—contrary to the facts—that most immigrants are in the United States illegally. The tightening economy also seems to be a major reason for the increasing anti-immigration sentiment." In his compelling 8-22 article, Mydans profiles Liu Jiang, the only person granted asylum when the U.S. turned back three ships carrying 656 other smuggled immigrants from China. The lone Christian on board, Liu claimed religious persecution. "'They beat me up because I am a Christian,'" Liu stated. "He said the other immigrants were his tormentors, mocking and threatening him because of his religion, and throwing his Bible into the ocean with the words, 'You and your things can go to heaven.'" Now that the *sturm und drang* mood of the Los Angeles riots has run its course, Mydans has the opportunity to apply his talents to other key topics affecting the nation's second-largest city.

Adam Nagourney
USA Today
★½

White House. Nagourney's pithy reports read quickly and easily. Although he rarely plumbs the depths of politics or policy, Nagourney provides sufficient coverage of White House affairs. An his 1-25 effort, Nagourney muses inconclusively on the missteps of the Zöe Baird nomination, squandering space on detail before pondering the question at hand. "How did Clinton—whose greatest skill might well be reading the public mood and who surrounded himself with campaign advisers whose careers were built on studying middle-class voters—fail to detect the time bomb he carted into the White House [with Zöe Baird]?" Nagourney's 2-3 piece on welfare reform notes Clinton's "decision to highlight the topic so quickly," but fails to mention that the President's full plate will likely preclude new legislation in the near future. Nagourney pops off a lightweight 5-17 review of the difficulty of getting Clinton to make a decision due to his insistence on soliciting one more option. Nagourney likens the President to TV's Lieutenant Columbo, who always has to ask one more question. Two efforts on Clinton's hiring of David Gergen, 6-8 and 8-2, provide sufficient accounts of the public relations and political value of the appointment,

but offer little new. In a 9-28 report, Nagourney falteringly assesses Clinton's performance in his first speech to the UN General Assembly. The speech, which "seemed less grand than promised by his advisers in recent weeks, offered his clearest description yet of when the world needed to intervene in trouble spots, and what needed to be done now to deal with potential threats to global order. But Clinton grew murky when discussing exactly what role he saw the United States playing in world disputes." Well, is it clear or murky? And Nagourney's superficial 10-7 review of Clinton's most recent decisions on Somalia leaves more issues unanswered than resolved. Although informative, Nagourney's TV-style news accounts need more context and analysis.

Sonia Nazario

Los Angeles Times

★½

Social issues. Moving from *The Wall Street Journal* at the beginning of the year, Nazario adequately covers social issues of both national and local concern. She personalizes her stories by quoting ordinary people, which gives readers an immediate feel for the subject. Her moving 5-2 obituary portrays local hero Rev. Bennie Newton, a black ex-convict-turned-preacher who protected a Latino man during a mob beating in the 1992 riots. Newton also employed other ex-convicts in his business and preached in county jails. Nazario quotes Chaplain Bob Macdo: "'Every prisoner from Pelican Bay to San Quentin knew who Bennie Newton was.'" In her 6-5 piece, Nazario thoroughly explores the topic of women police officers, discussing their work methods and success rates as officers. Female officers, she notes, tend to employ verbal alternatives to brute force and assist male officers in learning these practices. One male police officer says of his former partner, a woman, "'She taught me how to de-escalate rather than escalate situations....I haven't had a fistfight in five years.'" In two articles, 8-19 and 9-4, Nazario writes succinctly of the travails of immigrant janitors. She illustrates their workload with well-chosen detail, noting that one worker cleans 46 bathrooms every day. Nazario also reports insightfully on child abuse. In her 3-28 piece, she highlights the overlooked yet serious danger of placing abused children with relatives, a practice on the rise as "a cheaper alternative to foster care." The problem, Nazario states, is that "because child abuse is often learned from a parent, many relatives also turn out to be child abusers." Although her keen analysis of grisly topics often justifies her use of gruesome detail, Nazario's 10-30 piece on homeless squatters, co-authored by David Ferrell, treats hearsay as if it were fact. One homeowner living in the area of the squatters "remembered...how some of the neighborhood boys found a severed human head down in Pickens Canyon a few years back; how a dead body turned up in the same area, maybe 10 years ago." Such vague comments leave the reader to assume that squatters committed these crimes. Nazario's lengthy 4-19 article on local residents bringing gifts to police stations following the verdicts in the second Rodney King trial meanders as she goes overboard quoting everyone in sight. Quiescence may be rarer than an earthquake in Los Angeles, but that doesn't make it news.

Jack Nelson

Los Angeles Times

★½

Washington bureau chief. For all his years of experience as a political reporter and as head of the Washington bureau, Nelson has little to offer. His boyish enthusiasm for the administration comes through in inappropriate ways, making some of his dispatches suspect. Showing his remarkably pro-Gore slant in a 3-15 piece, Nelson predicts that Gore's influence in the Oval Office may exceed that of other Vice Presidents. Nelson gushes that "the relationship [between Gore and Clinton] has grown even closer since they took office, further strengthened by the friendship that developed between Hillary Clinton and Gore's wife, Tipper. In fact, the Clintons and Gores have become social friends, dining together and recently taking in a show at a bluegrass-music club." In his comprehensive 8-8 report, Nelson decries the "meaner" political divisions, which he paints as purely partisan and indicative of the "rancor" and "mean-spiritedness that now pervades the political process in Washington." Despite this fine article, he has to backtrack a mere six weeks later, 9-25, when, at a *Los Angeles Times* breakfast session broadcast on C-SPAN, he finds Senate Minority Leader Bob Dole [R-KS] surprisingly accommodating in remarks on health-care reform and NAFTA. Although noting the turnaround, Nelson fails to closely examine what caused it. The remainder of the year proves rote. In his 1-19 dispatch, Nelson adequately documents a day in the life of an incoming president. At least his 5-16 apologia for Clinton and his troubles contains some insights. "If he is to rekindle public enthusiasm for his programs, Clinton must find ways to dominate the public debate, instead of leaving the field open to critics and skeptics, as he often has this spring." In a barely passable 7-8 effort, Nelson reviews the criticisms expressed by the G-7 summiteers toward Teheran. C'mon, Jack, you can do better than this.

Gustav Niebuhr

The Washington Post

★★½

Staff writer, religion. While he provides solid accounts of major religious events, Niebuhr also digs into offbeat areas. His 8-15 article succinctly relates the highlights of Pope John Paul II's trip to the U.S. "In his speech, delivered on the third day of his third U.S. visit, the pope went well beyond a simple defense of traditional teachings. He lamented the scandals of child abuse by priests and condemned U.S. urban violence, finding its cause in both individuals and society. In speaking against abortion, he called on abortion opponents also to help the down-and-out." After the mass deaths of Branch Davidians in Waco, Texas, 5-4, Niebuhr looks for answers from former members of other cults. He finds one who "believes that what led him into cult membership was an ancient affliction, the sin of pride—the belief that mere mortals can usurp God's role and change the world." Niebuhr does not shy from controversial religious issues. His intriguing 4-25 story reports that "many homosexual Christians are taking a fresh look at Scripture and coming up with new interpretations of age-old stories. The result is a brand new field: gay theology." One gay chaplain, Niebuhr notes, understands the friendship between David and Jonathan "as a homosexual relationship." Niebuhr also quotes a former Jesuit. "'Christianity is not the enemy,'" he says, "'the institution [the church] is the enemy. Let's take back Christianity.'" In his 8-22 story on another provocative issue, Niebuhr examines changing terminology in the church. "Now Jesus' ancient title [Lord] is coming into question, as some see the word itself as laden with negative meaning. Individual churches, hymn writers and liturgists have already moved to replace 'Lord' with a range of gender-neutral titles, including Redeemer, Comforter, Friend and Christ." Displaying his interest in non-Western religions, 9-28, Niebuhr engagingly profiles Buddhist monk Thich Nhat Hanh. "What matters to his listeners here is his approach: His teaching is non-sectarian, the concepts expressed simply, the whole event shorn of rigorous physical discipline." With his own ability to convey religious trends simply and directly, Gustav Niebuhr—a distant relative of Reinhold Niebuhr, the great theologian and social critic—remains one of the better journalists on this beat.

Timothy Noah

The Wall Street Journal

★½

Washington, environment. Although he often gets to the guts of his topics, Noah maintains an uncomfortably close proximity to his sources and tends to report stories that appear ready-made for him. Debunking the incoming administration's claim that lobbyists would play no role in preparing new cabinet nominees, 1-7, Noah writes, "The only real difference between these lobbyists and their Republican predecessors during the Reagan and Bush administrations is that the Democrats are making a greater effort to be discreet about their role." Ingratiating himself with a key player on his beat, 4-1, Noah defends Kathleen McGinty—the 29-year-old head of the White House Office of Environmental Policy—who participated in a meeting in which she came across as unprepared and immature to a group of oil executives. "McGinty has shown a greater mastery of environmental issues than of the politics surrounding them." Yet, according to Noah, McGinty went straight from law school to then-senator Al Gore's legislative staff, making her a purebred product of the political system. Reporting from Columbia, South Carolina, 6-24, Noah perceptively captures the "pigment problem," as he felicitously calls it, of U.S. en-

vironmental groups. "The culture gulf couldn't be wider between the Sierrans who this month journeyed in their Hondas and BMWs to this town to meet their counterparts in a local environmental-justice group called Jesus People Against Pollution." Astutely calculating that an EPA study finding passive smoke a carcinogen is more a legal than a medical story, 1-6, Noah states, "Its ultimate impact will depend on the eagerness of the incoming Clinton administration to tackle the issue and the ability of lawyers to exploit a potentially lucrative new area of liability." While he delivers the goods on some unchallenging subjects, Noah would do well to exercise his discerning eye on some less obvious stories.

Martin F. Nolan

The Boston Globe

National politics. Nolan has a perfectly awful year on the national scene, his efforts often disjointed and devoid of insight. His local reporting, however, shows both style and substance. In his strange 1-20 "On Politics" column, Nolan tries to position Washington as a voracious city devouring its impermanent residents, presumably those in the administrations which come and go. He maintains that "the fundamental question at each inaugural is whether a new president changes the entrenched interests of the enduring culture here or whether permanent Washington changes him." However, with lines like "The K Street monster resembles Hannibal Lecter, pondering how all this innocence will taste with some fava beans and a nice Chianti," it's tough to get through. Nolan's blathering 3-4 compare/contrast of Clinton and FDR makes no sense whatsoever—and stumbles under the weight of pompous pronouncements. "The bond market and even the stock market have eschewed ideology for profit." Huh? In a scattered 4-19 composition, Nolan attempts to connect the Rodney King case to the Kennedy assassination, among other things, and then to police officer Stacey Koon's position of authority. Nolan does little to link these events coherently. He proves more adept on local politics. In a 5-5 essay, Nolan examines how Boston Mayor Raymond Flynn's appointment to the Vatican has left mayoral candidates short on policy pronouncements. "The candidates had planned to think great thoughts by 1995. An accelerated timetable has left them flatfooted in their base camps, pondering mostly geographical strategies." And Nolan's 8-26 story on the new clout of Hispanic voters displays both fine reporting and solid statistics, as he finds that "Mission Hill outvoted Beacon Hill." His 10-12 feature on the redesign of City Hall, however, is mistimed. Surely with the mayoral race coming down to the wire, Nolan has more to talk about than this. Much more at home in Boston than in Washington, *Globe* editors should keep him there.

Barbara Opall

Defense News

★★★½

Washington staff writer. One of the best defense writers in the business, Opall crafts brilliant reports on weapons proliferation, the international arms trade, and aircraft and ballistic defense technology. In her excellent 1-18 story on recent Defense Department successes, Opall writes insightfully, "In two years, and in spite of the typically glacial pace of U.S. weapon development and procurement, U.S. forces have been able to fine-tune an already formidable fighting capability through software upgrades, enhanced intra-service cooperation and implementation of some of the lessons drawn from Operation Desert Storm." Opall's shrewd 2-15 report chronicles the Israeli decision to include the F-15E fighter plane in procurement competition with the F-16 and F-18. "Israeli sources said they always have been interested in the F-15E, but the aircraft's high cost and U.S. administration reluctance to release technologies had disqualified it from consideration." Opall continues to shine in her 3-15 dispatch, in which she comments on efforts to resuscitate an element of the Strategic Defense Initiative (SDI). Despite Republican support for the new program, she points out, it will likely die without backing from the Clinton administration. Opall offers a fascinating peek into the world of high-tech arms sales with a superb 5-3 report on negotiations to sell F-16 fighter aircraft to Taiwan. Generous, unspecified offsets were offered to assuage Taiwanese legislators after they "objected to the relatively high cost of the older-model F-16 A and B planes and the refusal of the United States to transfer technology along with the sale." In her absorbing 6-21 piece, Opall chronicles the shift from the several current ballistic missile defense programs to a single new Tactical Agile Missile (TAGM) development program. If spending for the TAGM receives approval, she reports, the Pentagon hopes to save money by consolidating development and production costs. In her compelling 10-18 story on NAFTA, Opall finds that the feeling among defense contractors mirrors that of many industries. "NAFTA will enable us to drive our costs down and grab hold of new markets." Consistently producing riveting and engaging articles on the international arms trade and on state-of-the-art defense technology, Opall truly graces the pages of *Defense News*.

Richard N. Ostling

Time

★★½

Religion. Well-sourced and balanced, Ostling covers both spiritual trends and the politics of religion. His 4-5 story on the efforts of various churches to adapt to a new market of customers builds on a compelling premise—that churches are bending too far from their traditional models in order to attract the growing number of baby-boomers of restored but uncertain faith—yet in searching for an answer yields only vague observations. "Though strict, doctrinaire religion might seem to drive away the tolerance-minded boomers, liberalism fares even worse. When the faith replaces firm claims to truth with a spongy, homemade folk religion, younger members seem to take it as an invitation to look elsewhere." Ostling's 10-4 review of Pope John Paul II's encyclical on right and wrong discovers no surprises in its content, but expresses uneasiness with its tone. "While John Paul's list of social and sexual malevolences comes as no surprise, the sweeping nature of his condemnation as well as his demand of obedience are certain to send tremors through the ranks of the church's liberal wing....There were rumors that the document would be couched in terms of papal infallibility, making opposition impermissible. While that has not turned out to be the case, dissent is virtually forbidden." Amidst growing concern within the Catholic church about the sexual misconduct of priests, 7-5, Ostling zeroes in on the crux of the dilemma. "The church's role as the dispenser of forgiveness has hampered and may continue to intrude on its ability to deal with the problem [of pedophilia]. Says a church official in Rome: 'When a man comes in either admitting to or accused of inappropriate behavior, what can you do?...Often he is contrite, bewildered and offers all the requisite assurances that it won't ever happen again. Unfortunately what we're learning from scientific research is that pedophilia is a recidivist activity, so it probably will happen again.'" In his 12-6 profile of John Cardinal Ratzinger—considered the number two man in the political and spiritual hierarchy of the Church—Ostling captures the overwhelming power of his subject. "Ratzinger's behind-the-scenes interrogations and investigations exert a subtle chill on Catholic intellectual life. His actions imposed an 11-month 'penitential silence' on Leonardo Boff, Brazil's exponent of liberation theology....They also led to the removal of Charles Curran, a proponent of birth control, from teaching theology at the Catholic University of America." Treading on turf other reporters consistently avoid, Ostling offers insightful and dispassionate analysis of spiritual and institutional church matters.

Ronald J. Ostrow

Los Angeles Times

★★½

Justice department. Chronicling the turmoil at Justice, Ostrow delivers useful and serviceable reports. Yet the complexities of the long-term effects of the raid in Waco, Texas, the William Sessions probe, and Janet Reno's leadership seem out of his reach. He renders a sensible 1-17 recounting of the allegations made against FBI Director William Sessions due to misuse of office privileges. Ostrow offers a brief aside on what the incoming administration plans to do—which is nothing—as "some [aides] had privately expressed the belief that Sessions, 62, would voluntarily step down in the next year or so." His 2-1 effort, co-authored by Douglas Frantz, basically provides a forum for unnamed sources within the FBI to air their gripes against Sessions. The pair does, nonetheless, carefully examine different points on the whole fuss. Ostrow improves his coverage of the endgame, his 7-17 roundup of Sessions's imminent dismissal even containing some

strategic implications of the firing. In a 4-20 dispatch, Ostrow seems numbed by the events in Waco, examining adequately Janet Reno's cleanup after the torching of the Branch Davidians' compound. With his 5-16 review of Janet Reno's early performance, Ostrow buys into the conventional wisdom of the day but adds interest by examining how the Attorney General might spend her political capital at Justice. Finally, he finishes the story with a straight-faced 10-3 piece on the delayed release of a report on the affair. Ostrow notes that the release of the document has been delayed because it contains conversations from wiretaps within the compound, and that this information will be used at the trial of the survivors. Hence, the information can't be released. In a brisk, competent 8-11 dispatch, Ostrow and co-author John Broder detail the contents of the pieces of the letter found at the bottom of Vince Foster's briefcase. The pair reports that Foster was on anti-depressant medication prescribed by an Arkansas doctor. Always informative, Ostrow just needs to provide a little more depth and context.

Andy Pasztor

The Wall Street Journal

★★

Pentagon. Rather than breaking new ground, Pasztor devotes his energy to covering on-going domestic defense issues. His accounts, in turn, seem pedestrian this year. In his 9-13 report on the failure in a key test of the seriously overbudget C-17 cargo plane, he writes, "McDonnell Douglas Corp.'s C-17 transport, with years of cost overruns and technical problems, incurred yet another potential setback during ground tests of the plane's wings last Friday." Pasztor also reports ably on the Pentagon's continuing investigation of improper activity among defense contractors. Pasztor's 8-2 dispatch on Grumman's alleged overcharging for NASA hardware yields an important fact. "Prosecutors are considering seeking felony charges covering not only Grumman's dealings with NASA but wrongdoing involving the earlier Navy contracts and influence-peddling by former Grumman Chairman John O'Brien." Following up several years of his coverage on "Operation Ill Wind," the Pentagon's investigation of bribery among many defense contractors, Pasztor succinctly wraps up the story in a 9-24 article that places it in historical perspective. "For the government, a Litton plea would end Ill Wind on a high note, without a single major corporate target of the probe contesting government charges in a trial. Long before investigators decided to take action against Litton...Ill Wind had become the most sweeping probe of military bribery and influence-peddling since the Teapot Dome scandal of the 1920s." In his 8-30 effort, co-authored by Jeff Cole, Pasztor covers Defense Secretary Les Aspin's plans for downsizing the military and its potential effect on private industry. "While some existing programs are bound to shrink under Mr. Aspin's proposal, for many companies it may be the only way to retain top-notch scientists, engineers and at least a stripped-down manufacturing base during a period of severe Pentagon budget cuts." But despite these occasional bursts of insight, Pasztor's enthusiasm for Pentagon issues seems to be waning.

Robert Pear

The New York Times

★★½

Health care. A legendary reporter—at the office early and late, reading, reviewing, and working the phones—Pear moves from covering defense to health-care reform, his daily reports often making the front page. Perhaps because of his preoccupation with breaking news, however, he fails to probe the feasibility of and desire for reform. In his detailed 3-18 effort on the legalities of federal approval of Oregon's health-care reforms, Pear oddly enough fails to convey much about the reforms themselves, leaving the reader wondering whether the government has taken the right position. His 2-18 examination of Medicare identifies key problems in the program but fails to connect them to health-care reform. In his 4-19 story, co-authored by David E. Rosenbaum, on the potential cost of President Clinton's proposed health-care plan, Pear puts the amount at no more than $90 billion annually; other sources predict $100 billion, at least. He supplies solid information in his 5-5 dispatch explaining that the Congressional Budget Office still doesn't know how much the stripped-down version of Clinton's vaccine program will cost. "The administration never recommended a specific way to pay for its proposal, saying it would offer suggestions later as part of a comprehensive plan to revamp the nation's health-care system." Pear's careful 7-8 story reports data from a *New England Journal of Medicine* study that found higher mortality rates for the poor, but he points out that the nature of health care isn't the only factor influencing these rates. Pear returns to the topic of health-care reform costs in a 10-12 effort on how the administration hasn't produced an actual piece of legislation because the plan's numbers don't add up in a way that will be politically marketable on Capitol Hill. Unasked—and unanswered—is whether Clinton-style health-care reform should be undertaken at all. Perhaps this gifted journalist will examine this fundamental matter in 1994.

James M. Perry
The Wall Street Journal
★★★

Washington. Not missing a beat with the change in administrations, this veteran reporter files stories laden with information and cogent analysis that benefit from his years of experience. In his 1-28 essay examining the role of the new First Lady, he and co-author Jeffrey Birnbaum make a shrewd observation. "Like Eleanor Roosevelt, Mrs. Clinton will be in the eye of the storm—criticized for her own actions and singled out as the most vulnerable target for hurting her husband." Perry expertly crafts thumbnail sketches, 5-19, of three Clinton policy whizzes—Andrew Cuomo, Ellen Frost, and Thomas Lovejoy—supplying information about their backgrounds and what they hope to accomplish. Although obviously moved by the depth of emotion expressed by some of Vince Foster's colleagues, Perry keeps a circumspect, professional distance in his 7-23 report on Foster's suicide that indulges in neither speculation nor emotion. In his detailed 9-23 dispatch, Perry takes a look back at the American Medical Association's big fight in the 1940s over adding health care to Social Security. "The battle to bring compulsory, nationalized health care to the American people is the longest, nastiest, costliest legislative struggle in history. Now, with President Clinton's proposal, it has reached a new, and possibly decisive, climax." Perry rounds out the year with excellent reports on the nation's two pivotal gubernatorial elections. He paints a sharply defined picture of the craziness of the Virginia race, 10-15, highlighting several major issues—something political reporters often overlook when colorful personalities are involved. And his solid 11-1 look at the contest between Gov. Jim Florio [D] and Christine Todd Whittman [R] in New Jersey provides an insightful account of the electorate's potential response to slick campaigning. "With voters grumbling that hardly any of the candidates seriously addressed their concerns—most of the job-seekers followed to the letter the strategies outlined by their handlers—low turnout was thought to be a big worry in all the big races." As difficult as parachute journalism can be, Perry makes it work.

Timothy M. Phelps
Newsday
★

Supreme Court. Although one of the two reporters to break Anita Hill's allegations against Clarence Thomas in 1991, Phelps is no legal beagle. Lacking expertise in the field of law, he settles for gathering a range of opinion and relaying it to his readers. His fine 1-10 effort exemplifies this approach: Phelps gets a broad array of viewpoints on the legal issues surrounding a *Soldier of Fortune* classified ad that led to a hired killing. And he crafts an effective 3-20 review of the political makeup of the Supreme Court as Justice Byron White announces his plans to retire, but he ignores substantive legal issues. Rather than probing the views of Lani Guinier in his light 5-23 profile, Phelps gauges how upset both Democrats and Republicans are over her views. While his 6-15 portrait of Ruth Bader Ginsburg digs up interesting details—such as the friendship between her husband and Ross Perot—it provides little information on her judicial philosophy. In a 6-20 follow-up, Phelps reveals his own biases in describing what worries him about Ginsburg: two of her closest friends are Antonin Scalia and Robert Bork. He offers another profile of Ginsburg, 7-19, but again skimps on her judicial record. Phelps's 10-4 effort superficially recites upcoming cases on women's issues, such as sexual harassment. A month later, he performs a purely political examination of the decision on *Harris v. Hardy*, in which the Court ruled unanimously that "women do not have to

prove psychological or other injuries to win damages" for sexual harassment charges. Further, Phelps shows no interest in the legal implications, except to note that lawyers think it won't stop frivolous lawsuits. Hampered by this disinterest in—if not ignorance of—legal issues, Phelps can't rise above the pack.

Art Pine

Los Angeles Times

★★

Washington. A versatile reporter, Pine moves easily from one story to the next, constructing solid overviews of issues confronting the administration. His most substantive work concerns military downsizing. In a 3-12 effort on a Westinghouse plant in Baltimore, which converted from military to commercial production "without help from the federal government," Pine cuts to the heart of President Clinton's latest defense-industry panacea. "The thrust behind Thursday's effort [to release $1.4 billion in defense conversion funds] appeared to be political, designed to divert attention from an announcement expected today outlining the Administration's recommendations for military base closings in 1993." Pine follows this up with a fascinating 4-5 report on how the government impedes conversion, taking a navy air base in Beesville, Texas, as a case in point. "Like many communities are finding across the country, the biggest challenge in the base-closing nightmare is...getting the government to turn over the property so the community can put its recovery plan into action quickly enough to reduce the economic impact of the closure....Efforts to obtain an 'interim' lease to enable commercial tenants to use portions of the base pending final disposition ran into difficulties that added months to the transfer process. And new legislation concerning the Pentagon's liability for environmental damage has slowed the process even more. As a result, the Chase Field project already has lost three prospective tenants, with an estimated 100 to 300 new jobs." Pine's work on other military issues, while serviceable, often lacks the detail and flair of those two articles. In an informed 1-31 discussion on the pros and cons of removing the gay ban in the military, Pine carefully examines the ease—and difficulty—of instituting change. Although providing only a peripheral evaluation of overall strategy in Somalia, 6-12, he thoroughly reports on how the UN forces responded to the ambush that killed 23 Pakistani soldiers. Similarly, Pine's 7-3 update, while providing important background on the skirmish that cost the lives of three UN peacekeepers, offers no real exploration of strategy. And he delivers a solid, though simple, 10-2 report on the official request that Admiral Frank B. Kelso be dismissed over the Tailhook controversy. As a *Wall Street Journal* veteran, Pine remains much sharper on the business—rather than on political or strategic—aspects of defense.

Dana Priest

The Washington Post

★★

Health care. New to this beat at the *Post*, Priest turns in a solid portfolio on health-care issues. Like so many reporters covering this subject, however, she does not question the need for major reform, but merely reports events and trial balloons as they come along. In her 2-23 review of eldercare reform, Priest barely examines the proposal or the reaction of those whom it would affect. She does not talk with health-care con-

KAL - CARTOONISTS AND WRITERS SYNDICATE © 1993.

sumers other than representatives of the AARP, who aren't necessarily representative of the elderly population. In her 3-9 "Health Care Primer," Priest carefully outlines the effects that the rules and potential changes in health care would have on the consumer. "Although conventional private-practice medicine would continue to exist, the designers of managed competition believe most people would be enrolled in 'managed care' type plans, such as health maintenance organizations, because traditional 'fee-for-service' medicine would become relatively more expensive." In her 4-10 effort, Priest gets the jump on fleshing out Clinton's idea of a "health security" card—not unveiled officially until September. "With a health security card, an individual could change or transfer health plans at the workplace or in the local satellite office of the health insurance cooperative, which might be located in a shopping mall....The card would also assist in streamlining administration and reducing paperwork." Priest's 6-9 dispatch provides important data on the administration's trial balloon of a report card both for different HMOs and for plans operated by the government. She supplies an enlightening 7-14 report on which organizations—in order to better lobby on health care—give to which PACs that in turn give to which candidates. Short on context, however, Priest's report fails to mention which lobbyists prove most successful. And in her detailed 10-9 roundup, she discusses economics, noting that "[Clinton's health-care] package seems to shift a couple billion dollars a day." With her information and insight, Priest is a reporter whose star is on the rise.

Paul Proctor

Aviation Week & Space Technology

★★★

Northwest U.S. bureau chief. Returning to the United States from Hong Kong, the talented Proctor continues to provide strong coverage of aviation trends and developments worldwide. Based in Redmond, Washington, he often zeroes in on issues facing Boeing's commercial aircraft operations. Proctor's absorbing 2-22 report explores the burgeoning market in China and Hong Kong for Heliservices—a Hong Kong company offering helicopter charters—and for the helicopters they use. Proctor finds that the "company is prying open a new market in cross-border charters to China and planning a shuttle between downtown and Hong Kong's new Chek Lap Kok airport." This market, Proctor notes, seems sure to grow as unification between Hong Kong and China gets closer. In his solid 3-15 synopsis of USAir's operations strategy, Proctor finds that after two years of downsizing, "the airline is starting to see the results...while other U.S. and international carriers just now are slashing operations." USAir's early moves to stem red ink, Proctor discovers, have ensured that aircraft orders with Boeing face no danger of cancellation. Delivering a detailed 4-19 update on the Boeing 777, he reveals the meat behind improvements in design. "Use of digital, three-dimensional interactive design techniques has cut re-work and factory floor changes by more than 50 percent compared to the 767." These production and design changes, Proctor notes, allow customization for each airline, and may cut production costs significantly. In his far-ranging 10-4 report on aeromedical service operators and their reaction to the Clinton administration's health plan, Proctor shows that his beat extends beyond Boeing. He reports that if "Congress recognizes the value of quick-response helicopters in saving lives, reducing hospital stays and covering rural areas, the new health care plan could be a boon." However, Proctor points out, aeromedical services companies refuse to take legislative chances, and are reducing costs and increasing the efficiency of their services. Proctor makes the transition to the Northwest bureau smoothly. Continuing to deliver superb reports on the state of commercial aviation, Proctor's forays into aeromedical transport showcase his versatility.

Paul Quinn-Judge

The Boston Globe

★★★

National security. A veteran foreign and diplomatic correspondent, Quinn-Judge views national security issues from various angles, lending both depth and dimension to his work. Even his spot news reports generally contain a tidbit of strategic value. In his solid 1-18 spot dispatch, Quinn-Judge places the U.S. attack on Baghdad in strategic context. Some American allies, he contends, partic-

ularly Islamic states such as Turkey, grumble about the U.S.'s trigger-happy nature when it comes to attacking Muslims in Iraq. This stands in stark contrast to American unwillingness to intervene and defend them in Bosnia. In a prescient 2-26 dispatch, he renders a sharp explanation of why Somalia might become a "Lebanon-style quagmire" for American soldiers. "U.S. troops are facing what seems, on the surface, to be a haphazardly organized bunch of tattered street fighters with no motivation other than a mild narcotic known as qat. As such, they have tended to be dismissed as an occasionally lethal but generally minor irritant. But the gunmen have many advantages over the well-trained and superbly equipped Americans. They are fighting on their own terrain and have no lack of weapons. They are totally indistinguishable from those around them. And the Western troops facing them know little if anything about their language or customs, to say nothing of their leaders' plans and ambitions." Similarly, Quinn-Judge incorporates opinion on strategy in a cogent 10-5 report of the skirmish in which 12 U.S. servicemen died and General Mohammad Farah Aidid captured Officer Michael Durant. Quinn-Judge provides snapshots of life in Sarajevo after a year of siege, 4-5, the most telling images in this evocative story describing the relaxed multiethnic communities before the war, and the deep schisms now that will likely last for years. Although he gets plenty of facts for his 9-2 essay on the latest military reduction and reshuffling of personnel, Quinn-Judge fails to glean information from either military officials or strategic experts on how cutbacks might affect national security or world peace. Such omissions aside, however, Quinn-Judge usually hits the mark.

Robert Reinhold

The New York Times

Los Angeles. Writing both news and features, Reinhold emphasizes the politics underlying Southern Californian culture and economics. Although at times he reveals his own views, he avoids partisanship and preaching. In his fascinating 3-16 report, Reinhold explains that petitions to place the gnatcathcer, a tiny bird, on the endangered species list could lead to years of litigation and render valueless privately owned land. At the same time, he notes, environmentalists recognize that the long-term solution to species survival may lie in preserving habitats in which threatened creatures live. As a result, "developers, conservationists and Federal and state officials are working together to preserve an entire ecosystem, rather than haggling over emergency measures prescribed by the Endangered Species Act to save single species." As experts foresee the end of the California droughts, 2-25, Reinhold reports the formation of strategic alliances among competing interests vying for their share of runoff from the snowpack, which provides water to the state. "Water authorities in thirsty Southern California found themselves in league with their arch enemies in Northern California and the environmental movement to fight the farmers, who consume more than 80 percent of the available surface water." In a thinly veiled 4-7 attack on L.A. mayoral candidate Richard Riordan, Reinhold writes, "A bundle of energy and contradictions, Mr. Riordan has bought his way into Los Angeles politics with a combination of charm, determination and money." Rather than explore issues, Reinhold merely cites one pundit who claims that if Riordan wins, "'the next mayor may be another white male establishment figure.'" In a lofty summer series assessing the future of Southern California, Reinhold posits, 8-24, that this region "will demonstrate whether it will be possible to transform the American economy from one based on cold war military spending to one based on peace." He includes startling statistics—roughly half the 2 million immigrants entering the U.S. each year come to Southern California—and evocatively quotes Nathanael West. "'Where else should they go but California, the land of sunshine and oranges? Once there, they discover that sunshine isn't enough.'" Reinhold's wide-ranging and resourceful reporting results in stories as diverse in subject matter as in quality.

William C. Rempel

Los Angeles Times

★★★

Staff writer. With an engaging style, Rempel pens detailed and dramatic accounts of issues ranging from the investigation of the World Trade Center bombing to the alleged soirees of then-Governor Bill Clinton. In his 3-22 story of how ATF agents pieced together enough clues to make a quick arrest in the Trade Center bombing, Rempel chillingly describes the blast's immediate impact. "A seven-ton steel beam, secured with welds and rivets, was ripped away and launched like a giant, crude arrow. Fifty feet across the parking chamber, it slammed through a brick wall that collapsed onto the last lunch shared by four maintenance workers in the locker room on the other side." Drawing on recent success stories from a new strategy for battling drug cartels, 7-4, Rempel masterfully reveals the techniques used to follow the money instead of seizing drugs. "In an investigation that would be a trial run...Customs Service Agents identified the biggest cash depositors in [Manhattan zip code 10036]. They found the New York Telephone Co., *The New York Times*, major Times Square retail stores—and Luis Roges, a small-time Cuban gold wholesaler in the jewelry district. 'We found records of $90 million in cash deposits, and we looked at each other and said: 'Who the hell is this guy' said Customs Service Investigator Thomas McMahon." In his 12-21 tome, co-authored by Douglas Frantz, on allegations made by Arkansas troopers of Clinton's extra-marital activities, Rempel yields considerable information, but struggles to distance himself from his sources. He makes solid use of public records—which seem to corroborate the troopers' stories—but shows little of the narrative confidence which distinguishes his other work. His precise 11-7 account of the Clintons' dealings with failed thrift-operator James McDougal, again co-authored by Frantz, balances the White House denials with terrific first-hand information provided by McDougal himself. Of the alleged interview where Clinton jogged to McDougal's office to ask him to hire his wife Hillary, Rempel writes, "McDougal said he recalled the event vividly because he was so uncomfortable in the meeting—not over the retainer issue, but because throughout the morning conference, Clinton sat sweating in McDougal's new leather desk chair, an expensive gift from his wife." Time and again Rempel brings to life the fruit of his exhaustive investigative work.

Spencer Rich
The Washington Post
½★

Department of Health and Human Services. During a year in which the health-care issue grabs center stage, Rich provides neither the information nor the insight to advance the debate. It seems that it takes all his efforts just to keep up. In his otherwise standard 2-13 dispatch, co-authored by Ann Devroy, Rich provides a fascinating tidbit from a Merck spokesperson who asserts that the high cost of children's vaccines results from a federal excise tax. Rich offers only the barest information in a 3-20 report on the approval of Oregon's health-care reforms, failing even to list what Medicaid in the state won't cover. In his superficial 4-7 account, he rehashes a Health and Human Services report that describes how Medicare will go belly-up in 1999. He recycles another report, 5-20, this one by the Economic and Social Research Institute, that supports a payroll tax-based health plan. Rich jumps the gun by sketching how such a system might work but doesn't examine any of the elements in detail. In his 7-8 effort, Rich tells the reader nothing beyond the *New England Journal of Medicine* studies on the linkage of death rates to education and income. In a respectable 10-20 article, he and co-author Thomas B. Edsall not only outline the General Accounting Office study questioning the savings of managed-care health plans, but provide various reactions to it. In his lightweight 6-11 essay on Hillary Rodham Clinton's speech to the centennial symposium of Johns Hopkins Medical School, Rich at least talks to some unnamed administration sources—instead of just relying on the text of her speech—but still offers little substance. Although a great deal transpires at HHS and in health policy, you'll find scant evidence of it in Rich's dispatches.

Paul Richter
Los Angeles Times
★★½

Staff writer, Washington. Richter provides no-nonsense dispatches chock-full of information, and he shows signs of developing a talent for political analysis. In his curt, but sufficient, 1-13 report on the incoming President's restructuring of his campaign promises, Richter notes that "Clinton and his staff began trying to lower expectations about his plans

even before he won the election." Richter crafts an effective 7-10 essay on Clinton's use of policy incentives to woo California and thereby capture its electoral votes in 1996, contending that "as the California economy has continued to sputter and the effects of the defense contraction have become clearer, it is apparent that the Administration's goals for the state are going to be more difficult to achieve than it had appeared six months ago." In his 2-11 review of the President's first town-hall meeting, Richter praises Clinton's telegenic talents, observing sharply that "with his relaxed command of the issues and his ability to discuss complex problems in terms of ordinary citizens' lives, Clinton demonstrated that the mantle of the presidency has only added to his mastery of the town meeting format." Richter's tight 5-28 dispatch ably conveys Clinton's defensive posture at a "sometimes prickly" town meeting after Hairgate and Travelgate. Culling information from different congressional sources, 4-29, Richter solidly outlines the difficulties Clinton might have with the scaled-down national service program. And his well-rounded 6-15 report of Clinton's nomination of Ruth Bader Ginsburg provides a balanced view of the press conference announcing her selection, as well as reaction from various lobbying groups. However, in his emotional 9-17 account of the White House Rose Garden meeting between the Clintons and 15 people (out of 700,000) who wrote them letters on the health-care plan, Richter stops just short of crossing over into a public relations effort. Politics has been quite a switch for this one-time business reporter. For the most part, Richter has adjusted nicely.

Steven V. Roberts

U.S.News & World Report

★½

Senior writer, Washington. Roberts pens broad overviews that suffice as newsweekly fare, but are only a shadow of the dispatches he used to turn out for *The New York Times*. His 3-22 effort on Rep. Ron Dellums [D-CA] fails to capture either his vibrant personality or his views. Roberts then takes a bleak 4-26 look at Los Angeles. Yet for all the detail he provides in outlining the tensions, he scarcely looks at the "concerned" black middle class that he mentions briefly or offers any solutions to the problems plaguing the city. In his strange 5-3 essay on David Koresh and the Branch Davidians, Roberts vainly attempts to link Waco with Bosnia. "Waco and Bosnia. David Koresh and Slobodan Milosevic. One driven by religious zeal, the other by nationalist blood lust. But these two places, and these two men, present civilized people with basically the same questions: How does society deal with a messianic personality who resists all attempts at persuasion and pressure? What should people make of the leader who laughs at their attempts to halt his limitless yearning for power or paradise? What happens when a madman repeatedly calls their bluff?" While the questions may be provocative, Roberts makes no attempt to provide answers. His 6-28 essay doesn't quite capture Ruth Bader Ginsburg, perhaps because he tries to classify her as either a centrist or liberal. In his superficial 8-2 effort examining the political implications of a potential indictment of Rep. Dan Rostenkowski [D-IL] in the House Post Office scandal, Roberts never addresses in detail the substance of the charges. He argues speciously that because Rostenkowski has so much money in his campaign fund, he wouldn't bother with the comparatively small amount of cash involved. Really? Roberts does note, however, that "if Rostenkowski is indicted, he must step aside as Ways and Means chairman, and the result could be chaos for Clinton's domestic agenda." On the whole, it seems that Roberts prefers to coast at *U.S.News*.

Paul M. Rodriguez

The Washington Times

★★★

National and congressional investigations. Since the story broke in 1992, Rodriguez has been a leading source on the House Post Office scandal and the investigation of Rep. Dan Rostenkowski [D-IL]. He covers new developments assiduously and thoroughly. In his 3-8 report, he pinpoints the political aspects of the probe. "Complicating matters is the uncertain status of the chief prosecutor in the case, Mr. [Jay B.] Stephens, a Republican appointee who could be removed from office any day and replaced by a Clinton administration nominee." Amassing all the details in a sharp 7-20 dispatch, Rodriguez relates the plea of former House Postmaster Robert Rota and his agreement to testify "about a conspiracy with at least two unnamed congressmen to embezzle public funds." One "is said to be" Rostenkowski, the other, former Rep. Joe Kolter [D-PA]. In two revealing reports, 7-21 and 7-23, Rodriguez comes up with the data on the potential release of information by the House Postal Task Force and the final decision to keep this data private. "Mr. Rostenkowski's attorney's had placed at least one call to an unnamed Justice Department official and sought to delay the Rota plea agreement until after a joint House-Senate conference committee completes work on President Clinton's $500 billion budget package." Rodriguez later delivers a respectable 8-5 review of Rep. Ernest Istook's [R-OK] attempt to "force the ethics committee to investigate embezzlement and other improprieties at the House post office." In a series of tough dispatches, 10-12, 10-13, and 10-21, Rodriguez keeps on top of the missing Rostenkowski files of "possible ghost employees" on the Congressman's staff. His 10-20 report announces that, although "full details" are forthcoming, "the grand jury is looking at the relationship between Mr. Rostenkowski and several of his political associates, with whom he has had business and other dealings. 'There's a lot of interest in the flow of money' to several of Mr. Rostenkowski's campaign and political action committees and 'deals involving' local and federal legislation, the source said." Rodriguez sticks to the story as few other reporters do.

David Rogers

The Wall Street Journal

★½

Washington. Aspiring to provide the inside angle on Beltway players and personalities, Rogers concentrates on the human side—the emotions and psyches—of his subjects in his frequent contributions to WSJ's "Politics and Policy" column. Although revealing at times, Rogers struggles to convey the broader significance of his subjects. In his rich 9-24 piece on the fund-raising-oversight activities of Rep. Bob Carr [D-MI], the new chairman of the House appropriations panel that controls transportation funds, Rogers uses Carr's trip log in Florida to show the relationship between power and campaign contributions. "In Jacksonville, Mr. Carr met with city airport and transportation officials before a luncheon fundraiser at a downtown club; the event was organized by the local counsel for the transit authority and brought in about $10,000." Sketching a composite picture of the Clinton team, his 1-21 piece co-authored by Rick Wartzman finds some irony in the highly educated group with wallets bloated from the boom of the last decade. "Mr. Clinton seems to have imposed some standards that he is finding tough to meet. At a Detroit rally last fall, he lambasted the leveraged buyouts of the 1980s in which 'the people that were in the middle shuffling the paper made off with millions of dollars, and the American people got the shaft.' Yet weeks later, he appointed an economic team that included lawyers and Wall Street financiers who had profited by just such transactions." Such imaginative insights are nowhere apparent in Rogers's 6-10 profile of House Majority Leader Richard Gephardt [D-MO], which reads like campaign literature. "Mr. Gephardt's attitudes are deeply rooted in his background. From his mother, he inherited an almost religious optimism. His late father, a milk truck driver between stints in insurance and real estate, taught a harder-edged resentment of the 'big shots' who controlled his fate, an anger that still surfaces in the Congressman's voice." Caught up in the flamboyance of Rep. Fortney "Pete" Stark [D-CA], chairman of the House Ways and Means health panel, 10-19, Rogers fails to offer a single comprehensible clue about where the central character in any health-care reform might lead. "Mr. Stark rarely misses a chance to put down the Clinton administration's health team. And even on his best behavior, he can't resist taking a bite out of the White House staff or 'goody two-shoes ...team-player' Sen. Jay Rockefeller [D-WV], his Democratic counterpart on the Senate Finance Committee." Lacking focus or a significant news hook, too much of Rogers's work relies on over-stylized and insignificant biographical tidbits.

Larry Rohter

The New York Times

★★½

Miami bureau chief. With his clear, straightforward style, Rohter provides balanced and comprehensive coverage of Florida issues that have national—and international—implications. Af-

ter 2 1/2 years on the beat, he has gained an impressive understanding of the competing factions in Miami's large Cuban population. His groundbreaking 6-27 piece reveals that "new voices calling for a more flexible attitude toward...Castro's Communist Government are emerging...and challenging the hegemony of established groups" —chiefly Jorge Mas Canosa's anti-Castro Cuban-American National Foundation. He adds, prudently, 10-6, that "moderate exiles say they are fearful that events on the island are developing faster than Washington's ability to absorb them." In his 8-8 piece, Rohter carefully weighs the various options for Puerto Rico—statehood, independence, or continued commonwealth status. The upcoming plebiscite, he writes, "comes at a moment when Puerto Ricans are being sharply reminded of their second-class colonial status....They watched impotently as the Clinton Administration and Congress, intent on reducing the budget deficit, hacked away at the corporate tax exemptions that have been the backbone of the local economy for the last 40 years." Rohter's 9-16 article succinctly captures the tension caused by the murder of Gary Colley, a British tourist who was killed at a highway rest stop east of Tallahassee. "Galvanized by the blizzard of negative publicity around the world...the authorities in Jefferson county, where Mr. Colley was killed, began a dragnet aimed at young blacks with criminal records, a move that immediately generated controversy." Rohter also displays a knack for tracking down the offbeat story. His 7-25 piece exposes a "network of legal exemptions from bankruptcy claims that have led Florida to be dubbed...'debtor's paradise.'" Rohter reports on one of these exemptions—"a state law [which] prohibits the seizure of a person's legal residence in bankruptcy proceedings, regardless of the value of the property." With thorough reporting and a concise style, Rohter ably provides out-of-towners and out-of-staters with an illuminating view of the Sunshine State.

Jeffrey Rosen

The New Republic

★★

Supreme Court. As *The New Republic*'s "courtwatcher" for the past two years, Rosen has become worthwhile reading for those who follow the high court and things judicial. Unfortunately, he too often reminds readers that he applied to all nine Supreme Court judges for a clerkship, and sometimes his prose descends into legalese. A sympathetic critic of the new administration, Rosen knows the law but also does fresh reporting, often crafting well-reasoned arguments. In his 4-12 article, Rosen criticizes retiring Justice Byron White because he lacks "constitutional vision." Rosen shows how White was influenced at Yale Law School by Myers McDougal, "the last great legal realist." McDougal, Rosen points out, believes that judges, in deciding cases, should consciously take into account societal attitudes. The enterprising Rosen interviews the now-86-year-old McDougal, who praises his former student. Well, someone has to praise White in this downbeat piece. Rapping the Clinton administration for its "affirmative action mentality" and "apparent lack of interest in legal philosophy," Rosen argues that the White House should think first and foremost about judicial philosophy as it searches for White's successor. He supplies a short list of names for the President, 5-10, concluding presciently with his personal favorite, Ruth Bader Ginsburg. His comprehensive 8-2 piece treats the split between feminists like Ginsburg, who argue for absolutely equal treatment for women, and "difference feminists" like legal writer Catharine MacKinnon, who argue for special treatment. In reference to abortion, Rosen writes, the latter "focus on what *is* unique about childbirth. They advocate special treatment for pregnant women based on their premise that men and women are not 'similarly situated' because of their reproductive differences." The Court applied this same premise in 1974, Rosen points out, to permit discrimination against pregnant women—effectively rejecting Ginsburg's equal treatment view. In perhaps his best work of the year—and also his briefest—Rosen analyzes the Court's confused religion-clause jurisprudence, 3-29. Advocating "a neutrality test" for church-state cases, Rosen contends that it "would give appealingly clear answers to the most controversial questions of church and state." As Clinton names more judges (and maybe some more Justices) to the federal bench, and as the nature of the government's legal arguments change under the Democratic administration, Rosen can be counted on for sharp and timely analysis.

David E. Rosenbaum
The New York Times
★

Washington. Although he less frequently and less blatantly abuses the term "news analysis" this year, Rosenbaum, the *Times*'s main chronicler of the 1993 budget battle, contributes little to readers' understanding of either the complex budget process or its important economic implications. He's more comfortable detailing the political haggling, as he does in his 5-23 report, a colorful account of the behind-the-scenes deals being struck by the administration. On economics, however, Rosenbaum's neither instructive nor dependable. Despite stating, 6-23, that "no one can predict accurately what the deficit will be five years from now," he obviously forgets this point six weeks later when he writes with confidence, 8-3, that the President's proposal "should make the deficit significantly lower over the next five years than it otherwise would be." Complementing this vague generalization with a partisan potshot, Rosenbaum continues: President Clinton "stepped up with real deficit-cutting proposals based on real numbers—not the gimmicks and black boxes of the Republican years." Clinton, of course, like his Republican predecessors, engaged in budget gimmickry. This sleight of hand includes the redefinition of income as Family Economic Income (FEI), which goes well beyond the traditional measure of a family's taxable income by adding such things as tax-exempt interest, employer contributions for health plans and life insurance, and "imputed rent" (the amount of money a family would take in by renting out their house). Although such a measure could potentially add tens of thousands of dollars to a family's "income," Rosenbaum never mentions FEI in any of his dozens of articles on the budget. His fall coverage of the congressional debate over NAFTA emphasizes the glitz of politics while skimming the nitty-gritty economics. Typical is his 11-18 report on the House's approval of the trade agreement, which devotes an inordinate amount of space to sketching the emotional polarization over this issue, but little on NAFTA's potential economic impact. Those looking for an engaging read on the dog-fights that occur as economic legislation moves through the congressional blender will probably enjoy Rosenbaum's lively descriptions. However, those interested in understanding the legislation under consideration will be sorely disappointed.

Howard Rosenberg
The Los Angeles Times
★★★

Television. Smart and perceptive, Rosenberg crafts stylish reviews of TV shows and trends, producing columns both witty and quotable. In his 9-15 tribute to the late actor Raymond Burr, he aptly describes the "trademark, predictable confession sequence" of the old "Perry Mason" series as "TV's caviar of camp." In his 5-20 criticism of the heavy hype over the final episode of NBC's popular series, "Cheers," Rosenberg states, "If one word characterizes TV-driven popular culture, it's excess—the steroidal massing that comes from going too far, artificially swelling something beyond what's natural." Noting with disdain the proliferation of newsmagazine shows, 8-20, he derides KCAL's "Live in L.A.," remarking "This is a case of the format sucking the brains from the individuals, rendering them Stepford Hosts." Going beyond TV as popular culture, Rosenberg examines the medium's impact on news and events—as in his 11-11 coverage of a televised NAFTA debate. "The giant sucking sound you heard Tuesday was not Mexico drawing away U.S. jobs. It was [Al] Gore and [Ross] Perot having Larry King for dinner." In his startling 6-4 article, Rosenberg draws attention to the disturbing trend in broadcast journalism for foreign and even domestic news to be reported *off* location. He points out that it sounds as if the reporter is on the scene, until the moment the byline is given. Rosenberg notes a few examples: In the premiere edition of the "CBS Evening News" with co-anchors Dan Rather and Connie Chung, a story on bloodshed in Bosnia was produced in New York; and one on firebombings in Germany was produced in London. When correspondents work at a distance from the events they cover, Rosenberg contends, it is "more likely that the reporting will be shallow." He further notes with alarm "the kind of

crossover between reporting and editorializing that TV reporters are increasingly allowed to include in the tags of their stories." In two pieces, 5-28 and 7-1, Rosenberg argues that TV violence does not beget real-life violence, but he fails to address psychological and sociological studies that support the connection. Such lapses, however, prove rare. Tuned in to both TV and the outside world, Rosenberg provides the caviar of critiques.

Thomas B. Rosenstiel

Los Angeles Times

★½

Media. Rosenstiel's most informative columns focus on one of the central themes of his new book, *Strange Bedfellows*: the impact of the "new media" on politics and on politicians' efforts to control the news. Unlike his multifaceted book, however, Rosenstiel's work this year seldom offers more than a single main point, a point that often shifts with his own point of view. In his lengthy 5-16 piece, he looks at how the "kids" running the White House communications corps are "bypassing the old media, the national press corps, in favor of the new media, Larry King, town halls and satellite technology." Rosenstiel scornfully puts down these twentysomethings for their "arrogance," for their naiveté, and for viewing "their inexperience as a strength." Obsessed with computers and video screens, he opines, these "techno brats" care little for substance in their quest to control the image and thereby "control...the agenda." Rosenstiel undermines this convincing critique in his 5-30 profile of—or rather, tribute to—David Gergen, Clinton's new adviser. Instead of manipulating the media like the techno brats, this "moderate...intellectual...political technician" shines at "orchestrating news coverage." Get the difference? Because Gergen is competent and approachable (and respects traditional media), Rosenstiel applauds his efforts to shape the headlines. He notes conservatives' suspicions "that Gergen was too cozy with reporters"—a suspicion this puff piece supports. Such coziness becomes downright worshipful in his 7-14 article elevating Gergen toward "the pantheon of presidential 'wise men' who left a mark on their times." Even overlooking this hagiography, what is the reader to make of such phrases as "Republican-like skill" and, in light of the 1992 campaign, "Republican-style unity"? Such caveats aside, Rosenstiel quotes an impressive array of sources, and he can provoke thought. Commenting, 8-31, on Clinton's second local satellite press conference, "one curious trend emerged: The smaller the news organization, the more policy-oriented the question. The larger the local news organization, the more political the question." Such provocative nuggets confirm Rosenstiel's legitimate fascination with the "new media."

Michael Ross

Los Angeles Times

Capitol Hill. Ross fashions overviews that seldom get beneath the surface of events. Since he doesn't dig, sometimes he comes off plain disinterested in his subjects. In his 1-23 effort, Ross relates a serpentine tale of wrongdoing on President Reagan's allegedly providing covert aid to rebels in Laos during the 1980s. However, he fails to sort things out from documents now available, leaving the entire issue murky. Ross reveals little in his 3-3 take on the "testy exchange" as Ross Perot testified before Congress. He crafts an accurate, but light, 5-12 political review of the ending of the GOP Senate filibuster over the Motor Voter Bill. Although he adds color to his utilitarian 6-25 dispatch on the end of the supercollider by quoting an unnamed critic who calls the project a Tyrannosaurus Rex roaming through "Jurassic Pork," Ross just can't get excited about it. In a superficial 7-3 summary of President Clinton's non-opposition to the French-Japanese refinancing deal for Vietnam's loans to the IMF, Ross fails to probe the larger implications. Conversely, his well-rounded 10-13 dispatch on the Somalia debates between Clinton and Congress culls insightful quotes from Representatives who are getting negative feedback from constituents. Still, he looks less at the fine points of the policy than at the breakdown of the votes. Ross might benefit from a greater interest in Washington.

David G. Savage

Los Angeles Times

★★½

Supreme Court. Improving dramatically on this beat, Savage files substantive dispatches on the Supreme Court and on legal issues in general. In his 2-

25 effort, he meticulously explains the potential effects of the asset-seizures ruling on confiscation of properties purchased with drug money. Savage delivers a balanced 4-20 examination of the case of Margaret Kelly Michaels, a day-care worker whose conviction of child molestation was overturned because the testimony of the children may have been coached. In a clear-eyed, sharply defined 5-22 dispatch, Savage cuts through the muck to give examples of how Lani Guinier's ideas on race and voting might be implemented and how her nomination will be affected by conservative complaints. And his lively 7-22 review of Ruth Bader Ginsburg's testimony before the Senate Judiciary Committee notes her succinct comment on women and abortion. "'Men are not similarly situated. They don't bear the children.'" Savage pens a clear 8-27 review of the proposed change in the Habeas Corpus Act, which "would reverse a recent Supreme Court ruling that declared inmates facing execution are not entitled to an eleventh-hour hearing to submit 'newly discovered evidence of actual innocence.'" Although lacking in-depth analysis, the article yields a vast amount of information. Savage's solid 10-2 effort looks at the impact Clinton's health-care plan will have on malpractice insurance for doctors and hospitals. Going the extra mile by examining a broad range of ideas on the subject, Savage concludes that "none of [Clinton's] proposals would dramatically lower costs for the health care industry." Savage has come into his own on this beat.

Jeffrey Schmalz
The New York Times
★★½

Before his AIDS-related death on November 6, 1993, at age 39, Schmalz had pioneered a new and controversial domain of mainstream journalism—issues affecting gays and lesbians. Covering such topics as the ban on gays in the military and opposition to gay rights by religious conservatives, he provided detailed accounts that sometimes evinced his own sympathies. Schmalz will be most remembered for bringing the AIDS story to the front pages of *The New York Times*. His 6-13 profile of Dr. Nicholas Rango, former coordinator of AIDS policy in New York State (and who would die of AIDS four days after Schmalz) reveals the connection between the personal and the political in the gay community. "[Rango] is at once the administrator and the administered, the bureaucrat fighting AIDS on the grand scale and the gay man fighting it alone in his hospital bed." Schmalz tellingly quotes Rango. "'We all live on the edge of a volcano. It's just that when you have AIDS, your volcano is more active than other people's volcanoes.'" In his 5-7 piece on a Hawaii Supreme Court decision that recognized gay marriage, Schmalz notes that "the court has tended to use the State Constitution to impose broader rights than those interpreted...by the United States Supreme Court." He thoroughly discusses the possible implications of this case. "Each state recognizes marriages performed in another state. That means gay couples married in Hawaii would have to be recognized as married couples in other states." Schmalz's 4-27 piece, which lays out several tough challenges facing the gay-rights movement, comes too close to cheerleading with a concluding pep talk by Rep. Gerry Studds [D-MA]. "'[Those who attended April's gay-rights march] left transformed: proud and self-respecting...that's what will make for true political power.'" Schmalz's last article, a posthumously published 11-28 *Magazine* cover story called "Whatever Happened to AIDS?" begins: "I am getting weaker. Time is running out." After interviewing numerous people in the vanguard of AIDS research and policy, Schmalz writes of his increasing despair both at his own fate and at the frustrating search for a cure for AIDS. He also mourns the waning strength of the ACT-UP movement, which has been literally depopulated by AIDS deaths. Providing a readable primer on the conflict over different avenues of scientific research, Schmalz goes on to describe a strained moment in an interview with Kristine Gebbie, the national AIDS policy coordinator. "I asked Gebbie what she says to someone with AIDS—in other words, what she says to me. And for one brief moment, there was a glimmer of realization that delay means death." In a 5-24 *New York* interview with Edwin Diamond, Schmalz admits that he writes "with a bit of the voice of a gay man." Although that voice sometimes shaded his work, it was a voice undeniably heartfelt and professional, and one that will be deeply missed.

Eric Schmitt

The New York Times

★½

Pentagon. Focusing on the controversy over gays in the military, Schmitt files respectable and unbiased day-to-day reports on this volatile issue. Despite his high productivity, however, he fails to provide the reader with a sense of the larger issues involved. In his 1-13 dispatch on the ban, Schmitt quickly reviews the facts and gathers some quotes to conclude that gay activists refuse to cut Bill Clinton any slack on the issue. In his astute 4-1 account of the Senate Armed Services Committee hearings, Schmitt renders some useful insight. "The most provocative moments of the four-hour hearing came when speakers and senators sought to determine whether a unit's cohesion would be damaged just by its members' knowing that a fellow soldier was homosexual or if it would take overt homosexual behavior to cause disruption." Unfortunately, Schmitt doesn't offer anything conclusive either way. In his revealing 5-11 report, he boards a submarine to survey servicemen and women on the question of gay shipmates. While a majority support the ban, he finds a "'substantial minority,'" in the words of Sen. Sam Nunn [D-GA], who oppose it. On 5-12, Schmitt finds the first hint of the institutionalization of a "don't ask, don't tell" policy on gays in the military. Although he says the Clinton administration opposes the permanent use of this supposedly temporary compromise, Schmitt offers no evidence of Clinton coming up with anything better. Again, he provides a quick but respectable 8-21 review of the problems of prosecuting—or reprimanding—the accused men in the Tailhook case. Prosecutors, Schmitt explains, "fear that alcohol impaired memories, a code of silence among many pilots and scanty physical evidence may produce only a handful of convictions." In a spot 10-6 dispatch from the press briefing on Somalia, Schmitt doesn't address the deeper strategic concerns of military intervention. But he does relate a graphic account of how it took fresh troops nine hours to reach U.S. servicemen—a delay resulting in at least a dozen deaths. Although direct and clear-sighted, Schmitt could deliver in-depth reports if he asked more in-depth questions.

Elaine Sciolino

The New York Times

★★★

Washington. Breaking major news and providing insightful analysis, Sciolino's dispatches continually illuminate Washington's most pressing foreign policy issues. In easy-to-read and informative articles, she astutely examines the processes behind Clinton administration actions. Her 2-8 piece deftly assesses Clinton's foreign policy priorities. "The Administration, despite its early attention to crises in Bosnia, Somalia, Haiti and Iraq, has already begun to characterize the fate of Russia as the country's most important national security problem in the next decade." Sciolino further defines this subject, 6-1, adding a shrewd insight into the workings of the Clinton presidency. "Because of Mr. Clinton's determination not to become engulfed by foreign policy, he has taken what some senior officials describe as a two tier approach to the world. On top there is Russia, where he is applauded for being just as engaged as he is on health care....Below that is the rest of the world, which Mr. Clinton largely delegates to his national security advisor W. Anthony Lake and to [Secretary of State Warren] Christopher. The approach there has been largely to manage what the Administration inherited, to put a Clintonesque stamp on foreign policy in words, perhaps, but not yet in behavior." Writing about the conflict in Yugoslavia, Sciolino offers a cogent 5-12 analysis of why the U.S. and Europe have failed to devise a common approach to Bosnia. "Mr. Christopher was sent to Europe not with a plan of action but with only Mr. Clinton's general 'direction,' which was open not only for discussion but also for amendment. Mr. Clinton also ordered Mr. Christopher not to talk about the Administration's preferred strategy in public, which allowed the Europeans to fill the void by picking it apart." Sciolino ends the year, 12-21, chronicling a flaw in U.S. policy toward Russia, which may have led to election victories for extremist anti-reformers. "The Clinton Administration's top Russia specialist said today that the surprisingly large support for foes of reform in Russia's parliamentary elections last week showed that there had been too much emphasis on remaking the economy of Russia and not enough on improving the daily lives of its people." Here, as in many of her ground-breaking reports, Sciolino is right on target.

Gerald Seib

The Wall Street Journal

★½

Washington "Capitol Journal" columnist. Moving from the national security arena to politics in Washington, Seib offers sometimes-naïve work that falls short of his insightful writing in years past. He crafts a stock 1-13 dispatch on the founding of Empower America, whose mandate is "to seize intellectual leadership of the conservative movement in the wake of the Reagan and Bush years." Seib lists who's who at the organization, but neglects to relate what the group will actually do. Echoing Sen. Daniel Patrick Moynihan's [D-NY] essay on the decline of civility and the death of the social order, Seib canvasses other opinions to craft a rather discouraging 3-17 column. In his 4-14 essay, he finds Empower America's Jack Kemp to be the embodiment of a new kind of conservative—one who supports social policy but not the NRA. "This debate isn't so much about whether Mr. Kemp is sufficiently conservative, but whether he's the right kind of conservative to suit some activists. For Jack Kemp stands at the fault line of a much broader debate about the future of the conservative movement." Because Seib views the chances of a big GOP gain in 1994 Congressional seats through only the perspective of President Clinton and the Democratic party—rather than through the issues voters care about—his 6-9 analysis falls short. In his flawed 9-28 dispatch on the Virginia and New Jersey gubernatorial races, Seib sets up gun control as the winning issue, but then tries to cover himself. "It is entirely possible, of course, that for most voters concerns about guns today will give way to bread-and-butter economic issues by Election Day." Shrugging off Ed Rollins's admission that he bribed black ministers to sway their congregations from voting for Gov. Jim Florio [D-NJ], Seib simply accepts this as a fair campaign tactic. Without his foreign policy beat, Seib proves a far less compelling writer.

Jerry Seper

The Washington Times

★★½

Justice Department, drugs. Covering the new Justice Department, the Branch Davidian story, and the Madison Guaranty/Whitewater matter, Seper proves a prolific writer whose strength lies not in news analysis but in reporting—even advancing—the daily story. Few Justice reporters can match his law-enforcement sources, which enable him to break major stories. In his 1-31 dispatch, Seper aptly describes the heart of the problem of the second Rodney King trial in Los Angeles. "The key to the government's case, say lawyers familiar with it, will be the prosecution's ability to prove intent. Federal prosecutors must show that the four officers intentionally deprived King of his constitutional rights." Seper's 3-29 effort reports key statistics on drug convictions as compiled by the Justice Department's Bureau of Justice Statistics—49 percent of those arrested on drug charges are convicted—but Seper fails to place these statistics in a larger policy context. Two stories best demonstrate Seper's knack for the daily story: On 6-25, he details Attorney General Janet Reno's precedent-breaking decision to allow congressional interrogation of career Justice lawyers suspected of undermining prosecutions in environmental cases during the Bush years; and on 10-9, he reports Justice's internal review of the Department's role in the 51-day siege near Waco, Texas. One might think Seper's beat would keep him busy enough, but on 9-7 he files a superb A-1 story—reported nowhere else—on then-Governor Clinton's program to reinvent Arkansas state government. Seper shows that the program resulted in a significant loss of experienced personnel, produced only minor cost savings, and reduced the state government's ability to operate and deliver services. As the Madison/Whitewater story heats up at year's end, Seper becomes a reporter to watch, as his stories often make the front page. In his most notable scoop, 12-20, he breaks the news that Whitewater records were removed from the office of White House lawyer Vince Foster just hours after his suicide in July. On this ongoing story, as well as much else, Seper—pronounced with a long "e"—is no sleeper.

Tom Shales

The Washington Post

★★

Television. Forget the middle ground, Shales either loves it or hates it—and his reviews of TV

shows and personalities are often unabashed paroxysms of that love or hate. He repeatedly shows his contempt for newscaster Peter Jennings, whom he calls "hoity-toity," 1-21, and "Sir Blab-a-Lot," 9-14. Conversely, his love for CBS's "60 Minutes" renders his 11-13 article a drippy puff piece. Indulging in boundless poetic license, Shales invents words and employs expressions to the point of distraction. In his 3-15 piece on TV's offerings during a snowstorm, he remarks that his TV cable remained operational "no matter how much snow snowed or sleet slat." And his 10-23 column describes some Groucho Marx comments as "even ribalder" than others. Putting his extreme dislikes to good use, Shales pans such gratuitously violent TV movies as "River of Rage," 10-2, which he calls a "torturous wallow." But a rabid revulsion against Earth Day programming skews his judgment, 4-22, when Shales describes the HBO documentary "Earth and the American Dream" as a "75 minute illustrated tantrum." Curiously, Shales contradicts himself when he then calls one segment entertaining and well-done and the conclusion "grimly persuasive." In a rare detour from his typical love-hate dichotomy, Shales pens three articles on newscaster Connie Chung, 5-18, 6-1, and 6-17, toward whom he has only a cool feeling. Maintaining an open mind, he provides one of his more imaginative insights. "Perhaps one reason some of us find Connie Chung so compelling on TV is that she always seems to be right on the verge of developing a personality." While Shales's writing often suffers from being too cute, he *can* score with his inventive phrases and loose colloquialisms. In his smart and snappy 9-5 review of the new season's TV shows, Shales finds "Harts of the West" "forced, fey, and aw, phooey." Steven Spielberg's "seaQuest DSV," he quips, features "occasional ludicrous pop-ups from Darwin the darling Dolphin who, no kidding, talks. Him say: "seaQuest DSV' all wet—get my agent.'" Like the medium he covers, Shales turns out fast-paced and amusing fare that often lacks depth.

Walter Shapiro

Esquire

★★

White House. A former *Time* essayist, Shapiro has turned to portraiture in the self-proclaimed "Magazine for Men." Unlike his work at Time, Shapiro's probing profiles often prove insightful. His intriguing July exploration of the relationship between President Clinton and the media exemplifies this insight. "A near-lynching can leave lifelong rope burns, so, of course, Clinton cannot forget that his 'friends' in the media helped put a noose around his neck over Gennifer Flowers and his draft record. Beyond New Hampshire, other stories during the campaign wounded Clinton's ego—particularly the pieces about his Arkansas record that seemed to portray him as just another quasi-corrupt cracker politician. The result is a President so thin-skinned that he even snapped at the ever-innocuous Bryant Gumbel: 'Since when are *you* so worried about being fair?'" Shapiro adds shrewdly that "in an era when correspondents are given wide latitude for interpretation, never underestimate the psychological factors that influence coverage. News analysis is astonishingly subjective—a function of mood, climates of opinion, and, yes, how well one's best lines went over at last night's dinner party." In his August essay, Shapiro attempts to debunk various myths about Hillary Rodham Clinton, his quick prose verging on the sardonic. "When it was time to go, Hillary and I still had our differences. She views rooting for the Cubs as a metaphor for hope, while I regard it as a symbol of futility. And I find her sincerity too sugary. (When she lapses into earnest autopilot, the temptation is to shake her or feel for a pulse.)" Although the reader doesn't quite come away knowing the First Lady, Shapiro does uncover some of her complexities. His September profile cum evaluation of Vice President Al Gore seems oddly void, considering the sprightliness of Shapiro's other portraits. The reader gets neither a sense of Gore nor of what he's been doing. Now that John Taylor has moved to *Esquire*, following *New York* editor Edward Kosner, Shapiro will have serious competition on the political beat.

David Shaw

Los Angeles Times

★★½

Media. Shaw is one journalist other journalists talk to—in fact his articles often seem like a round-table discussion among old friends. Combining provocative quotes with keen insights, Shaw produces a splendid three-part series, 9-15, 9-16, and 9-17, on the roller-coaster relationship between President Clinton and the press. "Clinton's media coverage has been so schizophrenic over the past seven months that looking at it is a bit like watching a pornographic movie—he's up, he's down, he's in, he's out, with (as Meg Greenfield of the [*Washington*] *Post*, notes) 'a lot of moaning and groaning and hugging and kissing in-between.'" After describing the increasing pressures on the White House press corps, Shaw does something unique: he humanizes journalists against the backdrop of Washington. Journalists are people, he explains, and they respond negatively to inconsiderate treatment—such as phone calls not being returned, the closing of the White House briefing room, and Clinton's chronic lateness. Combine this treatment with the idea that this "administration stumbled and fumbled so often in the early going that if the White House had been a restaurant its *plat du jour* would have been flounder," and you get an avalanche of negative press. Shaw shows that compromise, such as on gays in the military, can thus be framed as weakness, a capitulation on principles, rather than as an act of statesmanship or pragmatic politics. He further explains how media coverage—whether fair or not—affects public perception, which in turn influences Congressional action, White House policy, and national affairs. This deft analysis that describes the process and explains its significance is sadly lacking in Shaw's other major series, 3-31 and 4-1, on the growing decline of the public's trust in the media. While he recites a litany of reasons for this growing distrust, Shaw dismisses the fact that a recent poll he cites reveals that *88 percent of the public* say that the media is doing a *good* job. That signifies far more of an endorsement than Shaw would have his readers believe. He notes shrewdly that the decline of the public trust in the media is part of the overall decline of trust in other major institutions. But is the diminishing of trust in the media far greater or less than that of these other institutions? Because Shaw fails to ask this key question, he leaves the reader in the dark and the series becomes a grand muddle of talking heads. Nonetheless, Shaw, with his overstuffed Rolodex, remains one of the savvier media critics around.

Jeffrey L. Sheler

U.S.News & World Report

★★½

Religion. A careful writer, Sheler provides balanced accounts of religious events and controversies. Although his editors do not always allot him generous space, Sheler manages to turn in solid, sometimes excellent, work. His 2-1 sidebar to a story on the ban on gays in the military manages to report fairly on the teachings of both scripture and tradition. He concludes that while "a handful of [Jewish and Christian] groups condone homosexuality outright," most "walk a narrow line—standing firm against homosexual conduct but seeking to accept and minister to homosexual persons." In his 4-12 epitaph on *Christianity and Crisis*, a magazine that ceased publication in March, Sheler relates its origins, editorial concerns, and declining fortunes—all in just four paragraphs. Given similar space, 9-13, Sheler reports the adoption of a code of ethics by the Parliament of the World's Religions that "essentially condenses the Ten Commandments...into 'four irrevocable directives.'" Displaying a strong sense of irony, Sheler concludes that "the new commandments don't seem to have the binding effect of the old: The document makes no mention of God." His 5-31 story on the hajj, the journey to Mecca that Muslims make at least once in their lifetime, reports how Islam's holiest city has been modernized—but at a cost. For example, the tradition of insistence on equality among those making the pilgrimage has changed, Sheler notes, with the rich now staying in fancy, first-class hotels. In Sheler's finest work, a 12-20 cover story, he tackles the question of "Who Was Jesus?" Concisely surveying the two-centuries old quest by scholars for the historical Jesus, Sheler employs a balanced set of sources to report the state of that search today. He finds that "it appears to most scholars that Jesus probably did perform some miracles," and he is struck by the "historical corroboration" of one of the "most astounding of Jesus's reported miracles"—the account of the raising of Lazarus from the dead. While Jerusalem, the site of this reported miracle, was destroyed by the Romans in 70 A.D., Sheler notes that it was later re-

built and renamed by the Arabs who settled there. They call it "'the place of Lazarus.'" "'Why would they change the name of the town," Sheler quotes a professor of ancient history asking, "unless something spectacular happened there?'" This story demonstrates that Sheler has the stuff when he's given the opportunity. Maybe *U.S.News* will let his light emerge a bit more from under the editorial bushel.

Robert Shogan

Los Angeles Times

★★½

Politics. Now off the rigorous campaign trail, Shogan pens few articles, but they are thoughtful and informative. They focus on his special area of expertise—political strategy. In his astute 5-10 assessment of President Clinton and Congress weighing the political risks before deciding on military intervention in Bosnia, Shogan makes a keen observation. "There is nothing insidious about Commander in Chief Clinton making political calculations as he ponders his moves in Bosnia. Unless he can generate public support for U.S. involvement there, or anywhere else, such a commitment is bound to be short-lived." Shogan's 5-23 dispatch reviews who's thinking what on realignment within the GOP, as well as the party's strategy of returning to grass-roots politics. And while he doesn't pick Ruth Bader Ginsburg as a potential Supreme Court nominee in his 6-8 analysis of Clinton's selection strategy, Shogan cogently defines the political requirements. "White House strategists are counting on the announcement of his choice...to reinforce Clinton's much-ballyhooed claim to be a born-again centrist and to reassure the middle Americans who helped send him to Washington. It will also be intended to dispel memories of the series of fiascoes that have plagued his presidency, most recently the failed nomination of Lani Guinier as the Justice Department's civil rights chief. However, by choosing Babbitt—or some other white male such as Federal Appeals Court Judge Stephen G. Breyer, whose name is also being mentioned—Clinton risks further estrangement of minorities, women and other Democratic liberals already furious about his handling of the Guinier nomination." In his 7-6 evaluation, Shogan neatly encapsulates liberal fears about Clinton. "All that liberals are likely to get under Clinton, in the view of many analysts, is leftover benefits from middle-class programs, or what amounts to 'trickle-down' liberalism. To add to their woes, liberals believe they have become convenient scapegoats for the President's public perception problems." Shogan's 8-10 examination of the New Jersey gubernatorial race disappoints. By concentrating mostly on superficial issues, such as advertising and promotional differences, Shogan confuses strategy with public relations. Uncharacteristically, the article proves a rare misfire in a decent year for this veteran political observer.

David Shribman

The Boston Globe

★½

Washington bureau chief and "National Perspective" columnist. Although moving from *The Wall Street Journal*, Shribman doesn't change his style. Still too top heavy on analysis, he often fails to add insight or information. Shribman seems to excel when he gets out and does his own reporting, which enables him to cover unique angles and choice details. In a poignant 7-23 essay, he takes the unusual step of positioning Vince Foster's speech to the graduating class of the University of Arkansas Law School as a kind of suicide note. Shribman reports that Foster spoke bitterly of the need to protect one's reputation—for once a reputation is lost in the legal profession, it's gone forever. A substantive 10-12 dispatch from Canada examines how Jean Chretien is courting Canadian voters. Further, Shribman designs a plausible scenario of how Clinton might pull the rug out from under the conservatives (which is, of course, what came to pass). But efforts like these appear seldom. In his 1-14 column, Shribman says only that, as an outgoing president, George Bush's air strikes on Iraq come as a surprise. And in his superficial 4-23 look at the media's treatment of the Branch Davidians and Waco, Texas, Shribman reviles the press for making judgments. However, he then makes a judgment himself by exonerating the administration of any culpability. Describing a split in the powerful coalition of the "religious right," 8-6, Shribman provides no conclusive detail of where reformer Ralph Reed would lead the movement should he be able to guide the Christian Coalition away from such "traditional values" issues as abortion and gay rights. Shribman waxes poetic on the Middle East peace accord, 9-14, but despite the gentle prose he fails to move the reader. As with most of Shribman's work, he could pack more punch with some sturdy reporting.

David Silverberg

Defense News
Armed Forces Journal International
★★★

Washington staff writer. An expert on the international arms trade, Silverberg delves deeply into the politics and economics behind defense procurement decisions. Because he understands the intricacies of weapons systems, his reports—both in *Defense News* and, after his late-year job change, in *Armed Forces Journal International*—contain a high level of technical expertise. In his 2-8/14 *DN* article, he reports on the natural inclination of Third World nations to acquire some of the high-tech weapons that proved such a success during the Persian Gulf War. Military officials in these countries were so impressed, he notes, that they "are now seeking air and ground-based low-cost precision weapons or at least the means to make the weapons smarter." In his 4-5 piece, Silverberg finds the U.S. arms-export policy being pulled in different directions. Commerce Secretary Ron Brown advocates a strong official presence at the Paris Air Show, while Defense Secretary Les Aspin seems hesitant. "Participation in air shows has been the subject of contention," Silverberg notes, "with critics charging [that] the [Defense Department] subsidizes private defense contractors." Silverberg successfully captures the essence of the administration's dilemma—weapons sales should be more closely regulated but increased economic growth through exports is also desirable. In his 5-24 report, Silverberg brilliantly addresses the changes proposed for the Defense Department's acquisition team to prepare officials "to grapple with the United States' concerns over economics, proliferation, technology and the environment." He explains that the changes only make sense if the Defense Department, rather than the State Department, takes a leading role in these areas. Silverberg's riveting 6-28 article emphasizes the slowing pace of technological improvements in U.S. submarine forces. The end of the Cold War, he writes, has led to declining defense budgets with less money spent on such improvements. It also has shifted the likely site of any future submarine operations. Silverberg reports that "the United States in particular is having a difficult time adjusting to warfare in the shallow seas of the Third World compared with deep-water operations during the Cold War." An outstanding analyst of defense-trade issues, Silverberg uncovers the essential elements of a story and ably ties international defense trade issues to U.S. political and economic concerns. He should be a great asset to *AFJI*.

Glenn Simpson

Roll Call
★★

Washington. In addition to keeping tabs on congressional committees and votes, Simpson breaks one of the hot stories of the year for partisan conservatives. *The Wall Street Journal* reprints on its 6-28 op-ed page his initial *Roll Call* bombshell that reveals House Speaker Thomas Foley's [D-WA] "flipping" of stock issues. "By any investment standard," Simpson states, "the success of Speaker Tom Foley, who uses only minimal capital, has been phenomenal." Simpson, however, fails to turn up any real evidence of impropriety on Foley's part. Following up this scoop with a dutiful 7-1 report of Foley's denial of wrongdoing, Simpson finishes the story in a 7-29 effort detailing the partisan bick-

ering. The article also reports Republican efforts to determine if Foley's financial advisor treated his investments differently—and if so, why. Simpson also covered Sen. Bob Packwood [R-OR] and the various charges, such as sexual misconduct, lodged against him. In his superficial 9-27 effort, Simpson never questions the propriety of four House members, including Rep. Pat Schroeder [D-CO], attending—and in Schroeder's case co-hosting—a fund-raiser to help pay the legal bills of Packwood's accusers. Simpson offers professional and detached work in his 10-25 story on the flap over the Packwood diaries. And in his 10-28 article, he's among the first to ferret out new evidence. "The dispute over the Packwood diaries is based mainly on the presence of potential new charges....Packwood's attorneys acknowledged the existence of potential new allegations against the Senator and the possible need for an inquiry into those matters." Despite additional allegations that the diaries might contain evidence that Packwood used his congressional contacts to land his ex-wife a job, Simpson's 11-4 dispatch reports that rather than wait for a legal ruling on the diaries, the Senate Ethics Committee may go ahead with the current investigation. With the energy and smarts of a detective, Simpson emerges as an up-and-comer on the political scene.

Ronald Smothers

The New York Times

★½

Southeastern U.S. Gallivanting from city to city across the South, Smothers may be stretched too thin. Although he provides adequate overviews, he seldom digs deep on any single issue. In his 1-9 portrait of a young girl with AIDS, who moved to Lakeland, Florida, for its warmer climate, Smothers describes how a chilly reception drove the family back to Maine. "What has happened to the family vividly illustrates the difficulty of living with AIDS: the shame of a sister who tried to be anonymous in her new school; the bubbly denial of a first grader...; the frustration of parents whose choice about where to live could not, ultimately, be based solely on what was good for a child." Unfortunately, Smothers provides few details on the harassment itself. In his 10-18 piece, Smothers travels to Memphis to explore the largely-black city's aim of merging with its largely-white suburbs. Some urban leaders oppose the idea because it could dilute black voting strength, but the mayor, who is black, and many white residents support the plan. Although Smothers tosses around reams of statistics, he fails to quote any actual residents—except for a few academics and city leaders—of Memphis or the surrounding area. In his 4-16 article, Smothers sets the scene as the Supreme Court prepares to hear the "serpentine" redistricting case from North Carolina. "*Shaw v. Reno* will be argued amid a cacophony of 'friend of the court' briefs both from national political parties and from civil rights, civil liberties and conservative groups." Carefully explaining the background of the dispute, Smothers notes that the "case is as tortured and convoluted as the district lines themselves." Not all his allusions work so well. Smothers's live-from-the-scene 9-2 account of Hurricane Emily in Buxton, North Carolina, gets cluttered with clichés—a fishing boat carried inland "looking like some beached whale"—and simply odd analogies—a survivor "sounding like some storm-tossed Willy Loman as he surveyed the clutter." Perhaps Smothers just needs to settle down.

Rochelle L. Stanfield

National Journal

★★½

Education, housing, urban policy, government affairs. With one of the broadest beats in the business, Stanfield skillfully follows the Clinton administration's plans to "reinvent government" on all fronts and highlights the politics of funding for each domain. Although she relies on optimistic buzzwords—reinvent, revitalize, redistribute, redesign, and reform—she digs deep to uncover the complex factors affecting congressional slices of the governmental-aid pie. In her succinct and hard-hitting 5-22 column on new urban-development grants, Stanfield shows the gap between the rhetoric of change and the business-as-usual manner in distributing federal aid to cities. "In President Clinton's empowerment zones, New Democracy runs smack into Old Politics....The soul of reinventing government is its competitive nature, the idea of rewarding those who take the initiative....Designation as an empowerment zone [is supposed to] be the prize in a competition among disadvantaged communities." Yet, Stanfield finds, "it's the consensus among urban politicians...that the five big-city designations will be awarded politically." Although sometimes drier when writing on education, Stanfield deftly covers the issue of youth apprenticeships in "Hire Learning," 5-1, education reform in "Learning Curve," 7-3, and the Chapter 1 compensatory education package in "Making the Grade," 4-17. She displays an impressive command of her multifaceted beat, and a surging tide of ideas and opinions fills her articles. However, she often releases a flood of figures in the millions and billions, failing to place them in context of the overall budgetary and national economic picture. Occasionally short on background, Stanfield alludes to a long-standing schism between the two teachers' unions, the NEA and the AFT, 3-20, by saying "maybe they aren't adversaries after all." Although noting that the NEA and the AFT compete for members and belong to different international federations (now joining forces), she gives no information on how the rift between the two unions developed. In fact, she often neglects to provide historical background before the 1970s, or even 1980s. But give her some time on this beat—with her strong "learning curve," the talented Stanfield will no doubt soon be "making the grade."

Barbara Starr

Jane's Defence Weekly

★★★

International security affairs. With authoritative sources, including Defense Secretaries Dick Cheney and Les Aspin, Starr employs a taut writing style that make her an authority on international security issues and Pentagon strategy. Her 1-9 article treats departing Secretary Cheney's opinions on the future size of the U.S. military and his differences with the policies of his successor, Secretary Aspin. Cleverly juxtaposing these differences throughout the article, she reports, "Cheney said he is arranging a meeting with Aspin to discuss the transition, but he doesn't expect to change Aspin's mind on further defense cuts, which Cheney opposes." Starr examines Aspin's statement, 3-17, that the conflict in Russia between hardliners and President Boris Yeltsin's reformers could slow the pace of defense cuts in the U.S. "Aspin reiterated that Yeltsin retains control of nuclear weapons, but he noted that arms control accords were signed with the reformers in power." Starr finds the implications clear—if Yeltsin falls, arms control accords will be worthless, and a new, expensive arms race could result. Starr's 9-4 interview with Aspin provides an excellent overview of the Pentagon's "bottom up review," which foresees a force structure that "would allow the USA to win two regional conflicts, but the fight will be constrained by airlift and sealift." She also provides useful details of planned cuts. In her 12-4 article, Starr reports on the resurrection of a 1985 plan, designed by Senate Armed Services Committee Chairman Sam Nunn [D-GA], to enhance allied participation in weapons research and development programs. Early disappointments led to what she calls a "period of inertia" in the program. "To get increased funding," she reports, "the Pentagon will have to demonstrate that it and the allies are serious this time." With her insightful reporting and continued access to Washington policy makers, Starr shines as one of the best defense reporters in Washington.

Peter Steinfels

The New York Times

★★★½

Religion. A thorough reporter and clear writer, Steinfels crafts solid stories on the news of the day. Hard to beat as an analyst of religious events and trends, he writes an every-other-Saturday column in the news pages that seldom fails to elevate the *Times*. In his 2-3 profile of Billy Graham, Steinfels comprehensively treats the career of "America's pastor," discussing his evangelical crusades as well as his relations with presidents of both parties. "In his preaching," Steinfels writes in a sentence that captures the essence of Graham's ministry, "he cites the world's many ills but generally avoids endorsing specific solutions—except faith in Christ." Tracking events involving the Branch Davidian compound near Waco, Texas, Steinfels illuminates the related subjects of millenarianism, 3-3, and the Book of Revelation, 4-25. He concludes the latter by questioning whether "the authorities who conducted the siege outside Waco had really recognized how deeply those inside might have believed that the last book of their Bible pro-

vided a script for the last hours of their lives." Steinfels also reports on non-mainstream religious happenings, such as his 4-16 piece on the annual meeting of the Women-Church conference in Albuquerque, "one strand of a larger movement of religious feminism." In a thoughtful 3-8 article following the arrest of what the news media called an "Islamic fundamentalist" for his alleged role in the bombing of the World Trade Center, Steinfels reflects on whether that term "illuminates or obscures the complex realities of militant religious movements." In some of his finest reporting of the year, 5-7, Steinfels examines American Muslims, charting their growing political and social impact in the U.S. "The most likely effect," he contends, "...will be to bolster the forces of social conservatism on issues like sexual permissiveness, support for parochial schools and gay rights." Superbly reporting the Pope's visit to the United States, 8-12, 8-15, and 8-16, Steinfels offers perhaps his best Saturday column of the year, 8-21, inspired by the media's "myopic" coverage of the visit. With the press focused on divisions among Catholics and the subject of abortion, he notes, "much about the Pope's visit and his message was obscured.... Those who reported and commented on the Pope's messages could have paid attention, not only to his specific condemnations of abortion, euthanasia and urban violence but also to his underlying moral diagnosis...the loss of belief in objective truth and in universally valid principles of morality." The spirited Steinfels is not only a fine religion writer but a good media critic, too.

Laura Sessions Stepp

The Washington Post

Staff writer. Stepp's reasoned forays into generally unambitious topics in the "Style" section of the *Post* could appear in any run-of-the-mill magazine on the supermarket checkout line. Many of her columns provide information for parents on child-rearing issues, such as teen parties and alcohol, 4-2, an easy-to-read book series, 4-16, and how to teach values, 6-8. While often readable and sometimes useful, she could express her ideas in far fewer words. In her inane opener to a 1-12 piece on the pessimistic views of teenagers, Stepp writes, "If there is one group of people who need that touted and tenuous thing called hope, it's today's adolescents." Dismissing the serious mental-health issue of depression, she focuses on such lighter fare as opinion polls of teenagers and "expert" child-guidance advice. There is a pattern to her articles: Stepp presents a mundane subject from everyday life, quotes dozens of everyday people to whom the subject relates, interviews the "experts," and then shifts into an advice-giving mode, in the manner of many self-help or "pop-psychology" books. Much like these books, Stepp's columns often fall short on information and place more emphasis on personal testimony than on findings from legitimate research studies. Of all the topics Stepp covers, her 8-17 article on kidnapping proves the most irritating in its lack of data. And this could have been an important and informative piece. Most abductors are acquaintances, Stepp shows, citing an array of sources, and she focuses on drawing a profile of the typical acquaintance/abductor and describing new approaches to educating the public. She provides a few statistics on "short-term, less-serious abductions"—whatever that means—and missing children, but she makes no further attempt to examine the demographics of the crime. She adjures parents to talk to their children and "use actual incidents in the news." However, she sketches only one incident, and it remains unsolved. Stepp meets with clear success in one endeavor this year—her 5-27 piece lambasting the local Ticketmaster for its policy of keeping the service-and-handling charge when refunding tickets for a canceled performance. She then reports victoriously, 7-16, that Ticketmaster has changed its policy to provide full refunds. While her material sometimes makes for entertaining reading, Stepp will have to tackle bigger game (and do so with more firepower) if she is to shine.

John Taylor

New York

Esquire

★★½

Politics. At *New York* magazine for most of the year, Taylor reveals occasional insights—and even flashes of brilliance—in his assessments of the political scene. He only needs to deliver this kind of performance more consistently. In his 1-25 *New York* effort, Taylor describes how

New York City Mayor David Dinkins curries favor with certain constituencies, citing Dinkins' support for gays marching in the St. Patrick's Day parade as an example. "As is so often the case in such situations, the rhetoric of multiculturalism is in part a calculated political tactic." Crafting a superb 4-26 critique of the coverage of the Clinton administration, he perceptively analyzes the media. "Once upon a time, journalists liked to brag about their 'sources.' Now they are more inclined to brag about their 'take'...—the perception, the judgment—[which] has superseded the 'source' as the primary status denominator for political correspondents....A common complaint throughout the past year has been that CNN and C-SPAN have circumscribed the traditional media, depriving them of their former news-gathering function. Faced with a future of dwindling relevance, the print media, in particular, have developed coping or survival strategies. One has been to shift from news to analysis." His 6-14 essay, in which Taylor takes a long time to say very little about the significance of David Gergen's appointment as Clinton's senior counselor, reads like a compendium of other people's opinions. Similarly, Taylor supplies heavy detail on the Tyler Bottoms custody case, in which a Virginia grandmother won custody of her grandson largely because her daughter is a lesbian. Yet he fails to examine the legal issues and implications of this ruling. In his strong 11-1 effort, which includes a keen assessment of the New York City mayoral race, Taylor sets the stage for the next step in urban, and perhaps American, politics. He asserts that voters "will respond less to ethnic appeals than to appeals to cultural values that transcend ethnicity." Having followed *New York* editor Ed Kosner to *Esquire* at year's end, Taylor should prove an asset there, as he would anywhere.

Stuart Taylor Jr.

The American Lawyer
Legal Times
★★★½

Senior writer. In both his articles and his columns, Taylor showcases his tremendous reporting and astute analytical skills. He loads his pieces with examples that clarify complex legal matters or that advance his point of view. In his dry but thoughtful May *American Lawyer* article, Taylor endorses a tort-reform measure proposed by U.S. District Judge William Schwarzer that would encourage serious offers of early settlement by either side. "Under the Schwarzer proposal," Taylor explains, "either plaintiff or defendant in any federal case... could serve a written offer of judgment on the opposing party at any time. If the offeree refused, and then failed to do better after proceeding to final judgment, the offeror would be entitled to recover its reasonable post-offer attorney's fees and costs, within certain limits." In his 11-29 *Legal Times* column, Taylor defends Solicitor General Drew Days III for refusing to support a lower court interpretation of a child pornography statute before the Supreme Court. "The tapes [which show clothed teenage girls engaging in various, non-sexual activities] were clearly designed to pander to a certain kind of pedophile," he reasons, but "...the legal question...was whether Congress *had* criminalized the possession of such tapes, with the clarity required by the Constitution, when it barred receiving and possessing pictures of 'minor[s] engaging in...lascivious exhibition of the genitals or pubic area.'" Taylor challenges Congress to pass a soft-core child-pornography statute banning films "'designed for the purpose of eliciting or attempting to elicit a sexual response in the intended viewer,'" as one Representative has proposed. In his March *TAL* article on Zöe Baird's downfall as attorney general nominee, Taylor pens a vigorous and articulate account of the Nannygate affair. "Zöe Baird should never have been picked as attorney general. She was ethically fit for the job. But she was unfit for the *symbolic* role of ultimate champion of the rule of law, given the public perception—simplistic, half-wrong, but unavoidable—that she had scoffed at laws enforced by the Justice Department." Relying on statistics and common sense, *LT* 1-10, Taylor argues against "three-strikes-and-you're-out" sentencing laws. "If California had managed to identify in advance and keep in prison *all* of the parolees who committed murders last year, it would have reduced the state's total of 4,000 murders by a little more that 1 percent....And while 44 murders by parolees is 44 too many, note that 4,189 Californians died in traffic accidents last year." Offering ac-

cessible and enriching perspectives, Taylor dependably applies engaging prose and compelling arguments to current legal issues.

Robin Toner
The New York Times
★

Domestic policy, Washington. Although Toner occasionally provides an inside political nugget, she offers little substantive information on such important issues as social security and health care. Lacking both experience and expertise, she is in way over her head on this critical beat. In her 2-7 dispatch, Toner pulls out all the stops to show lobbyist power in the face of a threat to social security. However, she provides too little information on the proposed one-year freeze in Social Security cost-of-living increases. Toner's sketchy 4-6 review outlining the public's response to President Clinton's ideas on health care opens with a questionable assessment. "Fired by a sense of crisis, a majority of Americans say they are willing to accept substantial changes in their health-care system, including government price controls, new taxes and longer waits for non-emergency appointments." Toner then adds briefly that "the survey found numerous signs of confusion and ambivalence toward some of the trade-offs that health-care reform may mean." Whoa. Toner gives no explanation of how both statements could be true. Instead, she seems content simply to recount the numbers without examining them too closely. Crafting a mushy 5-21 examination of the risks and complexity of health-care reform, Toner relies too much on secondary sources. And her awful 10-12 profile of Sen. Sam Nunn [D-GA] suffers a similar plight, as she recycles old quotes from an August 1992 interview. Toner also notes that Nunn hates the media's pseudo-psychoanalysis of him—and then proceeds to pseudo-psychoanalyze him. In her 9-19 report, she traces the strategy behind the selling of health-care reform, but never assesses the value of what the administration has compiled to date. And Toner's surprisingly substantial 6-3 profile of Sen. Daniel Patrick Moy-nihan [D-NY], the new head of the Senate Finance Committee, doesn't quite capture how he might shepherd Clinton's economic package through the Senate. Moreover, she does not even remotely attempt to assess the merits of the package itself, but instead sticks to the politics and the players—and does fine with that. But on Toner's beat, that's less than half the story.

Pat Towell
Congressional Quarterly
★★★

Senior writer, defense and foreign policy. Few reporters cover the legislative workings of this area as thoroughly and colorfully as Towell. The reader always learns something from his insightful and informative dispatches. In his exceptional 1-30 report on the issue of gays in the military, Towell compiles views from all sides of the aisle in all branches of government. Going beyond the "don't ask, don't tell" catchall phrase in the major papers, he infuses his 6-26 piece with the relevant detail on the proposed policy change. Towell rounds out his coverage with an excellent 7-24 evaluation of the politics behind the issue and the immediate impact of the new policy. "For all the fanfare and denunciations, President Clinton's effort to liberalize the military's ban on gay soldiers will do no more or less than this: It will make life a little easier, and less risky, for homosexuals intent on belonging quietly to an organization that remains determined to bar homosexual conduct." In his sharp 2-27 assessment of Defense Secretary Les Aspin and the effect his heart problems may have on his job performance, Towell notes wisely, "Aspin's illness also may have delayed his progress in the most subtle task he faces: Winning the confidence of the 1.6 million men and women in the armed forces. He comes to that challenge weighted down by the baggage of a reputation early in his congressional career as a gadfly who was dismissive of military traditions." Towell crafts an excellent 5-8 political profile of new House Armed Services Committee chairman Ronald V. Dellums [D-CA]. "It is a position of potentially great institutional authority that could give him tremendous leverage in defense policy debates. Yet, so great is the gap between where he would lead and where Congress seems ready to go, that if he pushes too hard, he could wind up a figurehead whose ostensible authority yields little true clout." Although less colorful in a series of dispatches on defense appropriations, particularly 9-25 and 11-6, he covers the subject clearly and competently. One of the stars at *CQ*, Towell always makes the most of his assignments.

Liz Trotta
The Washington Times
★½

Press veteran Trotta has a flair for rendering visual imagery in her coverage of media and politics. Unfortunately, her tendency to take cheap shots and her failure to produce insightful analysis often overshadow her narrative talents. In her 1-23 inaugural commentary, Trotta's conservatism turns to bitterness and name-calling. She draws an engaging picture of "a diversity orgy," only to become hostile, describing the new White House staff as resembling "nothing less than a UNICEF greeting card." More convincing in her caustic 2-16 criticism of the media, Trotta concludes that "the press will do anything to believe it is in control, molding opinion, moving and shaking, but this is an exaggerated and grotesquely amplified self-image that takes little note of its ultimate reliance on what will play in Boise." Such perspective, however, appears infrequently in Trotta's disjointed and rambling political reports. Unnecessary photos accompany her 8-24 comparison of the personalities of Gov. Jim Florio [D-NJ] and Republican challenger Christine Whitman, for Trotta's vivid depictions offer far more than any snapshot. "While Mrs. Whitman looks as though she belongs on a country club terrace after playing 18 holes, Mr. Florio's demeanor suggests he might be more comfortable at the tables in Atlantic City." While her prose amuses, Trotta fails to produce any insight into how either candidate might govern during the next four years, and she provides only a muddled account of New Jersey politics. Stating that Florio is "beset by warring factions within his own party," she proceeds to report how Republican Jersey City Mayor Bret Schundler has supported Whitman. Perhaps she could explain how these two points are related? Trotta succeeds in her reports on the New York City mayoral campaign. In addition to colorfully describing the candidates, she knowledgeably outlines the myriad problems facing the city. Trotta exhibits a special understanding of how the race issue plays above and beyond campaign rhetoric, 7-26, noting that "there is a profound sense of hostility between the haves and have-nots, an acute awareness of class distinction that often erupts into racial strife." If she could deliver such articulate analysis with greater frequency, Trotta might add weight to her dramatic narrative.

Karen Tumulty
Los Angeles Times
★★½

Washington. Tumulty packs ample information and insight into her tightly written dispatches. She and co-author Marlene Cimons craft a balanced, substantive 1-23 report on President Clinton's action on abortion *and* the pro-life rally on the Capitol steps. In doing so, the pair gathers many relevant details—such as the turnout of an estimated 75,000 pro-lifers, 5,000 more than the year before—that other papers tended to downplay. Tumulty and co-author William J. Eaton fashion a smart 2-19 dispatch, signaling early potential problems with the President's economic package among House Democrats. "The issue was one of balance—only by making deeper cuts in federal spending, [Democrats] contended, could Clinton's proposed tax increases be made palatable to American voters. Despite the characterization of Clinton as a new kind of Democrat, they worried that he had left their party vulnerable to the old tax-and-spend accusations that have drawn political blood in the past. Once the details of the package become clear, some said, early support may evaporate quickly." Tumulty truly understates her 6-29 profile of Sen. Daniel Patrick Moynihan [D-NY]. "Even in the Senate, an institution with a venerable tradition of eccentrics, Pat Moynihan stands out." And she perceptively examines Moynihan's relationship with other lawmakers both on the Senate Finance Committee and on its House counterpart. In her original 7-5 effort, Tumulty takes the vote on the Hyde amendment as a cue to examine the effect that newly elected minorities and women have on the House of Representatives. After probing both the current trends, Tumulty shows how these may herald further changes as the "price of diversity." She pens a crystal-clear 9-30 breakdown of the politics of Hillary Rodham Clinton's health-care reform. As Sen. James M. Jeffords [R-VT] becomes the first Republican to announce his support, Tumulty incorpo-

rates a vivid account of the First Lady's second day of Senate testimony. In her 10-3 effort on the FBI's annual crime report, Tumulty presents the information relevant to her Los Angeles readership but, uncharacteristically, she probes the report's trends only briefly. Quickly evolving into a top-notch political reporter, Tumulty's star is on the rise.

Ralph Vartabedian

Los Angeles Times

★★★

Washington. An essential cog in the *Times*'s coverage of the defense industry, Vartabedian provides informative dispatches that cover important angles other reporters often miss. In his 1-27 report, he gets the dope on an internal 1989 memo which reveals that then-Attorney General William Barr personally opposed the "federal False Claims Act, which empowers individuals to sue contractors on behalf of the government and share in any monetary awards" over fraud on defense contracts. This fine interim update relates directly to southern California, because, as Vartabedian notes, "virtually every major defense company has been sued under the False Claims Act." Vartabedian's 9-13 follow-up on this law focuses on the whistle-blowers themselves. However, the story lacks sufficient detail on why these people came forward, or why some lost everything in the process. In his 2-19 effort, he goes beyond the story of Boeing's elimination of 28,000 jobs. Vartabedian points out that this means Northrop will probably cut back as well—since they make Boeing 747 fuselages, which will no longer be needed in such large numbers. And crafting an excellent 3-30 wrap-up of the decision by the Hughes Corporation to close a California missile facility, Vartabedian makes an insightful observation. "The decision ranks among the largest transfers of aerospace jobs out of the state since the trend began in the mid-1980s. More ominously, it undercuts one of the state's last remaining strengths: retaining its wealth of science and engineering talent." In a solid 6-8 roundup, Vartabedian keeps on the story by examining a UCLA study that found half the workers laid off in 1989 had either relocated or not found work. He notes that this results in a drain of both the tax base and the intellectual capital of southern California. In his fascinating "The Enemy Within" series, 7-11, 7-12, and 7-13, Vartabedian reveals how the end of the Cold War has dramatically changed the way the defense industry does business by broadening the criteria for a secure environment. An employee, he notes, can be dismissed for having a foreign-born spouse, or for being Asian-American, or if the company doesn't like his or her looks. Vartabedian has a sharp eye for policy and its consequences.

Edward Walsh

The Washington Post

Chicago bureau chief. Having covered the Windy City for more than two years, Walsh writes credibly and with descriptive flair. He also produces a steady stream of original work. In his crisp 1-5 article, Walsh summarizes the early complaints against the nation's first black woman senator, Carol Moseley-Braun [D-IL]. "In the nine weeks since she defeated Republican Richard Williamson, Braun has suffered a dizzying series of sometimes self-inflicted wounds that, in the words of one of her supporters here, has resulted in a 'tremendous squandering of goodwill and resources.'" In his detailed 7-30 report on the Midwest flooding, Walsh notes "The cleanup task facing Portage des Sioux and the other inundated river towns...seems almost insurmountable. The water is everywhere, surrounding the houses, covering the few vehicles left behind and lapping against the graying tombstones of a cemetery at the edge of town." Walsh's grim 4-22 piece starkly portrays the end of the 11-day uprising at the Southern Ohio Correctional Facility. "The surrendering inmates, some in short-sleeved T-shirts, were led into raw, 30-degree cold and a steady drizzle from gloomy skies to cross a football field between two long lines of Ohio state troopers armed with rifles and shotguns....[The process] was agonizingly slow." Reporting on a controversial proposed settlement of a lawsuit brought by the Chippewa Indians against the state of Minnesota, 2-28, over hunting and fishing rights on the Mille Lacs Lake, Walsh fails to provide the whole story. Although he interviews government officials, politicians, tourist-business owners, and hunters, he quotes no one from the Mille Lacs reservation. Walsh's amusing 1-17 article surveys reactions to the firing of Chicago Bears football coach Mike Ditka. Many Chicagoans talk gruff like Ditka, Walsh notes, "including the man who was known as Da Mare, the late Richard J. Daley, and his son, Da Mare II, Richard M. Daley, who called a news conference to lament the ouster of his friend, Da Coach." With a solid feel for the nation's heartland, Walsh provides Midwestern tales that make even a world-weary *Post* audience gather round.

Kenneth T. Walsh
U.S.News & World Report
★½

Senior writer, Washington. Not much extraordinary appears in Walsh's coverage of the new administration. Although his best efforts remain his sprightly features, they often suffer from a paucity of information. In his 3-15 dispatch on how Bill Clinton is facing up to potential troubles dealing with the military, Walsh notes, "the president plans a charm offensive soon to try to repair some of the damage. In coming weeks, he will visit the Pentagon for a get-acquainted session and is expected to tour at least one military base outside Washington to show how much he values the armed forces." Unfortunately, Walsh doesn't get very specific about how this "charm offensive" might work. He details the Clintons' effort to establish a family life for daughter Chelsea, but this 5-10 feature sounds as though it could have been written by the First Lady's press secretary. In his silly 6-28 exercise, Walsh describes Clinton's method of governing by "instinct," without once citing a named source. If, as he says, Clinton "stubbornly refuses to reveal his thoughts," how does Walsh know? He takes an effective 8-2 look at the difficulties of the fishbowl life that administration officials must lead and how it helped to drive Vince Foster to suicide. Although he neglects to look at the ups and downs of White House policy, he provides a solid and dignified evaluation of the failures and successes of the administration in staffing. In his superficial 10-18 review of what's wrong with Clinton's approach to foreign affairs—particularly with regard to Somalia and Bosnia—Walsh finally addresses policy. However, he overgeneralizes: "Confusion" and "altruism" don't really stand out as specific flaws that mean anything—even when Walsh tries to explain them. His intriguing 7-19 profile of Vice President Al Gore is, alas, short on substance. Like so many of his colleagues, Walsh insists on covering the Democratic administration's personalities instead of its policies.

Daniel Wattenberg
The American Spectator
★★½

Relying on fact and incisive commentary, Wattenberg rises above the purely political to provide a fresh perspective for his conservative audience. Rather than seeking the next Watergate or chasing every tabloid scandal, he opts for depth, challenging views commonly held among the media and the Beltway elite. In his detailed February account of Secretary of State Warren Christopher's former tenure in the Carter State Department, Wattenberg slams Christopher's "litigational approach" to foreign policy as "barely distinguishable from appeasement." Citing numerous examples of Christopher's so-called blunders—such as his belief that the Iranian Revolution was the overthrowing of colonial rule rather than the establishment of a theocracy—Wattenberg holds him "as responsible as anyone for cutting America's interests loose from their strategic underpinnings in the late 1970s." This probing account questions the widely held opinion that the appointment of Christopher—whom he calls both a "naïf" and an "apologist"—is "not a cause for serious worry." His thorough August investigation into the Waco fiasco provides a credible and convincing explanation of the events surrounding the ATF/FBI siege and assault of David Koresh and his followers. Wattenberg contends that, faced with both sexual harassment charges and possibly hostile appropriations hearings, the ATF sought to improve its image by fabricating a case and then staging a raid on "this white, male, sexually predatory, patriarchal, tax resisting, gun loving religious nut." Wattenberg disappoints, however, when he turns to rhetoric to support his otherwise provocative arguments. In his January piece, he exposes former Sandinista Luis Carrión Cruz's acceptance as a fellow at Harvard's Kennedy School of Government. While Wattenberg effectively criticizes the use of U.S. tax dollars to fund the education of foreign officials linked

to torture and terror, his argument falls short when reduced to ad hominem attacks on Carrion's intellect. Wattenberg cites, for example, a detractor who calls him a "'dunce.'" Similarly, he trivializes his June account of the U.S. Chamber of Commerce's "budding romance with the Clinton administration" by characterizing one top official as "a bilious bureaucratic Iago." Although his rhetoric amuses and occasionally strikes a nerve— as in his December reference to sympathizers of Lorena Bobbitt as "sharia feminists" —Wattenberg's arguments prove most convincing when he is reflective, not reflexive.

Bernard Weinraub

The New York Times

★★½

Hollywood. After years of covering the White House, Weinraub stirs humor, realism, and insight into his reports on the business of entertainment. In his 1-28 article on the Sundance Festival in Utah, he goes beyond the screen to reveal the talk behind the films. "If there's a consensus this year it's that the movies here, as in Hollywood, are not better than ever. Younger than ever, perhaps, but not better....This year's showcase somehow proves that many of the twentysomething film makers, while technically proficient, may not have the vision or life experiences that can enrich a film." At the Golden Globes, 1-25, Weinraub delivers the kind of gab readers enjoy when actress Emma Thompson tells him, "'Darling, I've never felt like a movie star. It's the one thing I'm not. I keep trying to make sure my tights don't fall down.'" But Weinraub is no mere gossip, as witness his 4-5 report on Hollywood's financial problems. "Crédit Lyonnais had hired [Michael Ovitz's talent agency] C.A.A. to help manage its deeply troubled, if not disastrous, $3.1 billion entertainment portfolio. This includes the bank's control of Metro Goldwyn Mayer, once a great studio." Pursuing what exploded into a Hollywood power struggle, 5-3, Weinraub concludes, "It is a measure of Mr. Ovitz's weight in Hollywood that he has received many calls from studio executives and rival agents privately supporting him." In his 8-1 *Magazine* piece, Weinraub muses on the switch to his new beat. "I covered the White House for a while under Reagan and Bush. And now I cover Ovitz and [Disney president Jeffrey] Katzenberg. It hasn't been an especially difficult transition." With flair and charm, Weinraub informs readers of the politics and power plays surrounding the entertainment industry. And he's happy to remind readers how much he enjoys his beat.

Michael Weisskopf

The Washington Post

Staff writer. Writing comprehensive profiles of lobbyists and their efforts nationwide, Weisskopf documents their strategies and their spending. Making his most controversial statement of the year in a 2-1 story on the religious right, he calls the followers of evangelists Jerry Falwell and Pat Robertson "largely poor, uneducated and easy to command." The *Post* issued a correction the following day, and Weisskopf himself later called using the phrase "an honest mistake." Weisskopf's 5-10 article investigates the inner operations of the American tobacco lobby, exposing some cracks in its normally unified front. "Some farmers are now planning to sit out a fight over unprecedented increases in cigarette taxes, sought to finance health care reform, because the industry is using more and more cheap foreign tobacco." The tobacco lobby remains strong, however, as Weisskopf shows in his 7-10 report on the distribution of tobacco products to minors in Washington State. "Marlboro vans, customized and painted to teenage tastes, have started to park near high schools....One measure of the tobacco lobby's clout is its effectiveness in states such as this one so far from the tobacco patch of the South." Despite his revealing articles, Weisskopf sometimes pulls his punches, perhaps to maintain ties with his sources. He shows restraint, 11-12, when reporting that the government-funded Small Business Association published 200,000 brochures promoting President Clinton's health-care reform bill and donating 10,000 copies to the Democratic National Committee. "The SBA outlay of $82,000," Weisskopf lightly muses, "apparently falls within the narrow statutory limits on executive branch lobbying with appropriated funds. But the pamphlet is unusually political for the SBA." Reporting on NAFTA, 9-28, he observes that "Few issues have united U.S. companies the way NAFTA has....So far the 'giant sucking sound' from the south that [Ross] Perot predicted for NAFTA has come from the suites of lobbyists and PR agents vacuuming in funds from U.S. firms and the Mexican government to push the pact." Although he sometimes makes sense of the tangled special interests that can make or break a new law, Weisskopf's articles would prove more informative—and penetrating—if they also examined the aftereffects of some of the most intimidating lobbying efforts.

Isabel Wilkerson

The New York Times

★

Chicago. More interested this year in quotes than truth, Wilkerson overstuffs her straightforward reporting with talking heads. She offers firsthand accounts of daily life in the Midwest but rarely challenges her sources, and seems content with common wisdom and academic insight. In her 8-20 back-to-school piece from flood-ravaged Elwood, Kansas, Wilkerson obsesses over a school forced to set up in a church. "There is a cross in the back of the eighth grade classroom, fourth graders pass a bulletin board about the Temptations of Jesus to get to their room and near the fourth grade blackboard is the exhortation on gray construction paper: 'God has a plan for you.'" She presses the church-and-state conflict with a local education official. "'It's best you not ask,' said Dale Dennis, assistant commissioner of the Kansas State department of Education. 'They're doing what they have to do. Pretty near everything is destroyed. It looks like a nuclear attack over there.'" Although she saw that devastation, Wilkerson asked anyway. In a rambling 7-18 reminiscence of flood devastation, Wilkerson quotes an aquatic ecologist, the Civil War writer Shelby Foote, and various academics, but no one unschooled in soundbites. "'I think we as moderns tend to think that geological and meteorological changes have stopped,' said Bruce Michaelson, a professor of English...'that volcanoes will no longer erupt, that hurricanes will no longer come off the coasts and the great rivers of the world are going to stay quietly in their banks so we can cruise them in our boats and barges.'" Her shallow 8-15 analysis of the portrayal of African Americans on film and TV reaches an unremarkable conclusion. "It seems a black movie or television show is not considered 'authentic' without a rap score, a slack-shouldered teen-ager and drugs, violence or some other social ill. Reality is the new buzzword. But some blacks in television ask, whose reality?" Missing is a discussion of what African Americans themselves like to watch on television. In her revealing 6-2 effort on urban race relations, Wilkerson profiles Karen Gunn, a black Chicago woman employed by a Korean community group to mediate between Korean business owners and local black residents. "What Ms. Gunn and her supervisor, [Inchul] Choi, hope to do is to get the Koreans, who have faced discrimination themselves from the Japanese and from the white Americans, to see they have things in common with blacks." With an obvious affinity or contempt for her sources, Wilkerson unfairly forces readers to either accept her perspective or dismiss the pieces out of hand.

Curtis Wilkie

The Boston Globe

★★½

National politics. Always informative and often insightful, Wilkie provides clear-eyed views of Washington politics. In an extensive 1-17 look at Bill Clinton and his long affiliation with Washington, Wilkie debunks the mythology surrounding the incoming President. "Clinton posed as an outsider only when it was expedient to do so during the campaign, and even though he comes to Washington after 12 years as governor of a poor, rural state that President Bush characterized as the 'lowest of the low,' Clinton is an ultimate insider. He is as familiar with the political folkways of Washington as the hoariest veteran of Congress. 'This is a place that is not in any sense strange to him,' says Anne Wexler, a prominent Democratic lobbyist who was a White House assistant under Carter. 'He knows everybody in government, and he kept up his relationships over the years.'" In his 5-30 dispatch, Wilkie gathers reminiscences of the late Robert Kennedy, who, with typical Bostonian hyperbole, he compares to St. Paul. Despite such flights of fancy, he renders a useful political profile, even if it doesn't quite capture the complexity of the man. Wilkie's jumpy and disorganized portrait of Rep. Barney Frank [D-MA] also fails to convey the depth of its subject. In his 9-3 essay, Wilkie tries to

pin the changing landscape of urban politics on the new rules drafted by the Democratic party—in the wake of the 1968 Chicago convention—that diminished the power of big-city mayors to deliver votes. Although the piece is provocative, Wilkie fails to explore too many other factors. A correspondent in Lebanon during the early 1980s, he draws eerie parallels, 10-10, between the events in that country to those in Somalia. "In each case, American troops were hailed as a force for stability when they arrived in the country only to wind up hunkered in a defensive position after U.S. policy makers took sides in conflicts involving local warlords. And just as opposition in Congress rose with the number of casualties in Lebanon in 1983, President Clinton is under pressure from Congressional leaders troubled by the deteriorating situation in Somalia....Policy makers again have allowed events to transform U.S. forces overseas from peacekeepers to parties to a conflict not only foreign but so complex in its factionalism that it is unfathomable to most Americans." This kind of effort showcases what Wilkie—an experienced and capable journalist—can do.

Michael Wines

The New York Times

★★★

Washington. As Wines excels at ferreting out salient detail on major issues, even his overviews offer more specifics than features penned by his fellow reporters. Each story always contains a tidbit or two that only Wines has found. He crafts an in-depth 1-16 account of both the contents of George Bush's diary and its significance to the Iran-contra investigation. In his colorful 3-3 account of Ross Perot and his testimony before a joint House and Senate committee on streamlining government, Wines carefully avoids poking fun, but misses none of the eccentricity of the situation. "Mr. Perot came to Washington today, trailed by a throng of cheering, laughing applauding acolytes, to give Congress the road-tested message that when you get right down to it, the Government's problems are all very simple. It bore all the earmarks of a Frank Capra movie until one lawmaker began suggesting that he was long on pomp and arrogance, and short on solutions." Wines sharply covers the budget battle—from his solid 5-26 political summary of who's lining up where and how Clinton's swaying votes, to his wonderful 5-28 description of the political brawl in the House. "The House of Representatives spent 10 hours today giving President Clinton's budget the full benefit of the deliberative process. It may have been democracy at its best, but it was not pretty. On the contrary, the flocked and brass-trimmed House chamber was less a legislative arena than a movie-set bar room, a place where one cowboy makes a sneering remark, a second throws a punch and suddenly everyone is firing six guns and hitting friend and foe alike over the head with liquor bottles and chairs. It was ugly; it was hyperbolic; it was personal." Despite the Dowdish sound, Wines provides a great deal of information and successfully places the reader at center-stage in this next-best-thing-to-C-SPAN feature. His solid 8-6 review details the last-minute congressional wrangling for votes on the budget. With an evocative 11-3 dispatch on the fight in the Senate over Sen. Bob Packwood's [R-OR] diaries, Wines makes Packwood seem both human and tragic, culling a perceptive quote from Sen. Trent Lott [R-MS] who sums up the way many Senators feel. "In the end, the vote will not be based on ethical or legal questions, but on the politics of the moment. Do you want to be perceived as having voted for a cover-up?" With his sharp eye for detail and his astute analytic skill, Wines adds considerably to the public's knowledge.

Bob Woodward

The Washington Post

★★½

Assistant managing editor for investigative news. His reputation always preceding him, Woodward has one of the most influential bylines around. Although he uncovers no bombshell scoops, and offers nothing as his 1992 series on Dan Quayle and the Bush economic program, he turns in a solid portfolio of which any reporter would be proud. In his 1-5 effort, Woodward explains why Clinton's nominees are getting an easy ride. The FBI, he reports, is under a deadline imposed by the incoming administration to get things done fast. Instead of the normal 30 days for the background checks, Clinton aides have cut the time in half, and in some cases reduced the time to 6-12 days. "One source said that numerous questions raised by [Ron] Brown's past lobbying and business ventures would keep a dozen FBI agents busy for a month if all questions were to be answered fully. But sources said [Clinton transition counsel for nominations and confirmations James] Hamilton said that deadline was inflexible because the Senate Commerce Committee planned to begin confirmation hearings Wednesday." Woodward crafts an informative and detailed 2-21 profile of new Defense Secretary Les Aspin, finding out what makes him tick. "He is told that some who know him best and longest find that his compulsive proclivity for rumination and analysis leaves them wondering about his fundamental values." In a thorough 5-23 examination of the late Justice Thurgood Marshall's papers on the Webster decision—which came close to overturning *Roe v. Wade*—Woodward and coauthor Benjamin Weiser provide a fascinating look at the internal workings of the Supreme Court. They report that Chief Justice William Rehnquist circulated draft opinions on *Webster v. Reproductive Health Services*. "But in the last 10 days of the term, Justice Sandra Day O'Connor—the critical fifth vote—declined to agree with Rehnquist's language attacking *Roe*, forcing him to back off in his fifth and final draft." In an 11-6 *TV Guide* piece, Woodward, the investigative print reporter, profiles Mike Wallace, the investigative broadcast reporter. "The real Wallace has never been as tough as his one-dimensional reputation. In his 25 years with '60 Minutes,' Wallace has never been Sam Spade. He is not really an investigative reporter who digs in and immerses himself in one subject for a long time until he thinks he understands it. Though Wallace can make people squirm, he basically lets people tell their story." And therein lies one key difference between print and broadcast media. Although not a fully satisfying profile, Woodward's cogent observations make up for his shortcomings as a portraitist. Twenty years after Watergate, Woodward remains one of the top investigative reporters.

Kenneth Woodward

Newsweek

★★

Religion. Showing maturity and wisdom in his reporting, Woodward offers large doses of analysis and opinion. In his 5-17 article, he minimizes the notion that politically conservative Christians exert much influence over the public schools. "Apart from a few local battles—most of them over sex education—there is no evidence that the religious right is capable of capturing the nation's schools.... If the religious right really had muscles to flex, their power would show in the churchgoing citadels of the South and Middle West." Woodward's 11-29 article attempts to demonstrate "that while religion pervades the American landscape, only a minority takes it seriously." Despite the damage inflicted on the Catholic Church by sex scandals in the priesthood, Woodward's hyperbolic 7-12 assessment of the 2,000-year-old institution seems rather premature. "The long-term damage to the church...is still incalculable. Even before the current spate of scandals broke, the number of vocations to the priesthood was in steep decline. Today's priests may outlast the scandals, but the image of the priesthood may never be as bright." Woodward also explores human ethics, 2-22, discussing the need for guidelines in dealing with the medical and commercial uses of aborted fetuses. "Science does not advance in a moral vacuum," he notes. "What limits, if any, should be observed when experimenting with human fetuses? Does a mother who aborts her fetus have the moral right to...have any say at all about the disposition of the body?...Now factor in the profit motive." Woodward's strong faith in ethics propels his most moving piece, a 4-26 tour of the new Holocaust Memorial Museum in Washington, D.C. "The doors of the elevators are gunmetal gray; they open and shut heavily, like the doors of an oven....On the [museum's] third floor the story lunges dizzyingly from purgatory to hell. Silence is needed to assimilate what happened—and to realize that mass extermination is a recurring nightmare." While he won't satisfy those seeking the latest on hot topics, Woodward's sometimes iconoclastic views on religion and ethical issues often provoke.

★ BUSINESS & ECONOMICS ★

Alan Abelson

Barron's

★★

"Up & Down Wall Street" columnist. Authoring *Barron's* front-page feature each week, Abelson provides a commodity in short supply in financial writing—namely, wit. A master of turning the clever phrase or tossing out the *bon mot*, he serves as the chief supplier of jocularity for a humor-starved (or, perhaps, humor*less*) financial community. His talents considerable, Abelson seldom fails to enthrall or enlighten the reader. Describing corporate belt-tighteners whose jobs involve downsizing—i.e., firing people—he remarks, 5-3, "For a lot of companies that partied madly in the 'Eighties, it has been a very long morning after. And they've concluded with ineluctable logic that the best cure for a corporate hangover is to reduce the number of heads." Despite his column's name, Abelson comments on developments in Washington as well as on Wall Street, and the challenge to reading him is to get through an entire piece without laughing out loud. Contemplating the Vice President's "reinventing government" plan, 9-6, he irreverently proclaims that Al Gore "has set on reinventing the Leviathan. To what end? you may well ask. The possible answer has evoked considerable speculation in various organs, none of them vital, like *The Washington Post* and *The New York Times*." Some weeks find him whimsically overbearing—his propensity for puns leading him, 8-23, to label Wall Street's bull market "Moo-rasic Park"—but never so much so that he doesn't entertain. Even little asides showcase Abelson's ability to amuse. In his 4-26 column he sarcastically declares that Brazil "has long been a global pacesetter in the economic sphere. It has no peers in its ability to keep inflation soaring, and it is the acknowledged leader in running up foreign debt." In his 3-8 piece on the World Trade Center bombing, he wickedly quips about the suspect, "He's from the Middle East, the cradle of civilization and more recently the graveyard of civility." While Abelson's columns usually mention some new financial development or key player, they often serve more as structures that he adorns with witticisms. Read Abelson for the gleeful, almost bawdy, cynicism with which he impales Wall Street prognosticators and government do-gooders. For this alone, *Barron's* is worth picking up each week.

George Anders

The Wall Street Journal

★★★

Health, medicine. Sticking to the business side of health care and seldom exploring the arguments raging in Washington, Anders gives readers a break from the flood of stories detailing the Clinton health plan. Although he may discuss topics at play in the political arena, his pieces ooze business and not policy. In his shrewd 12-1 piece about the trend toward mergers by hospitals, Anders writes, "The flurry of hospital consolidation is partly a response to President Clinton's proposals for health-system reform, as well as more-immediate pressures to reduce costs and deal with declining occupancy rates." By laying off the Clinton plan, Anders provides superb coverage of issues under-reported in 1993. His 5-6 front-pager on Hill-Rom, the nation's largest hospital bed maker, offers insight into rising health-care costs. Advances in outpatient care have cut the need for beds, so bed makers churn out more advanced, costlier products, and then must convince hospital administrators of their necessity. "In the medical equipment business, almost everything, from hypodermic needles to computerized imaging machines, is the subject of high-powered marketing, rapid technological breakthroughs and equally rapid price increases." Tracking innovations in medical technology, 9-30, Anders writes of a rural Kentucky hospital's instantaneous access to big-city experts. "The little hospital will begin using special BellSouth Corp. telephone lines to flash X-ray images to a big hospital in Louisville, where radiologists will provide immediate readings of the films." The process, Anders concludes, will save thousands of dollars in courier fees and thousands of hours each year. Anders files few non-health pieces, but those he does rate very high. His 1-29 front-page look at the California Public Employees' Retirement System hits hard at the hubris and hypocrisy of Dale Hanson, the head of the mammoth pension fund. Anders notes that Hanson, a shareholder activist, "whizzes around the U.S. goading corporate directors," while leaving operations back home unattended. Anders deftly chronicles the sorry investment record of a man who loves to lecture company directors for poor performance. By keeping his focus on health and business issues and not getting bogged down in Washington politics, Anders avoids the arcane, sometimes alarmist, reporting that has tarred other reporters' work.

Edmund L. Andrews

The New York Times

★★★

Communications. With a thoroughness seldom found in other journalists, Andrews keeps readers keyed to the constant struggles involved in building the information superhighway. Of all the battlefields where the communications revolution is being fought, Andrews reports from what might be the most contentious arena—Washington, D.C. Prowling the meeting rooms of Congress and the corridors of the FCC, he files strong stories on the attempts by government regulators to bring unbridled technologies under their purview. The most intriguing part of Andrews's work is the way he peers into the crystal ball. In his fascinating 9-20 article exploring the ramifications of the government's decision to auction off a huge slice of the radio spectrum, he hazards, "Wireless phones could replace a high percentage of those now tethered to copper wire. That could be a mixed blessing, freeing people from their desks yet chaining them to their jobs... [with] computerized systems that can automatically track a person's movements anywhere in North America." More to the (fiscal) point, Andrews writes in a 9-27 follow-up, the government hopes to raise untold sums from the airwave auction. "It is, literally, the $10 billion question....Fueled by torrid demand for cellular telephones and other mobile communications, licenses for space on the radio have become the hottest parcels of real estate in the country." Though "reporting" on news still years down the road, Andrews doesn't neglect today's events. Describing the precipitous decline in business seen by "900" phone-number services, 4-21, he smartly explains, "The chat lines, dating lines, astrology services, sweepstakes and contests...have all seen their popularity decline as the novelty fades and newer technologies like computer bulletin boards come into wider use." Time and again, the authoritative Andrews writes with clarity, recognizing the different angles to an issue. In profiling Hughes Communication, a Colorado-based company hoping to use satellites to beam TV signals to mini-dishes in homes across America, 12-15, Andrews shows why this company of the future may already be behind the times. He points out that Hughes's competitors, "cable operators, many in league with telephone companies, are spending billions to upgrade their networks to offer hundreds of programming choices, plus something the Hughes system will not offer: two-way 'interactive' capabilities." Balancing his day-to-day coverage of official Washington's maneuverings with comprehensive assessments of their significance, Andrews rarely leaves readers with unanswered questions.

Ken Auletta

The New Yorker

Media, entertainment. Ehancing his broad-picture coverage of the media and entertainment industries with inside reporting, Auletta sometimes spreads himself too thin. His disjointed stories stem from his attempts to tackle diverse subjects that often don't mesh very well. In his 3-15 piece on the future of network television, Auletta fragments the story into profiles of various TV heavyweights. He further blurs his focus on treatments of interactive computing and Coca-Cola's acclaimed polar bear commercials. Auletta's inability to bring them all together winds up puzzling the reader, and while good insights abound, they must be mined like diamonds. "In the pursuit

of lower costs, all three networks have reduced the number of their foreign and domestic [news] bureaus in recent years, and have come to rely increasingly on international picture services, local stations' news, and free-lancers to supply pictures and reports....The networks save money, but they also end up vouching for the accuracy of news they don't control." In his markedly better 8-2 piece about CNN, Auletta deftly analyzes the global network's vulnerbilities in the wake of a BBC/ABC agreement to pool resources and compete with Ted Turner's Goliath. "[Turner] knows that CNN is open to attack from competitors on at least three fronts: it is not yet truly international; it is not local; it has so few overseas partners that its distribution system is stretched thin." Auletta also focuses on the print media. In his pedestrian 6-28 story, he dissects the upheaval at *The New York Times* initiated by publisher Arthur Ochs Sulzberger Jr., giving a fly-on-the-wall account of staff meetings in which acrimonious battles are fought over the paper's direction. However, his treatment on the contentiousness between the company's business and editorial sides begs for elaboration. Auletta remains more comfortable writing about the picture-driven media of TV and film. A glowing 2-22 pre-Paramount-bid profile of home-shopping guru Barry Diller sets the stage nicely for Auletta's 10-4 look at the battle over Paramount, in which Diller emerges as a key player. On the other hand, Auletta yields stiff 2-1 treatment of the networks' courtship of David Letterman. While divulging details of the negotiations, such as NBC's offer to eventually dump Jay Leno and give "The Tonight Show" to Letterman, the story ultimately falls flat. Still, Auletta's got the skills. Now he just needs focus.

Kenneth Bacon

The Wall Street Journal

★★★½

Banking. Opening a window to the highly charged and contentious banking industry, Bacon offers readers a peek at developments in Washington's corridors of power. In a year which sees a self-described "New Democrat" in the White House promise deregulation of the industry, Bacon guarantees bankable coverage as administration officials clash swords with cautious legislators. Barely three weeks into Bill Clinton's term, 2-16, Bacon reports how the President, "facing a congressional counter-attack against the banking industry's pleas for regulatory relief, will concentrate on administrative, rather than legislative, efforts to increase bank lending." Bacon reports in his 4-30 story that the comptroller of the currency is instructing bank examiners to ease "'overly restrictive'" regulations as they go about their appointed rounds. Later in the year, 7-14, Bacon reports a rapprochement with Congress which hints at new laws watering down banks' community reinvestment rules to eliminate paperwork and red tape. "The basic elements of the proposal have been public for months," he writes, "because the administration has discussed it with Congress in an effort to win quick passage." Stumbling somewhat, Bacon does not follow up this mention of the proposal's legislative prospects, nor does he gauge the response of key congressional figures. Despite this rare lapse, Bacon consistently provides stellar reporting of banking matters. In his 8-11 piece, he draws readers' attention to the fact that the FDIC's Bank Fund—$7 billion in the hole two years ago—now contains nearly $7 billion, a fact that both government and banks point out to emphasize the industry's health. In his 12-14 story, Bacon details how banking policy is made—or, in this case, not made—on the banks of the Potomac. "Congress has ended its year without passing any major banking legislation, and Citicorp had a front-row seat for the inaction," Bacon nimbly writes. He exposes how lobbyists for Citicorp—the only bank to have a fully-staffed office of influence-peddlers—"spend most of their time blocking and blunting changes that could hurt Citicorp's extensive credit-card operations, student-loan business or ever-broadening financial-services offerings." By furnishing vigorous coverage of both the banking industry and its government overseers, Bacon has established himself as one of the stars at *The Wall Street Journal.*

Aaron Bernstein

Business Week

Workplace editor. A forceful and passionate writer, the unabashedly liberal Bernstein appeals to proponents of government management of the economy. His commentary pieces read little different from his news stories, in which he argues strongly for both resurgent unionism and a higher minimum wage. In his 3-22 essay, Bernstein addresses the latter point. He contends, without substantiation, that minimum-wage opponents concede that initial employment setbacks would "be outweighed as rising wages force companies to...improve productivity—and eventually create jobs requiring higher skills that raise the standard of living." He further adds, "Minimum-wage critics have trouble countering such logic." Bernstein's focus on the economy always turns to government first. In his 8-16 story, he cites the fact that a 16-year-old girl couldn't get work from an underfunded federal summer-jobs program as proof that the economy is faring poorly for teens. While that may be true, the inability to land a government-funded job hardly ranks as a serious barometer of economic health. He suggests, 7-12, that mandated benefits and other labor costs have negligible effects on job growth. As proof he quotes the CEO of the 17,000-employee Home Depot Inc. as saying the company won't stop hiring because of medical benefits. Bernstein presents a superb 8-30 profile of Ron Carey, the reformer who bucked the entrenched leadership to become president of the Teamsters Union in 1992. Some Teamsters, Bernstein explains, distrust Carey because he stands to "inherit $350,000 from the sale of UPS that his father, a former UPS driver, bought in the 1930s.... Carey says the windfall won't affect his stance in the [UPS-Teamsters] talks. But the story has been spread by allies of R.V. Durham, a North Carolina Teamsters leader who ran against Carey." Even though the causes he defends come as no surprise, Bernstein refrains from providing predictable justifications for them. A firm defender of the union cause, which is all too rare among business writers, Bernstein often presents articulate and compelling commentary.

"I don't know what the hell happened—one minute I'm at work in Flint, Michigan, then there's a giant sucking sound and suddenly here I am in Mexico."

Harry Bernstein

Los Angeles Times

★½

Labor. A throwback to an earlier era of labor-management relations, the gruff Bernstein provides acerbic commentary on union issues. In his 8-15 piece on President Clinton's nominee to head the National Labor Relations Board, Bernstein implores the Senate to confirm William Gould IV and "ignore the forces of reaction that want to eliminate unions and let corporate moguls rule their domains with little or no 'interference' from workers or their unions." He heaps further scorn upon these "right-wing, anti-union" forces by branding them "rabid." A brutal wordsmith, Bernstein pens columns dripping with acid, and one senses that Bernstein would rather open old wounds than address issues facing labor today—like unions' role in health-care reform, or their declining membership levels. A TV show on UAW giant Walter Reuther, 2-1, leads Bernstein to cite bitterly a Machinists union survey finding "that unions and workers are generally ignored by the electronic media. Even prostitutes outnumber machinists—union and nonunion—on television by a 12-to-1 margin." A proponent of strong government direction of the economy, Bernstein approaches job creation the way a tinkering mechanic does an engine—twist a knob here, change a plug there, tighten this valve, and *bin-*

go! He argues in his 3-2 effort that the government must "increase the penalty on employers who work their employees more than 40 hours a week, thereby creating more jobs." He uses his 10-21 column on federal job training programs to argue that "without a new and substantial source of revenue—meaning a progressive tax hike—we aren't likely to get the jobs we need to revive our own economy." A good foot-soldier, Bernstein labors in the NAFTA fight, 2-16, rallying those who would "derail the treaty former President Bush and his aides concocted to help corporate America, regardless of the harm it does to workers." After congressional approval of the trade pact, 11-21, he gloats at the near defeat of "what should have been a lead-pipe cinch to pass." While he wears his politics on the rolled-up sleeve of his workingman's shirt, Bernstein seldom fails to entertain or to present perspectives not often seen in the daily press.

John M. Berry
The Washington Post

Economics. Berry's assessments of macroeconomic trends continue to be a mixed bag of conventional generalizations and occasional insights. Despite the inconsistency of his work in 1993, he has become one of the most reliable chroniclers of remarks made by Federal Reserve Chairman Alan Greenspan—an important and surprisingly rare skill among Fed watchers in the press corps. Accurately portraying Greenspan's reaction to President Clinton's budget proposal, 2-20, Berry carefully notes that while the Chairman praised deficit-reduction efforts, he refused to embrace the plan's details. In his 3-21 article, Berry resists the popular misconception that Greenspan had guaranteed easier money if Clinton's economic package stifled growth. "Treasury Secretary Lloyd Bentsen has said without equivocation that no deal for lower interest rates has been struck between the administration and the Fed." Other writers overlooked these important remarks. Providing an in-depth exploration of the Fed's attention to gold, 9-8, Berry reports for the record Greenspan's widely ignored testimony. "'Essentially what the gold price reflects is a concern about the purchasing power of currency or money.'" In his 9-22 dispatch, Berry emerges as one of the only journalists to investigate the mystery behind low interest rates, although his analysis proves far from the cutting-edge. Indeed, when Berry attempts to examine monetary or fiscal policy, he often falls short. In his 1-3 summary of how Clinton might influence the economy, Berry merely compiles generalizations implying that policy has little effect. In another predictable report, 4-30, Berry skims the sharp decline in economic growth during the first three months of 1993. While offering enough quoted sources, Berry misses an opportunity to explore the reasons behind this striking development. Similarly, in his 11-3 article on bonds, he treats theory as fact, reporting that "the yield curve is saying that investors believe stronger growth means higher rates." Berry has his strengths and weaknesses. Turn to him for strong reporting on the Federal Reserve, but don't rely exclusively on his analysis of fiscal or monetary policy.

Peter Brimelow
Forbes
★★½

Senior editor. Fiercely pro-market, Brimelow has a knack for bringing statistics to life, at least those that support his perspective. With his sharp intellect and contagious enthusiasm, he shapes forceful arguments, but his evident desire to indoctrinate readers borders on zealotry, especially when he covers socioeconomic topics. Joined by frequent co-author Leslie Spencer, Brimelow embarks on a politically incorrect 2-15 discussion contending that "'diversity' can conflict with merit." There's no missing the article's mission—to reveal the dark side of affirmative action. Although the estimates on the direct costs of "quotas" are startling—$17 to 20 billion nationwide—some of the methods used to calculate these figures indicate that the pair might have constructed an equally potent argument in favor of affirmative action. "Hyperbolic?" is the question Brimelow and Spencer ask when they label the National Education Association (NEA) the "National Extortion Association" in a 6-7 investigation of its heavy-handed lobbying. While perhaps an appropriate question, they interject highly loaded language between their substantial analysis and historical material. Such potshots as "the NEA's streak of left-wing looneyism" undermine their genuine insights about how economic resources currently get diverted from productive activities. Although less rancorous, equally conservative commentary permeates their sophisticated 1-4 scrutiny of the widely publicized study of racial bias in mortgage lending record of the Federal Reserve Bank of Boston. Brimelow and Spencer's claim that equal default rates among whites and minorities reveal that lenders weeded out applicants by credit risk—and did not engage in discriminatory activity—raises important questions, but asides such as calling the study "an excuse for more social engineering" detract from the article's credibility. Effectively comparing economic data, Brimelow delivers a less emotional 3-15 analysis of how the growing government share of the economy does more damage than swelling budget deficits. Similarly, his 7-19 dissection of gloom-and-doom reports about the growing federal debt reasons that as long as the debt isn't monetized and bond markets remain healthy, no financial Armageddon is imminent. A lively writer with a distinct point of view, Brimelow always warrants a read as long as one takes his occasional excesses with a grain of salt.

Samuel Brittan

Financial Times

★★½

Assistant editor. Cerebral, precise, and historically astute—Brittan consistently hits the mark in his "Economic Viewpoint" essays. A theoretician's writer, he renders the major economic debates accessible to newspaper readers—at least those with patience to sift through economic analysis thick with data. Devoting many words to the U.K. budget, 3-25, Brittan advises against new taxes. "It is better to avoid levying ever-heavier taxes on one group of citizens in order to make ever-high interest payments to another and overlapping group. The sooner the burden can be transferred to monetary policy, the better. In the meanwhile, the U.K. government should adopt a less cavalier attitude to the debt interest rate burden." But hedging between supply-side and Keynesian logic, 2-25, Brittan absolves fiscal policymakers of responsibility. "If higher public spending or lower taxes cause output to grow more quickly, then the [debt trap] theorem does not hold. Debt interest rises, but so does the real national income and government revenues with it." This assumes that higher spending and lower taxes work through the economy in a similar fashion, an issue hotly debated. Working on the broader European canvas, Brittan continues to glorify the European Rate Mechanism (ERM), even though England's recovery began after its break with the ERM. His 7-29 column attributes England's low inflation and more flexible labor market to interest-rate increases and "the [John] Major-[Norman] Lamont insistence on sticking to ERM membership for two years." Brittan, however, makes no effort to persuade critics who argue that England's war on inflation, in the name of ERM membership, caused unemployment, thus "softening" a demoralized labor force. In a similar vein, 6-10, he argues in an uncharacteristically alarmist tone that "the ERM may have had its fault lines, but these are nothing compared with the defects of unbridled currency nationalism." Yet Brittan offers no evidence of such a scenario unfolding. Searching for a more independent institution than Germany to play the anchor role, 11-11, he suggests the European Monetary Institute. But amid these musings, he overlooks the formula proposed by President Bush in 1992—a basket of commodities, including gold. Still, even armchair economists who don't agree with Brittan will find his unique brand of sophisticated economic commentary provocative and enlightening.

John Byrne

Business Week

★★

The von Trapp Family Singers would probably feel right at home reading Byrne's work week in and week out: It's all peaks and valleys. Traipsing through his pieces on corporate management will leave readers either nodding their heads in admiration or scratching them in confusion. In his expert 9-20 look at McKinsey & Co., the highly regarded management-consulting firm, Byrne evenhandedly penetrates the "McKinsey Mystique." Former McKinsey consultants, he notes, recently vaulted into the top spots at American Express, Westinghouse, and IBM. "Measured by the number of alumni who have captured corner offices, McKinsey is by far the most influential consulting firm in the world....McKinsey's most profound impact on business comes in its official role as corporate doctor to at least half of the 500 largest U.S. corporations, as well as many of the most elite foreign giants." Exploring the firm's famously selective hiring process along with the mind-boggling work demands placed on the chosen, Byrne offers readers a sobering glimpse at perhaps the most exclusive corporate club on earth. This quality reporting, however, never shows up in "The Virtual Corporation," his incomprehensible 2-8 cover story about the future of management. Full of fluff and bereft of details, Byrne's vision should not be confused with advertising megaguru Jay Chiat's similarly futuristic "virtual agency" workplace. Alluding to a more diversified production system, Byrne touts "adaptability," "trust," and "excellence" as the keys to business success in the 21st century—as if these ideas are new. In his weak 2-15 offering in the wake of the executive sackings at American Express and IBM, Byrne rather speciously forecasts that corporate America will depose dinosaur CEOs for being too feeble to hack it in the fast-paced, global marketplace. "Call it the Elvis Effect," he quips, "this phenomenon of generational change [is] marked by the Clinton-Gore victory." But Byrne climbs back to the top with a scathing 7-19 assessment of Harvard Business School. As *BW*'s business school expert-in-residence, he skewers the venerable institution, likening it to IBM—once monolithic and now tottering—as he details the school's attempt to reevaluate its mission. In this withering assessment, he gives the business to the famous business school. With Byrne you get a heads-or-tails reporter who wins about half the time, but one with the skills to definitely improve the percentages.

Christopher Byron

New York

★★★

"The Bottom Line" columnist. With forceful prose and quirky humor, iconoclast Byron takes on Washington, Wall Street, the Middle East, and the media with equal relish. He meticulously backs up his arguments with hard facts, and his impressive reportorial skills lend weight to his sardonic pieces. In his 1-11 article, Byron explores the cottage industry set up by grassy-knoll types to influence the fourth estate. "There really is such a thing in this country as a conspiracy industry—complete with gullible journalists, headline-hungry congressmen, and 'circular sourcing' experts who confirm one another's claims." Noting the deluge of Iran-Contra exposés, Byron remarks, "The main thing all these books have in common is the similarity of their sources—largely private investigators and washed-out spooks who keep turning up over and over again." Skepticism Byron never lacks. His 1-18 story, "While Wall Street Slept," gleefully skewers the financial soothsayers blindsided by IBM's demise. "If you want to know what the biggest and most embarrassing scandal on Wall Street is these days, it's not the latest insider-trading mess or penny-stock fraud. It's the egg-on-the-face failure of 99 percent of Wall Street's analysts to have foreseen the coming carnage at IBM....What they missed was shocking." Byron directs much of his firepower at the Clinton administration, 3-8, and he painstakingly details why the President's economic proposals may not work. "The real problem with unemployment in the U.S. is that the people now losing their jobs are from companies like IBM and Boeing, or in industries like defense that are going through painful readjustments. And no amount of short-term stimulus will bring these people back to work under any circumstances." Byron is one of the few journalists to sound the alarm, 3-29, on Assistant Treasury Secretary Alicia Munnell's scholarly proposal to tax pensions. "These investments aren't taxed for a simple and—one would assume—obvious reason: The government wants to encourage *more* such investment, not less." Fortunately for Bill Clinton, Byron doesn't expend all his energy blasting the administration. Casting a wary eye wherever he looks, Byron can be depended on to give readers the Bottom Line.

John Carey

Business Week

Washington. With the change in presidents, Carey benefits from the Clinton administration's focus on issues within the beats he usually covers—the pharmaceutical and high-tech industries. Unfortunately, Carey reveals his politics a little too often, and while long an excellent reporter, his work this year seems less balanced. He joins President Clinton in demagoguery over soaring drug prices, 3-8, instead of carefully reporting the contentious issue of price controls. Although he states that "considerable evidence suggests that well-designed price constraints wouldn't have to be a prescription for disaster," the "evidence" he presents—mainly comparisons with Canada, Britain, and France—is questionable, and he fails to examine competing evidence against controls. Scarcely less slanted in his coverage of technological industrial policy, Carey flavors his pieces with hearty doses of old-fashioned mercantilism, in which the government manages the battle with foreign competitors. Touting large subsidies for targeted industries, 10-18, he lauds Clinton's shift from Bush policies "perceived as ready to sacrifice American competitiveness on the altar of free-market fanaticism." Carey views the international economy as an arena in which whole nations butt heads and where American businesses work on the same team, yet he fails to consider that these businesses must also compete with each *other*. Carey ascends with his superb 5-10 cover story that takes readers on a fascinating journey to the cutting edge of technology. "In telecommunications alone, replacing poky electronics and copper wires with photons can boost capacity of transmission lines 10,000 times. The same approach could make today's computers the equivalent of Model Ts....One day, optoelectronics will have fomented a revolution as far-reaching as that wrought by the silicon chip." In his captivating 7-26 piece, Carey reports a promising antibody being developed by Bristol-Myers Squibb to combat cancer. Researchers don't claim to have found any "silver bullets," he notes, but the antibodies "may be aimed true enough to slow cancer in its tracks." In pieces like these, Carey's vision and savvy stand out. But as the political winds shift in Washington, Carey would better serve the reader by reporting the new policies rather than advancing them.

Laurie P. Cohen
The Wall Street Journal
★★

While Cohen, like colleague Bruce Ingersoll, produces pedestrian solo pieces, she can deliver hard-hitting, worthwhile stories when teaming up on a double byline. Fortunately, she spent much of 1993 jointly reporting major stories. Cohen's contributions to uncovering the New Jersey municipal-bond scandal helped to topple the governor and draw congressional attention to modern-day graft. In several May stories, she and co-author Michael Siconolfi describe how underwriters procure state and local bond-issue business not through competitive bidding, but by paying off politicians. Their 5-21 front-page profile of Richard P. Poirier Jr., a Lazard Frères partner who drummed up business by ingratiating himself with Garden State politicos, exposes the ethos behind acquiring bond work. "An investment bank's political relationships and contributions often play a larger role in the selection of underwriters and advisers than do skill and qualifications for the assignment." In an 11-30 effort, Cohen and co-author Thomas T. Vogel Jr. showcase Ken Dart, "a foam-coffee-cup tycoon" whose family holds 4 percent of the Brazilian national debt. "Mr. Dart, 38, isn't a particularly sympathetic character," they state. "He comes across as curt, haughty and secretive. His father, W.A. Dart, is all that and litigious besides....[They] rule the family business and investment empires with two iron fists." Although Brazil wants to restructure its debt, they note, the stubborn magnate will not accede. In a solid 2-11 feature, co-authored by Alix M. Freedman, Cohen details how the cigarette industry's PR experts labored for years to quash knowledge of any link between smoking and disease. Although this momentous story provides mounds of evidence of longtime cigarette-industry dissembling about the hazards of smoking, an accompanying report lambasting cigarette companies' courtroom strategies seems a scurrilous attempt to tar the industry. Cohen and Freedman unduly chastise tobacco companies for using hard-nosed tactics to defend themselves in multi-million dollar lawsuits. Motivated more by contempt for tobacco companies than by any study of particular accusations lodged in court against them, the pair assaults journalistic standards by ignoring basic principles of civil justice, such as the burden of proof resting with plaintiffs and the right of defendants to defend themselves. The first story deserves high praise, this supplementary polemic only scorn. Nevertheless, Cohen clearly makes waves, especially when writing in tandem.

Alison Leigh Cowan

The New York Times

★★★

New York. Coating numerous stories with a wisp of whimsy, Cowan uses 1993 to expand her coverage beyond the seldom-scintillating world of accounting. In switching beats, she scores in several fields—from executive pay to executive misconduct. In her 5-21 story, Cowan reports the startlingly high $21.6 million salary package that the small, Connecticut-based Citizens Utilities paid its chairman, Leonard Tow, in 1992. "One way to look at it," she writes, calling on her grammar-school skills with considerable aplomb, "is that more than 800,000 Citizens customers in 13 states who get their electricity, water, gas and telephone service from Citizens paid an average of $26 last year to provide Mr. Tow's pay." Cowan follows up the story with a noteworthy 7-11 look at Citizens, broaching with fairness the politically sensitive topic of executive pay. By keeping her contacts in the accounting world, certain key stories fall into her lap. In her 6-23 article, she reveals big news from a numbers-crunching giant. "In the final year of his three-year stint at the top of Coopers & Lybrand, Eugene M. Freedman is setting the stage to extend his stay." The potential for controversy looms, Cowan notes, because the 61-year-old "Freedman was elected chairman in 1991 largely on the strength of his business-getting skills and a campaign promise that he understood that his age disqualified him from serving more than one term." Much of Cowan's appeal derives from her skill with words—such as her 9-9 description of a decrepit, outmoded Ohio steel mill as "arthritic." Such verbal acumen enhances her serious stories and enlivens the more frivolous ones. When a Chicago lawyer, facing disciplinary charges for falsifying travel vouchers, blames his peccadilloes on having to visit Philadelphia too often, Cowan offers a pithy 3-2 summation. "In a world where criminals have been known to blame their acts on everything from rock music to Twinkies, it was only a matter of time before someone accused of financial misconduct would come up with the ultimate white-collar crime: too much business-travel made him do it." Despite switching gears from her 1992 beat, no one can accuse Cowan of being a no-account journalist.

John Crudele

New York Post

½★

Business columnist. With a conspiracy theorist's mentality, Crudele uses his commentary pieces to level charges of duplicity at some of the highest reaches of the U.S. government. Two agencies consume almost all of Crudele's energy: the Federal Reserve Board, which in his view wields undue power over the economy; and the Department of Labor, which he says deliberately distorts employment figures. In his 12-6 piece, Crudele writes that public utterances by Fed Vice Chairman David Mullins prove "what the Fed has never admitted before—that it participated in post-crash strategy after 1987, and had an active role." Frenzied suspicion of the Fed constitutes an article of faith among grassy-knoll types. Although Crudele raises some legitimate points—after all, the Fed won't release transcripts of its meetings, and up until this year, it denied even having such records—he repeats his charges with such mind-numbing regularity that they displace other fields of inquiry. Also ridiculous is his mantra about how the Labor Department fudges jobs data to hide poor economic performance. For instance, in his 10-11 piece on the latest figures, he states, "Those 156,000 jobs that the government said were created in September included 74,000 so called 'bias' factor jobs—meaning the Labor Department was guessing that someone was hiring these workers but couldn't prove it." Crudele raises a good point, but beats it into the ground seemingly every other column. If imitation is the sincerest form of flattery, then Crudele surely loves his own work, for he possesses the annoying habit of reminding readers that he has told them something prescient in previous columns: "As I've said before," 6-4; "As I've reported repeatedly," 8-6; "As anyone who reads this column should know," 10-11; "I've brought this subject up before," 11-22; "As I mentioned before," 12-6. Crudele can apparently type with one hand while patting himself on the back with the other. Instead of concentrating on these typewriter gymnastics, Crudele ought to worry about finding some more issues to treat—he's just about worn out the two he always uses.

Damon Darlin

Forbes

★★★

Los Angeles. Coming to *Forbes* from a stint as *The Wall Street Journal*'s Seoul bureau chief, Darlin brilliantly covers a range of subjects, from small business to marketing to international commerce. A lively writer, he brings both wit and verve to his stories. In his 10-11 piece on bounty hunters who track down stolen shopping carts to the tune of $3 million annually, Darlin gives readers the inside track on this latest southern California growth industry. "Despite [supermarkets'] efforts, like declaring February 'Return Shopping Carts to the Supermarket Month,' the shopping cart count continues to rise. Carts go AWOL because they are used as wheels for folks who don't have cars." In "Highbrow Hype," 4-12, he alerts taxpayers to a toy-maker's profitable advertising gambit—having PBS sponsor and produce a show starring their Thomas the Tank Engine while the company retains marketing rights. With the "imprimatur" of public television, Darlin explains, sophisticate parents snap up toy trains, books, and clothes for their tykes as healthy, less commercial alternatives to Mutant Ninja Turtles. Meanwhile, he notes, the toy-maker makes a mint while spending no money on promotion. Darlin tackles weightier issues, too, adding a twist to the media's coverage of health-care reform. His 9-13 piece profiles one potential beneficiary of a national system—ambulance companies, who presently collect on only 60 percent of their bills. Darlin's *Journal* experience in Seoul pays high dividends for *Forbes* in the form of excellent pieces focusing on Asia. Korea's booming stock market, Darlin shows, 2-15, may not be as lucrative for non-Koreans as one might think. "In almost all companies, foreign investors can own no more than 10 percent of a company's shares....Once the ceiling is hit, a foreigner can buy stock only from another foreigner....The result is a two-tier market: one price for Koreans, another for foreigners." In his amusing 5-10 offering, Darlin details the problems resulting from the proliferation of "cause" ribbons. "Washington, D.C. eco-extremist Jeremy Rifkin uses Kelly green ribbons for his fight against beef, but the Rainforest Action Network uses that color in its fight to save lauan trees in Indonesia." To Darlin goes the blue ribbon.

Susan Dentzer

U.S.News & World Report

★★

"On The Economy" columnist. Dentzer's weekly feature is misnamed. It should be called "On *Washington* On The Economy," as Dentzer confines her coverage of economic issues almost solely to activity within the Beltway. What's Clinton doing on this, or Laura Tyson on that? Must we tax Social Security benefits? Can we cut entitlements? Dentzer reports not on the economy at large but on government and its economic proposals, which she does creditably. Tackling the health-care saga, 5-24, Dentzer writes that the Clintons "are assembling a complex jigsaw puzzle of health reform that constantly rearranges itself as each piece is changed. And the most drastic rearrangement will be felt as Clinton settles the last and biggest question—how to sock businesses and the public for the cost of his sweeping plan." Dentzer's 3-15 piece, "The Case for a Stimulus Package," doesn't make one, but her 7-12 article on the administration's court battle over NAFTA provides shrewd insight and clearly states her view. "The higher courts may yet put a stop to [Judge Charles] Richey's folly, overturning his decision. But America will still have to figure out how to keep legitimate environmental issues from blocking its ability to lead the world." Using a chatty Q&A in her 3-8 piece, Dentzer makes a sophomoric attempt to explain the rationale behind the government taxing Social Security benefits. "I've heard that Social Security isn't even part of the federal budget, and that it hasn't contributed to the deficit at all." she writes. "So why are seniors being picked on?...You're correct to imply that raising taxes on benefits won't cut the budget deficit per se. But it will improve the nation's fiscal outlook in other important ways. How so?...Raising these taxes will push back the date at which the [social security] reserves will be exhausted and will lessen the size of future payroll-tax hikes." On the rare occasion when Dentzer breaks free from Washington, she acquits herself well. Two pieces datelined Tokyo, 7-19 and 7-26, offer an astute glimpse at how Americans view—and should view—Japan. "Many Americans think of Japan as a free-market giant—free for Japanese firms, at any rate—but, in fact, its economy is choked by thousands of regulations." Dentzer blames these regulations on "Japan's formidable government bureaucracy." Unfortunately, she provides little analysis of the *American* economy in her pieces, confusing it with government policy dictated by politicians huddled in Washington. When she expands her vision beyond the banks of the Potomac, Dentzer can log competent and sometimes perceptive articles.

Kathleen Deveny

The Wall Street Journal

★½

Marketing. While the fresh and engaging Deveny tracks marketing trends, she yields her most enjoyable work in frequent contributions to the *WSJ* "Marketscan" feature. The ingenious, column monitors data provided by Information Resources Inc., a company that uses computer technology to record which products are flying off store shelves and across check-out-line scanners. In her 2-23 story on a resurgent health food trend, Deveny writes, "They're baaack....America's craving for snacks that seem helpful—but don't taste like it—has helped turn granola bars into one of the 10 fastest-growing products in the supermarket." The computer records show, 9-7, that liquid diets are making a booming comeback. The dubious Deveny, however, seems given to a kind of grotesque fatalism. "In fact, chocolate lovers will probably always outnumber successful dieters. Despite boomers' decade-long preoccupation with health and fitness, America remains one of the fattiest nations on earth." Always sticking to the numbers, Deveny interprets for readers what the market is saying. On the changing face of backyard barbecues, 5-27, she writes, "Supermarket sales of prepared barbecue sauces inched up by a mere 1.8 percent during the 52 weeks ended April 18. Sales of hot dogs fell by 5.7 percent, while relish sales slipped 3.4 percent. Sales of hamburger buns were flat." While the usefulness of these articles may be questionable, they might help *WSJ* readers fare well on "Jeopardy." Alex Trebek: This city consumes the least amount of barbecue sauce per capita in the United States each year. Contestant: What is Green Bay? That's right. Aside from "Marketscan," Deveny files intriguing stories, such as her 11-24 piece examining how successful "Texas" can be in a product's name. Her 11-4 feature chronicles the recent travails of the Big Three. Writing not about cars but coffee, she reports that Procter & Gamble, Kraft General Foods, and Nestlé all missed out on the recent boom in gourmet coffees. "For years, the top coffee marketers have focused more on building brand names than on creating better brews." In trying to play catch-up, Deveny writes, "Efforts to reach coffee connoisseurs have largely fallen flat." While her efforts rarely fall flat, seldom do they provide anything significant. In piquing readers' curiosity with stories about the way Americans live, work, and shop, Deveny usually provides a pleasant diversion from the more weighty matters discussed elsewhere in the *Journal*.

Judith H. Dobrzynski

Business Week

★★★½

Senior editor. The grave changes at IBM occasioned by the computer giant's Wall Street nosedive ensures a full plate for Dobrzynski this year, and the highly talented, longtime *BW* fixture feasts on the events. In her sharp 2-1 indictment of CEO John Akers, she calls for his ouster, citing the company's wretched performance as ample justification. "For all the restructurings, personnel shifts, and product initiatives, the world's biggest computer maker still resembles nothing so much as a flailing giant unable to extricate itself from the mire of outdated strategy and culture." Akers resigned two weeks later. In numerous reports, Dobrzynski chronicles IBM's search for a new CEO, with her 10-4 cover story profiling Akers's replacement, the former RJR Nabisco head Louis Gerstner. Now charged with cleaning the company's Augean stables, "Gerstner must mount a cultural revolution at IBM: He must convince 250,000 employees in 140 countries to change the way they think and act. It's the toughest job in Corporate America today." With penetrating analysis of happenings in America's boardrooms, Dobrzynski reveals why her work remains a cut above that of her competitors: She's got vision. With a wide-angle lens focused on both corporate management and boards of directors, she urges a fundamental rethinking of the way American business does business. In her 2-15 piece, she suggests transforming tedious annual shareholders' meetings into venues for dialogue between investors and corporate leaders. Dobrzynski decries the reliance of companies' boards on the power and personality of the CEO and advocates greater control over decision-making by directors. "Many directors give short shrift to a key duty: regularly appraising the CEO's performance, formally and specifically....While they're at it, board members should evaluate directors' performance to make sure each is contributing." Boardroom deadweight, she notes, 8-2, compounded Big Blue's woes and led to its current crisis. But oak-paneled boardrooms and leather-backed chairs aren't Dobrzynski's only concern. Every so often she turns her attention to the art world, a subject under-reported by others. In her 6-14 piece on the biennial exhibition of new art at the Whitney Museum in New York, she notes the show's "hard-to-sell works," like unwieldy sculptures or video-art. "If it's an omen, the contemporary art business is in for rough times." An artist in her own line of work, Dobrzynski paints vibrant pictures and the occasional masterpiece at *BW*.

Tom Donlan

Barron's

★★½

"Editorial Commentary" columnist. The intellectual legacy of John Stuart Mill lives at *Barron's* in the person of Tom Donlan. Like Mill, he embraces free markets chiefly because they embody and emphasize the notion of natural personal liberty, with which government, accordingly, has little right to interfere. Precisely this principle separates Donlan from other free-marketeers who crunch numbers and quote statistics to prove the practical advantage of their creed that "markets work." That's not to say he doesn't subscribe to this idea. In his 2-1 essay, the economic-Darwinist Donlan writes coldly, "The Invisible Hand of the economy has recessions for the same reason Mother Nature has ice ages—to determine which of its creatures have evolved and which needs a little push into extinction." Still, liberty excites Donlan's passions most. One of the rare individuals to defend bureaucracy, 9-13, Donlan shudders at Vice President Al Gore's proposal to streamline government. "Efficiency in government is the first requirement for tyranny," he warns. "We look forward to the day when most people...can declare that the government has done nothing for them or to them or with them or against them." The predictability of his libertarian positions never clouds his wry musings. Observing the proliferation of Indian-run casinos—made legal because of Native Americans' sovereignty on their land—Donlan notes a cruel twist, 10-18. "It is ironic. The people who were defeated by imported alcohol and disease, then corrupted by the paternalistic reservation management of the victors, now are allowed by a fatuous legalism to erect institutions to corrupt their oppressors." One could hardly expect Donlan to refrain from hurling a few barbs at the new administration, and indeed he does so, with relish. In his amusing 5-31 commentary, he asserts that the Clintons' tonsorial excesses open the First Family to charges of hypocrisy. "The lady who lives at 1600 Pennsylvania Ave. spends $275 on a hairdo, and her husband spends $200. These are people who profess to believe that one of the big things wrong with our country is that their fellow citizens spend too much on doctors." In a field low on classical liberals, Donlan helps fill the void while bringing a whit of wit to his economic philosophy.

Rudi Dornbusch

Business Week

½★

Economics columnist. A professor of economics at MIT, Dornbusch has replaced columnist Alan Blinder, who joined the Clinton administration. Considered influential by many politicians, Dornbusch's perspectives should be read if for no other reason than to know what type of gibberish policy-makers digest. But he should not be considered a reliable source of information. In his 6-21 column, for example, Dornbusch distorts Federal Reserve Chairman Alan Greenspan's words, stating that the Chairman has cut a deal to ease monetary policy in the event that Clinton's budget proposal stalls the economy. "The Fed will be there to soften the fall with appropriately easy money. Greenspan can be relied on to hold up his part of the deal." Such irresponsible and inaccurate assertions can undermine confidence in the Fed. Dornbusch's columns are also a bundle of contradictions. He is a free-trader who eschews free-

market solutions. His 4-26 and 11-8 "Viewpoints" support NAFTA and GATT, respectively, while other columns encourage government intervention. To "boost U.S. growth," Dornbusch's 3-1 piece touts realignment of Asia's "chronically undervalued" currencies. Yet, illogically, realignment could mean stifled growth in U.S. export markets. "In the past 30 years the [Asian] region has averaged six percent growth per year....Now Asia should accept a major appreciation of its currencies." Although Japan has succumbed to this formula and now faces recession—a development that has curtailed U.S. exports to that country—Dornbusch does not consider the possible impact of this economic cycle. In the same vein, his 7-19 column endorses quantitative targets for market-access backed by sanctions against the Japanese. This ignores the fact that per capita, the Japanese import more U.S. goods than the U.S. does Japanese goods. And despite recession and the fall of virtually every European currency before the European Rate Mechanism, Dornbusch advises more of the same in his 3-29 article on the teetering French franc. "If the finance ministers in Germany and France declared their agreement to defend a fixed parity whatever the cost, the massive deterrence of such an accord would make the franc as good as the mark in a split second." Well, that certainly didn't work for the British pound. Readers looking for solid economic analyses will not find them amid Dornbusch's incongruous assessments.

Ann Reilly Dowd

Fortune

★½

"Politics and Policy" columnist. When Gertrude Stein said of Oakland, "There's no there there," she could have been referring to Dowd's earlier efforts. While still somewhat shallow, Dowd's work has improved, and occasionally she offers provocative and penetrating insights. In her superficial 1-11 introduction of Bill Clinton's new economic advisers, Dowd provides a paragraph or two on Donna Shalala, Lloyd Bentsen, Robert Reich, and others, each followed by a flattering remark from some member of the Washington establishment. "The records of the new Cabinet are mostly reassuring," she concludes, skating on the surface. In her 3-22 piece, Dowd commits the mistake of many others—attributing blanket support for the President's plan to the high-tech industry. She is too impressed by the fact that Apple CEO John Sculley sat at the First Lady's side during the State of the Union speech, a ploy which drew howls from many in Silicon Valley. Her illuminating 5-3 profile of the new National Economic Council chief Robert Rubin provides insight into how the former Goldman Sachs $26-million man will shape policy. "He chafes at the notion of being 'a link with the business community.' He does not share the opinion of many business leaders that tax increases are too large and spending cuts too small in the Clinton economic plan. Though price controls are dirty words to most business people, Rubin is willing to entertain the possibility of using them as part of health care reform." In her strong 8-9 piece detailing the changing face of lobbying, Dowd reveals that the way to get things done in Washington is to target not the denizens of Capitol Hill but rather their voters. "The cost of winning a congressional seat is so high...and the limits on PAC contributions are so low... that all money buys is a ticket to the show. What counts are constituents." Let's hope Dowd scratches beneath the surface to produce more fine stories like these.

Peter C. Du Bois

Barron's

★★½

"International Trader." Keeping readers apprised of developments at stock exchanges the world over, Du Bois acts as a clearinghouse for information on international markets. Collecting figures from nearly every locale where shares are bought and sold, he reports the results to the swarms of American investors searching for places to park their money. A typical intercontinental market report from Du Bois reads like this 9-20 entry: "Overseas bourses generally fell last week, with Europe (10 off, five up) narrowly underperforming the Pacific Basin (seven off, six up)." Replete with charts, the International Trader publishes the comparative performances of the major exchanges, focusing also on the world's emerging markets. For the most part, his coverage of global securities keeps track of equities, with little emphasis on debt. Charged with reporting the immediate past, Du Bois generally lets others peer into the future. Lending a good portion of his column to worldwide investment experts, he provides a showcase for those who make their livings prognosticating. Like Ted Koppel buttonholing his guests, Du Bois pens a running dialogue. "Why are French voters likely to throw out their socialist government and embrace the center-right again?" he asks not-so-rhetorically, 3-1. "Mainly because they want change, [economist J. Paul] Horne says....[But] what can a new government do for the French economy? 'Very little this year,' says Horne. 'It's almost impossible to get the economy moving before the fourth quarter.'" Although Du Bois defers to the experts for analysis on Latin American and European issues, he is more willing to venture alone into Asia. "The Philippines certainly doesn't sound like the kind of place that would drive investors in droves," he reports, 4-26. "It had a series of natural disasters over the past few years, and a severe shortage of electricity continues to plague the local economy. Yet the country's luck is about to change....One reason for optimism: Substantial new power generating capacity is being added." By no means sexy, but certainly the kind of news the casual investor might like to know about an emerging market. With his Rolodex stuffed with phone numbers of investment experts worldwide, Du Bois offers the comprehensive global perspective for investors anxious to experience a little financial multiculturalism.

Jack Egan

U.S.News & World Report

★½

Investing. Like a protective parent, Egan holds the hand of the naive personal investor with a few thousand dollars to spend. He offers nuts-and-bolts advice—along with a healthy dose of caution—and although quite predictable, he warns investors against running into Wall Street lest they be run over by a bear. Skeptical about the market's prospects despite the money flowing into stocks, Egan prudently notes, 7-5, that this money "has come from individuals bailing out of bank accounts because of the lowest interest rates in nearly three decades. Without better alternatives and eager to raise returns, individuals have been shoveling big money into stocks, primarily by buying shares of equity in mutual funds....Given the glut of cash, it seems more likely that stocks will first go higher before they go lower." Offering little forecasting, Egan usually adds a caveat, as in his 10-18 story on why biotech stocks might bounce back from a big bust. "It's still hard for investors—even sophisticated investors—to follow biotechnology stocks. Every company has a good story or it wouldn't be out there. You need to know a great deal about science and the drug approval process to vet claims and follow developments." Egan frequently utters the old refrain that a lengthy bull run has blinded many first-timers from recognizing the vagaries of the market. "It's easy to start believing you're smart," he writes, 9-20. "In fact, you've mainly been lucky." Preaching a brand of wary pessimism, Egan concerns himself with showing novices the attendant risks to dabbling in investing. Every now and then, however, he breaks from this mold and writes something thought-provoking, like his 3-29 piece on President Clinton's plan to sandbag the Student Loan Marketing Association in favor of direct loans. Sallie Mae has traded publicly for 10 years and done well. That, says Egan, bothers Clintonites who want "to prove that a reinvented government can sometimes do a better job than the private, or in this case, the quasi-private sector....Sallie Mae's sin may be its entrepreneurialism. Reformers resent [its] turning a solid profit." But such keen analysis comes rarely. Wary of sticking his neck out, Egan covers his rear by telling investors to cover theirs.

Stuart Elliott

The New York Times

★½

"Advertising." The chatty Elliott beguiles with his flighty dispatches from the capricious world of advertising. Usually constructing his column with a handful of small, unrelated news nuggets, Elliott prepares Cracker Jack for the mind—always fun, seldom edifying, and often yielding cheap prizes. He blends trade news, which provides little value to the average reader, with information about new ad campaigns or industry trends. Taking a big-picture look at the business, 1-14, he describes the trend toward "niche marketing or market segmentation, which, inelegantly put, slices a nice fat bologna into increasingly thinner pieces in

hopes of satisfying additional appetites." Inelegantly put, indeed. Levi Strauss, he continues, "is a master at that; basic Levi's jeans begat a closet full of denims for younger, older, fashion-conscious and fad oriented consumers." Like the industry he covers, in which a hip idea gets used and then discarded, Elliott dispenses witty, frivolous banter in his role as industry towncrier. He reports on Burger King switching accounts, 10-21, which he says it does "practically at the flip of a Whopper." This action "sets up, you should pardon the expression, a feeding frenzy among other agencies." Elliott abstemiously reports the merger of two New York firms, Mezzina/Brown and Wills & Evans, 6-30, calling the move "paradigmatic of continuing consolidation as the advertising industry enters the fifth year of its most serious slump since perhaps the 1930s." But hard times don't dampen spirits too long, either at the *Times* or on Madison Avenue. In his 11-8 story about the controversial commercials sponsored by the Health Insurance Association of America, which blast the President's health-care proposal, Elliott quips, "Bill and Hillary are lashing out at television commercials starring a couple named Harry and Louise....Those hoping the White House was condemning the Taster's Choice coffee couple will be disappointed." Some readers may be disappointed with Elliott's breezy column, as he rarely provides anything substantial. In applying brisk treatment to a superficial industry, Elliott delivers little else but entertainment.

Geraldine Fabrikant
The New York Times
★★★½

Mergers & acquisitions. Fabrikant's lucid style enables her to make complex issues understandable without patronizing her audience. Her top-notch daily coverage of the late-year Wall Street war for Paramount Communications made her byline intimately familiar to *Times* readers, nailing down her spot in the ranks of esteemed business journalists. From the earliest autumn announcement of cable colossus Viacom's plans for purchasing Paramount to a Christmas-season court decision placing the deal in jeopardy, Fabrikant seldom strays far from the action. In her 9-13 feature, she asserts that Paramount chief Marty Davis, anxious to help lead the convoy down the information superhighway, has for years "been on the prowl for a deal that would create a media powerhouse in an industry dominated by giants." What makes her coverage of the Paramount affair so impressive is her foresight of industry change. She displays this vision in her 2-10 report about Southwestern Bell's acquisition of two cable systems in the D.C. area. More significant than the particulars, Fabrikant recognizes the deal's importance as a bellwether for the next wave of the communications revolution. "Both industries [telephone and cable] want to use their elaborate networks to provide movies on demand, hundreds of channels of television programming and on-line electronic libraries. And advances in technologies, blurring the distinctions between what the two industries can do, have set off a Darwinian contest." In a particularly prescient 5-30 profile of the head of Tele-Communications Inc., John C. Malone, she observes that this Ph.D. must be up to something. "He is spending billions of dollars to upgrade his cable systems to deliver TV's exotic new products....In repositioning himself technologically, Dr. Malone is also moving aggressively into cable's high-end premium services, which face less regulation" in the aftermath of new rules designed by the FCC. When Bell Atlantic and TCI announce a merger, bearing out Fabrikant's story on

Malone's grand vision, 10-13, she notes that "ranked by assets alone, [the new company] would deserve to be showcased as the sixth largest company in *Fortune* 500's annual list of largest American companies." With an eye for the telling detail and a breadth of vision unusual in a daily news reporter, Fabrikant impresses with absorbing articles and acute analysis.

Paul Farhi

The Washington Post

★★★

Cable industry. Uncertainty surrounding re-regulation of the cable television industry left Farhi's dance card full in 1993. The year saw new rules promulgated by the FCC in the spring and implemented by fall, leaving enough time to survey the results. Farhi's yearlong documenting of the cable saga merits praise for thoroughness and trenchant analysis. Writing the week the FCC unveils its new regulations, 5-5, Farhi informs the reader of the sweeping scope of the government's recipe for cable operators. "The product of six months of bureaucratic endeavor, the new rules are contained in a forest-felling, phone book-sized stack of documents of...stunning complexity....This also is only the first cut. The FCC has promised to add additional language to the regulations by the end of the year." In his revealing 10-14 profile of Tele-Communications Inc. mogul John C. Malone on the day after TCI and Bell Atlantic stunned the world by announcing plans to join forces, Farhi details Malone's—and cable's—puissance. "[TCI] owns the wires that provide cable television to nearly 1 of every 4 households of America. TCI also has a share in many of the popular cable networks (CNN, Discovery, Black Entertainment Television) that run over these wires." Despite his stellar work in dozens of cable stories, Farhi embarrasses himself in recounting the controversy over whether cable operators would pay to carry networks' signals. "The three big networks," he writes, 6-17, "have all said that the powerful broadcast stations they own and operate throughout the nation will seek cash payments—setting up a gigantic game of chicken." Updating the story three months later, Farhi writes, 9-10, "The so-called 'retransmission consent' negotiations have been compared to a giant game of chicken." By himself, that is, for he cites no sources. But such minor miscues seldom mar his usually fine work. In two excellent pieces, 3-18 and 3-23, Farhi probes troubling spending irregularities by the Freedom Forum, the non-profit charitable organization headed by former Gannett chairman Al Neuharth. In the latter story, Farhi uses 1991 tax records to show that "the Freedom Forum spent nearly 70 percent more on administrative and operating expenses, such as salaries and travel, than it did on charitable contributions, gifts and grants." Farhi uncovers lavish holiday junkets and ostentatious office suites enjoyed by Neuharth and friends. With such superb, hard-hitting stuff on the cable industry and other topics, let's hope no one regulates Farhi.

Christopher Farrell

Business Week

★★★

Business. Farrell has emerged as one of the truly thought-provoking writers tracking the business beat. With an ability to see the big picture, he always presents more than bare bones or hackneyed analysis. And Farrell issues provocative statements, always coupled with facts and figures. Making a seldom-heard claim in his 7-5 commentary, Farrell maintains that passage of NAFTA will *increase* immigration from Mexico because Mexicans will be able to afford the move. He then implores the U.S. not to shut out immigrants for fear of harming global trade. In his 6-21 piece, "The Price of Open Arms," he reveals an often overlooked point in the debate over immigration. "Most immigrants, legal and illegal, are highly productive workers. That's why they came to the U.S....It's also true that illegal aliens actually pay a sizable amount of taxes. The problem: Most of the costs, such as schooling and education, show up at the local level, while most of the tax revenue goes to the federal and state governments." A new angle on the global economy receives his attention in an excellent 4-19 effort on multinational corporations' efforts to hedge their risks in volatile currency markets. Examining why the economic growth of industrialized nations has stalled relative to Third World upstarts in Asia and Latin America, 8-2, Farrell contends that communism's demise prompted military downsizing, which hurt both the U.S. and Europe. Farrell believes that be-

cause of America's passionate free-market ethic, this adversity will particularly benefit the U.S. economy. "Facing vicious competition at home and abroad, American companies have been investing in new technologies and overhauling the workplace. America has gone further than any other industrial country in deregulating its financial services, airlines, telecommunications, and trucking industries. The result: Even traditionally sheltered industries have been compelled to restructure to meet new price competition." This trend, he reports, 5-24, extends even to academe. Wary of further raising skyrocketing tuition, which at private colleges rose 9.2 percent per year between 1980 and 1992, "a growing number of universities are embracing the restructuring mantra and hacking away at administrative and faculty bloat." More incisive than ever, Farrell has begun to display the verve and sophistication at which his reporting always hinted.

Tim W. Ferguson

The Wall Street Journal

★★½

"Business World" columnist. With his weekly California-based missives, Ferguson emerges as Tuesday's treat on the *Journal's* op-ed page. More than simply bringing a West Coast perspective to economic issues, he drapes them in a free-market viewpoint. Reporting on an anti-NAFTA protest at the Port of Los Angeles, 8-24, he notes wryly, "A mini-rally...against free-trade at the busiest commercial harbor in the U.S. obviously had elements of contrast." His status as a longtime Golden State observer leaves Ferguson uniquely positioned to criticize Gov. Pete Wilson [R-CA], but in his 6-18 column, he lets the chief executive—a pariah to some conservatives who find him too moderate—off the hook. "If Gov. Wilson is to be faulted for a pinched vision of the creative political possibilities of a free-market approach, he is also to be defended in the context of its fiscal calamity. He entered office with state spending on one of its steroidal highs, with built-in escalators and a rapid growth in the number of beneficiaries." Yet, such departures from orthodoxy constitute exceptions to the rule for Ferguson, an articulate libertarian conservative whose focus extends beyond the borders of California. In his 10-12 piece leading up to the ballot-box battle over zoning in Houston, he lauds the last major American city unfettered by property restrictions. "Nonzoning is not a goblin that leaps out every few blocks. Traditionalists say the city's approach is largely to credit for what one doesn't see: sizable slums. Blighted areas certainly exist, but not on a par with Chicago or Philadelphia or even Atlanta." Not every Ferguson article touts the virtues of entrepreneurial capitalism and deregulation. In a solid 5-25 piece on alleged racial bias in mortgage lending, Ferguson chronicles Federal Reserve Governor Lawrence Lindsey's views on the issue by going straight to the source—Lindsey. "[He] takes the results [of a Federal Reserve study]—17 percent turndown of blacks vs. 11 percent of comparable whites—at face value and is encouraged: They indicate to him that in only six cases out of 100 do blacks suffer discrimination, and that means the profit motive is gradually overcoming deep historical bias." While the conclusion is debatable, Ferguson supplies the facts. With more reporting like this to bolster his sermons, Ferguson could join the upper echelons of conservative scribes.

James Flanigan

Los Angeles Times

★

Business columnist. More the advocate than the reporter, Flanigan, under the guise of providing news analysis, chooses sides and lectures from on high. He provides biting and incisive commentary that's better suited for the editorial page than the news page. And Flanigan, a devoted free-trader, argues eloquently for NAFTA and GATT. He issues his 11-13 piece with the NAFTA vote looming. To illustrate the importance of passing the trade agreement, he uses the example of Volkswagen, which, he claims, atrophied after unions blocked it from expanding operations into the U.S. "The truth is there would have been no 'export of jobs,' as we see from the success of Japanese car plants here. Instead, there would have been jobs created in both the United States and Germany as parts were shipped back and forth and two-way traffic built up. Commerce is not a zero-sum gain." Flanigan mocks his opponents. "Otherwise-intelligent people cling to the fiction that the talents and riches of the world's largest economy will flow into the teacup of Mexico's economy....The truth is, Mexico is developing because 60 percent of its people are under age 25 and they are through living in penury." *The truth is...* Flanigan uses this phrase too often, particularly when he's expressing not a fact but an opinion. Applying equal levels of passion to another contentious issue, immigration, he writes, 8-15, "We'll get nowhere blaming our problems on immigrants, who have always come to this country because it offers more opportunity for individual development than any other nation on earth." Despite his free-trade sentiments, Flanigan pleads fervently for increased government intervention in the economy. To bolster employment, 10-20, he urges "workfare and even make-work jobs." In his 12-12 piece, he implores government to charge full speed ahead in mandating electric cars. And in his 6-27 story, he calls for funding the space station despite its high costs. "In our admirable concern for budget deficits, we should not be shortsighted." Insulting, articulate, maddening, thoughtful, biased, polemical—all reasons that make Flanigan fun to read. But don't be deceived. Flanigan remains more a banner-waver than a news reporter.

Jerry Flint

Forbes

★★

Senior editor. Readers might reasonably expect the Michigan-born—and eponymously named—Flint to provide stellar coverage of the auto industry. But in 1993 he prefers to leave careful monitoring of the Motor City to others. His stories often intrigue and instruct, but can lack the hard reporting of strong news coverage. And although he competently conveys his major points, more digging might round out his automobile reports. Positively bullish on Chrysler's prospects, 4-12, Flint assesses plans to cut back production to boost profitability. "That makes sense. It boils down to preferring to build two cars at a profit rather than three at a loss." One of Flint's best auto stories comes not from Detroit, but from Cincinnati, where, in a 2-15 piece, he profiles two brothers who manufacture anti-terrorism cars. Business remains good as long as violence and strife remain prevalent worldwide. "One man's terrorist is another man's business opportunity, and [the O'Garas] are exploiting the opportunities in terrorism beautifully....Over 90 percent of the O'Garas' revenues are booked from sales overseas; more than half the brothers' vehicles go to the Middle East." Flint impresses when off the auto beat. Profiling Epner Technology, a barely surviving New York gold-plating business with 40 employees, 3-1, Flint examines a vital and under-reported segment of the American economy. "To paraphrase Humphrey Bogart ...the problems of a little guy in Brooklyn don't count for much compared with the big-time woes of IBM, GM and American Express. But those same little guys may tell us more about the spirit that drives this market economy." Epner nearly went bankrupt making watchbands during the digital watch's heyday, Flint notes, but with a lot of sacrifice, it converted its operations to handle infrared light reflectors in autos, and today scrapes by. Normally a calm, sober reporter, Flint takes on fellow journalists who stress the pain of corporate downsizing. In a scathing 4-26 rebuke, he writes, "Newspapers, lusting after Pulitzers, know that stories about suffering impress contest judges more than articles about people coping tolerably well." Armed with statistics, Flint claims business belt-tightening has actually been good for workers who took early retirement or were bought out, and that joblessness has been much more severe in other recessions. "As to unemployment, remember it peaked at under 8 percent and is down to 7 percent now. The peak was 11 percent in the downturn a decade ago." If he were to get this punch into his Detroit coverage, Flint might upgrade *Forbes*'s treatment of the auto industry.

Randall W. Forsyth

Barron's

Capital markets editor and "Current Yield" columnist. Although his recent work hasn't been as stellar as in years past, Forsyth remains one of the best debt-market analysts in the U.S. With good sources on Wall Street *and* at the Federal Reserve, he can be counted on to accurately reveal the closely watched ponderings of the nation's monetary policy-makers. Indeed, of all the bond writers, Forsyth proves the most capable of offering original analysis of the forces driving the nation's interest rates to historic lows. Like his counterparts, however, he slips into pre-

dictable assertions that answer few of the most important questions surrounding this development. For example, in his 9-6 piece, he agrees, without extended thought, that a contracting economy is good for bonds. "Bill Clinton is proving to be the best friend the bond market ever had....[His administration] pushed through a tax increase that has depressed consumer expectations and slowed growth." Yet, Forsyth fails to question why both the debt and equity markets are rallying in tandem—a state that could not exist if contraction was behind the long bond rally. Despite such disappointments, Forsyth remains *the* source for ahead-of-the-curve information on the Fed. On 7-26, he provides the most in-depth assessment of Chairman Alan Greenspan's announcement that the Fed will no longer use monetary aggregates to steer policy. In this and other columns, Forsyth illustrates his cognizance of the Fed's increasing attention to gold, a crucial shift missed by many. With the price of gold skyrocketing, 5-24, he offers the strongest account found anywhere of the key April and mid-May meetings of the Federal Open Market Committee (FOMC). Talking with crucial players and reading between the lines, he discerns: "The import of the price of gold goes beyond the bullion market, [Fed Governor Wayne] Angell contended. To quote from his own dissent in the March FOMC minutes, Angell 'believed that a clear signal of the committee's commitment to price-level stability would stabilize the price of gold along with the exchange value of the dollar and thereby provide a climate for further reductions in long- and intermediate-term interest rates.'" Sophisticated investors just can't find this type of information elsewhere.

Milt Freudenheim

The New York Times

★★★

Medicine, health. A year in which the President proposes an overhaul of the nation's health-care industry provides medical writers with numerous opportunities to stand out or stumble. Few meet the challenge of covering the controversial topic better than Freudenheim. Unlike reporters who amplify the idea of a health-care crisis to make reform more palatable and those who deny a health-care crisis exists, Freudenheim takes a more sober approach. His best work, from the middle of the year on, focuses on corporate America's nervous anticipation of the unknown. This imaginative writer refers to the Clintons and the drug companies "exchanging verbal thunderbolts," 9-30, and forecasts a "riptide of price competition" in pharmaceuticals, 7-21. Rather than studying the details of President Clinton's proposal, Freudenheim concentrates on the broad effects the plan will have throughout the private sector. His 9-19 feature examining the changes medical care will undergo assesses the winners (health-plan network doctors, primary-care physicians, nursing homes, lawyers) and losers (physician-specialists, hospitals, biotech and pharmaceutical companies), and captures the bitterness of some of the latter. "For many resentful physicians, George Orwell was only a decade off in predicting Big Brother would rule in 1984." In his 10-31 piece on Bill Gates's Microsoft empire, Freudenheim discusses the computer company's health-care policy. "Beside the usual types of medical coverage...Microsoft's 10,000 predominantly young employees—the average age is 32—are also allowed to select naturopathic treatment, which rejects the use of medicine." More than just the health-care plan shows up on Freudenheim's radar screen. Discussing possible FDA approval for one Alzheimer's-disease drug, 3-22, he demonstrates how, in the desperate world of terminal illness, the most promising prospects can only do so much. Very few patients witnessed any significant improvement from taking Cognex, Freudenheim notes, and even mild improvement appeared in less than half of those tested. "Cognex was credited with delaying mental deterioration associated with Alzheimer's for at least 12 months in about 40 percent of those able to take a stiff daily dose." A no-nonsense reporter, Freudenheim's vigorous coverage of the health-care reform saga adds immeasurably to the reader's knowledge.

Jonathan Fuerbringer

The New York Times

½★

New York. Fuerbringer evinces a blind devotion to the idea that good economic news always proves bad for bonds, and bad news always proves good for bonds. No matter what information has to be ignored or twisted to fit this highly debatable idea, Fuerbringer finds a way to do it. A bear throughout the impressive long-bond rally, he predicts the worst no matter what the news. Thus when the 30-year bond hits 6.93 percent—a new low—Fuerbringer sounds the mantra in his 2-23 piece. President Clinton's deficit-reduction plan, he claims, "is positive for the bond market because slower growth means that there is less chance that inflation will begin rising again soon." Yet, the debt and equity markets rose in tandem in May, when the long bond returned to 6.97 percent—after inching into the 7 percent range. With the Dow also rallying, Fuerbringer only offers this lame 5-20 explanation. "A rush of relief washed over the bond market yesterday, as the worst fears from Tuesday turned out to be wrong yesterday." Similarly, when the long bond tumbled below the 6.5 percent level on the same day that the Dow surged more than 15 points, 8-10, Fuerbringer writes that "the 30-year bond seemed to take on a life of its own." If the market direction doesn't fit his conventional guides, he just makes up something. Note his 10-29 explanation when the long bond rallied and the Dow rose more than 23 points following a government report showing higher than expected gains in the Gross Domestic Product. "It was not exactly clear why traders and investors ultimately chose to be positive about the report, which showed that the gross domestic product rose at an annual rate of 2.8 percent, after adjustment for inflation. It may have been that inflation...was up just 1.8 percent....Or it may have simply been relief that the growth did not turn out to be stronger." Creative, huh? In hindsight, as the long bond closed the year in the 6.3 range, Fuerbringer's constant skepticism and shallow, automaton-like analysis rang as hollow as ever.

James Gerstenzang

Los Angeles Times

★½

International trade. Moving to this beat from the White House, Gerstenzang has proven neither a great wordsmith nor analyst, providing only adequate news treatments from 1600 Pennsylvania Avenue. And while he yields serviceable work on trade, he shows little flair for the subject. In his nostalgic 1-3 article on George Bush's final presidential trip to Russia to sign an arms-control treaty, Gerstenzang covers only Bush and not the actual treaty. So he leaves the reader teary-eyed, but not well informed. In his 2-5 effort, he merely rewrites a recent National Research Council report in saying that the long-predicted AIDS epidemic will not spread to low-risk communities. Although he cuts against the grain, his echoing of the contention that "the disease will have only limited impact on much of the nation" seems naïve given the massive burden that both AIDS care and research will place on any major health-care reform effort. On NAFTA, 3-17, Gerstenzang fails to specify plainly the obstacles holding up the talks, preferring to speak in generalities. He does, however, credibly survey the political aspects of the accord. Similarly, his 5-20 effort adequately reports the latest trade-gap numbers but contains minimum detail on cause and effect—and even less on the economic impact of NAFTA. The article demonstrates that Gerstenzang lacks a sophisticated reading of the complexity of the U.S. economic picture. He offers a solid 6-13 overview of the last few conflicts that may impede the announcement of a trade policy at the Tokyo summit. While he offers little new, Gerstenzang neatly compiles most of the relevant data. His 7-1 piece outlines Judge Charles R. Richey's ruling that the U.S. government must complete an environmental study of NAFTA before it can implement the accord. Although the dispatch contains a full summary of the political implications, it does not address the economic or environmental ones. Somehow, Gerstenzang always leaves out a critical piece of the puzzle.

George Gilder

Forbes ASAP

★★★★

"George Gilder's Telecosm." One of the most articulate proponents of free-market economics alive, Gilder astounds with the breadth of his vision as he applies the tenets of Adam Smith to the information revolution. With his acute ability to recognize the implications of dramatic technological advances, Gilder emerges as tantamount to a prophet heralding the coming of a new society. A capital writer and a capitalist cheerleader, Gilder anchors *ASAP*, the publication that bills itself as "A Technology Supplement to Forbes Magazine."

Of the imminent changes in the cellular industry, 3-29, he writes, "When the convulsion ends later this decade, this new digital cellular phone will stand as the world's most pervasive PC. As mobile as a watch and as personal as a wallet, these...will recognize speech, navigate streets, take notes, keep schedules, collect mail, manage money, open the door and start the car, among other computer functions we cannot imagine today." Versed in techno-jargon, 9-13, Gilder translates the fantastic but erudite ideas poised to change society. "The coming age of bandwidth abundance in glass and in air [which will allow more space for more channels] converges with an era of supercomputer powers in the sand of microchips. We should build our systems of the future—the cathedrals of the information age—on this foundation of sand. It will not disappoint us." He also takes his futuristic outlook to more conventional efforts, as in his devastating, and slightly condescending, assault on Paul Kennedy and his best-selling *Preparing for the 21st Century*. In a 2-25 *Wall Street Journal* book review, Gilder brands the Yale professor a latter-day Malthus, but, "since Mr. Kennedy is a beloved liberal historian, it is unreasonable to ask him to keep up with leading-edge science, technology and economics.... Biotech boggles all speculations about food scarcity and population explosion. The danger comes from an enervated academy that is foisting its nihilist futilities and social fads on the world." Bringing back memories of Gilder's 1980 opus, *Wealth and Poverty,* his July piece for *The American Spectator* crows about the "success" of his supply-side ideas during the 1980s. Touting that time as "the decade when tax rates were cut in fifty-five nations," Gilder also emphasizes his disagreement with capitalist boosters who assert the moral neutrality of free enterprise. Gilder grippingly argues that values like humility and servility, and not love of money, motivate the capitalist. "I do not say that there are no greedy capitalists, only that the inner dynamic of capitalism is orientation towards the needs of others." Unlike some conservative icons who've grown stale with the passage of time, Gilder, with his almost mystical belief in the virtues of capitalism, continues to challenge and impress.

Howard Gleckman

Business Week

Washington. Trying to lend extra weight to his reports by demonstrating a mastery of the lingo used by policy wonks and administration insiders, Gleckman indulges in "in-the-know" arrogance that sometimes gets in the way of relating the facts. In his 6-28 assessment of a change in the President's attitude, he writes confidently, "Clinton's upbeat tone marked his passage from econo-pessimist to cheerleader. Some observers give new mediameister David R. Gergen, who learned happy talk at the knee of Ronald Reagan, credit for the shift." Unfortunately, the piece then degenerates into lines like "go-go talk from the President could become a self-fulfilling prophecy," whatever that means. His 1-25 cover story on the Clinton presidency fares better, perhaps because, like so many *BW* stories, it is written by committee, with Gleckman as chief author. Amid the flood of Clinton profiles during inauguration week, this article stands out with provocative commentary on how the former governor's experience in Arkansas has shaped his governing philosophy, leaving him without a grand vision. "Unlike traditional [activist] Democrats...Clinton sees the economy as a creaky machine plagued by a hundred different problems. His motto: Talk big. Think small." During the President's campaign to raise taxes, Gleckman and co-author Nancy Peacock turn their sights on a related issue—blasting the complexity of the tax code. Their 4-19 effort reports the huge amounts of money companies pay annually just for tax compliance, and chides Clinton for failing to alleviate the situation. "His proposed investment tax credit and his plans to raise taxes on U.S. businesses operating overseas will make the nightmarish code even more complicated." Gleckman shines with his 6-14 "The Technology Payoff," another article-by-committee in which he directs the efforts of four other *BW* scribes. Looking at how the technology boom has changed the workplace and the marketplace, he reports a revolution not so much technological as schematic. "It's the sweeping changes in management and organizational structure that are redefining how work gets done"—and which Gleckman predicts will lead to "a new era of economic growth." With tempered tone of these joint offerings and the confidence he exudes in his solo pieces, Gleckman's star may be on the rise.

Kevin Goldman
The Wall Street Journal
★★½

"Advertising." As the Journal's main man on Madison Avenue, Goldman patrols a beat that carries with it a license, if not an imperative, to be witty. Like the subject they cover, advertising reporters seek to be short, lively, and painfully to-the-point. While often droll, Goldman breaks the mold, filing less biting, slightly more contemplative, reports than his rivals. In his year-end 12-28 story on the advertising bombs of 1993, he notes the unfortunate tack taken by one corporation. "The year started with an odd mix of ads that failed to communicate AT&T's consumer discount plan—no small feat for a company in the communications business." Goldman distinguishes himself from his fellow ad journalists by concentrating on news that would be of interest to readers *not* in the business. During the hype created for the final episode of "Cheers," 5-20, Goldman attempts to explain why America may never again produce a sitcom so beloved by the public (and by advertisers). "The programs on now that have a chance to last many seasons are far different from 'Cheers,'" he remarks, notably "Murphy Brown" and "Roseanne." "They rely on catty and nasty humor, playing down warmth in favor of putdowns and zingers"—precisely the kind of humor that alienates, rather than broadens, audiences. In the wake of the Tailhook controversy and amid the gays-in-the-military debate, 2-1, Goldman describes the Navy's efforts to change its image by focusing its ad campaign solely on one group. "With a relatively small budget compared with ad spending for major consumer products, the Navy decided to storm the MTV generation at its favorite beachhead: MTV itself." While Goldman writes with considerable charm and effect, he avoids the obnoxious glibness that could haunt him in the event of a mistake. His 5-25 story about the Pep Boys auto-parts chain begins, "Manny, Moe & Jack... are headed for the unemployment line," but a correction days later notes the company has no plans to shelve its popular cartoon symbols. Oh well, nobody's perfect. Still, Goldman produces a valuable commodity, pumping out Madison Avenue news tailored to *all* the *Journal*'s readers.

Steven Greenhouse
The New York Times
F

Economics. Whether from ideology or ignorance, Greenhouse puts out many market-jarring distortions of reality. Granted, he's still new to the beat, having returned from Paris only two years ago. But no matter what the reason, the "reporting" that appears under his byline cannot be trusted. Typifying the egregious misrepresentations that pervade Greenhouse's work is his 2-20 report, which purportedly recounts the testimony of Alan Greenspan before the Senate Banking Committee. Greenspan, he writes, "a Republican and a staunch conservative, endorsed Mr. Clinton's proposal to cut the budget deficit." The videotape, however, reveals Greenspan did no such thing. But because the impression had created such concern in the debt markets, Greenspan was forced to clarify his position throughout the year. Congressional transcripts reveal he told policy-makers that he had "eschewed getting involved in the details of the composition of the budget. I have hopefully stayed away from being supportive of any particular vehicle that has come before this Congress, whether it be the President's or other initiatives that have come before either house of the Congress." Undeterred by the facts, Greenhouse once again twists Greenspan's words, 7-21, writing that the Chairman "used his testimony to badger Congress to approve the administration's plan to cut the deficit." A review of the transcript, however, reveals that when Representative John LaFalce [D-NY] congratulated Greenspan for his "warm endorsement of the basic budget plan submitted by President Clinton," Greenspan replied: "I know you are being a little facetious, but let's put it on the table, I was endorsing nothing." In yet another example of his fumbling, irresponsible journalism, Greenhouse writes, 9-16, that Fed Vice Chairman David Mullins and Governor Lawrence Lindsey believe it would be unwise to lower interest rates because "it could encourage a speculative bubble in stocks and bonds." Even though neither policy-maker is quoted as saying such a thing, Greenhouse has the gall to follow-up on 9-

20 with quotes from the President's economic advisors denouncing the Fed for these silly bubble ideas. Greenhouse even reports that "traders said the central bankers' remarks helped push down the bond market late last week." It's possible, however, that Greenhouse's shoddy reporting was the real culprit. Greenhouse moved to the State Department in January 1994. Perhaps Greenhouse will fare better in foreign affairs than he has in economic ones, which come to think of it, proved foreign enough to this correspondent.

John Greenwald

Time

½★

Senior writer. In over his head on the business and economics beat at *Time*, Greenwald seldom explores in any depth the economic effects of the price controls, taxes, and tariffs that he covers. He often falls back on ideological instincts to mask the fact that he lacks a grasp of fundamental economic principles. With Greenwald, reporting takes a back seat to advocacy, as in his 2-15 piece examining new sources of government revenue. He "concludes" from the outset that Americans don't pay enough for gas and that selfish interests—oil companies, coal companies, labor unions, and others—conspire to block any increase. Questionable statements like "a 5 percent sales tax on energy would raise about $18 billion a year and cost the average family about $100 a year in higher gasoline and electric bills" stand unsupported. His 3-8 treatment of the Clintons' fusillade against the pharmaceutical industry suffers from "he-said-she-said" reporting and proves equally one-sided. In response to the Zöe Baird fiasco, Greenwald writes an informative 2-1 piece on what couples with nannies must do to comply with the complicated tax laws. "Conscientious families must fill out five federal forms a year on behalf of each worker. State and local filings can add to the burden. Overwhelmed families may seek help from accountants, who will gladly handle the paperwork for about $500 a year for a child-care worker." Greenwald's 2-22 "Nanny Outing" merely regurgitates the original. And his 8-9 examination of the steel industry is simply confused. Although he claims that "in their relentless decline since the 1950s American steel giants have become a symbol of the country's lost industrial might," Greenwald details innovations that have made steel production more efficient. This poorly conceived lamentation gives no evidence to suggest that production has declined over the past few decades. His lengthy "How Long Will the Bull Run?" 5-17, answers that question by concluding that the stock market is a crapshoot and no one really knows for sure. This is news? Greenwald wastes his time with most of his efforts. Don't let him waste yours.

Lisa Gubernick

Forbes

★½

Senior editor. Reading Gubernick feels like leaving the restaurant still hungry. You scratch your head and ask, Is that all there is? Gubernick dishes out appetizer journalism when her readers would be better served with the entrée. This is not to say she can't provide a tasty morsel once in a while. In her informative 4-26 piece on Value Village and the used-clothing industry, Gubernick ably shows the thrift business as big business. Value Village buys goods collected from charities, paying by the pound. "Once the goods are delivered, sorters go through each bag, picking out usable items. Clothing judged too worn or too stained is packed into separate bales and shipped for sale in Third World countries....After five weeks unsold merchandise also makes its way to Africa and South America." Her incisive 3-29 story on a pioneer project in interactive TV concludes with a caveat encouraging investors to pass this opportunity by. "There are no signs that the big outfits that pumped money in earlier will come up with much more. We don't think much of the system itself, but we'd rather become a customer than a shareholder." But even these, her best stories, leave the reader little to chew on. Although she displays good reporting instincts, Gubernick treads too lightly on the subjects she covers, usually entertainment and communications, and her contributions seem more suited for *USA Today* than *Forbes*. Her 7-19 story detailing Egypt's attempts to boost tourism—its "biggest source of hard currency"—in the face of a terrorist campaign falls woefully short. She writes about official efforts to sell the country as an Eastern Mediterranean land, rather than part of the volatile

Middle East, but doesn't offer much else. Various pieces on movie moguls or production studios miss their mark because they reveal so little, and her 8-2 treatment of the used compact disc controversy proves eminently forgettable. A delightful writer and solid reporter, Gubernick's got the ingredients, but she'll need to work a little harder to improve the cooking.

Udayan Gupta

The Wall Street Journal

★½

Venture capital and small business. In the first year of Clinton's presidency, Gupta's antennae track onto issues of how the new administration's policies will affect small-business financing. However, his reporting and analysis don't cut as sharply as in previous years, as colorless writing and uninspired coverage mark his efforts. Gupta focuses on the biotechnology industry for much of 1993, but his dispatches seem sluggish. Reviewing the industry's response to Clinton's proposed health-care reform, 5-25, Gupta writes, "The entire biotechnology industry is under a cloud. But small biotechnology industries are the hardest hit. With no products and no revenue, they need steady access to the capital markets. The drought they now face threatens their plans for research and commercialization —and, for some, for their very existence." For all his sky-is-falling frenzy, Gupta barely scratches the surface of the problem, 10-8, when addressing a report that shows private biotech funding in the first nine months of 1993 jumped 75 percent over the amount raised in the same period a year earlier. Examining the diversification of financing for all small businesses, 10-15, Gupta writes, "Sources of start-up financing are proliferating, from networks of wealthy individuals to state-sponsored funds with mandates to promote economic development. Though the pool of capital available for new businesses may not be any bigger than a decade ago, the greater variety of financing sources, with different missions and outlooks, makes it more likely a venture will find money somewhere." Though investigating these sources makes for fascinating reading, he fails to address the question of banking deregulation so critical to the financing debate in 1993. Gupta does his best work gathering news about small business start-ups, digging up nuggets of information for *The Wall Street Journal*'s "Enterprise" feature. He reports, 6-1, that New England's Shawmut bank will create a separate unit to handle financing for the smallest of small businesses—those with less than $2.5 million in revenues. Exploring the success of minority entrepreneurs in his 2-19 story, Gupta notes a shift away from corporate paternalism. "Today, corporations are likely to view the purchase of goods and services from minority-owned firms less as the end of an obligation and more as the beginning of a long-term relationship." Though his legwork yields some choice information, Gupta often fails to capture the excitement and fascination of the subjects he reports.

George Hager

Congressional Quarterly

★★

Budget. Blending solid reporting with evenhanded analysis, Hager upholds *CQ*'s standards as he confidently details the tax and budget matters hashed out in Washington. In his 3-20 overview of the early proceedings on Capitol Hill, he insightfully shows how legislative tactics devised by Democrats on the House Rules Committee stymied Republicans. GOP confusion over how best to combat rival Democrats produced nothing but bickering and chaos, he argues, leaving a weakened opposition during debate on President Clinton's budget proposal. "At the end of the day, Republicans had agreed only that they did not like Clinton's plan, against which they voted unanimously." Hager's 9-11 reliance on budget figures supplied by the supposedly independent Congressional Budget Office will rankle Republicans who have long charged the CBO favors its Democratic sponsors. Nevertheless, Hager walks a fairly even line between the parties in covering the skirmishes on the banks of the Potomac. With his 8-7 story, he compares the new Clinton budget plan to George Bush's infamous 1990 budget deal, noting they contain many of the same provisions and were written by the same Democrats in Congress. Hager, however, fails to follow up on this observation. Concluding that the plans differ little, the next logical step would be to examine the results of the 1990 budget deal—a step he doesn't take. But Hager suc-

ceeds with a number of stories examining how the budget process works. In his 1-2 story on contentious entitlement programs, he writes that politicians consider Social Security "the 'third rail of American politics'—touch it and die." And in his 12-11 feature, Hager notes the power of the unelected in Washington. Subcommittee chairmen of the House Appropriations Committee "must reckon with a force whose powers in some ways seem to rival their own—a senior professional staff beholden only to the full committee chairman, men whose average tenure on the committee is some 20 years." Expect big things from Hager in 1994.

Kathleen Hays
Investor's Business Daily
★

New York bureau chief. Despite historically low interest rates, low inflation, and a recovering economy, Hays continues to use her news reports to criticize the Federal Reserve's handling of monetary policy under the direction of Chairman Alan Greenspan. She reproaches the Fed for not having done all it can to jump-start the economy. Such analysis ignores the Fed's mandate, which is not economic growth but price stability. Though the second half of her 1-6 report on Fed policy proves fairly balanced on the debate between monetarists and supply-siders, Hays editorializes that the Fed is "an extremely bad driver in its conduct of monetary policy....Some worry, however, that if the Fed does not set some definite monetary guideposts to steer by...it may repeat past mistakes." This theme emerges often in her reports. Hays calls the Fed "rudderless," 9-22, and cites a long list of what she calls "missteps that the Greenspan Fed has made." Once again, her arguments indicate she blames the Fed for slower growth and favors a return to traditional policy guidelines. Such advice is highly inappropriate in a news report. Despite her blunt criticism, Hays touts the benefits showered on the economy by lower interest rates, 3-4, saying they may offset the higher taxes proposed by President Clinton. However, her simplistic assessment uses many words to explain basic concepts. Similarly, her 12-13 report on the .2 percent rise in November's Consumer Price Index (CPI) constitutes standard fare—a technical comparison of the ups and downs of the CPI. She does, however, pepper the article with some useful quotes from Fed Vice Chairman David Mullins. "'There is no compelling evidence at this time that inflationary pressures are building,'" Mullins says, "'...[but] there are some other early warning signals that are twitching, or starting to twitch,' like rising gold prices and bond yields." If Hays had the insight to read between the lines of such subtle Fed statements, she might understand the importance of this last comment, and recognize the very specific guideposts steering monetary policy.

Diana B. Henriques
The New York Times
★★★½

Financial writer. With her name on the marquees of a couple of 1993 media blockbusters, one could excuse Henriques for acting like a Hollywood star. Yet all signs indicate that this Texan will continue her workhorse ways, a prospect unlikely to please the U.S. Department of Agriculture. Her 5-23 investigation of rigged bidding practices sets the stage for an explosive October series that reveals a corrupt farm bureaucracy. In three groundbreaking articles, 10-10, 10-11, and 10-12, Henriques and coauthor Dean Baquet deny the Agriculture Department the Grade A seal of approval, exposing massive fraud and corruption. The duo reconstructs a paper trail thousands of pages long to show, among other things, that the Department permits "politically powerful agriculture companies caught rigging bids, fixing prices and defrauding Government programs" to continue participating in lucrative federal programs. Such practice, Henriques and Baquet note, violates a 1986 executive order issued by Ronald Reagan. Court documents and FOIA files obtained by the *Times* "highlight how sprawling bureaucracies like the Agriculture Department, one of the Federal Government's biggest departments, can become so powerful that they defy Federal policies and even ignore the direct orders of Presidents." A related 10-10 story questions the efficacy of a subsidy program designed to boost wheat exports, noting that "after 1988, wheat exports declined, falling below the levels that prevailed before the program started." In her other starring role,

Henriques chronicles the exploits of Steven Hoffenberg, the crooked Towers Financial Corp. CEO and springtime suitor of the *New York Post*. With considerable legwork, Henriques uncovers past perfidy by Hoffenberg, who bilked some investors, and her 3-9 story describes his duplicity in denying any connection to a California nursing home. "The connections are there, however, scattered through state health, property and corporation records in Virginia, California and Delaware. The [address of the] shell company that took title to the nursing home...is a suite in an elegant apartment building on East 58th Street in Manhattan. The concierge at the building identified the suite as Mr. Hoffenberg's." And that's just one of many irregularities uncovered by Henriques in her outstanding and exhaustive coverage of the Hoffenberg episode. Henriques's success proves that talent, along with hard work and persistence—the main weapons in an investigative reporter's arsenal—can pay big dividends.

Tom Herman

The Wall Street Journal

★★

"Your Money Matters" and "Tax Report" columnist. While many business journalists fancy themselves oracles akin to the investor Peter Lynch—or at the very least Kreskin—and boldly proclaim where the markets will go, Herman prudently refrains and lets the experts do the forecasting. His 5-13 piece rings typical of this brand of reporting. "Economists argued that the producer price increase [of .6 percent in April] probably represents nothing more than a one-month fluke and will eventually be viewed as the latest in a long line of phony inflation scares." Backing this up by talking to financial analysts, Herman warns readers that the conventional wisdom on the Street may not be all that wise, and his 1-22 article offers a potent dose of populism. "Looking for an easy way to make money betting on interest rates? Find out the consensus forecast among leading economists—and then bet against it." This caveat comes courtesy of a ream of statistics casting doubt on the very predictions Herman reports daily. This, his other "job," involves playing advisor and handholder, allaying taxpayers' fears of the new levies by supplying tips on avoiding their sting. In his 9-24 effort, Herman walks the reader through the laborious process of requesting a certain refund occasioned by the new tax laws. "Use the worksheet on page 21 of the 1992 Form 1040 instructions. Substitute your full-year payment total for the half-year figure on the first line. Use 100 percent instead of 50 percent on line five of the worksheet." A bit tedious, but instructive. Some advice is simply basic. "Remember," he writes, 8-4, "...never to make any investment decision solely on the basis of tax considerations. That can be an instant formula for disaster." Quipster Herman notes, 3-12, that while "refinancing your mortgage can be a royal pain...the savings"—because of rock-bottom interest rates—"can be princely." This crowning advice may not be worth a king's ransom, but, like much of Herman's solid counsel, is worth checking out.

Bruce Horovitz

Los Angeles Times

★½

Marketing. Bringing the Southern California angle to coverage of sales and services, Horovitz often turns out entertaining stories. However, this may be due more to his subjects than to his efforts, which sometimes prove only adequate. Horovitz relies far too heavily on quotes, which detracts from the good ones he assembles. His 9-9 sto-

ry on J.C. Penney's minority-outreach campaign drowns in a sea of citations. But hints of progress do occasionally appear, dispersed throughout such stories as his 2-23 effort on marketing aimed at gays. He mentions that one Texas catlogue "offers leather wallets guaranteed to have been stitched by lesbians living in Lake Tahoe. Each wallet has etched on it, 'Handcrafted by California Women.'" In his 3-30 piece on the infomercial phenomenon, Horovitz humorously notes the problems encountered by late-night hawkers. Many people, he writes, are "frightened to order anything from an industry that sells everything from spray-on hair to bee pollen that supposedly helps people shed weight, rid allergies and, of course, reverse aging. But even as the infomercial industry insists that its reputation has greatly improved—with the likes of Volvo, Kodak and Ross Perot now on board—the sleaze factor is always lurking." In his smart 12-7 story, Horovitz reports why Southern California, which has seen much of its movie-production business leave for Florida, must now contend with the fashion-photography industry following suit. "While Miami is embracing the new business, Los Angeles and neighboring cities seem to be pushing it away. Los Angeles County has nearly 100 separate jurisdictions, each with its own film and print production bureaucracy. But for all practical purposes, a single permit will suffice in Dade County." For every solid story, however, Horovitz writes one that disappoints. In his 11-16 piece on the fur industry's efforts to boost its sagging image, he notes that the Fur Information Council of America "plans to print a booklet aimed at convincing skeptical teen-age girls that it's ethic- ally OK to wear furs." Ethiically OK? Like, just because he writes about teenagers, you know, doesn't mean he has to sound like one. Many other stories cry out desperately for more detail. This can make reading Horovitz—a delightful writer with a sense of what's hip and what isn't—frustrating.

Bruce Ingersoll

The Wall Street Journal

★★½

Trade, transportation. Judged solely on his own byline, Ingersoll probably rates a star and a quarter: Nearly half his stories—and almost all of his blockbusters—come through joint efforts filed with other *Journal* reporters. But this master of the double-byline manages to affix his name to some stellar works. In the heat of the NAFTA battle, Ingersoll and co-author Asra Q. Nomani pen a remarkable 11-15 profile of South Carolina textile-king Roger Milliken. They call Milliken, the secretive, but highly effective, anti-NAFTA leader, "the Howard Hughes of the U.S. protectionist movement; a publicity-shy billionaire who has been quietly bankrolling the campaign against NAFTA." The pair shines light on this veteran of the trade wars, whose behind-the-scenes maneuverings complement the public pronouncements of Ross Perot. Ingersoll's finest story, a 4-13 look at the new regulatory enthusiasm in Washington, co-authored by Bob Davis, shows the uncertain approach to government regulation after 12 years of Republican rule. The piece shrewdly notes Clinton's reluctance to touch certain industries, such as financial services and communications, while meddling in others. "The feds will even monitor whether cable companies answer customers' phone calls within 30 seconds." The comprehensive story also yields some surprises. "Some industries may welcome a dose of regulation. Biotech companies think that they can better allay consumer concerns about eating genetically engineered food if their products pass government muster. Fish and seafood processors hope that FDA regulation will be seen as a federal seal of approval." Curiously, most of Ingersoll's solo efforts—such as his 5-17 story on the government's attitude toward maritime policy, which falls short on details—prove only about half as good as his joint efforts. These lone ventures simply lack the punch of his tandem stories, although his 5-14 piece on U.S. aviation policy qualifies as an exception. Here Ingersoll notes how European countries like France and Germany plan to stifle American competition by diplomacy. In their eyes, "the ideal agreement is the very one that the Clinton team is trying to get the British to liberalize. They particularly covet provisions in the 1977 agreement that strictly limit how many U.S. carriers fly where, when and how often." Covering the Whitewater imbroglio, Ingersoll picks up steam at year's end with an astute solo piece, 12-17, and with co-author Jeffrey H. Birnbaum, 12-21. But getting a better read on Ingersoll will be tough until he goes it alone more often.

Bernice Kanner
New York
★★½

"On Madison Avenue." It takes a lot of stamina to keep up with the frenetic world of advertising, but Kanner does so with aplomb. Tireless legwork helps her track up-to-the-minute happenings on Madison Avenue, and she also keeps an eye on broader developments in marketing and business. In "Grand Hotel," 1-11, she focuses on a (very long) day in the life of Martin Anker, a concierge at New York's swanky Ritz-Carlton. Apprenticing with Anker, Kanner reports some of the more bizarre requests the hotelman fields whenever the phone rings. "'Where can I buy a gargoyle?' [someone asks.] Anker recalls a florist he thinks might know where one can be purchased. We recommend a pet hotel for a bichon frise, tell a caller he can eat lion meat at [the] New Deal [restaurant], and arrange a delivery from Pizza Villagio." In her 5-31 effort, Kanner describes New York City's efforts to woo filmmaking business back to the Big Apple. "Permits for shooting and scouting in New York are way up since the eight-month boycott by major studios in 1990-1991 almost shut down the industry. Credit the unions with this turnaround: Under their new contract they're paid a third less." But Kanner's bread and butter remains the ad world, a subject she handles with élan as she keeps readers abreast of the maneuverings of Madison Avenue's established kingpins and up-and-comers. Her 2-1 story tells of the newest account landed by the guy who thought up Wendy's "Where's the Beef?" and Little Caesar's "Pizza, Pizza." His next challenge is the as-yet-unnamed clear beer from Miller's. Never losing sight of advertising trends, 9-27, Kanner reports on marketers' recent embrace of country music warblers to hawk their wares. "Madison Avenue has latched onto Nashville because the heartland has become hip. In the past few years, 'country' has gone from a southern phenomenon to a mainstream one. Country music's market share has almost doubled since 1990." Fast and loose—like the industry she covers—but still informative and reliable, a Kanner column seldom fails to pique a reader's interest.

Peter T. Kilborn
The New York Times
★★

Labor. Like most major newspapers in the U.S., *The New York Times* provides scant coverage of organized labor and working-class activity. Even though the "paper of record" boasts dozens of business reporters and publishes a hefty business section daily, union and labor affairs—unless a major strike or scandal occurs—seldom make it into print. When they do, they usually carry Kilborn's byline. Kilborn's 6-3 piece spotlights a 25-year-old union organizer in California, while his 6-6 story focuses on several Cal Tech grads who can't find jobs. In a 9-5 Labor Day weekend piece titled "A Labor Day Message No One Asked To Hear," Kilborn declares, "For all but the elite, work holds less promise, less purpose, less security and less dignity than it did a generation ago." Unfortunately, Kilborn throws out this statement to stand on its own. Surveying the grim economic prospects of the once-thriving Lynn, Massachusetts, he adds, "This is the city where the General Electric Company was born a century ago. But its factories this Labor Day invite suspicions that the company might not be here much longer. Weeds grow in the fissured asphalt of the plants G.E. has closed around town, and most gates to the ones that remain open are chained shut because the gatekeepers have been dismissed." In his prescient 3-15 story examining the new "disposable" workforce, Kilborn tracks a surprising trend. "Many companies have adopted a form of workforce management to compete in the world market. They keep a core of managers and valued workers whom they favor with good benefits and permanent jobs. They take on and shed other workers as business spurts and slumps." Kilborn's artistry remains the profile, a style of journalism which permits him to skirt broad questions about politics and policy by honing in on the very particular experiences of a handful of individuals. In perhaps his best profile of the year, 9-26, Kilborn grimly portrays five Midwestern families struggling to survive under the current health-care system. "During the summer Mrs. Coen had a long bout with bronchial asthma, requiring three series of antibiotic treatments. In October she faces surgery to remove a cataract, the latest in a succession of serious eye ailments." The sometimes-maudlin Kilborn adds, "[Mr. Coen] and his wife were relieved to hear the President promise them help with long-term care." With his emphasis on workers and not management, Kilborn provides a perspective seldom seen in the *Times*.

Jerry Knight

The Washington Post

★★½

Finance. Rebounding from a poor year in 1992, Knight emerges as one of the most feared reporters in the nation's capital. His relentless digging and hard reporting yield biting exposés of Beltway improprieties. Leading the *Post's* late-year look into the allegations of influence-peddling swirling around Commerce Secretary Ron Brown (since cleared by the Justice Department), Knight files a groundbreaking 11-27 feature on a business partner of Brown's who, owing the FDIC millions from another failed venture, stiffed the feds but still contributed large sums to the Democratic party, then headed by Brown. Fixing his sights on Rep. William Jefferson [D-LA], 9-28, Knight details how the freshman Congressman arranged a meeting with top Treasury officials to appeal a decision forbidding his former law firm—still paying Jefferson for buying him out—from contracting with the Resolution Trust Corporation (RTC). Why the ruling? Because, Knight explains, the firm failed to disclose to the government that Jefferson, while partner, had defaulted on $780,000 in loans from failed S&Ls. "It is politically sensitive not only because a member of Congress is involved but also because it has produced a direct conflict between two goals of the Clinton administration—eliminating irregularities by RTC contractors and giving more business to minority-owned firms." In his terrific 11-21 piece, Knight unveils a nefarious source of funds for state and local politicians—contributions from municipal-bond underwriting companies. Competitive bidding for business, Knight reveals, seldom occurs. In 1992, "more than 80 percent of all municipal bond offerings were sold in negotiated deals...[in which] local officials pick the firm they want to sell their bonds and then negotiate the interest rate." While Knight excels with investigative features, his other efforts often fall short. In his 4-23 story on Republicans still running federal agencies due to Clinton lethargy, he bungles notions of the separation of powers. "Congressional Democrats are frustrated because they have been waiting 12 years to get control of these agencies," he states, "and the Republicans are still calling the shots." Yet Democrats in Congress have no more constitutional authority over executive-branch agencies than they did during Republican administrations. Still, Knight weighs in as a top-notch investigator who shines when piercing the armor of federal officialdom.

Robert Kuttner

Washington Post Writers Group

BusinessWeek

The American Prospect

★★½

Economics. A liberal, Keynesian economic commentator, Kuttner wields influence in political circles. Although government guidance of the market shapes all his analysis, he constantly puts a new spin on this core belief. Those who don't agree with his brand of economics, however, may be disappointed by many of his arguments, which try to persuade with rhetoric rather than historical evidence. His 1-18 *BusinessWeek* column, for instance, advises that "the preferred macroeconomic policy is stimulus now, best led by public investment, followed by gradual deficit reduction after growth is back on track." Yet, Kuttner offers no data to buttress his assertion that such a policy path would result in the high-growth, low-deficit environment he predicts. He gushes, 4-5, over the Council of Economic Advisers assembled by the Clinton administration, declaring it "a team that could revolutionize not just economic policy but also the economic profession." Later in the article readers learn the reason for Kuttner's unbridled glee—all members advocate government intervention. Far from revolutionary, that position was last in vogue during the Carter administration. Health care, a topic Kuttner follows closely both in his columns and as coeditor of *The American Prospect*, dominates his 11-15 *BW* column. He argues that productivity gains can't be measured in medicine, but conveniently ignores the extraordinary medical advances made in recent decades. Common sense dictates labeling these advances as productivity gains, even though they don't measure as easily as auto-assembly advances. At his persuasive best in his 7-26 column, Kuttner hearkens back to his interesting work in 1992 on the fallacies that guide deficit-reduction mania. One such fallacy, he writes, "is the old monetarist claim that the public deficit and long-term interest rates are closely linked....[But while] public deficits were enormous during World War II... long-term rates remained at 2.5 percent." Notice the effective use of historical evidence—it's a technique Kuttner might use more often in his economic analysis. On other subjects, such as Attorney General nominee Zöe Baird's nanny troubles, Kuttner, in a 1-22 *Washington Post* piece, emerges as a feisty and persuasive commentator. "One had hoped that the coming of age of the feminist legal titans like Hillary Clinton and Zöe Baird signaled a new agenda of concern for women's issues and children's issues—and not just the equal right of women to become yuppie power-lawyers alongside men." Shrewd and entertaining, Kuttner remains an influential writer on Clintonomics.

Jeffrey M. Laderman

Business Week

★½

Associate editor. Earnestly bullish, eminently entertaining, but seldom comprehensive, Laderman focuses his attentions almost exclusively on mutual funds. In his aptly-titled 1-18 cover story, "The Power of Mutual Funds," he provides a comprehensive account of a relatively recent investment phenomenon that has helped fuel a bull market. Shrewdly noting how these funds have altered the economic landscape, Laderman quotes a Federal Reserve official as saying they fundamentally change how the Fed measures the money supply. "In many ways," Laderman adds insightfully, "the funds have evolved into America's alternative banking system—freely moving capital around in ways that banks, still hobbled by an antiquated regulatory structure, can't." But while this overview demonstrates thoughtfulness, Laderman's week-to-week coverage falls short. A strong 1993 market validates his enthusiasm, and at year's end he sees no end to the good times. "The most fitting symbol of the stock market today is neither bull nor bear, but bunny," he writes cutely, 12-27. "You know, the rabbit in the battery commercial, the one that keeps going and going and going." His rationale, however, rests on shaky ground. Incessantly trumpeting low interest rates, Laderman blindly assumes they will continue, a claim based more on whim than evidence. Seldom considering the role of the Federal Reserve Board—just four mentions all year—he never speculates on signals sent by President Clinton that the White House will try to assert authority over the Fed in 1994. Sadly, Laderman's articles reveal little other than ardor for a rising S&P 500. Straying every once in a while from the mutual-fund beat, he gets mixed reviews. His lucid 7-19 look at variable annuities ranks as one of few stories dishing valuable information to readers, but a confusing 8-23 piece on corporate America's stock-buyback trend fails to explain why so many companies have chosen to rein in equity. And the introduction to his 4-12 quarterly wrap-up seems highly dubious. "It was a first quarter full of surprises. The new President proposed raising taxes—and the public embraced the plan." Embraced? Despite his often informative articles, lines like this should command this occasional reaction to his byline: Laderman? Later, man.

Richard Lawrence

The Journal of Commerce

★★½

Trade. With the solemn, almost grave, reporting style preferred by editors at the paper founded by Samuel F.B. Morse in 1827, Lawrence keeps a sober eye on the commerce front. He monitors developments in the Uruguay Round of the GATT negotiations, feeding his readers the latest reports from the battlegrounds of international trade. As the U.S. wraps up a GATT agreement in December after feverish negotiations with France, Lawrence assesses its chances of hurdling the next barrier—ratification by Congress. In his solid 12-16 front-page article, he reports that in the wake of losing on NAFTA, free-trade opponents, bitterly conceding defeat, remain unlikely to force a showdown over GATT passage. However, this piece yields an intriguing bit of information that Lawrence does not explore: He writes that the U.S. Chamber of Commerce—despite its longtime devotion to free trade, and its surprising 1993 rapprochement with the Clinton administration—is withholding its support for the GATT agreement touted by the White House. For the most part, however, Lawrence presents thorough treatment of trade issues, penning pieces chock-full of facts and statistics without bogging down in minutiae. His helpful 12-13 feature reports one of the European Union's chief contentions imperiling GATT—the U.S. automotive efficiency laws and a luxury-car tax that the EU says unfairly target its imported cars. "Altogether, [the EU] says, European carmakers pay about 90 percent of the combined gas guzzler and luxury car taxes and fuel economy fines that the U.S. government collects annually...[though] European car imports have only about 4 percent of the U.S. market." Tracking GATT negotiations earlier in the year, Lawrence reports, 2-2, on hardball U.S. efforts to restrict government purchases of EC products. And in his 9-27 piece, Lawrence shows why tariff phaseouts on machinery and equipment could prove a boon for U.S. firms. "A zero tariff agreement would be essentially a 'free ride' for U.S. farm equipment manufacturers, since the United States years ago stopped charging duties on farm equipment imports....The European Community, [John Deere's] largest export market, charges import duties on farm equipment ranging from 3.5 percent to 9 percent." Not just Eurocentric in his pursuit of trade stories, 4-15, Lawrence details the formulating of the "patchwork of free-trade agreements encompassing nearly all of Latin America and the Caribbean." Those seeking better information on developments in worldwide commerce should trade up to Lawrence.

Doron P. Levin

The New York Times

★★★

Detroit bureau chief. The Israeli-born Levin keeps his gaze focused squarely on the American auto industry. Ably combining incisive commentary and crisp reporting, he drives the *Times*'s car coverage on eight cylinders. In his 6-16 story about Honda losing market dominance, Levin details the fall of the auto industry's titan. "The company, once so canny, was caught flat-footed in the fast-growing markets for minivans and four-wheel-drive sport-utility vehicles, which many Americans now buy as a substitute for cars." In his superb 1-17 article, Levin examines the impetus for this trend. "Federal fuel efficiency and safety regulations are less stringent for mini-vans, sport utilities and pickups than they are for cars." Levin leads *Times* coverage of one of Detroit's biggest personnel stories—the saga of a heralded executive who jumped ship from General Motors to Volkswagen. In one of the earliest reports of the courtship of José Ignacio López de Arriortua, a fabled cost-cutter in his short stint at GM, Levin declares, 2-25, "It is clear why VW would want Mr. López: the auto maker is the sales leader in Europe, but its costs are among the industry's highest. VW's profits, therefore, have been weak." Largely avoiding the battle over NAFTA waged so furiously on the Michigan battleground by both labor and management, Levin does broach the topic in a 12-17 piece about Ford's announcement to build compact cars in Mexico. "Ford's plans will touch off a series of production shifts in Mexican, Canadian and American factories, [the company said], resulting in the creation of the equivalent of 550 jobs in the United States and Canada, and 300 jobs in Mexico...vindicat[ing] the stance of the supporters of the trade pact, who had argued that the agreement would add jobs, especially for the automotive industry." Though keeping track of which direction the Motown winds blow, Levin leaves coverage of the UAW-Big Three labor talks to others under his command. But when he turns his attentions to a particular issue, Levin can be counted on to furnish thoughtful, reliable reporting from the banks of Lake Erie.

Josh Levine

Forbes

★★½

With confidence and grace, Levine chronicles companies caught at the crossroads—those businesses faced with the choice of adopting new marketing strategies to meet consumers' changing tastes or holding out and risking possible extinction. As the economic climate continues to shift from the free-wheeling 1980s to the uncertain 1990s, Levine capably tracks the "life-or-death" decisions companies must make to compete. In his 5-10 effort, he wields a light touch in revealing the extraordinary lengths to which Coke and Pepsi must go to combat the Snapple iced-tea threat. Snapple, which Levine calls "one of the pioneers of the so-called new age (read expensive) sodas," hit the bull's eye with a ready-to-drink product that actually tastes like the real thing. "The canned versions that [Pepsi's] Lipton and [Coke's] Nestea have marketed for years tasted only faintly reminiscent of the genuine article, and sales reflected it." Levine describes in fascinating detail the battle strategies and advertising campaigns in a high-stakes global beverage war. Switching from cans to snifters in his 9-13 article, Levine engagingly tells of the problems encountered by makers of pricey cognacs. "Prized for slow sipping after dinner, preferably by a roaring fire with a trusty Labrador at one's feet, cognac doesn't fit the way many people live anymore." Highlighting a particularly irksome point for companies like Rémy Martin, Levine asks, "How do you broaden your image without destroying the elite image that is the soul of your business?" A charming writer, Levine, in his 11-22 article, delicately depicts the scantily clad waitresses at Hooters restaurants as "lightly swaddled." He goes on to recount advertising gambits openly seeking to offend politically correct sensibilities—a female-owned lingerie company using two large door knockers in its ads, or a barbecue sauce commercial celebrating carnivorism. "The folks busy saving spotted owls," Levine remarks, "probably aren't slathering slabs of meat with barbecue sauce and tossing them on the grill anyway." Whimsy comes easily to Levine, but he manages to keep pace with more serious developments. His 10-25 collaboration with Nancy Rotenier on the $200 billion industry in counterfeit goods—from clothes to auto parts to critical nuclear reactor equipment—should strike fear into most readers. Fortunately, with Levine you get the genuine article.

Marc Levinson
Newsweek
★★

Business. At his best when he sticks to reporting, Levinson provides sturdy and occasionally original articles on business and economics. His most impressive piece, 8-9, takes an unconventional look at the dumping charges made by so many U.S. companies against overseas manufacturers. Citing numerous examples, this eye-opening report reveals that foreign companies increasingly level this same charge against U.S. companies. The long-term implications? "In 1991, the European Community found [Monsanto] guilty of dumping U.S.-made sweetener and tacked on a duty of nearly $13 a pound. 'Our main competitor does not operate with such a duty leveled against it,' says a company spokesman. Soon Monsanto won't either. It will cut exports and open a NutraSweet plant in France next month." In his equally solid 6-28 dispatch, Levinson reports press leaks coming from the Federal Reserve where "discretion is a cherished habit." The facts prove fresh and carefully reported, and he explains their market impact and the possible motivations that prompted them. As Louis Gerstner, Jr., formerly of RJR Nabisco, takes the helm at the troubled IBM, Levinson provides a sound 4-5 analysis of the strengths and weaknesses he brings to the computer maker, as well as the unique challenges the new CEO will face. "Perhaps the biggest question is whether Gerstner knows enough about the direction of the information industry to shape IBM's future....A demanding manager, Gerstner is given credit for bringing in topflight executives at RJR. 'He knows what he doesn't know,' insists an associate." When Levinson steers toward economic analysis, he tends to forget the reporting side of the journalistic equation. In a mediocre economic overview co-authored by Rich Thomas, 2-22, he strings together all the handy generalizations and clichés on worker productivity, deficit-reduction, economic stimulus, and so forth, but does little digging of his own. Levinson should capitalize on his reporting strengths and leave the economic generalizations to others.

Larry Light
Business Week
★½

Corporate finance editor. A lack of depth marks Light's stories, too many of which come in at about half a page. This pattern marks a retreat from years past, in which thorough reporting was his hallmark. In his 8-23 story, Light touts the stocks of life-insurance companies as big

winners down the line. "The chief reason is demographic. The aging baby-boom population is thinking about retirement, so annuity sales are soaring." But that, coupled with stability of the industry, constitutes the sole reason cited. A few more would be helpful. A sidebar lists five insurers to keep an eye on, four of which by year's end had dropped in price, three of them considerably. In his 3-1 commentary, Light turns his attention to small businesses. "These incubators of growth," he states, "created 80 percent of the [new] jobs in the 1980s." Light decries cowardly banks for refusing to lend money to risky though potentially burgeoning businesses, choosing instead to reap small, secure gains from Treasury bills. "They prefer to fund the federal deficit rather than nurture job-generating small private enterprises that will benefit them and society in the long term." While some criticism here proves justified, describing banks' motives as "prefer[ring] to fund the federal deficit" ranks as silly. Light fares better reporting on specific players in the business world. In his 7-12 profile of financier Saul Steinberg, Light notes criticism the insurer has received from investors over his high salaries and big loans given to family members—important items now that he's thinking about floating new stock. In an 11-29 update on Donald Trump's attempt to return from the financial grave, Light playfully captures the semi-solvent mogul's ambitions. "The relentless Donald Trump is suddenly eager to show that, when it comes to deals, he's still the artist. True, his easel and brushes remain in hock." But Light's skeptical portrait, while long on style, runs short on details. A mixed year, Light alternates between illuminating and obscuring his subjects.

Thomas W. Lippman

The Washington Post

★½

Energy. Though Lippman covers energy, he spends much of his own this year on Vietnam, where he served as the Post's Saigon bureau chief in 1972-73. Talented and tenacious, Lippman zeroes in on Harvard researcher Stephen J. Morris's controversial discovery in Soviet archives of a document allegedly proving Vietnamese deception concerning American POWs. In a series of articles, 4-13, 4-14, 4-15, 4-22, and a 4-25 op-ed piece, Lippman challenges the validity of Morris's claim, accusing the researcher of dissembling in order to justify fiercely anti-communist views. "He has consistently criticized the government of Hanoi," Lippman writes, 4-25, "which he has accused of territorial expansionism, repression, duplicity and allegiance to Stalinism." But Morris shoots back, contending in the Autumn *National Interest* that Lippman hid facts about the background of one of his major sources, which had it been revealed, would have damaged the source's credibility. The controversy, although not settled, harmed Lippman's reputation. Numerous other stories focusing on Vietnamese-American relations, unrelated to the Morris imbroglio, distract Lippman from providing the excellent assessments of the energy scene that he filed in 1992. In his 3-21 piece, he touts Sacramento's new "nuclear-free" identity, following its 1989 vote to close the inefficient Rancho Seco nuclear power plant. Lippman, however, does not explore the economic feasibility of Sacramento's alternative energy sources. And he mars a 1-11 profile of outgoing Energy Secretary James Watkins by failing to identify the environmental groups whose scathing report on the Energy Department Lippman extensively cites. Moving beyond energy for much of the year, Lippman files several commendable stories on ethnic and religious tensions in the Middle East. His provocative 7-26 article traces U.S. support for anti-Soviet Afghan rebels during the 1980s to the rise of Muslim fundamentalism allegedly responsible for the World Trade Center bombing. "Through Pakistani channels, the CIA provided weapons, money and training for the Afghan insurgents," Lippman writes after consulting diplomatic and administration sources. "These young men learned about military tactics, weapons and explosives. Retaining their zeal and their skills long after the last Soviet troops pulled out...they have become a recurring threat to other nations, including the United States." Lippman also gets raves for a 10-18 report on Saddam Hussein's crackdown on Shiite rebels in the country's marshy southern region, where bulldozers are "constricting huge dikes to cut off the flow of water to the area." This foreign-affairs coverage, filed from Washington, salvages the year for Lippman. But readers have good reason to wonder whether the lights are dimming on Lippman's once-stellar energy coverage.

Carol Loomis

Fortune

★★★★

Board of editors. Despite penning just a half-dozen articles, Loomis remains as superb as ever, consistently meeting the high standards she has established over many years at *Fortune.* Casting a watchful eye over the land roamed by America's corporate giants, she has shown a knack for forecasting the downfalls of big-time corporate CEOs. The year saw shaman Loomis correctly predicting the ousters of IBM's John Akers and Kodak's Kay Whitmore, 1-11 and 5-31, respectively. Once the ax falls on Akers, 2-22, Loomis trenchantly analyzes Big Blue's blues and what the next chief must do to rescue the foundering company. While virtually every business writer in America has tackled this question, Loomis's assessment ranks among the best. Journalism's Monday morning quarterbacks uniformly blasted IBM for sticking too long with its mainframe computers instead of switching to PCs, but Loomis refutes this conventional wisdom. "It's easy to see why IBM resisted shifting from a mainframe mentality. Even as they decline, mainframes and their svelter cousins, minicomputers, are by far the most profitable part of its business." Offering insights that transcend her rivals' hackneyed carping about the IBM "bureaucracy," Loomis examines in abundant detail the particular circumstances that brought an American icon to its knees. She broadens this analysis in "Dinosaurs?" her spectacular 5-3 cover story chronicling the fates of three corporate titans—Sears, IBM, and General Motors—which in the early 1970s ranked among America's top five companies. None ranks in the top 20 today. Loomis shows why it's harder to stay at the top than to get there. She details the common ills afflicting these three companies, notably the mistakes made, the steps not taken, and the arrogance of being on top, which led them to underestimate rivals and misread competitors. IBM, for example, bought a 20 percent share of chip-maker Intel for $640 million in the 1980s and sold it a few years later, "cheerfully pocketing a gain and apparently never thinking about what larger profits it might be relinquishing. The shares IBM held would today be worth $3.6 billion." Loomis also investigates one company, General Electric, which successfully avoided these pitfalls to remain at the pinnacle of the business world. With her ability to recognize issues broader than the particulars of a given story, Loomis, who picked up a Gerald Loeb Lifetime Achievement award in June, stands at the pinnacle of business writing.

John Maggs

The Journal of Commerce

★★★

Trade. In a watershed year for international trade liberalization, Maggs adroitly reports the give-and-take as the U.S., Mexico, and Canada work out the chinks in their NAFTA armor. He alternates between solid reporting and astute analysis, providing *JC* readers with top-notch coverage of one of the year's most contentious issues. In his 2-3 effort, Maggs keeps his audience apprised of apparently questionable details in the pact. Revealing the underbelly of the hastily-written agreement, Maggs reports that NAFTA will maintain Mexico's 20 percent tariff on flat glass, protecting a Mexican company that already dominates world flat-glass production. Concentrating on the nuts and bolts, Maggs's stories illustrate the advantage of substance over style. In his 11-8 front-page feature on the Capitol Hill battle for votes over NAFTA, Maggs perspicuously describes how pledges from an increasingly desperate President escalate with the clock running out. The promise Clinton gives to build extra warplanes in one wavering Congresswoman's district spurs Maggs to note, "Until now, the examples of government largesse to get NAFTA votes have been relatively modest. Special interest trade provisions in the bill implementing the NAFTA do little more than call for studies or let off steam about alleged unfair trading practices." His 7-1 treatment of the June court-order requiring environmental-impact studies of NAFTA could leave some observers scratching their heads. He quotes "one former trade official as saying NAFTA is dead if the ruling stands." Yet, when the ruling is overturned three months later, he states, 9-

27, that it "was never a practical threat to the agreement....It [only] created a public relations nightmare for the administration." Fortunately, even though the latter claim remains unexplained, such incongruities appear rarely in Maggs's work. In his wry 6-22 analysis of the turns taken on NAFTA by Clinton, who had earlier amended the pact to assuage Democrats, Maggs writes, "Yet, as Ross Perot and others have stepped up their campaign against NAFTA recently, Mr. Clinton has found himself defending the trade agreement with the same arguments the Bush administration used to argue that side agreements were not necessary." With the NAFTA wars over, readers must eagerly await what subject the talented Maggs will cover next.

Maggie Mahar

Barron's

★★★★

Senior editor. One of the best in the business, Mahar rarely runs with the pack. A savvy, thorough reporter, engaging writer, and perceptive analyst—what more could a reader ask for in a journalist? She often plays the contrarian, spotting important trends and unearthing valuable new information. In her 6-14 column, Mahar questions Wall Street's hammering of Sallie Mae stock following the Clinton administration's threat to take control of the nation's student-loan business. Seeing beyond the panic, she soberly examines the emerging legislation and finds that "even if Clinton's version passed and the government one day managed to finance 100 percent of all student loans, Sallie Mae would still be looking at a potentially enormous business servicing those loans....Even Sallie's congressional critics suggest that Sallie is likely to emerge the winner." Shaking up the commercial real-estate bears, 10-14, Mahar reports that the market is at a "turning point." She bases this surprising analysis on dogged reporting, which turns up oodles of statistical evidence and well-placed industry observations. By the end of her exhaustive investigation, readers will likely take seriously her prediction that "real estate could well provide a better return than stocks, T-bills or bonds over the next five years or so." Mahar's byline pops up in *New York* 4-26, where she provides an illuminating and balanced discussion of the nation's changing healthcare system. Exploring many angles given scant attention elsewhere, Mahar assesses whether the current managed care proposals will mean better quality or simply controlled costs. An outstanding profile writer, Mahar talks with Arthur Levitt, Jr., the new chairman of the SEC. Taking readers well beyond the highlights of his career, *Barron's* 11-22, Mahar captures the essence of his political character, his disposition toward regulation, and his skills as a consensus builder. "Levitt's reputation for 'seeing both sides of a question,'" Mahar writes, "frequently places him on a verbal seesaw." Indeed, by the end of the essay, Levitt himself has admitted that he's no deregulator, preferring self-regulation to government regulation. Mahar always gets to the heart of the matter.

Thomas McArdle

Investor's Business Daily

★★★

New York. A dogged reporter who consistently manages to uncover important new facts on key economic stories, McArdle delivers original, high-yield articles. In his thorough 3-2 report, he reveals that tax levies on corporate profits have soared more than any other type of tax in recent years. One source notes that "corporate profit taxes at all levels increased 126.1 percent from the recession year of 1982 to 1992....According to the General Accounting Office, the effective corporate income tax rate skyrocketed from 18.6 percent in 1986 to 32.9 percent in 1989." These compelling statistics have surfaced nowhere else. His heavily researched 4-30 analysis of the different economic forecasting styles of the Congressional Budget Office (CBO) and the Office of Management and Budget (OMB) also proves an eye-opener. Shedding light on the CBO's numerous forecasting mistakes, McArdle gathers persuasive evidence that politics might be guiding President Clinton's embrace of the CBO's "morose scenario" of two percent long-term economic growth. In another top-notch effort, 9-16, McArdle profiles political up-and-comer Gov. Carroll Campbell [R-SC], one "of the handful of GOP governors seen as serious candidates to challenge President Clinton in 1996." Citing Campbell's numerous accomplishments in crisp, economical fashion, McArdle gives an informative snapshot of this Republican dark horse. His two-part series on the crisis of the underclass, 11-10 and 11-11, is provocative, although McArdle supports his argument—that crime and other woes of the inner city are caused by cultural attitudes as much as by economic conditions—more on opinions than on actual studies. The latter piece opens with the question: "How do the poor go about reacquiring the middle-class values that they need to function independently, but which they have lost over the last 30 years?" Fortunately, the rest of the piece forgoes editorializing and gets down to useful analysis of programs that have improved inner-city neighborhoods and the lives of welfare recipients. This series typifies McArdle's work, which provides both policymakers and the average reader with enough perspective and information to enter a productive policy debate.

Robert McGough
The Wall Street Journal
★★★

Mutual funds. Reporting a beat that proves one of the biggest investment stories of 1993, McGough splits his roles between news reporter and money manager. His study of the equities markets extends only to mutual funds, which absorbed a tidal wave of investment dollars in 1993 and whose progress he regularly chronicles. Furnishing much news-you-can-use for small investors, McGough steers them through the complicated, labyrinthine world of exotic funds. In his 9-24 story on the emerging-market fad, he notes the "daunting" number of such funds to choose from, and offers a bit of sound investment advice. "Always remember: Wild gyrations in value are the norm, not the exception....For many small investors, a broadly diversified international fund—holding stocks mostly from developed markets, but having some investments in emerging markets as well—may be enough exposure to these wild and woolly investments." McGough excels with his 3-23 piece examining investors' rush to get into hot mutual funds that have announced they will soon close. "A look at the past performance of closed funds shows that many hot funds stumbled after closing, lagging behind the stock market as well as their still-open competitors." Companies close popular funds, he notes, because excessive cash makes them difficult to negotiate in the small-stock arena, so an announcement of closing might mean that a hot fund has already become slightly unmanageable. McGough's ability to make sense of the myriad world of mutual funds, where seemingly dozens of new funds pop up every day, comes as welcome relief to investors attracted by the funds' supposed simplicity. McGough also has a firm grasp of the international scene. In his 12-14 article, he demonstrates how currency tumult produced a strong yen, which in turn "added about 15 percentage points to Japanese-stock funds' returns this year." Not entirely self-reliant, McGough serves his audience by regularly interviewing investment experts, like the Duke Business School professor, 10-5, who boldly advocates putting as much as 60 percent of one's portfolio into risky foreign markets. Considering the explosion in small-investor popularity enjoyed by mutual funds in recent years, the news market cries out for someone who can keep abreast of the wealth of fund information and cornucopia of investment possibilities. By parceling out comprehensive coverage and solid investment counsel, McGough fills the void.

David Moberg
In These Times
★★★

Senior editor. Bringing adroit analysis to his coverage of labor and economic issues, Moberg is a large part of the reason why *In These Times* is threatening to usurp *The Nation*'s role as *the* voice of the American left. Keeping readers abreast of new developments in organized labor proves Moberg's chief strength. In his solid 4-19 article, he examines the divergent stands on health-care reform taken by various labor groups, along with their plans to influence the Clinton package. The United Auto Workers advocate a single-payer system like Canada's, Moberg observes, while the AFL-CIO balks at eliminating private insurance companies. Moberg's "Striking Back Without Striking," 4-5, relates the novel strategies unions are using to force management's hand without resorting to walkouts. Running savvy PR campaigns that put public pressure on management has won concessions, he notes, such as the one conducted by workers at the Staley Manufacturing Company in Decatur, Illinois. Moberg also writes of slowdowns where Staley workers "use their

detailed understanding of how the factory functions to reduce the plant's output by nearly one-third." Reviewing NAFTA's environmental and wage side-agreements, 9-6, Moberg explains that President Clinton can't placate the left because the deals "have no teeth. They barely have gums." While applauding the Family Leave Act, 2-22, the first piece of legislation Clinton signed, Moberg asserts that it doesn't go far enough. "Let's get brutally realistic. By the standards of what other industrialized countries provide...this legislation is chump change." His 3-22 analysis of Clinton's plan to lift the U.S. out of recession will surprise socialists and supply-siders alike. "Whatever their merits, his deficit-reducing measures—tax increases and spending cuts—will create a 'fiscal drag' on the economy later this year." While Moberg sometimes stumbles—his 6-14 piece arguing that a high-speed rail network should be a national imperative gives no reason why we need it—more often than not he delivers. Sharp and provocative, the talented Moberg is one to turn to in these times of changing economic and labor conditions.

Gretchen Morgenson

Forbes
Worth
★★★½

Executive editor. Fidelity Investments hits the jackpot by wooing Morgenson to its fledgling publication late in the year. *Worth*, which will be published 10 times annually, would have a difficult time finding a finer business reporter. The former stockbroker earns her 1993 rating on the strength of her work at *Forbes*, where she pens not one but two of the year's superlative business articles. In her outstanding 8-16 cover story, Morgenson uncovers securities shell games on NASDAQ. She ferociously tears apart the self-promotion and hype floated by proponents of this small-issue, over-the-counter market. Detailing scams by which NASDAQ brokers use the o-t-c technology to fleece investors, Morgenson reveals tricks like "trading ahead of customer orders" for their own accounts, a process barred on most other exchanges. She claims this up-and-coming market, used primarily for trading smaller issues and touted by many as the future's alternative to exchanges, has stacked the deck in favor of traders who enrich themselves at the expense of clients. Exhaustive research and superb reporting paint a damning picture of faceless, computerized trading, and in perhaps her most convincing argument, she states, "Note this: Merrill, Bear Stearns, Morgan Stanley, Charles Schwab, Dean Witter, even Sherwood, are listed stocks. None trades o-t-c. The folks who know the market best seem to prefer the exchanges." Another brilliant cover-story, 5-24, gives a hint of the sweeping technological changes destined to revolutionize American commerce. She predicts that shop-at-home buying—aided by computers, modems, and TV—will transform daily life and overthrow the established commercial order. The entire idea of the store, she notes, is changing, "fast becoming a place where people kick the tires, lift the lid on a washing machine or listen to the sound of a stereo speaker—and then go home and call an (800) number to order the same item at a discount of 40 percent." Describing the big-picture technological possibilities, like credit-card slots and bar scanners in the home, Morgenson identifies the winners (consumers, techno-buffs, Federal Express) and the losers (salespeople, wholesalers, shopping-mall operators). She even posits that President Clinton, too, could be out of luck if the technology wave advances quickly enough,

upending the retail industry and throwing people out of work on his watch. In her debut in the November *Worth,* Morgenson examines the alarming industry ties of the new president of an association of state securities regulators. Here, as throughout the year, she proves that Fidelity made a worthy choice in hiring Morgenson.

Alan Murray
The Wall Street Journal
★½

Washington bureau chief. With his new responsibilities as bureau chief, Murray has less time for writing these days, as he only occasionally contributes a column to Friday's "The Outlook." Time constraints on research and reporting have taken their toll; he provides wishy-washy analysis, and though he raises worthwhile questions, he rarely comes through with concrete answers. A long-time deficit hawk, Murray devotes several columns to scolding the Clinton administration for insufficient spending cuts in its budget, 2-22, noting that "among the least questionable items counted as 'spending cuts' in the plan are $21 billion raised over the next four years by taxing Social Security benefits, $11 billion saved by shifting from long-term to short-term debt, $24 billion in reduced debt-service costs, at least $6 billion in new 'user fees,' and more than $80 billion in spending cuts over four years that were required...under the 1990 budget agreement. Take those away, and the net spending cuts virtually disappear." Yet, after such an effective thrashing, he offers no support for his conclusion—that Clinton's budget "begins to tilt government spending in a direction that will do more to help long-run economic growth." On productivity growth, Murray provides a weak 4-12 assessment that at least offers an interesting comment from Federal Reserve Chairman Alan Greenspan. "'Low rates of inflation,'" Greenspan says, "'tend to be associated with relatively high productivity growth.'" Pondering the benefits and drawbacks of the administration's proposed jobs summit, 7-19, Murray takes a firm stand smack in the middle of the road. In contrast, he clearly has convictions about health-care reform. His 8-30 column asks pointedly: If health-care reform "is the key to conquering the budget deficit...why do we need new taxes to pay for it?" Following up, 10-18, Murray notes that the administration's proposed caps on health-care premiums could prove too stringent in practice. "The President contends the cap will merely squeeze out waste and inefficiency; but the legions of skeptics worry it may cut deep into the fabric of the health care system, causing huge disruptions." A few credible examples and estimates to support his argument would have made this an excellent article. As Murray learns to juggle the responsibilities of his new position, he will hopefully find more time and energy for his columns.

Sylvia Nasar
The New York Times
★½

Economics. With the presidential election over, the egregious distortions that pervaded Nasar's work in 1992 have all but disappeared. She's still prone to an editorial comment here and there, but overall she concentrates more on the facts. Her 2-19 "economic analysis" of President Clinton's proposal to raise the tax rate on corporations from 34 percent to 36 percent explores several fresh angles. "What is more worrisome to economists is that in a global economy populated by huge multinational corporations, raising corporate tax rates could actually reduce the Treasury's take by encouraging companies to report less income here and more in tax-friendlier nations." As for the investment tax credit—meant to offset the negative side of the corporate tax—Nasar notes that it is only temporary and, thus, may have limited impact. Although her 8-16 article, "Despite New Budget, Fed Is Unlikely to Ease," puts to rest disquieting rumors that the Federal Reserve had struck a deal to loosen monetary policy if Clinton's budget deal stalled the recovery, she editorializes in her opening lines. "Despite Americans' fears that higher taxes and spending restraint will crimp economic growth, the committee is not likely to provide the kind of quid pro quo—easier money for tighter fiscal policy—that the Bush administration received in the fall of 1990." Nasar presents no evidence of such a quid pro quo, except to say that the Fed lowered rates after the 1990 budget passed. While she offers nothing especially new in her 9-17 primer on why economists favor NAFTA, her emphasis on the economics rather than the politics of the deal proves refreshing. Nasar uses facts to throw a cold dose of reality on the hyperbole that characterizes the NAFTA debate. "The Mexican economy is roughly the size of the Los Angeles economy, amounting to no more than four percent of the United States's gross domestic product," she notes. "Just as Los Angeles could not absorb a large portion of the new investment in the United States, neither can Mexico." Continuing on a similar theme, 11-12, Nasar eschews generalizations and brings to light specific studies on the price of protecting jobs with trade barriers. One study suggests that "the price of protection amounts to $170,000 a year per job saved." Thoughtfully including observations from those who disagree with such estimates, she notes their wide acceptance among economists. More careful and more balanced this year, Nasar delivers improved reporting.

William Neikirk

Chicago Tribune

★★

Washington, senior writer. Having covered economics since the 1970s, old-timer Neikirk has lived through and reported on many an economic trend and development. As a result, his articles teem with historical data. Despite his years of experience, however, there's an unevenness to his work; he often indulges in rhetorical flourishes, disregarding the facts. The quality of his coverage on the health-care debate, for example, remains inconsistent, as his 3-14 and 9-19 articles reveal. Although deftly surveying the history of insurance coverage since the 1950s, he peppers the first piece with alarmist, undocumented statements. "The health insurance system that the vast majority of Americans rely upon...is in the process of imploding." The second article, on the other hand, provides an even-handed, fact-rich analysis of President Clinton's health-care proposal. Neikirk really does his homework here: He asks tough questions and gives praise where due, while pointing out contradictions, weaknesses, and flaws when he finds them. Neikirk occasionally hits the mark as a reporter, but he's more suited for commentary. As a regular on *The Journal of Commerce*'s editorial page, Neikirk puts in his two-cents on national economic debates. His witty 3-12 critique of "Clinton's Pliant Economic Plan" observes, "Such profound flexibility has not been witnessed...in a long, long time, maybe not since the days of Lyndon B. Johnson, when government policy could be summed up in one word: Negotiation." The opinion contains some meaty tidbits on the BTU tax but ultimately proves more clever than informative. Similarly, Neikirk observes that although Commerce Secretary Ron Brown has moved Herbert Hoover's portrait out of his office, 4-16, the Clinton administration has been unable to shake the former President's mind-set, especially with regard to the jobs bill. "To my mind, it seems too wedded to a blue-collar past with its emphasis on production. It does not seem to provide enough resources, nor enough support, for the only economic safety net left in our economic system anymore, education." Unfortunately, Neikirk fails to support his intriguing thesis with enough data. Back on the pages of the *Chicago Tribune*, 7-14, he urges Clinton to take a more visionary stand on free trade, and offers the President sound advice when he urges him not to allow Ross Perot's "island mentality" to fester, saying it would be a strategic and tactical mistake. This is Neikirk at his best—commenting on national issues with style and vigor.

Peter Norman

Financial Times

★★½

Economics editor. A perceptive financial analyst, as well as a precise, no-nonsense reporter, Norman covers the European and global economy. He appears on both *FT*'s news and opinion pages. Exploring the mammoth economic power of the nine largest foreign exchange markets and global pension funds, 5-4, Norman points out that their daily net turnover is "much higher than the total non-gold reserves of all the industrial countries." While noting the benefits of these markets, Norman recognizes the challenges created for governments whose monetary authorities must deal with this emerging power. Turning to the Tokyo G-7 meeting, Norman provides a thorough, yet compact, 7-8 assessment of the "Quad agreement," which he describes as "a potentially far-reaching tariff-cutting deal which could unblock the long stalled Uruguay Round of trade liberalization talks." His 9-6 piece provides an enlightening overview of the new thinking in the wake of the near collapse of the European Rate Mechanism. "The...realization that freely flowing capital movements could undermine any attempt to rebuild the old structure have prompted a growing interest in those countries that manage their domestic monetary affairs through inflation targets." Unfortunately, Norman uses the terms "price stability" and "inflation targets" interchangeably, ignoring the fact that price stability also implies avoidance of deflation. Examining the evolving relationship between the U.K. Treasury and the Bank of England following a half-percentage point cut in the bank base rates, 11-24, Norman writes insightfully, "An important consideration for [Chancellor of the Exchequer Kenneth] Clarke and the Bank was to divorce the rate cut from day-to-day politics." With such political and economic insights, Norman's precise, thorough articles are always worth reading.

Floyd Norris

The New York Times

★★½

"Market Watch" columnist. Readers of the Sunday *Times* have come to enjoy Norris's whimsical ponderings from his perch on the front page of the financial section. He ruminates on both Wall Street and the economy at large, shattering in the process the conceit of members of the former that they necessarily control the latter. A healthy dose of skepticism, requisite of any good Wall Street-watcher, 9-26, leads him to furnish one of the best assessments of the craziness spawned by QVC's and Viacom's competing courtship of Paramount. "Whatever happens, Paramount shareholders will wind up with stock in a company with cable operations, just when Wall Street thinks that is a good idea. Too bad for them." Naturally, Norris casts a ray of this skepticism toward Washington, though not as severely as the many writers who savaged President Clinton's economic blueprint. Nonetheless, Norris has doubts. In a savvy 3-14 column, he questions the capital's strange view of "the bond market as a barometer of the nation's health," noting that "the lowest interest rates in this century came during the Great Depression." The paucity of space afforded Norris each Sunday places grave limitations on the product he delivers, and his confines—about 500 words—sometimes restrict him to quick generalizations, such as his 8-1 remark on the European currency crisis. "Having had the pound forced out [of the Exchange Rate Mechanism] last fall—at a huge cost to the Bank of England and similar profits to currency traders—many in Britain would love to see a similar fate befall the haughty French." On other occasions, Norris uses the space wisely. In his 6-6 examination of Citibank's gift of sports tickets to big depositors, he deems the perk "the 1990s equivalent of free toasters for aging yuppies." The move indicates to Norris that Citibank "wants more deposits and will spend money—U.S. Open tickets are not free—to get them....It is a straw in the wind that does not point to lower short-term interest rates." The brevity of his column forces Norris to spell out his argument quickly and articulately, a challenge he meets more often than not.

Peter Nulty

Fortune

Board of editors. Only occasionally descending from the Board to author dispatches on the economy, Nulty may have left behind his days as a full-time soldier of *Fortune*. He files stories less than once a month, which means subscribers need seldom encounter his shallow coverage and superficial analysis. Writing about *Fortune*'s newest inductees to the National Business Hall of Fame, 4-5, Nulty's praise for one honoree—auto executive Lee Iacocca—seems to miss the mark. Iacocca's business acumen and stories of his meteoric rise at Ford are the stuff of legend. Yet Nulty hypes the government bail-out of Chrysler as Iacocca's crowning achievement. "Can any salesman," the opening sentence begins, "confront a greater challenge than trying to sell damaged goods to a hostile customer?" Nulty's other pieces, mostly generic profiles of publicly traded companies, lack sufficient depth. His 7-26 look at the new Westing--house chief skims the surface and barely addresses the nuts and bolts. Tackling Sensomatic Electronics Corp., the company that dominates the market for anti-theft devices, 5-3, Nulty writes of a surprising CEO who "fights hard—but not too hard. Keeping competitors alive, he believes, helps his own team stay on its toes." Nulty, however, fails to examine this fascinating point in much detail. Similar lack of detail mars his lengthy 2-8 piece on organized labor's attempts to combat declining numbers. "Labor's realists are well aware that having a Democrat in the White House won't rid them of their two biggest problems—foreign competition and their own rotten public image." Combating these problems has led to schisms within unions, a point Nulty notes with inadequate elaboration. He hits the mark, though, with a solid 11-1 story showing how technological innovations make upgrading computer systems extremely risky for many companies. "Comes a day when upgrading reaches a limit....Then your system has hit a wall. It's time to start all over." The exorbitant cost of revamping a system, Nulty points out, raises the stakes for companies that play computer-roulette. "Indeed, the survival of some companies may depend on how well they handle this transition." One fine piece, however, cannot redeem the inadequacies of Nulty's other work.

Bridget O'Brian

The Wall Street Journal

★½

Airlines. The Houston-based O'Brian plays tour-guide for Dow Jones, directing readers and investors through the turbulent skies of the cutthroat passenger-airline industry. While she dexterously handles the bread-and-butter stories—who's been fired, who's been hired—she fails to display a broader vision of the industry's direction. And when she tries venturing into uncharted territory, the results prove disappointing. She misses her flight with a 7-12 front-page story examining a predatory-pricing suit leveled against American Airlines by weak sisters Continental and Northwest. Quickly expanding the scope of the article, O'Brian examines the nature of predatory-pricing complaints and considers them in the context of other industries. She then comments on evolving legal interpretations of the charge. "The courts have become less inclined to protect competitors and more concerned about the immediate interests of consumers"—an unexplained statement, which makes it difficult to see why the court would entertain this suit, since "immediately" slashed consumer prices are the point of contention. In stories where she sticks to discrete issues without trying to branch out, O'Brian fares better. She smartly explains in her 6-25 feature why Delta Airlines, which shelled out millions to buy Pan Am's transatlantic routes, faces stormy weather. "Business travel to Europe has stayed weak, especially in and out of Frankfurt, Delta's biggest European hub. And Frankfurt's costs are high. Preparing a plane there for a flight costs more than $7,000, far higher than the $1,650 in London." While O'Brian's pieces do not reflect much overall sense of broader industry themes, she applies precisely that kind of analysis to the banking industry. In one of her very few stories unrelated to the airlines, 12-16, she describes the changing nature of banking as banks tighten their own purse strings. "To attract customers to the remaining branches and boost profitability, banks are following the lead of retail stores and supermarkets—they're redesigning their outlets." But her mind doesn't stray far from the skies, since she explains, "Some industry observers...suggest that banks may shift toward a hub-and-spoke system, something akin to the airline industry." When it comes to her own field, however, O'Brian needs to get her head out of the clouds and show she can deliver the same kind of probing coverage.

Scot J. Paltrow

Los Angeles Times

★★★½

Wall Street. With meticulous reporting and fine-grained analysis, Paltrow has emerged to anchor business coverage at the West Coast's leading daily. He manages to teach readers—and the Gotham City financial press—a thing or two in almost every article. His 9-22 story on the return of merger-mania—highlighted by the quest for Paramount Communications, entertainment's Holy Grail—explores why a return to 1980s-style takeovers doesn't loom imminent. He reports executives on the Street as thinking "there is little likelihood of a fresh wave of hostile raids of the type in which companies that were minding there own business...suddenly found themselves 'in play.'" Paltrow's acumen becomes especially evident, however, in his 1-31 article on the resignation of American Express head James Robinson. Focusing on the "dramatic display of the growing power of disgruntled shareholders," Paltrow identifies the subtle ripples of a trend unnoticed by many rivals. "The decision to step down was an apparent response to Wall Street's clear negative reaction after American Express' board voted Monday to let Robinson stay on as chairman." By playing up the broader implications of the move—the democratization of the decision-making process, as registered on the Big Board rather than in the chummy confines of the boardroom—Paltrow amazes by offering shrewd analysis of the story almost as it occurs. The jewel in Paltrow's crown, though, comes courtesy of the opprobrium resulting from Prudential-Bache Securities' limited-partnership scandal, which bilked thousands of investors in the 1980s. Busy covering the aftermath of the company's settlement of a class-action suit, he still finds time to write the definitive narrative of the scandal, a mammoth two-part feature, 6-22 and 6-23. Recounting how brokers pushed these high-risk partnerships, Paltrow writes, "Just what were investors buying, though? Far from 'a piece of the rock,' the [partnership funds] were run by a tiny Louisiana company...[that] earlier had failed in oil and gas exploration efforts"—precisely the work the company was doing for Prudential. A new star in Hollywood, look for the name Paltrow not on marquees but on stories rich in news and analysis.

Peter Passell

The New York Times

★★

"Economics Scene" columnist. Back on track after a disappointing 1992, Passell takes readers slightly beyond standard economics, gathering a variety of opinions and data on the issues of the day. His unflattering analysis of the nation's bankruptcy laws, 4-12, presents some fresh options for reshaping Chapter 11, including a proposal to allow senior creditors to exchange their IOUs for stock. In one of his best efforts, 4-22, Passell examines the U.S. bullying of Japan, pointing out through a variety of sources the pitfalls of the Bush and Clinton administrations' heavy-handed trade policies. Casting a skeptical eye on the appreciation-of-the-yen solution, he credibly challenges the conventional thinking on the Japan-U.S. relationship. Passell offers sound economic advice to West Bank Palestinians, 9-23, warning against isolationism and protectionism, which, he says, will only lead to wasted resources. "There is already talk...of spending hundreds of millions of dollars improving the port in Gaza, in spite of the existence of a deepwater port a few miles up the coast in Israel." Following the signing of GATT, Passell offers a solid 12-15 primer on trade. For readers who have followed the wrangling over this agreement, Passell's report may seem facile, but for those unfamiliar with the pact it provides a useful guide. Constructing an illuminating defense of the IMF's decision to compare nations' incomes according to purchasing power rather than the exchange value of their currencies, 5-27, Passell clarifies the advantages of this complex shift. When he applies fresh thinking to a familiar subject, Passell's at his best.

Jonathan Peterson

Los Angeles Times

★★

Los Angeles. Offering lively, sometimes dynamic, dispatches from Southern California, a battleground where the recession still smolders, Peterson provides compelling work on varied subjects. In his 2-15 story, he compares the Clinton economic plan of a stimulus package married with tax increases to "two seemingly contrary if coexisting parts, almost like Siamese twins that don't like each other." Unfortunately, he smothers his local pieces with too much anecdotal reporting, such as his 2-22 article on the effects of President Clinton's tax package on San Bernadino residents, and his 12-21 story on defense downsizing in El Sugundo. Both these stories would benefit from greater attention to the larger picture, for Peterson's work improves when he adopts a national scope. His excellent 8-18 front-page feature examines the implications of the federal debt, noting its role as "a national punching bag," though few grasp its dangers. "By virtually all accounts it is a financial albatross and threatens increasing turmoil in the coming years. But agreement ends there. How much debt would trigger a panic is unknown." In a similarly strong 9-4 article, Peterson examines the media's propensity to rely on questionable statistics in taking the economy's pulse. "Virtually every week, the media turn a new statistic into a prominent news story. When the revision comes later, even whopping changes may get little notice." He cites several examples, such as the 1992 campaign. "Bush was widely accused...of overselling the national recovery, a charge buttressed by some of the data available at the time. But [recent] findings suggest the economy was picking up steam...and racing forward by autumn [of 1992]—more in line with Bush's claims." But deficiencies riddle some of his pieces. An otherwise compelling 7-30 profile of Council of Economic Advisers chief Laura Tyson omits mention of her study at MIT, the repository of liberal economic orthodoxy and chief rival of the Chicago school. And in his 2-24 effort explaining the administration's techno-policy, Peterson contends that the Clintonites are building on the legacy of GOP predecessors. "Aides to [Presidents Reagan and Bush]...came around to the Democrats' idea that more government investment in commercial technology was appropriate." This statement begs for elaboration: Which aides wanted to invest in what technology? But Peterson displays enough of a forceful style and inquisitive manner to suggest that a promising future awaits both him and *LAT* readers.

William Power

The Wall Street Journal

★★½

"Heard on the Street" columnist. Power's frequent contributions to "Heard on the Street," the daily feature of financial scuttlebutt, have helped solidify its position as a must-read. Rather than limiting himself to just the parochial personnel questions of which hotshot landed at what firm, Power tackles substantive matters concerning the health of the markets. And instead of turning in articles that are the picture of sobriety, he infuses his pieces with an almost impish charm. In his 5-10 effort, he examines what has come to be any up-and-coming company's kiss of death—being touted as "the next Microsoft." Acquiring this moniker will usually boost stock prices before sanity sets in. "The latest stock to ride the Microsoft magic carpet," Power muses, "is 3DO Co., a multimedia start-up company that has everything an investor would want—except revenue, profit or even a product to sell." Part of Power's job entails telling readers which way the winds blow on Wall Street, which he does by profiling the players and their stock picks. In his 12-17 piece, he draws a pithy picture of one perennial pessimist, Floridian Douglas A. Kass—"the Bear of Boca"—who is so confident of impending doom that he suggests bailing out of stocks in bullish brokerage firms. Kass's company "recommends selling (in alphabetical order) Alex. Brown, Bear Stearns, A.G. Edwards, Inter-Regional Financial...and on and on—basically the U.S. brokerage industry." When plummeting stock prices force an unusually rare withdrawal of an initial public offering for the restaurant chain bearing the name of an NBA legend, 2-17, Power shoots the perfect lead sentence: "Wilt Chamberlain took his ball and went home yesterday." His humor augments his articles, seldom precluding him from dispensing keen observations. In his 8-24 article, Power lends an ear to Wall Street's pariahs—short sellers—who've been flattened by the prolonged running of the bulls. "The shorts' argument is that stock prices are being yanked upward artificially by the trading tactics of mutual funds and other big investors." While Power doesn't think there was a second gunman, he concurs with these outcasts on the question of whether mutual funds can sustain the stock-market drive. With the media buzzing about the importance of the UAW-Big Three contract talks, 9-9, Power cautions investors against overlooking the important negotiations further north between Chrysler and the Canadian Auto Workers. "A Canadian walkout this year would be particularly bad news for Chrysler," he notes, "because some of its most profitable products are built there." While this Power is hardly the "ultimate aphrodisiac," readers can count on this Street-smart journalist for vital information.

Michael Prowse

Financial Times

★★½

"On America" columnist. The deliciously provocative Prowse offers the British daily an intellectual, almost effete, look at life in "the colonies." He brings an outsider's haughtiness to his commentary, which can both madden and enlighten. A sometimes-devotee of classical liberal economics, Prowse occasionally marginalizes himself by touting prescriptions for the nation's economic ills offered by the libertarian Cato Institute. His 6-1 and 8-23 columns read like paid advertisements for books published by Cato. In his 1-8 feature on worldwide political trends, he declares, "Do not be surprised if ideas that seemed to die with the passing of the Reagan/Thatcher era reappear in new—and more outrageous—guises within a few years. We have not, by any means, heard the last from libertarians seeking to 'empower' individuals by abolishing higher rates of tax, rolling back the welfare state and purging the economy of wasteful subsidies." Yet in his 2-22 and 4-13 columns, Prowse spurns the label of predictability, blasting President Clinton for taking a "timid" approach to taxes. In the earlier piece, he proudly recounts how his writings savaged England's 1987 tax cut. Prowse is indeed difficult to figure out. He comes across as a leader of the egghead brigade with his dense 12-20 dissection of neoclassical economic philosophy. The sketch accompanying his column, in which he looks like a chess grand master, does little to dispel the brainy reputation his writings impute. Nonetheless, he brings to his work a playful charm. Only a Brit could author a column about National Economic Council Chairman Robert Rubin entitled "President Clinton's Economic Jeeves." In this 7-12 piece, Prowse writes that in an interview, "I could not get him to express a really strong opinion about anything, even off the record. When asked for his personal views, he tended to reply by deftly outlining the president's policies on the topic in question." Sporadically deigning to author a news story from Washington, Prowse engages with his observations. Analyzing the White House's health-care task force, 5-13, he writes that, though still wedded to the idea, "it is chary of the language of managed competition, which was invented by right-of-center economists." While one shouldn't regard Prowse as the definitive observer of the American scene, the wry musings and keen insights of this somewhat-detached journalist make for compelling reading.

Jane Bryant Quinn

Newsweek

Personal investing columnist. Making her living as a spokeswoman for Common Sense, Inc., Quinn dishes out advice on how to handle one's nest egg and alerts readers to the basic rules of smart investing. Although she discusses trends and big stories, particulars are not her bag, and she seldom explores the financial markets in much detail. In her overly general 1-11 piece on strategies for the upcoming year, she writes, "As usual, the prudent investor should sample a little of everything. That way, you're sure to have a piece of whatever investments decide to go up." Not exactly inside information, but the kind of wisdom would-be investors should bear in mind. Quinn displays the disdain for Wall Street prognosticators fashionable among investment journalists, as she quips in her 10-18 column, "The chief function of stock-market forecasters is to make astrologers look respectable." Warning of brokerage snake-oil salesmen, she suggests that anyone with a little nerve, smarts, and a grasp of the fundamentals can formulate a solid investment plan. The trick, Quinn claims, is to recognize the obvious and act accordingly. In her 3-8 column, she instructs readers to refinance while interest rates are low. "Don't let this startling rate slide pass without restructuring your debt. Any loan can be rethought....Borrowers should seize the moment. If another moment comes next year, seize it again." And if another basic piece of advice enters Quinn's mind, she will surely relate it. Stocks or bonds? Buy or rent? The answers usually boil down to common sense, and Quinn notes the tips to take and traps to avoid. Highlighting the pitfalls in time shares, 7-12, she tells how a dream vacation spot can become a nightmare, because "a time share-resort is easy to join but tough to leave." Hence, don't rush in. As one of the nation's most popular financial advisors, Quinn offers logical and straightforward, if unchallenging, counsel.

James Risen

Los Angeles Times

Economics. Seasoned and confident after more than three years in D.C., Risen provides articles brimming with analysis. Yet, he's more comfortable assessing the politics of key economic debates than scrutinizing the economic arguments that shape them, as his 5-5 report on President Clinton's budget package reveals. Risen devotes plenty of space to the political impracticalities of pushing through tax levies and an expensive health-care program simultaneously, but provides nothing on the economic implications of either proposal. Verging on commentary, 8-9, his analysis of Clinton's budget takes everyone to task for resisting more spending cuts and tax increases. Yet, the inspiration for this scolding—that deficit reduction quick and deep helps the economy—remains hotly debated. A strong dose of skepticism guides his 9-12 and 10-10 assessments of the administration's health-care proposal. In a highly specific critique that lends credibility to his general statements, the latter piece questions the President's financing scheme. "As [Senator Daniel Patrick] Moynihan [D-NY] and other critics have noted, any fool can run numbers that will add up through a Lotus spreadsheet, but that doesn't make them valid or realistic public policy options." Zeroing in on the administration's victory in the House, which approved Clinton's $37 billion in spending reductions over a more austere $90 billion proposal, Risen offers an even-handed 11-23 overview with perspectives from both sides of the aisle. Once again, however, he leaves readers in the dark about the economic implications. Although Risen's talents keep improving, a greater focus on economics in the coming year will determine if he has risen to the peak of his abilities.

Mark Robichaux
The Wall Street Journal
★★★

Cable industry. A forceful and articulate writer, the perspicacious Robichaux brings a fresh outlook to a high-flying segment of the entertainment business that saw its wings clipped in 1993. He jumps headfirst into the controversy surrounding the surprising rise in cable rates after the government's regulation of prices went into effect in September. In his impressive 9-28 piece on the jump in rates Robichaux traces a path of industry legerdemain and dissembling. "Many cable companies worked to undercut the law," he explains, but part of the blame rests on the vagueness of the legislation. "Because the new law mainly regulates basic cable rates, systems can sidestep the impact by removing channels from the basic package to set up new, unregulated packages." Robichaux, thankfully, covers far more than just the regulation issue. In his 3-26 effort, he proclaims that American cable companies, having extended their tentacles across the country, "are seeking their manifest destinies across the seas." By invading Europe, he reports, cable firms are bringing ice hockey to Israel and country music videos to London. Robichaux hits the hustings to gather stories, reporting, from an industry trade show in San Francisco, 6-7, where talk of the electronic superhighway "and the someday era of 500 channels spills from the lips of all." Small niche networks already have formed to fill that space, "wait[ing] like jets in line to take off at the airport." In other trade news, 8-31, Robichaux reports plans for former Republican political operative Roger Ailes to take over as president of cable channel CNBC. While he notes that Ailes served as adviser to three GOP presidents, Robichaux fails to mention which three. But he makes up for this oversight by gathering a sharp Ailesian quote. "'I don't whine about working 70 hours a week,'" he tells Robichaux. "'It's what I like to do. I'm not new-aging myself to death looking at my navel.'" Neither, indeed, is Robichaux, whose coverage of the cable industry touches all the bases.

Hobart Rowen
The Washington Post
★½

Economics columnist. As the first journalist to receive a professional achievement award from the Society of American Business Editors and Writers, Rowen remains a respected voice in policy-making circles. Despite his 53 years as a financial journalist, however, he proves more surefooted discussing politics than economics. In top form, 1-14, Rowen exposes the spurned Paul Krugman's tirade against Robert Reich, Jeff Faux, and Amitai Etzioni, after the administration failed to select him for the Council of Economic Advisers. "Krugman added that [President] Clinton is making an 'effort to disenfranchise professional economists' in favor of 'pop internationalists' like Reich, Faux and Etzioni." But Rowan later plays the apologist for Clinton, 5-23, accusing a "hostile White House press corps" of unfairly labeling the President a failure. Here, Rowen wanders all over the place, opening with how the U.S. can't afford another failed presidency and closing by encouraging pressure on the Federal Reserve to handle damage control after tax increases. Savvy on the politics of NAFTA, 8-8, Rowen surprises by handing the President sound economic advice, and for once, he places both politics and economics in context. The pro-NAFTA forces "must convey to the public the essential facts....NAFTA will reduce the incentive of some manufacturers to move to Mexico because tariffs eventually will be cut to zero." When Rowen does immerse himself in economic analysis, he sometimes stumbles on conventional myths. "The bond market's judgment that the price of bonds will continue to go up is in reality a highly pessimistic assessment." he notes, 10-24. "It also may mean that the bond market anticipates a major deflation, tantamount to depression." How, then, does Rowen explain the surging stock market? He doesn't. Such questions Rowen often leaves unanswered in his work.

Howard Rudnitsky

Forbes

★½

Senior editor. Equipped with plenty of numbers and cold, hard facts, the no-nonsense Rudnitsky lays out his case with precision—and a little too much tedium. While the profits-to-earnings ratios, square-feet tabulations, dividend yields, and soft-drink-consumption calculations inform, they beg for more analysis. Explaining why international possibilities make him bullish on Coca-Cola and Pepsi, 5-24, Rudnitsky writes, "Overseas, unit volume is growing about 6 percent a year, versus 3 percent in the U.S. Coca-Cola already gets 67 percent of sales and 82 percent of its profits outside the U.S. Pepsi earns about a quarter of its profits abroad." Although the figures are relevant to his argument, the presentation needs refining—especially in clarifying why private-label soft drinks pose little threat to giants Coke and Pepsi. In his 8-30 report, Rudnitsky adroitly relates how pharmaceutical-giant Merck takes a blind leap into the future by acquiring Medco, a marketing and distribution firm. Though dubious of how safely Merck will land, he admires the company for not waiting to be pushed off the cliff like executives at IBM and American Express. On the rare occasion when Rudnitsky offers analysis, as in his 2-1 piece on Wall Street's odd enthusiasm for stocks of upscale chain restaurants, he illuminates and amuses. "These [outrageously high stock] prices make no sense, but then these are concept stocks. You aren't buying earnings or assets. Concepts are moonbeams. And who is to say what a moonbeam is worth?" In a 10-25 profile of David Wachs, CEO of Charming Shoppes, Inc., the company which owns Fashion Bug women's clothing stores, Rudnitsky reports the shrewd game plan of one company's attempt to expand in an apparel recession. "Not for Wachs the trendy woman with a fat pocketbook. She has too many suitors and she's hard to please. Wachs serves working women with family incomes of $30,000 to $35,000 whose husbands are most likely blue-collar workers. They may not be rich, but there are lots of them." Although such nuggets can be found in Rudnitsky's pieces, he too often hides them behind a wall of statistics and studies. One problem may be that Rudnitsky covers no particular beat. Perhaps when he finds a niche—and can stop relying so heavily on sheer numbers—Rudnitsky will expand his analytical abilities.

Kevin G. Salwen

The Wall Street Journal

★★½

Labor, "Labor Letter" columnist. A commendable financial reporter in past years, Salwen switches course in 1993 to follow the unions and pens reliable assessments on organized labor. Attending the annual AFL-CIO convention, he offers a pessimistic 10-5 report that painfully depicts the tired stewardship of America's powerhouse unions as the executive council ensures Lane Kirkland's reelection as president. "Then, the 35 mostly white, mostly male, largely over-60 members...will continue the same status-quo leadership that has presided over dwindling memberships in most of the 86 member unions." Rather than criticize Big Labor, though, most of Salwen's pieces reveal union maneuvering now that *sympatheticos* presumably inhabit the White House. As the unions thrust themselves into national policy debates with the expectation of a hearing from a friendly administration, Salwen furnishes coverage that often bests the trite stories filed by other reporters. By chronicling the unions' viewpoints rather than recycling worn assumptions, he digs up some surprises. He explains, 9-8, why many unions endorse Vice President Al Gore's "reinventing government" proposal even though it threatens to eliminate municipal union jobs. In his 9-22 story, he writes how "labor unions are salivating" over an employer-mandated health-care plan because it "will remove from the bargaining table the most contentious labor issue of the past decade." But Salwen casts a wary eye. "Obviously, it wouldn't be that simple. For one thing, many unionized companies already provide benefits more generous than the Clinton plan." In an effusive 5-5 profile of the new Labor Secretary, a glassy-eyed Salwen proclaims, "Bob Reich, thinker, has come to Washington," while in a 4-22 testimonial for a private job-training program—held out as an example for the Clinton administration—he omits information about recent *government*-sponsored training programs. Nevertheless, Salwen switches to his new beat with a fair degree of success, furnishing revealing glimpses into the revitalized labor movement of the 1990s.

Bill Saporito

Fortune

★★

Board of editors. In see-saw fashion, Saporito's work has its ups and downs this year. He remains a talented trend-spotter and well-connected business writer, but all too often he wears kid gloves when handling his subjects. His reporting excels when he worries less about access and more about the real story. For example, although he taps into his network to get behind-the-scenes details on the ousting of American Express CEO James D. Robinson, 1-11, he relegates discussion of the financial and managerial challenges ahead to the last paragraphs. Having followed Wal-Mart for several years, Saporito holds a key to all the executive offices, including that of CEO David D. Glass. His rosy 2-8 essay lauds the Wal-Mart chief—"self-deprecating...unprepossessing...absolutely at ease...his leadership unquestioned"—but offers no analysis of the company's inner workings. Far more effective when not so impressed, Saporito takes a hard 7-26 look at Kmart, which now plays second fiddle to Wal-Mart. Even though top-dog Joe Antonini refuses to talk to him, Saporito provides a much more illuminating report, as he turns a critical eye on his subject. "Retailing...is evolving into an asset battle, with big players bulldozing money by the ton to build and defend positions. Kmart cannot triumph on this ground with its current rate of return." In one of his trademark trend pieces, 9-20, Saporito ponders why men's suit sales are plunging as fast as IBM stock. He walks the reader through all the hows and whys, revealing the industry's coping mechanisms such as stocking more casual wear. When Saporito goes for the real story, he gets it; unfortunately, he does that less often these days.

Laura Saunders

Forbes

★★½

"Taxing Matters" columnist. With the zeal of a wartime correspondent, Saunders follows the volleys and shots in the ongoing battle between taxpayers and the IRS. Plainly siding with the taxpayer, she supplies hints to help trim one's annual tax bill and keeps the individual investor apprised of changes in the codes. "Beware of penalties," she warns ominously in her droll but deadly serious 4-12 investigation of the government's auditing practices. "As the Congress has stiffed the IRS for funds to audit taxpayers over the last two decades, it has handed the taxman an astonishing arsenal of penalties to punish scofflaws it does catch. In other words: We may not catch you, but if we do, we'll make you suffer." Most of Saunders's suggestions consist of commonsense stuff, but, then again, this quality may be in short supply among those cheating on their taxes. Especially funny are the real-life excuses she presents that people have given the feds, like the man who claimed his girlfriend burned his tax records in a bonfire when she caught him two-timing her, and of the traveling salesman whose cat tore apart his records while he was on a trip. Not merely a tax advisor, Saunders also keeps tabs on the machinations of lobbyists shaping the Clinton tax plan. She castigates the real-estate interests, 7-5, for strong-arming numerous special breaks from Congress. "Besides all the real-estate goodies in the tax bill, look at what *isn't* in there. The biggest no-show is any provision to tighten mortgage interest deductions, even for second homes or second mortgages....How to pay for this munificence in a time of budget austerity? The real-estate lobby gallantly offered to fund the changes by agreeing to a tax increase—on all of business." Still, Saunders's real value stems from the pecuniary pointers she proffers. Her 3-1 article highlights a recent IRS ruling—after the

"A question about the budget, Mr. President, and, as a followup, may I have a hug?"

courts forced the assessor's hand—which permits families to duck some high estate taxes and gift levies when passing along the family business. Playing accountant-in-residence at *Forbes*, Saunders provides helpful tax hints for all who tremble as April's Ides approach.

Michael Schrage

Los Angeles Times

★★★

"Innovation" columnist. Few observers of the fast and furious communications battles enjoy their jobs as much as Schrage. A research assistant at MIT, he focuses his deadly wit on major technological issues, dispensing badinage that often yields to sinfully amusing rebukes. Schrage, who appears every Thursday, never lets pass an opportunity to show where he stands. On the latest silicon-inspired fad to bolster the public schools, 5-6, he writes, "America's software entrepreneurs and investment bankers can scarcely wipe the drool off their double chins....Taxpayers and parents beware. Rather than improving schools, the computers-in-education technocrats are likelier to become the welfare queens of the Information Age." Cynicism, seldom in short supply—coupled with techno-jargon newspeak—overruns Schrage's 3-18 review of the entertainment industry's plans for the multimedia revolution. "Silicon Valley's digerati and Hollywood's more analog moguls now woo each other with the sort of passion you see only when the pheromones of Really Big Money are wafting in the breeze." In his 5-20 column, Schrage mocks the new-age frenzy over cable-phone mergers, lampooning "CEO Math. If you or I claim that 2 plus 2 equals 5, then we are destined for a tough time in life. When *Fortune* 500 CEOs assert that 2 plus 2 equals 5, however, it's called 'synergy' and they're hailed as visionaries." Schrage goes far beyond just lobbing withering attacks at business follies. "The contest between Paramount's prospective paramours," he notes, 10-7, "is important precisely because it reveals much about what drives the business of America's pop culture media: the personalities at the top....Today's awkward multimedia à trois of [QVC's Barry] Diller, [Viacom's Sumner] Redstone, and Paramount's Martin Davis affirms that, when you're a mogul, what you feel can matter far more than what you think." He claims that much of tomorrow's technology is being dictated by today's corporate egos. "The idea that these bids are irresistibly driven by tectonic shifts in the media landscape is simply false. These bids are driven by what the moguls claim will be tectonic shifts in media." On the firing of IBM's CEO, 1-28, he writes that "[John] Akers can fairly be faulted for not swiftly grasping the poisonous nettle." Whether doling out these piquant observations or hurling ribald sallies, Schrage has emerged as a thoughtful, clever, and extremely entertaining journalist.

Michael R. Sesit

The Wall Street Journal

★½

Markets. Sesit splits his time between monitoring international equities and compiling the daily Markets report. In the latter task he gives himself over to drab regurgitation of the previous day's activity, interspersing generalizations to explain its developments. They begin much like this very typical 7-27 example, co-authored by Anita Raghavan: "The Dow Jones In-

dustrial Average barreled to a new high as hopes of a German interest-rate cut sent investors on a shopping spree. Bond prices also rose, lending support to the stock rally, and the dollar ended mixed." The dollar, it seems, invariably ends "mixed." Apparently, the rigid parameters imposed on this daily feature, which reads more like a chart than a news story, preclude its authors from saying anything interesting. Sesit showcases his talents more effectively when he turns to the foreign stock markets, such as his analytical 5-19 piece, co-authored by Robert Steiner, suggesting that Hong Kong's stock exchange may be overheating. Since 60 percent of mainland China's exports go through the colony, the duo thinks that prospects for betting on China "may be waning, at least temporarily. First-quarter urban inflation in China stood at 16 percent. On the black market, China's currency, the renminbi, has fallen more than 25 percent against the dollar in the past year and is getting weaker." Moving west, 8-10, Sesit reports that many experts think the summer's changes in Europe's semi-fixed currency system "will lead to lower interest rates, faster economic growth and higher stock prices in Europe." A seeming inconsistency appears in two autumn stories. Discussing developing-market-mania, 9-24, Sesit states, "Given the listlessness of most Western economies these days, it's little wonder that emerging markets are becoming the darling of many investors." Little wonder indeed, except that one month later, in his 10-26 story, "Will European Stocks Stay Hot?" he marvels that with interest rates down, many European exchanges are up one quarter to one third on the year. Sesit's confusing take on the European scene detracts from his otherwise reliable reporting on international markets.

Michael Siconolfi

The Wall Street Journal

★★½

Wall Street. Who's up? Who's down? Who got the top job? Who got axed? The hirings and firings of Wall Street glitterati draw much of Siconolfi's attention. With considerable charm, he chronicles the personnel maneuverings among the big boys and girls of the Big Board. Commenting on how the marriage of Smith Barney to Shearson made two administrators' jobs superfluous, 3-19, Siconolfi writes, "The music has stopped in the Smith Barney-Shearson merger, and two senior brokerage executives are left with no chairs." Like several Dow Joneses, Siconolfi's best work comes when paired with other *Journal* scribes. In several July pieces, he and co-author Randall Smith track the travails at CS First Boston, and in September, the pair explores the quest for Paramount, adroitly detailing the furious scrambling by those trying to get a piece of the deal. "The bidding war," they note, 9-22, "...will deliver lucrative fees to those investment bankers who manage to play a part in whatever transaction ultimately takes place." Siconolfi also helps to expose the seamy relationship between politicians and underwriters fishing for municipal-bond work. With co-author Laurie P. Cohen, 5-5, 5-11, and 5-21, he uncovers dirt in the New Jersey Turnpike bond scandal, which soiled the image of Gov. Jim Florio [D-NJ]. The pair shows, for example, how a Lazard Frères partner ingratiated himself with the Governor's chief-of-staff in order to win bond business. In a 6-2 article, Siconolfi and co-author Constance Mitchell astutely examine the broader trends of "Muni Munificence." The two show how investment bankers donate to state and local pols, "hoping to be rewarded later with lucrative contracts to manage municipal bond offerings. By now, politicians have come to depend on the firm's money. They expect it. And they aren't shy about asking for it." Siconolfi also offers several top-notch solo reports, such as his superb 7-7 front page story on Merrill Lynch's attempts at a financial services empire and his 12-28 look at Prudential's settlement of a federal investigation. Whether starring or co-starring, Siconolfi has become a leading name on the *WSJ* marquee.

Allan Sloan

New York Newsday

Los Angeles Times Syndicate

★★½

"Deals" columnist. Readers who pick up the Sunday *Newsday* will tell you that Sloan is a funny guy. Sprinkling, if not plastering, every column with witticisms and jests, he comes off as the class clown. Comparing the President with his Vice President, 4-25, the wry columnist observes, "When it comes to tax returns, Al Gore is more interesting than Bill Clinton—possibly the only area of human endeavor in which this is true." How so? "For starters, eco-freak Gore gets a $20,000-a-year royalty from zinc-mining operations on his 88-acre farm in Tennessee." But guffaws pale in importance to what Sloan considers his serious vocation—keeping a sharp eye trained on developments in the business world, such as the turmoil at American Express and the purchase of Medco by pharmaceutical-giant Merck. Sloan wisely knows he doesn't have all the answers, and some of his better works conclude with questions, a skill he displays in his 11-7 roadmap of the information highway. Where others envision great things in the mini-merger-mania of 1993, Sloan warns that the year's celebrated info-marriages might really be moguls abandoning ship. "Would you rather sell alongside [Telecommunications Inc.'s John] Malone...and [Berkshire Hathaway's Warren] Buffet," he posits, "or buy along with the telephone companies and other arrivistes?" Seething bile at the prospect of Michael Milken's character resurrection, 12-12, Sloan notes that a judge presiding at the trial of an associate of the former junk-bond king found witness Milken, who testified, "much less credible than Ivan Boesky. That's an especially damning statement, because Boesky is to lying what Picasso is to painting." Unfortunately, Sloan often comes across as too flip and some of his metaphors seem strained. Of TCI's Malone joining the Bell Atlantic board, 10-17, Sloan writes, "Malone is used to roaring down the information super-highway in a Dodge Viper going 160 miles an hour, outrunning everything bigger than he is, and running over lots of competitors who are smaller. But at Bell Atlantic, Malone will find himself in the back seat of a four-cylinder Dodge Caravan trying to get up to 55." A flashy driver himself, Sloan provides nice views but should pay a little more attention to the road.

Randall Smith

The Wall Street Journal

★★★

Mergers & acquisitions. A distinguished reporter who had a subpar year in 1992, Smith returns to form as merger-mania sweeps the business world. The feather in his cap—coverage of Wall Street's war for Paramount—lends him the enviable distinction of penning the story *Journal* readers often seek first each morning. Toiling alongside *WSJ* teammate Johnnie L. Roberts, Smith logs countless hours in Delaware court chambers following the legal maneuverings of Barry Diller, Marty Davis, and Sumner Redstone. These efforts pay off handsomely as the duo provides stellar coverage of every move and countermove in the billion-dollar chess game. Witness their 12-13 report examining plans by Paramount's Davis to sway his board for Viacom before considering an offer by QVC Corp.'s home-shopping guru Diller. "Memos and statements filed in a suit QVC brought against Paramount...[show that] on numerous occasions, the board wasn't given a chance to weigh information that would have put suitor Viacom in an unflattering light—or made archfoe QVC's bid more attractive." Every day the pair's legwork uncovers information of, well, paramount importance to investors. Showing he understands the differences between 1980s- and 1990s-style corporate battles, 9-21, Smith writes, "In the takeover binge of the 1980s, cash was king. But now as a giant entertainment-industry takeover battle breaks out, stock has become the currency of choice." This revelation comes in handy later in the year, 12-20, as Smith hounds a financier suspected of buying chunks of Viacom stock in order to inflate the price and value for an old buddy—Viacom chief Redstone. The issue provokes interest, Smith writes, because "investors were using the stock prices of both Viacom and QVC to value their competing stock-and-cash bids for Paramount." In his 11-10 look at the investment banking firm Lazard Frères, Smith indulges his love for wordplay. "The cloud over Lazard's future has been that its biggest rainmaker, Felix Rohatyn, is 65 years old." A charming and clever writer, Smith displays a skill with words that never overshadows the substance of his work.

Paul Starobin

National Journal

★★½

Economic policy. With his gaze fixed on people inside Washington, Starobin offers glimpses of barons guarding fiefdoms on Capitol Hill, high priests con-

ducting secret rituals at the Federal Reserve, and brazen lobbyists twisting legislation for special interests. The *NJ* journalist searches for the cult of personality driving any issue. In his 1-16 story, Starobin gives one of the better accounts of how Bill Clinton engineered his drive to the White House with the help of Wall Street and Sen. Sam Nunn [D-GA]. Desperate to play a part in electing a president—any president—bigwigs on the Street (notably a cabal of heavyweights at Goldman Sachs) were primed to support Nunn, but when the Georgia Senator decided against running he persuaded them to back Clinton. Providing respectability and cash, Wall Street's wannabe kingmakers became one of Clinton's earliest, strongest, and most important sources of support. In this telling piece, Starobin shows that the largest impediment to winning high office may not necessarily be a lack of energy or ideas, but money. His 2-13 feature for *NJ*'s Hall of Shame, however, fares poorly. "The goal was to find things shameless *even by Washington standards*. This set the bar quite a bit higher than if the standard were the ordinary citizen's view of the matter." Starobin fails to clear that bar; his examples of unblushing behavior are *de rigueur*, standard fare inside the Beltway. One inductee probably should be congratulated, not damned. Starobin roasts John Zorack, a none-too-successful Washington lobbyist who duped producers of a "60 Minutes" segment on influence-peddling into portraying him as one of the capital's most powerful figures. Bouncing back with a 4-17 look at then-Apple CEO John Sculley reveling in his cozy relationship with Clinton and Co. while lobbying for the firm's interests, Starobin reveals, "A good deal of Sculley's energies in Washington are spent on resolving industry disputes in Apple's favor, in fact. If he's a high-tech Renaissance man, he's also the most important cog in his firm's lobbying machine." The focus on personality and relationships holds up in an 11-20 profile of Deputy Treasury Secretary Roger Altman. Starobin shows Altman torn between two masters: He must weigh loyalty to Clinton against loyalty to his immediate boss, Treasury Secretary Lloyd Bentsen, whose ideas about the nation's finances may not always parallel the President's. Kudos to Starobin for ably reporting how things get done in Washington. Now he must explain what they mean.

James B. Stewart

The New Yorker

★★★

Hiring Stewart ranks among editor Tina Brown's major coups in her inaugural campaign at *The New Yorker*. Whether explaining the massive defections of top talent from First Boston, 7-26, or the tumultuous succession struggle at American Express, 1-25, Stewart always has his eye on the big picture. And his highly placed, anonymous sources enable him to dish the inside dope on corporate America. Specializing in getting beyond press releases and public pronouncements, Stewart reports the thoughts and rationalizations of major decision-makers. In his 3-8 story on Michael Milken's day in court, he gives a fly-on-the-wall account of the legal sparring between prosecutors and Milken counsel Arthur Liman over the junk-bond king's plea-bargain agreement. The *Den of Thieves* author shows Liman and his client outwitting the feds in the back room negotiations that led to Milken's parole. In his 6-21 piece, "Death of a Partner," Stewart paints the picture of a prominent New York attorney whose brutal murder at the hands of a gay lover shocked family and firm. More interesting than the scandal, though, is the behind-the-scenes look at the Manhattan law firm Cravath, Swain & Moore. Stewart ably recounts the mores and quirky traditions of this prestigious firm by drawing on his experience as a member of the Cravath team years earlier. At the attorney's funeral, a "large block of seats at the front of the sanctuary remained empty, enclosed by velvet ropes. Then, as the organ swelled and the faint hush of whispered greetings among the mourners subsided, a procession entered from the rear. Marching two by two, uniformly clad in dark suits, ties, and white shirts, sixty partners...marched slowly down the central aisle in a procession known as the Cravath walk ....Their en-banc presence announced, as it had on so many occasions in the past, 'A partner has died; the firm lives.'" In his provocative 2-15 essay, Stewart deftly compares the relative fortunes of IBM and AT&T in issuing a call for renewed activist anti-trust activity under Clinton. Stewart's editorializing proves more appropriate for

The New Yorker than it was in his last job—Page One Editor at *The Wall Street Journal*. The liberation from Dow Jones suits his strong writing and reporting style, which makes anything Stewart produces both provocative and entertaining.

Bruce Stokes
National Journal
★

Trade/international economics. Do any real people in Washington speak to Stokes? How else to explain the fact that the overwhelming majority of sources in his articles hide behind the curtain of anonymity? An 8-21 profile of U.S. Trade Representative Mickey Kantor contains no fewer than 30 anonymous quotes, most attributed to "a Washington trade lawyer," "a trade association lobbyist," "a union aide," "a Washington lobbyist for Japanese firms," or the ubiquitous "Senate Democratic staff aide." These unnamed sources furnish no juicy gossip, controversial claims, or hot tips, and Stokes proves unable to fill in the blanks with keen analysis or prescient insights. All the reader basically learns about Kantor is that the blunt trade-hawk is trying to master the nuances of diplomacy. In his 3-27 piece on the Russian economy, Stokes seeks to pinpoint that nation's woes but gets bogged down in circular logic. "Political stability is obviously a prerequisite for economic revival....Without a functioning Russian economic system, continued political unrest is inevitable." His 3-13 effort praises Clinton for displaying an understanding of the global economy that his predecessor sorely lacked, but his derisive and casual dismissal of Bush administration trade policy undercuts his arguments. The *National Journal* wasted money on a plane ticket in sending Stokes to Tokyo to report on Japan's July elections. Banality abounds in his two pieces on the nation's political climate. "In the final analysis," he writes unremarkably, 7-24, "many experts here agree with their counterparts in Washington that the current Japanese political turmoil was unavoidable and that hoped-for political changes hold great promise." Stokes redeems himself, 8-14 and 9-18, with incisive pieces on the identity crisis at the World Bank. "Evidence of mounting problems with many of the far-flung projects financed by the Bank...worries even the institution's staunchest defenders. Its projects are coming under scrutiny because of their potential harm to the environment and because of past failures of Bank initiatives to reduce poverty." Unfortunately, this kind of work comes only in rare flashes. *National Journal* editors need to better learn how to stoke this reporter's journalistic fire a little more often.

Stephanie Strom
The New York Times
★

Retail. Memo to the *Times*: Get Walter F. Loeb on salary, pronto—and while your at it, take it out of Strom's check. As "the president of Loeb Associates, Inc., a retailing consultant firm," he appears as a source so often in Strom's pieces—upwards of a couple of dozen times in 1993—that it seems he's the only retail consultant in the country. This criticism aside, Strom offers straightforward assessments from Madison Avenue, as well as from warehouses and strip malls across the nation. In her sharp 6-20 piece, she speculates whether—with the advent of telemarketing—the newspaper industry's ad crunch may be permanent. "Retailers are the lifeblood of daily newspapers....So imagine the concern in the advertising offices of the country's major newspapers as one department store chain after another announces plans to explore selling its wares on cable television." No deep thinking here, but Strom provides reliable coverage of the fluid world of retail, an industry undergoing serious change as the computer revolution rolls forward. In her 6-2 article, she touts the newest entrant into the home-shopping race. "Insomniacs and shopaholics take heart. In little over a year, Macy's will be open day and night, 365 days a year, via cable television." Strom details the department-store giant's plans for starting its own channel to hawk its wares. Unfortunately, minor mistakes occasionally mar her work, such as her 10-1 story on the efforts of Barney's to draw shoppers to its two New York clothing stores. Barney's, however, has *three* Manhattan locales. And some stories seem simply peripheral, such as her 12-10 piece "exposing" the capricious behavior of catalogue retailers that accept Christmas orders as late as December 23. Strom's complaint? She vents outrage that they sometimes run out of popular items. In her 10-25 article about fashion designer

Donna Karan's planned stock offering, Strom rehashes quotes the designer gave to a different publication, without stating whether the *Times* even tried to contact her. While none of these items is too egregious, such careless journalistic practices ought to have no place at the *Times*.

James Tanner
The Wall Street Journal
★★★

Oil industry. The preeminent source for OPEC news in the American press, Tanner fills a void by keeping Americans tuned to happenings among the world's major oil producers. More than just tracking the numbers—the day-to-day fluctuations in prices and output—Tanner stays on top of developments in the turbulent Middle East that affect them. "Although oil prices generally have fallen around $3 a barrel since mid-October [1992]," he notes sagely in his 1-22 report on the previous day's market, "they rebounded yesterday in technically driven trading and in reaction to reports that a U.S. plane had fired on an air defense radar site in Iraq." Despite the oil glut, he reports in his 7-9 article that Iraq may be permitted to sell some of its reserves, a practice banned under the Gulf War settlement. Why would the UN allow that? "There have been suggestions that the UN now may be anxious to get Iraq to go ahead with the one-time oil sale because...if the Iraqi oil sale were made, the UN would receive 5 percent of the $1.6 billion, or $80 million, for monitoring expenses." Though not the liveliest writer—he at times displays what may be described as a flair for the drab—Tanner produces such solid reports on the oil markets that style can be overlooked. Perhaps his most daring writing surfaces in his 6-7 front-page profile of Kuwait. In the ruinous aftermath of the Gulf War, "the proud emirate, a founding member of the Organization of Petroleum Exporting Countries, even had to import fuel for domestic use. But today, Kuwait is not only an exporter again, it can produce almost as much as it did before the August 1990 Iraqi invasion." He muffs a 12-20 report on how new EPA rulings about reformulated gasoline will harm Venezuelan petroleum exporters. "Unlike U.S. refiners," he writes, "foreign firms wouldn't be able to use a formula based on their 1990 gasoline production to determine compliance." Why this specifically hurts the Venezuelans remains the reader's guess. Befuddling, however, is something the laconic Tanner can rarely be accused of on his OPEC watch. With an appreciation for how both the vagaries of global diplomacy and the spontaneity of international events can move the oil markets, Tanner offers on-the-mark accounts of petroleum politics.

Alex Taylor III
Fortune
★★★½

Detroit. Taylor finds himself in rare company as an auto-industry reporter who treats carmakers as players in a game with worldwide implications. In the increasingly global economy, the U.S. auto industry's importance is growing, a point usually overlooked by reporters whose focus rarely extends beyond the assembly lines of Detroit and nearby cities. In his 12-13 piece, he provides the definitive assessment of Japanese automakers' prospects, arguing that despite rough times, Japan is not the land of the setting sun for carmakers. "When sales accelerated in the late 1980s, every Japanese automaker looked like a superstar. Now that sales are skidding, they all look like chumps. In fact, the Japanese were never as strong as they seemed five years ago—or as vulnerable as they look today." Moreover, Taylor cautions not to count out companies such as Toyota and Honda "as Japan's auto industry evolves from lusty adolescence to quiet middle age." Keeping an eye on the world stage, 6-28, Taylor expertly tracks Ford's plans for a global blockbuster with its midsize Mondeo. "Building a world car—one that can be made and marketed around the globe—has been a holy grail for automakers because it should represent the ultimate in economics of scale." Such ambition, Taylor notes, entails huge roadblocks, from production problems to the metric system to cultural vagaries. "European buyers," for example, "prefer manual transmissions...and dislike air conditioning," while Americans are the opposite. Plus, there are other continents to consider. In his 6-14 piece detailing Honda's woes, Taylor reveals a downside to excessive corporate downsizing. "The company has prided itself on running the leanest organization in autodom," he notes, "so lean, maybe, that it couldn't respond quickly enough" to changes and challenges from competitors. In his 7-26 piece about electric cars, sales of which some states have mandated by the late 1990s, Taylor leaves no doubt as to what he considers gross folly. "Already it's clear that the much heralded [electric vehicles] will be severely limited. Drive time, for example, will be restricted to just 90 minutes or so at a maximum of 65 miles per hour, and even shorter periods if the air conditioner, heater, or headlights are also running. After that, owners will have to recharge the batteries for up to eight hours." Such advocacy, however, proves the exception, not the rule, in Taylor's evenhanded, comprehensive coverage of the auto industry. Motor City reporters should start taking notes from Taylor, one journalist who knows that stories don't all come from Detroit.

Rich Thomas

Newsweek

Chief economic correspondent. Almost any treatment on the economy from this veteran analyst is bound to contain one of two things—an impassioned plea for the government to tackle entitlement spending or a potshot lobbed at Ronald Reagan. In his 3-22 story, for example, he characterizes the Strategic Defense Initiative as "Reagan's flight of fancy," while in his 5-31 piece he warns that entitlements "threaten to devour all other government programs." But these biases aside, Thomas can be a solid source for what's happening on the economic front. Claiming, 2-8, that the "whole country is hungering for Clinton's leadership," Thomas generally displays skepticism about the new President's proposals. In his refreshing 2-22 analysis of Clinton's austerity program, he and coauthor Marc Levinson find the President downplaying optimistic economic figures that might render his plan superfluous. "For any other president, it would be a welcome gift. What can beat low inflation, falling interest rates and solid economic growth? But for Bill Clinton, the timing could have been better....Clinton must move fast, before those painful memories of recession fade." Much of Thomas's work dissects the Clinton tax-and-stimulus blueprints, providing a fair assessment of their chances of success in the world at large. He occasionally weighs in on other topics, too, such as Washington's rudderless approach to trade, 3-29. His best piece of the year, however, comes outside his main area of coverage. "Just as Safe at Any Speed," 5-10, details the National Highway Traffic Safety Administration investigation of GM, in which the government suggested a voluntary recall of the company's "exploding gas tank" pickups, based on evidence compiled in suits filed by personal injury lawyers—evidence the feds deemed insufficient to warrant an actual recall. At issue are fires caused by side-impact collisions. "The chances of an individual owner dying from this subset of fires is infinitesimal: a driver could spend 31,673 lifetimes before meeting such a fate, assuming he kept the truck for 15 years. Still, the NHTSA calculates that this tiny risk is fifty percent greater than the chance of a fatal fire in a Ford pickup during a similar accident....And it is this risk—in a truck basically as safe as Ford's—that has led the NHTSA to ask GM for a recall." If Thomas would only apply this kind of reporting to his economic stories, his byline would be the first thing to turn to each week.

James Treece

Business Week

Among the more soporific reporters in the *BW* stable, Treece nonetheless provides solid coverage of manufacturing and trade. He spends a fair amount of time traveling and his stories go far beyond the automotive industry in his hometown of Detroit. In his 10-25 piece, he describes his experience with a team of experts whipping through an Indiana auto-parts factory to improve efficiency as being on "the front lines in the battle for supremacy in world manufacturing." But some lines induce more sleep than thought. "We move parts bins, install a paint shield, and yank out old, unneeded equipment. By adding an air jet to cool the mounts' surface so workers don't have to wait as long to paint them, we halve in-process inventory." When the government offers a $30-million prize in a contest to design a more efficient refrigerator using fewer chlorofluorocarbons, 7-15, Treece reveals the cutthroat competition between the two finalists, Whirlpool and Frigidaire. The contest "illustrates a new twist on industrial policy," he notes insightfully. "Its backdrop is a movement among environ-

mental and other groups to use market forces and public-private coalitions, rather than litigation and laws, to promote social and environmental goals." His 2-22 examination of the $105-million verdict by an Atlanta court against GM in the sidesaddle gas-tank suit suffers from a superficial reading of the issue. Although Treece shrewdly reports that the company also faces trial "in the court of public opinion, with customers in the jury box," he dismisses the possible impact on those "jurors" of NBC's rigged footage in the "Dateline" story on GM pickups. In his 4-12 story, Treece observes how better-quality products—and increased pressure from the U.S. government—have led to an increase in Japanese purchases of American auto parts. Japanese carmakers, he notes, are modifying designs in order to do more business with Americans. "Rearview mirrors, for instance, are usually bolted to ceilings of Japanese cars but often glued to windshields in U.S. cars. Nissan's change to the U.S. approach for its new Sentra means a contract for mirror maker Donnelly Corp. in Holland, Mich." While seldom thrilling, Treece ranges far to keep the reader informed.

Louis Uchitelle

The New York Times

★★½

New York. In a banner year for the up-and-coming Uchitelle, original analysis seems to pour out of his PC as he better distinguishes policy-making rhetoric from reality. In his 1-17 examination of the budget deficit and its role in the U.S. economy, he demystifies the issue, asking provocative questions and providing edifying comments. "The deficit last year was equal to 4.9 percent of the $6 trillion...gross domestic product. That is well above the 2.9 percent in 1989, but is not considered high for a country emerging from...recession. The deficit hit 6.3 percent of GDP in 1983...and it stayed at 5 percent or more until 1987." A frequent observer of the Mexican economy, 4-22, Uchitelle ably explains the reason Wall Street money-managers have tripled their Mexican holdings since December 1991: high yields and political stability. While most of the press pack advocates easy money, Uchitelle pens a precise and well-sourced 6-23 view from the Federal Reserve. "'The logic is impeccable that inflation should not be a problem,' said David W. Mullins Jr., the Federal Reserve's vice chairman. '[But] if inflation were to become re-established in the minds of the markets, with no timely response from the Fed, that could be damaging to the economy.'" Fed governors suggested that Uchitelle's report helped firm the bond market. In his unconventional 11-14 assessment of NAFTA's impact on jobs, Uchitelle goes beyond the formulas and provides concrete examples that illuminate the complexities of international trade. Because of NAFTA, he explains, it will now be cheaper for Zenith's factories in Mexico to import 3 million tariff-free TV tubes from the U.S. than from Asia—thus saving 6,000 American jobs. Such valuable information and insight make Uchitelle an increasingly vital source on economic policy.

John Verity

Business Week

★★★

Communications. In a year that sees business writers analyze and overanalyze IBM's woes—targeting the company's excessive devotion to large, bulky computers—the talented Verity stands out as one reporter whose knee doesn't jerk at the mere mention of the word "mainframe." While not denying that sticking with the mainframe computer and scoffing at PCs laid low the corporate behemoth, the circumspect Verity notes a usually overlooked fact—mainframes still constitute a huge market. In his 6-7 story, he deftly relates the new sizzling competition among mainframe suppliers. "IBM has actually lost 17 [percentage] points off the 85 percent market share it held just four years ago. The reasons: inattention to increasingly specialized market segments and loss of technology leadership—exactly the same problems that have bogged down much of the rest of Big Blue." And in his 8-16 feature, Verity writes of the increasing use of mainframes to solve intricate work-place problems. "Conventional wisdom has it that the PC revolution is all but killing off the mainframe. But if the mounting rage for building alternate 'mainframes' is any indication, the high end of the computer market has life in it yet." Similarly refreshing is Verity's 8-30 commentary on AT&T's success, which offers less opinion than compelling analysis. By purchasing McCaw Cellular and the computer-manufacturer, NCR, Verity shows, AT&T staved off the crippling corporate aging process. "There's a lesson in all this: By addressing their problems the right way, even very large companies can successfully adapt to fast-emerging markets." In his 11-8 story, Verity examines the wisdom of the NCR purchase, noting that AT&T's triumphal foray into computers could falter. "Neither NCR's cost structure nor its marketing strength has kept pace with the market's wrenching changes." To meet the demands of a volatile market, Verity writes, NCR will undergo some changes. "A telling sign of the times: In the next few weeks, the name NCR may disappear." It was a few months, rather than weeks, before the name went—in early 1994—but Verity hit the nail on the head, all of which suggests that if you're searching for truth, look no further. His name, after all, is Verity.

Kirk Victor

National Journal

★½

Washington. Disappointing is the word to describe Victor's 1993 performance. Instead of showing off his considerable talents in analyzing Beltway politics with the change in administrations, Victor turns in efforts that flop as often as they succeed. In his 5-22 puff-piece profiling the painfully obscure Transportation Secretary Federico Pena, Victor raises sycophancy to new levels. Refreshing only as a diversion from the media's glorification of Attorney General Janet Reno, it reads like a passage from *Profiles in Courage*: "Pena quickly demonstrated a willingness to make tough calls, even over the opposition of powerful interests....[He] isn't one to duck controversial issues....[He] grapples with knotty and sometimes politically vexing transportation issues ....He's willing to tackle the tough ones." Unfortunately, Victor fails to supply evidence to justify this acclaim. Two mediocre attempts, 1-16 and 4-24, examine what public-interest advocates and unions hope to attain from the Clinton administration. Victor succeeds only in providing them a soapbox, and readers learn nothing because the pieces are short on specific legislative proposals. In one of his better efforts, Victor renders an 8-14 portrait of Richard L. Trumka, a new- style labor leader at the United Mine Workers of America. In addition to capturing Trumka, Victor gives fresh perspective to the changing union landscape. Tough times at the UMWA, aggravated by a coal strike in Pennsylvania, Victor notes, make Trumka's job anything but easy. "Victory for the mine workers is far from inevitable. Representing an ever-declining slice of the nation's coal production, they clearly no longer hold the keys to the country's energy needs." Victor's trenchant 7-3 look at the shipping industry's freight-undercharge crisis—in which bankrupt truckers haul "deep-pocketed shipp[ers]" into court on a spurious legalism, since invalidated by the Supreme Court—is the kind of story that built this *NJ* veteran's solid reputation over the years. Exploring the ramifications of a recent Supreme Court ruling limiting tax deductions for home offices, 2-13, he provides astute analysis and precise insight. He covers the reasoning behind the majority's decision—strict adherence to the Internal Revenue Code—and the argument of the lone dissenter, Justice John Paul Stevens. While this proves one of his best pieces of the year, Victor makes one glaring omission. He forgets to give the name of the case. (It was *Commissioner of Internal Revenue v. Soliman*). Still, past performance is a strong indicator that Victor should come back strong.

Matthew L. Wald

The New York Times

★½

Energy. Disgust for the gas-powered automobile fuels Wald's reports. In his 21st-century utopia, all cars will be electric, and his devotion to this voltage-driven buggy overwhelms much of his work—and his objectivity. In his 9-30 article, he merrily reports joint White House-Detroit plans to develop the voltage-powered car. And while he may question the efficacy of public-private partnerships—"Washington," he notes, "is not even certain what in its cold war-era bag of tricks would be useful to Detroit."—Wald pays scant attention to more important considerations, such as the practicality of the electric car. In his enthusiastic 7-11 endorsement of the battery-driven auto, he glosses over certain deficiencies, such as the fact it can't go very far and needs many hours to recharge. Other electric car enthusiasts—like *The Boston Globe*'s David Chandler—give these criticisms more play. In his 10-17 analysis of the energy scene, Wald writes, "Twenty years after the Arab oil embargo...after the nation's promise to itself to do better, some things have changed. Mostly they've gotten worse." But he skirts the issue of what these "things" are, and how they have "gotten worse." In his 6-20 article ostensibly touting railroads' future, Wald launches a polemical assault on today's drivers. "The private auto enjoys various subsidies, from the general tax dollars that go into road maintenance to the right to pollute the air to the use of the United States Army to keep Middle East oil fields out of hostile hands." The story, interestingly, contains no serious discussion of the merits of train travel. On topics less charged than the electric car, Wald yields provocative articles. In his 10-28 piece on the challenges facing New York City's next mayor, he explores landfills rapidly filling to capacity. Questioning an overly optimistic calculation by city engineers that the main dump will hold until 2030, Wald states that this "assumes the garbage pile on Staten Island can be built as steep as the city plans, making it one of the highest peaks on the East Coast, three times the height of the Statue of Liberty." His 10-31 feature gives a chilling account of the process of dismantling nuclear warheads in the aftermath of the Cold War. Technicians carrying out the job in the same plants where they built them "gently wheel bombs and warheads as if they were frail patients on hospital gurneys." But decent pieces like these may not get hearings from readers who, equating the Wald byline with cheerleading for the battery-powered auto, steer to another story.

David Warsh

The Boston Globe

★½

"Economics Principals" columnist. When Warsh stays focused, he's an enlightening commentator, but when he wanders—which he does frequently—he becomes muddled. His creative analogies can be effective, but not when he sacrifices the main point. Arguing against curtailing the independence of the Federal Reserve, 1-31, Warsh launches into the "cautionary tale" of IBM. The Japanese didn't bring down Big Blue, he notes, small U.S. companies did. Touting the "higher tolerance for decentralization" in the U.S., he warns against congressional tampering with the "highly diverse" system of control at the Fed. "Never mind Japan. The congressional assault on the Fed is something really to worry about." Although intriguing, Warsh does not flesh out the comparison between these two ideas. Warsh's odd 5-2 assessment of President Clinton's first hundred days compares Clinton to Icarus, but after a long, rambling essay on the President's marriage and social life, the analogy fails. Clinton "simply likes a little danger....He flies too near the sun." Huh? Much more effective, 6-6, he calls attempts to force Japan to accept trade targets "a profoundly bad idea," and eloquent arguments from trade experts support his stance. Following the parliamentary stand-off in Moscow, Warsh meanders through a wishy-washy 10-5 appraisal of capitalism Russian-style that tells readers nothing new. On the passage of NAFTA, 11-21, he argues that one winner emerged in the labor camp—Albert Shanker of the AFL-CIO's executive council. "'I thought we should have [handled trade relations] the way that Europe did...with Spain and Portugal, with more training, less dislocation and longer timetables.'" Making a strong point without the grand analogies, Warsh notes the AFL-CIO's anti-NAFTA campaign "bore little resemblance to Shanker-style argumentation....Instead, there was truculent opposition." Clearly intelligent, Warsh could use a stronger editor to temper his creative flourishes.

Gary Weiss

Business Week

★½

Markets, investments. Securing a rare interview with high-flying international investor George Soros highlights an otherwise fair year for Weiss. Because the rarely quoted, Hungarian-born billionaire's merest utterances set off bells in financial circles across the globe, that Weiss gains an audience with him is no mean feat. An 8-23 cover story, co-authored by Gail E. Schares, captures the Soros *esprit d'investing*: "Contrarianism combined with an analysis of economic cycles and market psychology have been the underpinning of Soros's investment style over the years." Though nearly fawning in places, this comprehensive profile of Soros capitalizes on the cooperation of "the man who moves markets," a subject the moneyman broaches. "I'm amused by my guru status," he says in an accompanying Q&A. "I acknowledge it. How can I deny it? [But] I think it is a passing phase." Usually, Weiss monitors the economy, taking the stock market's pulse and rendering a healthy diagnosis. "The likelihood of a full-blown blowout remains scant," he notes, 3-1, "because of the market's ace in the hole: [low] interest rates," which drive capital to stocks. His bullishness comes through again, in a 6-21 article on the small stock rally. "The market has yet to fall victim to that enemy of all bull markets: excessive euphoria. So the best advice is not to run for the escape hatch but relax and enjoy....It could last a long time." The continued running of the bulls down Wall Street in 1993 vindicated Weiss's unvarnished optimism, though his position seems more heartfelt than fully reasoned. He compensates with pieces like his 1-18 "Smart Money" column on Israeli bonds. While there's nothing wrong with letting your conscience guide some of your investing, Weiss argues, one shouldn't be fooled into thinking Israeli bonds double as particularly smart buys. When the institutional sales director claims they are "'competitive,'" Weiss shoots back, "But competitve with what? The Israeli-bond people prefer to compare yields with certificates of deposit. But bond investors generally look at the yeild of other bonds with comparable ratings and maturities." He notes that while "Israel has never requested a formal rating...Standard & Poor's has given the nation an implicit BBB-, the lowest investment grade. Weiss proves less trenchant with his 1-25 analysis of maneuverings at Salomon Brothers. Reporting the investment firm's impending rehiring of notorious arbitrage genius John Meriwether—fired after the 1991 Treasury Bond scandal—Weiss appears to have something hot. Why would they bring him back? "Time has passed. Tempers have cooled. And if there's a credo that Salomon's traders have always lived by, it's this: If it makes money, do it." But the firm does *not* do it; at year's end, the Salomon-Meriwether divorce remains intact. But a personnel move is not the worst call to blow. Weiss intermittently comes through with solid analysis to accompany his capable reporting of the financial markets.

David Wessel

The Wall Street Journal

★½

Washington. Although still struggling to break from the pack, Wessel succeeds more frequently than in the past. His reporting and analysis don't yet have an edge that distinguishes his work, but glimmers of originality do surface. He offers a surefooted 1-8 analysis of Bill Clinton's reassessment of campaign promises in light of "surprisingly" high deficit figures. Had Wessel questioned these estimates in light of falling interest rates, however, he might have foreseen the downward readjustment that occurred by year's end and exposed the President-elect's strategy. In his 4-8 article, Wessel provides a glowing profile of Treasury Secretary Lloyd Bentsen, but little that's newsworthy. An otherwise solid recounting of Federal Reserve Chairman Alan Greenspan's July testimony, 7-21, misses the significance of the Chairman's comment that the money supply "has been downgraded as a reliable indicator," treating this historic shift as just another detail. Joined by co-author Gerald F. Seib, Wessel packs a punch with his 9-22 piece on the administration's health-care strategy and the role of Ira Magaziner, senior adviser to the President for policy development. "The elaborate machinery of task forces and 'tollgates' Mr. Magaziner created was never intended to design a new health-care system. Rather, various advisers were marshaled to complete a vision that Mr. Clinton and the first lady, Hillary Rodham Clinton, had brought with them." Wessel's inventive 12-13 analysis of what distracts the nation from things that deserve attention merits reading, if for no other reason than for its feisty conclusion. "The political debate over health care, taxes and spending policy could be fought with facts and competing philosophies. The last few months suggest that, instead, it will be shaped by sophistry." This is the type of confident, original assessment readers crave.

Joseph B. White

The Wall Street Journal

★★★

Detroit deputy bureau chief. Winning both a Pulitzer prize and a Gerald Loeb award in

1993, White continues to provide superb reporting on the automaking industry in general and General Motors in particular. In his revealing 2-19 effort, he chronicles the fortunes of the once-indomitable automaker, which has recently fallen on hard times. White notes that many analysts believe GM has turned the corner since the hiring of CEO Jack Smith. "Recent events have marked a turnaround in confidence at an organization that made all the wrong moves for nearly a decade....Having steered GM away from the brink, Mr. Smith and his aides now are driving to overhaul everything about the company, from its culture to its cars." But as the year progresses, White points out the roadblocks impeding GM's path to financial health. Just as Big Three negotiators sit down with the UAW to hash out a contract, 6-23, White and co-author Neal Templin proclaim that of all the issues they will address, "nothing packs the explosive punch of GM's determination to adopt a...system that could enable it to shed more workers by the end of the decade than Chrysler Corp. employs today." When the talks produce a status quo pact that inhibits attempts to slash the workforce by "promis[ing] as much as 95 percent of full pay to laid-off workers—even those whose jobs disappeared as long ago as 1987," the duo shows in a 9-17 article why only competitors Ford and Chrysler will benefit. "They accomplished their own painful programs of cost-cutting and layoffs in the 1980s. Now [they] are gaining market share, returning to the black and rebuilding their balance sheets." White occasionally plays the field, extending his scope from GM to the industry as a whole. Covering the public-policy angle, he reports in a 3-23 article on a noteworthy Detroit speech given by Environmental Protection Agency chief Carol M. Browner to car-industry executives in which she pleads for cooperation. White notes that carmakers were flummoxed at the Clinton campaign's support for raising fuel-efficiency standards, and he interprets this speech as a passing of the peace pipe, a sign of "the Clinton administration's eagerness to reassure industry leaders that it is really pro-business at heart, notwithstanding Vice President Albert Gore's best-selling 'green' manifesto." On rare occasions, White zeroes in on other automakers. In a 9-21 feature, he

JOHN TREVER-ALBUQUERQUE JOURNAL © 1993.

and co-author Oscar Suris direct readers' attentions to Ford's big roll of the dice—a new model of an old favor-ite, the Mustang. They detail how Ford almost relegated Mustang to the scrap heap. "Never mind...that the Mustang belongs to an elite group of Detroit creations that have inspired romance, rock songs and riotous hormonal glee. In the brutal global auto industry of the 1990s, hormones take a back seat to cash flow." They go overboard, though, describing plans to "creat[e] a car that will make people dust off their old 'Mustang Sally' records and boogie into the showrooms." Such youthful enthusiasm aside, White drives home commendable auto coverage. Expect good things from the 1994 model White.

G. Pascal Zachary
The Wall Street Journal
★★★

Technology. On a beat that often finds him reporting from the cutting edge of computing and "technotainment," the San Francisco-based Zachary sets himself apart from fellow journalists whose focus rarely extend beyond the boundaries of a given story. With his compelling 5-26 feature, Zachary chronicles the agonizing process by which teams of codewriters at Microsoft labored to produce the best-selling Windows NT program. He draws a marvelous picture of the many dozens who toiled at solitary screens all day to write the programs people use on their PCs, revealing fascinating insights into an artistry spawned by modern times. "Writing code, far from being an exercise in rational deductionism, is more like hitting a baseball, programmers say. Two equally brainy people may sit down and try it; why one succeeds and another fails is as mysterious as art. Some of the best programmers have never been to college." Even when dealing with the mundane, Zachary never loses his grand perspective. In his knockout 3-17 feature, he shows how chipmaker Intel's shift of some operations to Ireland will affect white-collar employment in the years to come. "Intel's interest in bargain-priced engineers reflects a little-noticed but ominous trend: The professional class is facing the same kind of job erosion from global competition as the working class, though it is not as yet severe." For all the 1993 talk about losing manufacturing jobs to low-wage countries, this ranks as one of few stories to examine other effects of the increasingly global economy. In a 7-14 front-page article co-authored by Stephen Kreider Yoder, Zachary proves that part of seeing the big picture entails understanding that no one really has a clear view of the future. The pair turns a good article into an excellent one by milking some telling quotes from industry executives. "The deal makers concede that they don't know which products and services could turn into big markets. 'People know what the skeleton looks like, but they don't know what the muscles look like,' says Frank Biondi, chief executive of cable operator Viacom Inc. Intel Corp. Chief Executive Andrew Grove says that when speculating about what will be a hit, 'I don't know what the hell I'm talking about, really....We'll know the truth when we get there.'" Zachary's only fault is that in seeing the technological forest for the trees, he doesn't concentrate enough on those trees. Eschewing the meddlesome particulars that dominate the confusing stories of others, Zachary sometimes downplays them too much. In his 5-10 piece on Microsoft's Bill Gates meeting with IBM's Louis Gerstner, for example, Zachary delves into the significance of a partnership between the companies, but not into how the two companies might ally. Though concerned less with day-to-day news than with stargazing and wondering about the direction of the industry, this compelling reporter-by-the-Bay provides fascinating insight as the technological revolution rolls on.

★ SCIENCE & TECHNOLOGY ★

Lawrence K. Altman, M.D.

The New York Times

★★★

"Doctor's World" columnist. Despite being an M.D., Altman shies away from furnishing folksy, country-doctor advice. A reporter first and foremost, journalism's Marcus Welby covers his beat the same way other journalists cover City Hall—by keeping readers apprised of day-to-day developments in his field. In his 1-8 report, Altman monitors a potential calamity when the lone manufacturer of nitroglycerin, a drug used to battle angina, encounters production problems. He follows up with an astute 1-12 probe of a chink in the pharmaceutical industry's armor: What happens when the producer of a critical drug fails to meet demand? "Because many drugs are made by only one company, a serious manufacturing or financial problem could leave the United States vulnerable to a sudden disruption in the supply of a standard drug." This dilemma received scant attention in a year of scare stories about outlandish pharmaceutical prices. Altman provides a fascinating 8-30 piece on the last two remaining stocks of smallpox in the world, frozen in Moscow and Atlanta. "The execution of one of the biggest killers in history, the smallpox virus, is being planned for the end of [1993]....A last minute debate over whether the stocks should be destroyed or kept [for their scientific value] could lead to a stay of execution." In covering Washington State's Jack in the Box tainted-meat crisis, 2-9, Altman writes that "public officials have many reasons to be concerned about [the bacteria] E. coli....It can crop up anywhere from municipal water to apple cider to rare hamburgers, one of America's favorite foods. Doctors...can do little more than let the disease take its course." Altman also delivers solid reporting on AIDS and other deadly diseases, including a 4-30 story about how an expanded definition of AIDS will lead to greater numbers of cases reported. And his former work at the World Health Organization enables him to keep readers informed of international efforts to combat AIDS. Crystallizing complex ideas in terms the layperson can grasp, Altman excels as a no-nonsense reporter.

Natalie Angier

The New York Times

★★★★

Science. Once again, give Angier an 'A.' This Pulitzer Prize-winning science reporter struts her stuff, providing fascinating details that illuminate her colorful dispatches. Thanks to her clear and informative style, the average reader can understand and enjoy great breakthroughs in genetic research and amazing mysteries of the animal kingdom. In her intriguing 5-4 piece on fur pigmentation, she explores how different hues in "nature's mammalian palette" affect many bodily functions, such as hearing, sexual ability, and proneness to illness and obesity. In her 3-24 dispatch on "the most coveted treasure in molecular biology, the gene behind Huntington's disease," Angier carefully describes the nature of the disease, its means of transmission, and what the future holds for a cure. Probing the link between genius and madness, between creativity and mental illness, Angier's marvelous 10-12 report reveals that people in the arts tend to "oscillate between summit and abyss" more than those in other fields, concluding, "If in manic depression...artists list first starboard, and then port side on the blinding swells of the imagination, small wonder that upon returning, they distill paradox into beauty." Angier's extraordinary output this year ranged from a "fat drug" and gene therapy to gerbils and whales. But pin the blue-ribbon on her absorbing 8-31 piece on cichlids, one of the world's most bizarre and speciated fish. "Some species are bigger than goats, others fit in a thimble. Some are thick and boxy, others lean and long. They are brown or turquoise or every shade of a neon rainbow," Angier reports, and their eating habits vary just as widely: "a snail eater, a cichlid that feeds on fellow cichlids, a cichlid that eats only the eyes of other cichlids, another that exclusively sucks young cichlid fry out of the protective mouths of their parents." One scientist tells her, "'The standard idea in ecology is that there are various niches waiting to be filled. But cichlids seem to create their own niches.'" The same could be said for Angier. Thanks to her enthusiasm, energy, and insight, her byline always leads to treasure.

James R. Asker

Aviation Week & Space Technology

★★½

Space technology editor. Focusing on both science and politics, Asker authoritatively reports on the troubles that the U.S. space program faces on Capitol Hill. His solid articles analyze missteps by NASA and the response of a skeptical Congress—reduced budgets in the future. In his 1-18 article, Asker highlights an unexpected NASA success. Scientists using the "infamously flawed" Hubble telescope report the discovery of "what may be the farthest known galaxies and strong evidence that many stars are surrounded by disks of material that can form planets." These findings, Asker notes, have whetted scientists' appetites for the improved images that will come after repairing the Hubble's mirror. Against the backdrop of looming budget cuts, Asker's 3-22 article looks at problems in NASA's methods of awarding and overseeing contracts. Noting cost overruns on everything from the Mars Observer program to "a new toilet for the space shuttle," Asker reports on several proposed reforms, including closer scrutiny of contractors and "streamlined paperwork." He turns his attention to Mars exploration plans in a 4-12 piece that proves technically fascinating yet firmly rooted in today's fiscal reality. Asker summarizes NASA plans calling for a new approach to exploration that would lower costs but increase risks by eliminating system redundancies. And his 5-10 piece ably examines other cost-cutting approaches, such as redesigning the space station and even incorporating components of the Russian space program. Asker does note, however, that "officials familiar with Russia's space community say there is growing frustration with an on-again, off-again U.S. attitude about cooperation" that may prove to be a hindrance. In his 6-14 effort, Asker contends that the Clinton administration's plan to cut the budget of the space station "seems clearly at a point where any more efforts to delete hardware would create a facility of minimal value." Work like this shows that Asker can be a valuable source of inside political information on the U.S. space program.

Sharon Begley

Newsweek

★

Science. Although talented, Begley sometimes drowns her provocative work in personal conjecture and sloppy writing. Noting an idea broached by physicist Stephen Hawking in her 4-19 piece on quarks, she comments, "He means not merely a description of nature but an explanation of why it is this way and not some other. That is, did God have any choice when she made the cosmos?" While intriguing, this gratuitous reference to "God" and "she" has little to do with the science of the article. Begley inserts other distracting comments that are either vague or frivolous. "Models invoking 10 dimensions (the seven you don't see are rolled up inside the others; trust us) didn't exactly lend themselves to testing." Who's "us"? Begley later remarks that the mathematics of one calculation "are not fit for publication in a family magazine"—whatever that means. In her informative 2-22 cover story glorifying fetal-tissue research, Begley expresses hope that the wrenching issue might move beyond "politics" because potential scientific breakthroughs outweigh opponents' arguments. She carefully describes the different ailments—from Parkinson's disease to Huntington's disease to Hurler's syndrome—for which fetal-tissue research might yield treatment, explaining that such research even gives hope to sterile women. "If such a transplant can give a woman born without ovaries a chance to conceive, the abortion of one fetus can give life to a whole family of babies." In focusing on the science of the issue Begley all but ignores the ethical issues behind such research. Her enter-

taining, though somewhat confusing, 2-8 report on how to use the site of the washed-up Hanford nuclear facility in Washington State describes the clash between environmentalists who want to preserve the area as a wildlife refuge and farmers who see potential cropland. As to the dangers of growing contaminated food, Begley quips, farmers "promise not to irrigate with ground water that may contain strontium. And if they miscalculate? Maybe they'll stumble on a nouveau riche market: salad greens that glow in the dark." Her 6-14 cover story on the scientific possibilities of cloning DNA provides a fascinating treatment of a subject made topical by "Jurassic Park," and offers a glimmer of hope that 1994 might be a better year.

Jerry E. Bishop

The Wall Street Journal

★½

Science and health. Bishop's technical expertise can work against him, as this veteran correspondent tends to assume his readers will easily understand all his statistics and terminology. And sometimes he just doesn't provide enough of either. His 1-11 report on a Canadian study, which concluded that women who work the night shift are more likely to miscarry, proves inconclusive at best, as Bishop fails to address the *type* of work the subjects do. In his 3-17 article on a University of Michigan study examining the connection between smoking and longevity, Bishop stacks his story so thick with numbers that it becomes nearly impenetrable. In his 6-16 article, Bishop cites relevant details from a cholesterol study published in the *Journal of the American Medical Association*—but not enough to be really satisfying. While he raises the idea of good and bad types of cholesterol, he fails to define either for the reader. In one of his better efforts, 7-16, Bishop carefully details the "discovery" of the so-called "gay" gene. "The scientists [at the National Cancer Institute] said their research indicated there may be at least one gene that is inherited by a son from his mother that helps determine whether the son is predisposed to be heterosexual or homosexual. Presumably, a common version of the gene increases the likelihood that the son will be heterosexual while a less common version predisposes him to a homosexual orientation. The report left many questions unanswered, and scientists caution against drawing premature conclusions." Bishop also contributes with mixed success to the *Journal*'s "Mapping the Mind" series. In his 9-30 essay, he explores a "previously unknown connection between a spot in the brain that compiles images coming from the eyes and a library of images in the memory," but his disorganized discussions of various experiments with monkeys confuses the reader. Bishop better organizes his material in his 10-12 effort about how "in learning language, the brain doesn't simply build a mental dictionary. Instead, it sorts and stores words by grammatical category." Although he tackles fascinating subjects, Bishop doesn't always explain them clearly. Not all, or even most of his readers, know as much as Bishop does.

William J. Broad

The New York Times

★★½

Science. In the 11 years he has covered science for the *Times*, Broad has focused heavily on NASA and outer space. This year, however, he turns much of his attention to the ocean. In his illuminating 3-9 piece, Broad describes how undersea robots "are starting to scrutinize the ocean depths on behalf of basic science, promising to deliver a treasure trove of data from the planet's last, largest and most mysterious frontier." Scientists, Broad notes, expect robots to help find "millions of undiscovered life forms," and to monitor "abandoned nuclear warheads and submarine reactors, some 75 of which are now on the ocean floor." Although expensive—one robot runs $5 million—"robots cost far less than manned submersibles, are safer, and can stay down far longer amid the crushing pressures and inky darkness miles beneath the ocean's surface." Broad's brief but enlightening 12-19 article on the discovery of an ancient shipwreck off the coast of Louisiana provides a lesson in American history. "The vessel, El Cazador, or the Hunter, had been sent by Spain from its port in New Orleans to pick up Mexican coins for its holdings in Louisiana, with the aim of stabilizing their currency....She left Vera Cruz, Mexico, on Jan. 11, 1784, but never arrived back in New Orleans." A fishing boat, Broad explains, accidentally discovered the wreck when its nets got snagged underwater. "The raised net dropped hundreds of coins onto the...deck, all of them minted in Mexico City and most of them dated 1783." In his 9-7 look at how scientists are using computers to redesign parachutes, Broad peppers his facts with amusing anecdotes. "In 1802, [Andre-Jacques Garnerin] ascended in a balloon to an altitude of more than a mile and jumped with nothing more than a silk canopy. He landed safely. But his canopy had a tendency to swing so violently from side to side that he often had a bad case of motion sickness by the time he reached the ground." And Broad's fabulous 8-23 dispatch on the Navy's formerly top-secret system of underwater listening devices highlights a researcher who monitored a blue whale for 43 days. "Tracking whales is but one example of a heady new world just opening to civilian scientists after the cold war as the Navy starts to share and partly unveil its global network of underwater listening gear built over the decades to track the ships and submarines of potential enemies. The system is estimated to have cost $15 billion." With his splashy work this year, Broad shows that he is as much at home in the water as in the skies.

Malcolm Browne

The New York Times

★★★

Science. A longtime foreign correspondent, Browne has been enjoying a second career as a *Times* science writer, a position he fills ably. His early experience gives him an appreciation for daily news reporting sorely missing in those science writers who view themselves as liaisons between the scientific community and the public. In his 1-5 piece on the failure of a physics project in which 315 scientists attempted to gauge "the ultimate basis of material existence," Browne conveys how vastly more complex science is today than just a few decades ago. He also shows how this complexity shapes public perceptions about science. "In trying to ferret out ever deeper layers of nature's secrets, scientists are being forced to accept a markedly slower pace of discovery in many fields of research, and the consequent rising cost of experiments has prompted public and political criticism." Browne turns to astronomy in his stellar 5-4 story on a government plan to sell advertising on satellite "billboards in space." This proposal, he notes, sparked howls from the stargazing community. Just as comfortable on *terra firma* as in the heavens, Browne frequently draws on his extensive knowledge of paleontology. His 3-16 "Biologists Debate Man's Fishy Ancestors" covers the argument raging in the scientific community over which fish can claim man as a descendant—the lungfish or the coelacanth. And showing he can still turn a phrase, 5-25, Browne adds a new note to the international crusade against ivory. "The existing supply of ivory...is being depleted, and conservationists and elephant lovers hope it will grow scarcer still. But many pianists still swear by ivory, and swear at imitations." Reflecting on his career as a reporter in a 10-3 *Magazine* effort affords Browne the opportunity to wax philosophic. "Journalism helps its practitioners accept the ubiquity of death....It isn't that journalists fear death less than other people. It's just that we are a little more familiar with it than some, and we realize that despite its sting, death has its points." Upwards of four decades in journalism have left Browne with a keen sense of what makes a good story—and with a little wisdom as well.

Gene Bylinsky

Fortune

★★½

Science. With more than 30 years on the science beat, Bylinsky emphasizes quality, not quantity. Although he yields only a handful of stories annually, he writes them imaginatively and entertainingly, and consistently offers both knowledge and insight. In his 3-22 article, Bylinsky notes that, according to the National Institutes of Health, the amount of people walking (or not walking) around with chronic pain costs literally *billions* of dollars each year. Explaining that pain actually "suppresses the immune system and enhances the development of cancerous tumors," he describes new efforts to treat pain as a problem rather than a symptom. Bylinsky steps into the future with his 5-3 piece on computers you can talk to—and ones that even talk back. He notes that HAL, the verbal (and nosy) computer from the movie *2001: A Space Odyssey*, does not exist *yet*. However, at the rapid pace "speech recognition technology" is developing, Bylinsky

points out, such computers may be just around the corner. In "A Digital Adam," 11-1, he reveals how scientists combine cadavers and computers to create "a 3-D map of the anatomical universe." They "cut the frozen cadaver into four pieces," Bylinsky writes, "embed them in gelatin, and put each under a slicing machine called a cryomacrotome. It will shave away precisely one millimeter at a time; as each layer is removed, an overhead camera will automatically photograph the remaining cross section. The images will be digitized and combined with the scanning data to produce highly-detailed 3-D representation." Although the cadaver will be cremated, the corpse's memory "will live on in the form of 20 billion bytes of data stored on 35 CD-ROM disks." In a special Autumn issue, Bylinsky continues along the three-dimensional route by describing the many uses of 3-D computing. It can assist those playing the stock market, designing drugs, and even crash-testing. And the price to produce this 3-D technology has dropped from $8 million in 1976 to a mere $5,000 today. Like the technology he describes, Bylinsky's pieces are multi-dimensional and reward every reader who has an eye on the future. If only he wrote more.

David Chandler

The Boston Globe

★½

Science. Chandler's robust prose enlivens his stories, enriching the tenor of his quirky articles. Although his enthusiasm for unusual subjects can prove infectious, it sometimes clouds his objectivity. In four separate 5-24 articles on the prospects of the electric car, Chandler fervently reports that the future holds much promise because of government mandates to curb emissions. Writing excitedly of the day when cars will pull in to service stations to charge up rather than gas up, he touts one trial program teaming the federal government with the city of Atlanta. "By the time the 1996 Olympics open, they plan to have at least one out of every 10 gas stations so equipped, and at least one within 6 miles of any point in the metropolitan area." Chandler's ability to turn a phrase impresses but cannot mask inadequate reporting. His 9-26 piece artfully calls the scientists participating in the Biosphere II project in Oracle, Arizona, "the world's most high-tech peasants, subsistence farmers in a $250 million greenhouse." And despite energetically reporting all the scientific angles of the crew's two-year stay, Chandler provides no hints of the social experiment undertaken. The inspiration for some of his liveliest stories comes from outer space. His 6-14 article describes the challenge faced by UC Berkeley scientists, who are trying with radiotelescopes to pick up alien communications. "They have already begun the monumental task of searching for the equivalent of a distant whisper they hope exists in the middle of a very noisy crowd." After attending a conference on Martian exploration, Chandler crafts an intriguing 6-7 argument that a jaunt to the red planet may not be as expensive as critics allege. Rather than taking the space shuttle, he contends, the mission could use rockets, relying on "the resources of Mars, including the planet's thin air, to make fuel, oxygen and water, rather than transporting them from Earth at great cost." Although this article is absolutely fascinating, a touch more cynicism and a little more snooping would help.

Marilyn Chase

The Wall Street Journal

★★½

Health and medicine, San Francisco. Although moving easily from the world of drug companies to research and development, Chase seems at her best when she puts a human face on her statistical or drug-related information. In a 2-17 piece that has just the right balance of sensitivity, hard facts, and personal accounts, Chase presents the dilemma many women face when they seek alternative forms of therapy for breast cancer. "Peering out from a soft-brimmed hat that hides her new crop of post-chemotherapy hair, Peggy Cheung is a demure victor in a troubling battle. The 33-year-old accountant took on her insurance company and won the right to try a harrowing breast-cancer treatment that she was told might save her life—if it didn't kill her." In a short, but effective, 3-25 dispatch on HIV, Chase explains clearly that "according to a group from the National Institutes of Health, HIV is multiplying furiously in sequestered sites within the lymph nodes and related organs, such as the spleen, tonsils and adenoids." Illustrating the interaction between the scientific and financial communities, Chase crafts a fine 6-10 review of the development of an AIDS drug by a company founded by polio pioneer Jonas Salk. The drug, Chase notes, increases immune cells. However, because "scientists and stock analysts [are] unsure if the test results have scientific or commercial importance," the company's stock plunged 26 percent in a single day. Chase pens a grand finale to the *Journal's* "Mapping the Mind" series, 10-13, with a fascinating description of how the brain learns to control muscle movement. "When Stephen Lisberger watches an outfielder leap up and snag a fly ball, he admires the ballet-like performance and ponders it. 'The moment the ball is hit the outfielder's brain begins to receive visual inputs,' the neuroscientist explains. As the eyes track the ball, the brain begins computing its trajectory. Within milliseconds, millions of instructions are flashed to hundreds of muscles, telling each the exact degree of tension or relaxation required to start the body toward the spot where the ball will descend. A flood of signals feed back to the brain indicating whether each muscle is responding correctly. Finally, in a flurry of rapid-fire calculations that would outstrip the most powerful computer, the brain orders the muscles to propel the body upward and extend the arm. The gloved hand and the baseball arrive at exactly the same point in space and time." In successful efforts such as this, Chase humanizes science, making it both enlightening and entertaining.

Marlene Cimons

Los Angeles Times

★½

Health, Washington. In much of her work, Cimons simply seems to paraphrase press releases from the FDA and other government health organizations. Her 5-13 dispatch on the FDA proposing sun warnings on suntan lotions has a few enlightening statistics about the rise of skin cancer, but not enough details to really engage the reader. Another FDA piece recounting new rules to protect blood supplies,7-2, basically regurgitates Commissioner David A. Kessler's remarks on the issue. Cimons's 3-12 article on the debate over banning immigrants infected with HIV just hits the tip of the iceberg. The ban has been in effect since 1987, she notes, and "lawmakers supporting the ban had argued that allowing infected foreigners into this country would place healthy Americans at risk and could overwhelm the health care system." However, Cimons points out, a spokesman for the AIDS Action Council declares, "'Immigrants should be admitted—or excluded—on the same basis as everyone else. HIV status should not be a factor.'" Cimons's enjoyable 1-12 front-page story covers the trials and tribulations of the Secret Service and the presidents they protect. Although it reads like a school report, it reveals some amusing anecdotes about "the last line of defense." President Lyndon B. Johnson, she notes, "treated his agents like 'hired hands.' ...One rainy night at his ranch, Johnson put his dog Yukie out, screaming: 'Secret service! Throw Yukie back in when he's finished!'...The dog got quite muddy, so the agent on duty 'was delighted to follow the president's orders exactly....The next morning the President awoke to find the silk sheets on his bed quite a mess.'" Cimons's 8-25 front-page effort stands out as her best work. The National Institutes of Health conducted a drug trial on hepatitis-B patients using fialuridine (FIAU), a drug tested with limited success on hepatitis-B patients who also had HIV. But after the drug was administered, she explains, something went "horribly awry." Patients became deathly ill and the researchers could not figure out why. "'It's a tragedy,'" one scientist says. "'We feel horrible...for the patients....The fear that they must have been experiencing, knowing that their fellow members in the [drug] trial were getting sick, getting transplants, dying.'" When Cimons actually gets into her stories, they prove far more engaging than a press release.

Jared Diamond

Discover

★½

Science. By taking animated topics and wringing the life out of them, Diamond does little to dispel the notion that "science" and "fascinating" are mutually exclusive terms. The quirky subjects he covers can captivate, but his treatment of them, while informative, sometimes confuses and often bores. In his September effort, Diamond explores why the human female, unlike almost all others in the mammal world, conceals her ovulation. After noting the

result—that humans can have sex all the time—he offers some lascivious details. "Monogamous gibbon couples go several years without sex...[while] a female baboon emerges from a month of abstinence to copulate up to 100 times [and] a female Barbary macaque does it on an average of every 17 minutes, distributing her favors at least once to every adult male in her troop." Diamond then weighs down the text with mind-numbing prose. Few readers probably stuck around long enough to discover that "what it boils down to is that concealed ovulation has repeatedly changed and actually reversed its function during primate evolutionary history." A February piece details the threatened extinction of thousands of languages around the globe. "We hear much anguished discussion about the accelerating disappearance of indigenous cultures as our Coca-Cola civilization spreads over the world. Much less attention has been paid to the disappearance of languages themselves and to their essential role in the survival of those indigenous cultures." Diamond urges the U.S. government to protect languages the same way it protects endangered species. His most plausible argument, however, that knowledge of languages can be used to trace human development and migration, lies buried in a confused, if impassioned, plea for cultural diversity. In an entertaining May article, Diamond expends considerable energy explaining how different body parts are strong enough to withstand the stresses of the daily grind. Our tendons, bones, and organs stave off injuries because nature gives them just a little more toughness, on average, than they need. After all, Diamond asks, "would you really want to lug around unbreakable arms and legs twice as thick as they actually are?" An engaging March feature examines how isolated societies in Tasmania and nearby islands thrived for millennia, completely unaware of the rest of the world. But because Diamond seems torn between writing about the Tasmanian cultural experiences and condemning the European settlers who ultimately wiped the societies out, the story loses focus. While Diamond's articles brim with solid, sometimes provocative information, his delivery may impel readers to flip the pages.

Gregg Easterbrook

Newsweek
The Atlantic
★★★½

Contributing editor. When Easterbrook's byline appears, readers should stop and look. In a clear and engaging style, he offers compelling arguments on a range of scientific issues that invariably enlighten and entertain. Showcasing his wealth of information about American forestry, Easterbrook fashions an arresting 4-12 argument in *Newsweek* that a thriving logging industry and preservation of the spotted owl are compatible. In his 5-30 *Los Angeles Times* column on the "failed notions" of the Strategic Defense Initiative (SDI) and nuclear winter, Easterbrook portrays conservatives and liberals of the 1980s as emperors without clothes. With his lyrical narrative style, he describes how both concepts—an orbital missile destroyer and a global climate change induced by nuclear war that would cause extinction of human life—dodged scientific scrutiny before reaching the public, where each "fell on fertile ground." SDI was based on an idea for which "no laboratory tests had demonstrated any practical models," and nuclear winter was predicted by a rudimentary computer-modeling program that has since been discredited in the field of climatology. Easterbrook nonetheless concludes, "flawed and

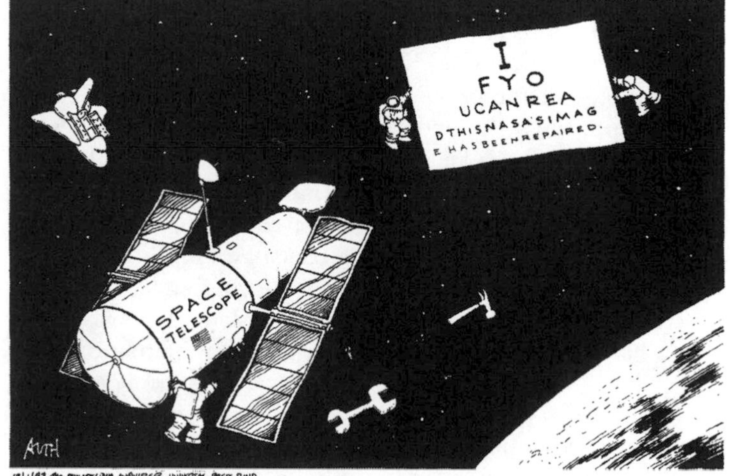

goofy as both ideas were, in the flawed and goofy realm of international events they combined to produce a tremendous benefit for society: nuclear arms reduction....This is a strange case where two wrongs actually did make a right." In his 6-20 *LAT* defense of violence in Steven Spielberg's "Jurassic Park," Easterbrook takes a refreshing jab at the furry dinosaurs "in the hideous, revolting, saccharine, contemptibly puerile and therefore, of course, wildly popular 'Barney and Friends' public television show." More importantly, he also attacks the "Back to Eden" faction of the environmental movement, which, he charges, inspires a distorted, utopian view of the natural world. In his July *Atlantic* article, Easterbrook tackles the complex subject of energy company deregulation, providing a breezy yet thorough account of the history and implications of new "free-market juice" policies. He relates with irony that "the environmental community, once ardently anti-utility, has qualms about power deregulation, though it might seem a deliciously satisfying revenge against the crowd responsible for acid rain and Three Mile Island." In all his work, Easterbrook adeptly combines scientific understanding, a keen sense of history, and thoughtful analysis of economic policy. His only shortcoming is that he doesn't write more.

Philip Elmer-DeWitt

Time

★★½

Science. Covering his beat with more verve than usual this year, Elmer-DeWitt is fast becoming one of the top writers in the science line-up at *Time*. Some of his dispatches, however, continue to sound alarmist. In his 3-22 piece on the interference to navigational equipment by CD players and laptop computers, Elmer-DeWitt points to the "tidal wave of concern" in the airline industry, but he voices too much apprehension to sound objective. "No planes have crashed and no lives have been lost—so far." Elmer-DeWitt also hits the panic button in his 5-17 story on the use in cows of genetically engineered hormones to produce more milk. But in his intriguing 11-8 cover story about human cloning, he addresses all the scientific and ethical issues surrounding the story, although he moralizes in his conclusion. "Technology tends to develop a momentum of its own. The time to discuss whether it is right or wrong is before it has been put to use, not after." Elmer-DeWitt focuses heavily on two subjects this year: "cybernetics," the science of communications and control theory, and the Internet, "the mother of all computer networks—an anarchistic electronic freeway that has spread uncontrollably and now circles the globe." In these areas, he shows his true passion, detailing his genuine excitement for what lies ahead in this cutting-edge technology. Elmer-DeWitt discusses "cyberpunk," 2-8, as "a way of looking at the world that combines an infatuation with high-tech tools and a disdain for conventional ways of using them." In his 12-6 piece, Elmer-DeWitt seems like a kid in a candy store as he describes all the delicious details of how the Internet works, its history, and potential uses for the future. He even explains the rules of "netiquette," or how to behave when interacting with others on the Internet. "Don't ask dumb questions....Don't type in all caps (IT'S LIKE YELLING)...indicate irony with a ;) (a wink sideways)," and, he might have added, signify a smile with a sideways happy-face :). Elmer-DeWitt's byline usually gives a :) whenever it is found.

Judy Foreman

The Boston Globe

★★★

Science, health, and medicine. With a keen eye for detail and a sharp ear for quotes, the talented Foreman vigorously covers medicine, aging, and health. In her superb 4-12 article on new treatments for strokes, she debunks the myth that strokes are "like bolts of lightning—devastating events that were over almost as soon as they began." Researchers have found that it takes hours, rather than mere minutes, for strokes "to wreak their full damage and that during this precious window of time several drugs now in testing may be able to stop the damage in its tracks." Following through, Foreman carefully explains the new drugs and techniques now being developed. Her brief 6-17 piece on treating hypertension argues that meditation works, but only to a small degree. "The fact that several mental approaches are approximately equivalent suggests that there is a placebo effect, the belief that what you're

doing to improve your health will work." Noting the increased risk of breast cancer in women who delay pregnancy, Foreman draws an odd conclusion in her 9-27 piece. "What is clear is that American women have split into two camps: less educated women who get pregnant early and more educated women who get pregnant late—or never." This puzzling emphasis on education—when all the evidence stresses age—detracts from an otherwise informative article. Foreman's 10-21 effort reports on a cream, the active ingredient of which is used in prescription asthma drugs. That it "melts" away fat from women's thighs sounds too good to be true. It may be: the facts show promise, but major research still needs to be done. In her most outstanding article of the year, 3-28, Foreman describes the wacky world of cryonics: "[being] frozen upon [one's] death for as long as it takes scientists to figure out how to thaw people and bring them back to the future." She quotes one detractor, who calls cryonics "'goofy beyond amusement. It's a movement that combines... screwy science and a secular lust for reincarnation with large-scale refrigeration technology.'" Still, her reporting on this technology won't leave readers out in the cold—with her cool style and polished prose, Foreman always fires up the reader's imagination.

John Horgan

Scientific American

★★★

Senior writer. Those who crave the latest scientific ideas and explanations should watch for Horgan's byline. He both fascinates and provokes. In his brief February essay, Horgan explores which scientific ideas are uniquely human and which may transcend mankind. "Are mathematical theorems and theories of physics universal truths, likely to be discovered by any beings given to pondering the nature of things? Or are they inventions, as much products of our idiosyncratic heritage and needs as eyeglasses or toasters?" Horgan concludes these inquiries with another question. "If we meet aliens, will they have the equivalent of the Golden Rule: Do unto others as you would have them do unto you?" Although intriguing, the piece is more a delicious appetizer than a full meal—the reader is left wanting more. In his fine March essay about a possible meltdown of the Antarctic ice cap—"several kilometers thick" in some places—Horgan cites findings of dramatic fluctuations in the past few million years. "If the...ice cap disintegrates, sea levels could surge by as much as 60 meters. 'New York' [one scientist remarks] 'is going to be underwater.'" In his June article, Horgan states boldly, "Eugenics is back in fashion. The message that genetics can explain, predict and even modify human behavior for the betterment of society is promulgated not just on sensationalistic talk shows but by our most prominent scientists." In his careful assessment of recent research, Horgan notes that although the evidence is far from conclusive, the news media showers far more attention on studies detecting links between genes and various diseases, behavior, and attributes than on studies that find no such links. His October cover story examines the predicted demise of the mathematical proof. "Mathematics, that most tradition-bound of intellectual enterprises, is undergoing profound changes. For millennia, mathematicians have measured progress in terms of what they can demonstrate through proofs—that is, a series of logical steps leading from a set of axioms to an irrefutable conclusion. Now the doubts riddling human thought have finally infected mathematics." The reason? Computers, which have opened up new realms of thought and made the concept of proof a matter of dispute. Horgan also crafts superb profiles of such geniuses as Linus C. Pauling, two-time Nobel Prize winner (March), John H. Gibbons, President Clinton's new science advisor (April), and Marvin L. Minsky (November), "a founding father of artificial intelligence." This field, Horgan explains, is dedicated to the proposition that "brains are nothing more than machines...whose abilities will someday be duplicated by computers." Horgan's intelligence—far from artificial—comes through in all his work, and makes *SA* worth the price of subscription.

Gina Kolata

The New York Times

★★★

Science and medicine. Tracking up-to-the-minute developments in health research and genetics, Kolata investigates scientific breakthroughs that could ultimately lead to cures for various diseases. She succeeds in making complex medical issues understandable, as in her 3-9 story on a new theory about how the AIDS virus operates. One strain of white blood cells, which revs up the body's immune system, decreases in HIV-positive patients, while another strain, which suppresses the immune system, remains unaffected. The body replenishes the more helpful cells—but not fast enough—and the unhelpful strain ultimately dominates. Kolata cleverly explains this complicated theory by likening the situation "to a bag with quarters [the unhelpful strain] and dimes [the helpful strain] in it and a tiny hole at the bottom that lets dimes slip through but not quarters. As dimes fall out both dimes and quarters are put back, but eventually, the bag will have almost nothing but quarters in it." Scientists, Kolata adds, are experimenting with drugs that aim to maintain the ratio of the two types of white blood cells. In her impressive 5-6 front-page feature, Kolata reports the discovery of a gene where 90 percent of those carrying it are sure to develop cancer. "Although the gene itself has not yet been isolated, the discovery is expected to lead within a few years to the development of a test to show whether a person carries the gene....People who know they have the gene [will] have regular tests to detect the cancer at an early stage, when in most cases it is likely to be cured." Kolata's 2-9 investigation into the scientific validity of the movie "Lorenzo's Oil," a "true story" about a miracle oil saving a terminally-ill child, merits praise for proving the film more fiction than fact. Interviewing the principals in the case, along with medical experts and parents of children with the same malady, Kolata shows that the "cure" had been unsuccessfully tested on numerous patients before Lorenzo. Addressing the ethical quandary produced by cloning human embryos, her 10-26 front-page story yields a provocative insight. "The spare embryos could also be sold, as sperm and eggs are now, to couples who could see from the already born child how the purchased embryo turns out." For fine coverage of health science, leave it to Kolata.

Margaret E. Kriz

National Journal

★★

Energy and environment. Kriz excels at imbuing the sometimes arcane issues involving energy and the environment with vitality and importance. She also attempts to put policy changes and proposals into a broader national context. In her 1-2 article, Kriz comprehensively examines the "striking changing of the guard" on the various congressional committees that oversee energy and environmental policy. "Much as President-elect Clinton represents the next generation of American politicians, so do the chairmen who will be taking over the three committees that shape environmental legislation....Four of the six congressional panels with major jurisdiction over energy and environmental issues [will now] have new chairmen." Though her flippant tone sometimes jars, Kriz uses her 2-13 piece to clearly define the desires of environmentalists. "The nation's environmental groups want nothing less than to be equal partners in establishing policy in the Clinton Administration." In her forthright 4-10 overview on the proposed BTU tax, Kriz reveals why the White House wants to levy it directly on local gas and utility companies. "Administration officials contend that it would be easier for the government to collect the tax from utilities than from millions of utility customers. But industry officials say that the President's real motivation is that he doesn't want to be directly identified with a line-item tax on customers' utility bills." In a typically enlightening dispatch on an obscure subject, 7-17, Kriz examines the problems with regulating water runoff, a primary source of pollution. "At the heart of the controversy is whether the federal government has the right to tell thousands of landowners what steps they must take to reduce the polluted runoff." And she yields a 10-9 article that spotlights the battle against time in deciding on how to dispose of nuclear waste. It's a dirty job, but somebody has to cover these kinds of issues—and Kriz does it better each year.

Michael Lemonick

Time

★★½

Science. Writing on subjects that have caught the nation's fancy, Lemonick splendidly covers pop science. Hollywood inspired his two best pieces in 1993. Amid the springtime dinomania sparked by "Jurassic Park," Lemonick chronicles

recent scientific developments, 4-26, that challenge long-held conceptions of the prehistoric creatures. "An avalanche of new evidence—from fossilized bones, dinosaur nests, eggs and even footprints, analyzed with such high-tech equipment as CAT scans and computers—has completely transformed scientific thinking about dinosaurs." How big, how old, how they lived and ate, whether they were cold-blooded—each of these questions, writes Lemonick, likely has a different answer than previously assumed. Another hit movie, "Free Willy," compelled Lemonick to investigate the save-the-whales movement, and his 8-2 piece yields some surprises. "The controversy over whether to save the whale...does not divide into neat ideological camps. Many whalers agree that some species need saving; many environmentalists—including [the Norwegian-based] Brundtland, considered one of the world's most conservation-conscious [interest groups]—think that some carefully regulated whaling is acceptable." Lemonick also handles less trendy subjects. In his 8-9 cover story on the Maya, co-authored by Guy Garcia, he describes recent archaeological discoveries in Central America. New findings, he shows, have radically altered earlier notions of the ancient Indian empire. "Among the first myths about this population to be debunked is that they were a peaceful race. Experts now generally agree that warfare played a key role in Maya civilization. The rulers found reasons to use torture and human sacrifice throughout their culture, from religious celebrations to sporting events to building dedications." Lemonick's forays into the world of hard science take him only to its fringes, as with his 11-1 report on the killing of the super-collider project. "It's tempting to call [its] demise the end of big science, but it would be more accurate to describe it as the end of big, bloated, bungled science....About all the taxpayers have for their $2 billion is a complex of buildings and 14.7 miles of tunnel under the Texas prairie." With his sharp eye and entertaining style, Lemonick makes science understandable and fun.

Jeffrey Lenorovitz
Aviation Week & Space Technology
★½

Senior international editor, Washington. Perhaps unfamiliar with the U.S. after a 13-year stint in Paris, many of Lenorovitz's stories this year lacked the perspective that better sources might have provided. While he capably covers meetings, his technology pieces often read like company brochures, missing the news behind the hardware. In his 4-5 story on the preparation of the Clementine 1 satellite to make 1994 flybys of the moon and a nearby asteroid, he produces overly technical work. "Two 370-gram, 7-watt star tracker cameras are integrated into the spacecraft. They have a 100-300-milliradian accuracy and a 29 x 43 deg. field of view." It's heavy going with no payoff. Fortunately, his straightforward 5-31 story in his series on the National Commission to Ensure a Strong Competitive Airline Industry captures the highlights of the meeting and hasn't a gigabyte or compression ratio in sight. "Under questioning from commissioners, witnesses admitted the financial community contributed to the problem by providing airlines with too much access to capital. 'The financial markets [said one witness] were, indeed, a bit undisciplined—but nobody had lost money in financing aircraft before.'" Lenorovitz provides an adequate 3-22 overview of the government's desire for a new primary launch system, but offers no industry response. Can the air force requirements be filled? Is there anything in development now? Lenorovitz fails to ask these key questions, so the reader never finds out. He also has a knack for making the fascinating dull. In his workmanlike 8-9 story on transforming Russian nukes into vehicles to launch communications satellites for corporate America, Lenorovitz begins the article with typical drabness. "Russia's primary design bureau for submarine-launched ballistic missiles is looking to civilian spin-offs as the means of generating revenue and keeping its work force employed." Despite considerable knowledge, Lenorovitz seems unable to muster enthusiasm for many of his assignments.

Thomas H. Maugh, II
Los Angeles Times
★★½

Science. Not confined to one beat, Maugh moves easily from one subject to another. One day finds him ably covering AIDS or genetics, the next poking around the ruins at Troy or the pyramids of Egypt. Exploring both the obscure and the familiar, Maugh always gets his facts—and his prose consistently entertains. In his 2-15 story on the growing incidence of relatives intermarrying, Maugh reveals two remarkable facts. "An estimated 20 percent of marriages worldwide are between individuals who are first cousins or more closely related....In India, uncle-niece unions account for 20 percent of all marriages." Maugh's informative 3-4 front-page report on a medical breakthrough details the discovery of the gene that causes amyotrophic lateral sclerosis—Lou Gehrig's disease—which afflicts victims in adulthood. This finding "opens the door to prenatal screening and the first effective therapies for the disease." Several June pieces, such as 6-1, 6-3, and 6-22, track the mysterious epidemic that swept Arizona and New Mexico in the late spring. Maugh concludes this series with a stellar 8-17 follow-up warning that much of the country is vulnerable to similar plagues. Latent viruses, he writes, lie waiting for some unusual occurrence—"like the heavy rainfall in the past two years that triggered a proliferation of rodents in the Southwest—to catapult them into an unexpected, and frequently deadly, encounter with humans." Hitting his stride on the archaeological trail, Maugh writes on digs in both Greece and Mexico and provides outstanding coverage of sites in Egypt. A secret chamber recently discovered in the Great Pyramid at Giza, he writes, 4-21, promises immense rewards—and perhaps the body of Pharaoh Cheops—when scientists and an enterprising filmmaker explore it with a robot camera in a planned March 1994 expedition. An 8-30 report on the work at Giza relates new understanding about the people who built the pyramids. "The findings cast doubt on the idea that the tombs were built by slaves or forced labor....Hard work was rewarded....Evidence from the tombs clearly shows that the overseers were workers who had been promoted based on merit." Maugh's keen grasp of diverse topics, many with global implications, helps anchor the *Times*'s solid science coverage.

John D. Morrocco
Aviation Week & Space Technology
★★★

Senior military editor. Covering a wide range of subjects, from political infighting at the Pentagon to the aeronautical details of the Bosnian airdrop, Morrocco showcases his remarkable technical expertise of military aircraft and systems. He is also an engaging writer. In his clever 2-8 article on the future of the U.S. Navy F-14 fighter aircraft, Morrocco reports that "the Navy can no longer afford single mission aircraft....The F-14 is already a multi-mission aircraft." For this reason, he notes, the F-14 will likely be revived for another generation. His well-researched 4-12 piece explores the technical-review dilemmas facing defense planners as they choose the next generation of tactical aircraft for the U.S. Planners, he explains, must choose between greater versatility and reduced capability across the board, or increased capability in fewer technical areas. Morrocco demonstrates his own versatility in a 6-28 report on the conflict among top Russian defense planners over whether to allocate funds for procurement or research and development (R&D). While Russia's official defense spending declined, Morrocco notes, "many defense factories kept on churning out more weapons than are on the domestic and foreign order books," using money earmarked for R&D and defense conversion to keep production lines open. Astutely delving beyond the headlines on Bosnia, Morrocco yields an informative 7-12 article on the airdrop operation. He details the allies' frantic efforts to re-fit C-130 cargo planes with additional protection against Serbian surface-to-air missile systems. He adeptly examines the confusion among Pentagon planners, 8-9, over how to proceed with next-generation procurement of such aircraft as the V-22 Osprey, pending a "bottom-up review" by Defense Secretary Les Aspin. During the Bush administration, Morrocco recalls, Defense Secretary Dick Cheney's consistent opposition to the Osprey program clashed with strong congressional support. As a result, "the program was not so much an acquisition program as it was a 'political pawn'." Morrocco makes technical topics more comprehensible than most of his colleagues. With his clear prose and thorough analysis, Morrocco pro-

vides strong insights on numerous topics.

Bruce Nordwall

Aviation Week & Space Technology

★★½

Avionics editor. Nordwall's probing style penetrates the technical jargon of the avionics industry, making accessible the latest scientific discoveries and aeronautic inventions. In his fascinating 1-18 report on advances in a new radar system developed by Swedish researchers, Nordwall clearly explains the promise of ground-penetrating synthetic aperture radar. The device "could give the military a tactical radar to detect forces concealed under trees and to locate objects under 5-10 meters of soil." Nordwall also explores potential civilian applications for this radar system, such as forestry and agriculture. Demonstrating his firsthand knowledge of the conversion of military navigation systems, 2-22, Nordwall convincingly underscores the significance of this equipment to the commercial airline industry. "The airlines hope to achieve Category 3 minimums, or the ability to see the runway from a decision height of 50 ft., without having to resort to costly autoland systems." He provides an exceptionally thorough 4-5 report on the difficulties encountered by American manufacturers of air-traffic-control equipment in their pursuit of foreign sales. "The world market is largely driven by cost. Political influence and in-country content are also more important [overseas] than they are to the FAA." Exploring the brave new world of mobile communications, 5-31, Nordwall argues that consumer markets may soon be available to defense contractors. But, he cautions, "defense companies will have to evaluate the market carefully because it will be highly dynamic and price-competitive relative to government contracting." Detailing the technical promise of a newly developed pressure sensor, 9-13, Nordwall explains its widespread applications in aircraft testing and its potential to detect wing ice in flight—thereby enhancing flight safety. A thorough reporter, Nordwall supplies an abundance—sometimes an overabundance—of detail that seldom leaves the reader wanting more.

Boyce Rensberger

The Washington Post

★★

Science. A prolific reporter whose beat varies from physics to biology to paleontology, Rensberger offers potluck science—you never know what you're going to get. Although sometimes light, he generally provides lively, satisfying fare. In a typical feature, 10-3, Rensberger captures the uproar in the scientific community over HBO's adaptation of Randy Shilts's "And The Band Played On." Many who worked in the early years of the fight against AIDS assailed the movie for allegedly promoting distortions and lies, such as a vitriolic attack on a discoverer of the virus. In reporting the controversy, Rensberger presents a comprehensive history from all perspectives. Turning attention to genetics, he reports, 2-22, on an innovation in DNA "fingerprinting" that can provide genealogical clues on the origins of tribes and ethnic groups. The process, Rensberger points out, constitutes "the genetic equivalent of Sherlock Holmes's trick of checking the mud on a suspect's boots. Just as a person carries evidence of his travels in the various muds on his shoes, an ethnic group carries odd bits of DNA codes picked up from other groups with which it has intermarried." Questions such as which African groups are the forebears of African Americans and whether all Native Americans are descended from a single Asian migration may be answered when scientists perfect the process. Unlike some colleagues, Rensberger refuses to get caught up in the hoopla surrounding the summer's blockbuster movie. "Would someone please turn off the 'Jurassic Park' hype machine?" he pleads, 6-28. "Director Steven Spielberg is just plain wrong, according to molecular and cell biologists, when he keeps claiming that his movie...is scientifically plausible." With appropriate skepticism, Rensberger details how the long march of time makes replicating prehistoric creatures impossible. "Extinction, in other words, is forever." Rensberger scours the globe to garner unusual stories, such as his 6-14 report on the newest mammal species—found in Vietnam—or his 4-15 dispatch on the Montreal Protocol's phaseout of chlorofluorocarbons (CFCs). Rensberger's flexibility enables him to dabble in various fields and subjects, usually with success.

Richard Saltus

The Boston Globe

★½

Medicine. Although he sprinkles his stories with enlightening details, Saltus covers his beat with a "just the facts, ma'am" approach, seldom departing from "who," "what," "where," and "when." In his superficial 1-23 piece on President Clinton's lifting of the ban on federal funds for fetal-tissue research, Saltus spends considerable time speculating about where the tissue will come from, but barely addresses the implications that lifting the ban might have for researchers and patients. His 10-26 article on embryo duplication, while intriguing, simply rehashes the call for ethical referees in the biomedical research arena. Cautiously optimistic in his 7-9 article, Saltus ably describes a "powerful anti-cancer drug, smuggled inside tumor cells by a 'smart bomb' protein that avoids normal cells [that] has cured human breast, lung and colon cancers growing in rodents, even when the cancer had spread widely." And Saltus's revealing 3-25 piece examines the process by which the AIDS virus in its early stages infiltrates the body. "Scientists have discovered that the AIDS virus, instead of going into an inactive period for a number of years, attacks the immune system from within, like a biological 'Trojan horse,' while remaining undetectable." In his regular "Medical Notebooks" feature, Saltus gives an "at your fingertips" guide to a wide variety of subjects, from cerebral palsy and schizophrenia to why the wealthy live longer and why exercise increases longevity. In his best effort of the year, 11-1, Saltus explores the discovery of pathways "that allow the outside of a human cell to communicate with the genetic control center in its nucleus. Discovering these pathways may open new possibilities for treating a variety of diseases, because the signals that zip along them sometimes mistakenly drive cells to malfunction—as cancer, arthritis, some mental disorders and allergies." Clear language and a step just beyond the facts make this piece captivating. Saltus should take that step more often.

Kathy Sawyer

The Washington Post

★★½

Space. With NASA suffering its worst year since the Challenger explosion in 1986, Sawyer tracks the story of the beleaguered space agency like a bloodhound. Her strong coverage of the agency's tumultuous battle for continued space-station funding allows the reader to follow the frequent shifts in the story. In her 2-13 report, she reveals that Vice President Al Gore has privately assured key lawmakers that full funding for NASA is in the works. However, she notes in a 2-19 column less than a week later that the Clinton administration has dropped the idea and called for cuts. Sawyer's 6-18 report encapsulates plainly: "Any savings envisioned under the president's plan depend on dramatic changes in NASA's management and culture, a 30 percent reduction in the space station work force, and stable funding at the hands of Congress." As Clinton and Congress parry back and forth during the summer, Sawyer evenhandedly follows the story to its conclusion, 9-9, never losing sight of the debacles that irk lawmakers. "NASA has suffered the devastating loss of its Mars Observer mission and a major weather satellite. As a result, congressional aides say, the agency will find it difficult to win approval for any new programs 'in the foreseeable fu-

Doonesbury BY GARRY TRUDEAU

ture.'" Chronicling the malfunction of a pricey satellite, 10-9, Sawyer zeroes in on a major contractor. "This is the fourth U.S. space flight failure in a two-month string....The losses—totaling an estimated $2.3 billion—involve at least three different government agencies but one corporate logo: Martin Marietta." Outer-space catastrophes and tenacious funding fights capture most, but not all, of Sawyer's attention. Reflecting on military downsizing, 9-27, she describes an espionage plane put out to pasture and now being used for research. "For decades of the Cold War, the sculpted black craft had dashed on demand across hostile borders around the globe, snatching photo images and electronic...intelligence for the president....Now the former spy plane has joined the ranks of cold warriors trying to make it as civilians." Credit Sawyer as one reporter who keeps her feet on the ground and head out of the clouds.

Keith Schneider

The New York Times

★

Environmental policy. Although he possesses fine reportorial skills, Schneider fumbles and bumbles his way through coverage of the government's environmental policies, often ruining a solid job with misleading analysis, sloppy organization, or simple omissions. In his 4-16 piece on Georgia Pacific's cutting a deal with the Interior Department to forego logging some of its land in order to preserve the habitat of endangered woodpeckers, Schneider heralds the cooperation between government and industry. But near the end of the story, he quotes Secretary Bruce Babbitt admitting that the agreement would do little to preserve the bird's numbers. "Mr. Babbitt said today...most of the 10,000 red cockaded woodpeckers in existence live in national forests and timberlands on military bases in the South. Thus, they are not affected by the agreement reached today." Schneider's garbled 3-17 effort reports on the new policy announced by Agriculture Secretary Mike Espy—at a highly publicized congressional hearing—to reform USDA inspection in the wake of Washington State's fast-food, tainted-meat scare. Yet Schneider fails to mention Espy until the middle of the story, and never gives the name of the hamburger chain—Jack in the Box—singularly responsible for the tragedy that led to four deaths, as well as the calls for reform. Bias infects his 9-16 report on divisions in the environmental movement over NAFTA. Schneider insinuates that groups favoring the pact have compromised their principles in order to curry favor with the White House. However, he gives no explanation of why lowering trade barriers amounts to a betrayal of the environmental movement. When Schneider applies his skills and avoids mistakes and bias, he pens cogent, timely pieces. He beat the competition, 2-2, in reporting EPA chief Carol Browner's plan to seek relaxation of a law banning most food pesticides, and hit the mark with a 4-19 report of a rift between Vice President Al Gore and the White House over the direction of environmental policy. When the mistakes glare less brightly, Schneider will begin to shine.

William Scott

Aviation Week & Space Technology

★★½

Senior national editor. One of the more versatile *AW&ST* writers, Scott covers aircraft and avionics technology as well as federal science policy, including defense conversion and the transfer of technology from the public to the private sector. Despite this broad range of subjects, he handles difficult technical and scientific issues with ease. In his brief but thorough 2-22 effort, Scott fully details a government report issued after a recent crash of a Fokker passenger plane. "The board's report," he writes, "included 15 recommendations such as modifying air traffic control procedures to reduce the time between deicing operations and takeoff." Such findings, Scott explains, should enhance safety for all civilian air transport. In his superb 3-29 article on the congressional debate over the future of Department of Energy labs, he draws a shrewd conclusion concerning federal-lawmaking in this area. "Legislation has the potential either to enhance U.S. economic competitiveness through technological leverage, or decimate the intellectual power houses that contributed so significantly to winning the Cold War." This, Scott argues, could potentially squander U.S. advantages in "critical technologies." In his 5-10 effort, Scott describes advances made in high-speed computer analytic tools utilized in B-2 testing. "More data were acquired on the first six flights of the B-2 program than were recorded throughout the F-16 fighter's entire life at Edwards AFB." Thus, the Air Force had more opportunity to improve the B-2 earlier in its life cycle. Scott's 6-7 article analyzes the new economic realities fostering cooperation between the government and the private sector. Somewhat caustically, he notes, "politicians and bureaucrats now recognize aerospace as a significant, positive contributor in the international balance-of-payments game," whereas previous decisions were based purely on U.S. strategic and defense interests. His brief but excellent 9-6 synopsis of findings by a panel of government and industry experts highlights the frustration felt by both sides at the slow pace of federal lab-technology transfers to the private sector. "Currently, the national laboratories are caught in a no-man's land between traditional nuclear weapons development roles and an uncertain future" cooperating with private industry. Scott's solid grasp of intricate details makes him essential reading for anyone charting the progress of defense technology conversion.

William K. Stevens

The New York Times

★

Science. Whether more professional or better-edited this year, Stevens shows less pro-environmental bias than in the past. Instead of long screeds on the crimes that humans inflict on nature, he now just throws in a line or two about the interaction between people and the environment. Only once does Stevens indulge himself, in an alarmist 1-26 dispatch on how farming, logging, and dams are destroying the ecosystems of the nation's rivers. Because he cites only two sources—one a Washington-based conservation organization, and the other a 1990 study from the Nature Conservancy—the reader does not get a balanced picture. Stevens fashions a neat 4-6 profile of Dr. Armen Takhtajan, a Russian botanist who "is attempting to sort out and formally classify the world's flowering plants on the basis of their evolutionary relationships." Despite the arcane subject matter, Stevens enables Takhtajan's enterprise to shine through. Two other excursions on botany, 5-11 and 6-22, carefully examine the ideas of translocation of endangered plant species and the controversy over genetically engineered plants. "Of the United States' 20,000 native plants," Stevens warns in the earlier piece, "about 4,200 are threatened with extinction, perhaps 750 of them within a decade." His 8-20 dispatch insightfully reports scientists' surprise regarding the fact that the amount of CFCs in the atmosphere has dropped rapidly, so much so that after the year 2000, "the ozone layer should begin a recovery lasting 50 to 100 years." While Michael Oppenheimer of the Environmental Defense Fund, whom Stevens quotes, thinks more should be done, Stevens steers clear from any noticeable bias himself. And in his eye-opening 12-21 effort, he explains how invertebrates—"the creepies, crawlies and squishies"—keep the earth livable by maintaining "the soil structure and fertility on which plant growth and thus all higher organisms depend." Stevens adds that "the world is experiencing a 'catastrophic loss' of invertebrate life as natural areas are destroyed and degraded." Like the worm in an apple, the reader must be watchful of this trend in Stevens's writing.

David Stipp

The Wall Street Journal

★★½

Science, Boston. Although Stipp sometimes strikes out in his day-to-day reporting, he hits home runs with his feature stories. His eye for unusual angles leads him to quirky stories that both amuse and intrigue. Two outstanding front-page pieces aim to poke holes in environmentalist credos. Stipp's 9-16 story contests the charge that lead poisoning poses the biggest environmental threat to children. "Removing lead paint in houses has become a booming business. And lead is fast replacing asbestos as the toxic tort king....But even as pressures mount to get the lead out, evidence is emerging that activists have overstated the threat. In fact, U.S. citizens' average lead levels have plummeted more than two-thirds since the mid-1970s, following bans on lead paint and gasoline." His outstanding 3-22 feature examines California regulations that label a pervasive natural substance as carcinogenic. "Crystalline silica, the primary ingredient of sand and rocks, looms as perhaps the scariest cancer demon

ever....Silica...makes up about a quarter of the earth's crust." Stipp notes that beach sand packaged for sandboxes in California now comes with warnings of cancer. And Stipp indicts environmentalists for endorsing the labeling of silica as carcinogenic despite their inability to scientifically pinpoint its toxic nature. "The official lumping of beach sand in the same category as carcinogens such as dioxin, critics contend, suggests as nothing before that the regulatory system tends to cry wolf when it comes to cancer." Stipp's seriousness can sometimes give way to more offbeat subjects. He shows this lighter side in his 8-18 story about killer cats terrorizing a small Massachusetts town, "a story Stephen King might have dreamed up—and rejected as too fanciful." In his 4-16 look at the mating habits of salamanders, Stipp provides a felicitous description of the amphibians. "Black, six inches long and spotted with bright yellow polka dots, they resemble baby alligators in overtight clown suits." However, his day-to-day reporting, particularly on genetics, fails to impress. Stipp, unfortunately, sticks to the narrow confines of these stories, providing little analysis and rarely commenting on broader implications. When the quality of these stories approaches that of his front-page efforts, Stipp will join the ranks of top-flight journalists.

Michael Waldholz
The Wall Street Journal
★★★

Pharmaceuticals and genetics. Waldholz distanced himself from many rivals by refusing to traffic in the hysteria over soaring pharmaceutical prices as the issue jumped to the fore in 1993. Covering the daily maneuverings of the nation's drug makers and President Clinton's price-control advocates, he provides accurate, factual accounts of their ongoing tug-of-war. In a rare appearance on the editorial page, 3-30, Waldholz superbly crystallizes the bumbling of the leading manufacturers. "The big drug makers have failed miserably to explain themselves to the American people. Fiercely competitive drug companies are accustomed to zealously guarding pricing policies, as well as almost everything else they do. It's no wonder that drug company executives have been unprepared and ill-equipped to parry price-gouging charges that have succeeded in tarring a business whose central objective...is about as worthy as any." Kicking off the *Journal*'s front-page series, "Mapping the Mind," Waldholz writes a fascinating 9-29 piece about a scientific study of emotions that attempts to decipher clues on the workings of the brain. "Powerful feelings such as hate, love, disgust, joy, shame, pleasure, envy, euphoria and guilt, difficult to define even in poetry, are nearly impossible to measure and dissect in laboratory settings." With the momentous discoveries in 1993 of genes for colon cancer, Huntington's disease, and Lou Gehrig's disease, Waldholz accurately credits the federally funded Human Genome Project for its hand in the breakthroughs—a point neglected by many other writers. He offers trenchant analysis, 3-24, on the discovery of the gene for Huntington's disease, which will soon lead to a test for determining if one carries it. "Whether to take the test, however, poses a dilemma for families haunted by the gene. For those who find they didn't inherit the gene, the test will provide immeasurable relief. But for those who discover they lost the genetic roll of the dice, the test will cause immeasurable distress, because there's no treatment for the disorder." In a 10-26 piece on the halt in the cloning of human embryos—due to ethical concerns—Waldholz does not go far enough in spelling out those concerns. For the most part, however, Waldholz delivers solid reporting on genetics to complement his stellar coverage of the nation's drug makers.

John Noble Wilford
The New York Times
★★★

Science. Wilford covers astronomy, archaeology, and paleontology with a zeal and enthusiasm rarely seen in a daily reporter. Remarkably, he's at home in all three of these diverse subjects. In his captivating 3-2 dispatch on how the moon helps to both stabilize the Earth's orbit and regulate its climates, Wilford muses, "although scientists did not say that a moonless Earth would necessarily have been lifeless, it would certainly have been a bleaker place—and not just for lovers and song writers." Drawing on his extensive experience, 8-24, Wilford places the communications failure of the Mars Observer in humorous perspective.

"So many Russian spacecraft in the 1960's experienced disabling communications losses as they approached Mars...that engineers in their frustration began imagining eerie extra-terrestrial forces. Scientists at the Jet Propulsion Laboratory often joked about the presence of a Great Galactic Ghoul preying on spacecraft in the vicinity of Mars." Two of his efforts on the repair of the Hubble telescope, 11-30 and 12-7, typify Wilford's style. The first clearly explains the shuttle mission's goals, as well as the political stakes for NASA; the second vividly depicts the astronauts' performance. No less colorful are Wilford's explorations of ancient worlds. In his marvelously written 4-20 dispatch, he reveals much about one of the "most controversial issues in paleontology today: the history of avian evolution and early flight." Wilford describes the "discovery of a strange new type of dinosaur....The 75-million-year-old fossil animal about the size of a turkey, was actually a flightless bird [some paleontologists] contend, and it perched firmly on the evolutionary tree as a transitional figure between certain carnivorous dinosaurs and modern birds." Wilford's wry humor comes through in his colorful 6-29 exercise demystifying the ruins of Teotihuacan, north of Mexico City. "Another aspect setting the civilization apart from most other prehistoric American cultures is the fact that its supreme deity was a goddess....In some less beneficent poses, the supreme goddess is associated with military imagery, heart sacrifice and destruction. Evidence of the mass sacrifice of more than 200 young soldiers has been discovered at the Temple of the Feathered Serpent. So much for earlier ideas of Teotihuacan as a peaceful theocracy run by priests." No matter which particular issue he explores, Wilford's fascination with his topics comes through clearly.

Ron Winslow

The Wall Street Journal

★½

Medicine. Focusing on medicine and the health-care industry, Winslow likes to toss around facts and figures—but his articles often lack depth. While considerable data flows through his 5-6 piece about "a group of health-care purchasers and providers [who] developed the first national standards for comparing the quality and performance of health maintenance organizations and similar health plans," the article ultimately falls flat. In his 3-25 dispatch, Winslow skims over all the aspects of a non-invasive technique to detect heart disease and notes that more testing must be done because the technique is not 100 percent effective. In his 7-22 article comparing atherectomy and angioplasty, he provides a checklist of the pros and cons of the two rival techniques for clearing the arteries that supply blood to the heart. In two pieces, 1-20 and 10-8, Winslow notes that hospitals and doctors are finally warming up to the idea of computers. The earlier piece reveals that doctors using computers instead of paper and pen can lower the cost of treatment for their patients by up to 13 percent. The computer shows the price of different drugs and tests and gives information that the pharmaceutical companies don't provide about their competition. Winslow's 10-8 article gives the low-down on the health-care industry's growing use of computers. "For most industries, upgrading computer technology is business as usual. But in health-care, it's a seminal event." Because much work is still done on paper or 3x5 index cards, "'most of the medical records in this country,'" one doctor remarks, "'constitute a fire hazard.'" Despite the wordiness of his 11-3 effort, this front-page article stands out as one of Winslow's better efforts. He discusses ways to reduce the cost of health care by rooting out steps that "add costs without improving results. The potential savings run to tens of billions of dollars a year." And Winslow's 6-23 dispatch on "medical centers that perform organ-transplant surgery [and] often charge patients or their insurers as much as three times what it costs to acquire the organs" begins strongly, but fizzles out at the end. Unfortunately, the same could be said for much of Winslow's work.

★ FOREIGN ★

Rick Atkinson

The Washington Post

★★½

Berlin. With the publication of *Crusade: An Account of the Persian Gulf War,* Atkinson moves to Europe, where he turns his considerable reporting and writing skills to the reconstruction of eastern Germany. He works hard to dig up little-covered stories, which he endows with broad implications. In his clever 8-18 dispatch on the effort to modernize the eastern German phone system, Atkinson contrasts the 1920s technology currently in use with the modern system replacing it. "Lights blink, switches clink, thousands of moving parts jiggle this way and that, giving the room a slightly wacky Rube Goldberg ambiance....The [new] room is quiet except for a pleasant hum. New fiber-optic cables snake across the floor, with new data lines and new junction boxes." As the primary work of Treuhandanstalt--the trust agency assigned to sell the 13,000 formerly East German state firms and factories—winds down, Atkinson's shrewd 9-26 piece highlights some of the few remaining bargains. "Investors with $600,000 to $2.5 million might consider the Havelberg cheese factory (specializing in Brie and Camembert), the Zwickau gold and silver jewelry foundry, or the Salzwedel meat and sausage plant, complete with 'blanching chamber' and 'emergency slaughterhouse.'" In one of his weaker efforts—a 12-21 profile of Rolf Kutzmutz, a former communist who narrowly lost a run-off election for mayor of Potsdam—Atkinson lets his subject slide on his political past. Atkinson also fails to press him on how he would achieve his stated goals. "Kutzmutz and most other politicians in his party profess to have shed their discredited Marxist doctrine for a more mainstream ideology not unlike that of the left-leaning Social Democrats. 'You can vote for me without turning red,' he told voters. 'My main promises are to work for affordable rents and to create jobs.'" During a brief stint in Somalia, 11-26, an agitated Atkinson blasts the creature comforts of the UN compound in which soldiers and aid-workers isolate themselves from the fury and despair on the streets. "There is electric power and a telephone network and a new sewer system. A $60,000 shark net erected Wednesday protects the beach. The general store peddles single-malt whisky, espresso machines and pornographic videos....A senior UN official estimated this week that less than $100 million of the $1.5 billion will be spent on genuine development assistance." Wherever stationed, Atkinson zeroes in on the telling detail that illuminates the larger picture.

P.T. Bangsberg

The Journal of Commerce

★★½

Hong Kong. With a broad range of knowledge and a highly discerning eye, Bangsberg consistently brings intelligence and common sense to his work. In addition to the standard *JC* fare of industry-specific stories, he drafts clever features on the Southeast Asian economic environment and its international implications. In his compelling 2-3 article on the grandiose Three Gorges project to dam the Yangtze River, Bangsberg provides awe-inspiring descriptions, as well as extensive statistical information. "Assuming it is finished, the dam will convert the boiling waters of the Yangtze into a placid lake hundreds of miles long. That will flood 60,000 acres that now produce 40 percent of China's agricultural output....It will [also] mean displacing more than 1 million people." Bangsberg's well-sourced 6-22 piece focuses on a Chinese government report criticizing joint ventures between Chinese and foreign businesses for not living up to their high promises. The article spells out the government's major complaints, which could lead to tightened regulation of such enterprises. As Bangsberg explains, the report denounces accounting tricks used by firms to get around a "two tier system" of monetary exchange whereby hard currency enters the country at one rate but, by law, leaves at a lower one. Piecing together signals and bits of information from the Chinese government, 12-6, Bangsberg relates that for the first time, the government plans to invite foreign construction firms to help rebuild the nation's massive public housing. The plan, he says, reflects profoundly shifting attitudes. "Liu Zhifeng, a vice minister in charge of reform, said the 'only way to alleviate the housing shortage is to make housing a transferable commodity. The only way to achieve that goal is to sell publicly owned housing or raise rents.'...The reform would change rent increases from symbolic to real." In a 6-11 effort, Bangsberg again deals with China's economic growth. Recognizing that "the prospect of high wages and foreign travel will be highly alluring" to poor Chinese from rural areas, the government intends to open 20 maritime academies over the next several years to supply the world with much-needed skilled seamen. The only drawback, Bangsberg finds, will be coercing flush farm boys back to sea after a few runs pad their pockets. Ensconced in vivid detail, Bangsberg's work enhances readers' awareness of growing enterprise in China.

Lionel Barber

Financial Times

★★

Brussels. Providing excellent detail, Barber's concise reporting shines when it includes a bit of analysis. His cerebral and demanding style appeals more to the expert than the general reader, as he confidently covers the intricacies of European economic diplomacy, including the myriad concurrent negotiations and the membership rolls of any number of European trade alliances. In his probing 3-15 article on U.S.-European Community trade negotiations, Barber provides the details of a major rift opening during procurement contract talks in which EC members claim they lack access to U.S. telecom and transport contracts. "The U.S. claims that bidding opportunities worth $16 billion were offered to EC contractors under the GATT government procurement code in 1990, compared with $7.8 billion in EC contracts open to U.S. companies. The EC agrees that in absolute terms the 1990 GATT figures confirm that the U.S. is more generous, but Brussels officials argue that the value of EC contracts open to U.S. companies rose sharply between 1985 and 1990, while the value of U.S. contracts fell over the same period." When currency speculators threaten to destroy the EC's exchange rate mechanism, 8-2, Barber shrewdly reports the perceived gravity of the situation. "The presence of politicians...showed that this time everyone grasped an essential truth. The latest crisis was too important to leave to the technocrats alone." Barber then presciently lays out the political repercussions of various measures the EC might adopt to control the speculation. In a darkly humorous but newsworthy 7-21 piece on the EC budget process, Barber shows how Community President Jacques Delors of France, ill and bedridden with sciatica, saves the day. "Summoned from his bed, Mr. Delors savaged the junior ministers present for being anti-Community and threatened to expose their greed to assembled reporters. Then after a performance worthy of Tammany Hall's finest, Mr. Delors...persuaded the rebel states to accept the new guidelines." In his pedestrian 12-3 effort, Barber flatly reports the significant news, for GATT watchers, that U.S. and EC negotiators are near a deal on farm subsidies in the latest GATT round. "In prospect is a deal providing improved access for U.S. and other farm exporters to Europe's market for grains, meat, dairy products and 'other specialty crops.'" Despite occasional dryness, Barber invariably shares with readers his tremendous grasp of European Community events.

John Battersby

The Christian Science Monitor

★★

Johannesburg. After efficiently setting forth an image or idea, Battersby uses elegantly simple and precise prose to develop his stories. However, he seldom offers contrary perspectives unless the topic obviously calls for them, nor does he attempt to enrich his presentation with commentary from observers or experts. In his 10-18 article on the awarding of the Nobel Peace prize to South African President F.W. de Klerk and African National Congress leader Nelson Mandela, Battersby shrewdly notes how important

the two men have become not only to each other, but to ending apartheid. "Until formal negotiations between the ruling National Party and the ANC got underway at the end of 1991, the fragile democracy process was almost entirely dependent on the relationship between the two leaders. When crises occurred—as they frequently did—all eyes would focus on the personal chemistry between the two men as they disappeared behind closed doors to seek a way out." Astutely recognizing that de Klerk represents a minority among heavily divided white Afrikaners, 9-24, Battersby describes a get-acquainted meeting between the right-wing Afrikaner group Volksfront (known as the AVF) and ANC leaders. "The major point of difference between the AVF and the ANC is over the status of an Afrikaner region. The AVF insists it must be almost autonomous in a loose confederal arrangement with other positions. The ANC and the government want the Afrikaners to accept a state under the ultimate authority of a federal government." In his 4-22 interview with UNITA general Arlindo Pena from Kuito, Angola, Battersby relays a Pena commitment that his rebels will abide by a UN-brokered cease-fire only if the governing MPLA accedes to his group's demands. "The MPLA want the resumption of humanitarian aid to be linked to a full and immediate cease-fire. UNITA's more gradual approach calls for a simultaneous suspension of hostilities and a resumption of humanitarian aid to UNITA-held and -besieged towns." Reaching back more than 150 years, 9-9, Battersby incisively contextualizes the specter of Afrikaners seeking protection from potential retribution by a black-ruled government in South Africa. "When the Voortrekkers packed their ox-drawn wagons and began a dangerous journey north from the Cape Province in 1836, they were embarking on a spiritual quest for self-determination that brought them into conflict with the country's black majority. Ironically, some of their descendants are looking to black-ruled states for refuge from what they see as an era of vengeance against the Afrikaner." Wittier than most of his reporting, this telling detail suggests an underutilized skill for Battersby to add to his repertoire.

Henrik Bering-Jensen

Insight

★

Seldom provocative, the strongly conservative Bering-Jensen consolidates a great deal of information acquired from other sources into lengthy, rambling surveys of international affairs. In his 2-8 article on the Clinton foreign-policy team, he recounts the diplomatic history of several key appointees and their positions on major issues with which they formerly dealt, mostly during the Carter years. Bering-Jensen derides Secretary of State Warren Christopher for his continued insistence that Carter-administration diplomacy won the release of the Iranian hostages. Providing no evidence, Bering-Jensen states: "Others have argued that it was the election of Reagan, rather than Christopher's persuasive powers or Iranian inhibitions about violating the international code of conduct, that ultimately persuaded them to release the hostages." Drawing from the experience of the Nuremberg trials, 3-29, Bering-Jensen takes three times more space than necessary to point out the reasons that an international tribunal hoping to prosecute war crimes in Bosnia fails practicality tests. Foremost among them, he argues, is "the mechanism for bringing the war criminals to trial." Regardless, Bering-Jensen concludes, despite all the talk, the UN doesn't seem overly committed to the idea. "[Former U.S. ambassador to the UN headquarters in Geneva Morris B.] Abrams, who assisted at the Nuremberg trials, noted upon his departure that the new commission so far has two attorneys and that at Nuremberg there were 1,170." In his 10-11 piece on the tenuous relationship between U.S. foreign policy and UN initiatives, Bering-Jensen highlights several previously published views on the issue. "The State Department, staffed with many Carter-era officials, is enthusiastic about the UN; some analysts say it has been uneasy about exerting American influence since the Vietnam War period. As *The New Republic*, which has supported Clinton with varying degrees of ardor, put it, the Clinton administration is 'uncomfortable or embarrassed or guilty about' the exercise of American power." Emphasizing the significance of GATT to world trade, 12-13, Bering-Jensen dullishly explores French opposition to the agreement, but renders it insignificant, considering the stakes. "If no agreement is reached by them, the talks will collapse—and that means the end of efforts to bring agricultural trade, intellectual property rights and a host of other crucially important issues under international regulation." With a dearth of original material, Bering-Jensen, despite his magazine's name, offers little insight.

Celestine Bohlen

The New York Times

★★

Moscow. With a solid grasp of the vast social and economic changes in Russia, Bohlen skillfully portrays everyday life among the poor, the rich, and the violent. She seems less intrigued, however, by the nation's political upheavals, which her pedestrian and voluminous dispatches do little to elucidate. In her 10-4 reports on the Yeltsin-Parliament conflict, for example, Bohlen meanders, as her focus wanders from bystander to participant to politician without reporting much memorable. In her 2-28 effort, however, she vividly chronicles the hopes and sordid living conditions of residents of one communal apartment about to be privatized and renovated for the nouveau riche. A film director who lived for twenty years in one room—sharing a bathroom, kitchen, and telephone with a hard-drinking policeman, an avant-garde artist, a cleaning lady, her juvenile-delinquent son, and their assorted spouses and guests—is happily moving out. "'All I want,'" he says, "'is to be able to walk into my own bathroom without having to wear rubber boots,' an oblique reference to the encrusted filth typical of a 'kommunalka.'" Bohlen's 7-31 article describes in mouth-watering detail how Russia's new rich spend their wealth. A jewelry salesman in downtown Moscow reports that $6,000 Cartier watches displayed in the morning sell out by lunchtime. Ably surveying the rise of "Russian mobsters" and organized crime —with gangland hits now common at midday—Bohlen highlights the incestuous relationship between the new capitalists and the criminal world. "Some of Moscow's best-known business executives, once hailed as the standard-bearers of a new era, are now fugitives, sought by the Russian police and prosecutors for defrauding the state or their partners, or both." Such sordid behavior also extends to politicians, one of whom, Bohlen notes, 3-28, accused Yeltsin of operating "'as instructed by Western intelligence services,' and suggested that he retire to the island of St. Helena, where Napoleon died in exile." With this kind of work, Bohlen displays her ear for the bizarre and reveals a bit of the crazy quilt of Russian political and social life.

William Branigin

The Washington Post

★½

Hanoi. More concerned with the official take on events than their practical effects, Branigin nevertheless reports solidly and efficiently from developing countries in Southeast Asia. His well-sourced 1-15 article on the breakup of the communist rebels in the Philippines provides plenty of details about the emerging factions, but never conveys the underlying cause of the division. Branigin inundates the reader with data in his uninspired and choppy 4-18 piece, written from Honolulu, on the rising demand for oil in Southeast Asia. He fails to show that the region's demand for oil will necessarily lead to a closer relationship between countries in Southeast Asia and the Persian Gulf, or why, as he suggests, this will create security problems for the U.S. Instead, he reports observations on the

China reacts to the awarding of the 2000 Olympics to Sydney.

oil situation by "experts" who speculate—as experts will—about the future price of oil and the wisdom of Indonesian and Japanese efforts to achieve energy self-sufficiency. Branigin seems onto something in a 2-3 report on Cambodian logging. "UN and diplomatic sources say the Phnom Penh government, which controls about 85 percent of Cambodia's territory, is responsible for a far greater volume of logging [than the Khmer Rouge] and has been violating the month-old timber ban with impunity." But the effort disappoints as Branigin never develops this promising ecological story beyond a one-line plot padded with quotes from anonymous "UN officials." Traveling to Hanoi, 7-28, Branigin describes nothing of Vietnam beyond what he sees traveling from the airport to the capital. Other than a few trite observations—"the ride is both instructive and fairly agreeable"—Branigin devotes this piece on Vietnamese infrastructure requirements to reviewing 20-year-old conditions under which the U.S. will lift its trade embargo, complete with how much the Senate spent on MIA investigations in 1992. A healthy dose of skepticism or controversy, even at risk of offending those providing him stories, would lift Branigin's efforts.

Marcus W. Brauchli

The Wall Street Journal

★½

Southeast Asia. Despite bouncing around the continent, Brauchli always seems to report at a safe distance from the real action. Readers are left wanting more. In his 6-2 story about modern piracy, he takes a boat ride in the Java Sea but ends up providing only bare speculation about who's behind the pirating. Brauchli throws out various theories on who supports the pirates. However, lacking even a sketch of the perpetrators, the speculation fails and the story falls flat. He gratuitously emphasizes an ecological angle to the story, noting that "the danger that such a vessel could slam into another ship or shore, perhaps with disastrous ecological consequences, is real." In his 4-15 piece on the role of once-shunned political leftists in Hong Kong, Brauchli profiles the Tsang brothers, who serve the Chinese government as advisers to local businesses. Brauchli implies that the cordial reception the pair routinely receives at business gatherings reflects tacit acceptance of their politics rather than a pragmatic response to their government ties, but he provides no evidence to back up his view. Brauchli's cumbersome 11-3 report on growing resentment among the rural Chinese population, as yet unbenefited by the prosperity in coastal areas, meanders from town to town and from economic to cultural concerns. Losing readers in obscure detail, Brauchli nevertheless conveys the spirit of the discontent. "With the fading of hard-line, antireligious communist government and the emergence of a more open, economically focused society, minorities who long were forcibly integrated into China's mainstream have started demanding greater respect for their separate traditions." In a detailed and amusing 5-10 report from Calcutta, Brauchli discovers a satellite television enterprise penetrating several Asian societies and cultures. "An NBC News crew, on assignment with Burma's Karen insurgents in the jungles along the Thai border, noticed a satellite dish set up near a mess tent. At first they thought it was a communications apparatus. Then, they heard music. Inside the tent, the guerrillas were glued to MTV." Despite his eye for the unusual, Brauchli rarely conveys a strong, substantive grasp of his subjects.

Ethan Bronner

The Boston Globe

Middle East correspondent. With an eye for the telling detail, Bronner combines even-handed reporting with a strong knowledge of his territory. He tracks down the right sources—including Yasir Arafat in a post-peace-accord interview—and needs only gutsier questioning to be among the best at his work. In his lyrical 9-14 portrayal of the East Jerusalem peace celebrations, Bronner describes "men on horses waving flags the size of bedsheets rac[ing] around a track while a drum corps marched," and notes amusingly that at a gathering of dignitaries, the words to the unfamiliar Palestinian national anthem had to be handed out so that everyone could join in. In his 10-24 article, Bronner observes Palestine's economic optimism as sometimes guarded and sometimes euphoric. One positive sign, he notes, is that land prices in parts of the West Bank have already quadrupled. Another "genuine reason for hope," Bronner adds, is the notable fact that more Palestinians—some 18 per thousand—complete college than any other Arab nationality. On 10-2, Bronner profiles a surprisingly debonair Fathi Shkaki—general secretary of the Damascus-based Islamic Jihad—who with others is attempting to form "an alternative PLO and fight the existing accord." But Bronner doesn't probe deeply enough to assess the viability or potential success of the new organization, nor does he press Shkaki, who blithely approves of suicide bombers and revenge murders of Israeli civilians. In his 10-31 interview with Arafat—dressed in "crisp fatigues, pistol on his hip and keffiyeh headdress folded smartly in the shape of Palestine"—Bronner sounds slightly awed and lets the PLO chief get away with stock answers. When asked about his ability to lead democratically, Arafat "compared himself to France's Charles de Gaulle, Israel's David Ben-Gurion and Egypt's [Gamel Abdel] Nasser, saying they too were leaders who controlled every detail of their countries." With Arafat presenting himself as a sensitive statesman, Bronner does little to balance the picture. In Bronner's 11-12 examination of press censorship in Jordan, he again fails to push hard enough. While aides contend that King Hussein "wants the system reformed," the London-based *Al Hayat* had been "banned three times in the past week." How earnestly the King is seeking reform never clearly emerges. What separates Bronner from peak performance is a sharpness that should develop with more experience on this beat.

James Brooke

The New York Times

★★½

Rio de Janeiro. Reporting mainly from Peru and Brazil, Brooke shrewdly balances his hard news reporting with the cultural, social, and historical undercurrents driving events. Although his pieces can run a bit long, his comprehensive focus generally enhances his work. Lighting the backdrop of a modern tragedy, 9-7, Brooke reveals the root causes of the war between gold miners and Indians raging along the Venezuelan border in Boa Vista, Brazil. He astutely finds much of the hostility the result of a "military style" government crackdown on squatting miners. "Evicting thousands of miners from Indian lands, the campaigns had a disastrous effect on the regional economy. Gold Street, once a thriving avenue of 55 gold shops, is now pockmarked with shuttered shops." In a quirky 7-13 look at the dangers of unnatural intervention in an ecosystem, Brooke ominously describes the proximity of a crocodile farm to a major inland waterway system in southwestern Brazil. Experts, he notes, predict the one-ton, 20-foot-long African crocodiles—imported from Zimbabwe to be raised for their hides—will inevitably escape their fortress-like confines. When that happens, Brooke adds, the colossal amphibians will wreak havoc on the environment. In his 1-25 article on the proliferation of diseases in Latin America, Brooke uninquisitively reports figures provided by hospital representatives and researchers vying for AIDS-relief funds. He casually cites the figure of one million infected people in the U.S. —a spurious number that hasn't changed since first reported by AIDS-awareness groups in the mid-1980s. But Brooke provides rich historical detail in his fascinating 8-15 article on land restitution in Brazil. Because of a clause in the 1988 Brazilian constitution, Brooke explains, the descendants of nineteenth-century fugitive slaves may gain title to lands settled by their ancestors. "In the Amazon, slaves escaping the cocoa plantations of Santarem started to flee up the Trombetas River in the early 1800s. After each armed incursion in pursuit, they retreated deeper into the forest, portaging their possessions around river rapids." Accentuating his reports time and again with this kind of pithy observation, Brooke's stories define for readers the character of the people he covers.

David Buchan

Financial Times

★★½

Paris bureau chief. With his facile style and attention to detail, Buchan adds flair to such soporific matters as the French social-security burden. This year he focuses most of his energies on the transition by the new French government headed by Prime Minister Edouard Balladur and his neo-Gaullist Rally for the Republic (RPR) party. In his 4-1 profile of the administration, Buchan portrays the new French leaders as strong supporters of the European Community. After probing the background of several officials, he speculates about their likely roles—and the potential turf wars—in the new government. "Mr. Edmond Alphandéry is effectively the country's new finance minister, but nominally only responsible for the 'economy,' with the word 'finance' excised from his title. This reflects the determination of Mr. Balladur, himself a former finance minister, to exercise a strong role on monetary policy." In his 4-14 article on the Bank of France struggle to keep its vast powers as it dissociates from the government, Buchan shrewdly argues that the bank will likely retain broad controls over monetary policy and banking regulation, mainly because the finance minister has long favored that policy. He reports, however, that a treasury official "has openly suggested that the central bank suffers from a potential conflict of interest between its job of controlling liquidity and its role of lender-of-last-resort." In his wise 5-11 analysis of the French social-security system, Buchan posits that the sorts of superficial reforms proposed by the Prime Minister will do little to alleviate the country's massive social-security debt. "The problem which Mr. Balladur is tackling is that France puts more of the burden of its welfare system on its active workforce than any other EC country.... This has given French employers a particular financial incentive to shed labor, so that 3 million are now out of a job." Noting that Mr. Balladur's popularity causes tension among his intra-party rivals, 12-21, Buchan captures the pointed rhetoric already flying two years before the 1995 presidential elections. "Mr. Jean-Louis Debre, deputy secretary general of the RPR and a die-hard backer of Jacques Chirac... yesterday criticized Mr. Francois Léotard, the defense minister, and Mrs. Simone Veil, the social affairs minister, for 'missing a fine occasion to shut up,' when in separate TV interviews on Sunday they praised Mr. Balladur's presidential potential." In his precise and articulate reporting, Buchan's profound understanding of French political tradition clearly emerges.

John Burns

The New York Times

★★½

Sarajevo. Chronicling the devastation of Bosnia, Burns reports with a steady, dispassionate voice. Although possessing a keen eye for the details that portray individuals, Burns seldom interviews the victims of war. Instead, he treats them anonymously as Muslims or Serbs. In his 8-8 profile of Ratko Mladic, head of the Bosnian Serb forces, Burns finds a man of "personal charm" and courtesy—and a liar. "Referring to allegations by the Bosnian Government that as many as 30,000 Muslim women had been raped, [Mladic] added: 'We would all have to be supermen to do this. We would have to be sexual maniacs worthy of an entry in the *Guinness Book of Records*.'" Burns then depersonalizes the situation by referring to government reports of rape rather than the charges of the many victims who have spoken to the Western press. His shrewd 7-11 dispatch notes that 1,500 people have been killed or wounded in Sarajevo in the two months since the UN designated it a "safe area." Burns finds the term both the butt of grim jokes and a sign of the growing resentment toward blustery and ineffective Western governments. "[Safe area]... has become a buzzword for Western hypocrisy....A woman [in a central market] shouted at a reporter: 'go away. You are all liars and cheats.' Children have begun to spit at the armored cars that Western reporters use to move about the city." Con-

veying the tragic drama of the downfall of the city of Srebrenica, 4-16, Burns focuses on a round of Serbian shelling that killed 14 children playing soccer. Although he talks to none of the witnesses or families, he poignantly captures the pathetic image of UN commander Gen. Phillippe Morillon making his way to Srebrenica for a heroic final stand. "When he was about 15 miles from the city, his armored vehicle was attacked by 300 Serbian civilians who hammered steel spikes into its bulletproof windows, slashed the tires, ripped off its radio aerials and United Nations flags and tried to dismantle its machine gun." Stressing the anxiety caused by a shoot-out between Sarajevo police and a well-known gangster, 10-31, Burns blames Serbian nationalists for the preponderance of violent crime in the city, but offers no evidence. "The costly resources that underpin the Sarajevo gang leader are smuggled into the city at night by Serbian gangs with links to political and military leaders on the Serbian side." Commendable for braving his horrific assignment, Burns would do well to occasionally paint some faces into his landscapes.

Steven Butler

U.S.News & World Report

★

Tokyo. Lacking insight and local perspective, Butler relies on statistics and lively writing to bolster his dispatches from various spots in Southeast Asia. His accessible prose makes for quick reading, but he avoids all the challenges that make for a compelling journey. Butler's 3-1 article on U.S. gains over Japan in the semiconductor industry contains all the relevant figures on American growth and Japanese decline, but never mentions that U.S.-Japan trade in semiconductors falls under a policy of *managed* rather than *fair* trade. This significant distinction means that outcomes of the semiconductor trade between the two countries are set by agreement rather than by the market. In his 8-2 report on the Japanese elections, Butler fails to probe beyond the numbers. The confusing election results beg further explanation; but, except for predicting instability, Butler offers only a few undeveloped and extraneous facts. "The average age of the new parliamentarians in the three new conservative parties is 49, compared with 57 for the [Liberal Democratic party]." Butler's lively 8-23 portrait of Toyota finds a car company overstaffed and over-specialized, with slowing demand and a strong yen raising the cost of its cars in the American market. Although the piece fairly portrays the numbers crunch at Toyota, Butler only alludes to the culture shock caused by the prospect of layoffs and shifting personnel in a society where absolute allegiance to a company has always been rewarded by a lifetime job guarantee and seniority-based wage increases. Butler's simplistic conclusion, while pithy, reveals his lack of sensitivity to the cultural issue. "Detroit's once beleaguered Big Three drove through Big Trouble not long ago and are just starting to get back on track; now it's time for many Japanese car makers to take a similar trip." Butler's reliance on economic statistics works well in his 11-22 series leading up to the Seattle summit of Pacific Rim nations. He notes shrewdly that the end of the Cold War and the economic expansion of Southeast Asian nations has tilted the scales. "In 1986, 42 percent of exports from the Four Tigers [Taiwan, Singapore, South Korea, and Hong Kong] went to the United States; by 1991, the proportion fell to 27 percent and the four economies' total trade more than doubled." While sometimes enlightening, Butler too often takes the view that statistics drive rather than follow events.

Steve Coll

The Washington Post

★★★

International. With his vividly written articles, Coll transports the reader to Turkish bazaars and Kazakhstan oil fields. Much more than travelogues, though, his dispatches examine political and economic forces that influence events half a world away. In his superb 3-7 report, Coll notes that ethnic clashes are not always about religion. "In a war where the spoils of conquest often are limited to family homes and loot seized from ethnic rivals, Serb fighters who took control of a swath of eastern Croatia are exploiting one of the richest prizes in the ravaged Balkans: active oil fields that once pumped 5,000 barrels of crude oil per day." Moving from crude oil to olive oil, Coll weaves a dense 10-31 story on Mafia informant Tommaso Buscetta, whose testimony helped convict many of Italy's most wanted. "[The informant] broke

down La Cosa Nostra's barriers of secrecy. He provided organization and membership charts. He explained codes and interpreted systems of decision making. But his most valued role...was as a kind of oracle. His account of the Sicilian Mafia as a hierarchical, monolithic, highly rational enterprise became known as 'the Buscetta theorem.'" Covering a string of bombings in Bombay, 3-22, Coll likens the terrorist actions to a germ eating away at the city's economy. "After several months of violence, the virus has deeply infected a metropolis that long prided itself on being an urban whole greater than the sum of it diverse religious and ethnic parts. It is threatening to reduce frenetic Bombay, often called 'a mini India,' into a divided polyglot of angry component pieces." Tackling the potential spread of nuclear arms in Central Europe, 5-15, Coll bluntly discusses the possibility of nuclear terrorism. "In the meantime, aspiring nuclear states such as Iran are shopping for opportunities, scattered smugglers are moving radioactive and sensitive nuclear-related materials to the West, and the original vision of a region free of nuclear weapons on Russia's borders is becoming more and more blurred." Few correspondents understand the international scene and its significance to American readers better than Coll.

Craig Covault

Aviation Week & Space Technology

★★★

Paris bureau chief. Bringing his expertise in aerospace technology to the Paris bureau, Covault provides excellent insight on international aerospace issues. He specializes in the former Soviet Union, particularly on the nature of future Russian cooperation with the West and on Russian technology's possible application to Western space projects. Carefully detailing the struggle in Russia between civilians and the military authorities over control of the space program, 2-1, Covault explains that at stake are millions of dollars in potential launch and cooperative revenues from Western countries and Japan. In his 3-15 report, Covault predicts that dissension could threaten future U.S.-Russian collaboration just when the Clinton administration, seeking to cut costs, is undergoing "a reexamination...of how greater synergy can be created between the U.S. and Russian [space] station programs." Extending the cost-cutting theme to Mars exploration, 4-12, Covault provides the reader with a vivid snapshot."Strong new international cooperation is needed to meld duplicative Mars efforts, replan strategy in light of the Soviet collapse and to mount effective missions in spite of the cost crisis affecting all the world's space agencies." Shifting venues, Covault displays his versatility and fine reporting skills in his 7-12 piece on the economics of defense. He reports allegations that British defense policy "had been dictated more by the British Treasury than strategy"—a problem, he notes, common to all Western countries in which the allocation of the "peace dividend" has taken precedence over military security. In his 10-4 report, Covault finds that budget concerns of European Space Agency (ESA) member nations have forced a reexamination of launch priorities. A formal strategy report, he states, will be issued to "give ESA flexibility to work with the U.S. and Russia on a revised [space] station design—but also to enable ESA to go it alone in manned flight if NASA or Russia falter." With more in-depth analysis and a sharper writing style, Covault has improved since 1992. No one else provides such astute coverage of the burgeoning international cooperation on space exploration.

John-Thor Dahlburg

Los Angeles Times

★½

Moscow. Except for rare examples, Dahlburg's writing lacks one of the two important ingredients expected of foreign correspondents—the insider's perspective or the outsider's analysis. Clumsy prose often clutters his reports, as in his 3-21 account of the political battle between President Boris Yeltsin and Parliament. "And, as a sort of booby trap to further undermine Yeltsin's waning legitimacy, before recessing one week ago, the Congress acted to set the wheels of the impeachment process turning if Yeltsin tried to unilaterally call a referendum, as he now has." Dahlburg repeatedly writes stories about Russia's power struggles and never analyzes the outcome should either side win. However, he produces several stories that effectively illustrate the nation's hardships. In his

6-6 article on Russia's flourishing drug trade, he notes, "Granted, the narcotics problems have not reached 'Miami Vice' levels. But many Russians see their country at the stage where America was in the 'flower power' era of the late 1960s, when marijuana, hashish, LSD and other drugs zoomed in popularity." In his prescient 8-22 story, Dahlburg foretells a strong electoral showing for nationalistic anti-reformists. "Two years after the Soviet Communist hard-liners tried but failed to seize control of the Kremlin, two years after Russia's president banned Communist activities on Russian soil, the Reds again are the biggest organized political force in the land." In the aftermath of the G-7 meeting in Japan, 7-10, Dahlburg assesses Russia's desire to join the West in trade. "But Yeltsin also came to Tokyo to urge a commitment by the G-7 to end restrictions dating back to the Cold War on Russian-produced goods. It is a potentially explosive issue in Russia, where many disillusioned citizens feel the West was happy to witness the fall of communism but does little to boost democratic and market-oriented change." When he sticks to features, Dahlburg provides articles worth reading.

Juanita Darling

Los Angeles Times

★★½

Mexico City. In a year when both sides of the NAFTA debate spout hyperbole and half-truths about Mexico, Darling digs beneath the rhetoric and finds a vibrant if troubled country struggling with its growing pains. Her lively, straightforward style complements her insightful reporting. In her 5-24 piece on the effects of recently implemented Mexican customs regulations, Darling recounts the anxiety among small-time importers with goods stuck at the Mexican border. She deftly balances the complaints of inexperienced business owners against the fact that anti-dumping regulations reflect further maturation of Mexican trade policy. "The freewheeling atmosphere that followed the easing of restrictions in the late 1980s and allowed small-scale entrepreneurs to build a flourishing cross-border trade has gradually been replaced by formal rules and procedures." In a keen twist, 8-21, Darling highlights Mexican concern about the concessions President Carlos Salinas de Gortari's makes to the Clinton administration in order to secure NAFTA. With elections looming, she writes, residents of towns dependent on the backflow of U.S. dollars claim Salinas will face repercussions if he agrees to construct border barricades that will further restrict Mexican crossing. An 8-23 piece on the Mexican cola wars, co-authored by George White, doesn't sufficiently follow through on the most interesting angle of PepsiCo's heavy reliance on local promotions to increase its market share—the difficulty of running giveaways in foreign countries. When prizes fail to arrive promptly, Darling notes, all Pepsi can do is apologize, prompting a company executive to comment, "'Eventually everyone did get their prizes, but in a small town this looks like fraud.'" Defying their roles in a patriarchal society, 6-29, Darling discovers Mexican women whose demand for better living conditions finally pays off. "Like women in other developing nations, poor Mexican women have found that to fulfill their traditional roles of caring for their families, they have to leave their homes and become activists....Last month, [activist Pilar] Lopez and her neighbors moved into their pastel pink houses and threw a party in the parking lot." Darling stays out of her stories but never seems detached. By reporting what she sees, rather than just what she's told, she presents an intriguing and multi-dimensional portrait of Mexico.

John Darnton

The New York Times

★★

London bureau. While short on articles that capture the Brits' plucky view of the world, Darnton capably analyzes the European scene. Though based in London, he isn't afraid to tackle larger issues that carry weight outside the British Isles. In his 3-4 interview with former Polish leader Gen. Wojciech Jaruzelski, Darnton sympathetically portrays him as caught between a world that no longer exists and a world that wants nothing to do with him. "Some still see him as a lackey for comrades in the former Soviet Union, someone who stepped in to do their dirty work in suppressing the mass movement for freedom and democracy that [Lech] Walesa's Solidarity trade union released." Darnton exuberantly covers

Britain's vote to ratify the Treaty on European Unity, 5-21. "Tonight's move represented the moment that Britain, often Europe's odd-man out, decided to throw in its lot with ancient enemies and work for a united region that would have greater weight in international commerce and world affairs." He pulls no punches in relaying the West's failure to intervene in Bosnia, 6-19. "After months of direct involvement in trying to broker an accord, the United Nations and the European negotiators in Geneva now seem to be simply providing a forum for [Serbian President Slobodan] Milosevic and [Croatian President Franjo] Tudjman to meet to ratify the respective territories won by their respective armies." His well-researched 8-10 article assesses Europe's rising tide of unwanted newcomers and the impact of immigrants on the continent since the beginning of the century. "The changes in the ethnic makeup of Western Europe are already irrevocable. For generations Pakistanis have lived in Britain, Algerians in France and Turks in Germany, and even though they are regarded by some people as alien, they are there to stay." Darnton delivers his best stories when he examines the big picture.

Giovanni de Briganti

Defense News

★★½

Paris bureau, European editor. An expert on Western European defense, de Briganti possesses a keen insider's perspective on post-Cold War military and political issues. He delves deeply into the implications of defense cuts and the manner in which militaries plan to cope with them. In his 1-18/24 report, de Briganti provides excellent detail and maintains a healthy skepticism on Dutch plans to cut defense spending while improving readiness through a "shift from a conscript force to a professional army, a key element in the government plan, [which] will allow a smaller number of military units to permanently be kept at full strength." De Briganti recognizes that the result may not be as positive as expected. He thoroughly analyzes the trade-offs between "guns and butter," 2-8/14, noting that the French are reducing military outlays "as part of a government plan to pay off the...$3.6 billion deficit run up by the national Social Security health-care insurance plan." De Briganti probes another aspect of defense cuts, 3-29/4-4, outlining the ongoing difficulties of funding the European Fighter Aircraft (EFA) program. Appropriated money will be spent by April, he notes, causing "a chain reaction that would halt payments to industry and thus stop development." This would make the EFA another in a series of military programs endangered by a lack of funding. De Briganti strikes a more hopeful chord in his intriguing 6-7/13 account of cooperation between European aircraft companies on a new civil-transport aircraft that "underscores the determination of European countries to increase cooperation despite repeated setbacks." Such cooperation is essential, he notes, in this era of budget cuts. De Briganti's insightful 11-29/12-5 report analyzes recent attempts—and failures—of European nations to come up with a common security policy. He finds that in spite of the appearance of resolve over military intervention in the former Yugoslavia, "Europe's threat to use force is accompanied by provisos and ambiguities that dilute its credibility." Providing a fine overview of important strategic developments throughout Western Europe, de Briganti's reports display a firm grasp on the argument for continuing U.S. cooperation with this region.

Judy Dempsey

Financial Times

★★★

Bonn. With street-level reporting on German employer-labor relations, Dempsey provides a useful backdrop to the monetary policy struggles of the European Community. Moving north this year from the former Yugoslavia, she masterfully defines the central issues of her stories. Dempsey gets to the crux of every debate, always allowing each side to offer its perspective. In her 1-25 article on the breakdown of talks between the German government and the public-sector trade union, Dempsey astutely reports that upward pressure on wages counterbalances pressure to cut interest rates for fear of spurring inflation above the current four percent rate. She concludes that the risk of pricing eastern German workers out of the market with pay increases gets offset by the stronger desire of workers to remain employed. "The consensus among economic institutes is that individual enterprises will opt for jobs and not income." In her trenchant 4-29 report on "massive backing" for an engineering-union strike in eastern Germany, Dempsey uses economic reality as the final gauge to explain why demands for a 20 percent wage increase may be excessive. "The employers are recommending about 9 percent, matching the region's annual inflation rate. Eastern German wages are about 70 percent of western German levels, but productivity lags behind western Germany by as much as 70 percent." Probing the matter of privately owned eastern German land expropriated by the Soviet government between the years 1945 and 1949, 8-25, Dempsey finds heated disagreement over recent German attempts to regain this property. "Lawyers [for those trying to win back family land] claim that documents recently obtained from Moscow show that the Soviet government never specifically made unification contingent on the 1945-49 land issue." Dempsey turns her attention, 12-21, to the strong showing by ex-communist candidates of the Party of Democratic Socialism (PDS) in Brandenburg's local government elections. She weakly reasons that the PDS will have a hard time expanding its influence to state and federal elections, because it must face opposing parties newly awakened to the threat of a political backlash. Dempsey speculates as to why the opposition may not be up to the task. "The Christian Social Union, the Bavarian based sister party of the [Christian Democratic Union], has already argued that the PDS is a worse threat than the far right....Yet recent statistics on the membership structure for some of the PDS...clearly show that it is hardline former Communist party members who are seeking refuge in the far right, rather than among the ranks of the PDS." Dempsey's thorough grasp of the popular waves rocking the German political and economic systems comes through clearly in her consistently shrewd reporting.

Michael Dobbs

The Washington Post

★★½

Moscow bureau chief. In his finely textured dispatches from Russia, Dobbs paints the picture of a nation stumbling into democracy and capitalism. His analysis of the nation's current problems, as well as the lingering impact of past debacles, makes for informative reading. In his 2-2 article, Dobbs expertly recounts how the fall of communism has enabled many Russians to enrich themselves at the expense of their nation's economy. "At a time when capital is desperately needed to revitalize the former Soviet economy, billions of dollars in Western hard currency earned by Russia from sales of raw materials is flowing in the wrong direction—back to the West." Dobbs's terse 3-22 article on the power struggle between Russian President Boris Yeltsin and Parliament concisely summarizes what's at stake in the conflict. "Yeltsin and the parliament are competing for the hearts and minds of three volatile constituencies—150 million long-suffering and apathetic Russian citizens, a vast bureaucratic apparatus that has traditionally been preoccupied with preserving its own power and privileges, and a disgruntled 2.7 million-member military that has spent the last five years in disorderly retreat from empire." In his penetrating 4-28 report, Dobbs vividly tells the tale of how, during a 20-year period beginning in the 1960s, the Soviet Union squandered its most important natural resource. "The story of the Samotlor oil deposit [in Siberia] is the story of the Soviet Union itself—a heroic onslaught against nature, great human sacrifice, epic miscalculations....In their haste to get the oil out of the ground, the central planners constantly cut corners. The extensive infrastructure needed for extracting oil efficiently—roads, pipelines, and gas-processing facilities—was never completed." Thoughtfully examining underlying causes, Dobbs yields a 9-5 article on the yoke of poverty and violence resulting from a vacuum of Soviet influence on the continent. "The road to disaster... is...represented by the former Yugoslavia. Here, the combination of an economic collapse brought on by the failed socialist system and the exploitation of nationalistic prejudices by former Communist apparatchiks determined to preserve their political power triggered an explosion of violence and hatred whose effects may spill over outside the Balkans." While sympathetically relaying the tragedy there, Dobbs does what he does best: portraying the troubles that still lie ahead for the former Soviet Union.

Bob Drogin

Los Angeles Times

★★★½

South Africa. Moving from Manila to Johannesburg late in the year, the talented Drogin continues to look beyond official government pronouncements and lay bare the grim realities of war. Rather than seeking justification for human suffering, he simply writes what he sees, and, although disturbing—at times gruesome—his compelling prose grips the reader. From an isolated town in war-torn Kashmir, 8-31, where in a violent rampage government troops killed seven people in retaliation for the death of one their own, Drogin conveys in staccato style not just the details of this incident, but the nature of warfare. "Like all wars, honest men fight on both sides. Atrocities are committed on both sides. And Orwellian double talk is used on both sides. One nation's terrorist is another's freedom fighter; one army's victory is another's massacre. Officials give one version of a battle. Insurgents give another. Victims yet a third. And somewhere is the truth. Only death is absolute." In his retrospective 2-1 interview with retired North Vietnamese army Colonel Huynh Ani, Drogin doesn't let his subject minimize the heinous crimes his troops committed during the 1968 Tet offensive. The colonel's troops, Drogin points out, were responsible for "the worst known atrocity of the war: Nearly 3,000 South Vietnamese soldiers, officials and civilians suspected of government sympathies were executed by the Communists and buried in mass

graves. Some were buried alive." When Ani offers a different version of events—"'Maybe these were people who were caught in crossfire'"—Drogin stands firm. "Pressed on the matter, [Ani] conceded that civilians were rounded up but said he doesn't know how many or what happened to them. 'The security people had the list,' he said. 'But in general, these people were taken away, not killed.'" In a personal and poignant 8-3 tribute, Drogin bids farewell to the Philippines, ably conveying the nation's pathos and tragedy. "The morning after the 1990 earthquake, then-President Corazon Aquino flew into Cabanatuan, where a high-rise school had collapsed....Although cries could still be heard from children trapped in the rubble, soldiers stood mutely....'Who's in charge here? Isn't anybody in charge?' the president angrily demanded. In four years I never found the answer." Drogin's riveting 11-24 article on the suffering of Angolans caught in the renewed fighting between the government and UNITA rebels explicitly emphasizes the human angle. "At Luanda's airport, Antonio Lucas Pinto, a tiny 10-year-old orphan, frantically hunts with other boys and men for grains of rice that spill on the oily runway from bags unloaded from UN relief planes. He is barefoot, caked with dirt, and his torn sweater and shorts are tied on with bits of string. 'There was a war, so I ran away,' he explained." Courageously venturing into the abyss of horror and despair, Drogin masterfully chronicles the human condition.

Steven Erlanger

The New York Times

★★★

Moscow. With his tireless legwork and shrewd analysis, Erlanger covers Russian politics on a regional level. He superbly picks telling quotes from politicians and civilians that reveal the confusion and frustration plaguing the no-longer-so-superpower. Relying on a series of public-opinion polls taken just prior to the April referendum, 4-18, Erlanger presciently notes that Russians long for order—

precisely the type that President Boris Yeltsin would impose after the autumn uprising five months later. "In their current mood of humiliation and pessimism, Russians are seeking some eager center, but they distrust the politicians who promise it. They yearn more for collective security than for democracy, for economic protection more than for economic opportunity." In his smart 8-22 analysis of Yeltsin's efforts to consolidate political support outside of Moscow, Erlanger astutely recognizes the President playing a dangerous game that could threaten the cohesion of the country. "Mr. Yeltsin is trying to use the regions to outflank Parliament and force new elections, but it is a risky strategy that simply encourages regional leaders to press for more autonomy than he can safely give." Erlanger brilliantly captures the frustrated citizens of Podolsk taking part in the democratic process, 9-23, by publicly debating whom to support following Yeltsin's dismissal of the Parliament. "A middle-aged man in a fraying suit stood to speak, twisting his hands. 'We must return quickly to the positions we occupied on Monday.'...There was loud laughter, at the apparent absurdity of the idea. 'And we should have simultaneous elections for President and Parliament,' the man continued, pressing ahead against the noise, then, suddenly out of anything to say, stopping, shrugging, then sitting down." In his probing 7-26 article, Erlanger makes a strong case that cynical politics lies behind a Russian Central Bank announcement that pre-1993 ruble notes would become invalid at midnight. "Diplomats suggested that the Central Bank's move, which is deeply unpopular and will discredit the Government, may have been coordinated with the lawmakers involved in the parliamentary session and was timed for a long summer weekend when few officials would be at their desks." Erlanger's thoughtful insight complements his thorough and far-ranging reports.

Mark Fineman

Los Angeles Times

★★½

Nicosia bureau chief. From tent cities in Mogadishu to the heart of the Baghdad war zone, Fineman skillfully covers the triumphs and tragedies of Africa and the Middle East. His sober dispatches tell the stories of people and nations under siege. In his urgent 1-26 account of a U.S. missile attack on Iraq, Fineman vividly conveys the tension. "It is one of those surreal moments at the cutting edge of the New World Order, the night President Bush will attempt to send his final 'message' to a dictator he hopes will listen 'loud and clear.' A U.S. warship in the Persian Gulf already has launched 40 cruise missiles at Baghdad. They're speeding above the Iraqi desert at more than 500 m.p.h. There's a news blackout on the ships in the U.S. fleet, but colleagues in Washington have just tipped several American journalists in the jittery press room at the Information Ministry that something is on its way." In his brutally honest 5-4 article, Fineman plainly spells out what's in store for the West in its efforts to tame and feed Somalia. "It is, according to many analysts, nothing short of a $1.5-billion, two-year experimental cure in a world spinning dangerously into a new age of regional instability and isolated anarchy—an attempt to forge the soldiers of more than 20 nations into a U.S.-assisted military force authorized, in effect, to act as a national army until Somalia is revived." Fineman, however, astoundingly tells the reader, 1-18, there may be more going on in this east African nation than meets the eye. "Far beneath the surface of the tragic drama of Somalia, four major U.S. oil companies are quietly sitting on a prospective fortune in exclusive concessions to explore and exploit tens of millions of acres of the Somali countryside." One of Fineman's best stories, 6-15, details an unholy alliance between Iraqis and Serbs. "At a time when rebel Serb forces in Bosnia-Herzegovina...were—and remain—a U.S. presidential order away from becoming an American military target, [Gen. Zivota] Panic sought advice from [Iraq], the world's experts in ground-zero survival." Fortunately for the reader, Fineman thrives at ground zero.

Peter Ford

The Christian Science Monitor

★★★

Jerusalem bureau chief. Ford's sharp reporting makes its point —and he always has a point— deliberately and convincingly. Using his quality sources, succinct style, and concise analysis, Ford often poses a vital question and then answers it. In his refreshingly clear 4-22 study, he sets that professional hook. "How can the wisdom...of the Koran be distilled for application in societies far removed from...7th century Arabia?" Quoting experts in Jordan, Sudan, Kuwait, and Egypt, Ford reveals that there are "almost as many visions of an Islamic political system as there are Islamic thinkers." Examining the question, "To what extent are democracy and Islam compatible?" 4-27, Ford digs beneath the stereotypes. The situation in Algeria, he notes, is what "everybody wants to avoid," but exclusion from the system is not the answer. "'When the social and political context in a country is normal and relaxed,'" says Ishak al-Farhan, the head of the Muslim Brotherhood in Jordan, "'the moderate interpretation of Islam will prevail. But when Muslims are oppressed, there will always be militants who see jihad (holy war) as the solution.'" In his 9-8 article on the Israeli-Palestinian negotiations, Ford coolly reasons, "Chief among the oddities that mark the nascent peace treaty...is one supreme irony: The deal would probably never have happened had it not been for those most bitterly opposed to it—Muslim radicals." PLO leader Yasir Arafat felt threatened, Ford contends, and was "in danger of becoming irrelevant, and the secular organization he heads was in danger of being swamped by Islamic militants with more popular credibility." As for the Israeli motivation, Ford quotes Danny Rubenstein, a commentator with the Israeli daily *Haaretz*. "'[Prime Minister Yitzhak] Rabin decided that the way to cope with the fundamentalists was to let the PLO do the job for him.'" On 9-20, Ford cites everyone from a Hamas supporter, "whose son blew himself up in a suicide attack against a Gaza police station last week," to the head of the Gaza Bar Association, to gauge the probability of continued Palestinian militancy. Ford then boldly predicts that "if Arafat reaches out to his Islamist opposition, as he is expected to do in order to bolster his leadership, the Islamists seem likely to reciprocate." With a keen ability to focus his reporting on a key issue, Ford makes journalism seem almost easy.

Damien Fraser

Financial Times

Mexico City. Masterfully packing information into concise, yet coherent, reports, Fraser routinely files strong stories based on solid analysis. In his 1-28 article, he warily recounts several changes made by Mexican President Carlos Salinas de Gortari to key election-oversight positions. Fraser sees danger but never firmly declares that the appointments suggest any wrongdoing. "With these moves," he notes succinctly, "the government has turned away from putting independent officials in charge of electoral organizations." Balancing tourism figures against popular hysteria regarding the safety of travel in Florida, 9-18 and 9-19, Fraser soberly and smartly reminds that "Florida has established a critical mass of highly competitive tourist services that offer some of the cheapest and best value accommodation in the world." In his shrewd 9-22 piece on the latest election reforms pushed through the legislature by President Salinas, Fraser clarifies the reforms before addressing their relative merit. He makes the case that the details of the reforms, such as high caps on donations, favor Salinas's Institutional Revolutionary Party (PRI), but he writes, "Put together with the changes passed earlier in his term, which included the drawing up of an accurate electoral roll, they make a repetition of the 1988 election, when fraud was widely reported, less likely." Fraser looks forward in his tightly packed 12-9 article profiling the policies of Luis Donaldo Colosio, most likely Mexico's next president. Fraser recognizes that differences between Colosio and Salinas may simply represent an extension of the PRI campaign to promote its election reforms without having to give up power. "Mr. Colosio's democratic proposals seem part of a campaign to assure the public his party can win cleanly. He promised that 'the PRI does not need or want a single vote outside the margin of the law.'" Fraser's balanced and comprehensive reporting on Mexican politics provides informative, compelling sketches of increasingly complex developments.

Peter Fuhrman

Forbes

International trade. Reading Fuhrman yields an education in the seamier side of international trade. His prose—usually simple and occasionally awkward—conveys an insider's knowledge of East-West trade.

In his fascinating 5-10 article, Fuhrman explains how gunrunners evade the arms embargo against Iraq. "Arms smugglers try to fool U.S. reconnaissance satellites, which track every single ship going to Iraq. After entering the Persian Gulf and once it gets dark at night, they paint the deck of the ship a different color. In the morning the satellite assigns the repainted boat a brand-new tracking number." In another behind-the-scenes account, 8-16, Fuhrman discloses marked corruption in Russia regarding U.S. grain donations. "Fraud is rampant. Russians involved in distributing U.S. wheat are illegally milling it into flour, which they then re-export to Central Asian republics." From the dark to the bright, Fuhrman warns Westerners, 9-27, that many aspects of the Russian economy are not as bad as many reports have suggested. "The strength of the Soviet Union's economy was greatly overestimated by many American politicians, scholars and the CIA—right up to its collapse in 1991. Now many of these same people are greatly overstating Russia's economic weakness." Russia's commercial space-launch industry, for example, demonstrates Russian competitiveness, as Fuhrman explains in his well-researched 10-25 story. "Now the Russians are coming, and the launch cartel is worried. In the first and only case where they were permitted to tender, the Russians won hands down." Fleshed out by a keen eye for detail, Fuhrman's insights on global trade make for compelling and provocative reading.

James P. Gallagher

Chicago Tribune

★★★½

Moscow bureau chief. With superb dispatches from Moscow, Gallagher provides a vivid panorama of life during and after communism. His basic news reports illuminate brilliantly and his feature articles enlighten even more so. In his 9-26 dispatch, Gallagher colorfully portrays the tide turning against the hard-liners barricaded inside the Russian White House. "The power is out, there's no water and the toilets don't flush. The people claiming to be the legitimate rulers of Russia spend their days shivering in dimly-lit rooms and their nights curled up on tables or the floor." In his penetrating 1-10 report, Gallagher reveals why people should care about an obscure group of Islamic Russians stirring up trouble across the continent. "With Moscow's hold on remote Russian areas growing weaker, the full impact of Chechnya's [a small Islamic enclave in the Caucasus Mountains] rebellion could be felt far beyond the Caucasus. Other independence-minded ethnic groups, including the Tatars, Bashkirs and Yakuts, are watching to see how the Chechens fare in their face-off with the Russian government." With a poignant 8-18 story on the fall from grace of one of Russia's formerly revered authors, Maxim Gorky, Gallagher provides an education on an evolving nation. "Worst of all for a writer who enjoyed almost idolatrous acclaim at the beginning of his career—when he was the voice of Russia's downtrodden proletariat—hardly anyone reads Gorky anymore." Gallagher continually supplies fascinating features, each with a payoff leading to a wider understanding of Russia. He interviews the Russians who knew Lee Harvey Oswald during the two years he lived in Minsk, 1-27. "But regardless of their personal opinions of Oswald, almost all of those who knew him do not believe he killed Kennedy, as the Warren Commission concluded." In his 4-5 article, Gallagher reveals baseball as an element of Russia's future. "Today, with communism routed and the country moving toward a market economy, baseball is being touted as a sport that helps young people develop the skills they will need for success in tomorrow's Russia." A dependable power-hitter, the talented Gallagher frequently slugs home runs.

Edward A. Gargan

The New York Times

★½

New Delhi bureau chief. While vividly portraying the Indian subcontinent as a generally dreary and dangerous place, Gargan offers little sense of daily life. He overemphasizes the level of support for the Bharatiya Janata Party (BJP), the fanatical, nationalistic Hindu opposition group—which he covers throughout the year. This tends to raise questions about Gargan's overall take on events. His 9-17 article on the resurgence of Hinduism as reflected in the supposedly strong support for this party betrays a rather outdated opinion of the Indian people. "[The BJP] has grown not merely by pointing to the weaknesses of the Congress Party, but more important, and more effectively, by pitting Hindus against Muslims, by appealing to widespread and deeply seated Hindu prejudices." As it turns out, the BJP alarms many voters and suffered significant losses in the November elections. Simplistically contrasting the "emerald forests, placid beaches and Buddhist traditions" of Sri Lanka with the effects of a decade of civil war, 5-3, Gargan deftly finds Sri Lankans unmoved by the assassination of President Ranasinghe Premadasa and 23 others. Reporting from a bunker-like office in a burned-out section of Srinaga, Kashmir, 5-19, Gargan eloquently profiles newspaper editor Khwaja Sana Ullah Bhat. "Through these three years [of violent rebellion] and during the decades that gave birth to the civil war, Mr. Bhat has chronicled the descent from paradise, as Kashmir was widely depicted, to the cataclysm of brutality that has engulfed the valley. Whatever hope he once retained for peace has long since been extinguished." In his 10-26 piece on the cost of order in Punjab, Gargan voices concerns both feeble and compelling over the oppressive police presence in the state. Still, these concerns are overshadowed by the bigger picture, which Gargan mentions only briefly and then ignores. The people of Punjab no longer live in fear of anarchic militant bands—the number of annual murders has dropped from 5000 to 500. "Its cities are once again alive, farmers are regularly in their fields after sundown....And for the first time in years, Punjab has been able to hold village elections in which large numbers have been willing to take part." Despite these obvious improvements, Gargan writes unconvincingly that "after a decade of bloodshed in which thousands have been killed, the atmosphere has changed. The anxiety of Punjabis is no longer driven by the Sikh rebels or gangs who have carried out killings in the past, but by the crackdown by the army and police." Reading several of his pieces, one gets the sense that Gargan could find despair and bleakness in Bermuda.

Francis Ghiles

Financial Times

★½

North Africa, based in London. Despite his superlative use of economic statistics, Ghiles's repetitive analysis of events in Algeria implies that not much changed there in the course of the year. While his stories shift in emphasis, they often echo the same themes and details. Ghiles does produce a smart 8-24 piece on the dismissal of Prime Minister Belaid Abdessalam, reasoning that the move comes too late to save the damaged Algerian economy. "Massive injections of cash into state companies which remain unreformed has turned a budget surplus equivalent to 2.4 percent of gross domestic product in 1991 into a deficit of 14.2 percent this year, and pushed inflation beyond the 30 percent mark." His informative but rather vaguely sourced 11-17 survey of the Algerian economy begins with general ruminations on the terror plaguing the country and then zeroes in on the crux of the misery. "The statistics are alarming: factories are functioning, at best, at 50 percent capacity; 84 percent of Algerians between the ages of 15 and 30 are without a job; 102,000 jobs were created annually between 1967 and 1990 when 234,000 were needed....The country imports $2 billion worth of food every year which amounts to more than two thirds of its needs." These numbers appear in various forms throughout his late-year work. Concentrating on the breakdown of social order in Algeria, 11-6/7, Ghiles highlights the danger posed by Islamic fundamentalists who would do away with plans to modernize the economy. "Many ordinary Algerians are deeply sickened by the growing violence on all sides, though among the crowd of younger unemployed many appear to look on the whole situation as a kind of wild thriller in which they tot up points." Relying entirely on economic figures of unknown origin, 3-3, Ghiles chronicles Tunisia's economic turnaround over the past six years. With the nation's liberal monetary policy encouraging foreign and domestic investment, Ghiles shrewdly predicts Tunisia's next hurdle. "Vested interests in the civil service and industry are now to be challenged by reforms aimed at raising industrial productivity, enforcing quality control and boosting exports." Despite these flashes of insight, Ghiles generally supplies specific information only in cases where figures apply. This detached reporting fails to provide adequate coverage of the day-to-day business and political culture of northern Africa.

Tim Golden

The New York Times

★★

Mexico City. Although Golden's voluminous reporting benefits from his keen observations, it suffers from his overly skeptical analysis. Too often he fails to provide general context to support his views, which gives his work a negative slant. In his 4-2 article on the spectacle of political infighting in Mexico, Golden reports from a convention of the Institutional Revolutionary Party. Contrasting the Yuppie demeanor of President Carlos Salinas de Gortari's party allies with the "ill-fitting polyester costumes" of the old guard. Golden observes, "[The battle between the new guard and the old] tends to be painted as one between the forces of democracy and those of darkness. But on their way to what they say will be a democratic future, the Salinastas have worked ceaselessly to strengthen their central control." The paradox begs further explanation, but Golden offers none. However, his insightful three-part series from Cuba, 1-11, 1-12, and 1-13, vividly portrays the endurance and suffering of the Cuban people. Golden provocatively reasons that further sanctions might only inspire resentment in people who generally look with hope toward the U.S. "As a beef substitute, a television chef recommends 'grapefruit steak.' Carefully remove the rind...season it, cover it with bread crumbs and fry. But in search of more solid food, several Cubans said they had eaten cats." In his 9-20 piece on election-law reform in Mexico, Golden argues that Salinas hasn't gone far enough, but he fails to lay out key points of the reforms, much less give a sense of what has or has not changed. This wispiness contrasts with an excellent 6-3 report in which Golden summarizes the weird counter-coup in Guatemala following President Jorge Serrano Elías's dismissal of Congress and suspension of the Constitution. "Why Mr. Serrano launched his palace coup in the first place and to what degree he initiated it or was pushed into it by the army was never entirely clear....According to Guatemalans close to the military, the commanders heard stronger and stronger arguments that by backing Mr. Serrano the army would squander what public support it had won since accepting the return of civilian rule in 1986." Despite these occasional bursts, Golden's hidebound disposition too often contradicts the context of progress displayed in his reporting.

Merrill Goozner

Chicago Tribune

Chief Asia correspondent. Writing as an omniscient observer, Goozner reports a wide range of issues from fresh and subtle angles. Although he relies too much on official sources and professional experts, Goozner sometimes captures popular images that reflect his broader subject matter. In his 7-2 article on the much-reported efforts of new South Korean President Kim Young Sam to reverse the corruption permeating many aspects of Korean life, Goozner cleverly seizes on the case of beauty-shop owner Ha Jong Sun. "Government prosecutors...accused Ha, 55, of being the bag lady in a bribe and kickback scheme in which mothers of three of the last four Miss Koreas paid up to 40 million won, or nearly $50,000, to boost their daughters' chances in the pageant." Despite the fierce anti-Western rhetoric emanating from the highest levels of the Malaysian government, Goozner's shrewd 1-14 survey paradoxically finds the Asian country, a cordial, if not friendly, environment for U.S. investment. Through compelling examples and figures, Goozner builds a strong case that American firms may be missing "a golden opportunity" to invest and locate in a burgeoning economy. Silent are voices of foreign business-owners conducting business in the country who might corroborate further the views of the U.S. ambassador to Malaysia and a think-tank director. In his fascinating 8-19 article, Goozner surveys a Japanese Shinto ritual celebrating the convergence of spiritual and political values. "The nation-builders of the late 1800s were rapidly creating a modern army, industries and government institutions needed to compete with the West. They wanted an institution capable of providing ideological unity to a people that had emerged late from a divisive feudalism. They turned to Shintoism and transformed its main symbols." In commemoration, Goozner finds, worshipers rebuild a shrine every 20 years as a symbol of "Japan's ceaseless effort to hold on to its native culture in the face of the overwhelming onslaught of Western in-

fluence." Wrongly concluding that the Liberal Democratic Party of Japan would survive its latest massive scandal, Goozner still manages a comprehensive 3-21 portrayal of the various interlinked forces that make up Japan Inc.—the government, the bureaucracy, and big business. Working hard to produce a populist ring in his reports, Goozner usually succeeds in writing for a general audience.

Clyde Haberman

The New York Times

★★★

Jerusalem bureau chief. Haberman covers Israeli politics so closely that anyone who reads between the lines of his reporting can get a jump on the general news. While his 8-17 news analysis doesn't predict the peace agreement, he reports presciently, "Some wonder if a meeting is inevitable between [Prime Minister Yitzhak] Rabin and [PLO leader] Yasir Arafat." And in his 10-14 article, Haberman presages the inability of meeting the December 13 deadline for the beginning of Israeli troop withdrawal. "Far from being mere technicalities, the specifics will determine the ultimate success or failure of the new relationship, and officials on both sides agree that they have not given themselves much time." Haberman also correctly points out that a key roadblock lies in resolving the question, "What is Jericho? The backwater town of 10 square miles, as the Israelis see it? Or the district of 146 square miles, as defined by Jordanian law and by the Palestinians now?" On 10-3, Haberman shies away from the real story when, after Israeli raids in the Gaza strip, he focuses on the verbal sniping between the PLO and Israeli officials rather than on Israel's motivation for the raids, which were seen by Palestinians as a "sign of bad faith." But he also demonstrates a healthy unwillingness to draw quick conclusions, as he shows by his 11-3 coverage of the Jerusalem mayoral election, which Rabin called a "test of his agreement...on bringing Palestinian self-rule to the occupied territories." Haberman calls the defeat of incumbent Labor Party Mayor Teddy Kolleck "a ringing statement by Jewish voters that they want their city to remain Israel's unified capital," but he concludes astutely that the election results fall short of a rejection of the accord. Haberman's broad knowledge of Israeli politics and culture informs his meticulous, if sometimes dry and slightly distant, reporting.

Joel Havemann

Los Angeles Times

★★½

Brussels bureau chief. Covering the European Community through the eyes of an economist, Havemann supplies provocative and well-researched articles that render the world economy a mélange of trading blocks and national interests. In his 3-3 article, Havemann discovers that an unexpected side effect of European unity is, in some instances, greater unemployment. "The European Community's new single market, by bringing down barriers to commerce among the 12 EC countries and dictating uniform product standards across Europe, has made it easier for companies to close their least efficient factories and consolidate production at the most efficient." Tracking a disturbing trend, 3-26, Havemann reports that five of the world's 15 largest oil spills have occurred in only the past several years. "No wonder the world's major ports have found it prudent to undertake their own tanker inspections. Rotterdam's six inspectors check about one-quarter of the ships that call on this port every year. They find that 80 percent to 85 percent of the vessels have at least minor defects that require correction. Of 433 tankers they inspected last year, 59 had sufficiently serious problems that they had to be detained." The economies of Europe face other difficulties as well, as Havemann's 8-31 piece brings to light. "Fraud is a mounting problem in just about everything the EC does. EC aid for Eastern Europe has been found as far afield as Egypt, for example, and the EC's poorer countries have collected aid for bridges and highways that have never been built." Havemann's amply documented 4-9 story on immigration in Europe and the rising tide of nationalism uses Antwerp as a microcosm for the EC as a whole. "Europe is home to bloodier rivalries, from civil war in the Balkans to seemingly perpetual terrorism in Northern Ireland. Belgium is no Yugoslavia, and Antwerp is no Sarajevo. Nobody has died here. Yet Antwerp's designation by the European Community as Europe's cultural capital has served to underscore that even Europe's traditional centers of commerce and learning are being washed by currents of bitterness and antipathy." Fanning out from Brussels, Havemann provides insightful analyses of business trends and economic issues throughout the continent.

Chris Hedges
The New York Times
★★

Cairo bureau chief. Surveying the Middle East with quiet efficiency, Hedges tracks down offbeat stories while covering the region's violent political outbursts. In one of his quirkier articles, 2-9, he reports that Kuwaitis have fallen in love with luxury American sedans. Using the cars as status symbols—and for courting—they "scoff at anything less than a V-8 engine....They gun their cars to speeds that reach 100 miles per hour or more, ignore stoplights and think little of darting the wrong way down a one-way street....And it is not uncommon to see five or six cars, each filled with young men, nosing their way like a school of fish behind a vehicle filled with young women." In his vivid 3-20 story from Yemen, Hedges visits one of the "squalid encampments," that are home to some "of the country's 14,000 lepers, banished from their villages by a populace that still views the disease as a curse reserved for thieves and miscreants." He calls "paltry" the government effort to both educate people about leprosy and to treat people infected with the now-curable disease. In a cogent 8-6 piece, Hedges reports the first meeting by an Israeli cabinet minister making contact with a PLO representative with the knowledge of the Prime Minister, thus "shattering one of Israel's most rigid political taboos." This meeting in Cairo, Hedges notes, "unleashed an acrimonious exchange in Israel between those who believe that the country must open direct negotiations with the PLO and those who believe that the state should have no contact with what they term a terrorist group." Hedges's 11-26 piece effectively depicts the wretched conditions created by unfettered state-run industry in Egypt, where "plants and factories spew waste directly into the Nile, damaging a river that provides over 95 percent of the country's water needs." But while Hedges mentions that this issue is playing into the hands of Islamic militants, he doesn't make a clear connection. In his insightful 12-19 article, Hedges reports from Egypt that "the re-emergence of Al Jihad—the successor to the group blamed for the assassination of President Anwar el-Sadat in 1981—has changed the rules of the game... threatening to sharply increase the level of violence." Backed by Iran, Hedges points out, "Al Jihad sees itself as a paramilitary group that must directly battle the government." While his reporting—at its best, descriptive and moving—sometimes suffers from a narrow focus, Hedges does offer solid analysis.

Fred Hiatt
The Washington Post
★★½

Moscow. The reader feels the cold, snowy slush under the feet of average Russian citizens when reading Hiatt's dispatches. In his expressive and textured stories, old women have "chapped red faces," while their husbands are "gaunt men in fur hats." One of Hiatt's best pieces in 1993, 6-6, details the saga of American citizens of Finnish descent who came to the Soviet Union in the 1930s to build the socialist dream. "But in the mid-1930s, Soviet leader Joseph Stalin began turning against the foreigners, accusing many—along with thousands of Russians—of sabotage and betrayal. Here, as throughout the Soviet Union, people began to disappear in the middle of the night." Hiatt makes a keen observation, 3-1, that Russia could be a wealthy nation if only it had the finances to tap its wealth of resources. "Russia is fabulously rich in natural resources, but decades of Soviet neglect, pillage and declining investment have left its industry and agriculture too feeble to exploit that wealth. The country therefore finds itself trapped in a vicious cycle that only Western aid or investment could break: It cannot earn enough dollars through exports to modernize, but without modernizing it will earn less and less." In his nicely understated 3-13 article on the war of wills between President Boris Yeltsin and Parliament, Hiatt simplifies the issue in two sentences. "Yeltsin has embraced the goal of a free-market democracy living in peace with its neighbors. Many of his opponents, while also supporting democracy, rue the contraction of Russia's empire and believe a Russian government should wield a stronger hand—in politics, economics and foreign policy." Trying to predict Russia's future is a near impossibility, as Hiatt superbly illustrates, 9-18. "Kremlinology was once the rarefied preserve of scholars who spent days gravely mulling over a single photograph or elliptical statement. Today, as the Russian government careens in a dozen directions at once without ever seeming to quite arrive anywhere, Kremlinology is an Alice-in-Wonderland sport for the brave, the foolhardy and the bemused." Consistently delivering the nitty-gritty, Hiatt gives the reader a front-row seat for the fireworks.

Murray Hiebert
Far Eastern Economic Review
★½

Hanoi. Emphasizing official perspectives on the burgeoning Vietnamese economy, Hiebert often lards his work with figures supporting obvious, broader points. His observations seldom convey distinctly Vietnamese characteristics, instead reflecting events common to most post-communist economic transitions. In an ill-reasoned 2-4 article, Hiebert cites cost overruns and bad planning in the construction of a power line to carry excess electricity from northern Vietnam to Saigon. Speculating that Vietnam may not be ready for the anticipated post-embargo influx of international funds, Hiebert recounts in full detail the shoddy planning and amateurish engineering plaguing the project. He finally acknowledges that "most developing countries find that their limitations often surpass their abilities to complete major infrastructure projects according to Western standards." In his disappointing 4-22 piece, coauthored by Susumu Awanohara, Hiebert unastoundingly concludes that Vietnam's crumbling social and physical infrastructures would benefit from foreign investment, and he uncritically relies on Vietnamese government officials for estimates of optimum levels. Reporting on the largest Vietnamese strike in 18 years, which, like all strikes, is illegal but tolerated, 9-2, Hiebert discovers that low pay—half the mandated minimum wage of $35 per month—and long hours are behind the walk-out. As the government formulates new policies to deal with a free-market economy, he adds, concern abounds about granting Vietnamese workers the right to strike. "Some officials fear the right to strike will scare off potential foreign investors." Hiebert's insightful 7-29 article on the fledgling legal system in Vietnam reveals both how far Vietnam has come in developing a modern legal system and why the process sets historical precedents. "Throughout most of Vietnam's history, the development of a legal system was given little priority. Like neighboring China, scholar-officials long ruled Vietnam by subordinating the will of the people to the authority of the emperor." Although generous in fresh detail, Hiebert's work would benefit from more non-governmental sources.

Theresa Hitchens
Defense News
★★½

Washington staff writer. Still equipped with her valuable European perspective, Hitchens moves this year from Brussels to Washington. Although she concentrates on military policy and international economic issues, she never misses the importance of underlying defense technology matters. In her intriguing 1-25/31 report, she examines U.S. efforts to bring NATO allies into an anti-missile defense program. Hitchens finds that the Strategic Defense Initiative Organization, now called Ballistic Missile Defense Organization, "had been trying to enlist European and allied participation in theater missile defense for years, but so far only the Israelis have been willing to commit technology and increasingly scarce resources." Failure to bring in new funding and technology from the allies may doom "Star Wars," Hitchens adds, but it will be a hard sell, especially with the demise of the Soviet Union. Her 3-8/14 article lucidly surveys ongoing defense conversion in Western Europe. Hitchens reports that the Swedes, in particular, are becoming much more aggressive in seeking international sources for research and development funding and in promoting their defense industry's products overseas. Her keen and insightful 4-19/25 analysis of the post-Soviet military in Eastern Europe reveals that a "key problem for the newly independent countries of Poland, Hungary, the Czech Republic and Slovakia is the fact that their armed forces were designed by Soviet generals in Moscow as pieces of a unified military machine." This will make it more difficult, Hitchens reports, to integrate these countries into a cohesive Western defense force such as NATO. In her penetrating 5-3/9 article highlighting the shortcomings of defense in the former Soviet bloc, Hitchens concludes that the Hungarians are looking to trade Soviet debt for Russian missiles. The war in neighboring Yugoslavia "has heightened Hungary's concern about its air defense gap," she notes, a gap that would be filled by the possession of Russian missiles. Her 10-18/24 dispatch on NATO's role in the Somalia relief program reports that the "NATO allies—especially the United States, Britain and France—have not only the military capability, but also the experience in command and control of large joint forces needed to manage peacekeeping missions that might involve combat." The move to Washington has obviously not weakened her grasp of issues confronting the nation's European allies. While expanding into defense technology, Hitchens continues her strong reporting of political issues confronting NATO.

David Hoffman
The Washington Post
★½

Jerusalem. Hoffman's strength lies in his acute, almost poetic, observations and analyses of the complex events in both Israel and the occupied territories. However, he often reports as if he's already a columnist on the op-ed page, with hard details and expert opinion missing. Hoffman insightfully uses the Gorbachev-era Soviet Union to frame his 11-28 assessment of the post-peace-accord Middle East. "Just as communism collapsed because of an inner exhaustion, so too have both Palestinian and Israeli societies grown weary...of the bloodshed and tension." He poignantly refers to recent violence as "a scream from the past, a violent outburst of the old thinking by men who will happily commit themselves to a lifetime of war." But when he concludes that the Arab secondary boycott of Israel has "eroded" because "Israel is practically bursting with salesmen and financiers anxious for the walls of hostility to collapse," he lacks solid evidence. In two articles, 1-21 and 11-7, Hoffman follows the plight of Russian emigré Raya Avilova and her sons to portray the struggles of new Russian settlers, whom some Israelis treat as outcasts. Hoffman's perfunctory reporting, however, falls far short of a moving profile, nor does it ever reach past the Avilova family to evoke the collective suffering of this community. "The Soviet refuseniks who fled to Israel in the 1970s," he notes, "eventually caught up with and even surpassed the economic status of longtime Israelis." While provocative, Hoffman offers no evidence to support this statement. In his 12-1 interview of Fares Hasouna, the deputy head of the preparations committee for the Palestinian police, Hoffman captures the confusion about security in the Gaza Strip during the transition. Although he concludes, "it is not known whether or how the Fatah police will be able to restrain the more militant Palestinians if they continue to attack Israeli targets," Hoffman provides no comment from Hasouna on this crucial point. Despite his strong analytical skills, Hoffman needs to dig deeper for the sources and facts that connect the dots.

David Holley
Los Angeles Times
★★★

Beijing bureau chief. Combining a discerning eye with articulate presentation, Holley stands out for his detailed reporting and incisive analysis. He steeps his judgments more in pragmatism than ideology, strengthening his arguments with observation rather than wishful thinking. In his 3-30 article, Holley points out the folly of speculating about the significance of record numbers of "no" votes cast against a party appointment at a Chinese parliament assembly, considering that no debate preceded the vote and that the delegates themselves were both surprised and amused by the outcome. If anything, he notes, the vote may benefit the Communist rulers. "By giving the impression that delegates enjoy at least a touch of freedom to vote as they please, it could help soften the repressive image that Beijing has had since the 1989 crackdown on China's pro-democracy movement." While numerous others botched and muddled the story of Japanese political reforms, Holley's knowledgeable 11-17 report methodically spells out the contents of the plan. "The set of four bills...attacks the endemic corruption of Japanese politics in two ways, by redesigning voting districts and by changing the rules for campaign financing." In addition to other provisions of the package, Holley provides a nice summary of a new phenomenon in Japanese politics—intra-party wrangling over details. Holley builds his 7-13 story around certain American images popular in China. Contending that "positive images of the United States are extremely widespread among ordinary Chinese," he laments that too often their impressions form from such sources as the television show "Dynasty." Unfortunately, Holley doesn't lend voice to common Chinese people, instead quoting an American teaching in China. But such lapses are rare. Contributing several pieces to a special 6-15 *Times* report from China, Holley shines with his feature story, "Ancient Power Steps Into Asian Spotlight." This compelling and intellectually honest piece warns that only one-third of the Chinese people benefit from the emerging market economy. "China is on the road to becoming two nations, politically united but economically divided." Nevertheless, Holley notes, if China succeeds at transforming to a market system, its economy, some experts predict, will grow to match that of the U.S. by 2020. With mature analysis and lucid reporting, Holley proves a captivating and dependable source.

Youssef M. Ibrahim

The New York Times

★★★

Paris bureau. Covering the many factions vying for power within the Middle East, Ibrahim provides the reader with a detailed road map of the region's people and their causes. By providing insight and texture, his reports go further than the typical coverage of Muslim fundamentalists, as shown in his lighthearted 2-3 story on the traditional garb worn by Islamic women. "Al Salam Shopping Center for Veiled Women is the powerhouse of Muslim fundamentalism chic in Egypt; a three-floor store in one of Cairo's finest suburbs, trying to sell solutions to the puzzle of how a woman can cover up from head to toe while preserving a sense of fashion." Bringing another little-known fact to light, 3-15, Ibrahim reports that not even fellow Arabs are safe from fundamentalists seeking to advance Islamic rule throughout the Middle East. "In a striking example of the power of Muslim fundamentalists, nearly 10 million Coptic Christians in Egypt, the largest religious minority in the Middle East and one of its most ancient, are under siege." Ibrahim's 6-29 dispatch astutely observes that Arab support for U.S. actions against Baghdad may be waning because of suspicions that the West has more than just military or security aims at stake. "Although few of them admire Saddam Hussein, there is a growing conviction in the Islamic world that the United States has adopted a double standard, rushing to use weapons against Muslims in Iraq, Libya and Somalia, but recoiling from similar actions against Christian Serbs and Croats committing massacres against Muslim Bosnians." In his well-balanced 8-25 report, Ibrahim provides a breakdown of the Palestinians' myriad factions and interests. "[Yasir] Arafat and the PLO are in trouble because the moment of truth for Palestinians appears over the horizon, and the vast apparatus of Palestinian movements—with its intellectuals, its revolutionaries, its masses living under Israeli occupation in the West Bank and Gaza or in refugee camps in the far-flung Arab world—are agonizing over the bitter choices ahead, which fall far short of minimal Palestinian aspirations of a decade ago." Ibrahim's success springs from his ability to illuminate obscure, offbeat details, while maintaining a strong focus on the major issues of war and peace in the Middle East.

Adi Ignatius

The Wall Street Journal

★★

Moscow bureau chief. Despite his eye for detail and ear for anecdote, Ignatius has trouble focusing on the big picture, and his most important pieces often suffer from a lack of context. During the autumn uprising in Moscow, he ran with the journalistic pack. His lengthy 10-4 summary of the revolt fails to ask key questions of the opposition, thus offering little beyond a Yeltsin-centric groupthink perspective. But Ignatius excels at penning compelling portraits. Showing he can break from the pack, Ignatius registers a penetrating 6-11 profile of Alexander Rutskoi, countering the popular one-dimensional image of the Russian Vice President as a faceless villain. Rutskoi comes across as both cultivated and human as well as the possessor of a large stable of pets, including "a terrier with a two-century pedigree and a rooster that perches on his shoulder and pecks at his mustache." Not surprisingly for a *WSJ* writer,

Ignatius's forte is business. His 5-13 piece on the Marc Rich company contains a succinct lesson in post-Soviet finance as seen through a single business transaction. "Here's how the deal worked. The company produced 70,000 tons of raw sugar from Brazil on the open market. The sugar was shipped... to Ukraine, where...it was processed at a local refinery. After paying the refinery with part of the sugar, Marc Rich & Co. sent 30,000 tons of refined sugar 6,000 miles east to huge Siberian refineries, which need sugar to supply to their vast work forces." The Siberians paid in oil, which the company then exchanged in Mongolia for copper, which was finally processed in Kazakhstan and shipped out to the West where it was sold, with the company realizing a hard-currency profit only several months after the transaction began. Ignatius also has a knack for spotting the unusual—and the sinister. His 2-18 piece on the "red-browns" describes the ties between former communists and right-wing, heavy-metal rockers. "A bizarre alliance is forming—between nationalistic former Soviet Communists, in their cheap polyester suits, and Russia's trash rockers, in black leather and chains.... 'We're opposition and they're opposition,' says [one conservative editor]. 'We need them and they need us.'" With these infrequent hits, Ignatius shows that he can complement his talent for detail with an analytical grasp of social trends.

Sam Jameson

Los Angeles Times

★★½

Tokyo. An articulate writer and solid reporter, Jameson emphasizes the political and social changes in Japan. His immense knowledge of Japanese culture surfaces in his insightful reports, which brim with practical information. Rather than relying on polls or pundits, 7-15, Jameson attends a less-than-enthusiastic rally led by the secretary general of the Socialist party. "Twenty people listened. Four female 'cheerleaders,' dressed in Girl-Scout-like uniforms, waved white-gloved hands to passersby. Nobody waved back. And after [Secretary Hirotaka] Akamatsu finished, eight people applauded—two fewer than the number of special police guarding the Socialists' No. 2 executive." When the state elections come, Jameson cogently assesses the results, 7-19, recognizing the strategically strong position of Morihiro Hosokawa as the head of a swing coalition. "So far, Hosokawa has refused to commit himself to a coalition with either side, although he did express interest Sunday night in heading an opposition coalition." Jameson's unconvincing 1-2 article purports to find bias against Japan's *burakumin*, or untouchable caste. Despite providing abundant and compelling historical detail, Jameson bases his analysis on incidents that happened a generation ago. Because many sources recount episodes from their childhood—rather than from recent experiences—the chronological distance raises questions about whether the report accurately reflects a modern social condition. In his 3-30 piece, Jameson liberally sprinkles skepticism into his report on the possibility of an economic miracle resulting from a united Korea. "Those estimates, which other analysts consider unrealistic, would give Korea a larger economy than Canada and one in the same league as Britain, Brazil and Spain." Despite some occasional unevenness in his reporting, Jameson, with his unique perspective, writes delightful, engaging, and informative stories found nowhere else.

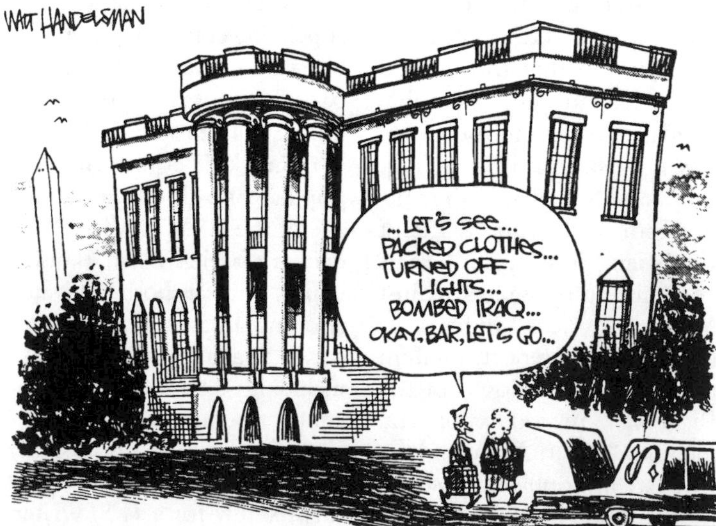

Clayton Jones

The Christian Science Monitor

★★★

Tokyo. Intelligent and insightful, Jones rarely misses with his well-researched, richly detailed reporting on the political economy of Southeast Asia. Covering mostly matters of policy, he relies heavily on official and often-quoted sources. In his 5-19 article on early Japanese maneuvering to dominate the burgeoning Vietnamese automobile industry, Jones effectively focuses on the experience of James Rockwell, one of the first American entrepreneurs to return to Vietnam. Rockwell, whose views figure prominently in the piece, claims the Japanese were nearly able to set their own automobile-industry standards. If they had succeeded, Jones notes, Vietnamese companies would have been totally dependent on Japan for both technology and equipment. Moreover, the Vietnamese would have been beholden to Japan for any future changes in their production techniques or styles. "For more than a decade, Japan has guided many Southeast Asian nations toward the goal of a regional industry that would manufacture vehicles and parts complementing each other along Japanese design." Rockwell, Jones explains, alerted the Vietnamese, who subsequently changed their approach to accommodate numerous suppliers. In his trenchant 11-10 survey of Laos, Jones finds that like most Asian economies racing toward unregulated open markets, the Laotian government is traveling the same road but in the slow lane. "Its leaders, who once suffered American carpet-bombing in jungle hideouts, want to prevent the social and environmental ills of rapid growth that they see in neighboring Thailand, Vietnam and China." With a discerning eye, 7-15, Jones assesses the Clintons' performance during their first trip to Asia. "Try as he might, [Bill] Clinton could not always get it right on this trip." The days of U.S. presidents getting unqualified respect are over, Jones finds. "No longer does a U.S. president carry the mantle of leader of the free world or spokesman for the healthiest economy. Asians are creating their own markets with each other, their own styles, their own security." In the first of a highly intelligent series on Asian security, 11-17, Jones discovers that despite a movement to buy up Cold War military surplus, Asian governments recognize the folly of mistrusting each other. "To cope with the new anxieties, many Asian nations are using preventative diplomacy, forming institutions for cooperation and 'confidence building' that, at the very least, keep historic and potential adversaries talking to each other." One of the key players in *CSM*'s resurgence, Jones masterfully balances his analysis and reporting, emphasizing each at just the right moment.

Henry Kamm

The New York Times

★★★

Geneva bureau chief. While continuing his incisive exploration of the aftermath of communism's collapse in Eastern Europe and Southeast Asia, Kamm produces a poignant tableau of human pain and suffering amidst hope. In his 3-27 story, he writes that Haiphong, Vietnam's largest port, "is operating at half or less of its yearly handling capacity" but "looks far more prosperous than it did before liberalization," primarily because "an extensive new private sector is providing second and third jobs," which are a must for those on government pay. Kamm visits a disillusioned Vietnamese doctor in Ho Chi Minh City, 5-6, who has treated an increasing number of teenaged prostitutes. "'We fought for freedom, independence and social justice,'" she says. "'Now all is money.'" A month later, 6-20, Kamm visits a rural village in Albania, where one family's meals consist mainly of "hot water poured over stale bread and salt to make a soup." Even amid such hardships, Kamm reports that while villagers say "material life was a little better in the Communist days...all rejected a return of the old." In his informative 11-17 story from Slovakia, Kamm maintains that "the millions of Gypsies of Eastern Europe have emerged as great losers from the overthrow of Communism and the end of the rigid controls that it imposed on daily life." He produces strong evidence to illustrate the openly hostile attitudes, such as the mayor of one town who "said selective killing of Gypsies was the only solution." But Kamm ends the story with an offhand mention of a positive development for Gypsies—"television programs and other encouragement"—that begs for more reporting. Kamm attains an interview with Czech Republic President Vaclav Havel, 12-10, and asks him about the intolerance of many Eastern Europeans for Gypsies. Concerning recent anti-Gypsy violence, Havel says, "'The impossibility of speaking openly about latent social problems and trying to resolve them under Communism...prevented the creation of true 'Civil Societies.'...I think in the Czech Republic we have created all the basic institutions of democracy....Now much more effort should be focused on building a civil society....This is what I see as the biggest challenge of our time.'" In his extensive travels across two continents, Kamm vividly conveys the impact on daily life and thought wrought by the vast political and economic upheavals of the past five years. With his ability to discover people on both the edges and the apex of society—and to place their ideas and attitudes in context—Kamm consistently delivers compelling articles.

Fred Kaplan

The Boston Globe

Moscow bureau chief. While he capably recounts the tangled web of Russian politics, Kaplan best displays his reporting skills in his finely textured accounts of everyday life in Moscow. He also manages engaging treatment of the nation's efforts to deal with burgeoning capitalism and the battle between haves and have-nots. As Kaplan notes shrewdly in his 8-19 piece examining Russia two years after the attempted coup, "For a country locked in a rigid order for the previous 75 years, disorder is not altogether bad." In his 6-6 article, he revels in the citizenry's new-found freedoms. "Most Muscovites are still stuck in low-paying state jobs, barely able to get by. But ever-growing numbers—certainly hundreds of thousands—are making, investing and spreading around money with a spirit of adventure, risk, freedom and tawdriness that would make desk-bound Western executives blush." But capitalism can also have a darker side, as Kaplan relates, 7-12. "Ever since President Boris Yeltsin legalized private trade, thousands, possibly millions of Russians have made big money, buying and selling and reselling. But almost none of Russia's new entrepreneurs have made their fortunes by *producing* anything....It is a situation of enormous controversy, with many fearing that Russia could turn into a colonial outpost—importing Western and Asian consumer goods but exporting only raw materials." Kaplan's 10-6 article examines the origins of the political battle that ended with Russian tanks blasting the Parliament. "The tank assault on the parliament building...may have clinched the end of a year-long power struggle over whether Russia should follow Yeltsin's policy of moving from socialism to capitalism or whether it should step back to a more state-managed economy, as favored by a majority of parliament." An able writer, Kaplan helps the reader wade through the many mixed signals coming out of a turbulent Russia.

Gregory Katz

The Dallas Morning News

★★½

Mexico City bureau chief. Exploring the social fabric of Mexico and the Caribbean, Katz can elucidate complex government policies as well as capture the struggle of everyday life. His accessible approach makes fine use of street-reporting skills and commonsense analysis, enabling him to tread much new ground. In his articulate 7-8 piece on the side agreements to NAFTA, Katz lays out all the intricacies that could slow passage of the agreement. "If the treaty is approved by the House and the Senate [in the U.S.], hundreds of details still must be worked out. Technical terms used in the treaty must be defined and U.S. regulations must be changed. This process can take another two months." In his riveting 1-25 portrayal of rural life in Haiti, Katz conveys the bleakness of the impoverished nation. "Each afternoon, the rail-thin women of Darguin trek a few miles to comb through the waste of a chicken-processing plant to fill their buckets with chicken entrails. They must pay about $1 a bucket for the privilege." Katz often complains about the coziness of the Mexican press and the administration of President Carlos Salinas de Gortari. The approach makes for for terrific irony in his fawning and folksy 12-3 tribute to Luis Donaldo Colosio, the man chosen to succeed Salinas. "Despite his exceptional grades, Mr. Colosio is not remembered in Monterrey as a nerd. He liked to dance, to play guitar, to go to the movies with his friends and to hang out in Sanborn's, a popular store and coffee shop." In his jargon-filled essay in the April *Esquire*, Katz manages one compelling point. Noting that cleaning the capital would re-

quire politically impossible measures—such as shutting factories and restricting the use of vehicles—he sarcastically intones, "But that would throw people out of work, and poverty, which can cause death by a dozen possible maladies, is an immediate threat, whereas pollution can cause only hypothetical deaths far in the future." Katz has a no-nonsense way of getting his message across.

Lincoln Kaye

Far Eastern Economic Review

★★★½

Beijing. Kaye's highly literate, icy precision substitutes exact detail for omnipotent conjecture. His reporting favors readers with a serious interest in the region over those content with a well-supported survey or argument. In his trenchant 1-28 article on the Chinese government's forthcoming efforts to slow the overheating economy, Kaye looks at the possible effects of the various initiatives the government might try. As he tirelessly points out, no one really knows, but what it may come down to is attitude. "Businessmen in [the city of] Wenzhou are betting that this time, mere rhetoric will not be enough to stop them. Yet it was little more than rhetoric that triggered the boom in the first place. At a word from [party chairman] Deng [Xiaoping] last January, the economy shook off the torpor of 'rectification' and rose to meet his call for double-digit growth." Building a strong case around the intricacies of GATT protocol, 3-11, Kaye finds China further from entry into GATT today than in January 1989. He clearly explains the barriers against China's acceptance into the GATT club and the historical vagueness about China's position—does it need to "re-enter" or "accede"? After laying out the reasons China is so anxious for fast-track approval, Kaye turns for an assessment to U.S. Trade Representative Douglas Newkirk, who has already been on the case for seven years. "'I'm going to be retired in seven years and I'm not sure that I'm going to be able to wrap it up —at the current pace.'" In his 11-11 article, Kaye lists general and specific reasons for skepticism about the Clinton administration's recently-turned-friendly overtures to Beijing. Most generally, he points out that no Chinese official stands to gain by reciprocating friendship with the West pending the death of Deng and the power struggle that will inevitably follow. In his poignant and touching 4-1 essay, Kaye captures the eerieness of spending the Tet holiday in Vietnam. "Thornbushes and creepers, trembling in the steady northerly windstream, all but obscure the underlying rubble of tin cans, rubber-tire sandals and canvas scraps. You practically trip over it before you even notice the half buried helmet." Week after week, Kaye provides the gritty detail from China and beyond, offering insights and observations often overlooked by his colleagues.

Bill Keller

The New York Times

★★★★

Johannesburg. With both comprehensive reporting and brilliant analysis, Keller always stays one step ahead of the pack. His sober and cerebral 2-19 account of the power-sharing agreement reached by the South African government and the African National Congress details the accord. Kelly carefully explains the hurdles negotiators faced convincing their respective groups of its benefit, and what each side conceded in order to reach a compromise. "The government has dropped its demand that regional powers and borders be permanently entrenched before elections....The congress, in turn, agreed that half of the assembly seats would be apportioned by regions, and that questions of regional power would require a two-thirds vote of those members." Rich with compelling economic information, Keller's eye-opening 6-17 piece on the corporate structure of South Africa reveals that 80 percent of businesses listed on the Johannesburg stock exchange are owned by four mega-companies. In anticipation of regulation by the multiracial government, Keller reports, the Sanlam Group—one of the four—plans to sell its Metropolitan Life insurance company to a black consortium. "Blacks may generally be poor, but they are numerous, [ANC Chief Economist Tito Mboweni] said, and they can buy into the economy, in something of the way that Afrikaners did, through black-owned pension funds or life insurance companies." Gallantly striving for balance in his 9-12 piece weighing the impact of sanctions in ending apartheid, Keller concludes that though the sanctions devastated the economy, the ancillary effects created tremendous pressure for change. "[One form of pressure] was to convert many South African business executives into grudging lobbyists for political reform. Alarmed by the prospect of endless isolation, bankers and corporate executives privately urged Mr. [F.W.] de Klerk to move faster, and publicly entered into their own dialogue with black leaders." In his astute 11-26 article on the future of Inkatha Chief Mangosuthu G. Buthelezi, Keller recounts the means by which the chief accrued tremendous power in the Natal province. He then lays out Buthelezi's options under a constitution that will cost the chief considerable personal power. Even though the Inkatha Freedom Party will likely emerge as the nation's main opposition group, Keller notes, it's not an easy road. "Some politicians who know Chief Buthelezi speculate that the Inkatha leader, faced with the options of waging insurgency or swallowing his pride, will do neither, but will decide at age 65 to retire, and turn Inkatha over to a successor." By tracking down the vital facts and placing them in fresh perspective, Keller consistently provides masterful coverage of South Africa.

Robin Knight

U.S.News and World Report

★★

European senior editor. Always searching for the underlying motivation, Knight manages a diverse portfolio of stories—from the sinister and desperate to the offbeat and amusing. Although constrained by the newsweekly format, he nonetheless articulates fresh perspectives. In his descriptive 2-1 article on why the Vance-Owen peace plan will likely fail to end the fighting in Bosnia, Knight explores the deep-seated anger of Bosnian Serbs in their makeshift capital of Pale, 10 miles outside of Sarajevo. Knight portrays how a paranoia stemming from their interpretation of the past contributes to their obsessive, single-minded struggle. "The Serbs have an emotional, myth-filled view of their own history, reinforced at every turn by wounded self-righteousness and a lasting sense of grievance at the outside world. What happened in 1389 or 1941 is as relevant as yesterday's firefight in the Drina Valley." In his bland but concise 11-1 piece, Knight analyzes the impotence of NATO and its prospects for the future. He focuses on the borrowed idea that, lacking a common enemy, NATO forthwith will face "'geo-economic' conflict"—the outbreak of hostilities over trade disputes. Effectively rebuffing those who argue that NATO's ineffectiveness in Yugoslavia offers an excuse to let the alliance disintegrate, Knight writes tersely, "But to say that NATO should be allowed to die is like arguing that police should be abolished because crime persists." Picking up the pace, Knight offers a crisp 10-4 interpretation of the prevailing attitudes among voters in Eastern Europe where years of economic hardship have inspired a backlash of support for ex-communists and other go-slow reformers. Far from giving up on the transition to market economies, Knight finds, the people of this region are simply expressing their despair. "Everywhere, there is a widespread desire for a Western, democratic and capitalist society but little consensus about how to build one....Inevitably, there is more gray than black or white in Eastern Europe today. Uncertainty is unsettling to people who have known only totalitarianism." In his humorous 7-5 account from Britain, Knight chronicles how sport debacles, weak government, and royal peccadilloes have battered national pride. "Actually the English positively revel in disasters. Mockery and self-deprecation are national sports; asked recently by pollsters what single thing about Britain gave them most pride, 39 percent could think of nothing at all." Knight's well-backed analysis makes for solid, if not always riveting, weekly reading.

Scott Kraft

Los Angeles Times

★★

Paris. Although in August Kraft moved to Paris from his position as Johannesburg bureau chief, his strongest efforts of the year remain his reflective analytical pieces from South Africa. The probing pieces he contributes from France lack the zip of his earlier work, but still reveal his intellectual prowess as he jumps right into complex issues of diplomacy and culture. In one of his final dispatches from South Africa, 7-23, Kraft presciently interviews several young economists in the African National Congress on the challenges facing the communist-based group as its turn to rule the country fast approaches even as its ideological foundation crumbles. "Gone is the

talk of nationalization and communism as means of uplifting the millions of impoverished blacks. Instead, ANC economists speak of creating incentives for private business, reducing government spending and letting the air out of bloated state bureaucracies." In his 6-27 piece from Mogadishu, Kraft notes a correlation between restored order and entrepreneurial activity. "It has been at least two years since Somalia has seen such a surge of healthy business activity. And though the free market is pretty raw here, sometimes resembling a 'Road Warrior' movie with Adam Smith in the lead role, it is functioning again nevertheless." In an effort to liven up his dullish 11-30 piece on French resentment of the U.S inflexibility on agricultural subsidies in the GATT negotiations, Kraft invokes yet another movie. "To make matters worse, Mickey Kantor, the U.S. trade representative and a man whose name may be better known in France than in America, 'admitted' that he had seen 'Jurassic Park' three times, according to the French press." Kraft's effervescent 9-28 piece on the glut plaguing the champagne industry notes that French farmers view the conspiracy of market forces as part of an eternal cycle. "The 30,000 people in the 300 small villages who earn their living in the industry are tough, stoic people for the most part; they and their ancestors have endured repeated invasions by foreign armies over the centuries. And, like farmers everywhere, they are accustomed to battles with nature and the marketplace." On his new beat, Kraft maintains his handy knack for imagery and metaphors. While that will help carry him until he develops a sharper eye for French life, Kraft should soon produce work to match his earlier efforts from South Africa.

Howard LaFranchi

The Christian Science Monitor

Europe. With his finger on the pulse of the European Community, LaFranchi moves smoothly from important issues in one member state to the next. His coverage of Europe, however, proves unnecessarily downbeat and rarely examines how Europe can improve its economy and political standing. In his 1-20 analysis of the European political scene, LaFranchi tells how the election of a vibrant American president has resulted in a case of leader envy among the French. "Voters are comparing Clinton—who is 46, of the post-World-War-II generation, a saxophone player, and who opposed the Vietnam war as a college student—with their own leaders, many of whom have been in power for most of the past decade, and feel a heightened desire for fresh faces in politics." LaFranchi's 5-12 article reports that the price of EC membership may be too high for some nations thinking of joining. "Of more importance, says [Sweden's minister of EC affairs Ulf] Dinkelspiel, will be the size of Sweden's financial contribution to the EC—especially as Sweden battles a recession and a huge budget deficit....The image of Sweden contributing heavily to the EC to pay for distant countries' inefficiencies and corruption is strong here." In his balanced 6-21 essay, LaFranchi analyzes whether Europe has the mettle to take the hard economic and political steps necessary to emerge from recession. "As Western Europe sinks deeper into its worst economic downturn in decades, the 12 countries of the European Community have reached a crossroads. They could either move toward more market protectionism, which would antagonize their American and Japanese trading partners, or anger their own populations by scaling back unprecedented levels of social protections." Postulating that the breakup of Yugoslavia also places a nail in the coffin of European unity, LaFranchi's well-thought-out 8-30 piece takes the pulse of Europe. "Having abetted Europe's plunge into its deepest pessimism since the 1930s, the conflict in the former Yugoslavia has revived old distrusts and revealed such political impotence...that the dream of a truly common European foreign and security policy has been pushed off far into the future—if not ended altogether." While this may be true, it would be gratifying if LaFranchi could—here and throughout his work—find a ray of hope in Europe's Herculean efforts to forge a political and economic alliance.

Christina Lamb

Financial Times

★★½

Rio de Janeiro bureau chief. Making excellent use of figures, Lamb effectively portrays the grim economic struggle in Brazil. She recognizes that politically motivated quick fixes of the economy have failed the country miserably over the past several years, and she critiques the fickle policies of the nation's new president, Itamar Franco, and his administration. In her straightforward 2-9 report on a pending meeting between Brazilian Economy Minister Paulo Haddad and IMF officials, Lamb smartly predicts that the new minister "is unlikely to get a warm reception....The rapid collapse of Brazil's last standby accord, agreed in January last year for $2.1 billion, followed that of nine letters of intent and two accords in the past 11 years." Noting the end of the honeymoon for President Franco, 2-12, Lamb carefully explains the reaction to the "check tax"—his proposal for taxing all fiscal transactions. "Demanding that the government sort out its finances and crack down on evasion, rather than increase taxes, the protesters called on the Senate to vote against the check tax and warned that it could result in price increases of as much as 50 percent." In her nicely detailed 8-12 article on the austerity measures aimed at stabilizing the Brazilian economy, Lamb has little optimism that legislators will soon get serious about cutting expenditures. "Spending pressures will increase enormously as campaigning gets underway for next year's congressional and presidential elections." In a comprehensive and enlightening 4-30 editorial on Franco's economic program and the effects of the nation's runaway inflation, Lamb cogently explains that inflation doesn't directly touch most people because 95 percent of private money in Brazil lies in bank accounts indexed to inflation. Therefore, she writes, Franco's uninspiring program—with its higher taxes and few spending cuts—has been well received. "The positive reaction to the plan centers on what it does not do, rather than what it does. There is understandable public relief at the absence of grandiose measures, given the disruption caused by the five shock plans imposed since 1986." While this trenchant style begs for longer pieces, Lamb's work offers a substantive account of the Brazilian government and economy.

John Lloyd

Financial Times

★★½

Moscow bureau chief. While he writes articulate stories, Lloyd presents acute analysis more than fresh information. His best pieces do not rely on anonymous or official sources but on what he sees going on. His keen 3-30 survey of the political self-immolation of Russian President Boris Yeltsin finds that the President appears either drunk or despondent—or both—before a Russian Parliament debate on a referendum over early elections. Lloyd notes the wearying effect on his supporters. "'The president's speech [the previous evening] made me bitterly disappointed,' said [Elena Bonner, widow of dissident Andrei Sakharov]. 'I have, do and will support the president, but he must be *our* president. I wanted him to say: we must continue the economic reforms; I wanted him to say: we will go by the voice of the people, we will have a referendum, and we won't allow any compromises.'" Lloyd comes down on the side of Yeltsin in the increasingly tense confrontation between the president-reformer and his hidebound legislature, but in his perspicuous 9-22 analysis, he deftly balances Yeltsin's words against reality. Lloyd writes that Yeltsin's speech dissolving Parliament both satisfies the World Bank and sends a clear signal that Yeltsin controls the KGB and the army. But looking back to the April referendum, Lloyd adds an equivocal observation. "That vote, surprisingly positive from a people wearied of political squabbles and economic decline, was followed by further squabbling (at a higher pitch) and further decline (at a faster rate)." A week later, Lloyd offers a terrifically descriptive 9-29 scene-setter from outside the Russian White House, where a small crowd braved the elements in support of the parliamentarians barricaded inside. "Two men purloined kitchen chairs, and one recited patriotic poetry into a microphone while the other held the crackling loudspeaker. The cold rain fell on bare heads and umbrellas....The stage was set for a confrontation." Despite pronouncing Yeltsin a brilliant tactician in the aftermath of the violent uprising, 10-5, Lloyd fails to convince that the Russian President intentionally allowed radicals into the streets to fire the first shots and instigate violence, thus enabling Yeltsin to crush them. Nevertheless, he keenly warns, "In removing Parliament [Yeltsin] has cut out a poison, but not yet cauterized the wound. If left to gape, it could fester well beyond Moscow. After the exhaustion of the past few days, he must gird himself to give new impetus to reforms which will produce no quick results, but without which the country could easily fall to the forces defeated yesterday." With his poignant and direct style, Lloyd consistently provides illuminating and comprehensive coverage.

Rick Lyman

The Philadelphia Inquirer

★★

Johannesburg. Lyman's sharply descriptive, though somewhat overwrought, prose reflects his efforts to offer a complete sense of the atmosphere in South Africa. Usually providing efficient, straightforward reports, Lyman shines when he focuses on compelling individuals who reflect the dramatic changes throughout eastern and southern Africa. His 6-13 profile of Malawi President Hastings Kamuzu Banda finds that after 28 years of one-man, one-party rule, Banda has compiled a treacherous book of intimidation tactics that he can turn to as he faces a referendum over whether the government should include opposition parties. The eccentric Banda, Lyman reports, has long shown a personal flair for authoritarianism. "With a kind of warped Victorian sensibility, Banda, who is believed to be in his 90s, has long forbidden men to wear long hair or bell-bottoms....Singing the Simon and Garfunkel song 'Cecilia' is against the law because the unmarried Banda considers it an affront to his 'official hostess' and longtime companion, Cecilia Kadzamira." Profiling Wilhelm Verwoerd, member of the African National Congress and grandson of the founder of apartheid, 5-16, Lyman deftly conveys the emotional forces preying on the soft-spoken philosophy student who speaks at ANC rallies. "'It is a liberating feeling to take this step and no longer be part of a fearful and threatened minority,' Verwoerd said. For his trouble, he has been called a 'traitor' by members of his family. Right-wingers have threatened his life. And his parents told him they felt 'like I had put a knife in their back.'" Observing the dramatic shift in reaction to the convening of the South African parliament, presumably the last dominated by whites, 11-23, Lyman writes, "Outside, instead of the now-customary march by tens of thousands of ANC supporters, the opening was greeted only by a rather lackluster gathering of about three-dozen right-wingers who were outnumbered and openly jeered by multiracial passersby." His verbose but characteristically descriptive 10-8 through 10-11 series on the U.S.-UN role in Somalia breaks little new ground, though the second installment, 10-9, lucidly profiles Gen. Mohammed Farah Aidid. "Aidid, 57, keeps his head slightly bent, as if deferentially, when he talks. His dark eyes peer through narrow slits and his voice is scarcely above a whisper. Bony, delicate fingers curl around the head of his walking stick....The clan leader is unwavering in his insistence on being the one, true, legitimate leader of Somalia—the general who, in his own mind, single-handedly vanquished former dictator Mohamed Siad Barre and earned a chance at power." Making liberal use of his literary skills, Lyman gives full flavor to his subjects.

Mark Magnier

The Journal of Commerce

★★½

Tokyo bureau chief. An amusing and perceptive writer, Magnier files cultural features and broad-based business stories, many of which focus on Southeast Asian shipping concerns. His efforts to portray Japanese life and society reveal an unapologetically American bias, which works because of its honesty. In his 6-6 feature on commuting via Japanese rail, Magnier explains that the sardine-like system operates at 200 to 270 percent capacity. But, according to rail planners, Magnier notes ironically, riders who now stand crammed shoulder to shoulder, "will be able to read newspapers by 2003 when trains will only be 180 percent overloaded." Relating his second effort of the day to board a packed train, Magnier opts for straight humor. "I now adopt the modified linebacker stance. Head down, feet set, shoulders braced, I surge forward....Dream on. You never even played peewee football and it shows." Magnier's precise chronology of events surrounding the breakdown of waterfront talks between Japan's harbor management and dock workers, 4-12, details a part-time strike in addition to deftly reflecting one of the idiosyncrasies of Japanese labor relations. Noting that five major ports will be affected by the work stoppage, he adds, "But in a strange twist, the port of Nagoya will remain open. Sources say this port is exempted because of strong personal ties between a key Japan Harbor Transportation Association executive and a [unionized] stevedoring company in the Nagoya port." Writing from Khabarovsk, Russia, 10-5, Magnier finds little local interest in Moscow affairs, as shortages of food have been replaced by shortages of money to buy abundant food. "In many other ways, the systemic changes are apparent. Farmers and other small business people now sell their produce out of small booths on the main street of Khabarovsk while the old deserted state-run stores behind them are sending workers into the street to try and attract customers." His smart 11-12 piece finds the U.S. government gearing up for intense lobbying against a Japanese law that would permit certain types of reverse engineering, whereby products are taken apart allowing other companies a view of how they work. Magnier reports that U.S. trade representatives see the law as a means to combat American manufacturers who dominate 70 percent of the $6.4 billion Japanese software market. Magnier's efforts to find fresh stories and perspectives complement his blunt and entertaining style.

Victor Mallet

Financial Times

★★½

Thailand. With an acute taste for local flavor, Mallet consistently provides street-smart insight from various cities in Southeast Asia. He emphasizes the results of policies rather than their political ramifications. Mallet's incisive 5-24 piece profiles the contenders in the first day of the highly successful Cambodian elections. Mallet observes that the candidates, many of whom are recently returned exiles, share a disdain for Vietnamese influence in their country. "Most recommend a free market economy but are otherwise vague on economic policy....The chief distinction between the leading contenders is over whether to isolate or destroy the Khmer Rouge or to attempt to accommodate them —as the UN did with so little success—in a new government." His slightly mocking 9-24 story of the U.S. embargo of Vietnam sheds little new light, but effectively reveals the impotence of continuing the trade ban. "Kodak films, Hewlett-Packard computer printers, and even Chef Boy Ardee canned ravioli (microwave-cookable version) are all on sale in Vietnam, although microwave ovens are almost unheard of." Mallet's highly articulate, if familiar, 2-11 story on the United Nation's $2 billion failure to restore order to the Cambodian countryside chronicles the constant and flagrant violence confronting the UN Transitional Authority in Cambodia (Untac). "In one particularly humiliating incident on a road north of Phnom Penh last month, unarmed Untac troops from Poland saw soldiers shoot dead the driver of a van that had failed to stop at a casual roadblock; then the Poles watched helplessly as the soldiers killed the two passengers in the van in cold blood." Traveling to the heart of Burma, 1-28, Mallet finds the once-quiet town of Mandalay reeling with prosperity and Chinese entrepreneurs. "The free trade boom has spawned a generation of flashy black marketeers; they smoke imported 555 cigarettes and drink Changlee beer brewed in the Chinese border province of Yunnan....They boast of their ability to buy police chiefs and immigration officers." Despite a tendency to cover much-reported stories, Mallet time and again provides a fresh perspective.

David Marsh

Financial Times

★★★

European editor. A consummate textbook reporter who sticks to what his source material yields, Marsh provides ample information on banking and finance. His experienced editorial hand enables him to move effortlessly between major points. His 3-5 profile of Japanese-born Kumiharu Shigehara, chief economist of the Organisation for Economic Co-operation and Development (OECD), examines the recent problems of the institution that failed to foresee the depth of the international recession. In this comprehensive effort, Marsh shows how others see Shigehara and discusses Shigehara's outlook for the OECD. "[Shigehara's experience] has also provided—besides an almost unnerving fluency in English and French and a lack of formality which belies his nationality—a good relationship with many top officials in the policy making world." Not wasting a word,

4-23, Marsh details the annual audit of the European Bank for Reconstruction and Development (EBRD), an audit that indicates the bank overshot its budget. "EBRD officials said yesterday that the difference between the sterling [the currency used to cover costs] and Ecu calculations partly reflect the impact of procedures for depreciation of capital spending. [They] said the discrepancy was also due to transactions carried out at the start of each year to translate the bank's income—denominated in Ecus, and accruing in a variety of currencies—into sterling for spending during the year." Recounting the significant findings of a United Parcel Service survey of European business owners, 11-9, Marsh trenchantly provides the textual accompaniment to a series of nine bar graphs. "The survey...points to widespread disillusionment with the effects of the single market program. However, there is relative confidence that plans to create a single currency will eventually produce results, despite the exchange rate mechanism upsets of the past two years." In his 11-12 piece on a speech by former Bundesbank president Karl Otto Pohl, Marsh moves briskly through the key points. "Mr. Pohl said the main issue facing Europe was combating unemployment and opening the west to the former eastern bloc. 'We can't solve these problems by establishing a monetary institution in Frankfurt.'" Thanks to his experience covering international banking and finance, Marsh can often interest lay readers in even the most arcane subjects.

Gary Marx

Chicago Tribune

Buenos Aires. Filing reports from Somalia to Bolivia, Marx provides rich analysis, and enhances his stories by altering his literary style to suit his topics. His inviting tone welcomes readers to the scene of an event and quickly brings them up to date. Shattering any illusions about life in a rain forest, Marx meticulously frames his 6-25 story about a small-town feud in Xapuri, Brazil, over who should run a foundation named for ecological martyr Francisco "Chico" Mendes. "It's hot, and things move slowly. This is the Amazon, an impoverished, lawless place where hard-up Brazilians from all over come to help themselves from nature's riches." Marx covers the action as Mendes's widow and members of the Xapuri's Rural Workers Union Mendes founded battle for control of his legacy. "Each side accuses the other of selling out to ranchers, duping the common rubber tapper and enriching themselves with money raised in Chico's name." Marx's unconvincing 3-15 analysis of Argentina's dramatic privatization of state companies ultimately fails as his mostly anonymous, critical sources oppose the sell-offs on ideological rather than economic or intellectual grounds. According to unnamed diplomats and economists he cites, "a government that sells its key industries is also abdicating its social responsibilities." Although his figures reflect that privatization has come at a cost, Marx offers no evidence that state ownership was better or even sustainable. In his 5-30 piece on the efforts of U.S. foundations to support a Brazilian co-op program, Marx finds growing frustration among the sponsors. The program provides financial incentives to keep rubber tappers in the forest cultivating Brazil nuts, he notes, "but the project has been plagued by financial and administrative problems that demonstrate the difficulty of applying international marketing strategies in a part of the world where most people don't understand—or reject—the concept of profit making." Proving that print media can match the drama of televised images, Marx's clever 1-14 report from Mogadishu brilliantly captures the turmoil and anxiety confronting U.S. marines. "A shot rings out. Then another. It's close. The marines peer from the sandbagged hotel and see someone about 50 yards away in a yellow shirt holding an AK-47. As he starts running toward a nearby house, Guerrero shouts: 'Let's get him.'" With his lively style, Marx successfully engages his audience, but sometimes fails when he oversells his point.

Robert Mauthner

Financial Times

Diplomatic editor. With his eye trained on diplomatic maneuverings, Mauthner thrives on his ability to provide telling information and assess intelligently the moves and statements of international policy-makers. Focusing most of his attention on Bosnia and Yugoslavia, he consistently interprets the myriad signals coming from all sides. In his 2-1 profile of Bosnian peace negotiators Lord Owen and Cyrus Vance, Mauthner finds two men who have worked together before—during the Carter administration—and who possess complementary personalities. Portraying Vance as the elder statesmen sitting stoically by, interjecting wisely when necessary, while the younger Owen keeps all sides talking, Mauthner salutes the pair for getting the belligerents in the Bosnian conflict to sit at the negotiating table for four weeks. In his outstanding 2-12 analysis of the Clinton administration's professed support for the peace process, Mauthner praises Clinton for dropping his campaign rhetoric about air strikes and for lifting the arms embargo. He smartly observes that "before an agreement can be enforced, however, it has to be reached. The U.S. administration, which has emphasized that it will not impose an agreement on the warring parties, may have to shed more illusions when it comes face to face with their slippery representatives." Recapping a fruitless meeting between Russia, the U.S., and Europe over the Bosnian situation, 5-24, Mauthner writes bluntly, "Communiqués usually try to put the most optimistic gloss on the outcome of the meetings which they describe.... The phraseology employed [from this one] is reminiscent of UN Security Council resolutions on the Arab-Israeli conflict, which have remained largely a dead letter for more than two decades." Relating the demands of the UN High Commissioner for Refugees (UNHCR) for the safety of relief convoys in Bosnia, Mauthner's 11-18 report reveals the fundamental shortcoming of diplomatic reporting: It relies on the words of diplomats, and often obscures as much as it reveals. Here an entire story on the threats of starvation in Bosnia comes from a UNHCR spokeswoman in London describing a meeting that took place the previous day in Geneva. The disturbing information easily sways readers, just as the UNHCR wishes, but taken alone presents an insufficient perspective. Fortunately, with his experience and knowledge, Mauthner usually provides deeper and more instructive pieces.

Hamish McDonald

Far Eastern Economic Review

★★½

New Delhi. McDonald's extensive knowledge of Indian politics and policy, along with his feel for the pulse of events, effortlessly meld in his consistently illuminating reports. At times, however, his myopic concern for the machinations of the government leaves unanswered questions about India's business culture that would fit neatly within his general themes. In his 8-12 article on Prime Minister P.V. Narasimha Rao's narrow victory in a no-confidence vote, McDonald perceptively observes that, "in the absence of firm leadership, the bureaucracy is dragging its feet and sometimes even sabotaging enterprises that fit the spirit of reforms." McDonald goes on to list several proposed reforms—such as the privatization of the banking system and the legalization of private airlines—that face immediate peril unless Rao pushes them strongly. In his 5-27 piece explaining the downfall of the Prime Minister, McDonald shrewdly portrays a leader of faltering political skills. "Rao should have been collecting accolades for pushing through a third reforming budget, with only minor concessions....Instead, MPs of the ruling Congress party went home to their electorates with near universal condemnation ringing in their ears." McDonald finds that members of Rao's party were split over whether to impeach a clearly corrupt Supreme Court justice. Rather than allow members to vote their conscience—which the Prime Minister feared would make him look weak—Rao had everyone abstain, thus making them appear as supporters of corruption. McDonald's incisive 4-29 piece on Indian bank reform reveals that the Reserve Bank of India understands the short-term risks of modernization. "The path to sound banking, however, is likely to be a tortuous one, both for the banks themselves and for the government, which cannot afford a sweeping bailout." Finally venturing into the streets for his 4-15 "Traveller's Tales," McDonald cheerfully discovers mayhem. "Two factors give New Delhi traffic its peculiar character. One is the unmatched variety of road-users, no less than 48 being listed in the regulations....As well as assorted vehicles traveling at all speeds, Delhi also has a wide variety of livestock in and out of harness: pony traps, bullock carts, and even camel-carts. Thousands of

cattle roam the streets...[and] mahouts walk their elephants to and from weddings and other entertainments....The other [factor] is the anarchy and aggression." This rich detail and refreshing levity suggest McDonald should get out more often, if he dares.

James McGregor
The Wall Street Journal
★★½

Beijing. Relying more on illustrative anecdotes than statistics, McGregor conveys rich, detailed stories on China. The irony and humor of a market system subverting the ideological foundation of a totalitarian economic system shine gleefully in his work. His 9-24 piece on the Chinese stock market—"trading is slow, prices are stagnant. The onlookers seem bored"—recounts the brief history of this paradoxical institution, revealing just how quickly the Chinese people embrace market concepts. "Of course, there will always be those for whom buying and selling stocks—even in the absence of securities laws—just isn't exciting enough. And for them there are the illegal futures trading shops that have been spreading rapidly along China's southern coast." Observing unrest on China's farms, 2-17, McGregor captures the continuing frustration among state officials and farmers over stagnating profits and productivity dating back to the land reforms of the early 1980s. In response to farmer complaints about bureaucrats squeezing their profits, McGregor shrewdly notes the advice of the Chinese agricultural minister. "Instead of taking money from farmers, local bureaucrats should find some other kind of work and thereby reduce the cost of government." McGregor then predicts that further modernization of agriculture would throw millions of farmers out of work. In a captivating 3-16 piece on post-Cold War Mongolia, where people are both starving and freezing, McGregor offers many vivid reasons for the country's degeneration to its current plight—"a below-zero Bangladesh." McGregor's literal modifiers add a light tone while conveying a grave situation at Power Plant No. 4 in the country's capital, Ulan Bator. "If this 600-megawatt rattletrap quits running, half the people in this city of 550,000 face freezing to death—and the entire country's gasping economy could finally suffocate." Offering a taste of the anxiety of doing business in semi-reformed China, McGregor pens a penetrating 6-2 article that defines in practical terms the effects of ill-conceived currency regulation. "Foreign corporations that are normally fastidious about the law are in the uncomfortable position of using the illegal black market or shutting down." Masterfully adding context and perceptive detail to his reporting, McGregor offers solid accounts of the business culture and practices in China.

Michael Mecham
Aviation Week & Space Technology
★★½

Asian bureau chief. Having moved from Bonn to Hong Kong, Mecham now surveys Southeast Asia, one of the hottest markets in commercial and military aviation. His "Load Factors Slip at Asian Carriers," 2-22, is misleadingly headlined—the reader may think the article covers the troubles facing Asian air carriers. Instead, Mecham offers a rather upbeat assessment of the prospects for these carriers. "Unlike their Eu-

WHAT GOES THROUGH A PRESIDENT'S MIND WHEN THE WRONG SPEECH COMES UP ON THE TELEPROMPTER?

ropean and U.S. counterparts, the OAA [Orient Airlines Association] members are seeing growth in passengers and freight accompanied by growth in net profits." Mecham points out that load factors are down and pressures from the West for market access have increased, but nothing justifies the pessimistic tone of the headline. In his engrossing 6-28 piece, he reports that Air Canada and McDonnell Douglas have come to an agreement to refurbish the former's fleet of DC-9's, a move resisted by McDonnell Douglas "because it wanted to sell new aircraft, according to one official familiar with the Air Canada talks." Mecham's brilliant 7-5 account of the recent Malaysian military aircraft purchase finds that "although a relatively small order by world standards...the Malaysian contest pitted the U.S. and Russian fighters against each other as never before and showed how intense competition is likely to be in the future." For countries struggling to keep their arms-industry production lines open, Asia will continue to constitute an important export outlet. His intriguing 10-11 report on the opening Vietnamese aircraft market recounts that "Air France has scored a marketing coup for itself and Airbus Industrie by supplying Vietnam Airlines with five A320 twin jets, helping the upstart carrier with flight crew and technical training and laying the foundation for a future equity partnership." With his grasp of the flourishing Southeast Asian market, Mecham captures the exciting potential of the region and its importance to aircraft manufacturers of the world.

Matt Moffett
The Wall Street Journal
★★★

Mexico City. With sketches drawn from Mexican life, Moffett masterfully portrays the practical aspects of larger political and cultural issues. Citing newly constructed shopping malls and roads rebuilt by citizens, he credits President Carlos Salinas de Gortari for providing the means for—and the Mexican people for seizing—these fresh opportunities. Moffett also glances nervously north across the border, whence the winds of fortune blow. Depicting communal spirit triumphing over bureaucratic ineptitude in the efforts to renovate the country's infrastructure, 1-8, Moffett deftly describes Mexico's National Solidarity Program as a highly successful plan to "ensure that the benefits from Mexico's free-market economic renaissance reach the very poor." Under the program, Moffett points out, the government delivers raw materials to crumbling neighborhoods, and—at a 30 to 40 percent savings over what it normally would cost—residents perform the work of repaving the streets or rebuilding the schools. Portraying Mexican enthusiasm for NAFTA in contrast to the historical animosity felt toward the U.S., Moffett makes a strong 4-20 case to support his simple observation. "U.S.-Mexico relations will soon get either a lot better or a lot worse. There is not much in between." Emphasizing the large extent to which President Salinas tied his future to passage of NAFTA, 1-22, Moffett warns that history shows Salinas entering a period of self-destructive temptation—the last two years of his term. "Since the late 1960s, the sad swan songs of Mexican presidents have included military massacres, stock market crashes, peso devaluations and street demonstrations over electoral fraud." Moffett also quotes a Californian with Mexican business interests who believes that, for now, Salinas seems to be hanging tough with his consolidation theme. Balancing his enthusiasm for opportunity with wise respect for an untamed beast, 9-24, Moffett incisively probes several factors of risk and reward for investors on the Bolsa, the Mexican stock exchange. "Many of the Wall Street analysts who serve as intermediaries between the market and the Mexicans are, for example, recently converted junk-bond or merger mavens. Sometimes an analyst's sole qualification as Latin American specialist is a certificate from Berlitz." With his strong experience and pragmatic approach, Moffett turns out consistently well-written and enterprising stories.

Molly Moore
The Washington Post

South Asia bureau chief, based in New Delhi. Moving in 1993 from Africa to Asia, Moore employs strong reporting skills that usually distinguish her crisply written features. Her political dispatches on Pakistan and other nations, however, often lack rudimentary detail and sufficient context. In her wispy 10-21 article on the daunting tasks facing President Benazir Bhutto, Moore altogether neglects economic issues, which will dominate the attention of Bhutto's incoming administration. Vaguely recounting findings by Pakistan's caretaker government, which ran the country for the preceding seven months and exposed the corruption of previous governments—including Bhutto's—Moore suddenly switches gears. "Bhutto also is under attack by women's rights organizations....Activists fighting for improvements in the treatment of women under Pakistan's Islamic codes charge that she did little to help women in her first period in office." In contrast, Moore's sharp well-sourced 4-29 piece on Pakistani drug trafficking reveals that its impact closely resembles that caused by the narcotics industry in Colombia. Despite the lack of financial and moral support, Pakistani officials, Moore writes, cite two reasons that infrastructure development provides the government's best hope of stemming the problem. "First, roads give access to police to enforce a ban on poppy growing and to close down heroin labs. And second, roads permit provision of services that encourage people to abandon the drug trade." Moore simplistically notes, 11-30, that modern developments—electricity, hospitals, and education—threaten the culture of Nepali Sherpas, an indigenous group of mountain dwellers. For sources, Moore cites a business executive living in Nepal who wants to preserve his old village for his kids to visit, and the chief abbot—and highest ranking lama in Nepal—of a rural monastery. About the latter, Moore astutely observes that "within arm's reach were a shortwave radio, the speakers of a portable stereo—and a black Harley-Davidson T-shirt bequeathed by a visiting trekker, now used to wrap a stack of religious documents." Before moving on to Asia, Moore yields an incisive and moving 2-13 article that captures the numbness of aid workers who venture into remote Somali villages. "[Christelle Breton] leaned over a 3-year-old boy, who looked more like a sack of bones and dry flesh than a human being....'But your baby will die in seven days if you do not go [to the hospital],' pleaded Breton. The mother shrugged and said through the interpreter, 'I have four others.' A frustrated Breton turned away from the hut. 'In the beginning I used to get so upset. But there is nothing I can do. The baby will die.'" As she gets to know her new beat, Moore might elevate her analysis to the level of her exemplary reporting skills.

Carol Morello
The Philadelphia Inquirer
★★½

Middle East. Reporting mostly on the effects of military and political battles in the region, Morello offers disturbing accounts of the tensions and hostilities between various groups. She usually succeeds in her efforts to humanize the daily and long-term effects of competing religious and political ideologies. In her instructive 6-9 article, Morello reports efforts by Egyptian citizens—concerned with their country's tarnished image abroad—to keep a Western reporter away from the scene of a highway bombing that injured 14 people, including passengers on a British tour bus. "The [bombing] also was a reminder that the battle between fundamentalists and the government is tearing Egypt apart. And that prospect frightens and shames many Egyptians." In her 7-30 piece on the acquittal of accused war-criminal John Demjanjuk, Morello carefully chooses her points. In so doing, she absolves his accusers. Several times Morello emphasizes the Israeli Supreme Court's finding that Demjanjuk probably was a death-camp guard, though not Ivan the Terrible, and she properly stresses that his release was a constitutional, not a moral, matter. "For the Ukrainian-born Demjanjuk, who is being kept in protective custody until he finds a country willing to accept him, acquittal on appeal brought no vindication of being judged innocent." Morello's 8-3 article describes the losses of life and property, as well as the political effects caused by Israel's bombing of several towns in southern Lebanon. The targeted towns were suspected of harboring Hezbollah guerrillas involved in rocket attacks on northern Israel. "Some residents who describe themselves as only lukewarm supporters of Hezbollah before the raids now say they are ready to enlist and seek vengeance." But, as Morello shrewdly adds, "In the narrow political sense, the seven-day operation [by Israel] apparently succeeded. The Lebanese army announced yesterday that...it would deploy troops in the south. The presumption is that the army will prevent Hezbollah...from firing on Israel during peace talks." Her well-balanced 12-2 article, filed from the Jewish settlements in the West Bank, portrays the growing tension following deadly outbursts by both sides in protest of the peace plan. "The violence that has cost 14 Jews and 31 Palestinians their lives since the peace pact was first made public has incensed and emboldened Jewish settlers who initially were stunned into inaction....In what is becoming a routine response to every attack on Jews, the Yesha Council of Jewish Communities in Judea, Samaria and Gaza called on all settlers to block roads in the occupied territories during the predawn hours today when most Palestinians go to work." Morello's gutsy reporting and keen analysis offer a rare, street-level look at the challenges of everyday life in the Middle East.

Ray Moseley

Chicago Tribune

★½

Chief European correspondent. Rarely venturing beyond the halls of power to see how people actually live, Moseley fails to convince readers that they should care about issues and events in Europe. Many stories barely scratch the surface and seldom use insiders as sources. His 2-8 story enumerating Europe's political and economic troubles is no more enlightening than last week's grocery list, but is notable for an absurdly prejudiced statement. "On the home front, the inept [Prime Minister John] Major government [in Britain] is facing some tough decisions on such questions as closure of mines and hospitals and possibly higher taxation. However it chooses to handle them, the government seems likely to continue bumbling along for the indefinite future." In his 8-15 story on cracks in European unity, Moseley employs obscure references and unexplained allusions to form a muddled metaphor. "The train of European Union that rolled out of the Dutch city of Maastricht in a festive mood in December 1991 has been attacked by bandits and has come to a grinding halt. The bandits, the notorious Currency Speculation Gang, came in with guns blazing and robbed the passengers blind before making their getaway, leaving behind a sour mood aboard the train." Huh? In his adequate 4-4 dispatch analyzing trade policy between the U.S. and Europe, Moseley catches the administration in a do-as-I-say, not-as-I-do situation with regard to protectionism. "The EC argues that corresponding U.S. trade policy is more restrictive than Europe's. It says the U.S. has a price preference in favor of American firms of 6 to 50 percent on government contracts." Though covering familiar territory, Moseley provides a worthwhile 4-7 tale that cautions against cutting too deeply into the military. "With the Cold War over, Western nations are beating their swords into plowshares at a rate that is beginning to alarm officials of the North Atlantic Treaty Organization." Despite these occasional flashes, Moseley would prove a more effective reporter if he spent less time in the press office and a little bit more on the street.

Caryle Murphy

The Washington Post

★★

Cairo bureau chief. Murphy, who won a Pulitzer Prize for her 1990 war coverage from Kuwait, does her best work on the street, where her strong reporting skills and extensive sources expose the guts of a story. Roving the non-Israeli Middle East, she hits full stride investigating the fallout of two violent terrorist events in Egypt. On 5-19, while exploring the militant Islamic Group's manipulation of a rural Egyptian village and the government's investigation of the shooting of five German tourists, Murphy quotes a government dentist on police torture. "'They hit people and rip out their fingernails. But I never heard of someone with their teeth smashed, especially a woman, maybe a man, yes.'" Murphy renders a thorough 7-9 profile of Sheik Omar Abdel Rahman's career as spiritual leader to violent Islamic organizations. Thanks to the World Trade Center bombing and American satellite news, Murphy notes, the sheik has emerged as "the best known symbol of Islamic protest politics in the West since Iran's Ayatollah Ruhollah Khomeini." Murphy visits a charismatic gun-toting governor, 6-29, to explore the return of Saddam Hussein's dominance in Shiite southern Iraq. Although she adduces strong evidence that rebel claims there are exaggerated, she offers little to support her list of assertions about government repression. Her claim that anti-government youths are "punished with detention or execution" particularly suffers from lack of evidence. Murphy's 11-22 piece masterfully recounts the story behind the Iraqi-ordered Bush assassination attempt in April. However, while the two main conspirators deny being tortured to confess, she overcautiously concludes that the trials "fall short of resolving the controversy." On 11-6, Murphy cites reasons why Arabs maintain the boycott of Israel but provides almost no evidence for her statement that the boycott has begun to "wither" as a result of the Israeli-Palestinian agreement. Although analysis is not her strong suit, Murphy can find the facts and tell the story.

Kim Murphy
Los Angeles Times
★½

Cairo. Perhaps stretched too thin covering various locales in the Middle East, Europe, and Africa, Murphy sometimes logs sketchy reports. She turns in her strongest work from her core region, the Middle East. She weaves choice quotes into her narratives, though her prose occasionally befuddles. In analyzing the Israeli-PLO peace agreement, 9-4, Murphy cogently notes that Yasir Arafat has his work cut out in selling a plan that offers "most Palestinians in the territories only limited autonomy...and leaves huge numbers of Palestinian refugees around the world with little or no hope of ever going home." In her 9-10 article, Murphy cleverly captures the mixture of cynicism and euphoria on both sides when she quotes a friend of Arafat's. "'I'm witnessing the rape of my rights, but I'm also witnessing history.'" In a courageous 2-22 outing, Murphy visits Hussein Moussawi, the belligerent leader of the Islamic Amal wing of the militant Hezbollah group, which now holds the biggest bloc in Lebanon's National Assembly. Moussawi tells her that Israel is an "'enemy we should be fighting, an enemy with whom dialogue is with the rifle, not diplomacy.'" In her 4-10 article about Sudan, Murphy crisply analyzes why the rebel Liberation Army has faltered this year, but, while she labels factionalism "most important," she never provides details. She competently describes the plight of Muslim refugees in Croatia, 6-22, but fails to present the big picture evenly. Although she quotes a Croat refugee as saying, "'We cannot possibly understand how Muslims in Bosnia are attacking Croatians who are giving shelter to their families,'" Murphy neglects to explain that Croatian forces had previously attacked Muslims. In both Lebanon and Bosnia, Murphy's unidentified sources—more than once an "aid worker" providing political commentary—occasionally seem weak and chosen without balance. Moreover, some of her sentences defy comprehension, such as in her 8-16 story on Sudan. "For much of a generation, the last half-decade has marked the loss of hope in what, in the middle of Africa, would already have been troubled lives." Despite such drawbacks, Murphy's deep awareness of the politics of the Middle East and nearby areas often makes for enlightening analysis.

Nathaniel C. Nash
The New York Times
★★★

Buenos Aires. Combining insightful analysis with common sense, Nash dependably produces logical and informative pieces. He comfortably reports from the gray area of life, where self-evident truths prove rare, and tough choices are made not between right and wrong but rather between ill-defined options that never stay the same for long. In his 11-2 version of the Peruvian economic miracle, Nash reports that, despite the country's political problems, $2 billion in foreign investment has flooded the country since President Alberto Fujimori began major economic reforms in 1990, compared to zero investment in the preceding five years. "Under Mr. Fujimori's regimen, Congress often rubber stamps his policies and the courts remain effectively under his control. Yet business often prefers a stable authoritarian climate to an unstable struggling democracy." Nash reports a similar story from Argentina, 7-25, finding that "the deep restructuring of the Argentine economy...stands out because it was accomplished during a period of democratic rule in which [President Carlos Saul] Menem has had a vocal, though often ineffectual, opposition." In his 5-11 dispatch, Nash writes that, despite the nation's newfound stability, many Argentines still struggle with the demons of the military dictatorship of the 1970s. With neither sentimentality nor lofty moralizing, he relates the story of children who were orphaned when their parents "disappeared." These orphans, he explains, were subsequently raised by their parents' killers or associates, and their grandparents now want them back. Crafting this compelling story of frustration, anger, and legal wrangling—and no easy answers—Nash brings the reader face-to-face with teenage children who must suddenly confront tragedies they never anticipated. And he delivers a lucid 6-21 assessment of the conflicting interests of loggers, Indians—and Mennonite farmers, "who have migrated here [and] have established farms that look like the countryside of Pennsylvania or Ohio." With all these groups vying for Bolivia's rain forests, Nash relates the economic, as well as ecological, exploitation in the region. Reporting that loggers removed $6 million in timber from Indian lands in the past two years, he notes, "But under pressure from government officials working with big logging interests, the tribal leaders have agreed to compensation of only $200,000." Indirectly, he raises the question of what would happen to the rain forests if Indians got fair-market value for the timber on their lands. Nash consistently shows his knack for reporting the hidden details and motivations behind significant events.

Robert Neff

Business Week

★★½

Tokyo. Always readable, Neff generally manages fresh stories and sensible, well-supported analysis. In his shrewdly tempered reaction to the election in Japan of the first government in 35 years not led by the Liberal Democratic Party, 8-16, Neff points out that expectations are pushing the stratosphere. "[New Prime Minister Morihiro Hosokawa] and his eight-party coalition are supposedly poised to enact electoral reform, overhaul the tax system, rein in bureaucrats, deregulate the economy, and make the consumer king. All of which means it's time for a reality check." In his sharp 4-19 piece, Neff reveals how, despite its denials, the Japanese Finance Ministry managed to halt the Nikkei's precipitous slide, at least temporarily. "By late September," he incisively reports, "[former Finance Minister and Diet member Yuji] Tsushima had also helped forge agreement among the Ministries of Finance, Health & Welfare, and Posts & Telecommunications to pump $25 billion in government pension, insurance, and postal-savings funds into stocks." Focusing on a would-be microbrewer long discouraged by Japanese minimum output requirements, 9-13, Neff finds a clear example of an individual who will benefit from Hosokawa's push to loosen the grip of the Japanese regulators. "Bureaucrats are proposing to liberalize or abolish 59 rules that restrict business activity, hamper market entry, discourage consumption, or keep prices artificially high. The bureaucrats delivered the list of suggested reforms to economic ministers...just 12 days after...Hosokawa ordered them to do so." Though modest by Western standards, 2-1, Neff discovers radical changes taking place at Japan Airlines Co. (JAL). The company aims to cut costs by $1.6 billion during the next year, which, Neff contends, will not be as hard as it sounds. "JAL's costly habits date back to another era, when it was a quasi-government airline and able to pamper employees. Consider: The airline still delivers pilots from their homes to Tokyo's distant Narita airport and back by chauffeur-driven cars. It often pays for flight attendants to commute by taxi at a cost of at least $150 per ride." Hovering around the big stories in Japan, Neff digs up anecdotes and details that portray values both distinctly Japanese and also shared by the West.

Bruce W. Nelan

Time

International. While he crafts flashy articles that brim with important detail and background, Nash's coverage of familiar, well-reported subjects sometimes seems stale. In his 9-13 dispatch, he provocatively contends that a successful Israeli-Palestinian peace hinges on revitalized West Bank and Gaza economies. "Poverty and hopelessness account for much of the rise of Islamic fundamentalism in the Arab world as well as bloodshed by those Palestinians who have nothing to lose. The deal will collapse unless the dreary lot of the Palestinians is rapidly improved." Nelan's 6-21 article on nuclear proliferation and the international dilemma of freezing membership in the nuclear "club" ends on a cogent warning for the U.S. "Washington could not, even if it wanted to, guarantee Arab states against Israel, India against China, Pakistan against India or Iran against

Iraq. Some of them have the bomb now, and the others will get it. In the years to come, the U.S. will have to choose very carefully where to engage its interests and its military forces. It may have its hands full just protecting itself." When a topic deserves extended coverage, Nelan willingly devotes the pages, as in his well-written 10-4 piece on the rise of Islam and his 11-15 article on possible expansion of NATO to include former Warsaw Pact countries. However, Nelan's main failing is his tendency to rehash old news and state the obvious. "The Cold War competition has evaporated, but the world has not necessarily grown safer," he remarks in his 7-5 analysis of political and industrial espionage. Later in the story, he observes, "The Soviet Union has dissolved, and while each of the now independent republics is easier to penetrate, there are many more of them." This occasional tendency to talk down to the reader duly noted, Nelan usually manages to impart valuable information.

Mark Nicholson

Financial Times

★★★

Cairo. With his organized and insightful reports from the Middle East, Nicholson offers solid factual accounts enhanced by keen analysis. And despite the highly charged political and religious beliefs driving many of the region's events, he maintains remarkable balance. As oil prices plummet beneath the target prices set by OPEC, 1-25, Nicholson smartly finds cheating by member states the primary cause. He reports that Kuwait—claiming it needs funds to rebuild—openly ignores its assigned output level, thus presenting an obstacle to OPEC's efforts to cut daily production by 1 million barrels a day. In his clearly written 8-24 piece on the announcement by Saudi Arabia's King Fahd of a new non-family council to oversee government affairs, Nicholson chills any suggestion of liberalization by the country's ruling structure. "The new Saudi council will be free to advise and criticize the government but has no legislative powers. Its creation falls well short of anything like a shift towards western-style democracy." Shrewdly recognizing what could be a reversion to Libya's days as a terrorist-supporting state, 12-21, Nicholson focuses on the international outrage over the disappearance in Egypt of a Libyan dissident—and resident of the U.S.—under apparently sinister circumstances. The case, he writes, "has raised serious concern among western governments that Colonel Qadaffi may have abandoned any attempts to curry favor in the west and is intent instead on reviving his self-appointed role as a maverick and dangerous nuisance." Nicholson's compelling 8-2 piece on the effects of Israeli bombing in southern Lebanon finds the slow rebuilding process under Lebanese Prime Minister Rafik al-Hariri continuing with remarkable spirit. "Indeed the manner in which the country united in opposition to the raids, and in its efforts to deal with the humanitarian crisis, surprised and impressed even local commentators....This unity, however, is a modest, albeit necessary, starting point for Lebanon's mammoth remaining task." With both his remarkable range and prudent analysis, Nicholson offers a valuable perspective on Middle Eastern affairs.

Colin Nickerson

The Boston Globe

Canada. Although he tends to oversimplify, Nickerson—who moved from Tokyo to Toronto this year—consistently delivers keen observations on a variety of subjects. Perhaps from lack of experience, however, his coverage of Canada lacks the sharpness of his work from Southeast Asia. Writing from the demilitarized zone between North and South Korea, 3-21, Nickerson deftly portrays the dangerous situation in the North caused by the collapse of the communist-bloc trading system. But, he warns, tightly-knit North Korea may not be ripe for the sorts of popular uprisings witnessed in Eastern Europe and even China. "North Koreans may be freezing, hungry and impoverished, but they are intensely nationalistic....Radios in the North have no tuning dials but are all set on the same government propaganda frequency. Lacking any other information, the populace swallows the hard-line preachings of the Kim dynasty hook, line, and sinker." Blaming only the Khmer Rouge, 4-18, Nickerson misses the sheer anarchy, documented by others, of the Cambodian countryside. Still, he provides vivid images of the fear inspired by incessant violence upriver from Phnom Penh. "That fear was almost palpable among the gazers who one day last week watched yet another body turn grotesque pinwheels in the muddy convergence of the Mekong and Tonle Sap Rivers....A Philippine army officer...implored Cambodian police playing cards in a river launch to retrieve the body. They shrugged, studied their cards." Unremarkably discovering economic survival in the allure of drug smuggling for underemployed Canadian fishermen, 11-8, Nickerson highlights their maritime skills. "Fishermen familiar with every treacherous shoal, tricky current and hidden cove along a stretch of coast would prove far more elusive quarry for law agents than drug runners from elsewhere who might possess nautical skills but no special knowledge of provincial waters." In his largely uninspired 10-26 coverage of the Canadian election results, Nickerson provides a vague survey of the results by region and party, but fails to illuminate any key themes—even in the dramatic victory by the Liberal Party. Suggesting the victory could "significantly affect trade relations with the United States," Nickerson goes on to point out that with NAFTA already passed through the Canadian Parliament, there isn't much the new government can do about it. Although he breaks little new ground, Nickerson has a knack for isolating compelling details that flesh out significantly his passable reporting.

Takasha Oka

The Christian Science Monitor

½★

Tokyo, columnist. With little regard for structuring an argument, Oka pens his arbitrary observations of Japan as if he were a passenger riding in a car with a broken radio—generously padding his conversation with not altogether related, but sometimes interesting, asides. A core intellectual point generally pops out of his pieces without warning, but usually to no great end. Oka oddly opens his 4-9 comparison of spirituality in Japan and the U.S. by relating a phone conversation between Japanese Prime Minister Kiichi Miyazawa and President Clinton regarding the Vancouver summit meeting between Clinton and Russian President Boris Yeltsin. Rambling on about present and past Japanese and American leaders' individual religious beliefs, Oka incomprehensibly concludes, "Does it matter if, say, Miyazawa does not acknowledge that Biblical 'secret place' where desires and ambitions are laid bare before God? Usually not. But it sometimes may. Recognizing this could be a real step toward understanding." What? In his miserably unfocused 4-23 effort, Oka comments on the changing relationship between Japan and the U.S. Discussing trade issues in terms of aid for the former Soviet Union, Oka unconvincingly likens Miyazawa's "major domestic commitment to reform the nation's creaky political structure" to "Clinton's task of restoring the U.S. economy to health and vigor." By relying on Miyazawa's strong rhetoric favoring reform and overlooking the reality—that Miyazawa had no intention to actually reform politics, as the results of the July elections would bear out—Oka bases his analysis on a shaky premise. In his concise and articulate 11-12 piece, he lauds improved relations between Korea and Japan. He points out that the warming may be Southeast Asia's best hope for dealing with the implicit threat of nuclear-weapon development by North Korea. "To combine firmness and patience is not easy when dealing with an unpredictable neighbor like Pyongyang. But that is what the situation requires. Elimination of resentment and suspicion between Tokyo and Seoul makes a joint approach to this question practical." In his 1-8 look at how Japan treats its citizens of Korean descent, Oka inappropriately—and inaccurately—compares their plight with that of Turks living in Germany. After all, Koreans in Japan face discrimination but they are not terrorized, firebombed, or otherwise molested. Although Oka notes the gradual dissolution of Japanese nationalism, he never makes a comprehensive point. Offering his opinions à la carte, Oka furnishes columns that make for light, inadequate fare.

Julian Ozanne

Financial Times

Nairobi. Although based in Kenya, Ozanne provides strong analysis on the Israeli-PLO peace negotiations and other events in the Middle East. He tends to intrude on his reports, however, disclosing to no useful benefit his sentiments about his subjects. His crisp 2-15 description from the Lebanese-Israeli border, where expelled Palestinians survive literally in limbo, repeats itself ("muddy hillside...rain-lashed hillside") and sounds suspiciously overblown.

"The deportees are kept alive with food smuggled through Lebanese checkpoints by sympathetic journalists and Lebanese villagers. Despite the rain and melting snow, and the scorpions which live under the boulders around the camp, the morale of the expelled Palestinians is high." In his 8-20 article recounting the failed Israeli military policies of the past, Ozanne adopts heavy anti-Israeli rhetoric to describe border tension between the Israeli army and Hezbollah rebels in Lebanon. "Just as the Jewish state was congratulating itself on last month's devastating seven-day offensive against Lebanese civilians, intended to curb attacks by the pro-Iranian Hezbollah militia, an increase in regional violence is back on the agenda." Recognizing the dominance of anarchy in Zaire, 1-30/31, Ozanne skillfully describes the deadly combination of events. "The portents of a fragile African nation heading inexorably towards chaos and civil war are unmistakable....A ruthless dictator unwilling to reform, an irreconcilable 18-month political crisis, the complete loss of control over law and order and the growth of tribal animosities and secessionist sentiments are breaking the country apart." Unafraid to take a stand on what he believes to be right and wrong, Ozanne registers better work on issues where his perspective drives his coverage.

Michael Parks

Los Angeles Times

★★★

Jerusalem bureau chief. With an eye for detail and a knack for drama, Parks tackles complex and controversial stories during his first full year in Jerusalem He delivers a gripping 9-14 reconstruction of the secret Oslo talks outlining Palestinian self-rule, beautifully capturing the night the monumental accord is signed. "As other members of the Israeli delegation went to their rooms...and their Norwegian counterparts left for home, [Israeli Foreign Minister Shimon] Peres and [Norwegian Foreign Minister Johan] Holst began quietly, almost on tiptoes, rearranging the furniture in the main hall....The Norwegian foreign minister laid a gold pen on each table." Four members of the PLO arrived "one at a time so they would not attract attention." This lengthy *tour-de-force* story on the eight months of clandestine meetings includes a cogent observation from an Israeli official who credits the accord's success to "'no media coverage, and thus...freedom to negotiate without our positions hardening through exposure.'" In his sharp 2-2 analysis of the "Americanization" of the Israeli political system—including open party primaries and movement towards both the direct election of a prime minister and the adoption of a bill of rights—Parks notes that the key to its success is that, rather than a single package, the reform is sliced into politically "doable phases." His 7-27 piece on the rift between the American Jewish community and Prime Minister Yitzhak Rabin's Labor Party government astutely points out that "it stemmed not only from divergent views on peace and how to achieve it, but also on sharply different perceptions of the relationship between Israel and the Diaspora." According to an Israeli official, fewer than one in five American Jews attend a synagogue, "'The balance has shifted.... American Jews need us...just as much as we need them and maybe even more.'" For his 11-14 story, Parks demonstrates the chaotic scramble for jobs in the new Palestinian territories. He cleverly uses the ironic story of a reluctant professor who is abducted by Yasir Arafat and assigned as the manager of the Palestinians' new economic development agency. Says one East Jerusalem economist, "'With everyone grabbing for power, Arafat finds those who refuse it all the more trustworthy.'" Again and again, Parks finds the story within the story—and then knocks home his point.

Quentin Peel

Financial Times

★★

Bonn bureau chief. Because he relies heavily on government reports and official spokespersons, Peel's success hinges on the quality of information contained in them, as well as the quality of reactions he tracks down. Nonetheless, his clever and engaging prose effectively conveys his thorough grasp of German financial matters. In his smart 2-11 article, Peel highlights the contradictions in an optimistic forecast released by the newly appointed German economics minister. The forecast, Peel notes, predicts zero growth—when most others foresee negative growth—for the German economy. Peel's sources point out that the prediction calls for substantial (and unlikely) improvement of the economy in eastern Germany. "Mr. Wolfgang Roth, economics spokesman [of the opposition Social Democratic Party], said there was no clear indication where the 5 to 7 percent growth rate in east Germany would come from, given the collapse of east German industry. As for zero overall national growth rate, that would require immediate reversal of the steady contraction [of the economy]." In his shrewd 5-14 analysis of the plethora of scandals shaking Germany's political parties, Peel convincingly argues that when politicians fall out of favor within their own parties, enemies use their smallest infractions to drive them from office. He finds several factors contributing to the recent spate of scandals: nearly all the disgraced politicians are perceived as liabilities in the 1994 elections; the German press has come to life, with several magazines competing to break investigative stories; and none of the outcast politicians has come to grips with the new politics of a unified Germany. In a flagrant example of press-release journalism, 12-14, Peel plugs a planned movie theme-park slated for construction in the Ruhr valley—an economically devastated region of Germany. "Now Bugs Bunny, Batman, and the Gremlins, not to mention the stars of Germany's biggest international war film spectacular, 'The Boat,' will seek to bring some good cheer—and jobs—back to the depressed industrial area." Citing economic figures, 5-17, Peel makes a strong case that representatives from the east and west will have to consider cuts to social-service programs during their second round of meetings. Lamenting the likelihood of higher taxes, Peel gives no sense of the tax burden on German wage-earners or corporations. Covering German economics as a beat, he necessarily files many stories that merely provide updates rather than explanations. When he allows himself analysis and observation, Peel proves unequivocally that he can shine.

Jane Perlez
The New York Times
★★½

Warsaw bureau chief. Reporting from Eastern Europe and the former Soviet Union, Perlez powerfully portrays the efforts of working people to improve their lives during the tortuous transition to new economic and political systems. In her encouraging 6-20 story, she profiles two entrepreneurs—a builder and a fashion retailer—who typify the ingenuity that gives Poland "Eastern Europe's most promising economy." Perlez notes that Poland's progress "has been prompted not by large-scale Western investment (which has, in fact, been disappointingly low) but by medium-sized Polish enterprises." Perlez reports, 7-4, that the Czech Republic is "reversing a policy of [President] Vaclav Havel to end arms exports." Assessing the Czechs' new pragmatism, Perlez writes that one official called Havel's arms policies "'naïve,'" claiming they were "'pushed upon the country by hypocritical Western powers.'" Her grim 7-17 account notes that "less than two years after it broke free of the Soviet Union, Ukraine is threatened by industrial protests, a steep decline in manufacturing output, hyperinflation and bitter quarrels with Russia over control of nuclear missiles and a strategic fleet." The core of the problem, Perlez concludes, stems from the refusal by Leonid M. Kravchuk, the conservative Ukraine President, "to introduce free-market changes along the lines of those in Eastern Europe or even in Russia." Perlez quotes a mine director forced to sell coal, worth $22 a ton on the world market, to the state for $9 a ton. "'Ukrainian independence, it's a mistake.'" Perlez detects a similar sentiment, 7-30, emanating from Slovakia. "Opinion polls showed that a majority of Czechs and most Slovaks were against the split [of Czechoslovakia]," she reports, and with unemployment expected to reach 18 percent, "Slovak national pride...has subsided into sullenness." In her 9-21 piece on Poland's elections, Perlez cuts to the quick. "As Poland grasped the sweeping swing to the left and the victory of the former Communists only four years after they had been flung from power, one lesson seemed clear: 40 years of Communism had ingrained expectations of social security that the new parties failed to provide." In surveying the desperate economic and social conditions confronting the former communist countries, Perlez captures both the pain and the hope.

Andrew Pollack
The New York Times
★★★★

Tokyo. A smart and highly skilled correspondent, Pollack

offers business-oriented reporting that brilliantly conveys both dominant and obscure features of Japanese culture. Every report contains outstanding detail and context, as well as explanations of how the subject reflects some uniquely Japanese characteristic. In his perspicuous 3-8 article, Pollack compares differences between the Japanese and American legal systems, as the former gradually adjusts to an orientation toward consumers rather than producers. A single example succinctly illustrates these differences. "The Japanese, who generally seek to avoid confrontation, do not like to sue. In the crash of a Japan Airlines Boeing 747 in 1985, the relatives of all 13 non-Japanese victims sued. But there were only 21 lawsuits representing fewer than 100 of the more than 500 Japanese victims." In his prescient 6-22 piece on the downfall of the Liberal Democratic Party, Pollack contends that the political shift represents not so much the prevailing winds of change, but rather a gentle breeze as the bureaucracy still writes regulations and laws. And while an increased emphasis on consumers in Japan bodes well for U.S. companies trying to compete there, he warns, "The political reform will sweep into power more quickly a new generation that is not as beholden to America as the generation that came of age during and immediately after World War II. That generation, which includes Prime Minister [Kiichi] Miyazawa, feels obligated to America for the role it played in Japan's recovery from the war and has been willing at times to bend to meet American demands." The cultural ramifications of Japanese companies converting compensation from a seniority pay-scale to a merit system ring clearly in Pollack's thoughtful 10-2 survey of this change. He finds the approach tepid and slow. "One of Japan's largest manufacturers this year started a merit pay system for workers at the general manager's level and above....But the company is keeping it a secret because it does not want to alarm younger workers." In his probing 9-12 article on automobile regulation, Pollack reveals the impact of government rules that force drivers of older cars to endure annual inspections of more than 100 items—after they pay about $600 to ensure passing. Pollack portrays this situation as a microcosm of the abuse that the bureaucracy inflicts on the population. As a result of these rules, he finds, Japanese consumers prefer to buy new cars, leaving their old ones for the foreign market. "Last year when the Russian circus returned to Moscow after a tour of Japan, 93 animals, including bears, leopards and parrots, were abandoned on the dock at Yokohama. There was no room for them because the ship was full of used cars bought by the crew." By using telling details and sharp analysis to consistently illuminate major issues and events, Pollack sets the pace for covering Japan.

Victoria Pope

U.S.News & World Report

★★

Moscow. Pope's enterprising reports on peculiar facets of post-communist Russia reflect the diverse cultures emerging from under the umbrella of totalitarian control. Although much of her work appears in collaborative efforts, she gets around on her own a good deal. Recognizing a "post-Soviet success story" in Kazakhstan, 3-8, Pope finds that President Nursultan Nazarbaev drives the free-market reforms of his country, which he rules nearly as a dictatorship. "Nazarbaev's adherence to old Communist ways has made his country a post-Communist success story, at least by comparison with most other former republics, which are sliding deeper into economic and political chaos." Her compelling 10-4 profile of Kirsan Ilyumzhinov, president of the Russian republic of Kamylkia, reflects the what's-in-it-for-me attitude of voters in Russia—and in many newly democratic nations. Superwealthy Ilyumzhinov promised every voter in his district $100 out of his own pocket if elected. Pope also notes that he bought off officials of state institutions to whom he did not want to answer. He simply offered higher-paying jobs to, among others, the local Supreme Soviet and the KGB. Pope quits early, however, barely scratching at the issues of Ilyumzhinov's apparent wealth and the manner in which his business interests might be affected by his political success. Riding the packed Moscow-Warsaw train with traders bound for the Polish streets — where they will sell basic necessities from Russia at a huge profit—Pope yields a vague 9-6 sketch on the economics and culture of the merchants. But

"Are there several doctors in the house, so we can have a little managed competition?"

in painting with such a broad stroke, she leaves basic questions unanswered. How (if at all) are the Russian traders organized? And why, as she reports, do Belarus border guards care enough to throw them off the train for carrying booze and cigarettes bound for Poland? Challenging popular western perceptions about Russian Vice President Alexander Rutskoi, 4-26, Pope finds the ex-fighter pilot more a victim of politics than ideas. "While the vice president is often portrayed as anti-Western, nationalistic or antireform, the truth is more subtle. Rutskoi and his allies oppose economic shock therapy and favor more cautious, Chinese-style economic reforms, but they do not seek a return to communism." Pope astutely recalls that Rutskoi's image problem first began when, widely perceived as a man of action, he pulled perilously close to Boris Yeltsin in popularity polls following the failed 1991 coup. Although she doesn't always provide fresh ideas or a full perspective, Pope's travels consistently open new windows of thought.

Bill Powell

Newsweek

★½

Tokyo. At his best, Powell challenges readers with his voice of opposition or new perspectives on issues; at his worst he resorts to lofty platitudes to mask a weak argument. In his well-reasoned 4-26 piece, he raises the unsettling possibility that the Clinton administration's offhand rhetoric about Japan's closed markets and the White House's growing emphasis on managed trade betrays ignorance about the complexity of U.S.-Japan trade relations. "Tokyo," he astutely argues, "isn't the terrible customer it used to be: while Japan's imports of U.S. grain, coal and soybeans are flat, it has developed a large appetite for advanced American merchandise. Last year Japan imported $3.8 billion worth of U.S. computers and electronic equipment, representing a 48 percent increase in five years." Powell's overwrought 5-24 portrait of the American-educated Masako Owada, chosen to wed Japan's crown Prince, portrays the match as a clash of hidebound tradition and cosmopolitan values. Powell vaguely reflects on how Owada may have come to agree to the marriage, which he frames as the most compelling angle of the story. "Owada will be a symbol for 21st-century Japan, to be sure. But the question only beginning to register, both in Japan and abroad, is a symbol of *what*? Is she—and symbolically, modern Japan—taking a step forward, or a step back?" Powell's 7-19 survey of President Clinton's performance during the G-7 summit, co-authored by Eleanor Clift, dramatically overshoots the evidence. "The Bill and Hillary show went global last week and the reviews, if not raves, were generally positive.... For Bill Clinton and his astute wife, Tokyo was like three good days on the campaign trail." Despite such praise, the only person quoted—a European diplomat—offers a more sober assessment. "'Everyone got to know your president better here, and that helped him.'" Powell's incisive 7-5 analysis of the breakup of the Liberal Democratic Party covers the personalities and the issues—but wrongly bets against the move to a single-seat constituency system. He speculates shrewdly, however, that the superficial reforms favored by many reformist politicians may not be sufficient. "Having started the reform ball rolling, they may not be able to stop it." Although he flourishes when he considers all the evidence, Powell tends to self-destruct by stubbornly sticking to story lines not supported by his reporting.

Carla Rapoport

Fortune

★½

European editor. Intermingling impressive statistics with often muddled or incomplete analysis, Rapoport covers both the slumping European economy and possible political solutions. This approach reflects her years in Japan, where the line between business and political interests remains far murkier, but her work never convincingly demonstrates the cause-and-effect relationship in the West between policy and prosperity. Overbearing with figures, Rapoport's 1-11 piece on European carmakers' efforts to prevent market penetration by their Japanese counterparts thoroughly surveys the key players. Yet, Rapoport never focuses on her premise. "If Europe makes a successful stand, that will be the result of good management, good luck, and good old-fashioned protectionism. Managers are producing better cars than ever, and many models are aimed squarely at the Japanese." The perspective of consumers —who will ultimately determine the degree of Japanese infiltration—is left unexplored. In her 5-3 piece on the economic problems facing Europe, Rapoport blames political systems disproportionately, offering hackneyed analysis of the effects of a jobless rate of 11 percent. "Such unemployment, on top of a rash of political scandals, has produced the virus-like gloom that infected so many Americans before Bill Clinton's election. But Europe doesn't have a place called Hope." The quality of this comment contrasts markedly with Rapoport's compelling economic overview. "Germany's stickiest structural problem is its high labor costs: an average of $40,474 per year for hourly workers, vs. $31,093 in the U.S. and $33,550 in Japan. Social benefits alone accounted for 45 percent of German workers' gross hourly compensation in 1991, compared with 27 percent in the U.S. and 23 percent in Japan." In her 10-18 piece on new Japanese investment abroad, Rapoport finds that with little cash available, Japanese firms offer experience to foreign joint-venture partners. "You won't find a single Japanese at Britain's Rover Group headquarters in Bickenhill, just outside Birmingham. But this company, whose origins go back nearly to the infancy of the world automotive business, owes its existence to Honda ....Rover estimates it contributed only 15 percent of the engineering hours [on its Accord knock-off called the 600] and saved $220 million, or 40 percent of the cost of bringing out a new model." Displaying both her weaknesses and her strengths in each of her pieces, Rapoport's dense style unfortunately makes it tough to get to the good parts.

T.R. Reid

The Washington Post

★½

Tokyo. With adequate but uninspired reporting, Reid adds little to the general understanding of Japan. His analysis wavers between blasé and faulty, and his voluminous contributions to a personal computing column suggest he's ripe for a new beat. To his credit, Reid presciently recognizes in his 2-2 piece that the demands by Ichiro Ozawa and Tsutomu Hata for political reform might represent more than infighting. "They might also indicate that a change of historical dimensions is in the offing for Japan's system of one-party democracy." But when, in June, the government falls, Reid yields an inadequate 6-20 report on the voter anger over the latest payoff scandal. Claiming that this pushed voters over the edge, Reid ignores the fact that voters reelected nearly all the officials tainted by recent corruption scandals. In an original—though unsubstantiated—take on the situation, he writes, "The drive for political restructuring got a major boost when the people of the United States—still Japan's role model—put their government in the hands of a 46-year-old president who had campaigned on the idea of 'the courage to change.'" Yawn. Reid's 3-15 "Style" piece on the "Malcolm X" trend sweeping Japan spuriously asserts that the prevalence of Malcolm X merchandise reveals more than successful marketing of a movie-cum-fashion. "Another basis for the admiration of Malcolm X is that many Japanese feel a vague sense of kinship with American blacks. The feeling comes from the sense that both groups have been victims of discrimination at the hands of whites." Even though the Japanese press kowtows pathetically before their imperial family, Reid's 10-21 piece on Empress Michiko's collapse from a possible stroke crosses the line of good taste with its inappropriately light tone. "The emperor and empress of Japan...have had a particularly strenuous year by the standards of Japanese royalty. They staged a lavish royal wedding in June for their son.... They became the first imperial couple ever to visit Japan's southernmost major island, Okinawa. Since August they have made two official trips to Europe." Reid reports on Japan as if he's covering Little League for a small-town paper—constantly boosting his team and writing what he thinks people want to read.

Sharon Reier

Financial World

★

Amsterdam. Writing business features exclusively, Reier packs her fawning profiles with relevant, but not necessarily enlightening, financial details. She allows her subjects—usually highly successful business leaders—to speak for and about themselves. They do this liberally, perhaps to the benefit of readers craving the voice of success, but a more critical approach, and perhaps a few dissenting voices, would add immeasurably to her work. In her amicable 2-2 profile of Royal Bank CEO George Mathewson, Reier finds the Scottish company's offshoot insurance operation growing dramatically faster than its banking business. Within days of his laying off 3,500 workers, Reier notes, Mathewson gave a $9.3 million bonus to the executive who came up with the insurance concept. Reier allows Mathewson to defend himself. "'If you look at it as a percentage of shareholder value [the executive] has created, it is a bargain,'" he maintains. Maybe so, but Reier might have looked at it some other way or dug a little deeper. Perhaps proving the efficiency of the markets, Reier's 10-12 article on the investment flooding the London real-estate market at a time of both plummeting rents and uncertain vacancy promises much but ends up a one-liner. Real-estate yields secured by long-term leases, she unremarkably discovers, prove higher than government bond yields. Reier's flattering 7-20 sketch of Alan Jackson, the Australian CEO of one of England's most successful companies, BTR PLC, finds virtually nothing to dislike about its subject. The story succeeds to the extent that Jackson relates what he looks for when considering a takeover—mostly a healthy balance sheet—but while Reier includes numerous references to Jackson's chilly reception by the London establishment, no concrete examples come the reader's way. Perhaps of necessity, Reier jumps around a bit in her 6-22 survey of the enormous Swiss chemical company Ciba-Geigy. Making several compelling points about the company's tenuous relationship with highly influential environmentalists, she notes that as the original producer of DDT, "Ciba has been spending a good part of its considerable $1.8 billion research and development budget...on innovations that will minimize environmental damage." Turning to the company's immediate business prospects, Reier adds, "Despite its large expenditures—near the top of the pharmaceuticals industry—Ciba-Geigy has no blockbusters in its pipeline, as [CEO Alex] Krauer readily admits." Despite reporting on these original characters, Reier's tendency to look at a balance sheet through the eyes of the corporation's officers results in analysis indistinguishable from an annual, high-gloss stockholder report.

Keith B. Richburg

The Washington Post

★★½

Nairobi bureau chief. Making good use of a wide variety of sources developed through energetic legwork, Richburg provides honest observations from Somalia that highlight many treacherous aspects of the enormous foreign presence there. His cynicism about the UN effort, however, grows throughout the year, sometimes tainting his reporting. In his disturbing and important 11-9 piece on Somali citizens killed in the cross fire of battles between UN troops and snipers or militia groups, Richburg sets an unfair standard for soldiers' conduct by questioning the wisdom of using troops to police city streets. He does so on the basis of an incident in which "Malaysians heard two sniper shots fired at their convoy of four armored vehicles, so the troops opened fire with automatic weapons," killing a CARE official and wounding six Somalis. The UN waffled in its account of the incident—blaming the death on Somalis—which Richburg rightly condemns, but he never proposes what the troops should do when fired on. In his prescient 1-30 interview of U.S. Gen. Charles Wilhelm, Richburg reports his subject's concerns. "The most important lesson from Beirut, Wilhelm said, was to avoid the danger of getting sucked into factional wars on the side of any clan or armed group. But the longer the Marines are here, he said, the greater the risk 'we could be drawn into it.'" Covering a black American mission to Libreville, Gabon, 5-30, Richburg gently but pointedly raises an uncomfortable contradiction. "While black American leaders were at the forefront of calls for immediate democratic reform in South Africa, when it comes to black Africa those same black Americans say it is not America's business to interfere—even when the victims are Africa's black masses." Richburg's shrewd 6-24 piece delves into the political maneuvering of Somali warlord Ali Mahdi Mohamed, who chose to deal with the UN differently than did his rival Mohammed Farah Aidid. "He signed every peace agreement put to him and has largely kept his word. And he ingratiated himself with the U.S. diplomats here, particularly former ambassador Robert Oakley, and never turned down an invitation to travel across town for a meeting at the American Embassy." As a result, Richburg speculates, Mahdi may emerge as the next president, with international backing. Although he sometimes comes across as unjustifiably critical of the UN mission, Richburg nevertheless conveys a deep understanding of contemporary Somali life.

Alan Riding

The New York Times

Paris. With his eye for compelling stories of international interest, Riding writes his best pieces with angles that offer instructive views of French culture, which dominates both political and economic decision-making. In his probing 9-18 article, Riding explores the reasons for the French film industry's opposition to GATT. "While France is eager to export its movies...its policy is essentially defensive, driven by its fear of the continuing advance of the English language and of what it refers to disparagingly as 'Anglo-Saxon mercantilist culture,' one, that is, that ignores 'true' culture in order to satisfy the whim of the masses." Ah, *plus ça change*... Continuing his coverage of GATT negotiations, 10-19, Riding reveals the competing sides of the French debate on how to ease subsidies of agricultural exports. Riding portrays the primary disagreement—which pits Edouard Balladur, the new French Prime Minister against Jacques Delors, the European Community President—as one between French political interests and international business concerns. "Bending to pressure from France's powerful farming lobby, both the Socialist government that was ousted in elections last March and Mr. Balladur's new conservative Government have threatened to block a global trade package unless the farm trade deal is renegotiated—a demand that Washington and the rest of the [European] Community have in turn rebuffed." In his disturbing 4-7 article on 72-year-old Kurt Werner Schaechter's efforts to pressure the French government into opening its World War II archives, Riding reveals that the entire French administrative machine—not just the Vichy government—was involved in Jewish internment. "One of the few documents that offers any opinion is a 1943 report on the Noe camp, 25 miles south of Toulouse. Noting that most of its prisoners were old, it states: 'The largest number of these are German Israelites who can be considered refuse of life and who are incapable of insuring their subsistence. Their permanence in the camp therefore responds to a necessity.'" Riding also shines in his provocative 3-21 exploration of the French psyche. "When the French close ranks with the farmers, they are fighting to keep alive the identity of all true French. Indeed, even in cities, the land never seems far away....Two-thirds of the population has a parent or a grandparent who was brought up *en campagne*. In Parisian homes, the cheeses or pâtés or wines of some ancestral *pays* will always be preferred over others." Covering France with an American's irreverent eye, Riding distinguishes between matters of French culture and those of international concern.

Eugene Robinson

The Washington Post

★★

London bureau. An astute judge of England's place in the world, Robinson delivers short, pithy articles. However, he does far more than just report the latest caustic comment to come from the Prime Minister's question-and-answer period. In his brief 7-6 article, Robinson explains why Britain continues to spend so much on defense. "With the end of the Cold War, British policy makers fear being pushed away from the inner circles of power by bigger, richer nations such as Germany and Japan. Hence, Britain has continued to shoulder an oversized burden of worldwide commitments." Continuing on this tack, 8-6, Robinson peers inside Britain's heart to reveal that for all its bluster, the nation may at last be realizing that the sun is finally setting on its once far-flung empire. "Politically, economically and culturally, Britain has long seen itself as one of the world's true heavyweights. But in the estimation of many observers—and in the nightmares of British policy makers—middleweight status is an increasingly accurate description." In his solid 2-22 article, Robinson portrays the government of Prime Minister John Major as constantly one step away from implosion. "Major may have survived the latest row over European union, but he is still backpedaling on a wide variety of domestic initiatives....With just a 21-vote majority in the 650-member House of Commons, he is hostage to any significant group of Conservative rebels who unite around an issue." Moving to examine Europe as a whole, 2-8, Robinson argues that the continent finds itself adrift because there exist no visionary politicians with a will powerful enough to unify the continent. "The architects of today's Europe hoped to build a new superpower that would strut confidently across the world stage. Instead, united Europe is adding up to considerably less than the sum of its parts, held back by what analysts call a debilitating lack of leadership." A capable political analyst, Robinson sheds light on Britain and its relationship to Europe and the world.

Keith M. Rockwell

The Journal of Commerce

★★½

Chief of European bureaus, London. In his stellar business and financial reporting from western Europe, Rockwell manages an engaging, almost conversational, tone. Rather than go for scoops, he sprinkles analysis throughout his reporting of stories that have usually been well covered. As the GATT negotiations move into their final months, Rockwell reports in his incisive 9-29 article that key officials, particularly Director General Peter Sutherland, are showing their hands. Sutherland, Rockwell notes, must pressure negotiators from the European Community and the U.S. to work from a draft agreement that only for a fleeting moment proved agreeable to both sides. In the effort, Sutherland "has become engaged in a sort of three dimensional chess match in which he must keep all nations on board without sparking a walkout by any of the major players." In his poignant 6-5 op-ed on the sacking of Chairman of the Exchequer Norman Lamont by the embattled British Prime Minister John Major, Rockwell emphasizes the political motivation behind the move, and notes that without Lamont to take his punches, Major himself may soon bear the wrath of his party's discontented. "Should the Prime Minister be unable to raise the level of his game to match the pace of political hardball all around him, the party will soon look elsewhere....The irony of all this is that, with at least four years to go before the next general election, the government has laid the foundation for the sort of low-inflation growth it always said was its main goal." Rockwell reports in his obtuse 11-9 article that the EC controls 16 percent of the world's high- and medium-technology market—down from 40 percent in 1965 and 23 percent in 1987. Rebutting solutions offered by others rather than making a case for how to improve the situation, Rockwell then stumbles to an obvious conclusion. "The bottom line is that European managers and workers are being paid too much, producing too little and taking too much time off." In his articulate and insightful 7-19 article on three "thorny issues" that will dominate the remaining GATT negotiations, Rockwell nicely circumvents the bluster and gets to the crux of the issues. "In the highly complex steel sector, for example, negotiators agreed in Tokyo to eliminate tariffs for most steel products. But the implementation of those duty cuts is contingent on negotiators reaching a deal in the parallel Multilateral Steel Agreement talks." Without being overly technical, Rockwell interweaves the concerns of commerce into his more general coverage.

David E. Sanger
The New York Times
★★½

Tokyo. Along with his comprehensive reporting, Sanger offers glimpses of Japanese idiosyncrasies that help to define the national character. Although he writes mostly of business matters, he portrays the workplace as a reflection of more general concerns and values. Sanger's 10-11 story of rebellious retailers selling discounted goods to consumers details the oppressive control that industries have long held over the Japanese domestic market and the efforts they're expending to maintain it. "[Discounting] is an experiment many companies, already squeezed by the recession, desperately wish would go away." Contrasting the strenghtened yen with the mid-1980s rise that thrust Japan to the head of the world economic class, 2-24, Sanger now finds concern among Japanese business leaders. In the past, he reports, Japan increased exports to battle recessions at home, but the record-strong yen eliminates that option. Furthermore, as the nation's corporate, job-for-life culture disintegrates, "no one expects the Japanese to go on a buying spree with their record-strong currency. And cheaper imports are not likely to impress many consumers here." Digging further into changes shaking Japan's corporate workers, 3-3, Sanger deftly exposes the tragicomic efforts of corporations to bump salaried managers from their payrolls. He writes that a 51-year-old lawyer "said he had been relocated to a basement office and then given no work. When he did not get the hint, the company dimmed the lighting week by week. He finally quit." Sanger's 6-19 article captures the grim drama leading to a vote of no-confidence and the downfall of the Liberal Democratic Party government headed by Kiichi Miyazawa. "The end came quickly, with no pretense of Japanese politeness or indirection." Although noting that factionalism long characterized the LDP, Sanger points out that past members have fallen back in line rather than split away, as several did this time. "The bolting from the party seemed a particularly heavy blow to Mr. Miyazawa." With an eye for the telling detail, Sanger sheds light on subtleties that add up to big change in the land of the Rising Sun.

Jacob M. Schlessinger
The Wall Street Journal
★★★

Tokyo. As Japan Inc. shakes from its foundations, Schlessinger keeps a steady hand to provide acute analysis of the nation's politics and economics. And he can masterfully distinguish between enriching detail and cumbersome trivia. Avoiding high-minded predictions, Schlessinger acknowledges the volatility in the Japanese government in his 7-30 political profile of new Prime Minister Morihiro Hosokawa. Noting the Japanese leader's mandate to reform the government, Schlessinger observes, "Mr. Hosokawa has outlined a fairly radical vision for a new Japan....But it isn't clear how much control Mr. Hosokawa will have over his fragile coalition." Schlessinger's 2-10 piece intelligently evaluates the standing of the U.S. in the latest verbal jousting with Japan over the trade deficit. "Japan still needs the U.S.—as an ally and as a marketplace—far more than the U.S. needs Japan...[but] as Japanese trade with Asia eclipses trade with the U.S., Japan may feel less dependent on the U.S. and thus more comfortable confronting the Americans." In his richly detailed 5-11 article on an American slot-machine maker's efforts to penetrate the Japanese market, Schlessinger offers a rare glimpse of the relationship between an industry group and its regulatory oversight agency. These two entities together establish rules about the minutest detail of legal machines. "The police, [the slot-machine maker] discovered, devise the specifications in consultation with the 18 members of *Nichidenkyo*, the industry trade association—which, incidentally, employs some retired police officers. Only members are told of the informal specifications....*Nichidenkyo*'s Catch-22 rules require that any new member be recommended by three current members—and have three years' manufacturing experience in Japan." An 11-19 piece, co-authored by Masayoshi Kanabayashi, deems the passage of a measure urging proportional representation a "critical first step" in reforming the Japanese political system. While they assess the ramifications of the measure, the pair never satisfactorily explains what other steps might follow. The writers do make clear that Japanese voters want more accountability, and that this effort aims to provide it. As the Japanese government's baffling overhaul could lead in any number of new directions, readers will do well turning to Schlessinger's comprehensive reports.

Serge Schmemann

The New York Times

★★★

Moscow. An erudite student of Russian history and literature, Schmemann offers cool commentary on fast-moving events. The grandson of an exiled Russian nobleman, his life might have been quite different if not for the Bolsheviks, and he tempers his broad perspective on Russia with a mild pre-revolutionary nostalgia. In his evocative 4-23 account prior to President Yeltsin's referendum, Schmemann wades out to the muddy town of Koltsovo, near his ancestor's estate, to get a feel for the attitudes of villagers. With his eye for detail, he vividly captures the atmosphere of a roadside gathering. "A local youth passing with a bucket of water...studies the assembly calmly for several minutes and then declares with a fervor that takes everyone aback: 'I'm going to vote for Yeltsin. The stench continues as long as the fish is rotting, and the others would only slow it down.'" Schmemann's 3-12 article ably analyzes the disputes between Yeltsin and Parliament. "The Constitution, amended more than 300 times by this Congress, is riddled with contradictions. Nobody knows, for example, what would happen if the Congress disbanded the Constitutional Court, which it can do with a two-thirds majority, and the court declared the resolution void, which it is empowered to do." Schmemann returns to this theater of the absurd, 3-23, to describe how the Constitutional Court interprets Yeltsin's decrees. "The chairman [of the court] declared that the court had neither the actual decrees nor other materials it had requested, but that it was working on its ruling nonetheless." In his 7-9 survey of Azerbaijan, Schmemann skillfully captures the nation's problems in a single sentence. "In less than two years of independence, this little republic by the Caspian has known war, elections, coups, pogroms, corruption, Islamic revival, resurgent Communists, international intrigue, economic chaos and the promise of...oil wealth." The problem, though, is that this overview is exactly that—an overview. Conversely, Schmemann's 10-7 piece amasses a suspenseful collection of vignettes that illustrate the misguided euphoria and subsequent letdown in the Russian White House before and during Yeltsin's assault. Here Schmemann shows Ruslan Khasbulatov pacing, as if in a trance as cannons boom outside. It becomes clear that a raised eyebrow in Moscow warrants almost more newsprint than a war in far-off Azerbaijan. Such Russocentrism typifies the entire press corps, however, and with his deep knowledge of Russia and his Russian ancestry, the talented Schmemann seems more entitled to it than others.

Uli Schmetzer

Chicago Tribune

★½

Beijing. While he competently describes scenes and chronicles life, mostly in China and Cambodia, Schmetzer tends to self-destruct through technical errors of style or fact. Portraying a grim reality in the days leading up to the Cambodian elections, he shrewdly notes in his 5-16 piece that no matter who wins, anarchy will reign in this country long torn by war. "Here in the wild Cambodian northwest, men buy their uniforms at the local market, shoulder their rifles and hire themselves out, often pretending to be Khmer Rouge guerrillas, Cambodian government troops or forces loyal to the former ruler, Prince Sihanouk....It is a war of nerves." Schmetzer struggles with his overwrought 7-11 story on a free-trade zone between Russian Siberia, northern China, and Mongolia. In one sentence, typical of this unfortunate piece, he attributes to the Chinese city of Harbin several human skills. "The capital of China's Heilonjiang Province, Harbin masterminded half of all of China's $2 billion barter trade with Russia last year and has cornered 10 percent of all Sino-Russian commerce for itself since 1989, when Mikhail Gorbachev came to Beijing to sign accords that ended 30 years of ideological rivalry." Schmet-

zer's poignant and revealing 8-29 article, on the other hand, movingly sketches the plight of young farmers in China's evolving economy. Risking nightly beatings and harassment, Liu Xia Jin, Schmetzer reports, lives on the streets of Guangzhou in hopes of picking up day-labor jobs. "Liu already has earned enough money to hire a tractor to plow his father's land. He also has bought enough bricks to build a house for the day when Xi, his girlfriend, will be his wife. But her father insists he wants 2000 yuan ($380) to compensate him for the food Xi ate while under his roof." In a rare 10-10 interview with Wei Jingsheng, one of China's most famous dissidents, Schmetzer conveys new Chinese attitudes toward freedom through the eyes of a man who conceived the idea but missed the gestation, having spent the last 14 1/2 years in jail. However, Schmetzer wrongly asserts that the 1989 student demonstrations at Tiananmen Square "nearly toppled the regime before troops ended their demands for reform with the massacre." Such overstatements only raise questions about the accuracy of lesser-known details reported by Schmetzer.

Stephen Seplow
The Philadelphia Inquirer
★

Moscow. Simplistic and confusing at times, Seplow can break some new ground but often fails to deliver reporting equal to his subject matter. While he typically provides the components of a compelling story, Seplow denies readers the necessary background explanation. In his muddled 7-28 piece on Ukrainians who take advantage of the Russian Central Bank recall of rubles printed before 1993, Seplow jumps indiscriminately between Russia, Ukraine, and a Ukrainian flea market, where a woman sells a chandelier. After several tries, careful readers will deduce that Ukrainians are buying old rubles at a large discount from fellow Ukrainians, who know the old currency will soon be worthless, and exchanging them in Russia for new rubles at full value. Unfortunately, Seplow makes the Ukrainian money the subject of his explanation—"The Karbonavetz notes...have been selling at 1 or 2 rubles on the black market, compared to 4 or 5 to the ruble, officially." Consequently, the reader must sort through the various exchanges in this process. Lifting the most telling bits of his 6-14 article from a Russian paper, Seplow surveys the brain-drain at the Russian foreign ministry, once one of the Soviet Union's most prestigious agencies. As many experienced diplomats are leaving for higher-paying, private-sector jobs, fewer young people are choosing a career in the foreign ministry owing to its dwindling reputation and budget. Seplow hits all (and only) the obvious points. "A major in international law who already has a part-time job with an American law firm here, [Max] Tikhonov said succinctly, 'Now everyone wants to make money.'" Rather efficiently getting to the crux of the matter in his 5-16 article on the debate over the Russian constitution, Seplow shrewdly recognizes President Boris Yeltsin flexing his muscle after a strong showing in the April referendums. "On successive days last week, he fired two top officials who failed to fully support his programs; moved forcefully to get his proposed new constitution adopted without much interference from Parliament, and forged new economic agreements with the former Russian republics in the Commonwealth of Independent States." Seplow gamely ventures to the city of Ufa, 11-29, to document considerable opposition to the emphasis on centralized control in Yeltsin's proposed constitution. It was here Yeltsin made "the often quoted declaration from his speech urging the people of Russia's 21 ethnic republics to 'take as much power as you yourselves can swallow.'" While doing commendable legwork, Seplow needs to do a little more homework to add more intellectual weight to his far-ranging dispatches.

Philip Shenon
The New York Times
★½

Bangkok bureau chief. Although he inundates readers with background information that lends a sense of completeness to his reporting on various Asian countries, Shenon rarely digs beyond the unsubstantiated proclamations of his sources. In his lengthy 5-10 article on the upcoming Cambodian elections, Shenon fails to convey the utter anarchy in the countryside well-chronicled by others, instead portraying each violent act as an event officially sanctioned by either the Khmer Rouge or the government. Presenting assertions by opposition leaders practically as proof, he writes, "Government officials have repeatedly denied any involvement in political violence or intimidation, although there is compelling evidence to suggest they are not telling the truth." Again focusing on official acts as the center of a society and culture, Shenon provides a repetitious—and incomplete—1-2 survey of Burma. Rather than examining the nation's economy—an odd failure considering the substantial Japanese interest in reopening trade channels—he concentrates excessively on the injustice of the oppressive 30-year-old military junta and the detention of 1991 Nobel Peace Prize winner Aung San Suu Kyi, who remains under house arrest for her efforts to reform the government. Efficiently but blandly, Shenon ties together several business angles, 8-23, to explain Rupert Murdoch's half-billion dollar investment in Star-TV, a pan-Asian satellite television venture. "Financial analysts say Mr. Murdoch will almost certainly use Star as a vehicle for rebroadcasting programs produced by Fox and Sky [other television companies]...which are thought likely to attract the sort of young, affluent audiences that major advertisers covet as much in Hong Kong as they do in Houston." In his shallow 5-2 article on the resumption of lumber trade between Cambodia and Thailand, Shenon reports Thai government plans to reopen checkpoints along the border so as to monitor the importation of manufactured timber from Cambodia. He overly emphasizes—in light of his scant evidence—UN concern that the lumber trade, which had been banned, will both subvert the election process by allowing parties to raise money and will lead to the ravaging of Cambodian forests. Although he writes adequately, always including official concerns and responses, Shenon misses the gray area where people live and work.

Nathaniel Sheppard Jr.

Chicago Tribune

★★

Central America. From month to month, Sheppard moves between Central American capitals to provide quirky reports on the many facets of post-Cold War adjustment. As he at times seems to bear ideological baggage from the political battles of the past 15 years, his analysis lacks the freshness of his reporting. Nevertheless, Sheppard distinguishes himself in a comprehensive five-part series, 6-13 through 6-17, examining the political and economic outlook for Central America's "fledgling democracies." Though repetitive, Sheppard reveals how the region became addicted to U.S. military aid during the 1980s and now struggles with adapting to peace. "After a decade of adventurism," he notes, 6-15, Honduras has all of the F-5 fighter planes it needs. But it doesn't have any good roads to its most fertile fields. It has a surplus of luxury cars but not enough food for a population shackled by poverty....The military budget is about $580 million, according to Sen. Carlas Sousa Coello, about 20 percent of the national budget." Sheppard breaks new ground with his 3-21 article on disabled veterans of the army and rebel groups convalescing together in El Salvador. The story says as much about human powers of forgiveness as about the Salvadoran situation. Unfortunately, Sheppard takes a ho-hum approach. "Guadron, Barentes and others among the 16 former combatants in the co-op said they quickly overcame distrust of each other and discovered they had found a healing process." Ambling through general criticisms of Violeta Chamorro's government in Nicaragua, 8-29, Sheppard eventually gets around to several devastating examples of how the government works against local development. "Last year, the finance minister approved a contract for a foreign company he represents to make Nicaraguan passports." Sheppard's lopsided 3-16 piece on the release of the Truth Commission's report about atrocities committed during the Salvadoran civil war makes no mention that the report finds culpability on *both* sides. Although the report says that the government and rebel forces each used murder and systematic intimidation to quell their enemies, Sheppard concentrates only on the government. He notes that it now refuses to take steps recommended by the report against army officials accused of atrocities. And he describes the commission findings as "a devastating United Nations report... that painted a chilling picture of El Salvador's government and military directing the repression and assassinations of government critics." While he certainly throws plenty of strikes, Shep-

pard's apparent willingness to sometimes doctor the ball raises concern.

John Simpson

The Spectator

★★★

Foreign contributor. Conveying his impressions from far-ranging travels as a BBC television producer, Simpson bluntly reports often overlooked detail from China to Bosnia. That he writes in the first person generally works for Simpson, detracting only in obscure stories where he bases his argument on unfamiliar or unsubstantiated observations. Making a strong 5-15 case for a tough stance against the Chinese government, Simpson smartly argues that the most important presence at Tiananmen Square went largely unnoticed. "Many of us who reported from the square during the demonstrations tended to focus on the students: they had ideas, they made the running, and they were educated and decent. We often ignored the rougher element, the fiercer and more alienated workers from the slums of Peking who hung around the edges of the demonstration....They were the proletariat, of whom Chinese political literature has so much to say; and now [that] there was a chance to get rid of Communism they were anxious to take it." Both personal and moving, Simpson's vivid 7-17 article on the subhuman conditions in Sarajevo reveals as much about the human spirit as it does about the toll of the siege. "An old woman sat on the floor, piling up a few logs cut from a small, possibly ornamental tree. Her dirty dress hung open at the neck, and did not hide her veined legs. She was all alone. Soon, with someone to talk to, she was weeping, her mouth open, the tears running down her seamed brown cheeks. 'That you should see me like this,' she wailed." In his 8-14 article, Simpson contrasts the thuggery and military amateurishness of the Bosnian Serbs with the feebleness and disorganization of the UN mission in the divided country. "When we stopped at the checkpoint the Serbs found a big wad of money on me, and tried to take it....Then our translator revealed that we were on our way to interview [Bosnian Serb President Radovan] Karadzic...[and] 'that I will give Dr. Karadzic a careful description of the way we have been treated here.' It worked, of course; with people like this it always does. The wad was handed back." Exhibiting tremendous confidence as a columnist, Simpson places humane and moral considerations above political or economic ones.

Daniel Singer

The Nation

★½

"Letter From Europe." Despite a verbose and academic style, Singer pens provocative interpretations of events in Europe. His arguments often build on original evidence or fresh perspectives. Amply chronicling the disarray of the European Economic Community, 1-25, Singer probes the collapse of the Exchange Rate Mechanism, providing incisive observations about the political and security interests of the member states. Conceding that some form of European Economic Community seems inevitable, Singer offers his suggestion for dissenters: Ignore frontiers and unite with the workers' unions and councils. In his articulate and inspiring 5-10 article, Singer shows he can turn a phrase as he attacks the shock-therapy reforms in Russia. "The Russian economy has been submitted to shock rather than therapy." Failing to build a case out of conveniently disturbing statistics, Singer resorts to elliptical prose in his rambling and disjointed 8-23/30 piece declaring capitalism a failure. Several times he introduces intriguing new thoughts only to skip abruptly to some vaguely related or muddled idea. "We are living in a system that, in its search for profits, is driven to raise productivity and to reduce the hours of work needed to create a commodity; it is also driven to invent profit-yielding jobs, a duty it finds increasingly difficult to perform. In any case it is a system intrinsically unable to set itself the task of abolishing the frontier between labor and leisure." Unfairly—and falsely—accusing the Western press of ignoring the legal questions of Yeltsin's attempts to overturn the Russian constitution, 10-11, Singer offers evidence that the formation of class underlies both sides of the debate over the future of Russia. "Very few years may be needed for the worker, technicians and the uncorrupted part of the intelligentsia to enter the stage as the defenders of their own interests, thus transforming altogether a battle that, so far, has been a test of strength between two gangs of would-be profiteers." With uneven success, Singer struggles gallantly to offer a realistic model for a socialist evolution.

Daniel Sneider
The Christian Science Monitor
★★

Moscow. Although Sneider details many sides of Russia's political imbroglio, he seldom portrays the big picture. His features, while well-researched, often fail to capture the split between Russian capitalists and apparatchiks. Sneider approaches his 6-30 story on Russia's hugely successful McDonald's from the unique angle of its suppliers, but does little more than mention who provides the ketchup and pickles. "McDonald's management has sorted out the entrepreneurial types among its suppliers and encouraged them to gradually take on production tasks. An example is Anatoly Revyakin, a former deputy director of a Moscow area 'sovkhoz' (state farm) supplying vegetables to the Kremlin elite, who now dreams of becoming the Heinz of Russia." In his intriguing 3-15 article, Sneider astutely diagnoses one of President Boris Yeltsin's main flaws—a tendency to walk away from unfinished political business. "For many Yeltsin supporters among the democrats, the president's angry walkout Friday from the Congress was an act of weakness, not strength. Each impulsive move, as happened when the Congress met last December, gives the hard-liners an opening." Trying to be cute in his 3-17 article on the importation of cheap Japanese cars to the Russian far east, Sneider instead talks down to the reader. "This is a tale about how decisions are made, and unmade, in Russia today. It is also about how much has changed, and how much has not, in this vast land. Our story begins far from the august capital of Moscow...." Sneider employs his historical knowledge of Russia, 3-26, to illuminate the conflict between Yeltsin and Parliament. "The situation is so familiar to Russian history that is has a name: *dvoevlastie*, or dual power. It refers to the period between the February Revolution of 1917, when the Czarist state was overthrown, and the October 1917 coup by the Bolsheviks, which established the Soviet Communist state. During that nine-month interregnum, power rested simultaneously in the liberal Provisional Government and the Socialist-led soviets." Framing his report with such context indicates a skill vastly underused.

James Sterngold
The New York Times
★★★

Tokyo. Concentrating mostly on business affairs, Sterngold reports on the Japanese commercial culture and its influence on the international community. Although lacking a significant analytical voice in his otherwise comprehensive coverage, he contributes several features that take on much broader themes. In his keen 5-24 feature on a challenge to Japanese imperial dogma, Sterngold exposes the paradox of a cosmopolitan society tightly gripping its historical myths. Japan's archaeologists, he finds, must constantly fight losing battles for permission to explore ancient burial cites as "the government restricts access to historical records that could illuminate what is fact and what is myth surrounding Japan's imperial family." Recounting failed efforts to stimulate the nation's slumping economy, Sterngold's straightforward 2-1 report on the cutting of the Japanese discount rate reveals the growing frustration and impotence of the Japanese government in fighting its recession. His comprehensive approach enlivens and enriches an otherwise bland subject. Interspersing hard data with rhetorical flourishes, 4-13, Sterngold brilliantly captures the belligerent debate between Japanese and Korean trade representatives over Japan's ever-growing trade surplus in Asia. He smartly notes that broader issues than trade figures come into play. "The problems created by Japan's surpluses are acute in South Korea, which is struggling to revive a faltering economy and is clearly feeling a touch of wounded pride in finding itself dependent on its ancient rivals." As the loose coalition of opposition parties now running Japan edges forward, Sterngold finds, 9-13, that all the group's efforts will concentrate on battling the deeply entrenched bureaucracy. Sterngold contends that the bureaucracy, which establishes Japan's oppressive business regulations, serves as the demon-du-jour, the national foe serving to unite the rest of the country. "Indeed if words were stone, the Government district in the heart of Tokyo would now be buried under a Mount Fuji of wrath."

Sterngold's facile pen and trenchant reporting consistently lift his voice above the chorus.

Lena H. Sun
The Washington Post
★★½

Beijing bureau chief. With her lucid style and original choice of subjects, Sun conveys her deep understanding of both the major and minor shifts in China's political economy. Despite being harassed last year by Chinese authorities, she dwells not on the nation's reactionary political forces but on the cultural and economic changes sweeping the country. In a quirky and revealing 5-31 piece on a Chinese entrepreneur who gets paid to think up names for children, Sun demonstrates how deeply the shift to capitalist thinking runs. In a nation where names often reflect "the prevailing political movement of the day," Jin Daochun assists parents in thinking up names that suggest "values of success and wealth rather than 'revolutionary ardor.'...[He] has founded a lucrative private business that specializes in providing names that he claims not only are unique, but also guarantee prosperity and a good life. His business is booming." Sun's 6-6 *Magazine* profile of Hong Kong's super-rich, with their high-toned business and social agendas, attempts but fails to portray their anxiety over the looming 1997 transfer from British to Chinese sovereignty. While none of the individuals she cites expresses particular anxiety, Sun nonetheless concludes, "To most of the monied class, however, 1997 conjures up an image of a Hong Kong depressed by communism, reduced, like Shanghai in the days after Mao's revolution, to drab impotence." Shrewdly observing, 7-27, that many Chinese believe the market will more effectively force political change than will any form of social unrest, Sun notes the hopeful political and economic climate on the mainland. "Unlike the changes that arose from senior leader Deng Xiaoping's economic reforms 14 years ago, today all pretense of 'socialism with Chinese characteristics' is gone. In its place is a full-scale embrace of capitalism." Sun smartly reports, 10-29, that a new tax policy separating federal and local taxes will challenge provincial autonomy and could be an effort to assure the cohesion of the nation once Deng dies. Oddly, Sun never mentions corruption among local bureaucrats as a burgeoning problem. Yet, such lapses prove the exception. With crisp analysis and healthy skepticism, Sun renders China more accessible, both as a nation and as a culture.

Anne Swardson
The Washington Post
★★★

Toronto. Working hard to convey the Canadian perspective, Swardson balances enriching quotes with telling observations. New to the assignment, she offers reporting and analysis that show a quick grasp of Canadian politics and culture. In her comprehensive 12-14 piece on the three-year-old predicament caused by barren fishing grounds off Aquaforte, Newfoundland—which forces much of the town to rely on public funds—Swardson finds a new threat to village life. "The crisis...is beginning to test the patience of the rest of Canada. The government and some of its non-Atlantic citizens are showing signs of impatience with the cost of maintaining the residents of Canada's poorest province." Her balanced and insightful 6-22 piece examines the Canadian health-care system largely from the vantage of Canadian experts. Focusing on both drawbacks and benefits of the system, she emphasizes that

many Canadians, including Roberto Iglesias, medical adviser to Quebec's Ministry of Health and Social Services, are beginning to wonder about its cost. "'It's not that the system is expensive in itself. The question is, can we afford it?' Iglesias said. 'It's not that we have a big car. The question is whether we can afford the insurance and gasoline.'" In her outstanding 11-23 essay comparing freedom of the press in Canada and the U.S., Swardson describes the trials of an Ontario husband and wife accused of the torture and murder of two girls, details of which the Canadian Courts have censored. Swardson reasons that the ban—because of the rumors and speculation that result—has added to the drama of the case. "News media [in Canada] are prohibited from reporting on any evidence presented at a bail hearing or preliminary inquiry, for instance, until the full trial has begun....And though the publication ban allowed journalists to discuss what they learned only with their editors, newsrooms are rife with gossip." Swardson finds a remarkable situation in Nova Scotia, 2-6, where after three years, officials have decided the social damage created by legalized gambling outweighs its benefits to government coffers. "Stories began appearing...about people who were dropping so many loonies [Canadian $1 coins] on video gambling that they did not have enough money for groceries or rent....'Is there anything wrong with saying a mistake was made?' [Premier Donald] Cameron asked in an interview. 'Although we didn't like losing the $40 million, decisions like that can't be made on dollars.'" By reporting Canadian stories as foreign stories, Swardson shows an unusual respect for the country and its people.

Andrew Tanzer

Forbes

★★★

Pacific bureau manager. Providing detailed information that relates to his subjects, generally entrepreneurs who have penetrated the Chinese market, Tanzer masterfully connects their experiences to broader business lessons. In his lucid 1-18 article on the proliferation of American fast-food establishments in Southeast Asia, he reveals that between 1990 and 1992, the number of people who ate fast food in the previous three months doubled to 42 percent. The big winner is PepsiCo's KFC restaurants, whose menu, Tanzer notes, provides an advantage. "Chicken is much cheaper and more widely available than beef in Asia's developing countries. It's a lot more familiar to Asian palates than the cheese topping on pizza. And it doesn't face any religious strictures, the way pork does in Muslim countries like Indonesia and Malaysia and beef does in India." In his intriguing and fast-paced 5-10 profile of Hong Kong clothing-magnate Jimmy Lai, Tanzer proves that "what sets him apart is the careful way he studied, then borrowed from, the formulas that had led others to success in retailing." Lai, Tanzer notes, acts liberally on the knowledge and experiences of other retailers, such as adopting "a point-of-sales computerized information system." Judging the Chinese capitalist boom irreversible, 8-2, Tanzer superbly assesses various aspects of the market from a purely business perspective. He addresses all the big questions raised by others, as well as several fresh ones directed to business readers. "Because the remnants of the socialist state still shower urban workers with huge subsidies, most of their income gains go right down to disposable income. For instance, Chinese families spend less than 5 percent of household income on housing, health care, education and transportation compared with 30 percent to 40 percent in other Asian countries." Hitting on several larger issues, Tanzer's 10-11 profile of Hong Kong native Paul Kan highlights the great rewards for entrepreneurs willing and able to navigate official China. With paging contracts in 36 Chinese cities at a 20,000 customer average, Kan, according to Tanzer, manages to circumvent a law against foreign ownership of telecommunications services. "[He] does this by dealing with the business units of non-telecommunications authorities, such as the People's Liberation Army and the Public Security Bureau, which are eager to cash in on surplus radio frequency they control." Extensive figures and details complement Tanzer's simple, almost folksy, style.

Paul Taylor

The Washington Post

Johannesburg bureau chief. With his rich insight and well-written reports, Taylor captures the complex relationship be-

tween government and people in southern Africa. Too often, however, he forgives individual acts of aggression as ancillary to the larger moral mission—the political dominance of the African National Congress. Mindlessly condoning violence in South Africa, his well-written but lopsided 4-18 piece celebrates the nation's disenchanted youth who boldly proclaim that armed insurgence and revenge represent the path of the future even in the face of free elections. While in many societies young people holding such volatile ideas might be termed impatient, immature, or worse, Taylor writes that "they are their generation's best and brightest—articulate, savvy leaders, most with positions in their local youth branches of the African National Congress, the Congress of South African Students or the South African Communist party." Taylor's trenchant 5-28 report from a parade during which a violent clash erupted between ANC marchers and Inkatha residents reveals how tensions between the two groups can quickly turn deadly. "Marchers and hostel residents alike were armed, and both groups ignored appeals by police and peace monitors to avert a confrontation. First taunts were exchanged, then gunfire. Thirteen people were killed in the confrontation, and 40 more have since died in follow-up and revenge killings.... More than 2,000 people have fled their homes in Tokoza and neighboring townships." In a mostly secondhand 3-23 account of the battle between UNITA rebels and the Angolan government for the city of Huambo, Taylor incisively sets the scene from this war-torn nation. "The killings of humanitarian workers are just one small part of a massive reign of terror, complete with an African version of ethnic cleansing, being inflicted on civilians by both sides." Contrasting the UN's success establishing peace in Mozambique with its failure in Angola, 10-24, Taylor deftly portrays the UN's Mozambique strategy whereby a UN trust fund essentially pays the expenses of turning combatants into political parties. Noting raised eyebrows as a rebel leader turns down two UN-subsidized houses before accepting a third on the condition that it be refurnished, Taylor finds the UN strongly defending its policy. "Far from admitting to any unease about such blandishments, the starved-for-success world body is touting its pragmatism as the best hope for reversing a painful losing streak in peace-keeping missions elsewhere." As the African economic and political puzzles keep changing, Taylor's sound reporting provides clues as to how and why.

Charles Trueheart

The Washington Post

Toronto. While not fully tuned in to his foreign beat, Trueheart files dispatches that break some new ground and offer bits of insight into the cultural ways of Canada. In his flat 4-1 piece on the changing demographics of Vancouver, a favored destination for immigrants from Hong Kong, Trueheart vaguely surveys the changing city. "Would-be entrepreneurs and investors with bank accounts to pledge are fast-tracked through the Canadian immigration process, with those from Asian countries representing a third of those settling in Vancouver." In his enthusiastic 9-7 profile of the radically anti-consumption, anti-advertising Media Foundation and its quarterly magazine, *Adbusters*, Trueheart giddily describes what comes across as a rather sophomoric endeavor. "Every day but Wednesday...editors and worker bees sit around thinking up ways to 'culture jam.' That is, to subvert, satirize and otherwise stick their tongues out at the beast that makes advertising the bane of daily life for millions around the world and mindless consumption our economic and social reason for being. That's as they see it, of course." In his 4-15 effort highlighting the cultural debate that accompanies the political debate over Quebec's Gallic identity, Trueheart tells the story of funeral-parlor owner Gordon McIntyre's testifying before a UN committee. McIntyre challenged the province's French-only laws, prohibiting English from being used on commercial signs. Although the UN agreed with McIntyre, Trueheart notes, the decision carries only symbolic significance. "The UN finding would not be binding, but it shines an embarrassing spotlight on Quebec's most inflammatory and divisive language law at a time when the province's leadership is preparing to haggle over it once again." In his astute 10-27 article on the Canadian election results, Trueheart finds that because the major opposition party—Bloc Quebeçois—exists to pursue the secession of the province, its leader faces a unique situation. "[Party leader Lucien Bouchard] said he would run a full-fledged opposition party rather than a single-issue one, but he eschewed residence in the opposition leader's official lodgings. 'We don't intend to settle in Ottawa,' he said. 'The presence of the Bloc in Ottawa is by definition temporary.'" Trueheart's coverage of Canada lacks any formidable punch, leaving readers craving more precise analysis.

Patrick E. Tyler

The New York Times

★★★

Beijing. Moving in the summer from Washington to China, Tyler quickly hits stride, offering fresh stories on topics ranging from film censorship to economic policy. In his 8-28 article highlighting both the Chinese and American sides of the debate over the legality of Chinese missile sales to Pakistan, this former Pentagon reporter presents evidence that ultimately favors the Chinese, as the Clinton administration's charge relies on recent changes in interpretation of a 1987 accord. "China and Pakistan have argued that any Chinese sales of parts or technology for M-11 missiles to Pakistan do not violate the missile proliferation accord because the M-11's range is less than the minimum of 300 kilometers, or 186 miles, covered by the agreement." In his precise 10-3 account of new Economic Minister Zhu Rongji's attempts to quell China's overheated economy and runaway inflation, Tyler explains just where the government turns to slow things down. "[Zhu] sent investigators to the provinces to gather information and to bully local officials who were circumventing Beijing's commands. He found some provinces building so many bridges, highways, ports and skyscrapers on concurrent schedules that they were driving material prices skyward and overloading the system." In a perceptive 10-17 interview with filmmaker Chen Kaige, whose "Farewell My Concubine" was banned and unbanned twice, Tyler examines the Kafkaesque task of working under a totalitarian regime in an identity crisis. "To be a film director in China today is to be a politician in the most dangerous sense, making political decisions about art and content in a vacuum. The vacuum is the one created by the Communist Party, which has taken an end-of-empire approach to censorship. The censors won't say what the rules are, and once they have banned a film, they won't even tell directors how to cut it to satisfy their objections. They simply ban films they don't like." In his smart 11-23 piece on Chinese abandonment of austerity measures, Tyler shrewdly remarks, "The throttle has already been opened, and foreign corporate investment continues to pour like water over Niagara. Signed contracts were a staggering $83 billion during the first nine months of this year and seem headed for more than $100 billion by the end of the year." Pulling off a seemingly effortless transition to his new beat, Tyler displays his consummate skills as a journalist.

Michael Vatikiotis

Far Eastern Economic Review

★★

Kuala Lampur. Vigorous and verbose, Vatikiotis exhaustingly covers the idiosyncrasies of Malaysia's political system. Moreover, he writes for a highly specialized audience, often calling on readers' prior knowledge of his subject. In his 4-15 article on potential successors to Prime Minister Datuk Seri Mahathir Mohamad, Vatikiotis provides extensive detail on the maneuverings and alliances but offers no explanation of the political structure of the country or the issues that distinguish the candidates. He makes clear the importance of the November elections. "Those who clinch the three vice-presidential posts will be viewed as likely successors to the current national leadership. Umno [United Malays National Organization] presidents typically serve as prime minister while deputy presidents become deputy prime minister." Vatikiotis furnishes a straightforward but soporific 8-5 piece on an Association of Southeast Asian Nations [ASEAN] security meeting in Singapore. Clumsily reporting the event, he says participants struggled to initiate substantive talks on various issues—such as collective security—but resolved little because of concern about maintaining the group's facade of cohesion. "One fear is that the focus on wider security issues could turn out to be controversial. This became evident in Singapore where the U.S. and China sparred with each other and the atmosphere... was marred by the fundamental differences between them." In a refreshingly populist 7-22 article, Vatikiotis discovers that rock music—even without irreverent or suggestive lyrics—offends Malaysian censors, and he points out that the nation's young musicians frequently leave for more open societies. "Industry sources say the criteria used by the censors are unfathomable. They once banned a song in Malay because it referred to the Indonesian airline Garuda. Another song by rock singer M. Nasir was banned because it used an English name." Surveying the results of the election that consumed much of his attention this year, 11-18, Vatikiotis focuses so narrowly on the speculation over who will follow Mahathir as Prime Minister, that he never explores what might happen if the expected successor, Finance Minister Datuk Seri Anwar Ibrahim, takes over. While serious Malayophiles might welcome the concentrated detail of his reporting, others might find Vatikiotis largely inaccessible.

Stefan Wagstyl

Financial Times

★★★

New Delhi. Resorting often and effectively to clever generalizations, Wagstyl authoritatively covers the political turmoil and social unrest in the Indian subcontinent. In his solid 1-22 article, Wagstyl shrewdly blames poor leadership by Indian President P.V. Narasimha Rao for the growing popularity of the nationalistic, radically Hindu, Bharatiya Janata Party. After referring to the party's platform and noting several instances of individual Hindus standing up to mobs to protect Muslims, Wagstyl thoughtfully concludes, "Many Hindus are appalled by such hate-filled talk and there has been no shortage of articulate condemnations of Hindu militancy." His probing 2-9 story of destitute Indians stealing electricity off the power line masterfully contrasts a country's need for more power facilities it can't afford with that of small communities for basic power they can't afford. Wagstyl recognizes a "Catch-22" situation, as the government frantically courts would-be bidders to build power generators in the country. "The cautious response is partly due to the huge scale of the proposed investments and partly to doubts about the government's ability to overhaul the industry's anti-commercial practices....The companies are worried because the electricity boards are controlled by local state governments, which use electricity supply as a political tool." Providing incisive background on the two main candidates in the Pakistani presidential election, 10-5, Wagstyl reports that both candidates are bound by the austerity measures, established by the current caretaker government with the approval of the International Monetary Fund. With these constraints thus limiting debate on economic issues, candidates have resorted to personal attacks. "The campaigns," he notes, "have not been short of vitriol, including charges of corruption, murder and terrorism." Wagstyl's cogent 5-14 piece from Punjab emphasizes the uneasy trade-off between social order and individual liberty as the state's police force has dramatically reduced the number of murders in the past two years—largely by wielding an iron stick. "There are doubts whether such an enforced peace can last unless the central government also tries to settle the grievances which first drove the militants to arms....Most Punjabis are less interested in [the police chief's] methods than in his results." By examining social and economic conditions as well as the ruling power structures, Wagstyl renders a balanced and revealing portrayal of Indian society.

Peter Waldman

The Wall Street Journal

★★★

Amman bureau chief. Reporting from the Middle East, North Africa, and the U.S., Waldman demonstrates a strong ability to cut to the heart of the matter. Almost presciently, 1-6, seven weeks prior to the World Trade Center bombing, he hits the streets in Brooklyn to investigate the controversial Sheik Omar Abdel Rahman. "Since moving to the borough of Brooklyn 2 1/2 years ago," Waldman writes, "the spiritual leader of Egypt's outlawed Jihad revolutionary group has brought the violent struggle against the enemies of Islam into the belly of the 'Great Satan' itself, the United States." In a 9-1 profile concentrating on the sheik's career in Egypt, Waldman skillfully assesses that, "after a lifetime of railing against the secular rule" of Egypt, Sheik Omar "now heads a movement that is shaking the government." With precision, Waldman notes that the sheik's "message to [his] followers is simple: The path to paradise is found through martyrdom. They must be ready to suffer as the Prophet Mohammed did. Sheik Omar preaches this message in the most powerful way imaginable: by seeming to live it himself." In his piercing 6-14 indictment of Egyptian President Hosni Mubarak's government, Waldman reports that "the U.S. has poured $30 billion of aid into Egypt [since the 1978 Camp David peace accord]—second only to the $40 billion for Israel....But the aid hasn't bought stability" because Mubarak's 12-year-old regime is "bedeviled by charges of corruption, brutality and ineptitude." After the U.S. attack on an Iraqi nuclear-processing facility, 1-18, Waldman coolly asserts that the act "is likely to compound the rage felt here toward Mr. Bush, and, increasingly, toward the U.S. itself." Waldman adds that "the hardships [caused by the United Nations embargo], coupled with despair over the likelihood that Saddam Hussein will hold on to power, has bred much deeper enmity for the allies now than after the war." In his 2-24 follow-up, Waldman concludes, "Though George Bush's parting shots at Iraq were militarily insignificant, the skirmishes have given the Iraqi dictator a bounty of ammunition in his war of words and images against the West." A hard-nosed reporter with strong analytical skills, Waldman extracts a clear, well-supported meaning from each investigation.

Patti Waldmeir

Financial Times

★★★★

Johannesburg. Acutely sensitive to the conflicting political and moral forces in South Africa, Waldmeir provides excellent dispatches that fairly and firmly cover the steps to representative government. She also astutely covers the political maneuvering underlying each step toward the transformation to majority rule. Waldmeir's detailed and penetrating 2-13/14 piece on the agreement to form a transitional multiracial government points out that while several crucial hurdles remain, the transition itself is inevitable. "It represents the most important step in the country's peace process since the release of Mr. Nelson Mandela in 1990 and the all-white referendum last year which endorsed President F.W. de Klerk's negotiating strategy." Attacking de Klerk in her shrewd 4-19 piece on the reactions of Mandela and de Klerk to the assassination of African National Congress leader Chris Hani, Waldmeir argues, "With his dark threats against 'radicals' (which he knows he cannot carry out without sparking civil war) and his frantic warnings of a descent into chaos, Mr. de Klerk has cut a somewhat pathetic figure in recent days. He may be president, but Mr. Mandela is South Africa's leader." Her brief but articulate 9-24 piece on legislation establishing a multiracial Transitional Executive Council makes the oft-neglected point that white South Africans welcome the step. "Passage of the bill marks the symbolic end of white hegemony and economic isolation. The transitional executive, which will bring blacks a share of power for the first time, will boost black morale, while the removal of 30 years of economic sanctions will help the morale of most whites." Probing the ANC's heavy-handed tactics in constitutional talks, 12-22, Waldmeir keenly exposes the ANC effort to split the Freedom Alliance—a coalition of conservative groups, including Afrikaners and the Inkatha Freedom Party—that opposes strong centralized power. While the ANC was being rebuffed in efforts to set up a bilateral alliance with the Afrikaners, Waldmeir reports, it was sending South African police to intervene in KwaZulu, an area inhabited primarily by Inkatha sympathizers. With incisive reporting and alert analysis, Waldmeir laces her stories with rich texture that always illuminates her subjects.

Tony Walker

Financial Times

★★

Beijing. Limited by oppressive state regulation, Walker usually interprets and quantifies information released by the Chinese government. His skilled efforts to read between the lines of the official Chinese press, occasionally interwoven with the local buzz, result in satisfying but vague conjecture about the government's actions and priorities. Walker offers extensive figures in his 2-12 portrayal of the booming Chinese economy. From these numbers, he smartly reasons that while government austerity measures may not be enough to slow down inflation, some unanticipated factors might eventually do the trick. "Infrastructure deficiencies in the power and transport sector may in the end prove the most effective break on fren-

zied development." Walker's amusing and insightful 5-14 piece on the desperate measures of Chinese officials to impress International Olympic Committee President Juan Antonio Samaranch points out that despite the friendly rhetoric, Beijing is waging a no-holds-barred propaganda battle to win the 2000 Olympics. "China's official *Outlook Magazine* almost certainly outdid its competitors in its praise for Mr. Samaranch. 'His achievements,' the magazine told its readers, 'are simply too many to count.'" And on one day, Walker adds, the *Beijing Daily* "carried almost nothing but 'Sama-stories' on its front and back pages." In his straightforward 8-18 piece on a Chinese austerity step calling for a freeze on state wages, Walker provides fine detail and analysis. Noting that more than 50 percent of Chinese state enterprises lose money, he explains, "Urban employees' wages have risen 21.7 percent in the first six months of this year compared with the same period last year. State-owned industry paid out...$7.24 billion in bonuses, 38 percent more than the same period in 1992." His hazy 11-16 wrap-up of what was to have been the most important Chinese Central Committee meeting since 1978 relies on the Chinese press and an unnamed Western official. Walker does well, however, explaining the conflicting interests of various factions at the meeting, which likely caused it to bog down. "Many officials also owe their party status to their association with industries which are having difficulty adapting to the demands of a market economy. These officials are fighting to preserve their fiefdoms." With his deep understanding of Chinese politics, Walker might make more of his reports by incorporating first-hand business information into his policy coverage.

Charles P. Wallace

Los Angeles Times

★½

Bangkok bureau chief. From various Southeast Asian capitals, Wallace's generalized reporting offers panoramic perspectives on compelling subjects—but rarely tantalizes the intellect. Banalities plague his writing, and too often important detail follows interminable qualification. In his 6-2 report, Wallace offers varied but familiar speculation about the reasons for the Cambodian government's protest about the fairness of elections. Losses at the polls, Wallace notes, would force it to share power with the opposition royalist party. "One Western diplomat noted that while the government's showing was quite respectable, it has ruled Cambodia for 13 years as a one-party state and was completely unprepared to share power....He said the problem lies in the provinces where local officials now serving the Phnom Penh government had lost their bids for seats and would hesitate to hand over power." Wallace's 7-27 article on Russian arms sales to developing Asian nations, such as Indonesia and Malaysia, warns that the availability of armaments from Russia and the uncertain balance left after the U.S. military withdrawal from the Philippines raises serious concerns. He provides telling detail but simplistic observations. "One feature of the new Russian sales in Asia is the lack of ideology in the transactions. Whereas in the past the Soviet Union strove to assist 'fraternal socialist' countries such as Vietnam or Syria, Russia's concern [now] appears to be cold cash." The region's tension rings clear in Wallace's grim reminder through a special 6-15 *Times* report on China. Citing past hostilities and a territorial dispute over oil-rich islands in the South China Sea, he argues that tension between Vietnam and China remains a threat to regional peace. "The end of the Cold War has helped resolve many of the conflicts in the region that pitted Communist countries against anti-communist ones. But it remains to be seen if former Communist allies can also end their historic antagonism and become good neighbors." In his riveting 4-22 piece, Wallace finds that mines injure thousands of people annually in formerly—and presently—war-torn regions, such as Cambodia, Somalia, and Afghanistan. Deftly exploring the issue from military, medical, and cultural perspectives, Wallace finds mines essential to modern warfare and nearly impossible to remove once planted. According to one source, "in a recent six-month period, all the mine-clearing by the United Nations and charity groups removed just 7,147 anti-personnel mines and 12 anti-tank mines. There were nine casualties, four involving supervising UN soldiers." While Wallace capably reports stories laid out before him, he would do well to dig deeper and uncover new ground.

Teresa Watanabe

Los Angeles Times

★★★

Tokyo. By offering fresh and revealing perspectives on the challenges facing Japan's hidebound political and economic cultures, Watanabe's trenchant reporting both elucidates and educates. She treats diverse subjects and ably reports the why and how of Japanese traditions before evaluating the prospects of change. In her 1-27 profile of Chad Rowan (a.k.a. Akebono), Watanabe finds it takes a massive girth, modest demeanor, and happy-go-lucky nature to produce the nobility, character, and power required to become the first foreign-born *Yokozuna*, grand champion of sumo. Her amusing piece plays on the contrast between a high-spirited, homesick American and the passive dignity that defines his sport. "After solemnly ending the practice session with a ritualistic circling of the sumo ring, Akebono clambered downstairs, turned up some rap music full blast and jammed wildly to the beat in his cotton kimono." Watanabe's well-organized and captivating 4-7 report on Japanese schoolyard bullying explores numerous examples of such behavior through the years, as well as the long- and short-term effects on students. Her well-reasoned, highly informative 7-16 report on the Japanese election goes far in explaining why the Japanese people tolerate the flagrant corruption resulting from its patronage system. The Confucian tradition, she reports, considers it ungrateful not to return something when you receive a favor. "As a result, even a political reformist such as [campaign manager Shinya] Tomomatsu is unsure where the line should be drawn between a virtuous custom and a corrupt practice. The quid pro quo that serves as a corruption yardstick in the West doesn't fit here, since the point of the custom is quid pro quo." Watanabe's tenacious 10-30 article astutely finds bid-rigging not just a bad habit but a century-old cultural tradition among Japanese contractors. In a bidding-cum-fixing process called *dango*, she reports, contractors "take turns at the trough so no one would starve, to subordinate personal interests for the good of the group." Watanabe points out that the recent entry of Japanese contractors into foreign markets has created demand for reciprocal access to the Japanese market. Coupled with increasing pressure from local contractors who feel mistreated by the system, Watanabe notes, the practice has drawn attention and criticism. Watanabe's reporting consistently reveals the benefit of understanding foreign systems before defining them with modish American vernacular.

Craig Whitney

The New York Times

★

Bonn bureau. Writing from the heart of Europe, Whitney rarely conveys an insider's knowledge of the region or its myriad troubles. And he launches too many articles with odd or cumbersome openers that do little to prompt further reading. In his 2-1 story on a defense industry scandal in Bonn, Whitney states, "This is such a small town that even political scandals don't usually meet the international standards set by Washington, London and Paris." Oh? In a 5-25 piece, he lets go another poorly constructed intro. "The one thing Serbian military and police authorities who govern here in Kosovo Province and the two million restive ethnic Albanians who resist them agree on is that if the war in the Balkans spreads here, the bloodletting will be worse than anything yet." Unfortunately, these initial handicaps get in the way of stories that dig into the problems of Europe—and especially Germany. In his lengthy 2-19 article on German reunification woes, he notes, "Only a year ago, in the midst of the now-vanished boom, it had not really dawned on western Germans that life might no longer be one annual salary raise after another and ever-shorter working hours." Whitney's 8-1 piece on German leadership within the European Community pursues an imaginative angle. "And for all the fears of Germany throwing its weight around, it has been the hesitancy and reluctance of Mr. Kohl and his Government to assert leadership that has most often surprised their European and American allies." Although he acknowledges Germany's most pressing problems—immigration, neo-Nazis, reunification—Whitney too often rehashes issues discussed many times over in recent years.

Carol Williams

Los Angeles Times

International. In her dispatches from a devastated Yugoslavia, Williams makes an indelible im-

pression vividly portraying a nation and region torn asunder. At her best covering the daily conditions of people caught up in events beyond their control, her stories convey the cold, fear, and hunger of the victims of war. In her 6-1 article, Williams focuses on the most innocent victims of all as she recounts the West's lack of response to cries for help from Sarajevo's embattled citizens. "The tiny, shrouded corpse of 10-month-old Vedad Hamzic joined a dozen battle victims in the Kosevo Hospital morgue Monday in what many in this disillusioned capital consider sadly appropriate testimony to the West's contribution to the Bosnian crisis." For her 7-25 *Magazine* story, Williams captures the despair of Bosnian women as they unwrap packages from the U.S. airdrop in hopes of finding anxiously awaited food supplies. "But on this late spring morning, the foraging mothers find a disappointing substitute for the usual life-sustaining alms. Instead of the cherished aluminum ration tins, their grappling is rewarded with men's shaving kits. In a town as achingly short of water as it is of shelter and food, the mini-bottles of lotion and after-shave and plastic-wrapped disposable razors seem more a mockery of the desperate, infested women than a hygienic pick-me-up, as the men's toiletries were meant to be." Williams infuses her 5-23 dispatch on a proposed peace plan for Bosnia with a sense of futility. "Thus, while the international community delves into the time-consuming work of translating its diplomatic tongue-lashing into action, Bosnia's defiant Serbs—emboldened by the outside world's reluctance to stop them—may press on with their deadly drive to create an ethnically pure, independent state." And how could the reader not be morbidly fascinated by the opening of Williams's 6-8 account of Serbian war crimes? "Hamed Celik's punishment for being a Muslim was to become a human minesweeper." The piece does not disappoint, as it chronicles systematic and institutional abuse of the civilian population. "The tens of thousands of Muslim men detained by Serbian gunmen in Bosnia last spring and summer have mostly been released, under pressure from Western human rights organizations....Survivors of some of the most heinous acts witnessed in Europe since the Nazi era... were exposed to abuse at the hands of criminal jailers who terrorized their prisoners with every weapon from psychological torture to summary executions." In her grim and gritty reports, Williams uses stark detail to illuminate the tragic

tapestry of the nation that was once Yugoslavia.

Howard Witt

Chicago Tribune

★★½

Moscow. Witt's articles put the reader smack in the middle of Moscow's Pushkin Square. From his well-textured accounts of Russian life and politics, you know he spends his days on the street reporting. In his 7-25 *Magazine* piece that draws parallels between the Moscow McDonald's and the Russian economy, he writes, "[Street] vendors drawn to McDonald's like pilgrims to a shrine offer books, fruit, candy, clothes, liquor—even condoms and inflatable sex toys—hoping that the restaurant's affluent clientele will still have room for something more, even after the apple pies....Three and a half years after it opened in a blaze of glasnost-era publicity, the Moscow McDonald's restaurant has settled into a delicate truce with the harsh, restive city that hosts it." At this time in history, Russia must be a dream assignment for a foreign correspondent, and Witt brings an obvious enthusiasm to his stories. "Russia is having a fire sale," he writes in his droll 3-21 essay on the privatization of government property. "The damaged goods are thousands of former Soviet factories, businesses, and stores warped and twisted by seven decades of ruinous socialist economics." Nevertheless, he finds the spirit of a waking bull among the generally flummoxed population. "When Yeltsin announced the voucher scheme on August 19—the first anniversary of the failed hard-line Communist coup attempt—he was greeted with a collective national shrug. How, many wondered, could a country of downtrodden proletarians possibly master the vagaries of a sophisticated stock market? Surprisingly well, the answer has turned out. 'I'm looking for a direct investment in an industry that promises a good profit and a stable dividend,' said engineer Vitaly Lodan, sounding like any prospective investor in the U.S." In his 3-22 piece, Witt vividly portrays the turbulent battles between President Boris Yeltsin, Parliament, and the courts. "The country may have a document called a constitution and a high court with jurists who wear black robes. But pique and passion, far more than precedent, are the dominant features of its budding legal system." Witt illustrates his point by interviewing one high court judge, who accuses Yeltsin of "urinating" on the Russian constitution. Witt also moves beyond Russia's borders to address issues in neighboring states, as evidenced by his 7-6 article focusing on Ukraine and its economic problems. "In Moscow, shoppers now wait in line to buy the latest Reebok sneakers. In Kiev, shoppers still wait in line to buy bread." Readers concerned with Russia's future should wait in line for Witt's articles.

★ COMMENTATORS ★

Russell Baker

The New York Times

★★★

"Observer" columnist. More than a humorist, Baker raises the absurd to an art form. Taking political correctness to the extreme, 1-26, he defines himself first as "a European-American," before adding: "I am a comparatively financially disadvantaged, square, married, heterosexual, comb-carrying, college-educated, hearing-impaired, Depression-generation, male European-American." Employing stuffy-nosed dialect, 3-9, Baker writes about his "reedy idcredible sufferig," announcing, "I hab a code." He addresses health-care reform briefly in a 9-28 list of marvelously unanswerable questions on the inanity of current events. "Speaking of the health program, why are lawyers (namely, both Clintons and most of the Congress) now in charge of inventing it? Doesn't everybody know that lawyers can't stop themselves from making everything so complicated that nobody can figure it out without hiring a lawyer? Wasn't the present income tax system designed by lawyers? Why do we have to suffer an April 15th experience every time we get sick?" Baker typically offers wisdom in his humor, smartly advising President Clinton on 6-5. "Cut out the talk about 'moving to the center.' No two people agree on where the center is. As a result, half your critics will say you've moved to the right of center and the other half will say you've stayed too far to the left of center. Outside the Beltway the audience for this kind of talk is slightly smaller than the audience for a lecture on the origins of the Peloponnesian War." In a 10-2 piece for Columbus Day, Baker crafts a pointed indictment of the conceit of today's intellectuals in deriding heroes of the past. "Last year's attacks on Columbus were denunciations of a human product of 15th-century European culture, but they were more than attacks. They were also celebrations of the superiority of the present culture. The modern custom is to stand in front of the mirror patting yourself on the back and loudly congratulating yourself on how thoroughly your moral superiority exceeds that of the old-timers of long-dead generations." Now gracing Alistair Cooke's "Masterpiece Theater" chair, Baker, thanks to his singular gift of treating serious, even tragic events and trends with gentle humor, has become an American institution.

Fred Barnes

The New Republic

★★★

"White House Watch" columnist. Few columnists had White House sources as good as those Barnes enjoyed during the Reagan-Bush era. Still cultivating sources in the Clinton era, Barnes remains a prolific and often insightful writer on the presidency and many other political topics as well. Examining the rhetoric of Bill Clinton's economic address, he concludes, 3-8, that the young President is "obsessed with emulating" the best of Reagan, but that the speech's real significance lay not in how he gave it but in what he said. Barnes takes a crack at spinning the spinner, 7-19/26, analyzing the effect of David Gergen upon the Clinton presidency. Here Barnes reports that Gergen is a "big advocate" of cutting the capital gains tax rate. In a superb 6-7 sketch of Sen. Bob Kerrey [D-NE], Barnes fleshes out the Nebraskan's politics and projects Kerrey's future as an anti-Clinton Democrat. And in his clever 11-8 piece on the politics of immigration, he highlights Clinton's eagerness to set the tone of the debate because "Republicans, sensing a political bonanza in economically insecure times, are ready to ride the immigration issue wherever it takes them, even at the expense of their image as an optimistic, inclusionary party." After citing the positive public response to Gov. Pete Wilson's [R-CA] call for eliminating benefits to illegal immigrants, Barnes draws a shrewd conclusion. "While Republicans seem unaware of the long-term dangers (not least to their own party) of fomenting nativism with this sort of rhetoric, Democrats have little in the way of a coherent response." *American Spectator* published Barnes's strongest effort, a controversial 5-93 critique of the "myth" that the United States has a "health-care crisis." Probing key aspects of the health-care debate, Barnes delivers a preemptive strike against the Clinton health-care plan—a big score for this incisive political writer.

Michael Barone
U.S. News & World Report
★★½

Informing Barone's work is the principle that re-election is the primary business of politics. While he stuffs his columns with data and insight, the quality of his analysis varies. In his 4-26 effort urging Bill Clinton and Al Gore to downsize the federal government, Barone notes that if they "want to take advantage of the political currents, they should take heed of the recent experience of governors: Those who cut spending and the size of the government work force are doing well; those who raised taxes and did not seriously slash public job rolls are in trouble." Here Barone conflates popularity with effective government. His 6-7 column wisely warns against finance-driven health-care reform. "There are two dangers inherent in ignoring the delivery side of health care. One is that many more Americans are served well by the current system than are poorly served by it. The other is that health care comes not from money but from people." Unfortunately, obscure precedents based on Robert McNamara's cost-benefit analyses during his years in the Pentagon muddle Barone's argument. Addressing what he considers the dilemma of Clinton's presidency, 6-14, he concludes: "the dominant ideas of the dominant wing of his party—the liberals—do not command approval of a majority of Americans." Eisenhower faced the same problem from the conservative wing of his party, Barone notes, and overcame it by building coalitions across party lines. Clinton, he suggests, should govern like Ike. In his 7-12 discussion of the Supreme Court ruling that North Carolina's 12th District is illegal, Barone makes excellent use of statistics. Pointing out that black candidates in the state run strongly among non-black voters, he surmises that the snaking 12th district was drawn as much to protect white incumbents as to create a black seat. A thoughtful columnist, Barone saturates even his weaker efforts with facts and information.

Robert L. Bartley
The Wall Street Journal
★★★

Editor. Bartley's influence stems largely from his intelligent, fearless editorship of the *Journal*'s editorial and op-ed pages. It's too bad his signed pieces don't appear frequently enough for him to acquire a large following; he's a strong writer, especially on economics. When Bartley does enter the world of byline punditry, he does best when he sticks to his strength, economics. On 2-24, he asks "whether the Clinton plan will, as advertised, 'grow the economy.' Two decades of experience...suggest that the Clinton proposals will not boost the economy but cripple it." He recommends "growing" out of the deficit, 3-4, through NAFTA and increased market efficiency—items on the wish list of most conservatives. Bartley looks beyond the current dollar fracas to point out, 4-29, that the dollar has the power to make or break the economies of other countries. "The dollar remains the keystone of the world's monetary system—as economists say, the *reserve currency*. It's the world *unit of account*, essential to facilitate trade. And it's the world's *store of value*, the preferred currency for liquid assets. If a store of value starts to look shaky, everyone tries to liquidate at once; with a confused unit of account, trade falters; the collapse of reserve currency can wreck economies the world over." In his 7-29 column, Bartley sharply observes what proposed taxes will do to both the entrepreneurial class and the rich. "Whether or not Macomb County resents the rich, the Beltway sure does. Entrenched *rentiers* always resent the entrepreneurial class." In his 9-23 discussion on conservatism, populism, and the 1992 presidential campaign, Bartley smartly argues that the future of American politics depends "on what is really on the Perot voters' minds. The heart of it is

not NAFTA or the deficit, but whether citizens can affect the political structure." Bartley finishes on a surprising note. "Politicians are wrong when they conclude the trick is fooling the people; we populists believe the trick is educating them." One wishes the byline of this populist-on-Wall-Street would run more often.

Tom Bethell

The American Spectator

★½

"Capitol Ideas" columnist. Although Bethell scatters a nugget or two in his monthly columns, it's sometimes work to find them, as he tends to wander from one subject to another in the same piece. In his January column, he moves from Gennifer Flowers and the then-governor's car in her driveway, to an exceptional description of the devastation in inner-city Washington, to Bill Clinton's economic policies and his fear that Clinton will cut the capital gains tax and be a two-term president. Bethell, guilty of unsportsmanlike conduct in favoring ideology over the welfare of the country, asks liberal commentators to keep arguing against cutting the capital-gains tax so the economy will suffer and conservative Jack Kemp will have an issue with which to drive Clinton out of office in 1996. Bethell's March observations of the inaugural are most potent when he discusses Clinton's plans for "sacrifice," because he's not simply griping about Maya Angelou's poetry but dealing with a substantive issue. Bethell reports, 4-93, on his meeting with Sen. Alan Simpson [R-WY] to debate the issues, particularly immigration, but Bethell's stream-of-consciousness style makes the information difficult to find. His dense August exploration of scientist Petr Beckmann's challenge to Einstein's theory of relativity sounds like a graduate class lecture and is misplaced in a "Capitol Ideas" column. Bethell fares better when dealing with real-life experiences, as he does in his October column, offering detailed examples of how tax laws, regulations, and incentives affect communities. Similarly, his reporting in *The Wall Street Journal* 7-23 shines, in that Bethell breaks news by reporting OMB figures on Clinton's budget expenditures and revenues. He provides no analysis in the piece, but the numbers pack a punch—something Bethell does only occasionally.

Sidney Blumenthal

The New Yorker

★½

Washington editor. One of Bill Clinton's biggest cheerleaders in campaign '92, this thinking-person's liberal has devolved into the administration's apologist. Who knows, perhaps Blumenthal is looking for a new job at 1600 Pennsylvania Avenue. Despite his connections, his insider views reveal little of importance about the first Democratic regime in more than a decade. Reporting more on style than substance in his 1-25 column, Blumenthal concentrates on personalities, as Friends of Bill wait anxiously to be tapped for government positions. In his 4-5 effort, Blumenthal recycles Jon Katz's idea of how the president can circumvent the Washington press corps and take his case directly to the people. Moreover, he adds little new to the body of work already penned on this subject. He mars an otherwise excellent 6-28 evaluation of David Gergen as cross-party advisor by veering off his subject to provide too much background on others who also influence Clinton, such as Mack McLarty and Harry Thomason. In his two-dimensional 7-5 portrait of Sen. Daniel Patrick Moynihan [D-NY], Blumenthal highlights the Senator's role in getting the Clinton budget plan through the Senate Finance Committee. Although mentioning that Moynihan is "known as a prophet and a gadfly," Blumenthal does not quote a single Republican on the committee or in the Senate about his stewardship. He relies instead on Democrats to explain what Republicans think—which is not the same thing. Following the suicide of Vince Foster, Blumenthal quotes an unnamed source alleging "'the town [Washington] has now killed somebody,'" but his 8-9 examination of the tragedy fails to illuminate. Blumenthal's best efforts came early—and late. His exhaustive 2-15 reporting on the nomination of Zöe Baird as Attorney General and her withdrawal because of the "nanny" controversy sheds light on how the Clinton White House works (or doesn't work). And in an outstanding 10-25 essay querying "Why are we in Somalia?" Blumenthal crafts the definitive history of recent U.S. involvement in that country. "In trying to relieve the famine, we plunged directly into the murderous cockpit of Somali politics....The humanitarian role could not have been more political. Preventing the recurrence of the crisis that had brought us into Somalia required nothing less than establishing a quasi-neocolonial United Nations trusteeship." When he traces the history of a subject, Blumenthal can shine.

Gloria Borger

U.S. News and World Report

★

"On Politics." As both a Capitol Hill reporter and regular columnist (she replaced the White House-bound David Gergen in July), Borger files well-reported pieces that lack insight and rarely break new ground. Too often she writes who's-in/who's-out articles that are only partly redeemed by her lucid style. In her 4-12 column, Borger reports that Sen. Bill Bradley [D-NJ], "the father of tax simplification," opposes President Clinton's planned investment tax credit. She cites an anonymous White House source as saying the President won't push the tax credit unless there's enthusiastic congressional support. But since this support does not exist, Borger writes, the plan will likely "vaporize." Borger concludes by citing Bradley's comment that he will support whatever the President decides. All of which means—what? In her 4-19 piece, co-authored by Matthew Cooper, the pair criticizes Republicans for "holding hostage the Democratic president's economic-stimulus package through parliamentary maneuvers." Such procedures as the filibuster, they claim, only diminish voters' regard for politics and politicians. "The key to Washington deal making," they conclude dullishly, "is to understand that even the self-proclaimed underdogs want to feed at the trough.... Americans are growing tired of waiting for both sides to get along." Borger's fawning 8-9 portrait of Rep. Kweisi Mfume [D-MD], the leader of the Congressional Black Caucus, suffers from her failure to cite a single Mfume detractor. One of her stronger efforts, 7-5, highlights the divisions within the Republican Party at a time of growing public dissatisfaction with the Democratic administration. "All this good news, however, has come too soon: Clinton's inauspicious start has caught Republicans unprepared....Unlike the productive post-Goldwater and post-Nixon periods of soul-searching, the chief product of this year's unexpectedly easy political ride is knee-jerk opposition." Although well-informed, Borger has yet to offer the kind of argument and insight expected of opinion columnists.

James Bovard

Freelance

★★★

Appearing regularly in *The Wall Street Journal*, Bovard's intelligent pieces on free trade condemn protectionist impulses of administrations past and present. Ever vigilant when other trade reporters let the wires do the work, Bovard broadens his beat this year to include taxation and property rights. His exceptional 1-28 examination of the steel industry and foreign dumping highlights the bureaucratic barriers enforced by the Commerce Department. The policy, he notes, "effectively erects a huge 'DO NOT ENTER' sign at the U.S. border...." In T*he New Republic* 3-15, Bovard argues that Bill Clinton has broken his vow to cut farm subsidies. "When President Clinton announced a sweeping agenda to reduce the deficit by almost $500 billion, the slashing of farm subsidies—one of the most blatant ways the government wastes money—was touted as an integral part of the effort. But once again the farm lobby has prevailed. For all of Clinton's tough talk, existing

farm program subsidies will almost double this year, from $9 billion to $17 billion, primarily in response to falling market prices for crops." In his 4-7 *WSJ* article, Bovard shows how the IRS stifles the growth of small businesses by forcing these businesses to reclassify independent contractors as employees, thus compelling them to pay payroll and social security taxes already paid by the contractor. In his 5-13 *WSJ* essay, Bovard contends that preservationists are gaining a strong hand in many communities across the country. Maintaining that "historic preservation itself has unfortunately become a pretext for mass confiscation," he details legislation pushed by preservationist groups that severely constricts what owners can do to renovate "historic" sites. He elevates a 6-9 *WSJ* discussion of Macedonian textile exports to the U.S. to an eye-opening report on the protectionist winds blowing in the new administration. Similarly, he looks, *WSJ* 10-15, at the implications of the administration's idea to restrict Canadian durum imports, which may "result in a Canadian rejection of NAFTA and a collapse of U.S. credibility in the GATT negotiations." Nobody covers these obscure issues as thoroughly as Bovard.

David S. Broder

Washington Post Writers Group

★★★½

Washington reporter and columnist. Broder is the best of an almost extinct species, the daily news reporter who doubles as an op-ed page columnist. In *The Washington Post* 2-24, he offers a devastating assessment of President Clinton's economic program. "Last Oct. 1...when the Bush campaign ran ads based on the calculation that Clinton could finance his campaign promises only by raising taxes on every family earning more than $36,600 a year, this is what the Democratic nominee said: 'It is blatantly false....' Last week Clinton, unembarrassed, put forward a revised program requiring tax increases the administration says will affect most families making over $30,000, one-sixth below the threshold George Bush had forecast. Clinton claims he has been forced to these steps by the unexpected $346 billion size of the deficit he inherited. But last July, he told *BusinessWeek* that deficits would approach $400 billion." Broder adds that "as administration officials have conceded, the higher tax bites actually begin at a figure closer to $20,000 than to $30,000." Broder gives smart advice to Clinton on trimming government waste, 1-13, urging the incoming president to expend "political capital" to meet his goal. He offers more wise counsel, 5-19, using his vast political knowledge to provide context and precedent for bipartisan cooperation between the White House and Congress, and urging the President to "invit[e] talented Republicans to join his administration." Perhaps Clinton listened—he hired David Gergen a few weeks later. Critical of Clinton's foreign policy, he supplies an incisive 10-13 evaluation of cabinet members, whose limitations the President should offset by considering the appointment of Republicans "who know their way around the world." Displaying his trademark fairness, Broder defends the President, 9-8, against media skepticism toward his economic ideas. He argues that "when [the news media's] managements start looking for ways to cut costs, we find it as hard as any auto worker to believe that the president is going to provide salvation by some new scheme he unveils." With his solid reporting and shrewd analysis, Broder remains one of the sager voices in Washington.

Patrick J. Buchanan

Tribune Media Services

★★

Off the campaign trail and back to writing (and sparring with Michael Kinsley on CNN's "Crossfire"), Buchanan has lost little of his fire and none of his belligerence. Whatever the subject matter, his efforts never lack for clarity. Buchanan gives the GOP a 1-21 pep talk in *The Wall Street Journal*, but says little new. In *The Washington Times* 3-10, he draws pertinent parallels between today's Russia and the Weimar Republic, concluding that Western aid cannot help Russia and that all President Clinton can do is watch the Yeltsin regime go up in smoke. Buchanan offers a savvy 6-23 review of Clintonomics, making a solid case for cutting the capital-gains tax. In his typically hard-hitting style, he argues that new tax rates on the rich proposed by Clinton will damage the economy. "Dressed up in the gaudy costume of progressivity and fairness, this is madness. Not only will these taxes retard the growth Americans want, they will abort the new jobs America needs." He assails New York City Mayoral candidate Rudolph Giuliani, 7-19, for toadying to gay activists. Arguing that such a tactic undermines GOP philosophy, he warns, "That way lies the Whigs." He does some solid reporting on Haiti, 10-13, examining the U.S.'s role and Jean-Bertrand Aristide's record. Buchanan's strongly articulated conclusion differs from that of most columnists and U.S. policy-makers. "We have battered a fragile economy, further impoverished the poorest people in the hemisphere, driven hundreds to their death in leaky boats, deepened the hatred and divisions in Haiti to a point where U.S. soldiers are at risk—all to restore a socialist ranter whose career was built on baiting the United States. To save Haiti for democracy, we have virtually destroyed Haiti....This sort of moral imperialism is one day going to make this country the most hated on Earth." Buchanan's supernationalist, street-fighter tactics, however, can turn to bluster. In his 8-4 attempt to exonerate accused war criminal John Demjanjuk, he relies on weak evidence—an Israeli guard smiling at Demjanjuk as he was released. Buchanan argues that an Israeli guard wouldn't smile at a prisoner that was guilty. C'mon, Pat.

Art Buchwald

Los Angeles Times Syndicate

★★

Buchwald's takes on the new administration in *The Washington Post* are more powerful (and funnier) than his observations on the state of society. His 4-13 dialogue between Woody Allen and his two psychiatrists over Soon-Yi Previn falls flat, both because of the distasteful subject matter and the sophomoric execution. Buchwald's strength still lies in poking fun at politics; he simply has more absurd material to work with inside the Beltway. In his 1-19 column, Buchwald's spin on the upcoming inaugural neatly captures the desperation of the job seekers and the despair of the defeated: "I have watched hardened veterans of an administration stumble out in the street handing out their resumes to anyone who would take them. I have seen men once charged with handling billions of dollars trying to get enough change from tourists to take the bus home." His moderately amusing 7-1 column has the CIA and FBI scour the country to find Bill Clinton's missing half-brother. "So far there have been no sightings," an agent tells the President, "although we have picked up two of your second cousins and an uncle you didn't know existed." Turning to health care, 8-17, Buchwald imagines a dialogue that countenances $25 cut-rate hernia operations and a long wait for any kind of care. Buchwald's funniest observations, however, concern the news media. Attributing a tragi-comic reason for press attention to Hollywood madam Heidi Fleiss, Buchwald argues, 9-1, that "this nation must have a scandal every month to make it forget guns in the street and the high cost of hernia operations." And his 6-29 description of the White House press corps is unforgettable. "The correspondents, male and female, are located in the White House basement and live in cages. They have hair all over their bodies, and twice a day someone from the press office comes down and throws them a banana. After eating the bananas they thump themselves on the chest and let out loud screams that can be heard in the Oval Office." Arguably, the only flaw in this analogy is that Sam Donaldson is no longer part of the White House press corps. Still, it shows that Buchwald finds his humor in things closest to home.

William F. Buckley Jr.

National Review

Universal Press Syndicate

★★

Editor-at-Large, *National Review;* syndicated columnist, Universal Press Syndicate. Having written his column since the 1960s, Buckley is at his best when he takes on a politician's thought, dissects a policy proposal, or analyzes a philosophical premise. Alas, under pressure to file his column three times a week, he sometimes runs out of good material or repeats familiar arguments. In his 8-4 effort, Buckley challenges President Clinton's "glib falsifications." Outraged that in a single speech the President could declare "no more something for nothing" and then proceed to announce how proud he was that the "federal government has been fighting alongside the people" in mitigating the damage from the Mississippi floods, Buckley points out that the victims of the disaster "are getting something for nothing"—namely, federal aid, courtesy of

taxpayers coast to coast. In his 8-9 effort, Buckley resourcefully takes an "Editorial Notebook" item written by *New York Times* editorial page editor Howell Raines and turns it into a column. The *Times* item, Buckley notes, contended that George Marlin, the Conservative candidate for mayor of New York City, "'is one of those who seem, as undergraduates, to have been force-fed the entire oeuvres of George F. Will and William F. Buckley. When he opens his mouth, their tired old complaints and nostrums come spewing out.'" As one might expect, Buckley has lots of fun with this characterization of his views. "The planted axiom here is that complaints ought to change every now and then with the season....But that assumption requires a flexibility in social attitudes that isn't easy to achieve. When I ran for mayor of New York (in 1965), people complained of crime. They still do." The same, he adds, continues to be true of welfare. Badly misfiring in his 11-5 column, Buckley charges that it was "a mistake for the Clinton people to decide to debate with Ross Perot," whom Buckley thought would outshine Vice President Al Gore. Seemingly out of material, he turns in a lazy 2-1 effort, as he pages through an issue of the *International Herald-Tribune*, commenting on whatever its columns disclose. He hyperventilates on the motor-voter bill, 2-11, failing to craft a cohesive argument. And he sarcastically derides the federal policy on drugs, 1-17, arguing weakly for the decriminalization of marijuana. Writing approximately 150 columns a year, Buckley still collects some big hits. They just come less frequently.

Stephen Chapman

Chicago Tribune
Creators Syndicate
★½

Alternately sensible, pedestrian, soaring, and incomprehensible, Chapman's column is a hit-or-miss event. He frustrates in a 2-17 *Washington Times* selection, in which he outlines problems with Social Security and Medicare. After suggesting possible solutions, he notes that his ideas "wouldn't solve the deeper problems afflicting Social Security: its long-run financial woes and the lousy return today's workers will get on their contributions once they retire." So why offer solutions? On a Senate proposal to limit campaign spending, *Chicago Tribune* 6-20, he doesn't approach the real heart of the matter until the column's end. Any such limit, he writes, favors incumbents because incumbents have so many free ways—such as franking privileges—to reach the electorate. Chapman derides the FDA, 7-11, for preventing drug companies from touting the medical benefits of their products unless the claim "reflects 'significant scientific agreement.'" While persuasively arguing that the FDA's bureaucratic lethargy in approving claims keeps important information from consumers, his solution that "the best way to assure that information gets out quickly is to allow its transmission by the people who stand to profit," seems naive at best and an invitation to hucksterism and abuse. In his imaginative 10-10 essay on the perils of U.S. military intervention in general and in Somalia in particular, Chapman notes that "Americans are safer than they could have dreamed a decade ago. The dangers we have most to fear are the ones we insist on seeking out." Chapman crafts a fine analogy in his cogent 5-13 argument that President Clinton's health-care plan will kill the patient. "Automobiles are a necessity of life, but not everyone has a car, and some people have crummy ones. They are expensive, siphoning off a large share of our resources. Making the market function is hard because these machines are too complex to be understood by ordinary people, who in any case can hardly negotiate with giant automakers. Here's a solution. First, the government ought to guarantee everyone a decent set of wheels. Secondly, motorists should get them through car purchasing cooperatives, which would insist that manufacturers offer high quality and low prices. Third, as a further brake on costs, Washington should restrict the amount spent on cars each year by all Americans. Sound weird? Then I have good news: Nobody is about to consider this approach to automobiles. I also have bad news: Bill Clinton is about to recommend it for health care." It is for these intermittent insights that Chapman should be watched.

Mona Charen

Creators Syndicate

A regular on CNN's "Capitol Gang," the conservative Charen relies as much on her keen intuition as clear-eyed logic to craft strong, well-written, but often predictable, columns. On Bill Clinton's first day in office, she launches a full-scale attack, *Washington Times* 1-21, assailing the new President for already breaking half a dozen promises, and pegging him as Jimmy Carter redux. Despite her considerable firepower, she says little that's original. She advances a solid argument, 4-12, that capitalism has not failed in Russia, mostly because it hasn't yet been tried, but she doesn't examine what measures might lead to a market economy. In her 9-1 *Chicago Tribune* piece, she deftly deflates Ross Perot's anti-NAFTA reasoning: "if American companies want to take advantage of Mexico's low wages, there is nothing to prevent them from doing so now. Moreover, low wages are only one factor companies consider. If low wages were the alpha and the omega of plant location, then Haiti and Bangladesh would be industrial giants." Two essays on the Baby Jessica case, *WT* 7-29 and 8-9, reveal her skill in dissecting social issues. Charen lobbies vigorously for emphasizing the welfare of the child over the rights of the parents, but saves her most stinging remarks for Daniel Schmidt, the biological father. Against the argument that Schmidt "had no knowledge of his paternity and therefore should not be deprived of the opportunity to serve as the child's father," Charen states, "Not so. Every birth father has notice that he may be a father when he has sex with the mother. If he is serious about his responsibilities, he should declare that fact during the pregnancy and certainly no later than a week after the birth. Dan Schmidt knew Cara was pregnant but did nothing to show interest in what was possibly his child until Cara had changed her mind about the adoption (a month later)." Charen abandons this solid reasoning in her 11-22 essay on rising illegitimacy in the black community by simply—and predictably—dismissing economic hardship as a possible factor. Charen is most challenging when least predictable.

Alexander Cockburn

The Nation

★★★

"Beat the Devil" columnist. Still the strongest voice on the far left, Cockburn seems reinvigorated with a Democrat in the White House to kick around. In the *Los Angeles Times* 1-24, Cockburn gives a tough appraisal of President Clinton and his philosophy: "Bill Clinton is a man of many tomorrows... 'Don't stop thinking about tomorrow' has become his mantra. He's even said he'd hang it as a sign in the Oval Office. The great thing about tomorrow is that it never comes, and by the time it does you can reschedule the rhetoric, claiming that it is necessary to adapt to new circumstances. Thus has Clinton rationalized his somersaults of the past month. Tomorrow is an endless alibi." Cockburn dishes more dirt on the administration in a particularly strong 4-5 critique of Clinton's foreign policy: "Welcome to the Clinton era. The Haitians have been brusquely betrayed, Cuban exiles pandered to and the Israelis bolstered in their forced transfer of Palestinians. Not bad for eight weeks." Cockburn reveals, 7-12, how Clinton may have allowed drug traffickers to use Arkansas as a pit stop. Two essays, *The Nation* 8-23/30 and 9-6/13, provide additional evidence of his solid reporting skills. In these pieces, he details how Clinton and Interior Secretary Bruce Babbitt have already alienated some environmentalists. Cockburn stands out as one of the few journalists with a clear-eyed view of the October events in Russia—and without a shred of Yeltsin romanticism. On the burning of the Russian parliament building and the suspension of the constitution, Cockburn brilliantly cuts to the heart of the matter, *Los Angeles Times* 10-5: "Economically, Russia remains stricken, plunged ever deeper into ruin by Yeltsin's team, coached by the same gang of international advisers whose failures in Poland recently prompted that nation's voters to give their biggest cheer to the former Communist Party." More trenchant than ever, Cockburn bids fair to keep Clinton well-informed of the desires—both domestic and foreign—of the far left. Welcome back, Alex.

Richard Cohen

The Washington Post

★½

Although often inconclusive, Cohen shows signs of improvement, soft-pedaling his emotions and relying more on logic and fresh information. However, he still fails to bring all his thoughts to a satisfying conclusion. In his 2-23 review, he addresses Bill Clinton's 1992

execution of an Arkansas murderer lobotomized after a self-inflicted bullet wound. Cohen can't bring himself to either condemn or praise then-Governor Clinton for executing a mentally-impaired person during the presidential campaign in order to appear tough on crime: "This willingness to subordinate almost everything to a political end is both impressive and troubling. It will either make Bill Clinton a great president or—if he oversteps himself—simply another slick politician whose most cherished principle is his own political advancement." He merely counsels caution on the possibility of using force in Bosnia, 4-27, although he candidly observes that "this has been the strangest of debates. It has been largely conducted by commentators such as myself, hurry-up experts on a part of the world about which many of us knew little until recently." In his 1-19 column examining Clinton's various options for handling Saddam Hussein, Cohen never quite defines how the incoming administration might dispose of him. He seems equally uncertain five months later. His 6-29 piece contends that Clinton's June raid on Baghdad was "sure-footed and adroit" but likely to accomplish "little" in terms of removing the Iraqi leader. Yet Cohen argues provocatively and decisively, 9-10, that in trying to build self-esteem, some multicultural curriculums quash all self-examination and doubt. "As with most things, the more you know, the more you realize you don't. There is hardly a successful person who, no matter what his or her talents and skills, does not down deep question his or her abilities." Cohen puts this in a new light.

E. J. Dionne Jr.

The Washington Post

★½

Making the transition this year from political reporter to editorial writer and weekly op-ed columnist, Dionne often neglects to examine all the angles of an issue. At other times he examines too many—perhaps because he knows so much—resulting in columns that go on too long. Author of the 1991 book, *Why Americans Hate Politics*, which President Clinton has publicly praised, Dionne sometimes sounds like a presidential adviser. His column seems designed to both reform liberalism and shape the direction of the Democratic party. While offering a fairly solid 1-19 review of the incoming administration's programs, he fails to evaluate how they would actually work. Dionne's 2-23 column provides a thoughtful discussion of the political balancing act Clinton must perform to get his programs enacted, but overlooks the economics. On 3-2, he defends Clinton's pursuit of "a new emphasis on work and family [that] is vital both to reconstructing liberalism and to achieving liberal ends." However, he drafts no blueprint for achieving this. Addressing the effort led by Al Gore to reinvent government, Dionne's 8-31 essay lists the various suggestions made in the Vice President's report, but offers scant analysis or interpretation. With mixed success, 9-21, Dionne answers the arguments put forth by conservative father-son duo Irving and William Kristol in their essays on the death of liberalism. "If I were a conservative, I'd be discouraged, too, and I'd be trying desperately to pick fights with liberals on crime and the two-parent family. The conservatives' problem is that most liberals aren't willing to be the punching bags anymore." His 12-7 column incisively analyzes the struggle between the White House and the Democratic Leadership Council to secure middle-class support while not casting off the poor. Despite its revealing insights, the wordiness of the article detracts from the argument. Although still developing his voice as a columnist, Dionne has many White House readers—including the occupant of the Oval Office.

Rowland Evans & Robert Novak

Creators Syndicate

★★★½

Although Evans went into semi-retirement in April, the Evans & Novak column continues at full speed. Identifying key players and events in the first months of the Clinton administration, this veteran conservative duo introduces realism and common sense to the public debate. Even before the inaugural, Evans & Novak reveal in their 1-4 column how Clinton, in selecting his cabinet, walks a fine line between diversity and a "quota system." Their observation gains momentum from inside sources who describe candidates being bumped because of their gender and ethnicity. The team performs a vital service in correcting the record, 2-24, on the press misinterpretation that Federal Reserve Board Chairman Alan Greenspan had endorsed Clinton's economic plan. Evans & Novak provide a cogent 3-1 analysis of the U.S. Chamber of Commerce's switch on Clintonomics. "The president has launched more than just another battle of the budget," they write, "but seeks to shape the political landscape for a dozen years into the future, as Franklin D. Roosevelt and Ronald Reagan did. Integral to his plan is not to defeat business interests but to make them heavily dependent on government for survival. While Republicans are trapped in their sterile, green-eyeshade discussions of budget cuts, Clinton is playing for the big prize. Business leaders are asked to join the president's campaign for a program that increases the burden of taxes and regulation. In return, they are offered government dependency: subsidies, protection and cooperation. The takers are not reticent. Detroit's Big Three, much of the Silicon Valley and beleaguered corporations like the Boeing Co. are rushing into dependency." A pithy 6-7 profile of David Gergen convincingly pegs him as a "courtier" rather than a politician or advisor, in that he's "short on innovative thought." With this in mind, Novak argues forcefully that Gergen's appointment won't make much difference in terms of policy. In his 9-6 examination of Clinton's three top concerns—health care, the budget, and NAFTA—Novak details the complex problems of each and reveals the chaos within the White House. Displaying in-depth reporting and incisive commentary, Novak seems uniquely gifted in maintaining his column's high standards even without his venerable partner by his side full-time.

Suzanne Fields

The Washington Times
Los Angeles Times Syndicate
½★

After a stellar 1992, Fields has slipped. Instead of challenging liberal orthodoxy—long her strength—she often simply echoes standard conservative doctrines. Attempting to use the case of Westley Allan Dodd—a criminal executed for raping and killing little boys—as a springboard in her 1-14 discussion on child molesters and prison sentences, Fields expends too much energy on Dodd and not enough on the broader issues and solutions. In a disorganized 2-11 attempt to dissect the ethical double-standard in Washington, she awkwardly links the difficulties of Zöe Baird and Kimba Wood to the problems of Bob Packwood. Despite the fact that Fields herself preaches the politically incorrect policy of abstinence, her 3-11 column derides the pro-chastity arguments of *Rolling Stone* editor Ellen Hopkins. Further, Fields impugns Hopkins merely because the latter has said that "teaching abstinence for teen-agers need not be a bad idea just because it's the province of right-wing crazies." In her 8-9 effort, she calls for an end to misogynistic lyrics in rock, rap, and pop music. Fields naively concludes that if young women told men that such music was a turnoff, "That would be the most powerful message of all." Since when have so many men responded to the word 'no'? A disappointing year.

Jack Germond & Jules Witcover

National Journal
The Baltimore Sun
★★

Germond & Witcover specialize in providing commonsense reviews of current events. Although this venerable team sometimes offers a flash of insight or a revealing fact, they too often have nothing new to say. Their well-written 1-30 evaluation of Bill and Hillary Rodham Clinton's working White House relationship adds little to the subject. In their intelligent discussion updating the abortion debate, 4-10, Germond & Witcover report the administration's announcement that it "will try to ditch" the Hyde Amendment. They demonstrate their reporting talents in a 6-5 investigation of United We Stand. The piece describes how Ross Perot is pulling the strings as the organization gathers both membership and political momentum. Exposing a potential consequence of redistricting, Germond & Witcover provide a shrewd 7-3 analysis of *Shaw v. Reno*: "One of the results of creating such a congressional district would be that one incumbent white Democrat would see the black share of his constituency drop from 26 to 9 percent and that another would see his share drop from 25 percent to slightly more than 13 percent. It would be no surprise if those Democrats turned out to be less responsive to black concerns. That's the way politics works." Few columnists have made this point so suc-

cinctly. While the pair does an admirable job in cataloguing the political boons of "reinventing government," 9-11, they do not confront the strong likelihood that some of Clinton's proposed programs, such as health care, will create more government. Although they seldom advance policy debates, their berth in the *National Journal*, the capital's political guidebook, makes Germond & Witcover essential reading.

Georgie Anne Geyer
Universal Press Syndicate
★½

While Geyer illuminates corners of the globe that other columnists leave shrouded in darkness, her analysis, particularly on economic matters, often falls short. In her 2-24 column, Geyer exposes the dire circumstances in Armenia. Unfortunately, she focuses only on the history and the politics of the country. Neglecting the economic policies that helped to bring about ruin, Geyer misses the opportunity to show how various policies might help remedy the situation. Her 8-14 effort is similarly hampered. Although Geyer firmly places the blame for Yugoslavia's ethnic splintering on the economic policies of the late 1980s, she neither details those policies nor attempts to map out how future, similar conflicts might be avoided. Geyer applauds President Clinton's proposals on illegal immigration, 7-29, and maintains that coming to the U.S. should be considered a privilege, not a right. She limits the utility of this dispatch, however, by failing to consider the more complicated issues of legal immigration as a logical next step. In her 10-12 report, she digs up quite a few nuggets from Haiti, foreseeing further chaos after authorities prevented a U.S. warship from docking: "One report, from a respected source, indicates that the army's goal is 'to create such havoc and instability that [President Jean-Bertrand] Aristide cannot be brought back,' thus convincing the world that only the army can maintain control there." Still, Geyer's lack of clear, insightful analysis on some of the subjects she elects to cover can lead to oversimplification, as shown in her 6-25 effort on the immigration crisis in Europe and the demands of the Third World. Her foolhardy prescription is simply for the West to "tell the Third World countries to deal with their *own* problems; that it is *they* who have no right to use the developed countries as a release for their own lack of discipline; and that they are poor because they have chosen not to do what is necessary to become rich and healthy, which is to curb their overpopulation and corruption and learn to create wealth." She never examines the role of the United Nations in encouraging Third World efforts at redistributionism, a topic Jeane Kirkpatrick covered in detail last year. Geyer needs to develop more economic expertise before crafting dispatches on these subjects.

Paul A. Gigot
The Wall Street Journal
★★★

"Potomac Watch" columnist. The generally conservative Gigot appears on the *Journal*'s editorial page more frequently (once a week) than anyone else. A thorough reporter and strong writer, Gigot often premises his column on some new idea, and while he tends to partisanship, his conclusions can surprise. In his 1-15 critique of Bill Clinton and the aides he had named so far, Gigot contends that "the emerging Clinton team may be 'diverse' (in gender and color) but perhaps not diverse enough in the thinkers associated with the ideas that made Mr. Clinton 'a different kind of Democrat.'" His 5-7 effort on Lani Guinier, the nominee to head the Justice Department post for civil rights, recapitulates arguments advanced a few days earlier in the *Journal* by conservative civil-rights lawyer Clint Bolick and adds little to the debate. Uncharacteristically, Gigot writes an anti-capitalist screed, 7-23, reviling House Speaker Tom Foley [D-WA] for making money in the stock market. Here he takes Glenn Simpson's *Roll Call* article a step further by implying Foley had done something unethical by merely investing his money, as millions of other investors do. Gigot, 9-10, doesn't join conservatives lining up against the nomination of Morton Halperin for a Pentagon democracy and peacekeeping post, but argues that Republicans should use Halperin's confirmation hearings to examine and debate Clinton's foreign policy. Gigot offers an exceptional 2-19 exploration of the politics behind Clinton's economic proposals. "He wants nothing less than to relegitimize the social-insurance state," Gigot notes, adding that the President has a good chance of succeeding. "Mr. Clinton's ally is the 'deficit,' which he is using to fan anxiety even in a growing economy." It is in political-economic commentaries like this that Gigot is at his best.

Ellen Goodman

The Boston Globe
Washington Post Writers Group
½★

Because Goodman does so little reporting, her commentary doesn't break new ground. Although her writing is passable and her analysis of information culled from other news sources occasionally interesting, she seldom says anything new or provocative. In her 4-18 dispatch on an anti-violence program that raises money to buy back guns from owners, Goodman doesn't report much on the program itself or its success in other cities. Instead she concentrates on how she *feels* about having contributed $200 to the program. Goodman offers little to the growing debate over the veracity of Anita Hill, contributing only a he-said/she-said deconstructionist 5-20 review of recent works. In her 6-17 essay, Goodman states during her visit to the UN conference on human rights in Vienna that "what is at stake here is values." This column aims more to inspire than to educate, but does neither. Goodman spins her wheels in her 7-4 description of the Navy's color-coding of harassment levels—red, yellow, and green—adding virtually nothing to the debate over where the lines of sexual harassment lie, in the Navy or anyplace else. She falls along conventional feminist-liberal lines in concluding, 10-7, that in the Hempstead, Texas, pregnant cheerleader case, fairness requires "benching the fathers." Goodman, however, clearly defines a solution for the girls. "We don't have to punish pregnancy but we don't have to celebrate it with pompoms at halftime." In a slightly stronger 2-6 contribution about the media's tendency to offer instant analysis on news as it happens, Goodman notes, "Newspapers that once tried to beat each other with stories are now as likely to compete with analysis." Such insightful comments appear only rarely.

Paul Greenberg

Arkansas Democrat Gazette
Los Angeles Times Syndicate
★★½

As former editorial page editor of the *Pine Bluff Commercial* and, since 1992, the *Arkansas Democrat Gazette*, Greenberg finds himself in the unique position of having watched and written about Bill Clinton since he was first elected governor of Arkansas. Importing his considerable knowledge of Clinton to his columns on the President and his administration, Greenberg frequently offers original insights. He derides the halfway measure of the Bosnian airdrop, *The Washington Times,* 3-3, putting the policy in context: "Once again Bill Clinton is taking an action calculated to please all (for a while) but one that may complicate matters for a long, long time." Greenberg reprises this critique of Clinton's foreign policy, 6-1, although he doesn't fully convince that Clinton must do *something* in Bosnia. In an otherwise conventional 4-29 list of what has surprised this long-time Clinton-watcher, he provides a memorable description of the President's style of governing. "He has been transforming the bully pulpit that is the American presidency into some vague graduate seminar." Greenberg also offers solid, if dull, commentary on racial issues, observing in his 9-1 review of the 1993 civil rights march that much of the black intelligentsia is still dedicated to solving yesterday's dilemmas. He packs a powerful punch, 1-15, with ringing observations about race in America, and the relevance of Martin Luther King, Jr. "The political success [of King] was not succeeded by a social and economic one.... The human struggle is not only against the elements or enemies, but, most telling, with and within ourselves." This provocative comment duly noted, it's a safe bet that because of his long tenure in Arkansas, Greenberg's primary utility as a columnist will stem from his expertise in all things Clintonian.

Meg Greenfield

Newsweek
The Washington Post
★★½

Newsweek columnist; *Post* editorial page editor. Greenfield's best work argues against the instant punditry in which her fellow columnists so love to indulge. She works hard to avoid that trap, incorporating historical perspective whenever possible. Sometimes, though, this technique can make her efforts seem ponderous and academic. In describing how important Hillary Rodham Clinton's job of just running the White House will be, Greenfield short-

circuits her excellent 1-18 *Newsweek* review of how far women have come in both the workplace and in the home. In her 3-15 piece, Greenfield fails to see the inconsistency of the First Lady's selling health-care reform on the talk shows—thereby engaging the electorate—and the elitism of the closed-door meetings of her task force. She builds an airtight case, 6-7, that the President and his staff should take full responsibility for travelgate. "This whole sorry episode is not about some arcane code of conduct that has been inadvertently breached by innocents who could not be expected to know its esoteric provisions....We are talking about the self-evident proposition that it is wrong for people in high office to use their authority and clout to publicly accuse others of criminal conduct or ethical improprieties without observing even the most elementary requirements of due process and fair play." In her 9-27 column, she uses the Middle East peace agreement to review media coverage of this and other "miracles": "What is so troublesome about this impulse to effusion is that it trivializes what may have been— usually were—serious issues, differences, quarrels that had to be overcome." In her breezy 8-30 review of what Americans want in a vacationing president, Greenfield shows her lighter, wittier side: "Considering the intensity of our conflicting emotions on these matters, Richard Nixon was probably our best president. He regularly went on vacation, as per our national instruction, but never looked like he was having a good time. This was ideal. And, crucially, Nixon never took his business clothes off, either. He was always dressed for nuclear retaliation." When taking a broader view of politics and history, Greenfield generally hits the mark.

William Greider

Rolling Stone

★★½

"National Affairs" columnist. While Greider seldom offers penetrating analysis, this biweekly, liberal columnist provides a provocative quote here or a memorable statistic there to inform and educate his youthful readers. In his 1-21 effort, he notes that 21 million Americans voted for term limits in 1992. "Like it or not," he observes, "...the idea of term limits is going to hang over politics in the Nineties like a giant scythe, threatening to cut down all who don't get the message." Greider's message is that Democrats had better turn the debate over term limits to one over campaign finance reform. Picking up this theme, 2-18, Greider attacks the special interests opposed to campaign reform but does not address some of their major concerns, such as limits on free speech. Greider cautions President Clinton, 4-15, against launching underfunded, misguided job-training programs and hammers the Labor Department for "failed experiments" of years past. Employers, he notes, used federal money to teach workers to wash dishes and flip burgers. This, he muses, is preparation for the 21st century? Other employers received funds up front to train workers, and then fired them the next day. Some even received subsidies to train workers they would have trained *without* the subsidies! Greider praises activists seeking programs directed toward high-wage, career-oriented job-training, but notes shrewdly that such programs are doomed "if the private economy continues to deteriorate." Perhaps because he does some real reporting, this is one of Greider's best efforts of the year. Still he takes a cheap shot at Dan Quayle, whom he bashes for bragging about his co-sponsorship of the Job Training Partnership Act of 1982. Sen. Ted Kennedy [D-MA], the other sponsor, emerges unscathed. Yet Greider is no party man. He attacks Clinton's national service bill, 6-24, as feel-good (rather than real good) legislation. And he criticizes the estimated costs of the President's health plan, 11-25, quoting one White House insider saying, ""These number are as squishy as any numbers on earth."' Greider scores a late-year coup with his revealing, if fawning, 12-9 interview with the President, whom he calls "awesome...impressive...authentic and powerful." Questioning Clinton on his perceived lack of convictions, the President responds: "I have fought more damn battles here for more things than any president has in 20 years, with the possible exception of Reagan's first budget, and not gotten one damn bit of credit from the knee-jerk liberal press, and I am sick and tired of it, and you can put that in the damn article. I have fought and fought and fought and fought...and you guys take it and you say, 'Fine, go on to something else, what else can I hit him about?' So if you convince them that I don't have any conviction, that's fine, but it's a damn lie. It's a lie." Greider indeed provokes a response.

Richard Grenier

The Washington Times

★★½

Grenier's manic, often barbed style is an acquired taste, not recommended to those who prefer polite commentary. He scores against both the administration and Hollywood, two of his preferred topics. In his 2-15 effort, Grenier takes aim at the New Age proclivities of the administration's denizens: "How would I bond with HHS Secretary Donna Shalala? It beats me how the president's facilitators achieve this cross-gender bonding. I say: Men bond with men, and women with women. That's what I say. Bond away. Hillary [Rodham Clinton] might prefer to bond with whatever female gets to be attorney general, for example. Donna Shalala is reported as saying that this human-resource stuff at Camp David was 'wonderful' and great 'fun,' so maybe she'll find someone to bond with too. Mind you, Miss Shalala isn't my personal idea of a fun bond. But tastes differ, of course." He skewers David Koresh in a 3-11 column on religion that is sure to offend someone, somewhere. "I've got a message from God, and He told me to pass it along. *I am the resurrection and the life, the alpha and the omega, the beginning and the end. He who believeth in me shall never die.* Now all this is useful. It gives me kind of a general direction. But I was hoping for something a little more specific, a little more like the kind of stuff God tells David Koresh down near Waco, Texas. Mr. Koresh gets highly precise instructions from God—like, do this, do that, surrender to the ATF, or don't surrender to the ATF." Grenier revisits and deconstructs such films as "The Last of the Mohicans" and "Poetic Justice," in *The National Interest* Winter 92-93, and the *Times* 8-8, respectively. He does this simply by juxtaposing Hollywood's vision with reality, and finding Hollywood's versions ripe with inaccurate history and insulting black stereotypes—including a psychotic preoccupation with sex and sexual imagery. Providing his own harsh imagery in describing what he sees as Bill Clinton's fatal flaw, 10-13, Grenier argues vigorously that the President doesn't "have the stomach" for foreign policy. As Clinton himself has said, he is a child of the '60s, who, Grenier notes, "did not believe in war, military force, soldiers, police or forcing anyone to do pretty much anything. They believed in 'flower power,' and put flowers in the rifles of the National Guardsmen sent to restrain them." This is classic Grenier—a writer who takes no prisoners.

Nat Hentoff

The Village Voice
The Washington Post
The Progressive

★★★

"Sweet Land of Liberty" columnist for *The Washington Post*; weekly columnist for *The Village Voice*, and contributing editor to *The Progressive*. An expert in First Amendment issues, Hentoff crafts well-written columns that explore both the nuances and impact of legal cases pertaining to personal rights. In *WP* 1-9, he draws a powerful comparison of the superprisons now in use to those that horrified Charles Dickens in the 19th century. "In Pelican Bay [prison in California]...nothing has been left unplanned. No sunlight enters the SHU [Security Housing Unit]. The prisoners are locked in their 8-by-10-foot cells 22 1/2 hours a day and [quoting an observer]... they 'never emerge without being handcuffed and in chains.'" In his 2-6 *WP* column, this veteran rights watcher discusses the subtleties that many other journalists missed in the debate on Wisconsin's hate crime laws. A 7-13 *WP* update on this topic argues convincingly against such laws, likening them to the police-state tactics in George Orwell's *1984.* His penetrating 3-16 and 3-23 *Voice* essays on the case of death-row inmate Leonel Herrera examine both the legal issues and the Supreme Court's refusal to hear the case on the basis of new evidence. Hentoff keeps his outrage in check long enough to present all sides, and then poses the question of the relevance of innocence in capital cases. In *TP* March, he defines the grounds for his reasoning on free speech and First Amendment issues, a good primer for those unfamiliar with either Hentoff's work or the subjects at hand. He places the University of Pennsylvania First Amendment case into context, *TP* August, making some incisive observations about race:

"[President Sheldon] Hackney and many other college presidents who also encourage black self-segregation on campuses are engaging in a form of paternalism....These black students are frustrated and angry, and we must understand that. Many are, indeed, frustrated and angry. But the answer is to do something real about the roots of the frustration and anger, not to treat these students as if they were 'special' people who have to be indulged in their unwillingness to take full responsibility for what they do. That's not respect for them. That's undervaluing them." Despite his fairly narrow focus, Hentoff remains one of the more compelling and provocative legal writers.

OHMAN · TRIBUNE MEDIA SERVICES © 1993.

Bob Herbert
The New York Times
★

"In America" columnist. A midyear *Times* acquisition from the New York *Daily News*, Herbert has yet to effectively address the issues of America, either at home or abroad. His distinct New York focus may be perfectly appropriate for the *News* or even a *Times* "Metro" column. It appears seriously misplaced, however, on the oped page of the *Times*. To make matters worse, Herbert's writing seldom makes his arguments and opinions clear. His weak 7-21 attempt to remind New Yorkers that Mayor David Dinkins isn't such a bad guy after all uses the flawed logic that, despite the disastrous three days in Crown Heights, Brooklyn, no riots erupted in New York following the Rodney King verdicts. Huh? Herbert spends most of his simplistic 8-25 column discussing the energy of the 1960s. Then, after talking to two twentysomethings who describe themselves as optimistic in a kind of '60s vein, he concludes that young people will lead this country. By failing to offer any opinion in his 9-1 column, Herbert diminishes the value of his excellent reporting on both the budget-driven deinstitutionalization of the mentally ill and the economic and social fallout of such actions. Given the information and bleak stories he presents, Herbert presumably opposes deinstitutionalization, but since he doesn't say so, the reader can't be sure. Nor does Herbert present any alternatives. Similarly, he does not use his atmospheric reporting from Bushwick, Brooklyn, 10-6, to make much of an argument. Herbert concludes dullishly that "crime, poverty, joblessness—these are issues that should be seriously engaged in the race for mayor of New York. It is not that Mayor Dinkins or Mr. Giuliani are expected to solve the problems, but they should be among the leaders in the search for solutions. It's hard to imagine that this will be the case when the tone of the campaign so far has been so low." Herbert has made it to the *Times*, but he should start swinging harder.

Christopher Hitchens
The Nation
★★

"Minority Report" columnist. This year a more restrained Hitchens proved to be a better columnist. Rather than bracing for a blast, the reader was able to look forward to at least a logical progression. Laced with his sharp British wit, Hitchens's 2-15 remarks on the inauguration score points, particularly with regard to his fellow journalists. "At least I wrote [my observations] myself, rather than pressing the 'Clinton/Torch/Uplift/Change' key that is now standard issue on all media consoles, and that allows for the sort of automatic composition that would make a Schlesinger blush." Hitchens urges U.S. action in a sensible, if emotional, 3-1 review of the *fatwa* against author Salman Rushdie, constructing a reasonable case for some kind of government action on the issue. He weaves interesting anecdotes and observations into his 6-21 take on China, Hong Kong, and most-favored-nation-status, but takes no clear position. Examining the legacy of the late Irving Howe, Hitchens argues convincingly in his 7-19 effort that history is the ultimate judge of all those who serve in public life—and that some judgments may surprise. Clearly outraged in his 8-9/16 column, Hitchens complains about the tenuous status of temporary workers. He uses as a case in point James Hudson, who died while cleaning the Lincoln Memorial in 100 degree heat. Hudson had been a *temporary* parks worker in that position for *eight years* but, because of his status received no death benefits. This piece would have been stronger had Hitchens taken into account the laws that lead businesses to hire in this manner, instead of merely noting, "it's increasingly common to redefine the term 'temporary' in order to get around our old pal the budgetary constraint." In his restrained 9-6/13 overview of the problems within the European Community vis-a-vis unification, he provides a British perspective, incorporating pertinent parallels from 9th-century European history. As always, Hitchens puts his own unique spin on things.

Jim Hoagland

The Washington Post

★★★

Relying on his reporting skills and knowledge of nations and governments around the globe, Hoagland has become one of the top columnists on foreign affairs. He offers fresh angles and insights on almost every subject he covers. In his informative 1-11 essay, Hoagland reveals that Bill Clinton is briefing himself on foreign policy by seeking out different sources for advice on international crises. Profiling the new Secretary of State, Warren Christopher, 2-14, Hoagland sensibly defines "the Christopher initiative" on Bosnia as "a problem-solving exercise undertaken by diplomatists." Though Hoagland fails to show that his own idea of sanctions would work, he makes a powerful case that the Christopher plan will not. "The U.S. initiative is a carefully composed diplomatic work of art, expressed in subtle shades of gray. Unfortunately, it is aimed at people who see their world and their struggle only in black and white." In his 4-22 essay, Hoagland puts nuclear testing in context. "At one level this is a seemingly technical decision involving warhead safety and reliability. But history, politics, diplomacy and military strategy intersect in resuming nuclear testing, which Congress had halted last month on a nine-month trial basis. The choice that Clinton makes will say a great deal about the nuclear world order he hopes to achieve beyond the Cold War and how he hopes to achieve it." Hoagland's 6-29 effort provides insight into Clinton's June raid on Baghdad: "By targeting the headquarters of Iraq's mukhabarat, Saddam Hussein's murderous secret service, Clinton chose a powerful symbol to establish his own commitment to helping the Iraqi people eventually end Saddam's bloody reign. Clinton struck a blow at the feared monsters of everyday life in Iraq." Hoagland excels at drawing unusual and persuasive analogies. He dribbles a basketball, 10-14, finding a valuable lesson in Michael Jordan's retirement from the sport while at the peak of his game—namely, that politicians ought to do the same. Hoagland finds quite a few—citing most of the present and recent heads of state in Europe and the U.S.—who would have better served their country (and their place in history) by stepping down earlier. Happily, Hoagland himself shows no signs of following Jordan's example.

Albert R. Hunt

The Wall Street Journal

★½

Former Washington bureau chief, now weekly op-ed columnist. Hunt has established a beachhead for his somewhat liberal views on the once-almost-exclusively conservative op-ed page—a major event for the financial daily. Unfortunately, Hunt's reasoning isn't always clear. In his 10-14 defense of Ron Brown, for example, Hunt argues that the Commerce Secretary "hasn't told the truth," but is innocent anyway. "The reason the charge probably is phony is that Mr. Brown is too savvy to take money from a stranger." Oh? Hunt's 1-19 column details a transition largely in disarray but maintains high hopes for the new President. He trumpets the abilities of Hillary Rodham Clinton and suggests the reasonable, if unoriginal, idea that the administration—just like the campaign team—must be anchored by a few key players. Supporting the idea of Sen. Bill Bradley [D-NJ] of using the Olympics to leverage with China on human rights issues, 5-25, Hunt overlooks one key point: The U.S. may grant most favored nation status for trade, but it does not run the International Olympic Committee. Hunt's most important contribution comes in a 2-17 discussion of the Clinton economic program. Here he offers invaluable advice to Republicans that they should not give an inch. "On many issues, including a broad range of foreign policy or national security matters, as well as such domestic initiatives as overhauling the welfare system or campaign financing and conceivably even health-care legislation, a bipartisan approach is both possible and preferable. But if the two parties are to stand for anything and the public is to be able to hold them accountable, the lines ought to be drawn sharply on the central economic issue, starting tonight. Thus, Republicans have that delicious opportunity to be blatantly partisan and responsible at the same time." The same could be said for Hunt, who veers back and forth between the two.

Molly Ivins

Fort Worth Star-Telegram
Creators Syndicate
The Progressive
★★★

Ivins's pithy assessments of politics and life at large crackle with broad Texas humor. Combining her talent for culling information with her razor-sharp wit, she throws a powerful knockout punch. One can imagine Ivins shaking her head as she hilariously relates her dreams over a lifetime of becoming an author, *The Progressive* January, only to realize that this puts her in the same company of Ivana Trump and Madonna. Her shrewd March/April *Mother Jones* profile smartly assesses HUD Secretary Henry Cisneros. After gently probing the reasons he chose the path to HUD, Ivins plainly states her opinions: "Cisneros has just made what I think is a major mistake by taking the cabinet job. It's not that he'll disappear into the fog of the D.C. alphabet. No, you'll see Cisneros in every ghetto and barrio in the country and on MTV as well. But he could have set his own agenda as the first Chicano U.S. senator from Texas, and who knows what after that?" With characteristically blunt prose, she reports on the passage of a heterosexual and homosexual sodomy law enacted by Texas legislators. Opines Ivins, *TP* August: "It's illegal for a prick to touch an asshole in this state." Her more serious work appears in her newspaper column. Ivins has the definitive word on Waco in her 4-21 effort, a powerful exercise from start to finish. "The FBI and Alcohol, Tobacco and Firearms agents responsible for this fiasco have no right to claim Koresh was unreasonable, that he wouldn't negotiate or cooperate, because they never tried it....When someone comes at you firing weapons, it is not an invitation to reasonable negotiation." In her 10-14 column, Ivins is fearless enough to take on Rush Limbaugh. "I'm a great believer in the American tradition of making fun of those who have power. Where I think Limbaugh misses the boat is aiming satire—traditionally a weapon of the powerless against the powerful—at powerless people. It's not the humor I object to; it's his targets. Women, children, dead people, the homeless and animals." Whether one agrees with her or not, Ivins's pen pierces both the brain and the funny bone.

John B. Judis

In These Times
The New Republic
★★

While attacking President Clinton from the left, Judis seems to be pulling back this year on hard-edged analysis, favoring instead succinct summaries that often read like primers. He maintains solid footing when discussing politics, but sometimes trips when it comes to economics and foreign policy. "Barely five months into his presidency," he notes, *In These Times* 5-17, "Clinton—like the last Democratic president—is bogged down in details. He is quickly losing his authority over Congress." Skewering Clinton for having "buckled under" to CEOs, bankers, and Wall Street on one issue after another, Judis highlights the President's backtracking on a promise to curb exorbitant corporate pay checks by denying firms tax deductions for salaries exceeding $1 million. "Last month the administration announced that CEO stock options would not be included in the $1 million limit. That's like setting a limit on gluttony, but excluding dessert." Judis can still turn a phrase. But sometimes the identical phrase appears in both his *ITT* and *The New Republic* columns. Indeed, a column in one publication often seems like a rough draft for a column in the other. His headier, more thoughtful *TNR* pieces focus more on policy issues, while his breezier *ITT* pieces stress the politics of an issue. "Rougher Trade," *TNR* 5-31, for example, describes the contents and details of NAFTA and connects the agreement to trade policy with Europe and Japan. "Gut Check," *ITT* 6-28, focuses on the Clinton administration's evolution (or, less kindly, about-faces) over NAFTA and its prospects for passage. Choose for yourself which type of article you prefer. In either case, avoid those on foreign policy (such as *ITT* 1-25, recommending tariffs to spur foreign investment), which tend to simplify and scarcely dig beneath the surface. Judis surprises in applauding Clinton, *ITT* 8-9, for "not exhaust[ing] his political capital in a fight over abortion and gay rights." He urges Clinton to emulate Reagan(!), who embraced the "high principles" of the far wing of his party (school prayer, abortion ban) but not "their practical agenda" so he could focus on his economic program. It is, after all, the economy, stupid.

Mickey Kaus

The New Republic

★★★

As a regular essayist and "TRB" columnist, Kaus has become one of the more versatile hitters in the *TNR* lineup. Armed with skepticism and insight, he not only smacks home runs but pokes timely and unexpected base hits. In his fascinating 2-15 exposé, Kaus courageously critiques Children's Defense Fund leader Marian Wright Edelman—the beloved "Saint Marian" to most of the press—for using children to expand welfare benefits when it's the parents who get the money. According to Kaus, Edelman knows that the younger (and whiter) you portray the victims, the more politically acceptable becomes their cause. Edelman comes across as shrewd, and so does Kaus. Exposing hagiography by the media is one of his strengths. Following Janet Reno's "disastrous decision" precipitating the bloodbath in Waco, Texas, Kaus denounces, 5-24, the disturbing (though popular) Washington habit of accepting responsibility while refusing, in the Attorney General's words, "'to engage in recrimination.'" Admit blame, don't look back, "and watch your polls rise. Truman + 'Donahue'=Absolution." But a little recrimination can be a good thing. "If a train crashes in Florida, there is no talk of sparing the engineers and switchmen. Would Washington reporters have applauded a Reno-like call to avoid 're-crimination' in the wake of, say, the Three Mile Island nuclear accident?" Bureaucrats and leaders, Kaus smartly concludes, should be held no less accountable. Dismissing the hubbub over Americans' enormous spending on health care, Kaus argues in "HMOphobia," 3-29, that heavy investment in physical well-being is a natural, indeed laudable, quality of an affluent society. "Which is the worthier choice: spending $15,000 to make somebody's life bearable for a few months, or spending $15,000 on a Mazda Miata?" Oversimplified, perhaps, but provocative nonetheless. In "Roe to Ruin," 4-12, Kaus urges moving the abortion debate out of court and into the legislatures. Despite his pro-choice leanings, he attacks *Roe v. Wade* as a bad legal decision. Privacy and autonomy, he notes *à la Bork*, are not Constitutional rights. "If judges are free to keep dreaming up new rights, pretty soon little will be left for voters to decide. One thing the Constitution *does* mention is democracy." Such iconoclasm makes Kaus a welcome voice in political affairs.

Michael Kinsley

The New Republic
Time

"Crossfire's" man on the left, Kinsley took a leave from *The New Republic* "TRB" column for six months. His post-sabbatical columns were often tasty but not very filling. While Kinsley, in his 2-1 essay, doesn't flinch from the task of listing politically unpopular tax increases and spending cuts to meet President Clinton's original promise to cut the deficit in half by 1996, he fails to offer a growth strategy. Reprising themes familiar to long-time readers of his column, Kinsley writes in *Time* 3-15, "A genuine line-item veto would require a constitutional amendment. But Congress could achieve the same result by agreeing to submit every appropri-

ation and tax item as a separate bill for the President to sign or veto." A fair point, but Kinsley does not address the unlikelihood of congressional agreement on separate-bill submissions. Kinsley recapitulates another familiar theme in his thoughtful defense of the War Powers Act, *TNR* 11-8, in which he argues that the 1973 law benefits democracy and the entire country by insuring congressional (and national) debate on the weighty matter of war and peace. The act also spreads the responsibility and potential blame for war among both the executive and legislative branches, which Kinsley contends is good, and what the Constitution's war-making clause—empowering Congress to declare war—originally intended. Although provocative, Kinsley takes liberties in proclaiming that "the flagrant violation of this [war-making] provision in recent decades is the biggest scandal in constitutional law." He rambles aimlessly, *Time* 7-5, on the nature of services, such as bellmen in hotels, querying, "Is this service valued for itself or only for the privilege of lording it over someone else?" And Kinsley pokes fun at Simon & Schuster for marketing the Bible in the same manner as its other books, but this 8-23/30 *TNR* essay, though pointed, lacks a broader context. In his 12-13 column, he claims that the problem with Clinton's healthcare plan "isn't too much government; it's too much politics." Yet this intriguing point gets lost in a dense, muddled argument. Perhaps a year without time off will improve Kinsley's work.

Jeane Kirkpatrick

Los Angeles Times Syndicate

★★

A former U.S. ambassador to the United Nations, Kirkpatrick writes forcefully about the UN. She spends more time analyzing UN policies and offering her opinions than in suggesting solutions to the world's problems. In her staccato fashion, Kirkpatrick supplies cogent analysis in the *Los Angeles Times* 1-17, examining the UN's trouble in deciding what to do about Bosnia. "The clash of national goals and strategies brings potential action to a standstill. The Security Council is like a committee and the United Nations Secretariat is like any other bureaucracy. Action is by consensus. Consensus is hard to build. Responsibility for UN action and inaction is so widely shared, so depersonalized that many ordinary moral and social disciplines disappear. Where everyone is responsible, no one is responsible." Kirkpatrick also provides unique perspective on the Bangkok Declaration, which rejected the idea that human rights are universal. She leads this 6-21 *New York Post* essay with an excellent definition of the sticking points of the New World Order: "With Marxism dead, the Cold War over and liberal democracy ascendant, the great ideological debates of the century have ended, but disagreement continues about the rights of citizens, the obligations of government and the appropriate role in these matters of what is routinely called the 'international community.'" Her strongest work vigorously critiques UN Secretary General Boutros Boutros-Ghali. In her stinging 2-1 *Washington Post* rebuke of him, she makes a strong case that his actions with regard to Israel and Bosnia have done little to improve either situation, and may have hampered settlement. Two tough essays, in the *LAT* 3-11 and the *NYP* 8-9, argue persuasively that "Boutros-Ghali continues his drive to make himself the world's commander in chief." Decrying his "power grab," Kirkpatrick posits plausible scenarios of what kind of disaster may follow if he succeeds. She provides a brutal, well-constructed assessment that Somalia is not an aberration in the trend toward nation-building, *LAT* 10-17. She offers particularly strong insight with "the coincidence of Boutros Boutros-Ghali's selection as UN secretary general" and "Clinton's acquiescence in Boutros-Ghali's unprecedented claim to 'command and control' forces acting under UN authorization." Kirkpatrick even proposes a sensible solution: "The simplest and best way to limit the United Nations' military interventions is to abide by the provisions of the UN Charter—and stick with conflicts that really pose a threat to international peace and security, avoiding civil wars and nationbuilding, neither of which the charter authorizes." With her sharp opinions and considerable experience, Kirkpatrick remains an important voice on UN affairs.

Joe Klein

Newsweek

★★★

"Public Lives" columnist. Klein's incisive discussions of social issues continue to distinguish his work. In his 5-3 review of President Clinton's first 100 days, Klein cuts the President considerable slack in noting that Clinton isn't easy to read, because "activism isn't easy." He's far tougher in his exceptional 1-18 examination of Clinton's apparent "squishiness" on social issues. This shortcoming, Klein notes, proves particularly evident in "the way Clinton selected his cabinet. Diversity is a fine thing. But mandating that the attorney general be a woman and that there be two Hispanics in the cabinet isn't diversity. It's a quota system. It perpetuates dependency, emphasizing the aggrieved status of the 'protected' groups, rather than the individual achievement or creativity." In his 7-5 article on the inner city, Klein effectively details the end of an era. "The liberal reform movement that supplanted the colorful, corrupt ethnic machines in the 1950s and 1960s has run its course....For the past 30 years, New York—to take the most egregious example—has spent too much of its resources 'trying to do the things a city can't do,' says Harvard sociologist Nathan Glazer, while it neglected 'the things a city can do.'" Klein's excellent 11-15 article on the New York City mayoral contest as seen through the prism of *The New York Times* is the dispatch of record. He shrewdly attacks the *Times* for lumping "all non-Caucasians" into a single group and failing to criticize certain black leaders so as to maintain the paper's "pursuit of a trendy disingenuous *correctness* on matters racial....The least responsible voices are given a respectful hearing—their anger is usually said to be 'understandable'—while the solid progress and social conservatism of the black middle class is too often ignored." With his hard-hitting commentary, Klein has become one of the top newsweekly columnists.

Morton Kondracke

Roll Call

"Pennsylvania Avenue" columnist. Kondracke's imaginative discussions of the world as seen from Pennsylvania Avenue seldom bore. Although his alternatives to White House policy tend toward the conventional, his clear reporting of the issues and his analytic skills enable him to offer occasional insights. In his intriguing 1-18 *Washington Times* essay, Kondracke describes the foreign policy theories of Harvard political scientist Sam Huntington, who warns that while many wars in this century have been "between ideologies," wars among the world's "major civilizations may be the dangerous wave of the future." Slamming the "military expansion of Islamic and Confucian states," Kondracke urges President Clinton to push for a stronger UN role in world affairs. With two savvy *Roll Call* efforts on the complexity of health care, 6-21 and 8-12, Kondracke examines the politics of the issue and its potential for passage in 1993. In the latter article, he explores a revealing critique of the actual program from economist Robert Shapiro, a former Clinton campaign staffer, and then puts Shapiro's expertise in context. The "price tag may be far too low. Many experts say that $50 billion can't possibly cover such a huge expansion in health coverage—Shapiro says $100 billion is a better estimate—and the President risks new allegations of 'Slick Willyism' if he tries to hide or underplay the burden on employers and taxpayers." In his blunt 10-7 evaluation of Clinton's crime plan, Kondracke argues persuasively that "the emphasis in presidential pronouncements has been on gun control as a solution—which is inexpensive, but also ineffective—rather than on securing the nation's streets, which costs money." Although he mentions some alternatives, such as outlawing handguns among minors and a separate prison system for hardened youths, Kondracke provides no evidence that these alternatives will work. In an imaginative 11-15 essay rich with examples comparing NAFTA to entry into World War II, Kondracke states succinctly, "Once again, this is a battle between isolationism and world leadership." In *The New Republic* 3-22, Kondracke gives impressions of the new Clinton-era Washington, in terms of restaurants, radio, and social events. On such items he thinks New York is better, but he still makes his living in Washington. After all, Pennsylvania Avenue offers far more political grist than Broadway.

Michael Kramer

Time

"The Political Interest" columnist. Finally getting out of his pundit's chair once in a while to do some reporting, Kramer

shows signs of modest improvement. In his 2-1 dispatch on Sen. Daniel Patrick Moynihan [D-NY], Kramer notes that as the new head of the Senate Finance Committee, Moynihan would be a key player in getting President Clinton's economic programs to the floor. Yet no one from the White House, Kramer reveals, has even contacted the Senator: "'Big deal,' says a top Administration official. 'Moynihan supported Bob Kerrey during the primaries. He's not one of us, and he can't control Finance like Bentsen did. He's cantankerous, but he couldn't obstruct us even if he wanted to. The gridlock is broken. It's all Democratic now. We'll roll right over him if we have to.'" Adds Kramer: "Those words reflect the arrogance of newfound power, and they are not the only example displayed by the Clinton Administration." Still, Kramer often stayed seated in his chair, dispensing pronouncements on various issues of the day. In a muddled 1-25 effort, he argues that the media should be critiquing Clinton on his style of changing policy, rather than his changing policy. Although he has a good point in noting that "if [Clinton] is right when he says that changing circumstances mandate changing views—and he is—he should say so and leave it at that," it takes Kramer too long to get there. He takes on the idea of national service, 3-22, but fails to examine the implications of his suggestion to broaden the program. In his 6-14 essay, he puts forward the provocative theory that Lani Guinier's confirmation hearings, far from provoking the confrontation Clinton so feared, might have been cathartic for the country's race relations. On 8-9, rather than examine the details of Clinton's proposed budget, he indiscriminately salutes the President for taking "an honest whack at the nation's deficit." But can Kramer really believe that a program of taxes now and spending cuts in 1996 constitutes an honest bit of deficit-whacking? He's neither particularly savvy nor enlightening on the Middle East peace process, 9-20, and without offering any evidence, Kramer buys into the myth that the current administration is responsible for bringing about peace. But it's easy to buy into media myths just sitting in a pundit's chair.

Charles Krauthammer

Washington Post Writers Group

★★½

A senior editor at *The New Republic*, Krauthammer writes thoughtfully and frequently on such disparate matters as foreign policy and today's culture wars. Although he seldom breaks news— Krauthammer does little reporting—he provides sharp and original analysis. In his *Washington Post* 4-9 evaluation of Clintonomics, he cogently argues that "the problem with Clinton is not that he is raising revenues. It is how he is raising them: with a massive expansion of state power into the inner workings of the economy. It is one thing for the government to milk the private sector for money to do what the government needs to do: defend the nation, support the poor, build the roads and rocket ships. It is quite another matter to entangle the government in the micro decisions of the private market." His 11-12 column maintains that "the best way of promoting development and erasing poverty abroad"—historically a goal of liberals—"is trade." Noting that most Democrats in Congress voted against NAFTA, Krauthammer accuses them of hypocrisy, a charge made by no other columnist. But he names only one anti-NAFTA liberal, Rep. David Bonior [D-MI]. Citing a few more names would have strengthened the piece. Krauthammer has no patience, 12-3, with Dr. Jack Kevorkian: "As they say in the Westerns, I'd give him a fair trial and hang him.... He wants to be a martyr to his cause. Let him....This is one physician-assisted suicide I would be loath to interrupt." Krauthammer contends that in a society in which killing oneself is fairly easy, "the last thing we should be doing is relaxing what stigma and disapproval still attach to suicide." In his finest effort of the year, "Defining Deviancy Up," *TNR* 11-12, Krauthammer picks up on Sen. Daniel Patrick Moynihan's [D-NY] thesis that the U.S. has dealt with the epidemic of deviancy—of criminality, family breakdown, mental illness—by defining it in such a way as to make it seem normal. Krauthammer argues that a complementary social phenomenon exists in which "the normal must be found deviant." Rather than serve as "a bedrock of social and psychic stability," ordinary middle-class family life, he contends, is now considered "a caldron of pathology, a teeming source of the depressions, alienations and assorted dysfunctions of adulthood." By redefining and wildly exaggerating genuine problems like child abuse and date rape, as well as elevating insensitive speech into "thought crimes," Krauthammer contends, society has distracted itself from confronting deeper and more pervasive criminal problems. "Defining Deviancy Up"—definitely a politically incorrect take on current social trends—shows Krauthammer at his analytic best.

Irving Kristol

The Wall Street Journal

★★★

Editor of both *The National Interest* and *The Public Interest.* With monthly contributions to *The Wall Street Journal*, Kristol yields incisive appraisals of political and social issues. In a brilliant 2-1 essay examining ideological shifting in politics, Kristol argues persuasively that "the beginning of political wisdom in the 1990s is the recognition that liberalism today is at the end of its intellectual tether." He explains that "the fact that it can win elections is irrelevant. Conservatives continued to win elections during 'the liberal century' (1870-1970); but, once in office, they revealed themselves to be impotent to enact a sustained conservative agenda. The tide of public opinion was too strong against them." Expanding on this idea in two essays, 3-24 and 5-12, Kristol dissects the stratagems and factions within each party and presents theories on how each might redefine itself to cope with a changing world. In his 6-14 column, he probes the moral questions of a welfare state and offers provocative ideas for overhauling the system. "The key to conservative welfare reform would be (a) to discourage young women from having an illegitimate child in the first place and (b) to discriminate between 'welfare mothers' and 'mothers on welfare.'" Welfare, Kristol persuasively argues, "should discriminate in favor of satisfactory human results, not humane intentions." In an offbeat yet effective 8-19 effort, Kristol shows that the counterculture of Bill Clinton's youth has helped to define his presidency. He notes that the pop-music themes of peace and brotherhood as well as other aspects of the 1960s, helped to shape the liberal orthodoxy. Indeed, they continue to do so, Kristol notes, as the ideology remains one of social consciousness in commanding concern for the downtrodden. In a sharp 10-12 condemnation of the Clinton administration's dodging of tough issues on health care, Kristol exposes flaws in the Clinton plan. He argues that it will ultimately result in "abolishing the private sector for medical insurance and medical treatment." The views of this leading neoconservative stand out as compelling, provocative, and Kristol-clear.

Donald Lambro

The Washington Times
United Features Syndicate

★★½

Chief political correspondent. Emerging as a prominent commentator on the nation's political economy, Lambro has a firm grasp on what, from a conservative's perspective, drives an economy: entrepreneurial capitalism. In his informative 1-18 account, Lambro examines several economic promises made during the campaign that Bill Clinton retracted or recast during the transition. Lambro uses his 2-1 column to identify flaws in Clinton's plans for health-care reform. "Does Mr. Clinton seriously believe he can restrict the prices that an industry charges and that the same quality products and services will continue to be produced in sufficient quantities in a vigorously competitive environment?" Adducing data from the National Center for Public Policy Research, 4-26, Lambro cites strong statistics to prove the obvious. "In 1990, half of all black families that were headed by a married couple had incomes of over $33,393—confirming that families that stay together are the best weapon against poverty." In a well-conceived 7-12 column, Lambro attacks some of the more popular media myths about trade deficits. "When the U.S. economy blossomed after the 1981-82 recession, our trade deficit with Japan grew sharply. Yet we experienced strong job growth and robust new business formation. The news media tried to make much out of the trade deficit, suggesting it was a cause for alarm. But the only thing the numbers meant was that our growing, affluent economy was buying more from abroad." Lambro contends, 8-5, that the Clinton administration is playing with the numbers to get its budget passed and that the battle is based as much on politics as on economics. He doesn't, however, thoroughly probe the implications of the budget's pas-

sage. Yet, with his sold reporting and outlook, Lambro remains an important voice at *The Washington Times*.

John Leo

U.S.News & World Report

★★★

"On Society" columnist. Monitoring America's halls of learning, Leo is ever on the lookout for the politically correct and the absurd. He consistently provides well-crafted critiques of modern curricula—and modern society. In his 1-18 essay, Leo superbly captures academic inanities; visiting the Modern Language Association convention, he hears one speaker "complaining testily about the 'white maleness of 'Jeopardy.''" In his 3-15 column, Leo perceptively explores the impact on both blacks and whites of "the free-agent scramble" by universities to lure minority students. "Diversity is no longer viewed as the expected byproduct of youngsters of all races and backgrounds striving to achieve. It's an end in itself, basically a quota system of group representation, with little or no talk any more about merit or standards. All this well-intentioned treatment has had a devastating effect on campus race relations." Leo takes on the "New Age approach to sports," 5-31, explaining that some schools no longer endorse team sports, "mostly because gym teachers think the games damage the feelings of children who aren't outstanding." He argues that "kids in a pick-up volleyball game are not learning the dangerous lesson that 'other people are obstacles to my success' ....They are simply playing, and perhaps learning something about cooperation, discipline and excellence along the way." In a 7-26 piece, Leo reveals how some policies in New York City help to create further anarchy in the streets, such as the refusal by Mayor David Dinkins to send fire department personnel into certain areas. Expanding a lively argument from Stephen Carter's *Culture of Disbelief* that elites have no use for religion in public life, Leo warns, 9-20, that when religion and religious groups are "undercut, all of society pays a price. Me-first individualism and 'choice' are no substitute for moral traditions." Although Leo's subject matter may be limited, his sense of cultural disorder invariably proves keen.

Anthony Lewis

The New York Times

"Abroad at Home" columnist. A passionate liberal, Lewis displays the talent to write powerful, airtight commentary. Occasionally, however, he undercuts his arguments by veering off on other subjects. In his 1-29 column on gays and the military, Lewis loses steam when he decides that the real issue regarding sex and the military is *not* sexual conduct, but, rather, the military's treatment of women. And he dilutes his 2-22 brief against Bill Clinton's position (and George Bush's policy) on returning Haitians to their country by praising Clinton for his speech to the nation on economic policy, a subject largely unrelated to his main premise. In a 3-5 piece arguing that the Serbian response may have warranted stronger U.S. action, Lewis forcefully critiques Clinton's policies in Bosnia, particularly the airdrop. He is less persuasive, however, in urging military force. Lewis reprises this theme in a ringing 8-13 condemnation of the failure to stop Serbian President Slobodan Milosevic when it was possible to do so. No one—not George Bush, James Baker, John Major, the European Community, NATO, or the UN—escapes this indictment. Although Lewis proposes bombing, he doesn't carefully explain how it would solve the region's complex problems. In a well-reported 7-23 column from Thailand, Lewis investigates the political implications of an economic boom—a growing middle class and movement toward lasting democracy in the Asian country. Unfortunately, he stops just short of applying these lessons to other nations with similar histories. In a solid, lawyerly 6-4 defense of Lani Guinier, he attacks Clinton for scuttling her nomination. Lewis answers her critics by examining closely the works in question and effectively using positions taken by the Bush administration against those critics. "She has explored possible alternative methods that would encourage 'cross-racial coalitions' and 'reduce racial polarizations.' One idea is cumulative voting...[which] is not a radical idea. It is often used for elections to corporate boards. The Bush Administration, under the Voting Rights Act, approved cumulative voting or a variant when adopted by 35 different jurisdictions. It also thought the act should prevent discriminatory official treatment of elect-

HENRY PAYNE - REPRINTED BY PERMISSION OF UFS, INC.

"BILL... YOU'VE BEEN INHALING..."

ed blacks, as does Ms. Guinier." Lewis's superb 11-29 piece focuses on the Justice Department's attempt to narrow a broad 1984 anti-pornography statute in order to make it both *stronger* against child pornographers and more constitutionally valid. His shrewd analysis reveals that the Clinton administration and the entire Senate ignored the facts, condemned Justice inappropriately, and engaged in "sleazy politics." When he zeroes in on a target, Lewis ranks among the very best in the business.

Christopher Matthews

San Francisco Examiner
King Features Syndicate
★★

Washington bureau chief. A former Carter speechwriter and Tip O'Neill spokesman, the gritty and combative Matthews relies on his Washington political experience to craft witty, and sometimes unpredictable, commentary. In *The Washington Times* 1-15, he reminds Bill Clinton that his mandate to govern is not as broad as the Washington press corps implies. In his smart 2-20 column, Matthews locates Clinton's split personality in the context of the multiple-personality Democratic party. "One is the moderate, Southern-sounding voice of the Democratic Leadership Council that Mr. Clinton once chaired. The other is the old, Big Labor, unreconstructed liberal growl of those who might think Walter Mondale had it dead right when he confessed to the 1984 Democratic Convention his hot plan 'to pay Mr. Reagan's bills.'" Why, Matthews asks in his sharp 7-29 assessment of gridlock, now that the Democrats control the White House and Congress and its various committees, do programs still back up? "The real traffic jam," Matthews writes, "comes, in fact, at the very beginning of the legislative route: when the folks in the West Wing and on the Hill have to decide just where it is this fantastic caravan called 'the Democratic party' wants to go." His dignified 6-25 tribute to Pat Nixon is all the more poignant, coming as it does from a columnist who spent his youth on the other side of the political aisle. After recounting the dramatic ups and downs of the former First Lady, he asks, "How do you assay such loyalty?" And Matthews is astute, 8-2, in picking up the threads left by the Clinton budget agreement and projecting how it will affect the GOP's chances to regain the White House in 1996. "The most vital Republican party is one that wins presidential elections by sticking to the issue that won for Mr. Reagan and Mr. Clinton both—the economy, stupid." Thanks to his knowledge of politics, Matthews's star is on the rise.

Mary McGrory

The Washington Post
½★

McGrory gets mushier and mushier in her assessments of Washington politics and the world at large. In her rosy 1-21 review of President Clinton's inaugural speech, McGrory says nothing of substance but manages to impart that, boy, did she like it. After the bombing of the World Trade Center, McGrory recycles some New York stories that convey atmosphere, but her 3-2 assessment shows she hasn't been to New York very often. "New York's big secret is that New Yorkers are nice to each other. They don't think a great deal of out-of-towners. It is the contempt of the Marine for the Sunday soldier." She's snide and humorous in her 6-6 effort ridiculing Clinton for hiring David Gergen. "Democrats are still in Gergenshock. The president's choice of a repairman who used to be Richard Nixon's ghost and Ronald Reagan's spinner has caused much bewilderment in his party. Why not Shields, they ask plaintively, meaning Mark Shields, David Gergen's PBS

sidekick. Shields is not as tall as Gergen, but he is funnier, and he's a Democrat." In her 7-27 column, McGrory captures the flavor of Sen. Carol Moseley-Braun's [D-IL] fight on the Senate floor to end government sanction of a Confederate flag insignia used by the United Daughters of the Confederacy. Her conclusion, however, that Moseley-Braun's strong performance may show her colleagues "the futility of opposing strong-minded black women"—and thereby bring about the confirmation of Joycelyn Elders—seems quite a stretch. McGrory's emotionally charged 8-15 appeal that the U.S. at least rescue the children from Bosnia suffers from her failure to adequately address what happens to these children once they get to the U.S., and then after the war is over. Nor does she offer much in the way of practical advice in her 10-14 piece on Clinton's foreign policy. "If he galvanizes the United Nations, rallies the Organization of American States, whips his Cabinet into line and faces down Congress, he can establish himself finally as commander in chief." McGrory seems to be dreaming more than thinking. Her sole value as a columnist lies in her ability to turn a phrase.

George Melloan

The Wall Street Journal

★

"Global Watch." Blunt to the point of being obtuse, Melloan offers unsubstantiated, and often unoriginal, observations on world events. Unlike other conservative columnists on his paper, Melloan seldom reports new information. His simplistic 12-20 piece on the alarming level of support for Russian radical Vladimir Zhirinovsky in the December election consists of a string of conventional, rather than provocative, rhetorical questions. "Why," he asks, "would anyone imagine that all the communists, who such a short while ago ruled the country, would just disappear overnight?" He follows such questions with trite assessments. "A lot of young Russians didn't vote, apparently out of disgust with politics and a focus on making their way in private endeavors independent of the state. But having seen that they had in effect defaulted to politicians like Mr. Zhirinovsky, many will most likely be less careless when the next parliamentary elections are held two years from now." His broad 10-18 swipe at the Clinton administration's alleged missteps in dealing with the military recounts several controversial policies but makes no effort to root out the causes or suggest solutions. Noting that such quagmires as Somalia and Haiti badly damage troop morale, Melloan recommends unremarkably that, "if the President is going to apply U.S. military might to relief efforts, nation building and the creation of world order, he and his advisers need to think more carefully about how to do these things." Oh. Offering no evidence to support his contrarian diatribe, 7-12, Melloan attacks the "enviro-radicals" for costing Americans billions of dollars each year with unnecessary and ineffectual regulations. Even when he makes a good point—such as questioning the chlorofluorocarbon-refrigerants ban meant to fight ozone depletion—he employs a sarcastic tone that grates and distracts. "If anyone had wanted to bother, they could have asked qualified researchers how much UV radiation sunbathers are actually getting. The U.S. National Cancer Institute, which has been taking measurements since 1974, could have told them that UV radiation reaching the earth had been falling lately, not rising." Confirming detailed reports that have been appearing for years in every paper, including his own, Melloan discovers flourishing industry in the Guangdong province of China, 3-15. "The new skyscrapers rising in such places as Shenzhen and the factories sprouting in the special economic zones will not transform the living conditions of nearly 1.2 billion people overnight. But some people now have a chance at a better life." In sum, a disappointing year for Melloan, whose tired analysis reflects a lack of effort, not skill.

Edward Mortimer

Financial Times

When writing on the European Community, few columnists possess either the depth of understanding or the intuitive sense of Europe that Mortimer regularly displays. His work on Europe's integration and the continent's complex problems consistently shines. In his insightful 1-27 evaluation of the 'new' Maastricht treaty, Mortimer reveals that there's *nothing* renegotiated or new in the treaty. He argues that the press and various pro-treaty European governments are playing it that way to encourage the Danes to vote yes. He crafts an exceptional 2-17 update, maintaining that "throughout its history the EC has been a brilliant conspiracy of Europe's governing elites. Each step forward in its history has been the work of an intergovernmental conference (IGC), at which national governments negotiated a treaty. Each successive treaty has amended or enlarged the preceding one." In a stinging 7-7 effort, Mortimer advances the provocative thesis that the pull of Europe and the EC has both accelerated and exacerbated the balkanization of Yugoslavia and Czechoslovakia. "Every nation or potential nation, if not every individual, starts to think how it could get in and how, above all, it must not be held back by association with less wholesome or unfortunate neighbors." When Mortimer tackles other subjects, however, he seems conventional. His 3-24 suggestions for helping Russia—debt relief and investment—seem not only obvious but largely avoid the complex currency issues. By detailing the drawbacks of legal foreign workers, Mortimer constructs a thoughtful 4-15 argument that illegal immigration benefits Europe. "Legal immigrants, enjoying all the rights accorded by the law to indigenous workers, cannot be sent home, and will soon be just as reluctant as indigenous workers are to do those 'dirty, dangerous and demanding' jobs. They will naturally expect the same wages and conditions as indigenous workers, and lose their main attraction in the eyes of employers." Mortimer's failure to examine basic human-rights questions, however, weakens his argument. In his 10-6 thumbnail sketch of the Council of Europe, a "club of democracies" for human rights, Mortimer confronts these questions. Yet in failing to adequately describe the council's functions, his suggestion that the council aid Eastern Europe remains unpersuasive. Although Mortimer speaks with less authority on non-EC matters, he remains the expert on European integration. With the EC likely to grow in importance in the coming years, Mortimer will be the source to turn to.

Michael Novak

Forbes

★★

"The Larger Context" columnist. The author of *The Spirit of Democratic Capitalism*, Novak supplies his "larger context" mainly in economic and moral-religious terms. He can be counted on to support free societies and free markets, as well as to insist upon the moral and religious foundations of liberty. Alas, Novak's columns, although few in number, sometimes seem repetitive. Praising Reaganomics in his 4-26 piece, he simply recycles his 1-18 theme that raising taxes on the rich will decrease the revenue they pay. Fortunately, the latter piece also contains a strong critique of the media's portrayal of the 1980s as "an economic failure," with Novak supplying information that suggests otherwise. For his 8-2 column, Novak crosses the ocean to Europe. The continent, he contends, "has lost its way," due in part to "the cost of its welfare state [and] growing armies of the unemployed —now over 19 million." Novak also stresses the continent's "moral deficiencies," but for evidence offers only that "[m]ore and more Europeans are complaining about the loss of ancient habits of self-discipline, punctuality, hard work, independence and honesty." Which Europeans and how many? Because Novak doesn't elaborate, such nostalgic musings reveal nothing. He is more persuasive in citing a London production of *Macbeth* as evidence of Europe's disconnection from "the classic sources of European culture." "*Macbeth* was played as if he were a modern weak man, a relativist, a pragmatist possessed of mad ambition; his stature was not moral, merely characterized by psychological quirks." In his 9-27 column, Novak relies on economic and social facts to question the U.S. government's "liberal social policy" of the past 30 years. While he commends the spending that cut by two-thirds the infant mortality rate since 1963, he finds that most other social problems have worsened. Unfortunately, Novak fails to consider that government policy may not be the only reason for such worsening conditions. In his 3-15 column, Novak makes the intriguing suggestion of promoting Radio Free Europe in Serbia. "RFE aims at minds, and surely minds are closer to the center of the evils in the Balkans today than any target that even the laser weapons of Stealth fighters can hit." Novak's passion for freedom remains his trademark as a columnist.

Thomas Oliphant

The Boston Globe

★½

Coasting in an off-election year, Oliphant hardly employs the strong analytic and reporting skills that distinguished his work in 1992. He merely states the obvious in arguing, 1-24, that responsibility for the flap over Zöe Baird falls squarely on the President's shoulders. Emotions rule in his 4-21 column on the second Rodney King verdict, in which Oliphant stops barely short of advocating justice by gut instinct, rather than by rule of law. His 10-6 commentary on the Russian parliament's revolt lacks both insight and nuance. In condemning the Reds who masquerade as parliamentarians and in blindly supporting Yeltsin without questioning the constitutionality of his actions, Oliphant simply follows the common herd of columnists. In his more convincing 6-16 report on Ruth Bader Ginsburg, he predicts she will be a candidate for consensus on the bench of the Supreme Court, though he doesn't explain what this consensus will mean. Instead of examining Bill Clinton's economic stimulus proposals, 2-17, Oliphant looks at the President's political strategy of pushing the proposals first through the House and then through the Senate—where the margin for error is much slimmer—so that the upper chamber would be vulnerable to charges of gridlock if it failed to side with Clinton. In his 8-29 column, Oliphant offers an apt football analogy to describe Clinton's style of governing. "The fullback had to accept several facts of life: He was going to get hit hard; he was unlikely to gain much yardage; he could at least look forward to giving as good as he got; the moments of glory were rare... [and] his lasting satisfaction was the quiet understanding that his work was essential to progress and to victory, for which he was not likely to get much credit....From the perspective of its first seven months, Clinton's fullback presidency seems a decent fit. The problems and forces he is bucking are all big and rough and cannot be avoided; one plunge cannot produce anything resembling solutions. Clinton is also a rookie and mistake-prone, but he keeps coming, and a certain grudging tolerance of the president's gritty persistence that is bordering on respect is becoming apparent." This imaginative observation shows that Oliphant still possesses reportorial and analytic muscles, but if he doesn't exercise them more frequently they will continue to atrophy.

P. J. O'Rourke

Rolling Stone
The American Spectator

★★★

International affairs correspondent for *Rolling Stone*, regular contributor to *The American Spectator*. O'Rourke's original reporting, irreverent humor, and crackerjack writing make for delectable reading. He never minces words or pulls his punches, whatever the subject. He also knows when to tone down the jokes, as in his 1-7 *RS* dispatch from Yugoslavia, giving the tragic stories he reports the solemnity they deserve. O'Rourke crafts a vivid 4-1 *RS* dispatch from Mogadishu, warning early that the humanitarian mission had long since evolved into something else, given the fact that guns appear to outnumber starving children. Revealing the intractability of this new problem, he concludes disturbingly: "There's one ugly thought that's occurred to almost everybody who's been there. I heard one marine private...put it succinctly. 'Somalis,' he said. 'Give them better arms and training and seal the borders.'" Characteristically blunt and amusing in *The Wall Street Journal* 9-23, he describes the inanity of having Bill Clinton, of all people, propose reforms on health care. "I also don't know why I'm supposed to take health advice from a man with an obsession with french fries, a waistline like a Beautyrest mattress, the jogging pace of a beached sea lion and the sleep habits of a teenage slumber party." At least, he adds, the President is open to criticism. "[First Brother] Roger Clinton may have some bright ideas. Socks may, too. Though the plan does not cover veterinary expenses. Yet." In his February *TAS* selection, O'Rourke offers a telling observation about the regeneration of the conservative movement. "We are also here to celebrate something else —our return to political opposition. Let's be honest with ourselves. What a relief to be on the attack again. No more gentle sparring with the administration." O'Rourke's list of "100 Reasons Why Jimmy Carter Was a Better President than Bill Clinton," *TAS* September, is simply hilarious. "Carter had governed a more important state. Carter had once held a job. He came from a more cosmopolitan hometown, and had a more charismatic vice president. It took Carter months to wreck the economy. It took Carter weeks to become a national laughingstock. Carter committed adultery only in his heart. And, if we know anything about female tastes, Carter was telling the truth about that." If this entry resulted from O'Rourke's barhopping, as the subhead proclaims, NBC should have hired him as Ted Danson's replacement on "Cheers."

Clarence Page
Chicago Tribune
Tribune Media Services
★

A former Pulitzer Prize winner, Page rarely moves beyond the ordinary to add fresh perspective. He makes a muted call for gun control, 1-13, as he examines recent violence in the Chicago area. His understated tone, somber as a churchman's, works superbly, but he only suggests conventional solutions. Disputing the allegation that Alex Haley may have made up some of his facts for *Roots*, Page argues, 3-10, for poetic license. "Mr. Haley's image survives like Teflon because of a larger truth: Whether Kunta Kinte existed or not, Mr. Haley's African ancestors did not come over on the Mayflower. Like other African-Americans, they are living evidence of a brutal institution whose legacy Americans are still trying to live down." In his cutesy and ultimately frivolous 5-16 'doctor's report' on the health of the Clinton presidency, Page offers a diagnosis of "George Bush Syndrome"—otherwise known as a lack of vision—and suggests better public relations as the prescription. Page's 6-2 examination of the appointment of David Gergen, which scarcely treats the packaging of the presidency that is Gergen's forte, warrants skipping entirely. His 7-11 defense of Joycelyn Elders falls short as he focuses on what each side is saying about her rather than on what Elders, herself, has actually said. In his 8-8 column, Page argues sensibly that if mandatory sentences are applicable, they should be applied no matter who the defendant is. Otherwise, why have them? This is one of Page's few columns to rise above the ordinary in a generally disappointing year.

Virginia I. Postrel
Reason
★★

Editor. Although her strong libertarian slant offers a refreshing perspective, Postrel's reporting and reasoning seem less incisive than in years past. Zeroing in on environmental controls, *Los Angeles Times* 1-26, Postrel tries to account for lost opportunities caused by various regulations, yet she doesn't lay the groundwork for her conclusion that "regulation is in fact hidden taxation. The jobs it 'creates' wipe out more valuable jobs and investment." In her sharp December *Reason* attack on President Clinton's health plan, she argues that price controls and rationing will inhibit development of new medical technologies. "You can indeed have 1965 health care at 1965 prices. But would you want it?" Although she effectively picks Clinton's plan apart, she offers no alternatives. What begins as a promising July essay on being "in the midst of an unacknowledged constitutional crisis," turns into a standard audit of lobbyists' roles. Her vapid October argument against Gov. Pete Wilson's [R-CA] proposal to deny citizenship to U.S.-born children of illegal immigrants turns merely on her contention that such legislation violates the principles of freedom. But Postrel is back in form with an excellent August/September treatise on Congressional attempts to censor violence on television. Challenging the Centerwall study concluding that violence on TV promotes violent behavior, Postrel argues effectively that it "*proves too much.* It doesn't prove that violence on television causes harm. It proves that television itself causes harm. Assuming his conclusion is correct, violent shows may have nothing to do with the shift. Television might disrupt family life in important ways, encouraging parents to pay less attention to kids or interrupting family conversations. It might undermine legal and parental authority. It might shorten attention spans and encourage instant gratification. Banning "Wiseguy" reruns or "America's Most Wanted" wouldn't affect any of these dynamics." This different take on the subject enriches the reader's understanding of the debate and shows Postrel at her best.

Wesley Pruden
The Washington Times

Editor. Pruden's caustic pen has been known simply to spew

conservative bile. Now that Pruden has been thrust into the role of loyal opposition, however, he must aim his barbed assaults at issues of substance if he is to be effective. His first effort under the new administration, 1-22, falls short, as Pruden merely reviles President Clinton for continuing George Bush's policy on Iraq, and then takes random shots at Rep. Barney Frank [D-MA]. In his 3-12 essay, he criticizes the President's reliance on focus groups and notes the fact that Harry Truman's famous buck doesn't seem to stop anywhere in the White House. Pruden warns presciently that, like Earl Long's voting machines, focus groups tend to give those who organize them the results they want, which will have a dangerous impact on Clinton's health-care policy. The Truman analogy gained currency later in the year, following Hillary Rodham Clinton's widely quoted statement that the buck on health care stopped with Congress. With the 'discovery' of Clinton's half-brother, Pruden crafts a sly 6-22 defense of the President's family tree. For a Southerner, Pruden argues, such discoveries aren't all that unusual. "The Father's Day story in *The Washington Post* on Sunday, about a brother who may have been sired by the father who died before the president was born, was fascinating stuff, just the kind of story that anyone born and bred in Dixie has heard, late of a muggy summer night with the frogs singing on the bayou bank, from an elderly aunt with a malicious sense of drama. Some of the stories are more lurid than others. Occasionally one of them is true." His 8-10 critique of the decision by Rep. Marjorie Margolies-Mezvinsky [D-PA] to switch her vote to 'yes' on the budget becomes downright nasty, as Pruden stops just short of arguing that women don't belong in Congress because they change their minds. What about *male* congressmen who flip-flop? In his revealing interview with Mexican President Carlos Salinas de Gortari on NAFTA, 10-12, Pruden includes a memorable quote from an unnamed Mexican about the fears of U.S. critics. "You are so terrified of us. I suppose you should be relieved that Haiti is not part of the treaty." It will be fun to see how Pruden grows into his opposition role—will he aim more carefully?

Anna Quindlen
The New York Times
★½

"Public & Private" columnist. Quindlen took a leave midyear to work on a book. Although readable and engaging, she writes more from the gut than from the head, the properties of a well-reasoned argument often escaping her. In her otherwise jumbled 2-17 essay discussing separation of church and state and the banning of gay marchers from New York City's St. Patrick's Day parade, she states bluntly that the parade is not a religious event. "The truth is that for many years the parade has been a polymorphous civic function with lots of bands, lots of bagpipes and a party-hearty atmosphere the likes of which you customarily encounter at the Theta Meta Beta house on Saturday night. It is about as prayerful as a darts tournament." Quindlen's touchy-feely 3-3 column casting journalism as the reporting of painful events is superficial. In her 4-25 attempt to deconstruct David Brock's *The Real Anita Hill*, she offers little new, except to argue that Brock's sources "fall into two categories: friends of Justice Thomas and anonymous detractors of Professor Hill. When Clarence Thomas supports black protégés, this is seen as praiseworthy; when Professor Hill is accused of favoring black students, she's a reverse racist." Quindlen returned to her column in October but seemed even more burned out. In her emotional, almost fact-free 10-7 effort, she urges U.S. withdrawal from Somalia based on seeing recent pictures of mutilated American soldiers. Quindlen also notes that she had originally favored intervention after seeing pictures of starving children. "But I was naive," she writes, thoroughly impervious to the dangers of basing foreign policy on images rather than on either analysis or solid reason (neither of which she offers). But at least she admits when she's wrong. In her 10-14 column, she casts the New York City mayoral race in context of a children's book, *The Stinky Cheese Man and Other Fairly Stupid Tales*. Unfortunately, "Fairly Stupid" seems the most succinct way to describe Quindlen's analysis.

William Raspberry
The Washington Post
★★★½

Raspberry is one of the few serious columnists who can write in the first person—and get away with it. Thanks to his strong reporting and careful consideration of contrary points of view, Raspberry writes consistently outstanding commentary. In his 1-13 effort, he considers the debilitating effects of racism on young blacks but argues that racism can also be an excuse for inaction. "The truth is that most of the things I say I'd do if I had the money are things I could at least *begin* doing right now. And for many of them (like getting in shape) money is an utter irrelevancy. And so it is with my young friends. Most of what they imagine they'd do but for racism they could at least begin to do now. And for much of it, racism might prove an irrelevancy." Raspberry's eloquent 3-1 description of the problems of welfare and rehabilitation cuts to the heart of the issue. "We keep trying to use welfare and prison to *change* people—to make them think and behave the way we do —when the truth is the incentives work only for those who already think the way we do: who view today's action with an eye on the future." His 6-7 column offers both effective criticism of President Clinton's handling of the Lani Guinier nomination and suggestions for improvement. "With political damage unavoidable, he should have done the right thing." Which is to say he should not have abandoned her or denied he had read her work. "As a result," Raspberry concludes, "he looks both weak and dishonest." In his 8-13 effort, Raspberry perceptively criticizes theories that homosexuality may be genetic, pointing out that in the long run, it really doesn't matter "in our search for rationality and justice. And despite the weight that many gays and lesbians give to the modest evidence of a genetic basis for homosexuality, I'm not sure they would want to follow the implications all the way. It's one thing to use science as absolution ('I'm not a bad person; I simply am what God made me'); quite another to acknowledge abnormality ('There's something wrong with me'). Yet, if you accept that our sexuality is designed to perpetuate the genetic pool, it's hard to see sexuality that cannot possibly have that result as other than abnormal. Science may yet prove me wrong, but it seems fairly clear to me that homosexuality and heterosexuality exist not as absolutes but as points on a continuum. Few people strike me as either perfectly straight or perfectly gay. If what I accept as a commonsense observation is true, it follows that sexuality involves at least some volition—more, no doubt, for some than for others." Raspberry is one of the best social critics around.

Paul Craig Roberts

The Washington Times
BusinessWeek

★★★

Few commentators can match Roberts in terms of his knowledge of economics (he has a Ph.D.) or his experience in government (he served in the Treasury Department in the early 1980s). This fullback of a writer leaves no doubt about his aim, making direct attacks from the right. Remarking, 2-11, on the implications of President Clinton's killing the Council on Competitiveness, "which worked with the Office of Management and Budget to make regulations cost-effective," Roberts contends that it may herald a dangerous trend in Clinton's governance. Boldly challenging the National Competitiveness Act, 6-22, Roberts states, "This act gives the federal government the job of providing startup capital to entrepreneurs. It establishes the U.S. Department of Commerce as investment banker for startup companies. All-knowing bureaucrats will allocate capital by making loans, purchasing preferred stock, and guaranteeing the dividends of venture capital companies. They will do this with taxpayer money, of course, thus completing the separation of risk and reward from accountability." One of the earliest and loudest critics of the Justice Department for its handling of the Branch Davidian situation in Waco, Texas, Roberts saves his harshest comments, 6-1, for Janet Reno, lambasting the Attorney General as "the woman who killed more people than Billy the Kid." In earlier columns, 4-22 and 5-7, he rebukes the government for violating the civil rights of the Davidians because of their unusual beliefs. A forceful writer, Roberts can be counted on as a consistent critic of government in general and of the Clinton administration in particular.

A. M. Rosenthal

The New York Times

"On My Mind" columnist. Less shrill and more thoughtful, Rosenthal's arguments seem better focused this year. But he still could use a good editor to polish his often dense and ponderous prose. In a cogent 1-8 argument on the relevance of history, Rosenthal constructs a convincing defense of the German government for banning the Nazi political parties apparently responsible for the abuse of foreigners. On 2-19, he zeroes in on the tax rhetoric in President Clinton's first two speeches, reminding his audience that entrepreneurs work for their gains. "The President must know that a lot of people did not even attain the $100,000 punishment level until the '80s and then only because of years of risk-taking and fruitful work, not tax manna. And he might have had the good humor to acknowledge that $100,000 is not all that guilt-laden an income if you do not have free government housing, limousines, weekend retreats, jogging tracks and household help." Three dispatches from India, 2-26, 3-2, and 3-5, showcase Rosenthal's excellent reporting skills. He indicts India's elected leaders for allowing different religious factions to polarize the country: "[Hindu nationalist group] Shiv Sena could have been put down in hours. The state and national governments behave like the Weimar reborn—disorganized, frightened, gutless." In his 6-1 column, he raises the voter-perfect objection to the appointment of David Gergen, assuming Gergen still belongs to the GOP. "If I had wanted to vote Republican in 1992, as I have whenever I wished, I would have done so. But Mr. Clinton convinced me it was time for the Democrats to show their new stuff. Fool that I am, it never entered my mind that Mr. Clinton would come to think so much of Republican positions that he would select as his top spokesman a man who had represented them so well for years. If he had told me, I might have chosen the real thing." His incisive 10-12 analysis of the drug situation in New York City looks behind the statistics and headlines to find a drug battle being lost due to politics. Rosenthal thoughtfully examines the Israeli-PLO peace process, 9-3, evoking the "heart-stopping risk" and calmly considering plausible scenarios of how the agreement might play out. Given his past tendency to side with Israel no matter what, Rosenthal's evenhandedness comes as a welcome surprise.

Mike Royko

Chicago Tribune
Tribune Media Services
★★★

Celebrating his 30th year in commentary by turning to tough issues, Royko the humorist gives way in 1993 to Royko the social critic. With vigorous logic and prose, his scathing commentary hits the mark almost every time. He is exceptionally pointed, 3-5, on the "slick public relations gesture" of putting Vice President Al Gore in charge of cutting waste. "Now Mr. Clinton expects Mr. Gore, who voted on billions of dollars in federal programs, to poke his head into government offices and say: 'My goodness, what are all you people doing here?'" Royko argues passionately for leaving in place the ban on gays in the military, 1-16, but he provides no solid evidence that lifting the ban will "affect morale and discipline" or weaken the nation's defense. He contends, again without evidence, that "gay obsessives... have an agenda: total social acceptance. And they are using the military ban as a blue chip in their poker game." In his 4-7 column, he provocatively compares the different media responses to the Rodney King beating and the murder of Barbara Meller Jensen, the first tourist killed in Florida in 1993. "Why the difference in emphasis? Because in the minds of those who run the news business, the Rodney King beating has social significance. It is about Rodney King, symbol of white cops beating up a black man. It is about oppression, victimization, economic and social deprivation, legal discrimination and just about any other -ion you want to toss in. But Mrs. Jensen? She's just a tourist who happened to be in the wrong place at the wrong time." Comparing everyday violence in Chicago to the rioting after the Bulls won the NBA playoffs, Royko is equally tough and illuminating, 7-6. The statistics, he reveals, are worse for a weekend "of normal behavior." In his 8-11 column, Royko goes after the priorities of some police departments: "The big crime news is that the Los Angeles Police Department, with help from the FBI and the Beverly Hills Police Department, has busted Heidi Fleiss, 27." Unyielding and often wry, Royko begins a more profound level of commentary for his next 30 years.

William Safire

The New York Times

★★★

"Essay" columnist. No columnist is a more diligent reporter, none pursues targets so zealously (and even too zealously), and none writes a better sentence. But even a master can get tired, and Safire's 1993 portfolio, while excellent, occasionally lapses. Two exercises on Iraqgate, 1-25 and 2-11, add little new information, as Safire renews his 1992 call for a special prosecutor to take over the case and provide the fresh details that he himself has not reported. He gives a sporting first-quarter report, 4-26, on President Clinton's first 100 days, shrewdly examining the long-term impact of his policies and criticizing both his judgment and approach. "The leftward lurch of the new President's economic proposals was a historic miscalculation; Clinton, who thinks it was merely a mistake in tactics, still doesn't get it: Americans are prepared to sacrifice for the next generation by reducing the deficit, not for this generation by continuing it." In his 8-2, 8-12, and 8-16 columns thoroughly questioning how the White House handled the tragedy of Vince Foster's suicide, Safire attempts to solve the puzzle, and considers the role played by the press. "Journalists have a job to do, and cannot pull their punches at wrongdoing on the assumption that high officials may be mentally ill." Safire makes no bones about how he feels about the Middle East peace agreement, 9-2: "It galls a pro-Israeli hawk to say this, but let's hope the slippery Arafat can deliver." He recognizes the historic, unprecedented opportunity afforded by events, and smartly acknowledges the true heroes. "Our State Department is emitting ludicrous little bleats suggesting that Warren Christopher was the hero because Israel kept him informed of the dealings and he didn't blab. But this is not our deal; it was truly worked out 'between the parties.'" In one of his most noted columns, 12-23, Safire disparages Bobby Ray Inman, the President's nominee for Secretary of Defense. Calling Inman "a flop...naif...and cheat," Safire recounts the single phone conversation he ever had with him when the "arrogant admiral" called him in 1980 to denounce a recent column. "I respectfully asked if he would entertain one question. Icily, the admiral informed me he never talked to the press, but what was it I wanted to know? I asked him how a grown man could go through life calling himself 'Bobby'; he slammed down the phone." Inman's subsequent withdrawal in January 1994—when he accused the press of a "new McCarthyism" and singled out Safire—no doubt delighted the former Nixon speechwriter. Few columnists have proved as consistently strong as Safire over the years; this punning pundit still shines like a royal, polished jewel.

Robert J. Samuelson

Newsweek

Washington Post Writers Group

★★

"Judgment Calls" columnist for *Newsweek*. While Samuelson's forte is commonsense economics, he sometimes writes well-considered pieces on the presidency and other political subjects. Mercifully for the overburdened reader, Samuelson specializes in short sentences. In *The Washington Post* 2-17, Samuelson suggests ways of raising revenue, such as taxing capital gains at death. Here he takes on the administration's economic program: "It is naive to think Clinton's proposals, if enacted, would constitute only a limited unraveling of the 1986 [tax] reform. By embracing high rates and selective preferences, he sanctions a new quest for tax breaks." Arguing that Clinton is no FDR, *Newsweek* 5-24, Samuelson usefully relates history neglected by most other journalists. "This is not the 1930s. We don't face an acute national crisis, but instead a chronic disillusionment....Government needs to retreat from jobs that it cannot do or aren't worth doing, while focusing on things that it might do and must do. Clinton disdains this difficult job of redefinition. Instead, he mimics the Roosevelt model by proposing new programs ranging from 'national service' to high-speed railroads. He's dissipating government's energies by expanding its responsibilities." Samuelson uncritically accepts the conventional wisdom on the current recovery, 6-7, observing that "what has also hurt growth is the legacy of the 1980s' debt." In his 8-2 effort, he tells of his personal experience with an HMO, relating it to the broader issue of health care. However, his failure to address how representative his experience might be limits the column's utility. In his strongest *Washington Post* selection, 10-13,

Samuelson argues strongly against the administration's plan to design a supercar that's affordable, lightweight, and gets 60-80 miles to the gallon. Although it "sounds like a great idea," he points out that while some ambitious government-industry ventures may succeed technically—the Manhattan Project, the Apollo Project—most fail commercially, such as synthetic fuels, the breeder nuclear reactor, and the space shuttle. They also gobble up vast amounts of money for which no one is held accountable. Like most of Samuelson's offerings, this one is accessible and to the point.

William Schneider

National Journal
Los Angeles Times Syndicate
★

"Political Pulse" columnist for *National Journal.* As CNN's poll analyst, Schneider bases much of his written appraisals on CNN's polls, often ignoring other types of data. His superficial 5-8 effort is typical, with CNN's poll numbers Schneider's only source of information. Having not actually spoken to anyone, he concludes: "People aren't afraid of Clinton's [economic] plan. They're afraid that he won't be able to get it passed." He again uses polls, 6-12, to discuss the pros and cons of President Clinton's governing from the center, observing sensibly, though unoriginally, that "it is always dangerous for a politician to antagonize his base supporters. Maybe they have nowhere else to go, but [the liberals] can still make a lot of trouble." Schneider limits two essays on the Clinton economic package, 2-20 and 3-6, by failing to address the economics and focusing only on how voters may react in the voting booth. Although he devotes half his 9-18 column to CNN poll results, Schneider offers succinct insights on the Israeli-PLO agreement. "The Administration's strategy is to play the role of fund raiser rather than sole investor. Clinton is seeking pledges of large-scale financial assistance from the Europeans, the Japanese, the Arab oil states and the World Bank to make sure the new Palestinian entity is economically viable. What's in it for them? The same thing that's in it for the United States, Israel and the PLO, namely, stability in the Middle East. Everybody has the same enemy—radical Islamic fundamentalism." Schneider strains credibility in his 10-9 exercise postulating Colin Powell for president in 1996, especially since Schneider admits that few know anything about Powell's politics or ideas. While he cites no numbers, one suspects that Powell's high poll ratings have been the impetus behind this weakly argued essay. Schneider should stop using the polls as a crutch, before his fine mind and analytic powers waste away.

Daniel Seligman

Fortune
★★★

"Keeping Up" columnist. Seligman combines exhaustive database searches and cogent, irreverent analysis to produce consistently informative articles. In his 2-22 column on "phony statistics" about health care—heart disease and strokes cost the U.S. $117.4 billion a year, schizophrenia $50 billion—he points out that "the data are wobbly....It tends to be most unclear what is being added up to arrive at the total." He writes that naturally, these "wobbly" numbers are the ones the media "continually fall for," helping to create an atmosphere of crisis. In his blunt 3-22 column on the problem with raising the minimum wage, Seligman provides a clear and precise example: "A guy who has saved or borrowed $100,000 to open a dry-cleaning store is not doing it because he gets kicks from pressing pants. He is greedily postulating that the store will give him a superior return on his money. But if politicians then come along and say, hey,

It doesn't have a damn thing to do with political correctness, pal. I'm a sausage, and that guy's a weinie.

wait a minute, your costs are going up and your return going down because the pimply teenager who delivers the pants needs $1 an hour more than you were assuming, and then he runs the figures again and some of the time decides not to proceed, so the acne kid is out of work again. Q.E.D." His 5-31 effort amusingly deconstructs Hollywood's portrayal of the evil businessman but ultimately goes nowhere. He attacks the Americans With Disabilities Act, 6-28: "nobody knew exactly what it meant. Well, nobody except the lawyers. What they instantly osmosed is that this arguably well-intentioned law would be a gravy train in 1992-93 and an even bigger bonanza in 1994 (when the cutoff goes down to 15 workers)." He then examines applications of the act where the lawyers might make out like bandits. Seligman consistently examines the consequences of legislation affecting the economy. He also offers a strong 10-18 critique of the bond writers. "Sad, is it not? Especially if one tends to think about these reports for seven seconds, the time estimated to set the bile flowing when the AP quotes a guy from Nomura Securities on the deeper meaning of the Treasuries' yielding under 6 percent and attributes to him the thought that this level is 'psychologically important, as the market is now free to test lower yield levels.' How the market got there in the first place if it was not previously free to test lower yield levels is one of the many questions not answered for the old folks." The irrepressible Seligman seldom disappoints.

Mark Shields

Associated Features

★½

What has happened to our favorite populist? Invigorated during campaign '92, Shields now seems greatly discouraged by the return to business as usual—or perhaps by the springtime departure of his TV sparring partner David Gergen to the White House. Whatever the reason, Shields, who appears regularly in the *New York Post*, doesn't deliver the commentary expected of this veteran political observer. His 1-20 effort, a compendium of various thoughts related to that day, such as the length of the inaugural speech as a measure of presidential success (Washington at 135 words, father of our country; William Henry Harrison at 8,000, dead a month later), is mildly amusing. Shields notes, 2-22, that with public confidence in government's ability to solve problems sagging dramatically, the Clinton administration is the do-or-die moment for liberalism—standard fare but well written. Shields provides a distinctively populist 4-13 evaluation of the difficulties that have bedeviled recent presidencies as well as the newest one: "five months [after the election], the national desire for change remains strong and as yet unmet. But the young president has lately diffused his message. As President Reagan's campaign manager, Ed Rollins, sees it, Clinton 'has not successfully defined himself or his mission to the country. He has good days and bad days, but too often he's in a Bush mode—reacting instead of acting.'" Shields examines the upside to Ross Perot, 6-22, reviewing the Texan's positive impact on politics, a persuasive and detailed exercise that's more like the Shields of yore. In his 8-11 essay on the budget vote, he simply salutes Senators and Representatives who voted 'yes,' but because he fails to analyze the package itself, he doesn't convince that a 'yes' vote was correct. In his 10-6 *Washington Post* assessment of the charges against Sen. Kay Bailey Hutchison [R-TX], Shields finds that the most serious charge concerns destruction of records, which he compares to a "third-rate burglary." But his concluding quote of Texas Democratic consultant Mark McKinnon, that "Bailey had better start thinking seriously of how to save her career," seems premature, as she's yet to be tried, much less found guilty.

Hugh Sidey

Time

★★

Washington contributing editor, "The Presidency" column and "Hugh Sidey's America." More and more, this polished writer's "Presidency" column seems like an exercise in nostalgia rather than a cutting-edge assessment of the men who occupy the Oval Office. While this tone may be appropriate for Sidey's "America" selections, it detracts from his news reporting and his Washington assessments. Few can match his elegant prose, however, which makes his selections among the best in the weekly. He excels at describing the ceremony of Ronald Reagan's receipt of the Medal of Freedom, 1-25, and of George Bush's last morning

in the White House, right up to the moment of Bill Clinton's taking the oath of office, 2-1. He also writes revealing portraits of the larger-than-life politicians of the late 1950s, 5-31, such as Eisenhower and LBJ. But in all these selections, Sidey never provides hard information. More novelist than analyst, his "America" efforts evoke a romantic vision of the nation rather than provoke thought or outrage. Sidey offers a poetic 3-8 lament of the death of the ranchers, squeezed out by government and environmentalists, but as usual, he's long on ambiance and short on an actual critique of the causes. Lucky enough to be given every little boy journalist's fantasy assignment, Sidey pens a charming 8-23 piece on freight trains, making Newark, New Jersey, the train's starting point, sound inviting and utopian. He offers little sentiment in his 9-27 essay conveying the atmosphere surrounding the handshake that changed history in the Middle East. Sidey paints the event honestly in a good supplement to the hard news accounts. "It was a triumphant but curious time for Bill Clinton. He deserved credit not for what he had done but for what he had not done. This agreement was the work of others over decades. Clinton had stayed out of the way in the last act and let it happen naturally. He did not posture or seek personal acclaim, but paid tribute to those who had long carried the heavy burden. Such acts are far too rare in the presidency, but they are just as much a measure of honor." Amid the mediocrity at *Time*, Sidey is a class act all the way.

Tony Snow

Detroit News
Creators Syndicate
★★

A former Bush speechwriter and media affairs aide, and before that *The Washington Times* editorial page editor, Snow returns to journalism by returning to another previous employer, *Detroit News*, for which he writes a twice-weekly column (now syndicated by Creators) out of Washington. As with most journalists who have cycled through government, Snow needed some time to recover his own voice. He writes succinctly but sometimes takes unnecessary swipes without sufficient evidence. In his 3-9 *WT* column, Snow highlights the flaws in President Clinton's economic program, offering plausible explanations for the reactions of different indicators. He cites the stock market as an example, reasoning that the positive signs may not be quite what they seem. "Businesses fear William Jefferson Clinton. They don't know whether to invest or hoard; hire or hold tight; laugh, cry—or jump." A weaker 4-23 *Boston Globe* effort outlining the pork in the budget could have carried almost any conservative's byline. Similarly, Snow's 5-31 mockery of Clinton over travelgate and hairgate adds little to the broader picture, and his contention in the *Detroit News* 7-12, that "allegations in this [travel] scandal dwarf those of Watergate" seems overdrawn. After Clinton's hiring of David Gergen to play spinmeister, Snow gives the President a timely tap on the shoulder, *USA Today* 6-3, reminding him that it's the ideas, stupid, not the image. This otherwise thoughtful piece suffers from a mean-spirited attack on Clinton, "a president who instinctively blames others for his troubles.... Voters do not like the president's style—the bitten lip, the theatrical silences, the practiced righteous replies." Snow unfairly accuses Clinton for using "Orwellian language," but amuses by saying he "governs like FDR with a pompadour." He provides a solid 8-5 *WT* dissection of the numbers behind the last several budgets, including Clinton's first. Sounding a partisan note on forced volunteerism, 10-5, Snow gripes that "students get credit for working at Planned Parenthood, but not at Operation Rescue." Snow's column picked up late in the year. In the *Detroit News* 11-18 and *The Washington Times* 11-22, Snow's probing pieces on potential conflicts of interest pertaining to Hillary Rodham Clinton's finances contain important, original reporting. Reporting, indeed, stands out as the strength of this young column—one to watch in 1994.

Thomas Sowell

Forbes
Scripps-Howard News Service
★★★

"Observations" columnist for *Forbes*, columnist for Scripps-Howard. The provocative, conservative Sowell clearly defines his challenges to administration decisions. His efforts would be richer, however, if he made his own recommendations more specific. His 2-15 *Forbes* essay contains solid, pointed analysis of the selection process employed by President Clinton in choosing his cabinet: "Demographic representativeness is seldom achieved in a multi-ethnic society without quotas, whether or not people are honest enough to call them quotas." In a well-rounded 3-9 *Washington Times* effort, Sowell thoughtfully examines the GOP's options as the opposition. "Much of the Republican leadership is too worried about its image to risk seeming to be obstructing the new president. They prefer to 'go along to get along.' They are 'pragmatists.' Pragmatism, however, is not always practical in the long run, if playing everything by ear on a day-to-day basis leads people to conclude that you don't really stand for anything—or at least not for anything that anyone else can figure out and depend upon." He follows this up with a dynamite 3-29 *Forbes* selection on the Clinton economic plan. "It is runaway spending which has produced the deficits and the growing national debt. Government receipts doubled in a decade, yet the national debt kept rising. There is simply no way that anyone can raise more money than Congress can spend, no matter what the tax rates are on the rich, the poor, or the other 90 percent of the population." In a succinct, memorable 4-93 *American Spectator* piece, Sowell answers some of the questions posed by multiculturalists. "'Why are the traditional classics of Western civilization written by dead white males?' Take it one step at a time. They are written by dead people for two reasons: First, there are more dead people than living people. Second, a classic is not something that is hot at the moment but something that survives the test of time." On the Baby Jessica case, *WT* 8-8, he argues eloquently that laws defining children as chattel and shuttling them from home to home ought to be changed immediately. Sowell's experience with computers, related in his 9-13 *Forbes* column, is something anyone who's ever come into contact with an IBM or a Mac can appreciate, a charming effort revealing his ability to poke fun at himself. This new side of Sowell enhances his work as a columnist.

Harry Summers

Los Angeles Times Syndicate

★★★

A retired army colonel, Summers is a valuable resource on defense issues. His impressive expertise on military life and strategy enables him to provide a deep understanding of the complex problems facing both the U.S. government and the international community. In his strong 3-11 *Washington Times* effort, Summers points out the dangers inherent in the erosion of military authority due to confusion in the upper ranks over the Bosnian airdrop. Surmising that the U.S. has both the equipment and the skill to carry out the mission flawlessly, but lacks the will to do so, he quotes a somber warning from Gen. Douglas MacArthur: "If you hit soft, if you practice appeasement in the use of force, you are doomed to disaster." In his 7-9 column, Summers characterizes the main arguments against women in combat as outmoded: "Women will be coming home in body bags. Women will be wounded. Women will be taken as prisoners of war. And the clincher: women can't stand the horrors of the battlefield." Army nurses, Summers notes, have been facing these conditions since 1861. His 8-5 piece ascribes a meaning to the combat decorations received by soldiers who served in Somalia. "What the military is saying loud and clear...is that 'peacekeeping humanitarian operations' are in reality small-scale combat operations." In a strongly worded 9-2 indictment of the neo-Cold Warriors on the left, Summers issues a bitter, cogent warning about using the military to create or rebuild countries. "'Nation-building' failed in Vietnam, and it will surely fail in Somalia and Bosnia as well. Political, economic and social institutions cannot be forged with force of arms." On these strategic issues, Summers remains a clear and vital voice.

Cal Thomas

Los Angeles Times Syndicate

★★

A publicly committed Christian and political conservative, Thomas addresses a wide range of topics—and his convictions usually show. In a well-organized 3-11 *Washington Times* piece, Thomas astutely addresses concerns over health care. After denouncing Hillary Rodham Clinton's closed-door task-force sessions, he details flaws in the health-care systems of other countries. A sweet (almost saccharine) remembrance of Pat Nixon, New York *Daily News* 6-24, illustrates Thomas's religious sensibility. "It might also be said that she defined a virtuous woman, of whom the

Bible says, 'her children will rise up and call her blessed.' Indeed, they have. And America was blessed by her life and example." Thomas, however, jarringly makes political use of her example, enlisting it in behalf of conservative causes. In his 7-11 *WT* essay on reviving GOP prospects, Thomas assumes, with no hard evidence, that the family-values issue is a winning one for the Republican party. Shrewdly contrasting George Bush with Ronald Reagan, he warns of the dangers of ignoring controversial issues in the name of pragmatism. "When politicians abandon principle, people with principle quickly abandon them." Thomas's empathy is evident in his sturdy 8-8 defense of Sen. Ted Kennedy [D-MA] after the release of Joe McGinniss' *The Last Brother*. "Even if everything in Mr. McGinniss's book were true (and much of it apparently is not, if one is to believe the testimony of those who witnessed the events or who interviewed those who did), the book speaks of a different man and a different time. People change, some for the worse, some for the better. Whatever can be said of the former Ted Kennedy, it is clear to me that he is no longer on the road to self-destruction." In his 9-19 essay, Thomas sharply notes the impropriety of the media's recruiting gays as reporters to get their perspective on gay-related stories. "The incestuous relationship between the press and groups who want to promote their political agenda has to stop....The profession will resemble Bosnia: a Balkanization of competing ideologies and a public that will no longer be able to separate facts from advocacy." Such moral concerns often distinguish Thomas's writings.

R. Emmett Tyrrell, Jr.

The American Spectator
Creators Syndicate
★★

Editor-in-Chief of *The American Spectator*, columnist for Creators Syndicate. Tyrrell's influence stems more from his editorship of *TAS*—now possessing the largest circulation of any political opinion magazine—than from his syndicated column. His great strength lies in his colorful, bold-thrust writing, which he displays regularly in "The Continuing Crisis," a prose cartoon of the previous month's news that opens the magazine and leaves no doubt about his politics—libertarian conservative. In his July column on the nation's fluctuating incarceration rates, Tyrrell supplies evidence showing "that the federal government does at least one thing right: the nation's prison population has reached an all-time high and the number of miscreants jugged by the federal prison system rose significantly faster than that of the states. Good going, fellows!" Unafflicted with solemnity—the disease of so many Washington pundits—Tyrrell always appears in a chipper mood. In his September piece, he describes his chance meeting with two high-powered Washingtonians. "On the evening of July 24, Drs. Donna Shalala and Joycelyn Elders, the administration's leading champions of the noble condom, were asked by the editor of this journal for an autographed condom as they passed his table at The Palm restaurant. Everyone laughed, but neither lady had one on her. Call it Condomgate!" Tyrrell's writing style—well showcased in his books on the respective "crack-ups" of liberalism and conservatism—proves less suited to the column format. In his March effort, he derides Bill Clinton's supporters at the inaugural but provides no reasons. And in his July effort, in which he calls the President and the First Lady "the spoiled brats of their generation," he recites everything either one of them has ever done that irritated him. Tyrrell opens his April column with the provocative premise that Clinton's economic package is "the progressives' version of trickle-down economics," but he only sneers at Clinton when some original reporting might have developed his point. Reporting, in fact, is too often missing from his columns. With some fresh information, Tyrrell could wittily engage the policy debates.

Ben Wattenberg

Newspaper Enterprise
Association

Syndicated to *The Washington Times*, Wattenberg's columns offer constructive and timely criticism of Bill Clinton, and this neocon Democrat proves to be an excellent predictor of where the new administration is going. In his 1-13 commentary, he realizes early the possibility that Clinton will govern according to a "Chinese menu" theory. "Jimmy Carter and George Bush used the 'Chinese menu' for policy formulation, picking 'one from group A,' and then 'one from group B.' That soon translates into the perception of a 'lack of coherent vision,' which is politically fatal. If Mr. Clinton doesn't stick to the themes that got him elected...he too might end up with a fortune cookie that will read, 'Sorry, this cookie has no message.'" As a member of the Commission on Broadcasting, Wattenberg offers suggestions for instituting a Radio Free China that carry weight, 3-10, although he has discussed this idea in earlier essays. In his shallow 8-12 column, he chooses to judge only the rhetoric of the budget deal, rather than the deal itself. Wattenberg, however, shows his form in a 6-18 piece, revealing the "dirty little secret" of Clinton's welfare reform: "What happens if a welfare recipient doesn't go to work? Based on the ideas propounded by Mr. Clinton, the only penalty would be a loss of the mother's share of Aid to Families with Dependent Children. Thus, the mother continues to receive her children's share of the AFDC grant. And food stamps. And housing grants. And Medicaid. And Women-Infant-Children benefits. And is eligible for about 70 smaller programs." On a similar note, he takes the administration to task on the issue of illegitimacy, making a persuasive 7-15 case that "as long as political America remains uncomfortable mentioning illegitimacy, we will continue to condone it. As long as we condone it, we will subsidize it." With his unique perspective, Wattenberg is one to watch as the next three years of the Clinton administration unfold.

Jacob Weisberg

The New Republic

★★½

Surveying Washington with both anger and skepticism, Weisberg shows more concern for the *method* of politics than the results. It's not whether you win or lose but how you play (or misplay) the game. In "Clincest," his devastating 4-26 cover story, Weisberg names names —more than 100 Friends of Bill—to reveal how the vast, interlocking web of friendships woven over the years by Clinton and pals has warped the integrity of the new administration. "Clincest is not just about the rise of conflicts of interest, as husband, wives, friends and former classmates promote each other's careers and advance in tandem, socially and professionally. It's about the increasingly cozy relationships between press, law, academia and government that now mark the Clinton era." This superb piece has force, but its analysis fails to fully convince. By not showing how the "Clintelligentsia" is significantly different from the hordes that descended on Washington when previous administrations changed hands, Weisberg cannot sustain his conclusion that "there's rarely been a time when the governing elites in so many fields were made up of such a tight, hermetic and incestuous clique." Weisberg proves better at exposing problems than at proposing solutions. Enumerating the glaring loopholes of both old ethics laws and proposed new rules, 2-1, he describes Republican PR. giants eagerly hunting out-of-office Democrats to lobby the new administration. "To date, no high official has ever been punished for post-employment influence-peddling." Weisberg's solution? "The easiest, cheapest and most effective remedy is shame." Is he serious? Bob Strauss brags about his deal-making phone call that netted him $8 million. Instead of shame, it probably brought him more clients. "True Fax," 7-5, ably defends the much-maligned Mary Matalin, noting that her notorious, anti-Clinton campaign press-releases uncannily predicted many of the new President's turnabouts in policy. Although a valuable corrective, the news that Clinton misled or over-promised during the campaign hardly surprises. Weisberg also sketches political portraits, some more successful than others. "Moyniham," 6-7, captures the "mercurial" personality of the New York senator, while "Hokey Okie," 6-28, reveals little about David Boren [D-OK]. Although Weisberg's conclusions sometimes outrun his evidence, he supplies a steady dose of provocative information.

Lally Weymouth

The Washington Post

★★½

Factoring in many angles, Weymouth's solid and detailed geopolitical overviews present a multifaceted picture of a complex world. She always enlightens, although sometimes inadvertently. Her 1-26 examination of how the change in administrations may affect the rebel groups in Angola—with the Marxist Popular Movement for the Liberation of Angola and its president Eduardo dos

Santos enjoying new access and with Jonas Savimbi and UNITA suddenly out in the cold—provoked a 2-16 rebuttal from Alfredo Salvaterra, alternative permanent observer of Angola for the OAU. Salvaterra offers a decidedly different perspective—and because of this debate, the reader comes away informed. Weymouth has long covered the Middle East, and her 9-12 effort showcases her expertise. "Rabin and Peres have seized the best available option. In so doing, they have turned the tables on both King Hussein of Jordan and President Hafez Assad of Syria. For a decade, Israel tried but failed to reach a peace agreement with the Palestinians through Jordan. In 1987 Peres—then prime minister—watched an accord slip away from him at the very last moment when King Hussein lost his nerve. As for Assad, he can no longer use the Palestinian card in his dealings with Israel. No longer can the Syrian dictator base his unwillingness to negotiate a treaty on the claim that he is morally committed to refraining from entering into a Sadat-style 'separate peace.'" Sometimes, however, Weymouth provides too much peripheral background detail, depriving herself of adequate space to build her conclusion. She crafts a strong 2-8 review of the civil war in Bosnia-Herzegovina, but after dwelling too long on the Russians, concludes obviously that "policy makers would do well to remember that it would be easier to get into Bosnia than to get out." Similarly, her 8-2 deciphering of the New York State report on the Crown Heights rioting is excellent. Yet, again, Weymouth leaves too little room to craft an effective rationale for the federal investigation she suggests. Although her 6-7 recommendation of the use of military force in North Korea seems abrupt, she superbly assesses the importance to this Asian country of the development of the bomb. "If Pyongyang develops a nuclear capability, this will alter forever the balance of power in Asia. In all likelihood, Japan will likewise opt to build nuclear weapons—leaving a nuclear China facing a nuclear Japan." Her sharp insights not-withstanding, Weymouth's effectiveness requires improved pacing.

George F. Will

Newsweek
Washington Post Writers Group
★★★

Few columnists can range over as many subjects, write as elegantly or as sharply, or draw on so extensive a fund of knowledge as Will. Given that he writes so many columns—100 for newspapers, 25 for *Newsweek*—it's not surprising that a few fall short. Will's 9-9 *Washington Post* effort, for example, outlines his concerns over the PLO-Israeli agreement but adds little to the wide body of commentary on the subject. Will exposes the subsidies granted peanut growers in a 6-6 story told in the form of a presidential fairy tale to his 11-month-old son who likes peanut butter. It might stick to the roof of your mouth, but it doesn't stick to the ribs. Fortunately, Will's portfolio for the remainder of the year is more palatable, and sometimes quite delectable. Opening fire with a memorable 2-11 lead, Will indicts President Clinton's policies from the get-go: "In his first radio address from the Oval Office, President Clinton said that 'for the last 12 years our leaders haven't completely leveled with us.' Make that 13." Similarly, he offers a vibrant 4-18 critique of Clinton's back-to-the-future politics. "The administration is on the cutting-edge of 30 years ago, the decade formative for the president and many of his people, the 1960s, when they were young and modern." Will pens a solid, inside-the-Beltway 7-1 profile of newly-elected Los Angeles Mayor Richard Riordan, providing a clear breakdown of how he got there and what he hopes to accomplish. Skillfully highlighting the pertinent issues of rebuilding after the 1992 rioting, Will also describes the constituency Riordan can summon to help resurrect the city. His intensely personal and moving 5-3 *Newsweek* tribute to his 21-year-old son, Jon, who has Down's syndrome broadens to a poignant appreciation of the human potential of those who might otherwise be dismissed. Will can also hit hard. His best for the year is his devastating 10-8 *WP* attack on foreign policy in as "colonialism-of-compassion," a critique widely applicable elsewhere. Will knew the phrase would create a stir, and it did. Clearly, when this prominent commentator has the will he finds the way.

PUBLICATIONS AND SYNDICATES

Publications

The American Prospect
P.O. Box 7645
Princeton, NJ 08543-7645
(609) 497-2474 (fax, no phone)

The American Spectator
2020 N. 14th Street
P.O. Box 549
Arlington, VA 22216
(703) 243-3733

The Atlantic
745 Boylston Street
Boston, MA 02116
(617) 536-9500

Aviation Week & Space Technology
1221 Avenue of the Americas
42nd Floor
New York, NY 10020
(212) 512-2000 - general
(212) 512-3507 - editorial

Barron's
200 Liberty Street
New York, NY 10281
(212) 416-2700

The Boston Globe
135 Morrissey Boulevard
Boston, MA 02127
(617) 929-2000

BusinessWeek
1221 Avenue of the Americas
39th Floor
New York, NY 10021
(212) 512-2000

Chicago Tribune
435 N. Michigan Avenue
Chicago, IL 60611-4041
(312) 222-3232

The Christian Science Monitor
One Norway Street
Boston, MA 02115-3195
(617) 450-2000

Chronicles
The Rockford Institute
934 N. Main Street
Rockford, IL 61103
(815) 964-5054

Commentary
165 East 56th Street
New York, NY 10022
(212) 751-4000

Defense News
6883 Commercial Drive
Springfield, VA 22159
(703) 642-7300

The Economist
U.S. office:
111 West 57th Street
New York, NY 10019
(212) 541-5730
U.K. office:
25 St. James Street
London SW1A 1HG
United Kingdom
44-71-873-3000

Far Eastern Economic Review
GPO Box 160
Hong Kong
582-580-4300 - general
582-508-4381 - editorial

Financial Times
U.S. office:
13 East 66th Street
New York, NY 10022
(212) 752-7400 - editorial
U.K. office:
Number One Southwark Bridge
London SE1 9HL
United Kingdom
44-71-873-3000

Financial World
47 West 34th Street, 3rd floor
New York, NY 10001
(212) 594-5030

Forbes
60 Fifth Avenue
New York, NY 10011
(212) 620-2200

Foreign Affairs
58 East 68th Street
New York, NY 10021
(212) 734-0400

Foreign Policy
2400 N Street, NW
Washington, DC 20037
(202) 862-7940

Fortune
Time-Life Building
Rockefeller Center
New York, NY 10020-1393
(212) 586-1212

Harper's
666 Broadway, 11th floor
New York, NY 10012
(212) 614-6508

Harvard Business Review
Harvard University
Boston, MA 02163
(617) 495-6182

Human Events
422 First Street, SE
Washington, DC 20003
(202) 546-0856

In These Times
2040 N. Milwaukee Ave.
Chicago, IL 60647
(312) 772-0100

Insight
3600 New York Avenue, NE
Washington, DC 20002
1-800-356-3588

Investor's Business Daily
12655 Beatrice Street
Los Angeles, CA 90066
(310) 448-6000

Jane's Defence Weekly
Jane's Information Group, Inc.
1340 Braddock Place, Suite 300
Alexandria, VA 22314-1651
(703) 683-3700

The Journal of Commerce
2 World Trade Center
27th Floor
New York, NY 10048-0298
(212) 837-7000

Legal Times
1730 M Street, NW
Washington, DC 20036
(202) 457-0686

Los Angeles Times
Times-Mirror Square
Los Angeles, CA 90053
(213) 237-5000

The Miami Herald
1 Herald Plaza
Miami, FL 33132
(305) 350-2111

Mother Jones
1663 Mission Street, Suite 200
San Francisco, CA 94103
(415) 558-8881

The Nation
72 Fifth Avenue
New York, NY 10011
(212) 242-8400

The National Interest
1112 16th Street, NW, Suite 540
Washington, DC 20036
(202) 467-4884
(202) 467-0006 - FAX

National Journal
National Journal, Inc.
1730 M Street, NW
Washington, DC 20036
(202) 857-1400

National Review
150 East 35th Street
New York, NY 10016
(212) 679-7330

New Perspectives Quarterly
10951 West Pico Boulevard, 3rd Floor
Los Angeles, CA 90064
(310) 474-0011

The New Republic
1220 19th Street, NW
Suite 600
Washington, DC 20036
(202) 331-7494

New York
755 Second Avenue
New York, NY 10017-5998
(212) 880-0700

The New York Review of Books
250 West 57th Street
Room 1321
New York, NY 10107
(212) 757-8070

The New York Times
229 West 43rd Street
New York, NY 10036
(212) 556-1234

The New Yorker
20 West 43rd Street
New York, NY 10036
(212) 536-5400

Newsweek
444 Madison Avenue
New York, NY 10022
(212) 350-4000

Policy Review
214 Massachusetts Avenue, NE
Washington, DC 20002
(202) 546-4400

The Progressive
409 East Main Street
Madison, WI 53703
(608) 257-4626

Reader's Digest
Pleasantville, NY 10570
914-238-8585

Reason
3415 S. Sepulveda Boulevard
Suite 400
Los Angeles, CA 90034
(310) 391-2245

Roll Call
900 2nd Street, NE
Washington, DC 20002
(202) 289-4900

Rolling Stone
1290 Avenue of the Americas
New York, NY 10104-0298
(212) 484-1616

The Spectator
56 Dougherty Street
London WC1N 2LL
United Kingdom
44-71-405-1706

Time
Time-Life Building
Rockefeller Center
New York, NY 10020-1393
(212) 586-1212

USA Today
1000 Wilson Boulevard
Arlington, VA 22229
(703) 276-3400

U.S.News & World Report
2400 N Street, NW
Washington, DC 20037
(202) 955-2000

Utne Reader
1624 Harmon Place
Minneapolis, MN 55403
(612) 338-5040

The Wall Street Journal
200 Liberty Street
New York, NY 10281
(212) 416-2000

The Washington Monthly
1611 Connecticut Avenue, NW
Washington, DC 20009
(202) 462-0128

The Washington Post
1150 15th Street, NW
Washington, DC 20071
(202) 334-6000

The Washington Times
3600 New York Avenue, NE
Washington, DC 20002
(202) 636-3000

Syndicates

Associated Features, Inc.
P.O. Box 7099
Fairfax Station, VA 22039
(703) 764-0496

Creator's Syndicate
5777 West Century Boulevard
Suite 700
Los Angeles, CA 90045
(310) 337-7003

King Features Syndicate, Inc.
235 East 45th Street
New York, NY 10017
(212) 455-4000
(800) 526-5464

Los Angeles Times Syndicate
218 Spring Street
Los Angeles, CA 90012
(213) 237-7987

Newspaper Enterprise Association
200 Park Avenue
New York, NY 10166
(212) 692-3700

Scripps-Howard News Service
1090 Vermont Avenue, NW
Suite 1000
Washington, DC 20005
(202) 408-1484

Tribune Media Services
64 East Concord Street
Orlando, FL 32801
(407) 420-6200
(800) 322-3068

United Features Syndicate
200 Park Avenue
New York, NY 10166
(212) 692-3700
(800) 221-4816

Universal Press Syndicate
4900 Main Street
Kansas City, MO 64112
(816) 932-6600
(800) 255-6734

Washington Post Writers Group
1150 15th Street, NW
Washington, DC 20071
(202) 334-6375
(800) 879-9794

★ BIOGRAPHIES ★

Abelson, Alan. *Barron's.* "Up & Down Wall Street" Columnist. B. 1925, New York, NY. City College of New York, 1946, BS, English/Chemistry; U. Iowa, 1947, MA, Creative Writing. *New York Journal American*, reporter, 1949-56. *Barron's*, reporter, 1956-65; ed., 1965-present; "Up and Down Wall Street" columnist, 1981-present. NBC-TV, "News at Sunrise," bus. commentator.

Abramson, Jill. *The Wall Street Journal.* Deputy Washington Bureau Chief. Harvard, 1976, AB, History and Literature. *Time,* stringer, 1974-76; Boston bur. manager/reporter, 1976-77. Chernoff, Silver & Associates (political consultants), researcher and chief writer, 1978-79. NBC News Election Unit, researcher, 1979-81. *American Lawyer*, sr. writer, 1981-88. *Legal Times*, ed., 1986-88. *WSJ*, 1988-present. Co-author, *Where Are They Now: The Story of the Women of Harvard Law 1974* (1976).

Allen, Henry. *The Washington Post.* Reporter. B. 1941, Summit, NJ. Hamilton College, 1963. *The New Haven Register*, 1966. New York *Daily News*, 1966-70. AP Dow Jones, 1970. *WP*, 1970-present. Author of *Fool's Mercy* (1982).

Alter, Jonathan. *Newsweek.* Senior Writer and Media Critic. B. 1957, Chicago, IL. Harvard, 1979, History. *The Washington Monthly*, ed., writer, 1981-83. *Newsweek*, assoc. ed., news media writer, 1983-86; sr. writer, 1987-91; sr. ed., 1991-present.

Altman, Lawrence K., MD. *New York Times.* Medical Correspondent. B. 1937, Boston, MA. Harvard, 1958, Government; Tufts, 1962, MD. *Morbidity & Mortality Weekly Report*, ed., 1963-64. *New York Times*, medical corr., 1969-present. Author of *Who Goes First? The Story of Self-Experimentation in Medicine* (1987).

Anders, George. *The Wall Street Journal.* Senior Special Writer. B. 1957, Chicago, IL. Stanford, 1978, Economics. *WSJ*, sr. special writer., 1988-present.

Angier, Natalie. *The New York Times.* Science Reporter. B. 1958. Barnard College, English/Physics. *Discover*, staff writer, 1980-83. *Savvy*, sr. assoc. ed., 1983-84. *Time*, staff writer, 1984-86. NYU, adjunct prof., 1986-90. *NYT*, sci. reporter, 1990-present. Author of *Natural Obsessions: The Search for the Oncogene* (1988).

Apple, R.W., Jr. *The New York Times.* Washington Bureau Chief. B. 1934, Akron, OH. Columbia, 1961. US Army, 1957-59. *The Wall Street Journal*, reporter, 1959-61. NBC-TV News, writer and corr., 1961-63. *NYT*, metro staff, 1963-65; Saigon bur. chief, 1965-68; chief African corr., 1968-69; nat. pol. corr., 1970-76; London bur. chief, 1976-85; chief Washington corr., 1985-92; Washington bur. chief, 1992-present.

Applebome, Peter C. *The New York Times.* Atlanta Bureau Chief. B. 1949, New York, NY. Duke, 1971, History. Northwestern, 1974, MS, Journalism. *Ypsilanti* (MI) *Press*, reporter, 1975-76. *Corpus Christi Caller*, reporter, 1976-77. *Dallas Morning News*, reporter, ed., columnist, 1978-82. *Texas Monthly*, sr. ed., 1982-86. *NYT*, Houston bur., nat. corr., 1986-87; Houston bur. chief, 1987-88; Atlanta bur. chief, 1989-present.

Archibald, George. *The Washington Times.* Congressional Investigative Reporter. B. 1944, Newmarket, Suffolk, UK. Old Dominion U., 1967, BA, Pol. Sci. and History. *The Arizona Republic*, editorial writer and columnist, 1967-73. Cong. aide, 1970s. Dep. Asst. Sec. of Education, 1981-82. *WT*, nat. corr., 1982-93; congressional investigative reporter, 1992-present.

Asker, James R. *Aviation Week & Space Technology*. Senior Space Technology Editor. B. 1952, Louisville, KY. Rice, 1974, Policy Sciences; MIT, Knight Science Journalism Fellow, 1987-88. *The Houston Post*, sci. tech. and space reporter, 1974-88. Freelance, 1988-89. *Electronic Business*, man. ed., 1989. *AWST*, space tech. ed., 1989-present.

Asman, David. *The Wall Street Journal.* "America's Watch" and "Manager's Journal" Editor. B. 1954, Hollis, NY. Marlboro College, 1977, BA, Anthropology. *Prospect Magazine*, ed., 1978-80. *Manhattan Report on Economic Policy*, ed., 1980-82. Freelance, 1982-83. *The Wall Street Journal*, 1983-present. Author of *The Wall Street Journal on Managing* (1990).

Atkinson, Rick. *The Washington Post.* Berlin Correspondent. East Carolina U.; U. Chicago, English. *WP*, gen. assignment reporter, 1983-85; dep. nat. ed., 1985-87; investigative reporter, 1989-91; Berlin correspondent, 1993-present.

Atlas, Terry. *Chicago Tribune.* Chief Diplomatic Correspondent. B. 1952, Washington, DC. U. Rochester, BA, Economics and Pol. Sci. *Chicago Tribune*, energy reporter, 1978-83; Washington bur., 1983-present.

Auerbach, Stuart. *The Washington Post.* Financial Reporter. B. 1934, New York, NY. Williams College, 1957, BA, Pol. Sci. Pittsfield, MA *Berkshire Eagle*, reporter, suburban bur. chief, 1957-60; *The Miami Herald*, reporter, columnist, 1960-66. *WP*, reporter, 1966-69; sci. and medical reporter, 1969-76; Beirut bur., corr., 1977; legal corr., columnist, 1978-79; New Delhi, India, South Asia corr., 1979-82; financial corr., 1982-present.

Auletta, Ken. *The New Yorker.* Media Columnist. B. 1942, Brooklyn, NY. SUNY-Oswego, BA, History. Syracuse U., 1965, MA, Pol. Sci. New York *Daily News*, pol. columnist. *New York*, pol. columnist. *The Village Voice*, pol. columnist. *The New Yorker*, media columnist. Author of six books, including *Three Blind Mice: How the TV Networks Lost Their Way*.

Ayres, B. Drummond, Jr. *The New York Times.* Mid-Atlantic National Correspondent. B. 1934, Nassawadox, VA. Virginia Military Institute, 1957, BA, English; U. Virginia Law School, 1958-59; Columbia, 1962, MA, Journalism. *The Richmond Times-Dispatch*, copyreader and reporter, 1959-62. *The Washington Post*, copyreader and reporter, 1963-65. *NYT*, Washington bur., reporter, 1966; Saigon bur., corr., 1968-70; Kansas City bur. chief, 1970-73; Atlanta bur. chief, 1973-78; Washington bur. corr., 1978-85; "Washington Talk" page, ed., 1985-87; mid-Atlantic nat. corr., 1987-present.

Babcock, Charles R. *The Washington Post.* B. 1944, Pittsburgh, PA. Ohio Wesleyan, 1966, History/Journalism; Fletcher School of Law and Diplomacy, 1967. *Louisville Courier-Journal*, 1970-75. *WP*, 1976-present.

Bacon, Kenneth H. *The Wall Street Journal.* Assistant News Editor. B. 1944. Amherst College, 1966, BA; Columbia, 1968, MBA; MS, 1968, Journalism. *WSJ*, econ. reporter, 1969-75; Pentagon reporter, 1975-80; econ. reporter, 1980-83; econ./foreign policy ed., 1983-88; health/education reporter, 1988-90; banking reporter, 1990-93; global financial reporter, 1993-present.

Baker, Russell. *The New York Times.* "Observer" Columnist. B. 1925, Loudoun County, VA. Johns Hopkins, 1947, BA, Eng. Lit. Baltimore *Sun*, reporter, 1947-54. *NYT*, Washington reporter, 1954-62; "Observer" columnist, 1962-present. Author of numerous books, most recently, *There's a Country in My Cellar* (1990).

Balz, Dan. *The Washington Post.* Chief Political Reporter. B. Freeport, IL. U. Illinois, BS; MS, Journalism. *National Journal*, assoc. ed. *The Philadelphia Inquirer*, reporter. *WP*, part-time asst. ed., 1974-77; asst. ed., 1978; dep. nat. ed., 1979; Austin, TX, nat. news corr., 1981-85; nat. ed., 1985-90; political reporter, 1990-91; chief political reporter, 1991-present.

Bangsberg, P.T. *The Journal of Commerce.* East Asia Correspondent. B. 1942, Syracuse, NY. TV/Radio, Buffalo, news writer, sub-ed., producer, 1959-60. UPI, sub-ed., ed., 1960-63. ABC Radio News (NY), sub-ed., 1963-65. *The Daily Telegraph* (London), asst. night ed., 1969-72. *The Birmingham Post* (UK), asst. ed., chief sub-ed., 1972-74. *Birmingham Evening Mail* (UK), man. ed., 1974-81. *South China Morning Post* (Hong Kong), asst. ed., 1981-83. *JC*, East Asia corr., 1984-present.

Barber, Lionel. *Financial Times.* Brussels Bureau Chief. B. 1955, London, UK. St. Edmunds Hall (Oxford), 1978, German/Modern History. *The Scotsman*, 1978-81. *The Sunday Times*, bus. corr., 1981-85. *Financial Times*, financial corr., 1985; Washington corr., 1986-92; Brussels bur. chief, European Community corr., 1993-present.

Barnes, Fred. *The New Republic.* Senior Editor. B. 1943, West Point, NY. U. Virginia, 1965, BA, History. *The Charlotte News & Courier*, reporter, 1965-67. *The Washington Star*, Supreme Court, White House reporter, 1967-79. Baltimore *Sun*, nat. pol. corr., 1979-85. "The McLaughlin Group," panelist, current. *Reader's Digest*, roving ed., current. *TNR*, sr. ed., 1985-present.

Barnes, James A. *National Journal.* Political Correspondent. Washington and Lee, 1978, BA, Russian Area Studies. American Enterprise Institute, research assoc. *The Christian Science Monitor, Washington Post*, contributor. Chief speechwriter for Treasury Sec. James Baker. *NJ*, pol. corr., 1987-present.

Barone, Michael. *U.S.News & World Report.* Senior Writer. B. 1944, Highland Park, MI. Harvard, 1966; Yale Law, 1969. US Court of Appeals (6th Circuit), law clerk, 1969-71. Peter D. Hart Research, vice president, 1974-81. *The Washington Post*, ed. page staff, 1982-89. *USNWR*, sr. writer, 1989-present. Co-author of bi-annual *The Almanac of American Politics*.

Barrett, Paul. *The Wall Street Journal.* Supreme Court Correspondent. B. 1961, New York, NY. Harvard, 1983, American History. *WSJ*, Philadelphia bur., reporter, 1987-88; Washington, Justice Dept. reporter; Supreme Court corr., 1991-present.

Bartley, Robert L. *The Wall Street Journal.* Editor. B. 1937, Marshall, MN. Iowa St., BA, Journalism; U. Wisconsin, MA, Pol. Sci. US Army, 1960. *Grinnell* (IA) *Herald-Register*, reporter, 1959-60. *WSJ*, staff reporter, 1962-64; ed. page staff, 1964-71; editorial page ed., 1972-79; Ed., 1979-present.

Begley, Sharon. *Newsweek.* Senior Writer. Yale, BA. *Newsweek*, editorial asst. in science, 1977-79; sr. editorial asst., 1979; asst. ed., 1979-80; assoc. ed., 1980-83; general ed., 1983-90; sr. writer, 1990-present.

Bering-Jensen, Henrik. *Insight.* Writer. B. 1951, Copenhagen, Denmark. Oxford, MA, Eng. Lit.; Stanford, International Fellow, 1981-82. Danish newspa pers, reviewer, 1977-85. *Insight*, writer, 1985-present.

Berke, Richard L. *The New York Times.* National Political Correspondent. B. 1958. U. Michigan, 1980, BS, Pol. Sci.; Columbia, 1981, MS, Journalism. Baltimore *Sun*, reporter, 1981-86. *NYT*, reporter, 1986-present.

Bernstein, Aaron. *BusinessWeek.* Labor Editor. UC-Santa Cruz, BA. UPI, London corr. *Forbes*, reporter. *BW*, editorial staff, 1983-85; labor ed., 1985-present.

Berry, John M. *The Washington Post.* Staff Writer. Wesleyan, BA. *Providence* (RI) *Journal*, reporter. *BusinessWeek*, reporter. *Time*, nat. econ. corr. McGraw-Hill News Service, corr. *Forbes*, Washington bur. chief. *WP*, financial staff writer, 1979-present.

Bethell, Tom. *The American Spectator.* Washington Editor. B. London, UK. Oxford, 1962, Psychology, Philosophy, Physiology. *New Orleans*, man. ed. *The Washington Monthly*, ed. *TAS*, contrib. ed., to 1988; Washington ed., 1988-present. Author, most recently of *The Electric Windmill* (1988).

Beyer, Lisa. *Time.* Jerusalem Bureau Chief. B. 1961, Lafayette, LA. U. Texas, 1983, Journalism. *Asiaweek*, Singapore, sr. corr., 1984-88. *Time*, staff writer; assoc. ed.; Jerusalem bur. chief, 1988-present.

Birnbaum, Jeffrey H. *The Wall Street Journal.* Political Reporter. B. 1956, Scranton, PA. U. Pennsylvania, 1977, BA. AP, stringer, 1977. *The Miami Herald*, reporter, 1977-79. *WSJ*, retail reporter, 1979-82; Washington bur., cong. reporter, 1982-present. Author of several books, including *The Lobbyist* (1992).

Biskupic, Joan. *The Washington Post.* Supreme Court Reporter. B. 1956, Chicago, IL. Marquette, 1978, BA; U. Oklahoma, 1986, MA; Georgetown, 1993, JD. *Tulsa Tribune*, State Capital bur. chief and reporter, 1985-87; Washington corr., 1987-88. *Congressional Quarterly*, legal affairs reporter, 1989-92. *WP*, Supreme Court reporter, 1992-present.

Bishop, Jerry. *The Wall Street Journal.* Deputy News Editor. B. Dalhart, TX. U. Texas, 1952, BA, Journalism. *WSJ*, copyreader, 1955-57; reporter, 1957-59; Washington reporter, 1959-60; science and medicine reporter, dep. news ed., 1960-present. Co-author of *Genome* (1990).

Blumenthal, Sidney. *The New Yorker.* Washington Editor. B. 1948, Chicago, IL. Brandeis, AB, 1969. "The Today Show" (NBC), pol. commentator, 1984. *The New Republic*, nat. pol. corr., 1983-85. *The Washington Post*, staff writer, 1985-89. *Vanity Fair*, contrib. ed., 1992. *TNR*, sr. ed., 1990-92. *The New Yorker*, Washington ed., 1992-present. Author of five books, most recently, *Pledging Allegiance: The Last Campaign of the Cold War* (1990).

Bogert, Carroll R. *Newsweek.* Acting Foreign Editor. B. 1961, Chicago, IL. Harvard, 1984, Social Studies. *Newsweek*, Beijing bur., stringer, 1986-87; Southeast Asia reporter, 1987-88; Moscow reporter, 1989-92; Moscow bur. chief, 1992-present. Author of *USSR: Collapse of an Empire.*

Boo, Katherine. *The Washington Post.* Assistant Editor. Columbia, Philosophy/Literature. Washington *City Paper. The Washington Monthly*. *WP*, Outlook section, asst. ed., 1992-present.

Boot, Max A. *The Christian Science Monitor.* Writer/Editor. B. 1969, Moscow, Russia. UC-Berkeley, 1991, History; Yale, 1992, MA, History. *The Daily Californian*, reporter/columnist, 1987-91. *CSM*, writer/ed., 1991-present.

Borger, Gloria. *U.S.News & World Report.* Assistant Managing Editor. Colgate,

1974. *The Washington Star*, 1975-78. *Newsweek*, chief congressional corr., 1978-86. *USNWR*, asst. man. ed., 1986-present.

Bovard, James. Freelance Writer. B. 1956, Ames, IA. Virginia Tech, 1976-78, General Arts and Sciences. Cato Institute and Heritage Foundation, policy studies. *The Wall Street Journal*, *The New York Times*, *The New Republic*, *Detroit News*, freelance contrib.

Branigin, William. *The Washington Post*. Southeast Asia Correspondent. B. Wiesbaden, West Germany. Ohio U., BS, Journalism. McGraw-Hill World News, Middle East corr. UPI, Paris corr. *The Washington Post*, Middle East corr., 1976-79; asst. foreign ed., 1979-81; Southeast Asia bur. chief, 1981-86; Central America corr., 1986-90; Southeast Asia corr., 1990-present.

Brauchli, Marcus W. *The Wall Street Journal*. Asia Correspondent. B. 1961, Colorado. Columbia, 1983. *WSJ*, Asia corr.

Brimelow, Peter. *Forbes*. Senior Editor. B. 1947, United Kingdom. U. Sussex (UK), 1970, BA, History; Stanford, 1972, MBA. Richardson Securities, Winnipeg, investment analyst, 1972-73. *Financial Post*, Toronto bur., staff writer, 1973-76. *Maclean's*, bus. ed., 1976-78. *Financial Post*, contrib. ed., 1979-80. Economic counsel for Sen. Orrin Hatch [R-UT], 1979-81. *Barron's*, assoc. ed., 1981-83. *Fortune*, assoc. ed., 1983-84. *Barron's*, contrib. ed., 1984-86. *Forbes*, sr. ed., 1986-present. *National Review*, contrib. ed., 1993-present. *The Times* (London), columnist, 1986-present. *Influence Magazine*, Toronto, contrib. ed., 1984-present. Author of several books, including *The Patriot Game: Canada and the Canadian Question Revisited* (1986).

Brittan, Samuel. *Financial Times*. Assistant Editor. B. 1933, London, UK. Jesus College (Cambridge), Economics. *Financial Times*, 1955-61. *The Observer*, econ. ed., 1961-64. Dept. of Economic Affairs, adviser, 1965. *FT*, principal econ. commentator, 1966-present; asst. ed., 1978-present. Nuffield College, research fellow, 1972-74; visiting fellow, 1974-82. U. Chicago School of Law, visiting prof., 1978. U. Warwick, prof. of politics, 1987-92. Author of numerous books, including *Capitalism with a Human Face* (1994).

Broad, William J. *The New York Times*. Science Reporter. B. 1951, Milwaukee, WI. Webster College (St. Louis), 1973; U. Wisconsin, 1977, MA. Industry Research Program, reporter, 1977-78; concurrently History of Science Dept., teaching asst., Anesthesiology Dept., research asst., 1977-78. *Science*, reporter, 1978-82. *NYT*, sci. reporter, 1983-present.

Broder, David S. *The Washington Post*. National Political Correspondent and Columnist. B. Chicago Heights, IL. U. Chicago, 1947, BA, Pol. Sci.; 1951, MA. *The Daily Pantagraph*, reporter, 1953-55. *Congressional Quarterly*, pol. reporter, 1955-60. *The Washington Star*, pol. reporter, 1960-65. *The New York Times*, pol. reporter, 1965-66. *The Washington Post*, pol. reporter, assoc. ed., nat. pol. corr., and columnist, 1966-present. Author of several books, most recently (with Bob Woodward), *The Man Who Would Be President: Dan Quayle* (1992).

Broder, John. *Los Angeles Times*. Staff Writer. B. 1952. U. Michigan, 1974, BA, Religion/Philosophy; MA, 1978, Journalism. *Cleveland Press*, photographer, 1973. *Kettering-Oakwood* (OH) *Journal-Times*, photographer, 1975-76. *Racine Journal-Times*, intern, 1977. *Detroit News*, photo ed., 1978; Lansing bur., staff writer, 1979-82; staff writer, 1982-85. *LAT*, bus. writer, 1985-87; Washington bur. staff writer, 1987-present.

Bronner, Ethan. *The Boston Globe*. Middle East Correspondent. B. 1954, New York, NY. Wesleyan, 1976, College of Letters; Columbia, 1980, MS, Journalism. Reuters, Madrid corr., 1981-82; Brussels corr., 1982-83; Jerusalem bur. chief, 1983-85. *BG*, urban reporter, 1985-87; legal affairs and Supreme Court corr., 1987-91; Middle East corr., 1991-present. Author of *Battle for Justice: How the Bork Nomination Shook America* (1989).

Brooke, James B. *The New York Times*. Brazil Bureau Chief. B. 1955, New York, NY. Yale, 1977, BA, Latin American Studies. Asst. to columnist James Reston, 1978-80. Stringer from South America, 1980-81, *The Miami Herald*, South America corr., 1982-84. *The New York Times*, metro reporter, 1984-86; West Africa bur. chief, 1986-89; Brazil bur. chief, 1989-present.

Browne, Malcolm W. *The New York Times*. Science Reporter. B. 1931, New York, NY. Swarthmore. AP, Vietnam bur. chief, 1961-65. ABC television, chief Indochina corr., 1965-66. *NYT*, 1968-present. Author, *The New Face of War* (1986) and autobiography *Muddy Boots and Read Socks* (1993).

Brownstein, Ronald. *Los Angeles Times*. National Political Correspondent. B. 1958, New York, NY. SUNY-Binghamton, 1979, BA, English Lit. Senior staff writer for Ralph Nader, 1979-83. *National Journal*, White House corr., 1983-87; West Coast corr., 1987-89. *Los Angeles Times Magazine*, contrib. ed., 1987-89. *LAT*, nat. pol. corr., 1989-present.

Buchanan, Patrick J. Tribune Media Services. Columnist. B. 1938, Washington, DC. Georgetown, 1961, AB, English; Columbia, 1962, MS, Journalism. *St. Louis Globe Democrat*, editorial writer, 1962-64; asst. editorial ed., 1964-66. Asst. to Richard Nixon, 1966-69. Speechwriter, special asst. to President Nixon, 1969-73. Consultant to Presidents Nixon and Gerald Ford, 1973-74. New York Times Special Features, syndicated columnist, 1974-78. Chicago Tribune-New York Daily News Syndicate, 1978-85. White House Dir. of Communications, 1985-87. "Crossfire" (CNN), co-host, 1982-present. Candidate for Republican Presidential nomination, 1992. Author of three books, including *Right From the Beginning* (1988).

Buchwald, Art. Los Angeles Times Syndicate. Columnist. B. 1925, Mt. Vernon, NY. *Variety*, Paris corr., 1948. *The New York Herald Tribune*, editorial staff, 1949-62. Los Angeles Times Syndicate, columnist, 1962-present. Author of numerous books, including, *Things I Don't Remember* (1987).

Buckley, William F., Jr. *National Review*. President. B. 1925, New York, NY. Yale, 1950, BA, Pol. Sci./Economics/History. Yale, asst. instructor, 1947-51. *American Mercury*, assoc. ed., 1952-55. UPI, columnist, 1962-present. "Firing Line" (PBS), host, 1966-present. *NR*, founder/ed.-in-chief/president, 1955-present. Author of 33 books, most recently, *Happy Days Were Here Again* (1993).

Burns, John. *The New York Times*. Toronto Bureau Chief. B. 1944, Nottingham, UK. McGill; Harvard, 1980-81, Russian; Cambridge, 1984, Chinese. *The Ottawa Citizen*. *The Toronto Globe and Mail*, reporter; Parliamentary corr., 1969-71; China corr., 1971-75. *NYT*, metro reporter, 1975; South Africa corr., 1976-81; Moscow bur. chief, 1981-84; Peking bur. chief, expelled 1986; Toronto bur. chief, 1986-present.

Butler, Steven. *U.S.News & World Report*. Tokyo Bureau Chief. B. 1951, New Hampshire. Sarah Lawrence, 1973; Columbia, 1976, MA; 1980, PhD. *Financial Times*, Seoul corr., 1984-86; Southeast Asia corr., 1986-87; energy corr., 1988-90; Tokyo corr., 1991-92. *USNWR*, Tokyo bur. chief, 1993-present.

Bylinsky, Gene. *Fortune.* Board of Editors. B. Belgrade, Yugoslavia. Louisiana State, Journalism. US Army. Newhouse papers, science reporter. *The Wall Street Journal*, science reporter. *Fortune*, assoc. ed., 1966-85; Board of Editors, 1985-present. Author of two books, including *Mood Control* (1978).

Byrne, John A. *BusinessWeek.* Senior Writer. William Paterson College (NJ), 1975, BA, Pol. Sci./English; U. Missouri, MA, Journalism. *Fairchild Publications*, London bur. chief, 1979-81. *Forbes*, Washington bur., assoc. ed., 1981-84. *BW*, management dept. ed., 1984-88; assoc. ed., sr. writer, 1988-present. Author of several books, most recently, *The Whiz Kids: Ten Founding Fathers of American Business and the Legacy They Left Us* (1993).

Byron, Christopher. *New York.* "Bottom Line" Columnist. Yale; Columbia Law. *Time*, foreign corr., London, Bonn; New York ed. Time Inc., "TV Cable Week," sr. ed., 1983. Citicorp Capital Markets Training Program, 1984. *Forbes*, asst. man. ed., law, tech., and annual industry survey, 1983-85. *NY*, "Bottom Line" columnist, 1989-present. Author of *The Fanciest Dive* (1984).

Cannon, Lou. *The Washington Post.* Reporter. B. 1933, New York, NY. Various Nevada and California newspapers, reporter. Ridder Publications, Washington bur., 1969-72. *The Washington Post*, pol. reporter, 1972-76; Los Angeles corr., 1977-80; presidential campaign corr., 1980; White House corr., 1980-89; Los Angeles corr., 1989-present. Author of several books, including *President Reagan: The Role of a Lifetime* (1991).

Chapman, Stephen. *Chicago Tribune.* Columnist. B. 1954, Brady, TX. Harvard, 1976, History. Freelance, 1976-78. *The New Republic*, assoc. ed./staff writer, 1978-81. *CT*, columnist/editorial writer, 1981-present.

Chase, Marilyn. *The Wall Street Journal.* Reporter. B. Los Angeles, CA. Stanford, 1971, AB, English; UC-Berkeley, 1973, MS, Journalism. *Arlington* (VA) *News*, reporter, 1974-75. *Arlington Journal*, reporter, 1975-76. *The New York Times*, stringer, 1976-78. *WSJ*, San Francisco reporter, 1978-present.

Chen, Edwin. *Los Angeles Times.* Science Writer. B. 1948, Nanking, China. U. South Carolina, 1970, BA, Journalism; Harvard (Nieman Fellowship), 1984-85. *LAT*, San Diego County Edition staff writer, 1979-81; legal affairs writer, 1982-85; asst. metro ed., 1985-89; Washington bur., science writer, 1989-present. Author, *PBB: An American Tragedy*.

Claiborne, William. *The Washington Post.* National Correspondent. B. 1936, New York, NY. Hobart College, 1959, English. *Rochester Democrat & Chronicle*, reporter, 1959-66. Long Island *Suffolk Sun*, city ed., 1966-69. *WP*, nat. corr., 1969-74; New York City bur. chief, 1974-77; Jerusalem, corr., 1978-82; New Delhi, corr., 1982-85; Johannesburg, corr., 1986-90; Toronto, corr., 1990-92; nat. corr., 1992-present.

Clift, Eleanor. *Newsweek.* White House Correspondent. B. 1940. Brooklyn, NY. Hofstra; Hunter. *Newsweek*, researcher, 1963-65; Atlanta office man., 1965-72; Atlanta corr., 1972-76; White House corr., 1976 85. *Los Angeles Times*, White House corr., 1985-86. *Newsweek*, Washington corr., 1986-92; White House corr., 1992-present.

Clymer, Adam. *The New York Times.* Chief Congressional Correspondent. B. 1937, New York, NY. Harvard, 1958, History. Norfolk *Virginian-Pilot*, 1960-62. Baltimore *Sun*, metro/cong. reporter, 1963; Moscow corr., 1964-65; Supreme Court corr., 1965-67; New Delhi bur., reporter, 1967-70; pol. reporter, 1970-76. New York *Daily News*, pol. reporter, 1977-83; polling ed., 1983-90; pol. ed., 1987-89; sr. ed., 1990; chief cong. corr., 1991-present.

Cohen, Richard. *The Washington Post.* Columnist. B. 1941, New York, NY. NYU, 1967; Columbia, 1968, MS, Journalism. UPI, New York staff, 1967-68; education and Maryland legislative corr., 1968-76. *The Washington Post*, Washington Post Writers Group, columnist, 1976-present. Co-author (with Jules Witcover) of *A Heartbeat Away—The Investigation and Resignation of Spiro T. Agnew*.

Cohen, Richard E. *National Journal.* Correspondent. B. 1948, Northampton, MA. Brown, 1969, History; Georgetown, 1972, JD. *NJ*, corr., 1973-present. Author of *Washington at Work: Back Rooms and Clean Air* (1992).

Coll, Steve. *The Washington Post.* Investigative and Projects Correspondent. B. 1958, Washington, DC. Occidental, 1980, English and History. *California*, contrib. ed., 1982-84. *Inc.*, contrib. ed., 1984-85. *WP*, feature writer, 1985-86; financial corr., 1987-89; South Asia bur. chief, 1989-92; London-based intl. projects corr., 1992-present. Author of four books, most recently, *On the Grand Trunk Road* (1994).

Covault, Craig. *Aviation Week & Space Technology.* Paris Bureau Chief. B. 1949, Dayton OH. Bowling Green State, 1971, BS, Journalism. *Urbana Citizen*, writer, 1971-72. *AWST*, sr. space ed., 1972-92, Paris bur. chief, 1992-present.

Dahlburg, John-Thor. *Los Angeles Times.* Moscow Correspondent. B. 1953, Orange, NJ. Washington and Lee, 1975, BA, Politics and Journalism. *Time*, Paris bur. intern, 1973. *Boca Raton News*, reporter/ed., 1980-81. *Elrop Magazine*, ed., 1983-84. AP, corr. and ed., 1981-90. *LAT*, Moscow corr., 1990-present.

de Briganti, Giovanni. *Defense News.* European Editor. B. 1954, Pisa, Italy. Institut d'Etudes Politiques, Paris. *Defense Edition*, ed. and pub., 1975-81. *Defence & Armament*, editor-in-chief, 1981-83. *Armed Forces Journal International*, corr., 1983-85. *DN*, European ed., 1985-present.

Dempsey, Judy. *Financial Times.* Berlin Correspondent. B. 1956, Dublin, Ireland. Trinity College (Dublin), History and Pol. Sci. BBC, analyst, broadcaster, 1983-85. *Irish Times*, East European corr., 1985-87. *FT*, Vienna corr., 1987-90; East European corr., 1990-92; Berlin corr., 1992-present. Contributor to several books.

Denniston, Lyle W. Baltimore *Sun.* Supreme Court Reporter. U. Nebraska, 1955, BA; Georgetown, 1957, MA, History and Pol. Sci. *Nebraska City News-Press*, reporter, 1948-51. *Lincoln Journal*, reporter, 1951-55. *The Wall Street Journal*, Washington bur., 1957-60. Prentice-Hall Inc., ed., law newsletters, 1960-63. *The Washington Star*, Supreme Court reporter, 1963-81. Baltimore *Sun*, Washington bur., 1981-present. Author of *The Reporter and The Law: Techniques of Covering the Courts* (1980).

Dentzer, Susan. *U.S.News & World Report.* Chief Economics Correspondent. B. 1955, Philadelphia, PA. Dartmouth, 1977, English Literature; Harvard, 1986-87, Nieman fellowship. *The Southampton Press/Hampton Chronicle-News*, reporter, 1977-78. *Newsweek*, sr. writer, 1979-87. *USNWR*, sr. writer/chief econ. corr., 1987-present.

Devroy, Ann. *The Washington Post.* White House Correspondent. U. Wisconsin, 1971, Journalism/Pol. Sci. Gannett News Service, political reporter, 1977-80; White House corr., 1981-85. *WP*, pol. ed. and White House corr., 1985-present.

Dewar, Helen. *The Washington Post.* National Staff Reporter. B. 1936, Stockton, CA. Stanford, BA, Pol. Sci. *The*

Northern Virginia Sun, reporter. *WP*, metro reporter, 1961-77; nat. staff reporter, 1977-present.

Diamond, Edwin. *New York*. Contributing Editor. B. 1925, Chicago, IL. U. Chicago, 1947, BA, Pol. Sci.; 1949, MA. Wire services reporter, Washington and Chicago, 1953-57. *Newsweek*, sr. ed., 1958-70. Television commentator, Washington, 1970-77; Boston, 1980-83. New York *Daily News*, assoc. ed., 1980-81. MIT, visiting prof., Pol. Sci., 1971-85. NYU, prof., Journalism, 1985-present. *New York*, contrib. ed., 1970-77, 1985-present. Author of several books, most recently, *Behind The Times: Inside the New York Times* (1994).

Diamond, Jared. *Discover*. Contributing Editor. B. 1937, Boston, MA. Harvard, 1958, biochemical sciences; Cambridge, 1961, PhD. UCLA Medical School, prof. of physiology, 1968-present. *Natural History*, columnist, 1988-present. *Discover*, contrib. ed., 1984-present. Author of *The Third Chimpanzee* (1992).

Dionne, Eugene J. *The Washington Post*. Editorial Page Writer. B. 1952, Boston, MA. Harvard, 1973, BA; Oxford, 1982, PhD, Political Sociology (Rhodes Scholar). *The New York Times*, metro reporter, 1977-80; Albany bur. chief, 1982; Paris corr., 1983-84; Rome bur. chief, 1984-86; chief nat. pol. corr., 1986-89. *WP*, nat. pol. reporter, weekly op-ed column, 1990-present. Author of *Why Americans Hate Politics* (1991).

Dobbs, Michael. *The Washington Post*. Foreign Correspondent. B. 1950, Belfast, Northern Ireland. U. York (UK), 1972, BA, Economics; Journalism School at Cardiff, Wales, 1973. *Hindustan Times*, 1974. Reuters, London, Rome corr., 1974-75. *WP*, special corr. in Yugoslavia, 1979-80; Eastern European corr., 1980-82; Paris corr., 1983-87; Moscow bur. chief, 1988-93; on leave, writing a book, 1993-present.

Dobrzynski, Judith H. *Business Week*. Senior Editor. B. 1949, Rochester, NY. Syracuse U., 1971, BS, Journalism. McGraw-Hill, Inc., San Francisco bur., 1973-75; New York bur., 1975-76. McGraw-Hill World News, Washington bur., corr. for *BW* and several other McGraw-Hill publications, 1976-79. *BW*, London bur., corr., 1979-83; New York bur., Corporate Strategies ed., 1983-85; assoc. ed., 1985-88; sr. writer, 1988-91; sr. ed., 1991-present.

Donlan, Thomas G. *Barron's*. Editorial Page Editor. B. 1945, New York, NY. Hamilton, 1967, English Literature; Indiana U., 1968, MA, English Literature; Princeton, 1978-79, Sloan Foundation Economic Fellowship. *Bergen* (NJ) *Record*, reporter, 1969-74. AP, New Jersey, reporter, 1974-78. *Barron's*, assoc. ed., 1979-81; Washington ed., 1981-91; editorial page ed., 1992-present. Author of *Supertech: How America Can Win the Technology Race* (1991).

Donohoe, Cathryn. *The Washington Times*. Reporter. B. Bronx, NY. Middlebury, 1958, American literature; Columbia, graduate study in Russian literature; American U., 1983-84, Journalism studies. Radio Liberty, New York, research and policy coordinator, 1963-74. Freelance, 1977-84. *The Potomac Almanac* (MD), reporter, 1985. *WT*, reporter, 1985-present.

Dornbusch, Rudi. *Business Week*. Economics Columnist. B. 1942. U. Geneva (Switzerland), 1966, Pol. Sci.; U. Chicago, 1971, PhD, Economics. U. Rochester, prof., 1972-73. U. Geneva, prof., 1974-75. U. Chicago, prof. of econ., 1975-present. *BW*, econ. columnist. National Bureau of Economic Research, research assoc. Institute for International Economics, advisory committee. Author of numerous books, including *Exchange Rates and Inflation* (1988).

Dowd, Ann Reilly. *Fortune*. Board of Editors. Smith; Northwestern, MS, Journalism. Sen. Larry Pressler [R-SD], press secretary. *Dun's Business Monthly*, sr. ed., 1983; *Fortune*, assoc. ed., Board of Editors, 1983-present.

Dowd, Maureen. *The New York Times*. Washington Reporter. B. 1952, Washington, DC. Catholic U., 1973, Eng. Lit. *The Washington Star*, editorial asst., sports columnist, metro reporter, feature writer, 1973-81. *Time*, corr., writer, 1981-83. *NYT*, metro reporter, 1983-86; DC reporter, 1986-present.

Drogin, Bob. *Los Angeles Times*. Johannesburg Bureau Chief. B. 1952, Jersey City, NJ. Oberlin, 1973, Asian Studies. Columbia, 1976, MS, Journalism. *The Lorain* (OH) *Journal*, reporter, 1973. United Nations Children's Fund, Indonesia, program assoc., 1973-75. *The Charlotte Observer*, reporter, 1977-80. UN Children's Fund, Cambodia, program officer, 1980. *The Philadelphia Inquirer*, reporter, 1981-83. *LAT*, staff writer, 1983-89; Manila bur. chief, 1989-93; Johannesburg bur. chief, 1993-present.

Easterbrook, Gregg. *The Atlantic*. Contributing Editor. *Newsweek*. Contributing Editor. B. 1953, Buffalo, NY. Colorado College, 1976, Pol. Sci.; Northwestern, 1977, MS, Journalism. The *Washington Monthly*, ed., 1979-81; contrib. ed., 1981-present. *The Atlantic*, nat. corr., 1981-86; contrib. ed., 1987-present. *Newsweek*, contrib. ed., 1986-present. Author three books, most recently, *A Moment on Earth* (1994).

Edsall, Thomas Byrne. *The Washington Post*. Political Reporter. B. 1941, Cambridge, MA. Boston U., 1966, Pol. Sci. *Providence* (RI) *Journal*, 1965. VISTA volunteer, 1966-67. Baltimore *Sun*, 1967-74; cong. corr., 1974-81. *WP*, pol. reporter, 1981-present.

Egan, Jack. *U.S.News & World Report*. Assistant Managing Editor. *Washington Post*, bus. writer, New York bur. corr. *New York*, bus. and investment columnist, 1973-84. *Personal Investor*, ed. and founder, 1984-85. *USNWR*, personal finance ed., 1985-93; asst. man. ed., 1993-present.

Egan, Timothy. *The New York Times*. Seattle Bureau Chief. B. 1954. U. Washington, 1980, Communications. *Seattle Times*. *Seattle Post-Intelligencer*. *NYT*, Seattle bur. chief, current. Author of *The Good Rain* (1990) and *Breaking Blue* (1992).

Elliott, Stuart. *The New York Times*. Advertising Columnist. B. 1952, Brooklyn, NY. Northwestern, 1973, Journalism; 1974, Journalism. Rochester, NY *Times-Union*, 1974-79. *Detroit Free Press*, marketing reporter, 1979-82. *Advertising Age*, New York bur., 1982-87. *Investment Dealer's Digest*, exec. ed., 1987. Gannett News Service, Washington bur., bus. writer, 1988. *USA Today*, New York bur., advertising, 1988-91. *NYT*, advertising columnist, 1991-present.

Elmer-DeWitt, Philip. *Time*. Associate Editor. B. 1949, Boston, MA. Oberlin, 1973, BA, English. McGraw-Hill, project ed., 1973-74. *Academic Press*, production ed., 1975-78. Freelance, 1978-79. *Time*, reporter, researcher, 1979-83; staff writer, 1983-90; assoc. ed., 1990-present.

Evans, Rowland, Jr. Creators Syndicate. "Inside Report" columnist with Robert D. Novak. B. 1921, White Marsh, PA. Yale, 1943, English. US Marines, Pacific theater, 1942-44. *Philadelphia Bulletin*, 1944-45. AP, Washington bur., 1945-55. *New York Herald Tribune*, Washington corr., 1955-63. "Inside Report" columnist with Robert D. Novak, 1963-present. *Reader's Digest*, roving ed., 1980-present. "Evans and Novak" (CNN), co-host. Co-author of several books, including (with Robert D. Novak), *The Reagan Revolution* (1981).

Fabrikant, Geraldine. *The New York Times.* Business Reporter. B. 1943, New York, NY. U. Wisconsin; Brandeis, 1964. Film ed., 1966-72. Freelance, 1972-76. *The Hollywood Reporter*, reporter, 1976-78. *Variety*, reporter, 1978-81. *Business-Week*, media ed., 1981-85. *NYT*, bus. reporter, 1985-present.

Fallows, James. *The Atlantic.* Washington Editor. B. 1949, Philadelphia, PA. Harvard, 1970, American History and Lit.; Queen's College (Oxford), 1972, Economic Development. *The Washington Monthly*, staff ed., 1972-74. *Texas Monthly*, assoc. ed., 1974-76. Speechwriter for President Jimmy Carter, 1976-78. *The Atlantic*, Washington ed., 1979-present. "Morning Edition" (NPR), commentator, 1987-present. Author of several books, including *More Like Us* (1989).

Farhi, Paul. *The Washington Post.* Reporter. B. 1958, Brooklyn, NY. UCLA, 1979, Communications. *Oceanside* (CA) *Blade-Tribune*, reporter, 1979-80. *Adweek Magazine*, reporter/ed., 1980-84. *San Francisco Examiner*, reporter, 1985-88. *WP*, reporter, 1988-present.

Farrell, Christopher John. *Business Week.* Economics Editor. B. 1953, Bethesda, MD. Stanford, 1976, History; London School of Economics, 1981. Janzway Research & Publishing, newsletter ed., 1980-81. "Business Times" (cable TV show), finance ed., 1982-85. "Business Times" (radio show), host/ed., 1984-85. "Sound Money" (nationally syndicated radio show), regular commentator, 1985-present. *BW*, ed., 1985-present.

Ferguson, Tim. W. *The Wall Street Journal.* Columnist. B. 1955, Santa Ana, CA. Stanford, 1977, Economics. *Orange County Register*, reporter, ed., 1977-83. *WSJ*, editorial features ed., "Business World" columnist, 1983-present.

Fialka, John J. *The Wall Street Journal.* National Security Reporter. B. 1938, New Ulm, MN. Loras College, 1960, BA; Columbia, 1962, MS, Journalism; Georgetown, JD, 1965. Nat. Petroleum Refiners Assoc., 1962-65. Baltimore *Sun*, 1965-67. *The Washington Star*, 1967-81. *WSJ*, reporter, 1981-present.

Fields, Suzanne. *The Washington Times.* Columnist. B. 1936, Washington, DC. George Washington U., 1957, BA, English Lit.; 1964, MA, Catholic U., 1970, PhD. *World Week*, staff writer, 1957. Freelance, 1965-73. *Innovations*, ed., 1973-84. *Vogue*, columnist, 1980-81. Los Angeles Times Syndicate, columnist, 1988-present. *WT*, columnist, 1984-present. Author of *Like Father, Like Daughter* (1983).

Fineman, Howard. *Newsweek.* Chief Political Correspondent. B. Pittsburgh, PA. Colgate, 1971, AB; Columbia, 1973, MS, Journalism; U. Louisville Law School, 1975-77; Georgetown Law School, 1978-80. *Louisville Courier-Journal*, 1973-77; Washington bur., 1977-80. *Newsweek*, pol. corr., 1980-present.

Fineman, Mark. *Los Angeles Times.* Nicosia Bureau Chief. B. 1952, Chicago, IL. Syracuse, 1974, BA, Journalism and Philosophy. *Chicago Sun-Times*, staff writer, 1974-78. *Allentown Call-Chronicle*, staff writer, 1978-80. *The Philadelphia Inquirer*, Asia corr., 1981-86. *LAT*, Manila bur. chief, 1986-88; New Delhi bur. chief, 1988-92; Nicosia bur. chief, 1992-present.

Finnegan, Philip. *Defense News.* Staff Writer. B. 1953, Omaha, NE. Carleton College, 1976, Modern European History; Stanford, 1977, MA, History; American U., 1991, MA, Economics. *Time*, North African corr., 1983-85. *U.S.News & World Report*, Central American corr., 1985-86. McGraw-Hill Newsletters, industrial and trade issues writer, 1986-88. *DN*, 1988-present.

Flanigan, James. *Los Angeles Times.* Staff Writer and Columnist. B. 1936, New York, NY. Manhattan College, 1961, History/English. *New York Herald Tribune*, copy boy, Paris edition desk, financial reporter, 1958-66. *Forbes*, staff writer, asst. man. ed., 1966-86. *LAT*, 1986-present.

Fleming, Thomas J. *Chronicles.* Editor. B. 1945, Superior, WI. Charleston College, 1967, BA, Greek; U. North Carolina, 1973, PhD, Classics. Miami U., prof. Charleston College, prof. Shaw U., classics prof. *The Southern Partisan*, founding ed., 1979-83. *Chronicles*, man. ed., 1984-85; ed., 1985-present. Author of *The Politics of Human Nature* (1987).

Flint, Jerry. *Forbes.* Senior Editor. B. 1931, Detroit, MI. Wayne State U., 1953, Journalism. *The Wall Street Journal*, Chicago/Detroit bureaus, 1956-57. *The New York Times*, 1967-73. *Forbes*, Washington bur. chief, asst. man. ed., sr. ed., 1973-present. Author of *The Dream Machine.*

Foreman, Judy. *The Boston Globe.* Science and Medicine Writer. B. 1944, Ft. Bragg, NC. Wellesley, 1966, BA, Anthropology/Sociology; Harvard, 1970, Education. *Lowell* (MA) *Sun*, City Hall reporter, 1970-73. *BG*, stringer, 1976-78. *The Times* (London), gen. assign. reporter, 1982-83. *BG*, sci./med. writer, 1983-present.

Forsyth, Randall W. *Barron's.* Capital Markets Editor. B. 1952, New York, NY. NYU, 1975, Economics; NYU Business school, graduate studies in finance and economics. *Bond Buyer*, asst. ed., 1972-76. Merrill Lynch, staff writer for market letter, 1976-80. Dow Jones Capital Markets Report, 1980-83. *Barron's*, Capital Markets ed., "Current Yield" columnist, 1983-present.

Fraser, Damien. *Financial Times.* Mexico City Correspondent. B. 1964, London, UK. Oxford, 1987, Philosophy; Harvard, 1989, MPA. *The Economist*, 1989-90. *FT*, Mexico City corr., 1991-present.

Friedman, Thomas L. *The New York Times.* Chief White House Correspondent. B. 1953, Minneapolis, MN. Brandeis, 1975, BA, Middle East Studies; St. Anthony's College (Oxford), 1978, MPhil. UPI, London/Beirut correspondent, 1978-81. *NYT*, bus. reporter, 1981-82; Beirut bur. chief, 1982-84; Jerusalem bur. chief, 1984-88; Washington, diplomatic corr., 1989-92; White House corr., 1992-present. Author of *From Beirut to Jerusalem.*

Fritz, Sara. *Los Angeles Times.* National Correspondent. B. 1944, Pittsburgh, PA. Denison, 1966, BS, Writing major. *Pittsburgh Press*, copy ed., 1966. UPI, Pittsburgh bur., 1967-71; Harrisburg, PA, bur. chief, 1971-73; Washington Weekend News, ed., 1973-75; nat. labor reporter. *U.S.News & World Report*, nat. labor reporter, 1978-80; chief White House corr., 1981-83. *LAT*, pol. reporter, 1983-90; Washington investigative reporter, 1990-92; nat. corr., 1992-present.

Fuerbringer, Jonathan. *The New York Times.* National Economics Correspondent. B. 1945, New York, NY. Harvard, 1967, BA, American History; Columbia, 1968, MS, Journalism. *The Boston Globe*, copy ed.; reporter; state house reporter; financial reporter. *The Washington Star*, reporter, nat. econ. corr., through 1981. *NYT*, nat. econ. corr., 1981-present.

Fuhrman, Peter. *Forbes.* European Bureau Manager. Tufts, 1980, BA, Chinese History; Cambridge, 1985, MPhil. *Forbes*, reporter, 1986-87; European corr., 1987-93; man. of European bur., 1993-present.

Fulghum, David. *Aviation Week & Space Technology.* Military Editor. B. 1944, Orange, CA. Angelo State U., 1974, BA, Journalism; Texas A&M, 1974-77, graduate studies in History; Georgetown, 1977-81, graduate studies in History. US

Navy and Army, 1962-69. *San Angelo Standard Times*, 1970-74. *U.S.News & World Report*, sr. writer, book div., 1981-83. Time-Life Books/Boston Pub. Co., sr. writer, 1983-85. Air Force Times/Army Times Pub. Co., assoc. ed., 1985-90. *AWST*, military ed., 1990-present. Co-author of several books, including *South Vietnam on Trial* and *A War Remembered*.

Fumento, Michael. *Investor's Business Daily*. Reporter. B. 1960, Urbana, IL. UNC-Ft. Bragg, 1982, Pol. Sci.; U. Illinois, 1985, JD. *The Washington Times*, legal affairs reporter, 1987. Denver *Rocky Mountain News*, ed. writer, 1989-90. *IBD*, reporter, 1991-present. Author of several books, including *The Myth of Heterosexual Aids*.

Gallagher, James. *Chicago Tribune*. Moscow Bureau Chief. B. 1941, Brooklyn, NY. Manhattan College; NYU, 1965, MA, English Lit. Teacher of high school and college, 1965-74. *Detroit Free Press*, 1974-77. *CT*, Moscow corr., 1977-82; science and education ed., dep. asst. man. ed., 1982-92; Moscow bur. chief, 1992-present.

Gelman, David. *Newsweek*. Senior Editor. B. Brooklyn, NY. Brooklyn College. *New York Post*, reporter, 1946-62. Peace Corps, Washington, African projects evaluator, dir. of special programs, 1962-68. *Newsweek*, assoc. ed., 1966-68. *Newsday*, ed., 1969-75. *Newsweek*, gen. ed., 1975-78; sr. writer, 1978-present.

Gellman, Barton. *The Washington Post*. Military Correspondent. B. 1960, Philadelphia, PA. Princeton, 1982, International Affairs; Oxford, 1988, MLitt. *WP*, metro reporter, 1988-90; military corr., 1990-present. Author of *Contending with Kennan: Toward a Philosophy of Moral Power* (1984).

Germond, Jack W. *National Journal*/Tribune Media Services. Columnist. B. Boston, MA. U. Missouri, Journalism/History. Jefferson, MO *Post-Tribune*. Monroe, MI *Evening News*. *Rochester* (NY) *Times-Union*. Gannett Newspapers, New York, Albany, and Washington bureaus, pol. reporter, 1953-69; Washington bur. chief, 1969-73. *The Washington Star*, asst. man. ed., chief pol. writer, 1974-81. Baltimore *Sun*, 1981-present. *National Journal*, "Inside Politics" columnist (with Jules Witcover), current. Tribune Media Services, "Politics Today" columnist (with Witcover), 1977-present. Co-author of several books with Jules Witcover, including *Whose Broad Stripes and Bright Stars? The Trivial Pursuit of the Presidency 1988*.

Gerstenzang, James R. *Los Angeles Times*. Staff Writer. B. 1947, New York, NY. Rutgers, 1969, BA, Pol. Sci. *The New York Times*, stringer, 1964-70. Elizabeth, NJ *Daily Journal*, summer 1968. UPI, summer 1969. AP, reporter, 1970-73; Southwest regional corr., 1973-77; White House reporter, 1977-81; White House corr., 1981-84. *LAT*, defense reporter, 1984-86; White House reporter, 1986-93; econ. and trade reporter, 1993-present.

Gertz, Bill. *The Washington Times*. National Security Correspondent. B. 1952, Glen Cove, NY. Washington College, English Literature; George Washington U., Journalism. *New York News World*, Washington corr., 1979-81. Paragon House Publishers, book ed., 1981-83. *New York City Tribune*, Washington corr., 1983-84. *WT*, nat. security corr., 1985-present.

Getlin, Josh. *Los Angeles Times*. Staff Writer. B. 1950, New York, NY. UC-Santa Cruz, 1971, BS, History. Columbia, 1972, MA, Journalism. Press secretary/speechwriter for San Francisco Mayor George Moscone [D], 1975-78. Press secretary/speechwriter for San Francisco Mayor Dianne Feinstein, 1979. *LAT*, staff writer, San Fernando Valley Edition, 1979-80; staff writer, 1980-83; staff writer, Orange County edition, 1983-89; New York bur., staff writer, 1989-present.

Geyer, Georgie Anne. Universal Press Syndicate. Columnist. B. 1935, Chicago, IL. Northwestern, 1956, BS, Journalism. *Chicago Daily News*, society desk reporter, 1959-60; gen. assign. reporter, 1960-64; Latin America corr., 1964-67; roving foreign corr., columnist, 1967-75. Los Angeles Times Syndicate, foreign affairs columnist, 1975-80. *The Washington Star*, columnist, 1980-81. UPS, columnist, 1981-present.

Ghiles, Francis. *Financial Times*. North Africa Correspondent. Oxford. *City Press*, reporter, 1974-76. *Euromoney*, reporter, 1976-77. *FT*. Euromarket reporter, 1977-82; North Africa corr., 1982-present.

Gigot, Paul Anthony. *The Wall Street Journal*. Editorial Board, Columnist. B. 1955, San Antonio, TX. Dartmouth, 1977, Government. *National Review*, ed. asst., 1978-79. *Far Eastern Economic Review*, reporter/ed., 1979-80. *WSJ*, reporter, 1980-82; Asia corr., 1982-84; *Asian Wall Street Journal*, editorial page ed., 1984-86. White House Fellow, 1986-87. WSJ, member editorial board and "Potomac Watch" columnist, 1987-present.

Glaberson, William. *The New York Times*. Business Reporter. B. 1952, Brooklyn, NY. Tufts, 1974, BA, Pol. Sci.; Albany Law, 1977; Columbia, 1982, MA. Westchester Legal Services, civil litigator, 1977-80. Matthew Bender, Inc., ed./sr. ed., 1980-82. *New York Law Journal*, reporter, 1982-83. *BusinessWeek*, ed., Legal Affairs Dept., 1983-87. *NYT*, bus. reporter, 1987-present.

Goldman, Kevin. *The Wall Street Journal*. Advertising Columnist. B. 1954, Brooklyn, NY. Boston U., 1976, Journalism. "Rolling Stone Rock Magazine," writer, 1981-83. *Variety*, TV corr., 1983-86. *Newsday*, TV corr., 1986-89. *WSJ*, TV corr., advertising columnist, 1989-present.

Goodman, Ellen. *The Boston Globe*. Feature Writer, Columnist, and Associate Editor. B. 1941, Newton, MA. Radcliffe College, 1963, BA; Harvard, Nieman Fellow, 1973-74. *Newsweek*, researcher, reporter, 1963-65. *Detroit Free Press*, feature writer, 1965-67. Washington Post Writers Group, columnist, 1976-present. *BG*, feature writer, columnist, 1967-present; assoc. ed., 1987-present. Author of several books, including *At Large* (1981).

Goozner, Merrill. *Chicago Tribune*. Tokyo Bureau Chief. B. 1950, New York, NY. U. Cincinnati, 1975, History; Columbia, MS, Journalism. *Hammond* (LA) *Times*, 1982-83. *Crain's Chicago Business*, 1983-87. *CT*, bus. reporter; Tokyo bureau chief, 1987-present.

Greenberg, Paul. *Arkansas Democrat-Gazette*. Editorial Page Editor. B. 1937, Shreveport, LA. U. Missouri, 1958, BA, Journalism; 1959 MA, History; Columbia, 1962, American History. *Chicago Daily News*, editorial writer, 1966-67. *Pine Bluff Commercial*, editorial page ed., 1962-92. Freelance Syndicate, columnist, 1971-present. *Arkansas Democrat-Gazette*, editorial page ed., 1992-present. Author of *Resonant Lives* (1991) and *Entirely Personal* (1992).

Greenfield, Meg. *The Washington Post*. Editorial Page Editor. B. 1930, Seattle, WA. Smith, 1952, BA, English; Newnham College (Cambridge), Fulbright Scholar, 1953. *The Reporter*, researcher, 1957-61; corr., 1961-65; DC ed., 1965-68. *Newsweek*, columnist 1974-present. *WP*, editorial page dep. ed., 1969-79; editorial page ed., 1979-present.

Greenhouse, Linda. *The New York Times*. Supreme Court Correspondent. B. 1947, New York, NY. Radcliffe College, 1968, BA, American Government. Yale, 1978,

MA, Law. *NYT*, asst. to James Reston, 1968-69; metro reporter, 1969-74; Albany, leg. reporter, 1974-75; Albany bur. chief, 1976-77; cong. corr., 1986-87; Supreme Court corr., 1978-present.

Greenhouse, Steven. *The New York Times.* Washington Financial Correspondent. B. Long Island, NY. Wesleyan, 1973; Columbia, 1975, MS, Journalism; NYU, 1982, JD. *The Chelsea News*, reporter. *The Westsider*, reporter. *Bergen* (NJ) *Record*, labor and econ. reporter, 1976. US District Judge Robert L. Carter, law clerk, 1982-83. *NYT*, copyboy, 1973; reporter, 1983-84, Chicago financial corr., 1984-87; Paris financial corr., 1987-92; Washington financial corr., 1992-present.

Greider, William. *Rolling Stone*. National Editor. B. Wyoming, OH. Princeton, 1958, BA, English Lit. and American Studies. *Louisville Times*, gen. assign. reporter, 1962-66; Washington corr., 1966-68. *The Washington Post*, gen. assign. reporter, 1968-79; "Outlook" section ed., 1979-80; asst. man. ed. for nat. news, 1980. *RS*, nat. ed., 1982-present. Author of several books, most recently, *Who Will Tell the People: the Betrayal of American Democracy* (1993).

Grenier, Richard. *The Washington Times.* Columnist. B. 1933, Cambridge, MA. US Naval Academy, engineering. *Agence France-Presse*, 1962. *Financial Times*, Paris bur., 1962-69. Group W Broadcasting, Paris, 1968-70. *The New York Times. Commentary. The American Spectator. The Washington Times*, columnist, 1985-present. Author of three books, including *The Marrakesh One-Two* (1983).

Grove, Lloyd. *The Washington Post.* Reporter. B. 1955, Los Angeles, CA. Yale, 1976, English. *Kansas City Times*, intern, 1976. *Corpus Christi Caller*, 1976-78. *Dallas Morning News*, 1978-80. *Vanity Fair*, contrib., 1986-present. *WP*, reporter, 1980-present.

Gubernick, Lisa. *Forbes*. Senior Editor. B. 1955, Los Angeles, CA. Bryn Mawr, 1978, English. *Securities Week*, 1981-83. *East Side Express*, 1983-84. *American Lawyer*, 1984. *Forbes*, 1984-present. Author of two books, including *Get Hot or Go Home: Trisha Yearwood, The Making of a Nashville Star.*

Haas, Lawrence J. *National Journal*. Correspondent. B. 1956, Brooklyn, NY. U. Pennsylvania, 1978, American History; Princeton, 1980, MA, American History. Shrewsbury, NJ *Daily Register*, reporter, 1980-82. *Pittsburgh Post-Gazette*, state house corr., 1982-83. UPI, Harrisburg bur. chief, 1983-85. *The Bond Buyer*, Washington corr., 1985-87. *NJ*, staff corr., 1987-present.

Haberman, Clyde. *The New York Times.* Jerusalem Bur. Chief. B. 1945, Bronx, NY. City College of New York, 1966, English. *NYT*, campus stringer, 1964-66. *New York Post*, 1966-68; 1970-76. *NYT*, "Week in Review" ed., 1977-78; metro reporter, 1978-82; Tokyo bur. chief, 1983-88; Rome bur. chief, 1988-91; Jerusalem bur. chief, 1991-present.

Hall, Jane. *Los Angeles Times*. Staff Writer. B. 1950, Abilene, TX. U. Texas, 1972, BA, English; Columbia, 1973, MS, Journalism. *TV Guide*, writer, 1974-81. *View Magazine*, editor-in-chief, 1981-83. *People*, television corr., 1983-88. GTG East, dir. of development, 1988-89. *LAT*, New York bur., staff writer, 1989-present.

Richard Harwood. *The Washington Post.* Editorial Columnist. B. 1925, Chilton, WI. Vanderbilt, 1950, English Literature/Russian Language. *Nashville Tennessean*, 1947-52. *Louisville Courier-Journal*, 1952-65. *WP*, reporter, columnist 1966-present. Co-author of *Lyndon*.

Havemann, Joel. *Los Angeles Times*. Washington Bureau Projects Editor. B. 1943, New York, NY. Harvard, 1965, BA, Mathematics. Portland *Oregonian*, gen. assign. reporter, 1965-67. *Chicago Sun-Times*, education reporter, 1967-73. *National Journal*, budget reporter, 1973-78, dep. ed., 1978-83. *LAT*, econ. reporter, 1983-84; projects ed., 1984-90; Brussels bur. chief, 1990-93; DC projects ed., 1993-present. Author of *Congress and the Budget* (1978).

Hedges, Michael. *The Washington Times.* National Desk Reporter. B. 1955, Muncie, IN. Northern Kentucky U., Communications. *WT*, nat. desk reporter, 1985-present.

Henriques, Diana B. *The New York Times.* Financial/Investigative Reporter. B. 1948, Bryan, TX. George Washington U., 1969, International Affairs; Princeton, 1981-82, Woodrow Wilson fellow. *Lawrence* (NJ) *Ledger*, man. ed., 1969-71. *Asbury Park* (NJ) *Press*, reporter, 1971-74. *Palo Alto* (CA) *Times*, copy ed., 1974-76. *Trenton* (NJ) *Times*, investigative reporter, 1976-82. *The Philadelphia Inquirer*, econ. corr., 1982-86. *Barron's*, 1986-89. *NYT*, "Wall Street" columnist, 1989-92; financial/investigative reporter, 1992-present. Author of *The Machinery of Greed: Public Authority, Abuse and What to Do About It* (1986).

Hentoff, Nathan Irving. *The Washington Post*. Columnist. *The Village Voice*. Writer. B. 1925, Boston, MA. Northeastern, 1946, English and Government; Harvard, 1960; Sorbonne, Fulbright Fellow, 1950. WMEX radio, producer, announcer, 1944-53. *Down Beat*, assoc. ed., 1953-57. CBS TV, "The Jazz Review," co-founder, co-ed., 1957-60. *The Progressive*, contrib., current. *The New Yorker*, writer, 1960-present. *The Washington Post*, "Sweet Land of Liberty" columnist, current. *The Village Voice*, writer, 1958-present. Author of several books, including *Free Speech for Me—But Not For Thee: How the American Left and Right Continually Censor Each Other* (1993).

Herbert, Bob. *The New York Times*. Op-Ed Columnist. B. 1945, Montclair, NJ. Empire State College, BS, 1989. *Newark Star-Ledger*, reporter/night city ed., 1970-76. New York *Daily News*, reporter, 1976-81; City Hall bur. chief, 1981-83; city ed., 1983-85; columnist, 1985-93. *NYT*, op-ed columnist, 1993-present.

Herman, R. Thomas. *The Wall Street Journal*. B. New York, NY. Yale. *WSJ*, Washington bur., intern, 1967; New York bur., reporter, 1968-69; Atlanta bur., reporter, 1969-74; New York bur., reporter, 1974-76. *Asian Wall Street Journal*, 1976-77. *WSJ*, econ. reporter, 1978-present. "NBC News at Sunrise," regular reporter.

Hiatt, Fred. *The Washington Post*. Moscow Co-Bureau Chief. B. 1955, Washington, DC. Harvard, 1977, BA, History. *Atlanta Journal-Constitution*, City Hall reporter, 1979-80. *The Washington Star*, reporter, 1981. *WP*, Virginia reporter, 1981-83; Pentagon reporter, 1983-86; Northeast Asia co-bur. chief, 1987-90; Moscow co-bur. chief, 1991-present. Author of one novel, *The Secret Sun* (1992).

Hiebert, Murray. *Far Eastern Economic Review*. Hanoi Bureau Chief. B. 1948, Manitoba, Canada. Goshen, 1970, BA, History; 1973, MA. *IndoChina Issues*, ed., 1980-86. *FEER*, Indochina corr., 1986-89; Hanoi bur. chief, 1990-present. Author of *Vietnam Notebook* (1993).

Hitchens, Christopher. *The Nation*. Washington Columnist. B. 1949, Portsmouth, Hampshire, UK. Balliol College (Oxford), 1970, Philosophy, Politics, and Economics. *The Times* (London) Higher Education Supplement, social sci. corr. "Weekend World," London TV, researcher, reporter. *The Daily Express*, foreign corr. *New Statesman*, writer, 1974-80. *The Times* (London) *Literary Supplement*, "American Notes" columnist, 1982-present. *The Spectator*, Washington columnist, 1981-86. *Vanity Fair*, contrib. ed. *The Nation,* columnist, current. Author, most recently of *For the Sake of Argument: Essays and Minority Reports.*

Hitchens, Theresa A. *Defense News.* Staff Writer. B. 1959, Somerset, OH. Ohio U., 1981, Journalism. Senator John Glenn [D-OH], intern, 1981. North Atlantic Assembly, intern, 1982-83. Inside Washington Publishers, 1983-88. *DN,* Brussels bur. chief, 1988-93; staff writer, 1993-present.

Hoagland, Jim. *The Washington Post.* Associate Editor and Chief Foreign Correspondent. B. 1940, Rock Hill, SC. U. South Carolina, 1961, Journalism. *Rock Hill* (SC) *Evening Herald,* reporter, 1960. *The New York Times* (Intl. Edition), copy ed., Paris, 1964-66. *WP,* metro reporter, 1966-68; Africa corr., 1969-72; Middle East corr., 1972-75; Paris corr., 1975-77; nat. affairs reporter, 1977-79; foreign ed., 1979-81; asst. man. ed. foreign news, 1981-86; Paris bur., assoc. ed. and chief foreign corr., 1986-present.

Hoffman, David. *The Washington Post.* Jerusalem Correspondent. B. 1953, Palo Alto, CA. U. Delaware; Georgetown, 1981, tutorial in economics. States News Service, 1978-79. *WP,* gen. assign. reporter, 1982-83; Jerusalem corr., 1993-present.

Holley, David. *Los Angeles Times.* Tokyo Correspondent. B. 1950, New York, NY. Oberlin, 1972, Chinese; Stanford, 1978, MA, Journalism. *Monterey* (CA) *Peninsula Herald,* gen. assign. reporter, 1979. *LAT,* metro staff writer, 1979-87; Beijing bur. chief, 1987-93; Tokyo corr., 1993-present.

Holmes, Steven A. *The New York Times.* Reporter. B. 1949, Brooklyn, NY. City College of New York, 1974. Yonkers *Herald Statesman.* UPI. *Atlanta Constitution. Time,* 1979-89. *NYT,* Washington bur., reporter, 1989-present.

Hook, Janet. *Congressional Quarterly.* Senior Writer. B. 1955, New York, NY. Harvard, 1977, Philosophy/Government. *The Washington Monthly,* intern, 1977. *Public Interest,* asst. ed., 1978-79. *Chronicle of Higher Education,* asst. ed., 1979-83. *CQ,* sr. writer, 1983-present.

Horgan, John. *Scientific American.* Writer. B. 1953, New York, NY. Columbia, 1982, BA, English; 1983, MS, Journalism. *IEEE Spectrum,* assoc. ed., 1983-86. *Scientific American,* sr. writer, 1986-present.

Horovitz, Bruce. *Los Angeles Times.* Marketing Columnist. B. 1952, Cleveland, OH. Colorado State, 1975, English. *Carmel Pine Cone,* reporter, 1977-79. *Industry Week,* assoc. ed., 1979-83. *LAT,* Orange County edition, staff writer, 1984-86; marketing columnist, 1986-present. Author of *Explaining Everything,* a book of poetry.

Hundley, Tom. *Chicago Tribune.* Jerusalem Bureau Chief. Middle East Correspondent. B. 1950, Brooklyn, NY. Georgetown, 1972, BA, English Lit.; U. Pennsylvania, 1980, MA, International Rel. *Middletown Record,* gen. assign. reporter, 1974. *Bergen* (NJ) *Record,* gen. assign. reporter, 1976-79. *Detroit Free Press,* City Hall reporter, 1980-83; gen. assign. reporter, 1984-85; special projects reporter, 1985-88. *Chicago Tribune,* nat. corr., Detroit bur. chief, 1988-90; Middle East corr., Jerusalem bur. chief, 1990-present.

Hunt, Albert. *The Wall Street Journal.* Executive Washington Editor. B. Charlottesville, VA. Wake Forest, BA, Pol. Sci. "The Capital Gang," moderator, 1988-present. *WSJ,* reporter, 1965-72; nat. pol. reporter, 1972-83; Washington bur. chief, 1983-93; exec. Washington ed., 1993-present. Co-author of several books, most recently, *Elections American Style* (1987).

Ibrahim, Youssef M. *The Wall Street Journal.* Energy Editor. B. 1943, Cairo, Egypt. American U., 1968, BA; Columbia, 1970, MA, Journalism. *The New York Times,* foreign corr. *WSJ,* energy ed., 1981-present.

Isikoff, Michael. *The Washington Post.* Reporter. B. New York, NY. Washington U. (MO). Capitol Hill News Service. States News Service. *The Washington Star,* reporter. *WP,* financial reporter; Richmond bur., reporter; nat. news desk reporter, 1981-present.

Jameson, Sam. *Los Angeles Times.* Tokyo Bureau Chief. B. 1936, Pittsburgh, PA. Northwestern, 1958, BS, Journalism; MS, 1959, Journalism. *Chicago Tribune,* copy reader, 1959-60; Tokyo bur. chief, 1963-71. *LAT,* Tokyo bur. chief, 1971-present.

Jehl, Douglas. *The New York Times.* White House Correspondent. Stanford U., 1984, BA, History; St. John's College (Oxford), 1987, Rhodes Scholar, MPhil., International Relations. *Los Angeles Times,* Washington bur., 1987-93. *NYT,* White House corr., 1993-present.

Judis, John B. *The New Republic.* Contributing Editor. *In These Times.* Senior Editor. B. 1941, Chicago, IL. UC-Berkeley, BA, Philosophy; MA Philosophy. *ITT,* foreign ed., 1976; Washington corr., sr. ed., 1982-present. *TNR,* contrib. ed., 1988-present. Author of several books, most recently, *Grand Illusions: Critics and Champions of the American Century* (1992).

Kamm, Henry. *The New York Times.* Roving Correspondent. B. 1925, Breslau, Germany. NYU, 1949, BA. US Army, 1943-46. *NYT,* editorial index dept. member, copy ed., 1946-60; International Edition, Paris, asst. news ed., 1960-64; foreign corr., 1964-67; Moscow bur. chief, 1967-69; Asia corr., 1969-71; roving corr., 1971-81; Rome bur. chief, 1982-84; Athens bur. chief, 1984-87; Central European corr., 1987-90; roving corr., 1990-present.

Kanner, Bernice. *New York.* Senior Editor. B. New York, NY. SUNY-Binghamton, English Lit.; MA, English Lit. *Advertising Age,* sr. ed., 1977-80. New York *Daily News,* columnist, 1980-81. *NY,* "On Madison Ave." columnist, 1981-present. CBS Morning News, corr., 1983-84. "Business Times" (cable TV show), marketing corr., 1984.

Kaplan, Fred. *The Boston Globe.* Moscow Bureau Chief. B. 1954, Hutchinson, KS. Oberlin, 1976, Pol. Sci.; MIT, 1978, MS; PhD, 1983. *The Absolute Sound,* audio reviewer, 1985-91. Washington *City Paper,* jazz critic, 1986-91. *BG,* nat. security, 1982-91; Moscow bur. chief, 1992-present. Author of *The Wizards of Armageddon* (1983).

Katz, Gregory. *Dallas Morning News.* Mexico Bureau Chief. B. 1953, New York, NY. U. Vermont, 1977, BA, Religion. *DMN,* Mexico bur. chief.

Kaus, Mickey. *The New Republic.* Senior Editor. B. 1951, Santa Monica, CA. Harvard, 1973, Social Studies. *The Washington Monthly,* ed., 1978-80. *American Lawyer,* sr. ed., 1980-82. *Harper's,* politics ed., 1982-83. Sen. Ernest F. Hollings [D-SC], speechwriter, 1983-84. *TNR,* West Coast corr., 1984-87. *Newsweek,* sr. writer, 1987-89. *TNR,* sr. ed., 1989-present.

Keller, Bill. *The New York Times.* Johannesburg Bureau Chief. B. 1949. Pomona College, 1970. Portland *Oregonian,* reporter, 1970-79. *Congressional Quarterly,* lobbying reporter, 1979-82. *Dallas Times-Herald,* reporter, 1982-84. *NYT,* domestic corr., 1984-86; Moscow corr., 1986-92; Johannesburg bur. chief, 1992-present.

Kelly, Michael. *The New York Times.* Washington Correspondent. B. 1957, Washington DC. U. New Hampshire, 1979, BA, History. Baltimore *Sun,* Washington bur., corr., 1986-89. Freelance,

1989-92. *NYT*, Washington bur., corr., 1992-present. Author of *Martyr's Day: Chronicles of a Small War* (1993).

Kilborn, Peter T. *The New York Times.* "Workplace" Correspondent. B. 1939, Providence, RI. Trinity, 1961, BA, English; Columbia, 1962, MS, Journalism and Economics. *Providence* (RI) *Journal-Bulletin*, reporter, 1962-63. McGraw-Hill World News and *BusinessWeek*, Paris corr., 1963-68. *BusinessWeek*, writer, asst. tech. ed., 1968-71; Los Angeles bur. chief, 1971-73; companies ed., 1973-74. *Newsweek*, sr. ed., 1974-78. *NYT*, Sunday business section ed., 1977-82; econ. ed., 1982-83; econ. corr., 1983-89; "Workplace" corr., 1989-present.

Kinsley, Michael. *The New Republic.* Senior Editor. B. 1951, Detroit, MI. Harvard, 1972; Magdalen College (Oxford); Harvard Law. *TNR*, man. ed., 1976; ed., 1979-81. *Harper's*, ed., 1981-83. *TNR*, ed., 1983-89. *The Economist*, "American Survey," ed., 1989. "Crossfire" (CNN), co-host. *TNR*, sr. ed., 1989-present.

Kirkpatrick, Jeane J. Los Angeles Times Syndicate. Columnist. B. 1926, Duncan, OK. Stephens, 1946, AA-Pol. Sci.; Barnard, 1948, AB; Columbia, 1950, MA; 1967, PhD; U. Paris Institute de Science Politique, French Govt. Fellow, 1952-53. George Washington U., research analyst, 1953-56. Georgetown, assoc. prof. of Pol. Sci., 1967-73; professor, 1973-78, Thomas & Dorothy Leavey prof., 1978-present. American Enterprise Institute, sr. fellow, 1977-81. US Rep. to United Nations, 1981-85. Los Angeles Times Syndicate, columnist. Author of several books, including, *The Reagan Phenomenon* (1983).

Klein, Joe. *Newsweek.* Senior Editor. B. 1946, New York, NY. U. Pennsylvania, 1968, BA, American Civilization. *Essex County* (MA) *Newspapers*, reporter, 1969-72. WGBH-TV, Boston, reporter, 1972. *The Real Paper* (Boston), news ed., 1972-74. *Rolling Stone*, Washington bur. chief, 1975-77; contrib. ed., 1975-80. *New York*, pol. corr., 1978-87; pol. columnist, 1987-92. *Newsweek*, sr. ed., 1992-present. Author of *Woody Guthrie: A Life* (1980), and *Payback: Five Marines After Vietnam* (1984).

Knight, Jerry. *The Washington Post.* Staff Writer. B. Iowa. Iowa State U. *Ames* (IA) *Daily Tribune*. *Des Moines Register*, reporter. *National Home Center News*, founding ed. *The Trenton* (NJ) *Times*, reporter, city, ed. *WP*, financial writer/dep. financial ed., 1980-present.

Knight, Robin. *U.S.News & World Report.* European Senior Editor. B. 1943, Chalfout St. Giles, UK. Dublin U., 1966; Stanford, 1968, MA, Pol. Sci. *USNWR*, London reporter, 1968-74; London bur. chief, 1974-76; Moscow bur. chief, 1976-79; African regional ed., 1979-81; Mediterranean regional ed., 1981-83; spec. assign., 1983-84; European sr. ed., 1985-present.

Kolata, Gina. *The New York Times.* Science Reporter. B. 1948, Baltimore. U. Maryland, 1969, MS, Mathematics; MIT. *Science*, copy ed., 1973-74; writer, 1974-77. *NYT*, sci. reporter, 1987-current.

Kondracke, Morton M. *Roll Call.* Columnist. B. 1939. Dartmouth, 1960, AB; Harvard, Nieman Fellow, 1973-74. *Chicago Sun-Times*, corr., 1963-77. *The Wall Street Journal*, columnist, 1980-85. "This Week with David Brinkley" (ABC), panelist, 1984-88. "The McLaughlin Group," panelist, 1982-present. *Newsweek*, Washington bur. chief, 1985-86. *The New Republic*, exec. ed., 1977-85; contrib. ed., 1987-present. "American Interest" (PBS), moderator, 1987-present. *RC*, columnist, 1991-present.

Kosterlitz, Julie. *National Journal.* Staff Correspondent. B. 1955, Chicago. UC-Santa Cruz, 1979, History. Portland, OR *Willamette Week*, bus. reporter, 1979-80. Common Cause, 1980-85. *NJ*, staff corr., health and income security, 1985-present.

Kraft, Scott. *Los Angeles Times.* Paris Bureau Chief. B. 1955, Kansas City, MO. Kansas State, 1977, Journalism. AP, staff writer, 1976-77; Kansas City corr., 1977-79; Wichita corr., 1979-80; nat. writer, 1980-84. *LAT*, staff writer, 1984-86; Nairobi bur. chief, 1986-88; Johannesburg bur. chief, 1988-93; Paris bur. chief, 1993-present.

Kramer, Michael. *Time.* Amherst, 1967, Pol. Sci.; Columbia Law, 1970. *New York*, city pol. col., 1970-76; pol. ed., 1979-87. *More*, editor-in-chief, pub., 1976-78. Berkeley Books, pub., 1978. *U.S.News & World Report*, chief pol. corr., 1987-88. *Time*, chief pol. corr., 1988-present.

Krauss, Clifford. *The New York Times.* Washington Correspondent. B. 1953, New York, NY. Vassar College, 1975, BA, History. U. Chicago, 1976, MA, History; Columbia, 1977, MS, Journalism. UPI, Mexico bur., 1977-79; New York bur., metro reporter, 1979-80. Freelance, Central America, 1980-81. Cox Newspapers, Mexico City, 1981-84. *The Wall Street Journal*, Central America/ Caribbean corr., 1984-87. Council on Foreign Relations, press fellow, 1987-88. Freelance, 1988-89. *NYT*, Washington corr., 1990-present.

Krauthammer, Charles. The Washington Post Writers Group. Columnist. B. 1950, New York, NY. McGill, 1970, Pol. Sci.; Balliol College (Oxford), 1971; Harvard Medical School, 1975, MD. Carter Administration, science advisor, 1978. Speechwriter for Vice President Walter Mondale, 1980-81. *The New Republic*, essayist, ed., 1981-88. *Time*, essayist, 1983-present. The Washington Post Writers Group, columnist, 1985-present. Author of *Cutting Edges: Making Sense of the 80s*.

Kristol, Irving. *Public Interest.* Co-Editor. *The National Interest.* Publisher. B. 1920, New York, NY. City College, 1940. US Army, 1940-46. *Commentary*, man. ed., 1947-52. *Encounter*, co-founder, co-ed., 1953-58. *The Reporter*, ed., 1959-60. Basic Books, exec. vice president, 1961 69. NYU, faculty, 1969-88. *The National Interest*, pub. *Public Interest*, co-ed., 1965-present. Author of several books, including, *Reflections of a Neoconservative* (1983).

Kriz, Margaret E. *National Journal.* Staff Correspondent. B. 1954, Chicago, IL. U. Illinois, Journalism; American U., MS, News Editorial. *Chicago Tribune*, municipal reporter; county govt. and courts reporter, 1976-79. Bureau of National Affairs, Inc., publications, staff reporter. *NJ*, staff corr., financial, energy and communications, current. Author of *Chemicals and the Community* (1987).

Kurtz, Howard. *The Washington Post.* Media Reporter. B. 1953, Brooklyn, NY. SUNY-Buffalo, 1974, English; Columbia, 1975, Journalism. *Bergen* (NJ) *Record*, reporter, 1975-77. *The Washington Star*, reporter, 1978-81. *WP*, investigative reporter, 1981-82; urban affairs reporter, 1982-84; Justice Dept. reporter, 1985-87; New York bur. chief, 1987-90; media reporter, 1990-present. "Reliable Sources" (CNN), frequent panelist. Author of *Media Circus: The Trouble With America's Newspapers* (1993).

Kuttner, Robert. Washington Post Writers Group. Economics Columnist. B. 1943, New York, NY. Oberlin, 1965, Government. *The Village Voice*, Washington ed., 1965-73. *The Washington Post*, nat. writer, 1973-75. US Senate Banking Committee, investigator, 1975-78. *Working Papers*, editor-in-chief, 1978-82. *The Boston Globe*, columnist, 1984-present. *BusinessWeek*, columnist, 1985-87. *The New Republic*, econ. corr., 1982-88. Washington Post Writers Group, econ. columnist, 1988-present. Author of two books, including *The Economic Illusion* (1984).

Labaton, Stephen. *The New York Times.* Washington Correspondent. B. 1961. Queens, NY. Tufts, 1983, Philosophy/Pol. Sci.; Duke 1986, JD; MA, Philosophy. *Newsday*, intern, 1981 & 82. *The Washington Post*, intern, 1985. *NYT*, reporter, 1986-87; New York bur., legal affairs corr., 1987-90; Washington bur., finance reporter, 1990-92; Washington bur., legal affairs corr., 1992-present.

Lambro, Donald. *The Washington Times.* Chief Political Correspondent. B. 1940, Wellesley, MA. Boston, 1963, Journalism. *The Boston Traveler*, reporter, 1963-68. UPI, Hartford bur., state pol. reporter; Washington bur., pol. corr., 1968-80. United Feature Syndicate, Washington investigative columnist. "The Washington Times Forum" (C-SPAN), producer and moderator. *WT*, nat. affairs ed., columnist, 1980-present. Author of *Land of Opportunity*.

Lancaster, John. *The Washington Post.* Pentagon Reporter. Stanford, BA, English. *Atlanta Journal-Constitution*, reporter. *The Des Moines Register and Tribune*, reporter. *WP*, metro reporter, 1986-89; Interior Dept. reporter, 1989-91; Pentagon reporter, 1991-present.

Lawrence, Richard. *The Journal of Commerce.* Reporter. B. 1928, New York, NY. RPI, Communications. McGraw-Hill World News Service, 1954-58. *Financial Times*, 1958-59. *Agence France Presse*, 1959-60. *JC*, reporter, 1961-present.

Lenorovitz, Jeffrey Mark. *Aviation Week & Space Technology.* Senior International Editor. B. 1952, Burbank, CA. UC-Northridge, 1974, BA, Radio/TV/Film and Journalism. City News Service, aviation ed., 1972-74. *AWST*, engineering ed., 1976-80. Paris bur. chief, 1980-84. European ed., 1984-92. sr. intl. ed., 1992-present.

Leo, John. *U.S.News & World Report.* Contributing Editor. B. 1935, Hoboken, NJ. U. Toronto, 1957, Philosophy. *Commonweal*, assoc. ed., 1963-67, *The New York Times*, 1967-69. *Trans-Action* (now *Society*), book ed., 1972-74. *The Village Voice*, founded the "Press Clips" column, 1974. *Time*, 1974-88. *USNWR*, columnist, 1988-present. UPI, columnist, 1991-present. Author, *How the Russians Invented Baseball and Other Essays of Enlightenment* (1989) and *Two Steps Ahead of the Thought Police* (1994).

Leopold, George. *Electronic Engineering Times.* Washington Bureau, Senior Editor. Columbia, 1984, MS, Journalism. *Electronics* Magazine, 1984-86. *Defense News*, 1986-93. *EET*, 1993-present.

Levin, Doron P. *The New York Times.* Detroit Bureau Chief. B. 1950, Haifa, Israel. Cornell, 1972, History; Columbia, 1977, MS, Journalism. *St. Petersburg* (FL) *Times*, police and bus. reporter, 1977-80. *The Wall Street Journal*, automotive reporter, 1981-87. *St. Petersburg Times*, Pittsburgh and Detroit reporter, 1987-88. *WSJ*, Pittsburgh and Detroit reporter, 1987-88. *NYT*, bus. and financial reporter, 1988; Detroit bur. chief, 1988-present. Author of *Irreconcilable Differences* (1989).

Levine, Joshua. *Forbes.* Senior Editor. B. 1953, New York, NY. Columbia, 1975, Comparative Lit.; 1976, MA, Journalism. *Marketing Week* (now *Brandweek*), ed., 1985-89. *Forbes*, 1993-present.

Levinson, Marc. *Newsweek.* General Editor. Antioch College, BA, History; Georgia State, MA, Public Administration; Princeton, MA, Public/International Affairs. *Time*, Atlanta. Bureau of National Affairs, Inc., publications, staff. *Business Month*, sr. ed. *The Journal of Commerce*, editorial dir., 1987-90. *Newsweek*, 1990-present. Author of two books, including *Beyond Free Markets: The Revival of Activist Economics* (1988).

Lewis, Anthony. *The New York Times.* Columnist. B. 1927, New York, NY. Harvard, 1948, English. *NYT*, deskman, 1948-52. *Washington Daily News*, gen. assign. reporter, 1952-55. *NYT*, legal reporter, 1955-56; Supreme Court reporter, 1957-64; London bur. chief, 1964-72; columnist, 1969-present. Author of three books, including, *Make No Law: The Sullivan Case and the First Amendment.*

Lewis, Neil A. *The New York Times.* Legal Affairs Reporter. B. 1947, New York, NY. Union College, 1968, Biology; Yale Law School, 1979, MSL. Pittsfield, MA *Berkshire Eagle*, 1969-70. *Bergen* (NJ) *Record*, 1971-76. New York *Daily News*, 1977-80. Reuters News Service, 1980-85. *NYT*, legal affairs reporter, 1986-present.

Lewis, Paul. *The New York Times.* United Nations Bureau Chief. B. 1937, London, UK. Balliol College (Oxford) 1961. *Financial Times*, Common Market corr., 1961-67; Paris corr., 1967-71; DC bur. chief, 1971-76. *NYT*, econ. corr., 1976-87; UN bur. chief, 1987-present.

Light, Larry. *BusinessWeek.* Corporate Finance Department Editor. B. 1949. Lafayette College, 1971, BA, English; Columbia, 1974, MS, Journalism. *The Camden* (NJ) *Courier-Post*, municipal reporter, 1974-75. *Bergen* (NJ) *Record*, bus. reporter, 1975-76. *Philadelphia Bulletin*, state govt. corr., 1976-78. *Congressional Quarterly*, pol. and econ. reporter, 1978-83. *Newsday*, govt. reporter and gen. ed., 1983-88; bus. reporter and ed., 1988-89. *BW*, Corporate Finance Department Editor, 1989-present.

Lipman, Joanne. *The Wall Street Journal.* Advertising and Public Relations Reporter. B. 1961, New Brunswick, NJ. Yale, 1983, History. *WSJ*, summer intern, 1982; real estate reporter, 1983-86; advertising and public relations reporter, 1986-present.

Loomis, Carol Junge. *Fortune.* Board of Editors. U. Missouri, Journalism. Maytag Corp., corporate publications, ed., 1951-54; *Fortune*, research assoc., 1954-58; assoc. ed., 1958-68; Board of Editors, 1968-present.

Lyman, Rick. *The Philadelphia Inquirer.* South Africa Bureau Chief. B. 1954, Gary, IN. Indiana U., 1976. UPI, reporter, 1977-78. *Kansas City Star*, reporter, 1977-78; suburban bur. chief, 1980; asst. city ed., 1981-82. *PI*, suburban reporter, 1982; film critic, 1983-86; New York corr., 1986-89; people ed., 1989-90; South Africa bur. chief, 1990-present.

Madigan, Charles M. *Chicago Tribune.* Senior Writer. B. 1949, Altoona, PA. Penn State; Roosevelt U. *Pennsylvania Mirror. Altoona Mirror. Harrisburg Patriot-News.* UPI, Philadelphia and Harrisburg bureaus. *Chicago Tribune*, reporter, 1979-80; nat. corr., 1980-83; Washington news ed., 1983-85; nat. ed., 1985-87; sr. writer, 1987-present.

Maggs, John. *The Journal of Commerce.* International Trade Reporter. B. 1962, New York, NY. Columbia, 1984, BA, English/Pol. Sci. Fairchild Publications, energy reporter, 1984-87. McGraw-Hill, Inc., nuclear energy newsletter, reporter, 1987. *JC*, 1987-present.

Magnier, Mark. *The Journal of Commerce.* Tokyo Bureau Chief. B. 1958, New York, NY. Columbia, 1981, BA, Lit. and Pol. Sci.; 1984, MS, Journalism. WNYW Metromedia-TV, 1981. Center for Population Communication, News and Publications Director, 1981-84. *American Shipper*, writer, 1984-85. *JC*, staff reporter, 1985-88; West Coast ed., 1988-91; Tokyo bur. chief, 1993-present.

Mahar, Maggie. *Barron's.* Senior Editor. B. 1949, Syracuse, NY. Yale, 1971, English; PhD, English. Yale, prof., English, 1975-82. Freelance, 1983-86. *Barron's*, staff writer, sr. ed., 1986-present.

Mallet, Victor. *Financial Times*. Southeast Asia Correspondent. B. 1960, Bonn, Germany. Merton College (Oxford), 1978, BA, English. Reuters, foreign corr., 1981-86. *FT*, Africa corr., 1986-88; Middle East corr., 1988-91; Southeast Asia corr., 1992-present.

Mann, James. *Los Angeles Times*. State Department Correspondent. B. 1946, Albany, NY. Harvard, 1968, BA, Social Relations; U. Pennsylvania, 1975, non-degree study in History and Economics. *New Haven Journal-Courier*, staff writer, 1968-69. *The Washington Post*, staff writer, 1969-72. *The Philadelphia Inquirer*, gen. assign. reporter, 1973-75. Baltimore *Sun*, Supreme Court reporter, 1976-78. *Los Angeles Times*, Supreme Court reporter, 1978-84; Beijing bur. chief, 1984-87; Washington, State Department corr., 1987-present.

Marsh, David. *Financial Times*. European Editor. B. 1952, Shoreham, UK. Queens' College (Oxford), Chemistry. Reuters, 1974-78. *FT*, econ. staff, 1978-82; Paris corr., 1982-86; Bonn corr., 1986-91; European ed., 1991-present.

Marx, Gary. *Chicago Tribune*. Buenos Aires Bureau Chief. B. 1957, Los Angeles, CA. Harvard, 1982, BA; The London School of Economics, 1984, MS, African Politics. *The Christian Science Monitor*, stringer, 1983. *Orlando Sentinel*, city reporter, 1984-88. *CT*, metro reporter, 1988-90; Buenos Aires bur. chief, 1990-present.

Mashek, John W. *The Boston Globe*. Political Correspondent. U. Minnesota, 1953, Pol. Sci. US Army, 1953-55. *Dallas Morning News*, local reporter, 1955-60; Washington reporter, 1960-64. *U.S.News & World Report*, Houston bur., 1964-70; Washington bur., cong. corr., 1970-74; White House corr., 1974-78; political ed., 1978-85. *Atlanta Journal-Constitution*, pol. and nat. corr., 1985-89. *BG*, political corr., 1989-present.

Mathews, Jay. *The Washington Post*. Reporter. B. 1945, Long Beach, CA. Harvard, 1967, Government/Chinese; 1971, MA, East Asian Studies. US Army, 1967-69. *WP*, metro reporter, 1971-76; Hong Kong bur. chief, 1976-79; Beijing bur., 1979-81; Los Angeles bur. chief, 1981-92; New York bur., financial reporter, 1992-present. Author of several books, including *Escalante: The Best Teacher in America* (1988).

Maugh, Thomas H., II. *Los Angeles Times*. Science Writer. B. 1943, Denver, CO. MIT, 1965, BS, Humanities; 1966, BS, Chemistry; UC-Santa Barbara, 1970, PhD, Chemistry. *Chemical Engineering News*, sci. writer, 1970-72. *Science*, researcher/sr. writer, 1972-85. *LAT*, sci. writer, 1985-present.

Mauro, Tony. *Legal Times*. Columnist. *USA Today*. Supreme Court Correspondent. B. 1950, New York, NY. Rutgers, 1971, Pol. Sci.; Columbia, 1972, MS, Journalism. *Gloucester* (MA) *Daily Times*, reporter, ed., 1972-76. *Camden* (NJ) *Courier-Post*, reporter, 1976-79. Gannett News Service, Trenton bur. chief, 1979; Supreme Court corr., 1980-present. *USA Today*, Supreme Court corr., 1982-present. *Legal Times*, Supreme Court columnist, 1987-present.

McGrory, Mary. *The Washington Post*. Commentator. B. Boston, MA. Emmanuel College. *The Boston Herald*, 1947. *The Washington Star*, book reviewer, 1947-54; nat. commentator, columnist, 1954-81. *WP*, columnist, 1981-present.

McGurn, William. *Far Eastern Economic Review*. Editorial Page Editor. B. 1958. Notre Dame, 1980, Philosophy; Boston U., 1981, MS. *The American Spectator*, asst. man. ed., 1981-83. *This World*, man. ed., 1983-84. *The Wall Street Journal Europe*, editorial feature ed., 1984-86. *Asian Wall Street Journal*, dep. editorial page ed., 1987-89. *National Review*, Washington bur. chief, 1989-92. *FEER*, 1992-present. Author of *Perfidious Albion: The Abandonment of Hong Kong 1997*.

McManus, Doyle. *Los Angeles Times*. Foreign Policy Writer. B. 1953, San Francisco, CA. Stanford, 1974, BA, History. U. Brussels, 1974-75. Citizens for Senator Alan Cranston, asst. field director, 1974. UPI, Middle East corr./Belgrade bur. chief, 1975-78. *LAT*, metro reporter, 1978-79; Beirut bur. chief, 1979-81; New York bur. chief, 1981-83; Washington bur., 1983-present. Co-author of several books, including *Landslide: The Unmaking of the President* (1988).

Mecham, Michael R. *Aviation Week & Space Technology*, Asian Bureau Chief. B. 1946, Los Angeles, CA. Claremont, 1968, Pol. Sci.; American U., MA, Communications. *AWST*, cong. ed., 1987-90; Bonn bur. chief, 1990-92; Asian bur. chief, 1993-present.

Melloan, George. *The Wall Street Journal*. Deputy Editorial Page Editor. B. Greenwood, IN. Butler U., BS, Journalism. *WSJ*, copyreader, 1952; reporter, "Page One" editorial staff, "Business" column ed., Atlanta bur. man., Cleveland bur. man., 1952-66; London corr., 1966-70; ed. writer, 1970-79; editorial page dep. ed., 1973-present. Co-author (with wife Joan Melloan) of *The Carter Economy* (1978).

Merline, John. *Investor's Business Daily*. Washington Correspondent. B. 1962, Detroit, MI. U. Michigan, BA, Philosophy. *The Times of The Americas*, asst. ed., 1985-86. *Consumers' Research Magazine*, ed., 1986-91. Radio America, commentator, 1987-91. *IBD*, 1991-present.

Methvin, Eugene H. *Reader's Digest*. Senior Editor. B. 1934, Vienna, GA. U. Georgia, 1955, BA, Journalism; graduate study in Law; US Air Force, 1955-58. *The Vienna* (GA) *News*, 1940-51. *Atlanta Constitution*, reporter, 1952. *Washington Daily News*, reporter, 1958-60. *Reader's Digest*, Washington bur., writer, assoc. ed., sr. ed., 1960-present. Author of two books, including *The Rise of Radicalism* (1973).

Moberg, David. *In These Times*. Senior Editor. B. 1943, Galesburg, IL. Carleton College, 1965, Philosophy; U. Chicago, 1972, MA, Anthropology; 1978, PhD, Anthropology. *Newsweek*, Los Angeles bur., 1965-66. *ITT*, sr. ed., 1976-present.

Moore, Molly E. *The Washington Post*. South Asia Bureau Chief. B. 1956, Lake Charles, LA. Georgetown, 1978, American Govt. *Lake Charles American Press*, pol. reporter, 1971-78. New Orleans *Times-Picayune*, education writer, investigative team, 1978-81. *WP*, Virginia politics, 1981-86; Pentagon, 1986-92; South Asia bur. chief, 1992-present. Author of *A Woman at War: Storming Kuwait with the U.S. Marines* (1993).

Morgenson, Gretchen. *Worth*. Executive Editor. B. 1956, State College, PA. St. Olaf College (MN), 1976, English/History. *Vogue*, asst. ed., personal finance columnist, 1976-81. Dean Witter, stockbroker, 1981-84. *Money*, staff writer, 1984-86. *Forbes*, sr. ed., 1986-93. *Worth*, exec. ed., 1993-present. Co-author of *The Woman's Guide to the Stock Market* (1981).

Morrison, David C. *National Journal*. National Security Correspondent. B. 1953, Minneapolis, MN. Columbia, 1978, History/Black Studies; 1982, MSJ. Center for Defense Information, sr. analyst, 1982-85. *National Journal*, 1985-present.

Morrocco, John D. *Aviation Week & Space Technology*. Senior Military Editor. Boston College, AB. London School of Economics and Pol. Sci., MA. *AWST*, mil. ed., 1986-89; sr. mil. ed., 1989-present. Author, *Thunder from Above* and *Rain of Fire*.

Mortimer, Edward. *Financial Times*. Foreign Affairs Editor. B. 1943. Balliol College. All Souls College (Oxford), Fellow, 1984-86. *The Times* (London), asst. Paris corr., 1967-70; foreign specialist, editorial writer, 1973-85. *FT*, columnist, foreign affairs ed., 1987-present. Author of several books, including *The World that FDR Built* (1989).

Moseley, Ray. *Chicago Tribune*. Senior European Correspondent. B. 1932, Marshall, TX. U. North Texas, 1952. *Rome Daily American*, man. ed., 1961-62; *Philadelphia Bulletin*, diplomatic corr., 1971-72. UPI, Europe, Africa, and Middle East news ed., 1974-77. *CT*, 1977-present.

Munro, Neil. *Defense News*. Intelligence Reporter. B. 1962, Dublin, Ireland. University College (Dublin), 1983, BA, History; King's College (London), 1985, War Studies. *Strategy and Defence*, 1983-84. Freelance, 1986-87. *Government Computer News*, Defense Dept. reporter, 1987-89. *DN*, 1989-present. Author of *The Quick and the Dead: Electronic Combat and Modern War* (1990).

Murphy, Caryle. *The Washington Post*. Middle East Correspondent. B. 1946, Hartford, CT. Trinity (Washington, DC), BA, History; Johns Hopkins School of Advanced International Studies, MA, Islamic studies. Freelance, Angola, 1974-76. *WP*, South Africa corr., 1977-82; Middle East corr., 1982-present.

Murphy, Kim. *Los Angeles Times*. Cairo Correspondent. B. 1955, Indianapolis, IN. Minot State, 1977, BA, Eng. Lit. *The North Biloxian*, asst. reporter, 1973-74. *Minot* (ND) *Daily News*, reporter, 1978-80. *The Orange County* (CA) *Register*, reporter, 1980-83; asst. metro ed., 1982-83. *LAT*, staff writer (Orange County edition), 1983-86; staff writer—civil courts, 1986-89; Cairo correspondent, 1989-present.

Murray, Alan S. *The Wall Street Journal*. Washington Economics Reporter. B. 1954, Akron, OH. U. North Carolina, 1977, English; London School of Economics, 1980, MS, Economics; Luce Scholar, Japan, 1981-82. *The Chattanooga Times*, bus. and econ. ed., 1977-79. *Congressional Quarterly*, intl. econ. reporter, 1980-81; 1982-83. *Japan Economic Journal*, Tokyo reporter, 1981-82. *The Wall Street Journal*, DC econ. reporter, 1983-present. Co-author (with Jeffrey Birnbaum) of *Showdown at Gucci Gulch* (1987).

Murray, Frank J. *The Washington Times*. Senior White House Correspondent. B. 1938, New York, NY. AP, Miami and Washington bureaus, various Florida newspapers, reporter, 1963-70. *The Washington Star*, night city ed., 1970-72. International Medical News Group, exec. man. ed., 1972-78. *Miami News*, city ed., 1978-79. *Medical Tribune*, editor-in-chief, 1979-81. *Florida Nursing News*, founding ed. and pub., 1981-85. Hollywood, FL *Sun-Tattler*, man. ed., 1986-87. *WT*, 1987-present.

Muwakkil, Salim. *In These Times*. Senior Editor. B. 1947, New York, NY. Rutgers, 1973, Pol. Sci. AP, Newark, NJ bur., 1972-74. *Muhammad Speaks*, Senior Editor 1974-77. Freelance, 1977-present. WVON-AM, Chicago, frequent talk-show host. "Our Voices" (BET), frequent commentator. Canadian Broadcast Association, frequent commentator. *ITT* sr. ed., current.

Nagourney, Adam. *USA Today*. White House Reporter. B. 1954, New York, NY. SUNY-Purchase, 1977, BA, Politics and Economics. Gannett Westchester Newspapers, 1977-82. New York *Daily News*, Albany bur., political reporter, 1982-86; Albany bur. chief, 1986-87; presidential campaign corr., 1988; political reporter, 1989-90. *USA Today*, 1990-present.

Nasar, Sylvia. *The New York Times*. Business Reporter. Antioch, BA, Literature; NYU, MA, Economics. Institute for Economic Analysis, NYU, asst. research scientist. Scientists' Institute for Public Information, dir. of energy programs. Control Data Corp., sr. economist. *Fortune*, assoc. ed., 1983-90. *U.S.News & World Report*, "Economic Outlook" columnist, 1990-91. *NYT*, bus. reporter, 1991-present.

Nash, Nathaniel C. *The New York Times*. Buenos Aires Bureau Chief. *NYT*, bus./financial copy ed., 1973-79; asst. to bus./financial news ed., 1979-85; bus./financial reporter, 1985-91; Buenos Aires bur. chief, 1991-present.

Nazario, Sonia L. *Los Angeles Times*. Urban Affairs Writer. B. 1960, Madison, WI. Williams College, 1982, BA, History. UC-Berkeley, 1988, MA, Latin American Studies. *El Pais* (Madrid, Spain), reporter, 1980. *The Washington Post*, intern, 1981. *The Wall Street Journal*, reporter, 1982-86; 1988-93. *LAT*, urban affairs writer, 1993-present.

Neff, Robert. *BusinessWeek*. Tokyo Bureau Chief. B. 1947, St. Louis, MO. U. Michigan, 1969, BA, Pol. Sci.; Missouri, 1974, MA, Journalism. *Pacific Business News*, reporter, news ed., 1975-76. *Kansas City Star*, reporter, 1976-77. *BW*, Los Angeles corr., 1977-79. McGraw-Hill World News, Tokyo bur. chief, 1979-83. *International Management*, man. ed., 1983-86. *BW*, International Edition ed., 1987-89; Tokyo bur. chief, 1989-present.

Neikirk, William R. *Chicago Tribune*. Senior Writer. B. 1938, Irvine, KY. U. Kentucky, 1960, BA, Journalism. *Lexington* (KY) *Herald*, asst. ed., 1960-61. AP, southern corr., chief economic corr., 1961-74. *CT*, econ. corr., 1974-77; White House corr., 1977; econ. corr., 1978-83; Washington bur. news ed., 1983-84; econ. corr. and Sunday columnist, 1984-88; Business section, asst. man. ed., 1988-91; Washington bur., sr. writer and columnist, 1991-present. Author of several books, including *Volcker: Portrait of the Moneyman* (1987).

Nelan, Bruce Woodward. *Time*. Senior Writer. B. 1934, Hammond, IN. U. Illinois, 1956, Journalism; Columbia, 1961, MA, International Affairs. Twentieth-Century Fox Movietone News, weekend news ed., 1959-61. Carnegie Endowment for International Peace, Director of Information and Education, 1961-65. *Time*, State Dept. corr., 1965-68; Hong Kong bur. chief, 1968-72; Bonn bur. chief, 1972-76; defense corr., 1976-78; Moscow bur. chief, 1978-81; nat. security corr., 1981-83; news ed., 1983-85; South Africa bur. chief, 1985-89; "World Section," sr. writer, 1989-present.

Nelson, Jack. *Los Angeles Times*. Washington Bureau Chief. B. 1929, Talladega, AL. Georgia State, Economics; Harvard (Nieman Fellowship), Politics, History, and Public Administration. Biloxi, MS *Daily Herald*, reporter, 1947-51. US Army, 1951-52. *Atlanta Constitution*, staff writer, 1952-65. *LAT*, Atlanta bur. chief., 1965-70; investigative reporter, 1970-75; Washington bur. chief, 1975-present.

Nicholson, Mark. *Financial Times*. Middle East Correspondent. B. 1960, Darlington, UK. Clare College, Philosophy; Carleton College, Journalism; Cambridge, Philosophy/Journalism. *New African Magazine*, writer/ed., 1985-86. *FT*, "United Kingdom" section ed., 1986-90; ed., reporter, 1990-91; London, Middle East corr., 1991-92; Cairo, Middle East corr., 1993-present.

Nickerson, Colin. *The Boston Globe*. Roving Foreign Correspondent. B. 1950, Cambridge, MA. Marlboro College, 1975. *BG*, northern New England reporter, 1980; roving Africa corr., 1983-88; Asia bureau chief, 1988-93; roving foreign corr., 1993-present.

Niebuhr, Gustav. Washington Post. Staff Writer. B. Arlington, MA. Pomona College, 1977, BA, History; Oxford, 1980, History. Pittsfield, MA *Berkshire Eagle*, 1980. *Atlanta Journal-Constitution*, religion reporter, 1986-89. *The Wall Street Journal*, religion reporter, 1989-92. *WP*, staff writer, 1992-present.

Noah, Timothy. *The Wall Street Journal*. National Correspondent. B. 1958, New York, NY. Harvard, 1980, English. *The New Republic*, writer, 1981-82. *The New York Times*, asst. op-ed. page ed., 1982-83. *The Washington Monthly*, ed., 1983-85. Freelance, 1985-86. *Newsweek*, DC corr., 1986-89. *The New Republic*, DC corr., 1989-90. *WSJ*, housing, urban affairs, and civil rights corr., 1990-present.

Nolan, Martin F. *The Boston Globe*. Reporter. B. 1940, Boston, MA. Boston College, 1961, History. US Army, 1963-65. *BG*, reporter, 1965-69; Washington bur. chief, 1969-81; editorial page ed., 1981-91; reporter, 1991-present.

Nordwall, Bruce D. *Aviation Week & Space Technology*. Senior Avionics Editor. B. 1936, Norfolk, NE. US Naval Academy, 1959, BS; 1966, BSEE. Naval aviator, squadron commander, and major program manager. Retired as Capt. *AWST*, avionics ed., 1986-93; sr. avionics ed., 1993-present.

Novak, Michael. *Forbes*. Columnist. *Crisis*. Editor-in-Chief. B. 1933, Johnstown, PA. Stonehill, 1956, Theology; Gregorian U. (Rome), 1958, Theology; Harvard, 1966, MA, History/Philosophy of Religion. *Forbes*, "The Larger Context" columnist, 1989-present. *Crisis*, co-founder; editor-in-chief, 1993-present. Author of numerous books, most recently, *The Catholic Ethic and the Spirit of Capitalism* (1993).

Novak, Robert D. Creators Syndicate. "Inside Report" Columnist with Rowland Evans, Jr. B. 1931, Joliet, IL. U. Illinois, 1952, English. US Army, 1952-54. Joliet *Herald-News*, reporter. Champaign-Urbana *Courier*, reporter. *The Wall Street Journal*, reporter, 1958-61; chief cong. corr., 1961-63. "Inside Report," columnist, with Rowland Evans, Jr., 1963-present. *Reader's Digest*, roving ed., 1980-present. "Evans & Novak" weekly interview show (CNN), co-host. "Capital Gang" (CNN) weekly program, panelist, co-exec. prod., current. Co-author several books, including (with Evans), *The Reagan Revolution* (1981).

Nulty, Peter. *Fortune*. Board of Editors. B. 1943, New York, NY. Wesleyan; Columbia, MA, International Affairs. *Middle East Monitor*, ed., 1970-75. *Middle East Journal*, asst. ed., 1970-75. *Fortune*, reporter, researcher; assoc. ed., 1976-90; Board of Editors, 1990-present.

Opall, Barbara A. *Defense News*. Staff Reporter. B. 1960, Uniontown, PA. American U., BA. *The Jerusalem Post*, staff reporter, 1982-86. American Israel Public Affairs Committee, director of media relations, 1986-87. Israel Broadcast Authority, broadcaster, 1992-present. USA Radio News Network, broadcaster, 1992-present. *DN*, staff reporter, 1988-present.

O'Rourke, P.J. *Rolling Stone*. International Affairs Desk Chief. B. 1947, Toledo, OH. Miami U. (Ohio), 1970, BA, English; Johns Hopkins, 1970, MA, English. *Harry*, ed., 1971. *The Herald*, feature ed., 1972. *National Lampoon*, assoc. ed., 1973-75; man. ed., 1975-77; editor-in-chief, 1975-81. *The American Spectator* and *Automobile*, contrib. ed. *RS*, 1981-present. Author of several books, most recently, *Give War a Chance* (1992).

Ostrow, Ronald J. *Los Angeles Times*. Staff Writer. B. 1931, San Francisco, CA. UC-Berkeley, 1953, BA, Journalism; 1960, MA, Journalism. *The Wall Street Journal*, West Coast reporter, 1956-60. Western Air Lines, news bur. man., 1960-61. *BusinessWeek*, Los Angeles bur., asst. ed., 1961-62. *LAT*, financial writer, 1962-65; Washington, Supreme Court reporter, investigative reporter, 1966-present. Co-author (with Griffin Bell) of *Taking Care of the Law* (1982).

Ozanne, Julian. *Financial Times*. Israel Correspondent. B. 1964, Nairobi, Kenya. London School of Economics, 1987, government. *FT*, Africa corr., 1988-93; Israel corr., 1993-present.

Page, Clarence. *Chicago Tribune*. Editorial Board, Columnist. B. 1947, Dayton, OH. Ohio U., 1969, Journalism. *CT*, reporter and asst. city ed., 1969-80. WBBM-TV, director of Community Affairs Dept., 1980-82; reporter, planning ed., 1982-84. "Lead Story" (BET), panelist. "Weekend Sunday" (NPR), biweekly commentator. *CT*, columnist and editorial board member, 1984-present.

Parks, Michael. *Los Angeles Times*. Jerusalem Bureau Chief. B. 1943, Detroit, MI. U. Windsor (Ontario), 1965, BA, Classical Languages and Eng. Lit. *Detroit News*, reporter, 1962-65. Time-Life News Service, corr., 1965-66. *The Suffolk* (NY) *Sun*, asst. city ed., 1966-68. Baltimore *Sun*, gen. assign. reporter, 1968-70; Saigon corr., 1970-72; Moscow corr., 1972-75; Middle East corr., 1975-78; Hong Kong bur. chief, 1978-79; Peking bur. chief, 1979-80. *LAT*, Peking bur. chief, 1980-84; Johannesburg bur. chief, 1984-88; Moscow bur. chief, 1988-93; Jerusalem bur. chief, 1993-present.

Passell, Peter. *The New York Times*. Economics Columnist. B. 1944, Pittsburgh, PA. Swarthmore, 1966, Economics; Yale, 1970, PhD, Economics. Columbia, asst. econ. prof., 1971-76. *NYT*, editorial board member, specializing in econ., 1977-present; econ. columnist, 1988-present. Author of two books, including *The Best* (1977).

Pear, Robert. *The New York Times*. Defense Correspondent. B. 1949, Washington, DC. Harvard, 1971, BA, English, History, and Lit.; Balliol College (Oxford), 1973; Columbia, 1974, MS, Journalism. *The Washington Star*, reporter, 1974-79. *NYT*, DC corr., State Dept., 1979-90; domestic corr., 1990-92; defense corr., 1992-present.

Peel, Quentin. *Financial Times*. Chief Correspondent. B. 1948, Woking, UK. Cambridge, Economics. *FT*, staff writer, 1975-76; Southern Africa corr., 1976-81; Africa ed., 1981-84; European Community corr., 1984-87; Moscow corr., 1988-91; Moscow chief corr., 1991-present.

Perry, James M. *The Wall Street Journal*. Political Reporter. B. 1927, Elmira, NY. Trinity, 1950, English. *Leatherneck Magazine*, 1946. *Hartford* (CT) *Times*, 1950-52. *Philadelphia Bulletin*, 1952-62. *National Observer*, 1962-77. *WSJ*, pol. reporter, 1977-85; London bur., 1985-86; pol. reporter, 1987-present. Author of several books, including *Barry Goldwater* (1964) and *The New Politics* (1966).

Pine, Art. *Los Angeles Times*. Washington Correspondent. B. 1939. U. Missouri, 1960, BJ; 1962, MA, Journalism. *Atlanta Constitution*, reporter, 1966; Washington corr., 1967-69. Baltimore *Sun*, reporter, 1969; Washington corr., 1970-77. *Washington Post*, reporter, 1977-81. *The Wall Street Journal*, Washington corr., 1981-87. *LAT*, Washington corr., 1988-present.

Podhoretz, Norman. *Commentary*. Editor-In-Chief. B. 1930, Brooklyn, NY. Columbia, 1950, English; Cambridge, 1953, English. *Commentary*. North America Syndicate, columnist, 1985-present. Author of six books, including *The Bloody Crossroads* (1986).

Postrel, Virginia I. *Reason*. Editor. B. 1960, Asheville, NC. Princeton, 1982, BA, English. *The Wall Street Journal*, intern, 1981; reporter, 1982-84. *Inc.*, writer, 1984-86. *Reason*, asst. ed., 1986-88; assoc. ed., 1988-89; ed., 1989-present.

Power, William. *The Wall Street Journal.* Reporter. B. 1961, Philadelphia, PA. Fordham, 1984, Media Studies. *The Wall Street Journal*, 1984-present.

Priest, Dana. *The Washington Post.* Staff Writer. B. 1957, San Louis Obispo, CA. UC-Santa Cruz, 1981, Pol. Sci. *St. Petersburg* (FL) *Times*. *WP*, asst. foreign ed., 1986-87; metro reporter, 1987-89; federal govt. reporter, 1989-present.

Proctor, Paul. *Aviation Week & Space Technology*. Reporter. B. 1952, Newton, MA. Syracuse U., 1970, BA, English; 1974, MA. *Professional Pilot Magazine*, exec. ed., 1980-84. *AWST*, 1985-present.

Pruden, Wesley. *The Washington Times.* Editor-In-Chief. B. 1935, Jackson, MS. Little Rock Junior College, 1955, History. *Arkansas Gazette*, 1952-56. Memphis *Commercial Appeal*, 1956-63. *The National Observer*, 1963-76. Freelance, 1976-82. *WT*, columnist, 1982-present; editor-in-chief, 1992-present.

Quindlen, Anna. *The New York Times.* Columnist. Barnard College, 1974. *NYT*, reporter, dep. metro ed., 1977-86; columnist, 1986-present.

Quinn, Jane Bryant. *Newsweek*. Contributing Editor. Washington Post's Writers Group, Financial Columnist. B. 1939, Niagara Falls, NY. Middlebury College, 1960, BA. McGraw-Hill, *Personal Finance Letter*, ed. and gen. man. *Insider's Newsletter*, assoc. ed., 1962-65; co-ed., 1966-67. Cowles Book Co., sr. ed., 1968. *BusinessWeek Letter*, editor-in-chief, 1968-73; gen. man., 1973-74. *Woman's Day*, contrib., "Money Facts" columnist, 1974-present. NBC-TV, News & Information Service, contrib., 1976-77. WCBS-TV, New York, bus. corr., 1979. CBS-TV News, corr., 1978-present. *Newsweek*, contrib. ed., 1978-present. Author of several books, including *Making the Most of Your Money* (1991).

Quinn-Judge, Paul. *The Boston Globe.* Washington Correspondent. B. 1949, London, UK. Trinity College (Cambridge), Modern Languages/History. *The Christian Science Monitor*, Moscow corr., 1986-89. *BG*, Moscow corr., 1989-92; Washington corr., 1993-present.

Raspberry, William J. *The Washington Post*. Washington Post Writers Group. Urban Affairs Columnist. B. Okalona, MS. Indiana Central College, BA, History. US Army, 1960-62. *Indianapolis Recorder*, reporter, photographer, ed., 1956-60. *WP*, columnist, 1960-present.

Reid, T.R. *The Washington Post.* Tokyo Correspondent. B. Baltimore, MD. Princeton, BA; George Washington U. Law School. *Trenton Times*, reporter; Washington bur. chief. *WP*, cong. affairs reporter, 1977-81; "The Federal Page" ed., 1981-83; Denver bur. chief, 1983-90; Tokyo corr., 1990-present. Author of several books, including *The Chip: How Two Americans Invented the Microchip and Launched a Revolution* (1985).

Reinhold, Robert. *The New York Times.* Los Angeles Bureau Chief. B. 1941, New York, NY. Johns Hopkins, 1962, Biology; Columbia, 1965, MS. *NYT*, sci. reporter, 1967-69; Boston bur., 1970-75; Washington bur., 1976-82; Houston bur., 1982-87; Los Angeles bur. chief, 1988-present.

Rempel, Bill. *Los Angeles Times.* National Correspondent. B. 1947, Palmer, AK. Pepperdine, 1969, BA, Journalism. *LAT*, suburban staff, 1973-76; waterfront reporter, 1976-78; state feature writer, 1978-80; Chicago bur. reporter, 1980-84; financial reporter, 1984-89; nat. correspondent, 1989-present.

Rensberger, Boyce. *The Washington Post.* Science Editor. B. 1942. U. Miami, 1964, Zoology; Syracuse, 1966, MS. *Detroit Free Press*, sci. writer, 1966-71. *The New York Times,* sci. writer, 1971-79. "3-2-1 Contact," head writer, 1979-81. *Science*, sr. ed., 1981-84. *WP*, sci. writer, 1984-88; sci. ed., 1988-present. Author of *The Cult of the Wild* (1977) and *How the World Works* (1986).

Rich, Spencer. *The Washington Post.* Staff Writer. B. New York, NY. NYU, BA, Modern European History; Columbia, MA, Russian/European History. *Congressional Quarterly*, writer. *WP*, asst. nat. ed., 1966; cong. reporter, 1968-69; Senate reporter, 1969-77; nat. desk, staff writer, 1978-present.

Richburg, Keith. *The Washington Post.* Africa Correspondent. B. Detroit, MI. U. Michigan, 1980, BS, Pol. Sci. London School of Economics, MA, 1984, International Affairs and Development. *WP*, Maryland politics reporter, 1980-83; education and gen. assign., 1984-86; Southeast Asia corr., 1986-90; Africa corr., 1991-present.

Richter, Paul. *Los Angeles Times.* Staff Writer. B. 1950, Schenectady, NY. Clark U., 1972, BA, History. Easton, MD *Star-Democrat*, reporter, 1974-76; ed., 1976. Charlottesville, VA *Daily Progress*, gen. assign. reporter, 1976-78. *LAT*, staff writer, 1981-84; New York bur., bus. reporter, 1984-91; Washington bur., 1991-present. Co-author, *California and the American Tax Revolt* (1983).

Riding, Alan. *The New York Times.* Paris Bureau Chief. B. 1943, Rio De Janeiro, Brazil. Bristol U. (UK), 1964, BA; Grays Inn, qualified barrister, 1966. Freelance, *Financial Times*, *The Economist* and *The New York Times*, 1971-78. *NYT*, Mexico corr., 1978-84; Brazil bur. chief, 1984-89; Paris bur. chief, 1989-present. Author of *Distant Neighbors: A Portrait of Mexicans.*

Risen, James. *Los Angeles Times.* Economics Writer. B. 1955, Cincinnati, OH. Brown, 1977, BA, History; Northwestern, 1978, MS, Journalism. *Fort Wayne* (IN) *Journal-Gazette*, reporter, 1978-79. *The Miami Herald*, reporter, 1980-81. *Detroit Free Press*, reporter, 1981-84. *LAT*, Detroit bur., staff writer, 1984-90; Washington bur., econ. writer, 1990-present.

Roberts, Paul Craig. Scripps Howard News Service. Syndicated Columnist. B. 1939, Atlanta, GA. Georgia Tech, 1961, Industrial Management; U. Virginia, 1967, PhD, Economics; UC-Berkeley; Merton College (Oxford). Economic counsel for Rep. Jack Kemp [R-NY] and staff economist for House Appropriations Committee, 1975-76. Chief Republican staff economist, House Budget Committee, 1976-77. Economic counsel for Sen. Orrin Hatch [R-UT], 1977-78. Asst. Secretary of the Treasury for Economic Policy, 1981-82. Center for Strategic and International Studies, William E. Simon Chair, 1982-93. Cato Institute, Washington, Distinguished Fellow, current. Institute for Political Economy, Washington, chairman, current. Hoover Institution, Palo Alto, CA, Distinguished Adjunct Scholar. *The Washington Times*, columnist, current. *BusinessWeek*, columnist, current. *Le Figaro*, columnist, current. *National Review*, contrib. ed., current. Scripps Howard News Service, syndicated columnist, current. Author of several books, including *The Supply-Side Revolution* (1984).

Roberts, Steven V. *U.S.News & World Report.* Senior Writer. B. 1943, Bayonne, NJ. Harvard, 1964, Government. *The New York Times*, research asst. to James Reston, 1964-65; metro reporter, 1965-69; Los Angeles bur. chief, 1969-74; Athens bur. chief, 1974-77; Washington bur., reporter, 1977-80; cong. corr., 1980-86; White House corr., 1986-89. *USNWR*, sr. writer, 1989-present.

Robinson, Eugene. *The Washington Post.* London Correspondent. B. Orangeburg, SC. U. Michigan. *San Francisco Chronicle*, reporter, 1975-79. *WP*, City Hall reporter, 1980; asst. city ed., 1981-84; city ed., 1984-87, South American corr., 1988-92; London corr., 1992-present.

Rockwell, Keith. *The Journal of Commerce.* European Bureau Chief. B. 1958, Boston, MA. Tufts, BA, Hist./Pol. Sci.; George Washington U., MBA, 1991. *JC*, editorial page ed., 1984-86; enterprise ed., 1986-87; intl. econ. corr., 1987-91; European bur. chief, 1991-present.

Rodriguez, Paul M. *The Washington Times.* National/Congressional Correspondent. B. 1951, Washington, DC. George Washington U. Bureau of National Affairs, Inc., publications, 1972-87. CNN, commentator, early 1980's. States News Service, 1988-89. *WT*, 1989-present.

Rohter, William Lawrence (Larry). *The New York Times.* Miami Bureau Chief. B. 1950, Oak Park, IL. School of Foreign Service, 1971; Columbia, 1971-73, School of Intl. Affairs. *Washington Post*, Style section reporter, 1973-77. *Newsweek*, Latin American bur. chief, Asian Regional Ed., 1977-84. *NYT*, reporter, 1984-87; Mexico City bur. chief, 1987-91; Hollywood corr., 1991-92; Miami bur. chief, 1992-present.

Rosen, Jeffrey. *The New Republic.* Legal Affairs Editor. B. 1964, New York, NY. Harvard, 1986, English and Government; Balliol College (Oxford), 1988, BA; Yale, 1991, JD.

Rosenbaum, David E. *The New York Times.* Washington Correspondent. B. 1942, Miami, FL. Dartmouth, 1963, AB; Columbia, 1965, MS, Journalism. *The St. Petersburg* (FL) *Times*, 1960-66. *Ilford Recorder* (UK), 1966. *Congressional Quarterly*, 1967-68. *NYT*, Washington bur., reporter, 1968-81; enterprise ed., 1981-84; Washington corr., 1984-present.

Rosenberg, Howard. *Los Angeles Times.* Television Critic. B. 1942, Kansas City, MO. Oklahoma U., 1964, BA, History; U. Minnesota, 1966, MA, Pol. Sci. *White Bear* (MN) *Weekly Press*, ed., 1965-66. *Moline* (IL) *Dispatch*, reporter, 1966-68. *Louisville Times*, reporter, 1968-70; TV critic, 1970-78. *LAT*, TV critic and nat. syndicated columnist, 1978-present.

Rosenstiel, Thomas B. *Los Angeles Times.* B. 1956, Redwood City, CA. Oberlin College, 1978, AB, English Literature; Columbia, 1980, MS, Journalism. *Jack Anderson's Washington Merry Go 'Round*, reporter, 1978-79. Palo Alto, CA *Peninsula Times Tribune*, reporter, 1980-82; bus. ed., 1982-83. *LAT*, financial reporter, 1983-84; media reporter, 1984-89; Washington bur., media writer, 1989-present. Author of two books, including, *Strange Bedfellows* (1993).

Rosenthal, Abraham Michael (A.M.). *The New York Times.* "On My Mind" Columnist. B. 1922, Sault Ste. Marie, Ontario. City College of New York, 1944, BS, Social Science. *NYT*, reporter, UN corr., 1944-54; India bur., 1954-58; Warsaw bur., corr., 1958-59; Geneva bur., corr., 1959-61; Tokyo bur., corr., 1961-63; metro ed., 1963-66; asst. man. ed., 1966-69; man. ed., 1969-77; exec. ed., 1977-86; assoc. ed., 1986-88; "On My Mind" columnist, 1986-present. GP Putnam, ed. at large, 1988-present. Author of *Three Witnesses*; co-author of three books, including *One More Victim.*

Ross, Michael. *Los Angeles Times.* Capitol Hill Correspondent. B. 1949, New York, NY. UPI, foreign correspondent, 1971-76. Ford Foundation Fellowship, Harvard, 1976-77. UPI, foreign desk ed., 1977-82; Peking bur. chief, 1982-84; Tokyo bur., sr. ed. for Asia, 1984-85. *LAT*, Middle East corr., 1985-89; Washington bur., 1989-present.

Rowen, Hobart. The Washington Post Writers Group. Columnist. B. 1918, Burlington, VT. City College of New York, 1938, BSS, Government and Sociology. *The New York The Journal of Commerce*, copy boy, reporter, 1938-41; Washington bur., reporter, 1941-44. *Newsweek*, Washington bur., 1944-65. *WP*, financial ed., 1966-69; asst. man. ed., 1969-75; econ. ed. and columnist, 1975-present. Washington Post Writers Group, columnist, 1975-present. "Nightly Business Report" TV show, commentator. "Washington Week in Review" TV show, frequent guest. Author of *The Free Enterprisers* (1964). Co-author of several books.

Royko, Mike. *Chicago Tribune.* Columnist. B. 1932, Chicago, IL. Wright Junior College. Air Force Base newspaper, ed., 1952-56. City News Bureau of Chicago, asst. day city ed., 1956-59. *Chicago Daily News*, gen. assign. reporter, 1959-76. *Chicago Sun-Times*, columnist, 1976-84. *CT*, columnist, 1984-present.

Rudnitsky, Howard. *Forbes.* Senior Editor. City College of New York, BBS. Moody's Investor Services, 1959-61. *Forbes*, statistical dept. chief, 1961-69; staff writer/assoc. ed., 1969-78; sr. writer, sr. ed., 1978-present.

Safire, William. *The New York Times.* "Essay" and "On Language" Columnist. B. 1929, New York, NY. Syracuse U., 1947-49. New York Herald Tribune Syndicate, reporter, 1949-51. WNBC-TV/WNBT, Europe and Middle East corr., 1949-51; US Army corr., 1951-54; producer, 1954-55. Tex McCrary, Inc., vice president, 1955-60. Safire Public Relations, president, 1960-68. Speechwriter and asst. to President Richard Nixon, 1969-73. *NYT*, "Essay" columnist, 1973-present; "On Language" columnist (*New York Times Magazine*), 1979-present. Author of numerous books, including *Freedom* (1987).

Samuelson, Robert J. *Newsweek.* Contributing Editor. Harvard, 1967, BA, Government. *The Washington Post*, bus. reporter, 1969-73. *The National Journal*, econ. corr., 1976; "Economic Focus" columnist, contrib. ed., 1981-84. *Newsweek*, contrib. ed., 1984-present.

Sanger, David E. *The New York Times.* Tokyo Financial Correspondent. B. 1960, White Plains, NY. Harvard, 1982, Government. *NYT*, college stringer; news clerk, 1982-83; technology reporter, 1983-88; Tokyo, financial corr., 1988-present.

Saporito, Bill. *Fortune.* Associate Editor. B. Harrison, NJ. Bucknell, BA, American Studies; Syracuse U. MA, Journalism. New York *Daily News*, 1978. *Chain Store Age Supermarkets* Magazine, sr. ed., freelance, 1982-84; *Fortune*, assoc. ed., 1984-present.

Saunders, Laura. *Forbes.* Senior Editor. U. of the South (TN), 1976, BA, English Language and Literature. National Fire Protection Association, Boston, editorial department, 1977-81. *Forbes*, reporter/researcher, 1981-82; sr. reporter-researcher, 1982-84; reporter, 1984-86; staff writer, 1986-89; assoc. ed., 1989-91; sr. ed., 1991-present.

Savage, David. *Los Angeles Times.* Staff Writer. B. 1950, McKeesport, PA. U. North Carolina, 1972, BA, Pol. Sci.; Northwestern, 1974, MS, Journalism. National Institute of Education, asst. to director, 1974-75. *EDUCATION, USA* (weekly newspaper), assoc. ed., 1976-81. *LAT*, metro reporter, 1981-86; Washington bur., staff reporter, 1986-present. Author of *Turning Right: The Making of the Rehnquist Court.*

Schmemann, Serge. *The New York Times.* Moscow Bureau Chief. B. 1945, France. Harvard, 1967, BA, English; Columbia, 1971, MA, Slavic Studies. AP, 1972-80. *NYT*, Moscow corr., 1981-84; Moscow bur. chief, 1984-87; Bonn bur. chief, 1987-92; Moscow bur. chief, 1992-present.

Schmetzer, Uli. *Chicago Tribune*. Beijing Bureau Chief. B. 1944, Stuttgart, Germany. Melbourne U. (Australia), BA, Journalism. *Sydney Morning Herald*, reporter, 1965-69. Reuters, Latin America corr., 1969-76; London corr., 1976-78. *CT*, freelance, 1981-85; Rome bur. chief, 1986-88; Beijing bur. chief, 1988-present.

Schmitt, Eric. *The New York Times*. Pentagon Correspondent. B. 1959, San Francisco, CA. Williams College. *NYT*, asst. to James Reston, 1983-84; reporter, 1983-90. Pentagon corr., 1990-present.

Schneider, Keith. *The New York Times*. Washington Reporter. B. 1956, White Plains, NY. Haverford College, 1978. Freelance, 1978-79. Wilkes-Barre, PA *Times Leader*, reporter, 1979. *The News and Courier* (SC), reporter, 1979-81. News service reporter, 1981-85. *NYT*, Washington bur., reporter, 1985-present.

Schneider, William. Los Angeles Times Syndicate. Columnist. American Enterprise Institute, Washington, resident fellow. Harvard, prof. of Government. *The Atlantic*, contrib. *Public Opinion*, contrib. *National Journal*, contrib. ed., current. CNN, pol. commentator, current.

Schribman, David M. *The Wall Street Journal*. National Political Reporter. Dartmouth, 1976, AB, History; 1977, Cambridge graduate fellow. *Buffalo Evening Star*, metro reporter, 1977-79; Washington bur., reporter, 1979-80. *The Washington Star*, society and pol. reporter, 1980-81. *The New York Times*, political reporter, 1981-84. *WSJ*, nat. pol. reporter, 1984-present.

Sciolino, Elaine. *The New York Times*. Washington Correspondent. B. 1948, Buffalo, NY. Canisius College (NY), 1970; NYU, 1971, MA, History. *Newsweek*, reporter, foreign corr., 1971-80; Rome bur. chief, 1980-82; roving intl. corr., 1982-84; *NYT*, metro reporter, 1984-85; UN bur. chief, 1985-87; Washington corr., 1987-present.

Scott, William B. *Aviation Week & Space Technology*. Senior National Editor. California State, BS, Electrical Engineering. US Air Force Test Pilot School; Officer Training School. Nine years active duty. *AWST*, sr. nat. ed., 1982-present.

Seib, Gerald F. *The Wall Street Journal*. National Political Coordinator. U. Kansas, BA, Journalism. *WSJ*, Dallas bur. reporter, 1978; Washington bur. reporter, 1980-85; Cairo corr., 1985-87; Washington bur., 1987; nat. pol. coordinator, 1992-present.

Seligman, Daniel. *Fortune*. Contributing Editor. B. 1924, New York, NY. NYU, 1946, AB, History. *The New Leader*, labor columnist, 1946. *The American Mercury*, asst. ed., 1946-50. *Fortune*, assoc. ed., 1950-59; Board of Editors, 1959-66; asst. man. ed., 1966-69. Time, Inc. Publications, sr. staff ed., 1969-70. *Fortune*, exec. ed., 1970-77; assoc. man. ed., 1977-89; contrib. ed., 1989-present; "Keeping Up" columnist, current.

Seper, Jerry. *The Washington Times*. Reporter. B. 1943, Los Angeles, CA. US Navy, 1964-68. *Chicago Enterprise-Record. San Gabriel Valley Tribune. South Bay Daily Breeze. The Tucson Citizen. The Arizona Republic. WT, 1985*-present.

Shales, Tom. *The Washington Post*. TV Critic. B. 1948, Elgin, IL. American U., 1973, Journalism. *DC Examiner*, entertainment ed. WP, TV critic, columnist, 1977-present. National Public Radio *Morning Edition*, film critic, 1979-present. Author of *On The Air!*, and co-author of *The American Film Heritage*.

Shapiro, Walter. *Esquire*. White House Correspondent. B. 1947, New York, NY. U. Michigan, 1970, BA, History; 1970-71, History, graduate studies. *Congressional Quarterly*, reporter, 1969-70. Democratic candidate for Congress (Michigan), 1972. *The Washington Monthly*, ed., 1972-76. Special asst. to Labor Secretary Ray Marshall, 1977-78. Speechwriter for President Jimmy Carter, 1979. *The Washington Post Magazine*, staff writer, 1979-83. *Newsweek*, gen. ed., 1983-87. *Time*, sr. writer, 1987-93; contributor, 1993-present. *Esquire*, 1993-present.

Shaw, David. *Los Angeles Times*. Media Critic. B. 1943, Dayton, OH. UCLA, 1965, BA, English. *Huntington Park Signal*, 1963-66. *Long Beach Independent*, reporter, 1966-68. *LAT*, reporter, 1968-74; media critic, 1974-present. Author of several books, most recently, *Press Watch* (1984).

Sheler, Jeffrey Lynn. *U.S.News & World Report*. Senior Writer. Olivet Nazarene College (IL); Grand Rapids Junior College (MI); Michigan State U., 1971, BA, Journalism; Georgetown, graduate study in Philosophy and Religion UPI, Chicago bur., 1971-72; Springfield bur., pol. corr., 1972-75; Western Michigan corr., Grand Rapids, 1975-77; Detroit bur., automotive writer, 1977-79. *USNWR*, Detroit bur. chief, 1979-80; Washington bur., assoc. ed., 1980-85; chief cong. corr., 1985-86; sr. ed., 1985-89; religion writer, 1989-present; sr. writer, 1992-present.

Shenon, Philip. *The New York Times*. Washington Reporter. B. 1959. Brown, 1981, English. *NYT*, clerk for James Reston, 1981-82; copyboy, financial desk, 1982-83; metro reporter, 1983-85; Washington reporter, 1985-present.

Sheppard, Nathaniel, Jr. *Chicago Tribune*. Central America Correspondent. B. 1948, Atlanta, GA. Morris Brown College, 1970, BA. *St. Paul Pioneer Press*, 1967. *Atlanta Journal-Constitution*, reporter, 1969-71. *The New York Times*, nat. issues, 1971-83. *CT*, gen. assign. reporter, 1983-84; Africa corr., 1984-86; Washington corr., 1986-90; Central America corr., 1990-present.

Shields, Mark. Associated Features. Syndicated Columnist. B. 1937, Weymouth, MA. Notre Dame, 1959, Philosophy/History. Campaign consultant for numerous politicians, including Senator Edmund Muskie [D-ME] and Boston Mayor Kevin White [D]. *The Washington Post*, editorial writer, 1979-81. Associated Features, columnist, 1979-present. CBS News, presidential campaign pol. commentator, 1984. Mutual Radio Network, daily commentator, 1984. WMAL radio, Washington, regular commentator, 1985-86. "Capital Gang" (CNN) weekly program, panelist, current. Author of *On the Campaign Trail* (1984).

Shogan, Robert. *Los Angeles Times*. National Political Correspondent. B. 1930, New York, NY. Syracuse U., 1951, Journalism and American Studies. *Detroit Free Press*, 1956-59. *Miami News*, telegraph ed., 1959-61. *The Wall Street Journal*, asst. ed., 1961-65. Peace Corps, evaluation officer, 1966. *Newsweek*, corr., 1967-72. *LAT*, nat. pol. corr., 1973-present. Author of several books, including *None of the Above* (1982).

Sidey, Hugh. *Time*. Washington Contributing Editor. B. 1927, Greenfield, IA. Iowa State, BS, 1950. *Omaha World-Herald*, reporter, 1951-55. *Life*, corr., 1955-58. *Time*, corr., 1958-66; columnist, 1966-69; chief contrib. ed., 1969-78; Washington contrib. ed., 1978-present.

Simpson, Glenn R. *Roll Call*. Senior Staff Writer. B. 1964, Paoli, PA. George Washington U., 1986, BA, Journalism. *Insight Magazine*, editorial asst., 1986-87; reporter, 1987-89; writer, 1989. *Roll Call*, staff writer, 1989-93; sr. staff writer, 1993-present.

Simpson, John. *The Spectator*. Foreign Affairs Editor. B. 1944. Magdalene College (Cambridge). BBC Radio news, sub-ed., 1966-70; reporter, 1970-72; Dublin corr., 1972-75; Brussels corr., 1975-77; Johannesburg corr., 1977-78; Television news, various positions, 1978-80. *The Spectator*, foreign affairs ed., 1988-present. Author of *In the Forests of the Night* (1993).

Singer, Daniel. *The Nation*. European Correspondent. B. 1926, Warsaw, Poland. *The Economist*, editorial staff, 1951-58; Paris corr., 1958-69. *The Nation*, European correspondent, 1980-present.

Smith, Randall. *The Wall Street Journal*. Reporter. B. 1950, Montclair, NJ. Harvard, 1972, Social Relations; 1977, MBA. US Navy, 1972-76. *New York Post*, City Hall reporter, 1977-80. New York *Daily News*, real estate reporter, 1980-81. *WSJ*, real estate reporter, 1981-83; institutional investing reporter, 1983-85; computer reporter, 1985-86; reporter, 1986-present.

Sneider, Daniel. *The Christian Science Monitor*. Moscow Bureau Chief. B. 1951, Washington, DC. Columbia, 1973, East Asian History; Harvard, MA, Public Admin. Freelance, Asia, 1975-82. *Defense Week*, Tokyo corr., 1985-86; Tokyo, special corr., 1986-90; Moscow, special corr., 1993. *CSM*, Tokyo corr., 1985-90; Moscow bur. chief, 1990-present. Co-author of three books.

Snow, Tony. *Detroit News*. Syndicated Columnist. B. 1955, Berea, KY. Davidson, 1977, BA, Philosophy. Bushiangala Secondary School (Kenya), teacher, 1978-79. *The Greensboro Record*, editorial writer, 1979-81. Norfolk *Virginian-Pilot*, editorial writer, 1981-82. *The Daily Press*, editorial page ed., 1982-84. *Detroit News*, dep. editorial page ed., 1984-87. *The Washington Times*, editorial page ed., 1987-91. The White House, Dep. asst. to President George Bush for communications, dir. of speechwriting, 1991-93. *Detroit News*, columnist, 1993-present. NPR, commentator, 1993-present. WAMU-FM, Washington, "The Diane Rehm Show," panelist, 1993-present.

Sowell, Thomas. Scripps-Howard News Service. Columnist. B. 1930, Gastonia, NC. Harvard, 1958, Economics; U. Chicago, 1968, PhD. Hoover Institution, sr. fellow. *Los Angeles Herald Examiner*, 1978-80. Scripps-Howard News Service, columnist, 1984-present. *Forbes*, "Observations" columnist.

Stanfield, Rochelle L. *National Journal*. Staff Correspondent. B. 1940, Chicago, IL. Northwestern, 1962, Journalism/Pol. Sci.; 1963, MSJ. Council of State Governments, ed., *State Government News*, 1963-66. Voice of America, Latin American desk, 1966-67. National Governors' Conference, press sec., 1967-70. Advisory Commission on Intergovernmental Relations, information officer, 1971-74. US Conference of Mayors, project director 1974-76. *NJ*, corr., 1976-present.

Stanglin, Douglas. *U.S.News & World Report*. Moscow Bureau Chief. SMU, BA, Pol. Sci./Journalism. *USNWR*, Bonn bur. chief, 1985-88; diplomatic corr., 1988-91; Moscow bur. chief, 1991-present.

Starr, Barbara. *Jane's Defence Weekly*. International Security Affairs Correspondent. Cal State-Northridge, 1975. Thousand Oaks, CA *News Chronicle*, 1975-76. Bureau of National Affairs, Inc., publications, 1976-77. *Platts Oilgram News*, 1977-79. *BusinessWeek*, 1979-88. *Defense News*, 1987-88. *JDW*, 1989-present.

Stepp, Laura Sessions. *The Washington Post*. Staff Writer. B. Arkansas. Earlham College (IN), BA; Columbia, MS, Journalism. *Charlotte* (NC) *Observer*. *Philadelphia Bulletin*. *Palm Beach Times*. *WP*, ed., staff writer, 1982-present.

Sterngold, James. *The New York Times*. Tokyo Correspondent. B. 1954, Detroit, MI. Columbia, 1980, MS, Journalism. Time-Life Books, freelance, 1978-80. AP, Hong Kong corr., 1980-84. *NYT*, bus. reporter, 1984-89; Tokyo corr., 1989-present. Author of *Burning Down the House: How Greed, Deceit and Bitter Revenge Destroyed E.F. Hutton* (1990).

Stewart, James B. *The New Yorker*. Reporter. B. 1952, Quincy, IL. DePauw U., 1973, BA, History; Harvard, 1976, JD. Cravath, Swain & Moore, New York, NY, lawyer, 1976-79. *American Lawyer*, exec. ed., 1979-83. *The Wall Street Journal*, legal writer, 1983-88; "Page One" ed., 1988-92. *The New Yorker*, reporter, 1993-present. Author of *Den of Thieves*.

Stokes, Bruce. *National Journal*. International Economics Correspondent. B. 1948, Butler, PA. Georgetown, 1970, International Affairs; Johns Hopkins, 1975, MA. Worldwitch Institute, 1975-82. National Public Radio, 1983. US-Japan Leadership Institute, 1987. *NJ*, intl. econ. corr., 1984-present. Author of *Helping Ourselves* (1981).

Strom, Stephanie. The *New York Times*. Reporter. B. 1963, Texas. Northwestern, 1985, Pol. Sci./History; Columbia, 1986, MS, Journalism.

Summers, Harry. Los Angeles Times Syndicate. Military & Political Affairs Columnist. B. 1932, Covington, KY. U. Maryland, 1957, BS, Military Science; US Army Command and General Staff College, 1968, MS, Military Arts and Science; Army War College, 1981. US Army, infantry squad leader, Korea; battalions and corps operation officer, Vietnam; negotiator, POW/MIA, US withdrawal terms from Vietnam; Army War College, MacArthur Chair of Military Research, 1974-85. Ret. as Col. *U.S.News & World Report*, sr. military corr., 1985-87; contrib. ed., 1987-90. LAT Syndicate, military & pol. affairs columnist, 1987-present. Author of *On Strategy* (1982).

Tanzer, Andrew. *Forbes*. Pacific Bureau Chief. B. 1957, Washington DC. Wesleyan, 1979, BA. East Asian Studies. Columbia, 1980, MS, Journalism. *Far Eastern Economic Review*, Taiwan corr., 1980-83. *Forbes*, staff writer, 1984-85; Pacific bur. chief, 1985-present.

Taylor, Alex, III. *Fortune*. Board of Editors. B. 1945, Greenwich, CT. Middlebury, 1967, History; U. Missouri, 1969, MA, Journalism. *Detroit Free Press*, 1977-80. *Time*, assoc. ed., 1980-84. *Fortune*, Board of Editors, 1985-present.

Taylor, John. *New York*. Political Correspondent. B. 1955, Japan. U. Chicago, 1977, Disciplines of the Humanities. *Newsweek*, 1980-83. *BusinessWeek*, 1983. *Manhattan Inc.*, 1984-87. *NY*, 1987-present. Author of several books, including *Circus of Ambition: the Culture of Wealth and Power in the Eighties.*

Taylor, Stuart, Jr. American Lawyer Media. Senior Writer. B. 1948. Princeton, 1970, AB, History; Harvard, 1977, JD. Baltimore *Sun*, reporter, 1971-74. Wilmer, Cutler & Pickering, attorney, 1977-80. *The New York Times*, Washington bur., legal affairs reporter, 1980-85; Supreme Court reporter, 1985-88. Princeton, visiting lecturer, 1988-89. American Lawyer Media, sr. writer, 1989-present. *Legal Times*, contrib., current.

Thomas, Cal. Los Angeles Times Syndicate. Columnist. B. 1942, Washington, DC. American U., 1968, Eng. Lit. NBC News, 1961-65, 1969-73. KPRC-TV, Houston, 1968-69, 1973-77. WTTG-TV, Washington, commentator, 1985-present. NPR, commentator, 1985-present. Los Angeles Times Syndicate, columnist, 1984-present. Author of several books, including *Uncommon Sense* (1990).

Thomas, Rich. *Newsweek*. Chief Economics Correspondent. B. 1931, Detroit, MI. U. Michigan, 1952, BA, English Lit.; U. Frankfurt/Main (West German), 1955, graduate studies; Yale, Poynter fellow, 1975. US Army, 1952-55. U. Michigan, teaching fellow, 1957. UPI, Detroit bur., corr., 1957-59. McGraw-Hill, public affairs dept., 1959-60. *New York Post*, financial ed., 1960-62. *Newsweek*, New York bur., writer, ed., 1962-70; Washington bur., chief econ. corr., 1970-present.

Toner, Robin. *The New York Times*. Washington Correspondent. B. 1954, Chadds Ford, PA. Syracuse U., 1976, Journalism and Pol. Sci. Charleston, WV *Daily Mail*. *Atlanta Journal-Constitution*, pol. reporter, 1982-85. *NYT*, Washington corr., 1985-present.

Towell, W. Patrick. *Congressional Quarterly*. Senior Writer. B. 1945, Washington, DC. Georgetown, 1966, BA, Pol. Sci.; Northwestern, 1968, MA; U. Illinois, 1975, PhD. Cal. State College, lecturer in pol. sci., 1972-75. *CQ*, 1975-present.

Trotta, Liz. *The Washington Times*. New York Bureau Chief. Boston U.; Columbia, MA, Journalism. *Chicago Tribune*, reporter. AP, reporter. *Newsday*, reporter. NBC News, CBS News, pol. and foreign corr. Gannett Foundation Media Center, fellow, 1989-90. *WT*, New York bur. chief, 1993-present. Author, *Fighting for Air—In the Trenches with Television News* (1991).

Tumulty, Karen. *Los Angeles Times*. Senior Writer. B. 1955, San Antonio, TX. U. Texas, 1977, BA, Journalism; Harvard, 1981, MBA. *San Antonio Light*, bus. ed., gen. assign. reporter, 1977-79. *LAT*, bus. writer, 1980-83; Washington bur., staff writer, 1983-88; New York bur., nat. corr., 1988-91; Washington bur., staff writer 1991; Washington bur., sr. writer, 1991-present.

Tyler, Patrick. *The New York Times*. China Correspondent. B. 1951, St. Louis, MO. U. South Carolina, 1974, Journalism. *The Hampton County* (SC) *Guardian*, ed., 1974. *The Allandale County* (SC) *Citizen*, ed., 1974. *Charlotte* (NC) *News*, reporter, 1974. *The St. Petersburg* (FL) *Times*, police and courts reporter, 1974-78. *Congressional Quarterly*, 1978. PBS, WCET-TV, Cincinnati, "Congressional Outlook," documentary series, host, 1978. *The Washington Post*, metro reporter, foreign affairs reporter, Middle East corr., 1986-90 *NYT*, Pentagon reporter, 1990-93; China corr., 1993-present.

Tyrrell, R. Emmett, Jr. *The American Spectator*. Editor-in-Chief. B. 1943, Chicago, IL. Indiana U., 1965, History; MA, 1967. *TAS*, founder, editor-in-chief, 1967-present. Author of four books, including *The Conservative Crack-Up*.

Uchitelle, Louis. *The New York Times*. Economics Writer. B. 1932, New York, NY. U. Michigan, 1954, English/Philosophy. *Mount Vernon* (NY) *Daily Argus*, reporter. AP, reporter, 1957-64; San Juan, Puerto Rico, Caribbean corr., 1964-67; Buenos Aires, Argentina, bur. chief, 1967-73; New York bur., energy ed., 1973-74; Newsfeatures, supervising ed., 1974-77; bus. ed., 1977-80. *NYT*, sr. bus. ed., 1980-97; econ. writer, 1987-present. Columbia, journalism instructor, 1976-90.

Vartabedian, Ralph. *Los Angeles Times*. Staff Writer. B. 1951, Detroit, MI. U. Michigan, 1973, BA, Journalism; 1976, MS, Economics. *Kalamazoo Gazette*, bus. writer, 1976-79. *Minneapolis Star*, bus. writer, 1979-81. *LAT*, staff writer, 1983-present.

Wald, Matthew L. *The New York Times*. Reporter. B. 1954, Cambridge, UK. Brown, 1976, BA, Urban Studies. *NYT*, Washington bur., news clerk, 1976-77; metro reporter, 1977-78; Stamford (CT) bur., 1978-79; Hartford (CT) bur., 1979-82; metro reporter, Boston bur., reporter, 1982-88; bus. reporter, 1988-present.

Waldholz, Michael R. *The Wall Street Journal*. Science Reporter. B. 1950, Newark NJ. U. Pittsburgh, 1972, BA, English Literature; 1973; MA, English Literature. *WSJ*, science reporter, 1990-present.

Waldman, Peter. *The Wall Street Journal*. Middle East Correspondent. B. 1961, San Francisco, CA. Brown, 1984, History. *WSJ*, high-tech reporter, 1986-88; Atlanta bur., 1988-90; Jerusalem bur., 1990-91; Middle East corr., 1991-93.

Waldmeir, Patti. *Financial Times*. South Africa Correspondent. B. 1955, Detroit, MI. Clare College (Cambridge); U. Michigan, MA, English. Reuters, corr., 1980-82; European Community corr., 1982-84. *FT*, Africa corr., 1984-86; dep. features ed., 1986-87; "Lex" columnist, 1987-89; South Africa corr., 1989-93.

Wallace, Charles. *Los Angeles Times*. Singapore Bureau Chief. B. 1950, New York, NY. NYU, 1970, BA, Communications and Fine Arts. Fawcett Publications, writer, 1970-71. UPI, 1971-81. *LAT*, staff writer, 1981-84; Beirut bur. chief, 1984-85; Amman bur. chief, 1985-87; Nicosia bur. chief, 1987-90; Bangkok bur. chief, 1990-93; Singapore bur. chief; 1993-present.

Walsh, Edward. *The Washington Post*. Chicago News Bureau Chief. B. 1942, Chicago, IL. College of St. Thomas (MN), BA, Pol. Sci./Journalism; Harvard (Nieman Fellow) 1981-82. American Pol. Sci. Association Congressional Fellow, 1967-71. *Houston Chronicle*, reporter, 1967-70. *The Catholic Messenger*, Davenport, IA, reporter/ed., 1965-67. *WP*, metro reporter, 1971-76; nat. news reporter, 1976-81; Jerusalem bur. chief, 1982-86; political reporter, 1986-90; Chicago news bur. chief, 1990-present.

Walsh, Kenneth T. *U.S.News & World Report*. Senior Writer. Rutgers U., BA; American U., MA, Communications. *Asbury Park Press*, copy boy. *New Brunswick Home News*. *Northern Virginia Sun*. AP, Denver bureau, 1972-75. *Denver Post*, Washington bur., chief political writer, 1975-84. *USNWR*, 1984-present. President of White House Correspondents Association, term 1994-95.

Warsh, David. *The Boston Globe*. Financial Columnist. B. 1944, New York, NY. *Pacific Stars and Stripes*, reporter, Vietnam War. *Newsweek*. *The Wall Street Journal*, bus. reporter. *Forbes*, bus. reporter. *BG*, econ. writer, financial columnist, 1978-present.

Watanabe, Teresa. *Los Angeles Times*. Tokyo Correspondent. B. 1957, Seattle, WA. U. Southern California, 1982, BA, Journalism/East Asian Languages and Culture. *Los Angeles Herald Examiner*, editorial writer, 1981-84. *San Jose Mercury News*, suburban education writer, 1984-85; Sacramento corr., 1986-87; national corr., 1988-89. *LAT*, bus. corr., 1989-90; Tokyo corr., 1991-present.

Wattenberg, Ben. Newspaper Enterprise Syndicate. Columnist. B. 1933, New York, NY. Hobart College, 1955, BA. US Air Force, 1955-58. Aide to Vice President Hubert Humphrey. Asst. to President Lyndon Johnson, 1965-68. Business consultant, Washington, 1968-79. Adviser, Sen. Henry Jackson [D-WA], 1972, 1976. Mary Washington College, Prof. at Large, 1973-74. Coalition for a Democratic Majority, co-founder, Chairman, 1972-present. American Enterprise Institute, Washington, sr. fellow, 1977-present. United Features Syndicate, columnist, 1977-87. Newspaper Enterprise Syndicate, columnist, 1987-present. *Public Opinion*, co-ed., 1977-present. Author of several books, including *The Birth Dearth*.

Weinraub, Bernard. *The New York Times*. Hollywood Correspondent. B. 1937, New York, NY. City College of New York, BA. *NYT*, copyboy, 1961-63; news clerk, UN bur., reporter, 1963-67; foreign corr., 1967-68; metro reporter, 1968-70; London corr., 1970-73; India corr., 1973-75; London corr., 1975-77; Washington corr., 1977-87; presidential campaign reporter, 1988; Washington, Los Angeles bureaus, corr., 1988-present.

Weisberg, Jacob. *The New Republic*, Senior Editor. B. 1964, Chicago, IL. Yale, 1987, Humanities; 1989, Oxford, Politics. *TNR*, assoc. ed., 1989-90; sr. ed., 1990-present.

Weiss, Gary. *BusinessWeek*. Markets & Investments Editor. B. 1954, New York, NY. City College of New York, 1975, BA; Northwestern, 1976, MS. *Hartford* (CT) *Courant*, reporter, 1976-81. States News Service, reporter, 1981. Network News, Inc., reporter, 1981-82; bus. ed., 1982-83. *Barron's*, 1984-present. *BusinessWeek*, 1986-present.

Weisskopf, Michael. *The Washington Post*. Reporter. B. Chicago, IL. George Washington U., BA, International Affairs; Johns Hopkins, MA, International Studies; Princeton, graduate studies; Middlebury College, graduate studies. *Montgomery* (AL) *Advertiser*. Baltimore *Sun*. *WP*, metro reporter, 1977-80; Beijing bur. chief, 1980-85; nat. news desk reporter, 1985-present.

Wessel, David M. *The Wall Street Journal*. Chief Economics Correspondent. B. 1954, New Haven, CT. Haverford College, 1975, Economics; Columbia, 1980 81, Bagehot fellowship in Business and Economics. *Middletown* (CT) *Press*, 1975-77. *Hartford* (CT) *Courant*, 1977-80. *The Boston Globe*, 1981-84. *WSJ*, Boston bur., 1984-87; Washington bur., chief econ. corr., 1987-present.

Weymouth, Elizabeth G. (Lally). *The Washington Post*. Columnist. B. 1943, Maryland. Radcliffe College, 1965, BA, American History and Lit. *The Boston Globe*, reporter, 1965-66. *Thomas Jefferson: The Man, His World, His Influence*, biography, ed., 1973. Freelance, 1977-83. *Los Angeles Times*, contrib. ed., 1983-86. *WP*, columnist, 1986-present. Author of *America in 1876, The Way We Were* (1976).

White, David. *Financial Times*. Defense Correspondent. B. 1948, Harrow, UK. Queens' College (Cambridge), 1970, English. Reuters, 1970-73. *FT*, Rio De Janeiro corr., 1975-78; Paris corr., 1978-83; Madrid corr., 1983-88; defense corr., 1989-present.

Whitney, Craig R. *The New York Times*. European Diplomatic Correspondent. B. 1943, Milford, MA. Harvard, 1965, French History and Lit. *The Worcester Telegram*, reporter, 1963-65. US Navy, public affairs officer, 1966-69. *NYT*, asst. to James Reston, 1965-66, metro news staff, 1969-71; Saigon bur. chief, 1971-73; Bonn bur. chief, 1973-77; Moscow corr., 1977-80; dep. foreign ed., 1980-82; foreign ed., 1982-83; asst. man. ed., 1983-86; Washington bur. chief, 1986-88; London bur. chief, 1988-93; diplomatic corr., 1993-present. Author of *Spy Trader* (1993).

Wilford, John Noble. *The New York Times*. Science Correspondent. B. 1933, Murray, KY. U. Tennessee, 1955, BS, Journalism; Syracuse, 1956, MA, Pol. Sci. *The Wall Street Journal*, gen. assign. ed., 1956, 1959-61. *Time*, contrib. ed., 1962-65. *NYT*, sci. reporter, 1965-73; asst. nat. ed., 1973-75; dir. of sci. news, 1975-79; sci. corr., 1979-present.

Wilkie, B. Curtis. *The Boston Globe*. Reporter. B. 1940, Greenville MS. U. Mississippi, 1962, Journalism. *Clarksdale* (MS) *Press Register*, 1963-69. *Wilmington* (DE) *News Journal*, 1971-74. *BG*, Washington bur., 1977-84; Jerusalem bur., 1984-87; reporter, 1987-present.

Will, George F. *Newsweek*. Contributing Editor. B. 1941, Champaign, IL. Trinity, 1962, BA; Magdalene College (Oxford), 1964, BA, Politics, Philosophy, Economics; Princeton, MA; PhD, 1967, Politics. Senator Gordon Allott [R-CO], staffer, 1970-72. The Washington Post Writers Group, columnist, 1971-present. *National Review*, Washington ed., 1973-76. "This Week with David Brinkley" (ABC), founding member of panel, 1981-present. *Newsweek*, contrib. ed., 1976-present. Author of several books, most recently, *Restoration: Congress, Term Limits and the Recovery of Deliberative Democracy* (1992).

Williams, Carol J. *Los Angeles Times*. Vienna Bureau Chief. B. 1955, Pawtucket, RI. U. Washington, BA, Journalism, 1977. *Bremerton Sun*, reporter, 1976-79. *Fournier Newspaper*, news ed., 1979-80. AP, writer, 1980-83; foreign/world desk, 1983-84; Moscow corr., 1984-88; Berlin corr., 1988-90. *LAT*, Budapest bur. chief, 1990-91; Vienna bur. chief, 1992-present.

Wines, Michael. *The New York Times*. Washington Correspondent. B. 1951, Louisville, KY. U. Kentucky, 1973, BA, Pol. Sci./Journalism; Columbia, 1974, MS, Journalism. *Lexington* (KY) *Herald*, reporter, 1974. *Louisville Times*, 1974-81. *National Journal*, reporter, 1981-84. *Los Angeles Times*, Washington bur., econ. corr., 1984-88. *NYT*, Washington bur., corr., 1988-present.

Witcover, Jules. *National Journal*/Tribune Media Services. Columnist. B. Union City, NJ. Columbia, 1949, BA; 1951, MS, Journalism. *Hackensack* (NJ) *Star-Telegram*, reporter, 1949-50. *Providence* (RI) *Journal*, reporter, 1951-52. *Newark Star-Ledger*, reporter, 1953. Newhouse Newspapers, reporter, 1954-68. *Los Angeles Times*, pol. reporter, 1969-72. *The Washington Post*, pol. reporter, 1973-76. *The Washington Star*, 1977-81. Baltimore *Sun*, 1981-present. *National Journal*, "Inside Politics" columnist (with Jack Germond), current. Tribune Media Services, "Politics Today" columnist (with Germond), 1977-present. Author of ten books, including *Marathon* (1977), and co-author of several books with Germond.

Witt, Howard. *Chicago Tribune*. Moscow Correspondent. B. 1960, Chicago, IL. Michigan, English Language and Lit. *CT*, gen. assign. reporter, 1982-86; Midwest corr., 1987; Canada corr., 1987-89; African corr., 1989-91; Moscow corr., 1992-present.

Woodward, Kenneth L. *Newsweek*. Religion Editor. B. Cleveland, OH. Notre Dame, 1957; U. Michigan, Law; U. Iowa, MA, English; U. Strasbourg (France), European Literature. U. Maryland, Overseas div., English instructor, 1959-60. *Time*, stringer, 1959-60. *Sun* newspaper group, Omaha, chief feature writer, 1962-64. *Newsweek*, assoc. ed., 1964-69; gen. ed., 1969-74; sr. writer, religion ed., 1974-present.

★ INDEX ★

C

D

E

F

G

H

I

J

K

L

M

N

O

P

Q

R

S

T